# Pre-reflective Consciousness

*Pre-reflective Consciousness: Sartre and Contemporary Philosophy of Mind* delves into the relationship between the current analytical debates on consciousness and the debates that took place within continental philosophy in the twentieth century and in particular around the time of Sartre and within his seminal works. In contemporary debates, so-called representationalists and self-representationalists are, once again, as Sartre did, evoking primitive pre-reflectivity for thinking about the nature of consciousness. Still, what they are not taking into account is that there are serious problems with assuming pre-reflectivity to be representational. Needless to say, philosophers do not dispute the subjectivity of the mental. The question is, rather, whether it is possible to take a third-person, objective stance towards mental states. What is, after all, the distinctive feature of mental states in a physical world?

Examining the return of the problem of subjectivity in philosophy of mind and the idea that phenomenal consciousness could not be reduced to functional or cognitive properties, this volume includes twenty-two unique contributions from leading scholars in the field. Asking questions such as:

- Why should we think that self-consciousness is non-reflective?
- Is subjectivity first-personal?
- Does consciousness necessitate self-awareness?
- Do we need pre-reflective self-consciousness?
- Are ego-disorders in psychosis a dysfunction of pre-reflective self-awareness?
- How does the Cartesian duality between body and mind fit into Sartre's conceptions of consciousness?

**Sofia Miguens** is a Professor in the Department of Philosophy of the University of Porto, Portugal.

**Gerhard Preyer** is Professor of Sociology at Goethe-University Frankfurt am Main, Germany.

**Clara Bravo Morando** is a graduate student (PhD, Philosophy) at the University of Porto, Portugal.

# Pre-reflective Consciousness
Sartre and contemporary
philosophy of mind

Edited by Sofia Miguens, Gerhard
Preyer, and Clara Bravo Morando

LONDON AND NEW YORK

First published 2016
by Routledge
2 Park Square, Milton Park, Abingdon, Oxon OX14 4RN

and by Routledge
711 Third Avenue, New York, NY 10017

*Routledge is an imprint of the Taylor & Francis Group, an informa business*

© 2016 Sofia Miguens, Gerhard Preyer and Clara Bravo Morando, editorial and selection matter; individual chapters, the contributors.

The right of the editors to be identified as the authors of the editorial material, and of the authors for their individual chapters, has been asserted in accordance with sections 77 and 78 of the Copyright, Designs and Patents Act 1988.

All rights reserved. No part of this book may be reprinted or reproduced or utilised in any form or by any electronic, mechanical, or other means, now known or hereafter invented, including photocopying and recording, or in any information storage or retrieval system, without permission in writing from the publishers.

*Trademark notice*: Product or corporate names may be trademarks or registered trademarks, and are used only for identification and explanation without intent to infringe.

*British Library Cataloguing in Publication Data*
A catalogue record for this book is available from the British Library

*Library of Congress Cataloging in Publication Data*
Pre-reflective consciousness : Sartre and contemporary philosophy of mind / edited by Sofia Miguens, Gerhard Preyer and Clara Bravo Morando. — 1 [edition].
pages cm
Includes bibliographical references and index.
1. Philosophy of mind. 2. Sartre, Jean-Paul, 1905–1980. 3. Consciousness. 4. Subjectivity. I. Miguens, Sofia, editor.
BD418.3.P74 2015
128'.2092—dc23
2015013241

ISBN 978-1-138-92581-6 (hbk)
ISBN 978-1-315-68114-6 (ebk)

Typeset in New Baskerville
by Swales & Willis Ltd, Exeter, Devon, UK

Printed and bound in Great Britain by
TJ International Ltd, Padstow, Cornwall

# Contents

*Notes on contributors* viii
*Preface* x

**Introduction: back to pre-reflectivity** 1
SOFIA MIGUENS, GERHARD PREYER, AND
CLARA BRAVO MORANDO

## PART I
**Foundation of the mental** 27

1 Why should we think that self-consciousness
   is non-reflective? 29
   MANFRED FRANK

2 Is subjectivity first-personal? 49
   TOMIS KAPITAN

3 Degrees of self-presence: rehabilitating Sartre's accounts
   of pre-reflective self-consciousness and reflection 66
   KENNETH WILLIFORD

4 Sartre on pre-reflective consciousness: the adverbial
   interpretation 101
   MARK ROWLANDS

5 Pre-reflective and reflective time-consciousness:
   the shortcomings of Sartre and Husserl and a
   possible way out 120
   GERHARD SEEL

## PART II
## I-knowledge, perception, and introspection    141

6  The zero point and I    143
   TERRY HORGAN AND SHAUN NICHOLS

7  A sketch of Sartre's error theory of introspection    176
   MATTHEW C. ESHLEMAN

8  A pebble at the bottom of the water: Sartre and Cavell
   on the opacity of self-knowledge    208
   PIERRE-JEAN RENAUDIE

9  Does consciousness necessitate self-awareness? Consciousness
   and self-awareness in Sartre's *The Transcendence of the Ego*    225
   DANIEL R. RODRÍGUEZ NAVAS

10 Perception and imagination: a Sartrean account    245
   URIAH KRIEGEL

## PART III
## Pre-reflectivity disputed    277

11 Do we need pre-reflective self-consciousness? About
   Sartre and Brentano    279
   ERIC TRÉMAULT

12 Sartre's non-egological theory of consciousness    298
   JOSHUA TEPLEY

13 The "of" of intentionality and the "of" of acquaintance    317
   ROCCO J. GENNARO

14 A "quasi-Sartrean" theory of subjective awareness    342
   JOSEPH LEVINE

## PART IV
## Body as a whole, the other, and disorder of the mental    363

15 Pain: Sartre and Anglo-American philosophy of mind    365
   KATHERINE J. MORRIS

16 Sartre, enactivism, and the bodily nature of
   pre-reflective consciousness 385
   KATHLEEN WIDER

17 The body is structured like a language:
   reading Sartre's *Being and Nothingness* 407
   DOROTHÉE LEGRAND

18 Basic forms of pre-reflective self-consciousness:
   a developmental perspective 422
   ANNA CIAUNICA

19 Ego disorders in psychosis: dysfunction of pre-reflective
   self-awareness? 439
   ANDREAS HEINZ

PART V
**Historical philosophical background** 453

20 Radical *Epokhè*: on Sartre's concept of "pure reflection" 455
   RAOUL MOATI

21 Sartre and Kierkegaard on consciousness and subjectivity 476
   IKER GARCIA PLAZAOLA

22 Invisible ghosts: *Les jeux sont faits* and disembodied
   consciousness 495
   JEREMY EKBERG

   *Index* 507

# Contributors

**Clara Bravo Morando**, Dr. phil., University of Porto, Departemento di Filosofia, Porto, Portugal

**Anna Ciaunica**, post doc., FCT Postdoctoral Fellow – Mind Language and Action Group, Institute of Philosophy, Porto, Portugal

**Jeremy Ekberg**, Associate Professor of English, Shantou University, Shantou, China

**Matthew C. Eshleman**, Professor of Philosophy, Department of Philosophy and Religion, University of North Carol, Wilmington, Wilmington, NC, USA

**Manfred Frank**, Professor of Philosophy emer., Eberhard Karls University, Tübingen, Germany

**Iker Garcia Plazaola**, Visiting Lecturer, University of Illinois at Urbana-Champaign, Champaign, USA

**Rocco J. Gennaro**, Professor and Chair, Philosophy Department/Phil of Mind/CogSci Area Editor, Internet Encyclopedia of Philosophy, College of Liberal Arts, University of Southern Indiana, University Blvd., Evansville, IN, USA

**Andreas Heinz**, Professor of Psychiatry and Psychotherapy, Klinik für Psychiatrie und Psychotherapie, Charité – Universitätsmedizin Berlin Campus Charité-Mitte, Berlin, Germany

**Terry Horgan**, Professor of Philosophy, University of Arizona, Tucson, AZ, USA

**Tomis Kapitan**, Professor of Philosophy, Department of Philosophy, Northern Illinois University, DeKalb, USA

**Uriah Kriegel**, Professor of Philosophy, Research Director, Jean Nicod Institute, Ecole Normal Supérieure, Paris, France

**Dorothée Legrand**, Professor of Philosophy, Chercheur CNRS, Archives Husserl, Ecole Normale Supérieure, Paris, France

**Joseph Levine**, Professor of Philosophy, Department of Philosophy, University of Mass, Amherst, MA, USA

**Sofia Miguens**, Professor of Philosophy, University of Porto, Departemento di Filosofia, Porto, Portugal

**Raoul Moati**, Assistant Professor, Department of Philosophy. University of Chicago, Chicago, USA

**Katherine J. Morris**, Fellow in Philosophy, Mansfield College, Oxford University, UK

**Shaun Nichols**, Professor of Philosophy, University of Arizona, Tucson, AZ, USA

**Gerhard Preyer**, Professor of Sociology, Goethe-University Frankfurt am Main, Frankfurt a. M., Germany

**Pierre-Jean Renaudie**, Post-Doctoral Researcher, University of Porto/ University of Lisbon, Portugal

**Daniel R. Rodríguez Navas**, PhD Candidate, Department of Philosophy, University of Chicago, Chicago, USA

**Mark Rowlands**, Professor of Philosophy, Department of Philosophy, University of Miami, Coral Gables, USA

**Gerhard Seel**, Professor of Philosophy, Institute of Philosophy, University Bern, Bern, Switzerland

**Joshua Tepley**, Assistant Professor of Philosophy, Saint Anselm College, Manchester, NH, USA

**Eric Trémault**, Dr. phil., Post-Doctoral Researcher, Archives Husserl de Paris, CNRS, France

**Kathleen Wider**, Professor of Philosophy, Department of Literature, Philosophy, and the Arts, University of Michigan-Dearborn, Dearborn Michigan, USA

**Kenneth Williford**, Professor and Chair, Department of Philosophy, UT Arlington, Arlington, USA

# Preface

The project which gave rise to this book developed in the context of a cooperation between the University of Porto and the Goethe University–Frankfurt am Main. The cooperation started in 2008 and involved the coordination, by means of common projects, of the research agendas of the Mind Language and Action Group (MLAG: Institute of Philosophy, University of Porto, Portugal; Principal Investigator: Sofia Miguens) and *ProtoSociology: An International Journal of Interdisciplinary Research and Project*, Goethe-University Frankfurt am Main (led by Gerhard Preyer). The first common project, Consciousness and Subjectivity (2008–2012; see Miguens and Preyer 2013) started from a shared concern about the generalization of a naturalized epistemology stance in current discussions on consciousness in analytic philosophy. Not only did we have doubts that naturalized epistemology could be the last word in epistemology, but we also believed that such a situation resulted in a blind spot concerning the natures of consciousness and subjectivity. When third-person approaches are dominant (and the proximity of much philosophical work on mind and language with cognitive science reinforces such orientation), issues concerning subjectivity are taken to be exhausted when problems regarding the place of consciousness in nature, or problems of language and first-person authority, are addressed.

Our second project, Pre-reflective Consciousness, took up issues where that prior, first project left them. We were interested in the shape of what we saw as a return of the problem of subjectivity in philosophy of mind, and we regarded the works of Elisabeth Anscombe, Héctor-Neri Castañeda, Roderick Chisholm, John Perry, and others, as examples. We were also interested in looking systematically at the history of twentieth-century philosophy. As a result we decided to explore the relations between current debates on consciousness within analytical philosophy (in particular the debate around self-representationalism) and debates taking place in continental philosophy around the time of Sartre, and in Sartre's work. In fact, one may consider early critiques of functionalism in the philosophy of mind in the 1970s to also be a symptom of the *return of subjectivity* in analytic philosophy of mind. A number of philosophers, with quite different backgrounds, converged around the idea that phenomenal consciousness could not be reduced to functional or cognitive properties. Such agreement later went under headings such as the "explanatory gap" or the "hard problem of consciousness." We took such agreement to concern not only—or not even necessarily—phenomenal experience, but also the pre-reflective structure of consciousness. That is the main topic of this book. One may see such a return to subjectivity as a renewal of what one of us calls "the Cartesian intuition," i.e., the intuition of the self-givenness of consciousness. It is under such light that a need arises to rethink borders between what counts as "inner" and "outer" when the nature of the mental is at stake.

This liminal question of boundaries is, namely, a question of whether the *inner* should be characterized as under the skin only. And it is also a question of whether there is indeed such a thing as an epistemic priority of consciousness of one's mental states in relation to knowledge of other minds and of the world. Along with the idea that the mental cannot be described from the outside only comes an analysis of pre-reflective (immediate) consciousness, an analysis which extends to phenomenal consciousness, to self-knowledge (as I-knowledge), and to the consciousness of time.

A general intention and policy of our common projects here, as it was already the case with the first project (*Consciousness and Subjectivity*: Berlin: De Gruyter, 2013), is to bring analytic, or analytically inspired, philosophers and phenomenologists working on the continent together alongside Anglo-American philosophers. We believe that discussions (e.g., discussions of the so-called mind–body problem), which have in many quarters of analytic philosophy become quite scholastic, can come alive once again once they are seen through the light of a different philosophical tradition. Furthermore, we believe that even if one shares a non-reductionist position in the philosophy of mind, this does not yet entail the option for a particular ontology. What is at stake, rather, is not opting for ontological dualism in epistemology and the philosophy of mind, but simply taking the explanatory gap seriously. Such was the starting point of the work that gave rise to the articles collected here.

We would like to thank all the contributors of the project, which has brought together authors from several countries, and in fact embodies a cooperation between Europe and the USA in the fields of Sartre studies and consciousness studies in a way we hope is mutually illuminating.

We would also like to thank many colleagues in Frankfurt am Main and in Porto for their helpful sensitive cooperation, as well as the Portuguese Fundação para a Ciência e a Tecnologia and the EU Erasmus Programme for financing Gerhard Preyer's lectures, and our meetings at the Institute of Philosophy of the University of Porto.

Sofia Miguens<br>
Gerhard Preyer<br>
Frankfurt a. M./Porto, January 2015

# Introduction
## Back to pre-reflectivity

*Sofia Miguens, Gerhard Preyer, and
Clara Bravo Morando*

> Ce qu'on peut nommer proprement subjectivité, c'est la conscience (de) conscience.
>
> (Jean-Paul Sartre 1943, p. 29)

### Pre-reflectivity and consciousness

Looking back at philosophy in the twentieth century is not merely a historical exercise, especially if such a retrospective is undertaken with a systematic intent. In this book, our starting point for looking back are current debates in the philosophy of mind,[1] in particular those around the pre-reflective foundations of consciousness. In those debates, so-called representationalists and self-representationalists[2] are, once again, as Sartre did, evoking primitive pre-reflectivity for thinking about the nature of consciousness. Still, what they are not taking into account (whereas it was very much discussed before) is that there are serious problems with taking pre-reflectivity (as *pour-soi*, or being for-itself) to be representational and thereby relational (Williford 2006a, 2006b; Kriegel 2009). Needless to say, philosophers do not dispute the subjectivity of the mental. The question is, rather, whether it is possible to take a third-person, objective stance towards (first-person) mental states. What is, after all, the distinctive feature of *mental* states in a *physical* world? In what follows, we will argue in favor of an answer that points to "pre-reflective consciousness." Pre-reflectivity means, first of all, that self-consciousness is not the result of reflection; rather, consciousness is "non-positional" consciousness of itself. This pre-reflectivity does not entail the identification of an object, such as an "I," which can then present itself as "myself"; rather, pre-reflective consciousness is a basic being and thus mental states are themselves conscious. If pre-reflective consciousness indeed has such features, then one should think of the mental as non-relational; there is no mediation to speak of here (one speaks, thus, of "*translucidité*": "transparency," "diaphanousness"). This way of thinking finds a particularly rich example in Sartre's early philosophy, namely in *The Transcendence of the Ego* (1931936/1937)—hence Sartre's centrality in this book. Sartre's approach, with its appeal to consciousness as activity, nihilation, and perpetual flight, might seem radically alien to contemporary philosophers of mind. If this book succeeds in its intent, we will have shown that this seeming distance between Sartrean and contemporary philosophy of mind is not a necessary division. Once one gets past the strangeness of Sartrean terminology, it should become apparent that what Sartre has to say, especially about consciousness in particular, bears upon contemporary discussions in very important ways.

To draw the argument in very broad strokes, we may consider that the concept of extruding thoughts (Frege 1918) and things (phenomenology) from consciousness was a very central, multistranded feature of philosophy in the last century. Extruding the "I" from consciousness is the mark of Sartre's early work. This is the background against which Sartre's philosophical context and method should be characterized and that is where we will start. Next, we will try to analyze what taking the *pour-soi* as the foundation of consciousness amounts to. Finally, we will look at *pour-soi—en-soi—valeur* relations and, thereby, at the question of freedom, focusing on *réalité humaine* as self-determination. We will then look with some detail at the contributions to this volume, and finally sketch the shape and the consequences of the idea of *pre-reflectivity* as the *structure* of consciousness and *inner framework* of the mental. Accepting such an idea would amount to a renewal of the research agenda in the philosophy of mind (and, in fact, not only in the philosophy of mind), and to reconceiving relations between subjectivity and objectivity. This is what is at stake in this volume.

The figures lurking behind Sartre's philosophical context are Descartes, Husserl, and Heidegger.[3] The way Husserl himself reads Descartes holds that the Cartesian doubt was not consequent enough, since it "left the rest of the world as result." A more radical conception of the Cartesian turn, i.e., of the idea that the foundation of epistemology lies with the subject's point of view (the "*cogito-axiom*"), was thus needed. Husserl own proposal—the *cogito cogitatum* of phenomenology—leads him to a transcendental "I" (an *Urich* or *reines Ich*). Then there is Heidegger, according to whose own anti-Cartesianism the *cogito-axiom* is not held to be self-grounded. Sartre positions himself in this context by going along with Brentano: according to him, the self-transparency of consciousness is a dependent condition deriving from its intentionality.

Brentano's concept of non-thetic consciousness is crucial for understanding such positioning. As (non-thetic) consciousness of itself, or immediate familiarity with itself, consciousness is not consciousness of *a* something (as consciousness of, e.g., a flower vase would be). Being conscious of *something* is, rather, the mark of thetic or positional consciousness. In thetic or positional consciousness, there is intentional orientation towards an object, which Sartre describes as *transcendent*—i.e., something different from consciousness itself. As non-thetic consciousness, consciousness is conceived by Sartre not as a position, but rather as a negation of itself. Plus, its condition of pre-reflectivity precludes any propositional knowledge (which Sartre speaks of as *connaissance*).

Sartre was particularly interested in an analysis of what he thought of as the "pre-reflective foundations" of the *ego cogito*. His critique of Heidegger, namely, takes place here and is basically as follows. Heidegger's *Dasein* analysis, designed as a straight "route to Being," simply leaves out the self and is thus contradictory. Heidegger's anti-Cartesianism has wrong premises: self-reference is not, and could not be, as it were, a reflex of the reverberation of things. Why would "ecstatic being" come back to me and not, for example, to my neighbor? The *ego cogito* is in no way exhausted by the *Dasein* analysis as a route to "being." It should, rather, be reinterpreted as giving a different—and more important—role to the self. Sartre's *réalité humaine* is an attempt at doing exactly that, and it steps into the realm of Heidegger's *Dasein* (in fact, the expression *realité humaine* is Sartre's translation of Heidgger's *Dasein*). Ultimately for Sartre, Heidegger—who, according to Sartre simply (and wrongly) suppresses consciousness from his consideration of the *Dasein*—ends up being significant mostly as evidence of a very much needed critique of Cartesian *instantaneism*. Cartesian instantaneism is the association of the *cogito* with time as an instant (*"la vérité d'un instant,"* as Sartre calls it in *L'Être et le néant*). There, Heidegger was right; Sartre too believes that "le cogito, instantané, ne peut fonder la temporalité" (Sartre 1948, pp. 49/367). The *réalité humaine* is *ecstatic* being, i.e., it is temporal in the sense that it extends from past to present to future. Hegel is, in fact, also relevant for Sartre here, since Sartre believes that any analysis of the structure of consciousness should take into account that a simple unit of consciousness does not disappear by (in Hegelian terminology) "being differentiated." That said for Hegel, Sartre definitely does not go along with anything like the (timeless) *absoluter Geist*, and the *absolute Idee* of Hegel's philosophy, or with Hegel's logicism (i.e., the idea that in his *Logic* are expressed the thoughts of God before he has created the world). This—represented as "absolute thinking" in Hegel's "system of absolute idealism"—Sartre sees as a "circle within circles."[4]

Moreover, Sartre's own regressive–progressive method is not a Hegelian dialectical method, in that philosophical systematization does not ever come to an end; rather, it is always open. *Valeur* is not accomplished by finite beings; it is not like Hegel's *absolute idea* or *absolute knowledge*. So, Sartre's ontology is a new type of ontology: at its center lies the existential project of a mundane subject. Such a subject is a concrete one, constituted by situations. The *réalité humaine* is ontologically characterized by pre-reflective consciousness, as well as by primary freedom. No matter how much Descartes, Husserl, and Heidegger influenced his thought, Sartre's epistemological and metaphysical point of view is no longer that of the Cartesian *cogito*, nor does it envision a conception of consciousness that could consist in either a pure *I* or a *Dasein* without a self.

2. Sartre makes a distinction between three types or modes of being: the *pour-soi*, the *en-soi*, and the *valeur*. If the *pour-soi* is, ultimately, the being conscious of a concrete subject, and the *en-soi* is the non-temporal being, *valeur* has a status similar to that of Kant's regulative ideas in his *Critique of Pure Reason* (1996). The question for Sartre is, then, what the relations are among *pour-soi*, *en-soi*, and *valeur*. The first thing to notice is that it cannot be that the *cogito* is familiar with itself by reflection. One who reflects can only perform the act of reflection if he is already pre-reflectively familiar with himself.[5] Here the idea that the *pour-soi* is not a substance comes in. The *pour-soi* is "spontaneous," "empty," and "self-transparent." Consciousness is always active; there are no degrees of consciousness. It is empty, because all content is outside it. It is a *néant d'être* (a nihilation). The *pour-soi* is conscious as such, because it is not dependent from the *en-soi*—rather, it is a negation (nihilation). This is not a matter of cognition epistemically directed at oneself. All contents–including the "I"—are, as it were, thrown out of consciousness. We could describe that by saying that the *pour-soi* is an operation of distinction of mental states which are immediately conscious. This does not contradict what Sartre calls his "ontological proof," which he takes to be evidence of what he calls the *transphenomenology of phenomena*. According to him there is no *noumenon*, no Kantian *Ding an sich*. The being of the phenomenon is a transphenomenality of being (Sartre 1943, pp. 14–16).

What is the being of consciousness? This question outlines the shape of Sartre's investigations. His answer is that the relative and abstract being of consciousness is not its own being. Although it grasps itself pre-reflectively and immediately, consciousness is always consciousness of *something*. This something is something external. Every thetic consciousness (*connaissance*) rests on a primary non-thetic consciousness (*conscience non-positionelle (ou non-thétique) de soi*). But it is what it is only when it is founded by the *en-soi*.

We see here the gist of Sartre's ontological proof of consciousness. Sartre considers consciousness as something which is without any identity. Only the *en-soi* is identical with itself. Sartre speaks of the interplay between the transphenomenality of phenomena and the *pour-soi* as the *reflet–reflétant* (*jeux de réflexion reflétant*). Once we recognize this, his claim to introduce a new type of ontology should be accepted. Sartre's example for a quasi-material component of the consciousness-dyad is *désir* (in German, "*die Lust*"): *Lust* is, by itself, a "*Lust*-consciousness" only. There is no dispute that there is a propositional knowledge of the environment in which we live. (McGinn (1989, p. 22), for example, has argued that Sartre is an externalist.[6]) The question, rather, consists in how we should interpret Sartre's hermetic *reflet–reflétant* and the role of pre-reflectivity therein.

3. Again, what are the relations between the *en-soi* and the *pour-soi*? Isn't Sartre in fact a dualist, interested in consciousness only (as the creator of being), while leaving nature simply aside? How can he call himself a materialist (a "monist materialist," in fact)? How can he be called an externalist? Sartre's ontology is a phenomenological description of the relations between consciousness—the annihilating activity, the *néant*—and the being from which consciousness depends—namely, the *en-soi*. In a sense, the shape of this ontology is definitely dualist: it is a dualism of the *en-soi* and the *pour-soi*.[7] This is the place where *consciousness of time* comes into play; the *reflet* is distinguished from the *reflétant* by the *néant d'être* (*vide absolu*, "absolute emptiness"). The hermetic *reflet–reflétant* is differentiated by time. Sartre's view is the following: it is a mystery, in Husserl, we can *have* protentions and retentions, whereas at the same time these are something *in* the past (Sartre 1943, pp. 52–153, 165). The *en-soi* is effective in my body, but not in the *pour-soi*. Would it then be the case that the *pour-soi* might shed its self-transparency? Although there is no real correspondence between the two, time *en-soi* comes to itself by means of time *pour-soi*. The dimension of time does not come to any end. They come together only in *valeur*, i.e., as a regulative idea (Kant).

This is where Sartre's views on freedom enter the picture. Sartre believes that free will and pre-reflectivity play together. As time-determined beings, we have the experience of free will through our decisions and projects. Yet our experience of freedom does not correspond to something in the world. We are in the world without any excuse, and we are existentially convicted to freedom (*condamnés à la liberté*). *Les jeux sont faits*. This does not contradict our freedom; rather, it is a piece of evidence towards our free *existential*-being.

We are back at Sartre's method in *L'Être et le néant* (1943). The *terminus a quo* of philosophical reflection is the existing subject himself, with his primary freedom. This has a direct connection with his trans-phenomenal being as a concrete subject. The pre-reflective *cogito* and the phenomenon of being are not distinct. The *pour-soi* is determined by that. The *terminus ad quem* is not an event in the world. It is the *project* constituted by *time*, which has no end. So this is what the *pour-soi* is: ecstatic being, a being of the *réalité humaine* that is determined by a lack of being.

This *réalité* is given in the *situation* of existence within which we, as humans, have the experience of freedom by our doings. This is precisely what is reflected in the method of *L'Être et le néant*. *Valeur* is the orientation of the "primary project" as self-determination. *Néant* is the being of project, the possibility of the existence in the world. Freedom of choice participates in the contingency of being and thereby in the *absurd*. *Le choix* is *absurde* because we, faced with choice, logically cannot effect a nondecision. This is what my own being is; this is the meaning of *ecstasis* as distance to myself. Therefore, the method of *progress* that begins with the pre-reflective *cogito* is both a *return* to myself and—at the same time—an *observation of the Other*, an observation through which this return to Self exists. Sartre's is a *concret* conception of subjectivity. This is in fact a critique of Heidegger's *Seinserschließung* in his *Sein und Zeit*, relating specifically to the *Zuhandenen*.

A conception of the social accompanies Sartre's ontology. Sartre's theory of the social starts with the elementary looking of *others upon me* (*le regard des autres*). We encounter others by reciprocal observation, yet these others are not primordially constituted (as it is in Husserl), nor is it a part of the *Dasein* as *Mitsein* in the world (as it is in Heidegger). For Heidegger, *Mitsein* is the existential constitution of the being in the world (*Dasein*) which is determined by *Sorge*. The difference here between Sartre and Husserl or Heidegger is that for Sartre the experience of the eyes of others upon me is transcendent: it is not my own domain. There is no direct connection between the *pour-soi* and others. Therefore I cannot reach and appropriate the consciousness of others. As such, there is no "other" nor "we" in the domain of pre-reflectivity. The connection of the *pour-soi* can only be a connection with my own body because the first instantiation of the *pour-soi* consists in my body, in that body as a whole. It is through my body that there is an existential borderline between myself and others—and this is a border which I cannot cross. *The other* is the border of my world; this, for Sartre, is a necessary limitation on my freedom. Sartre's view of freedom is very distinct from Heidegger's *Sein zum Tod*. For Sartre, birth and death are facts. He distinguishes between the "thought of death" and "finiteness." Finiteness is determined by the ontological structure of the *pour-soi* and the project of the self.

So, according to Sartre's theory of the subject, subjectivity should first be conceived as pre-reflective subjectivity. Sartre's ontology is that the being of the subject is, as it were, "given" to him, i.e., given by the objective external world. Subjectivity is thus pre-reflective (*non-positionelle*): "La subjectivité, c'est la conscience (de) conscience" (Sartre 1943, p. 29). The constitution of temporality *vis-à-vis* subjectivity and its project-structure corresponds to *valeur*. And *valeur* is not to *be* accomplished from the subject's point of view. Thus self-consciousness is not determined by being. Such is, then, Sartre's new type of ontology: an exploration of the *réalité humaine*, or in other words, a study of the connections between the *pour-soi*, the *en-soi*, and the *valeur*.

## The contributions

Part I of this volume, *Foundation of the mental*, brings together authors who see pre-reflectivity as a core condition of the mental, and of consciousness. To claim that pre-reflectivity is the foundation of consciousness is to claim that thetic consciousness is grounded on non-thetic consciousness. Non-thetic pre-reflective consciousness is conscious *as such*; it is not consciousness of something. It is its own immediate self-transparency.

Among contemporary German philosophers, Manfred Frank is a leading voice emphasizing the importance of pre-reflectivity as the foundation for a theory of mind. (Frank 2012, pp. 191–260; 2013, pp. 171–187; 2015, with reference to Brentano, Husserl, Heidegger, and Sartre). In Chapter 1, *Why should we think that self-consciousness is non-reflective?*, he brings together and compares Dieter Henrich's positions (formulated around "Fichte's fundamental insight") with positions of authors such as David Lewis, Roderick Chisholm, and Héctor-Neri Castañeda. These authors arrived at similar views in completely different contexts (the last of these were, namely, discussing the *de se* constraint, the "he himself" locution or quasi-indicators).[8]

Frank discusses and compares not only philosophers who bring pre-reflectivity into the philosophy of mind, such as Henrich or Castañeda, but also the so-called "separatists" (e.g., Ned Block and David Chalmers) and "anti-separatists" (Terry Horgan and Uriah Kriegel). (This classification refers to "phenomenal consciousness"—those who think that there is such a thing are called "separatists".) Although he believes that one-level accounts of the mental—and of consciousness—come nearer to what he sees as the good idea (i.e., pre-reflectivity), he criticizes not only higher-level conceptions of consciousness (David M. Rosenthal), but also one-level models of self-representation such as Kriegel's. He thinks that self-representationalists' condition of representation does not have the power to capture the discriminating structure of consciousness. The reason for this is that they do not take into account the *de se* constraint. In analyzing relations between *de re*, *de dicto*, and *de se*, one must conclude that *de re* does not imply *de se*. Mach's famous "shabby pedagogue" example is a well-known case of this. *De re* consciousness is not the foundation of consciousness; the questions of regress and circle (which are not to be conflated) are still posed. If *de re* does not imply *de se*, then the *de se* constraint should be satisfied for there to be self-ascription of mental states in general. The overall proposition is the following: I myself cannot self-ascribe mental states from an external point of view, that is, indirectly.[9] Once one takes the *de se* constraint seriously, the step to pre-reflective consciousness is evident. And Frank argues that pre-reflective consciousness is not a negative thesis only, but is in fact a feature of the structure of consciousness.

In *La transcendance de l'ego*, Sartre has distinguished non-reflective from reflective consciousness. He thinks the "I" and the "me" exist only in episodes of reflection. Still, a number of contemporary philosophers of mind see pre-reflective consciousness as a form of self-consciousness. In Chapter 2, *Is subjectivity first-personal?*, Tomis Kapitan argues for a distinction between subjectivity and first-person, or for a non-first-personal account of ipseity. Subjectivity is not primarily a question of self-consciousness. Although it is widely agreed that reflective consciousness goes along with expressions such as "mine" or "for me," this is a feature of reflective consciousness only, which is in fact first-personal. In order to defend Sartre, Kapitan argues that such first-person self-reference is bound to indexical reference expression and conceptualization. The content of primitive self-consciousness is, rather, a perspective structure (a perspectival array). In other words, Kapitan believes that the much discussed idea of *for-me-ness* conflates cognitive self-reference (I-knowledge) and immediate consciousness. But this pre-reflective, conscious lived experience, which makes conscious all mental states is not, he claims, first-personal.

Self-representationalism had the merit of bringing into philosophy of mind, with a systematic intent, the discussion of the pre-reflectivity of the mental. It followed Sartre in proposing that there is a "non-positional" self-consciousness. In Chapter 3, *Degrees of self-presence: rehabilitating Sartre's accounts of pre-reflective self-consciousness and reflection*, Kenneth Williford goes along with Sartre's idea of "non-positional" self-consciousness, in order to offer an interpretation of it in terms of pre-predicative self-acquaintance. Such proposal avoids serious problems which face other interpretations of Sartre's account of pre-reflective self-consciousness (as well as his account of the distinction between pure and impure reflection). Such problems were forcefully presented by, e.g., Kathleen Wider (1997). On Williford's interpretation, self-consciousness is not a matter of any sort of representation *sensu stricto*. It is independent of attention, conceptualization, and objectification. It is not a matter of intentionally aiming at an object that has to be revealed over time via profiles (*Abschattungen*). This view does not lead to any sort of regress: the only price to pay for taking such a view is to accept something like Russell's notion of direct acquaintance and some reasonable notion of the Given, and this is a price that Williford argues we should indeed pay. He closes by arguing that Sartre's claim according to which the Law of Identity (the universal reflexivity of identity) does not apply to the *pour-soi*, precisely *because* it is pre-reflectively self-conscious, is *de trop*. He does not deny the self-distancing operative in reflection and in other striking phenomena (for example, heautoscopy, depersonalization, derealization) which may be partly behind Sartre's claim. Rather, he believes we can conceive of such phenomena without denying the self-identity of consciousness, simply by appealing to consciousness' circular and projective structure.

Sartre thinks positional, or thetic, consciousness of an object is at the same time non-positional consciousness of *itself*. There is thus something like a pre-reflective consciousness condition of consciousness. In Chapter 4, *Sartre on pre-reflective consciousness: the adverbial interpretation*, Mark Rowlands argues that pre-reflective consciousness is an adverbial modification of an act of positional consciousness. He emphasizes that an adverbial interpretation of pre-reflective consciousness does not go hand in hand with an adverbial interpretation of phenomenal content. Pre-reflective consciousness should not be mistaken for phenomenal content.[10] Also, he believes that the adverbial construal of pre-reflective consciousness preserves Sartre's insight that consciousness is nothingness; it carries with it no commitment to a "substantial" sense regarding the consciousness that consciousness is directed to.

According to Sartre's conception of *réalité humaine*, the self-transparency of self-awareness is dissected and articulated by time. In fact, self-awareness is ultimately *consciousness of time*. It was Sartre's merit to recognize that "le cogito, instantané, ne peut fonder la temporalité."[11] Time gives consciousness its direction as a continuation of immediate (pre-reflective) consciousness: consciousness is not what it is and is what it is not (in Sartre's own terms). This is also the key for the understanding of consciousness of time, for time, like consciousness, also "is not what it is and is what it is not."

Gerhard Seel is one of the leading Sartre and Husserl experts among German philosophers.[12] In Chapter 5, *Pre-reflective and reflective time-consciousness: the shortcomings of Sartre and Husserl and a possible way out*, he emphasizes the difficulties of any theory of time. Philosophers usually quote St. Augustine's famous remark in *Confessiones* 11: "Quid est ergo tempus? Si nemo ex me quaeret, scio, si quaerenti explicare velim, nescio." St. Augustine's question was metaphysical or ontological. We had to wait until Husserl's *Vorlesungen zur Phänomenologie des inneren Zeitbewusstsein* (1893–1917) to understand that the question "How is time-consciousness possible?" is even more puzzling.

To explain time-consciousness one needs to presuppose a number of operations of the mind which are not conscious in a thetic way. What are these operations exactly? Most philosophers, contemporary philosophers included, have failed to solve this problem. They do not even see that there is a problem there or what the problem really is. Among those who came close to seeing the problem and solving it, Sartre and Husserl occupy a prominent place. Still, Seel argues, their theories are not satisfactory in many regards. After diagnosing the shortcomings of Sartre's and Husserl's positions, he introduces his own solution to the problem.

In Part II of this volume, *I-knowledge, perception, and introspection*, we bring together articles exploring influential ideas about the self-relating structure of subjectivity. Within the analytic tradition, some of these ideas were developed around the importance of the first-person pronoun and its role as an essential indexical, while others focus on the importance of the subjective point of view, the role of I-knowledge (or I-thoughts), or the nature of introspection.

There seems to be something important and distinctive about the first-person pronoun. Some have spoken of it as an *essential indexical*. A natural extension of this is that there is a corresponding kind of mental representation which performs such a function in thought—perhaps a first-person indexical term in the *language of thought*, perhaps a first-person, essentially indexical, imagistic or pictorial form of self-representation, or perhaps both.

In analytic philosophy of mind, many influential ideas regarding the self-relating structure of subjectivity have arisen in connection with phenomenal consciousness. Phenomenally conscious mental states are typically described as those mental states for which there is *something that it is like, for the experiencer,* to be in such a state.

A third further significant issue, which concerns certain perspectival aspects of conscious experience, is what Husserl called the experiential *zero point (der Nullpunkt)*. A very similar idea sometimes surfaces in discussions of mental representation in the analytic tradition—for instance, the notion of "scenario content" deployed by Christopher Peacocke.

In Chapter 6, *The zero point and I,* Terry Horgan and Shaun Nichols focus on two guiding questions. The first one is when, and why, are various cognitive tasks faced by humans accomplished in the sparser way, i.e., without the use of I*/me* mental representations? The second one is when, and why, are certain cognitive tasks instead accomplished in the less-sparse way, i.e., by deploying I*/me* representations? Horgan and Nichols address each of these questions in two complementary, mutually reinforcing ways. On one hand, they resort to phenomenological description, i.e., they put forward attentive introspective characterizations of certain aspects of conscious experience, which they hope will resonate with the reader. On the other hand, they resort to empirical and theoretical cognitive science.

The "what-it-is-like" aspect is often called *phenomenal character,* whereas the "for-the-experiencer" aspect is what they call *phenomenal subjectivity.* Horgan and Nichols argue that "phenomenal subjectivity"—the direct, non-representational presence of the experiential self in consciousness as the *me for which* one's conscious experience has a phenomenal character—is richly suffused with various interpenetrating *zero-point aspects*. These include the zero-point aspects of sensory-perceptual experience (in its several modalities), the zero-point aspects of voluntary-action experience (including the self-sourcehood aspect and the core-optionality aspect), the temporally layered zero-point aspects that figure in at least some instances of prospection and recollection, the zero-point aspect of ordinary self-involving desires, and the zero-point aspect (within the space of reasons) of both practical and theoretical rationality. Phenomenal subjectivity, Horgan and Nichols think, is essentially the same feature which, in the continental tradition, is sometimes called *pre-reflective self-consciousness,* or *pre-reflective self-awareness.*

What exactly is the privileged stance of the subjective point of view, particularly as it is involved in self-ascription of mental states? Self-monitoring, different versions of introspection (inner awareness), and inner sense are attempts at explaining privileged access to my own mental states. Fred Dretske and others have put forward arguments according to which introspection does involve a sort of "looking inward." The critique of this position in the Wittgenstein–Ryle–Sellars tradition is quite well known. But still, many naturalized epistemology approaches follow it. Sidney Shoemaker is a prominent critic on the inward-glance model. The idea is that all awareness is a thetic consciousness and directed at the external world. Inner awareness would be an "awareness" of oneself from an external and third-person point of view.

In Chapter 7, *A sketch of Sartre's error theory of introspection*, Matthew C. Eshleman considers four interpretations in the recent renaissance of the studies of introspection: those of: (1) pessimistic local skeptics; (2) open-minded general skeptics; (3) hesitant optimists; and (4) robust, non-egalitarian optimists. He clarifies the difference between two different kinds of non-egalitarian views and makes a minimalist case for the robust, non-egalitarian, optimistic interpretation. Toward the end, Eshleman opts for a reverse strategy: rather than pursuing questions regarding the epistemic warrant or how introspection operates head-on, he sketches a general error theory as a way of approaching the study of introspection.

Motivated by Sartre's early phenomenological writings, Eshleman maps the different kinds of basic errors people can make when thinking about thinking along such lines. Eshleman argues that introspective errors share a common core: namely that, when we think about our own conscious experience, we frequently try to adopt the perspective of another person. In our efforts to gain objective purchase upon ourselves we attempt to view ourselves as others view us, as if we could adopt a third-person perspective upon our own personal experience. Doing so, however, requires standing outside of one's own perspective, which is a little like pulling oneself up by one's own bootstraps.

Even so, those who accept that a third-person perspective necessarily fails to capture *essentially* first-person aspects of lived experience are, nonetheless, faced with a puzzle: what can it mean to take a first-person perspective on one's own first-person perspective? In response to this question, Eshleman argues for two claims: first, that such a proposition doesn't mean anything coherent, since doing so is impossible, and, second, that the very attempt to take a "point of view" upon one's own conscious experience motivates many—if not all—errors made in our introspective efforts to understand consciousness better. To Kant's complaint that philosophers have for too long mixed empirical with transcendental claims, Sartre effectively adds that philosophers almost inevitably muddle the first-person vs third-person distinction when theorizing about (embodied) consciousness.

In Chapter 8, *A pebble at the bottom of the water: Sartre and Cavell on the opacity of self-knowledge*, Pierre-Jean Renaudie sets out to criticize the presuppositions in Sartre's conception of self-knowledge. In particular, he wants to argue that self-knowledge must be understood as a way of dealing with one's concealment, rather then an attempt to overcome it. In *The Transcendence of the Ego*, Sartre explores the relations between the translucence of consciousness and the opacity of the ego. Renaudie wants to assess the consequences of this view for self-knowledge. He argues that such a relationship between translucence and opacity makes the pursuit of self-knowledge both necessary and impossible. Finally, he tries to address this paradox by drawing on Stanley Cavell's analysis of the relation between first-person narration and self-concealment.

One widespread interpretation of Sartre's *The Transcendence of the Ego* holds that Sartre requires self-awareness to be a necessary condition of consciousness. In Chapter 9, *Does consciousness necessitate self-awareness? Consciousness and self-awareness in Sartre's* The Transcendence of the Ego, Daniel R. Rodríguez Navas argues, through a close scrutiny of Sartre's *The Transcendence of the Ego*, that such an interpretation is incorrect. On the contrary, he defends the proposition that what Sartre is saying is that consciousness does not necessarily involve self-awareness. To make this argument, Rodríguez Navas brings into view the main philosophical implications of Sartre's position on the issue. If Sartre is right in thinking that self-awareness is a cognitive achievement rather than a necessary condition of consciousness, then this implies the inadequacy of any account of higher forms of self-awareness which takes as its starting point the assumption of a primitive capacity for self-awareness that is common to all conscious creatures by virtue of their being conscious.

Putnam's twin-earth scenarios make room for testing not only intuitions regarding indexicality, but also *disjunctivist positions* regarding phenomenal consciousness. Disjunctivist positions (e.g., John McDowell or M. G. F. Martin) are epistemologically externalist, and according to them the difference between veridical perceptions and hallucinations is a radical difference.[13] Their explanations have to be distinct. But how are we to distinguish between the phenomenology of perception and the phenomenology of imagination?

In Chapter 10, *Perception and imagination: a Sartrean account*, Uriah Kriegel argues against the traditional view according to which there is no categorical distinction between perception and imagination, but only modifications (for example, in degree of intensity and resolution). Kriegel looks back to Sartre's view in his *The Imagination* (1936), seeing there an alternative to the traditional views.[14] Sartre's view is that the image does not modify the intentional object, but rather modifies the intentional act.

Going against a "long Anglo-Saxon tradition," Kriegel concludes that Sartre convincingly argues that there is a categorical distinction between perception and imagination (pertaining to the manner in which the object is represented in consciousness), and that perception and imagination are phenomenally dissimilar.

In Part III of this volume, *Pre-reflectivity disputed*, we have gathered articles which are critical of Sartre's view of subjectivity, namely of his understanding of the *cogito axiom* and of pre-reflectivity as the core condition of mental states. They are followed by Joseph Levine's article (Chapter 14), which is an answer to these critiques.

According to Sartre, pre-reflectivity does not have an "I" as an occupant. His view does not, in principle, change in *L'imaginaire* (1940) and *L'Être et le néant* (1943). Sartre's conception of the transcendence of the "I" is not in harmony with the epistemological role that Descartes' *cogito axiom* attributes to it, or with Kant's conception of a *transcendental unity* of self-consciousness, according to which the "I think" accompanies all representation, which "all belong to one self-consciousness" (Kant 1996, B 132).

In Chapter 11, *Do we need pre-reflective self-consciousness? About Sartre and Brentano*, Eric Trémault claims that Sartre's conception of intentionality is in fact closer to Brentano's than to Husserl's. Both Sartre and Brentano think that sensory contents are intentional objects, and that all intentional acts are pre-reflectively self-conscious. Brentano was not a Cartesian thinker. According to Trémault, the agreement between Sartre and Brentano is due to an understanding of the Cartesian *cogito* according to which only intentional acts are self-evident. Trémault argues that if this understanding of the *cogito* is mistaken, then pre-reflective self-consciousness becomes useless. He turns to Husserl's understanding of the *cogito*, which is presented as the legitimate one, an understanding according to which sensory contents do not exist as mere intentional object.

Sartre's view is that the ego is not the subject of the consciousness. Sartre's theory of subjectivity starts without any ego; the ego is viewed not as transcendental, but rather as transcendent—just like any other thing in the natural world. In Chapter 12, *Sartre's non-egological theory of consciousness*, Joshua Tepley systemizes the two strategies for developing such a theory of the subject. First, in *The Transcendence of the Ego*, Sartre claims to show that there is no subject of consciousness and thus that the ego cannot be the subject of consciousness. Then, in *Being and Nothingness*, there is a subject of consciousness (the body-subject), but the ego and the body-subject as a substance are numerically distinct. Tepley's claim is that such non-egological theories of consciousness are untenable and that, *pace* Sartre, there is a subject of consciousness, and the ego is such a subject. "I" refers to an entity: it is something which has character as a conjunction of properties. Tepley argues that when Sartre identifies the ego with character, then the ego, and not character, is referred to with the word "I."

It is often argued that the expression "consciousness" is ambiguous, namely between state-consciousness and creature-consciousness. Explaining state-consciousness is explaining what makes a mental state a conscious one. Higher-order thought theorists, such as Rosenthal and others, claim to offer a theory of state-consciousness and thus to explain the distinction between unconscious and conscious mental states. According to this view, all conscious mental states are states of *consciousness of*. A higher-order thought is conscious by reflection or introspection; so, such thought itself is conscious by a higher-order thought. One idea is that, in order to avoid circularity and regress here, one should consider the first-order world-directed state as not, itself, being conscious. If this is not done, regress and circularity come back into the picture.

In Chapter 13, *The "of" of intentionality and the "of" of acquaintance*, Rocco J. Gennaro argues that the idea of pre-reflective non-positional consciousness is coherent with a version of higher-order-thought theory of consciousness. According to the "wide intrinsicality view," conscious states are intrinsic, relational, and self-referential. There is also an immediate and intimate relation between "meta-psychological thought" and "conscious mental states."

Gennaro explains pre-reflective awareness as appealing to unconscious representational self-awareness ("ubiquitous self-awareness"). Pre-reflective consciousness is representational and unconscious, in contrast to weaker forms of intentionality and acquaintance. Therefore, Gennaro concludes, Sartre would have been better off interpreting "pre-reflective self-awareness" as unconscious and representational, not as states of acquaintance.

Following Thomas Nagel's characterization of the subjective as "what-is-it-like-to-be," one finds two views: the "secondary awareness" and the "access" approaches. The distinction here is between reductionists (materialists) and non-reductionists (often non-materialists). In Chapter 14, *A "quasi-Sartrean" theory of subjective awareness*, Joseph Levine goes through a number of theories of consciousness that have been put forward in the last decades, each with something to say about what subjectivity is; he argues in favor of an account of what he calls the "for-itself," which is inspired by features of Sartre's theses in *Being and Nothingness*. He goes though the access-approach (Block) and the distinction between phenomenal and access consciousness with reference to M. Tye's PANIC (Poised Abstract Nonconceptual Intentional Content) theory, as well as the "secondary awareness approach" (Rosenthal). Rosenthal's higher-order thought account of consciousness is a reductive account. Another reductionist program is "first-order representationalism" (as presented by, e.g., Fred Dretske). For the first of these, conscious states are "states" one is conscious *of*; for the latter, they are states one is conscious *with*. Yet for neither are conscious states primitive. According to Levine, a reductive account simply cannot account for subjective and qualitative experience.

Levine also analyzes the neo-Brentanoism of self-representationalism (Kriegel 2009) as well as Gennaro's interpretation of Sartre, according to which subjectivity is a sort of secondary awareness. He then puts forward a Sartre-inspired theory of the "for-itself" which he believes is a better explanation of the transparency of mental states than reductionist representationalism.

One reason no reductionism will do as an account of consciousness is that every reductionism leaves out the temporality of consciousness. Sartre's view is that the *pour-soi* exists as a past only, and that it projects itself to the future as a "not-yet." The project is not to be realized; there is no ontic realization of the *valeur* as "regulative idea" (Kant 1996). The past as own existence of the *pour-soi* is brought by the body of the whole. It is this body, which is my body as a domain of my lived experience, that is the foundation of the achievement of the *pour-soi*. Therefore the mundane initial situation of the project of the *pour-soi* is the real distinction between the situation wherefrom the project is coming and the future whereupon the project is directed (the *valeur* ultimately). Bodily being connects the consciousness of time and the world time.

Part IV of the volume, *Body as a whole, the other, and disorder of the mental*, brings together contributions whose subject is the relation between the body and pre-reflectivity, the body and language, pre-reflectivity and the other, and pre-reflectivity and ego disorders. As noticed above, the *pour-soi* is also relevant for Sartre's social theory. The other (*l'autre*) is a boundary of my freedom; by it the project of the *pour-soi* experiences a limitation. The other is not a particular which we identify with singular terms and sortals. He is not someone whom I see and I have experience about; he sees and refers to me. There is a non-bridgeable existential distinction between me and the other. The *difference corridor* between me and you cannot be bridged.

In Chapter 15, *Pain: Sartre and Anglo-American philosophy of mind*, Katherine J. Morris attempts to bring Sartre into dialogue with Anglo-American philosophers of mind on the topic of pain. One problem here is that Anglo-American philosophy focuses almost exclusively on "acute" pain, whereas Sartre's focuses largely on "long-lasting" pain; neither has anything to say about "chronic" pain. Morris' main conclusion is that, although Sartre and Anglo-American philosophy may be able to converse around the periphery, the possibility of dialogue is severely limited because of fundamental differences in philosophical outlook. Specifically, this is the case with Anglo-American philosophers' commitment to naturalism and their consequent treatment of the body as *Körper* rather than *Leib*, as well as a presupposition of much Anglo-American philosophy of mind, *internalism*, a view which is in fact at odds with the fundamental phenomenological concept of being-in-the-world.

Enactivist philosophers of mind (such as, e.g., Alva Noë or Dan Hutto) see their view of mind as inspired by the work of Maurice Merleau-Ponty; they rarely, if ever, mention the work of Jean-Paul Sartre. They believe, as Merleau-Ponty himself did, that the author of *Being and Nothingness* has too often forgotten that the subject of consciousness is bodily. In Chapter 16, *Sartre, enactivism, and the bodily nature of pre-reflective consciousness*, Kathleen Wider argues first that such criticism is based on a mistaken view of *Being and Nothingness*. If one has a proper understanding of Sartre's work on the body and its relation to pre-reflective consciousness, Sartre can indeed himself be seen as another predecessor to the current enactivists. To offer further evidence of this predecessor status, she then examines the work of enactivist Alva Noë. She looks at his work side by side with Sartre's work in order to highlight the similarities in their respective analyses of perceptual consciousness, including the centrality of the role of the body in consciousness. She concludes by briefly suggesting how Sartre's analysis of consciousness could enrich and deepen the enactivist account.

In Chapter 17, *The body is structured like a language: reading Sartre's* Being and Nothingness, Dorothée Legrand brings from her reading of Sartre's *Being and Nothingness* the idea that the body is structured like a language. Language is a fundamental mode of being for others, and exhibits a twofold structure. A world with language is a world where separated terms are inseparable: oneself and another, speaker and listener—irreducible to each other, and as such jointly constituting speech as occurring between them (i.e., as being multivocal). It is this structure that the body incarnates. In particular, the caress is the language of desire, strictly speaking, in the sense that the caress occurs between separated terms which are thus made inseparable from each other. Through the caress, I am responsible for incarnating my transcendence in my flesh, thereby being simultaneously responsible for the other's transcendent incarnation, bound to remain inapprehensible. One's responsibility for oneself and others, therefore, is tied to the body as it is structured like a language.

In his famous analysis of shame, Sartre argued that my experience of the other is an experience that involves my own self-consciousness, that is, a self-consciousness in which I am pre-reflectively aware that I, as lived body, am also a *visible object* for another. In Chapter 18, *Basic forms of pre-reflective self-consciousness: a developmental perspective*, Anna Ciaunica argues that the standard way to cash out the notion of pre-reflective self-consciousness by contrasting it with its reflective, more elaborated forms fails to capture the role of *bodily awareness*. She draws on recent empirical findings regarding the developmental primacy of social versus visual perspective taking to provide a nuanced understanding of the notion of basic pre-reflective self-consciousness. She argues that at the basic developmental level, my being-for-others is not experienced as an external dimension of being, nor is it experienced as an existential "alienation" provoked by my encounter with the other. Rather, in my experience of the other, I am pre-reflectively aware that *we* (i.e., the other and I) are *co-subjects* of a shared experience. Ciaunica thus concludes that, at the most primitive level, pre-reflective self-awareness might be experienced as other-relatedness rather than self-centered or first-personal "for-*me*-ness."

The concept of pre-reflectivity of the mental may also be significant for the analysis of mental illness and psychotherapy. In Chapter 19, *Ego disorders in psychosis: dysfunction of pre-reflective self-awareness?*, Andreas Heinz claims that ego disorder (*psychosis*) can be explained by a disturbance of pre-reflectivity. Interpreting clinical phenomena, he shows that the absence of thought ownership (as in, e.g., thought insertion: there is an alien thought in *my* own mind), is a failure of pre-reflective self-reference. But how should it be conceptualized that the subject of my own experience cannot itself be an object of experience? Heinz refers to Helmuth Plessner, who claims to answer the question by making a distinction between "centric and eccentric positionalities." Heinz argues that Plessner's shaky distinction between "centric versus eccentric positionalities" required a pre-reflective self-awareness identifying my centric position. Failures in this embedment promote "inserted thoughts" and body movement under "alien control."

In Part V of this volume, *Historical philosophical background*, we gather articles which connect Sartre's thought with philosophers who were particularly important for its development. This is the case, namely, for Husserl, Kierkegaard, and Descartes. Sartre was very keen on the idea of a radicalization of the gesture of "phenomenological reduction" coming from Husserl's phenomenology. Sartre's critical approach to Husserl implies the necessity of radicalizing the phenomenological suspension of the natural attitude, in order to reach consciousness reflectively in its impersonal dimension. But at the same time, most passages of *The Transcendence of the Ego* about reflection are explicitly skeptical about any possible reflection that would be absolutely pure, i.e., able to reach consciousness in its impersonality.

Sartrean skepticism towards reflection has also led some important and influential Sartrean scholars to discredit the possibility of a pure reflection, in other words, a reflection that would be able to bracket off the ego. This reading of Sartre entails the conclusion that Sartre's account of reflection finally joins Husserl's theory, according to which the ego remains a transcendence of a particular kind that can never be suspended. Sartre argues that the foundation of psychology and epistemology requires that the traditional opposition between subjective experience and objective world be dissolved; however, Husserl's phenomenological reduction precludes this dissolution, because it precludes explanation of the experienced resistance of the world to our efforts.

In Chapter 20, *Radical* Epokhè: *on Sartre's concept of "pure reflection,"* Raoul Moati tries to show that a skepticism towards reflection leads Sartre in *The Transcendence of the Ego* to mobilize *non-reflective means* in order to reach consciousness in its impersonality. Therefore a reading of reflection according to which Sartre finally joins Husserl's theory is based on a misunderstanding of Sartre's concept of pure reflection. As a matter of fact, the fact that there is no reflection that does not imply the apparition of an ego within the field of the reflected does not imply in any way that pure reflection would remain, in Sartre's perspective, an unreachable ideal.

Moati tries to prove that the unavoidable apparition of the ego within the field of the reflected does not imply necessarily impure acts of reflection. It nevertheless implies a radical redefinition of the phenomenological reduction. Such a reduction cannot be understood any more as a deliberate and intellectual act of suspension of the natural attitude in Husserl's phenomenology, but as an undesired and existential suspension of our natural attitude in the experience of anguish.

Danish philosopher Søren Kierkegaard is the initiator of existentialism, the "philosophical tag" Sartre is most often associated with. Kierkegaard's impact on twentieth-century existentialism was strong. A challenge such as his is important for the contemporary scene of philosophy of mind—the idea is that there is no such thing as a complete theory of mind elaborated from the third-person point of view.

In Chapter 21, *Sartre and Kierkegaard on consciousness and subjectivity*, Iker Garcia Plazaola emphasizes the relevance of Sartre and Kierkegaard for identifying the blind spot of third-person view to consciousness and subjectivity in the naturalistic and materialistic theories of mind. According to Sartre, the primary mode of consciousness is pre-reflectivity; reflection comes later. Kierkegaard did not put forward a systematic study of being conscious. But we find a comparable anti-reflective turn in *The Concept of Anxiety* (1845) and *The Sickness unto Death* (1849), where he appeals to anxiety and despair to depict the first-person attitude.

Unlike most professional philosophers nowadays (analytic philosophers anyway), Sartre did not make a sharp distinction between his philosophical writings and his literary ones. His plays and essays are exemplifications of his philosophy. Human existence and self-determination are not scientific subjects of research and theorizing; existence, as a condition, cannot be described by scientific vocabulary or fall under scientific laws.

In Chapter 22, *Invisible ghosts:* Les jeux sont faits *and disembodied consciousness,* Jeremy Ekberg addresses Sartre's 1943 screenplay, which was screened at Cannes in 1947 (directed by J. Delannoy). After their death, the two protagonists of *Les jeux sont faits* are ghosts. They have no physical force, but rely more upon their reflective consciousness than upon their pre-reflective consciousness. The definition of the protagonists' situation is such that both persons are reflective, making them pure consciousnesses and therefore empowered to recognize psychically the real situation in their environment; however, they are unable to warn their loved ones and comrades of impending danger.

Sartre is saying thereby that reflection is not necessarily better when disembodied, and that, for its characters to create any meaning form themselves, they must have that Cartesian duality in perfect and natural balance. This strange and mystical state of existence is not the only reason the protagonists fail, however. Their failure to love each other enough to save themselves is the product of their focusing on their own projects rather than on loving each other enough to save themselves in accordance with the mysterious. But there is no definite end of everything, because "les jeux sont faits"—the die is cast. Therefore, every life is a failure. The film connects the subject's point of view with love, rebellion, and second chances, a point of view which is ultimately shown to be fiction. The definition of the situation is given as social frame by an authoritarian (fascist) political order as a closed system. This social frame serves as a substitute for other total institutions within which we are still free in our existential decisions. Through this, Sartre reminds one, whether intentionally or not, of the importance of the *thought* of freedom (Fichte) and not only of its reality (as this was put in the Hegelian philosophical tradition).

## The pre-reflective structure of consciousness

One may consider that there are two major, opposing, views of self-consciousness, egological and non-egological views. For the first view, consciousness is ultimately consciousness of a subject which refers to itself as an "I." Descartes, Locke, Leibniz, Kant, Fichte, the New Kantians, and the late Husserl would all fall here, as might, within contemporary philosophy of mind, for example, S. Shoemaker, J. Campbell, or Quassim Cassam.

For the second kind of view, the reflective pronoun "self" does not stand for an "I" or a person, but rather refers back to a "consciousness" which is conscious of itself. Such presupposed domain is an anonymous "field" (A. Gurwitsch) or the stream of consciousness (Husserl). Hume, Brentano, the early Husserl, Sartre, members of the Vienna circle, B. Russell (with the difference between *knowledge by acquaintance* and *knowledge by description*), Castañeda and G. Strawson would fall here.[15]

One may see as a recent result in Sartre studies the idea that Sartre is in fact quite close to Brentano. This would render necessary a re-evaluation of the relations between pre-reflective consciousness and I-knowledge (the *cogito-axiom*); the idea is that it is doubtful that the "I" is the result of reflection.

Why would one think that Sartre comes close to Brentano here? Brentano initiates an analysis of intentionality which takes intentionality to be identical with self-consciousness. He thus makes a distinction between "self-representation" (*innere Vorstellung*) and "self-observation" (*innere Beobachtung*). In other words, "inner consciousness" is a matter only of "accompanying" the perception of an object (internal or external), whereas in "inner perception" (*innere Wahrnehmung*), consciousness turns to itself, becoming its own intentional object (of reflection). The all-important thing here is that "inner perception" is not observation. Brentano's psychology is based on a faculty of inner perception, not on an objectification by observation. Therefore he named his psychology "empirical."[16]

For Brentano all intentional consciousness is accompanied by inner pre-reflective consciousness; only such pre-reflective consciousness can give rise to reflective self-consciousness. Thus, there cannot be, e.g., unconscious psychical objects. Pre-reflective self-consciousness is intentional consciousness; full-blown consciousness remains "secondary," and is subordinated to the appearing of the "primary" intentional object of perception.

The critique we can address to Brentano's conception of inner pre-reflectivity, as the basis of reflectivity, whether in the special case of the "I" or others, is that it somehow misses a true disclosure of the secondary object (to Brentano, a "judgment") about its own existence. For the same reason, pre-reflective self-consciousness is no more than a "simple representation" (*blosse Vorstellung*), and is also not a full-blooded inner perception or reflective self-consciousness.

However, pre-reflective self-representation is far from keeping an undifferentiated relation towards itself. Brentano does not hesitate to claim that pre-reflective self-representation is usually accompanied by an "affection" or an "affectional feeling" (*Gefühl*) of itself. Therefore for Brentano every self-reference to, or every inner self-perception relating to, lived experiences which is reflective is preceded by an intentional self-representation, where that primary sense of self or tacit selfhood is presented and even presumed as being the form of a secondary object, which is also affectional. The originary self-manifestation of consciousness is, from its very beginnings, articulated or inhabited by an affective and representational intentionality, which remains, however, subordinated to the appearing of a perceptive primary object that is the only thing that must occupy the subject in the first place. Nothing precludes the primary object from being the object of inner perception, and nothing precludes that inner consciousness which accompanies it from being the unreflected consciousness of a self-reflective consciousness. Brentano has paired an object to inner consciousness. Yet his designation ("secondary object") is misleading, because relation with an "object" is, precisely, relational.

At this point one might take the following global look at things. When one considers approaches to self-consciousness, a pursuit of something like Fichte's concept of I-knowledge is hopeless. Fichte analyzes what he calls "*unmittelbares Bewusstseyn*" (immediate consciousness) from the point of view of the "I" as an "*Anschauung des Ich*" ("*intellektuelle Anschauung*"; perception of the *I*, intellectual *Anschauung* (perception). This means he takes it to be an activity of "self-thinking" (*Selbstdenken*). The *I*-thought is therefore for him a matter of attention and thereby reflective. It should be mentioned that Fichte does not make the distinction between "immediate (primitive)-", "attentive-", and "self-consciousness" using the word "Anschauung" clearly—(self-consciousness = *I*).

Such a view can easily go astray and tend towards ontological idealism (Berkeley-style). As for Brentano, he does not put forward an adequate analysis of self-consciousness either; the secondary object and the priority of intentionality cannot explain the unity of consciousness (inner consciousness). Neither Fichte nor Brentano saw the place of the I-less self-consciousness in the theory of consciousness adequately.

Husserl's phenomenology also fails to give an adequate analysis of the relation between the pre-reflectivity of consciousness and I-knowledge. This is because Husserl, maybe contrary to better insights, takes as the priority for phenomenology the undertaking of an analysis of the I and of intentionality.

As for Sartre's phenomenological ontology, even if we agree with and want to pursue his insight regarding the pre-reflective structure of consciousness, we are confronted with the fact that Sartre does not acknowledge the phenomena of *de se constraint* and *indexical self-reference*. He claims to explain I-knowledge by appealing to pre-reflectivity, or starting from it. There is no functional equivalent of the *de se constraint* and the *indexical self-reference* in his ontology of the subject's point of view. And the same goes for Fichte.

One step to take at this point could be, for instance, to pursue Castañeda's "guise theory." The problem is that, although Castañeda considers the pre-reflective (anonymous) consciousness, he misunderstands self-consciousness as being constituted by reflection.

The self-representationalists have the virtue, with their *Same-Order Monitoring Theory*, of not distinguishing two numeric mental states characterizing consciousness. Still they unjustifiedly duplicate the representing and that which is represented; on the "paradoxes of subjectivity," see Williford et al. (2013). Self-representationalist accounts are in fact a variation of the Higher-Order Monitoring (Thought) Theory of R. Rosenthal (2005), even in the case of a Same-Order Monitoring (Thought) Theory. The problem here is duplication between the mental representant and what is represented.[17]

Consciousness involves non-conceptual state consciousness, a stream of consciousness (lived experiences), and I-knowledge. The idea of pre-reflective consciousness is that we cannot explain consciousness starting from prior non-conscious states. All mental states are conscious *as such* as non-conceptual states. Thus, they are not intrinsically relational. If one sees things this way, one accepts that the so-called "explanatory gap" is in fact deeper than assumed by the philosophical community: subjectivity is not just a feature of experience; it is present in every experience. It is not an object. This is where one might take the step of thinking of an *inner framework* of the mental (Castañeda). This would come out as a step against naturalism and materialism, but also scientific realism.

Sartre's enduring insight is that it is pre-reflective consciousness which makes mental states conscious as such. We have consciousness of mental states as non-mediated states. This is non-egological, pre-reflective, and anonymous consciousness, that is, non-indexical consciousness. So there is (a) consciousness of states, like, for example, acts, lived experiences themselves and (b) consciousness of propositional contents of these states/acts/lived experiences. The relation is between (a) and (b) the "consciousness as consciousness of *something.*" Intentionality should be reinterpreted from this point of view.

But a correction of Sartre's own epistemology might be also required. One way of formulating this is to say that Sartre did not accept something like a *noema*. When we turn epistemically to the *pour-soi* as the foundation of the mental states, we find that the content of intentionality (i.e., propositional attitudes) is not the entity itself. What we are immediately aware of in being aware of these contents is an intentional content, for example, believed, desired, wished, and hoped. Sartre's view is there is no object consciousness, but the *intentional object* only.

Also Sartre's repudiation of the existence of an "I" outside of consciousness should be corrected: the *de se* constraint has to be taken into account in the analysis of consciousness.

In self-referential consciousness of subjects, the *de se* attitude cannot be side-stepped and is not based on other attitudes.[18] The I-knowledge of the subject (*cogito-axiom*) is not a primary consciousness. I am conscious of myself immediately, i.e., the pre-reflective *cogito* is a condition of the Cartesian *cogito*. It should thus be accepted that the concept of *mineness* and *for-me-ness* is not more basic as the concept of *I* (*I-ness*) or *me-ness*. Subjectivity is not simply a first-person phenomenon only.

The primary instantiation of the self-reference of the *pour-soi* is therefore the objectification by the look of others upon my body as a whole.

This is evidence for the symbiotic relationship between myself and others as *facticity*.[19] Still, no consciousness can reach the consciousness of the other. This might be called the *difference corridor* between *ego* and *alter* as an existential foundation. The channel between them is reciprocal observation.[20] Free choice is an existential *one* as a decision in us-self as our fate and thereby "L'homme est une passion inutile" (Sartre 1943, p. 708). *Les jeux sont faits* should be read literally.

Pre-reflective consciousness and existential self-determination can also work as keys for understanding mental illness: for example, ego disorders in psychosis and self-deprivation appear as a disorder of pre-reflectivity. This could be also a new turn with respect to an existential psychology and therapy.

Arguing from Sartre's insight, one would hold that the structure of consciousness is no "subject–object relationship," nor is it primarily a direct epistemological relation (direct realism/externalism). The structure of consciousness is a structure of self-determination which is dejected by time and existential self-determination. We grasp all conscious states immediately or pre-reflectively. A misleading conceptualization was lurking in the model of inner perception and the secondary object; Sartre's insight is that this cannot be the case. Self-consciousness cannot be analyzed in the model of reflection and inner perception. Looking inward is going wrong. This has consequences for philosophy in general, and for theory of mind and consciousness in particular: there cannot be such a thing as a complete theory of mind from an external, or third-personal, point of view.

This has also consequences for epistemology, because there is no all-knowing observer, or interpreter. The reference to a finite observer (interpreter) does not exclude that there is at the same time an objective knowledge of the objective world in the dimension of shadowing up by our experiences.[21] Therefore a reinterpreted version of Sartre's early philosophy goes along with a *dual or polar epistemology* with connects both an ontological realism and an epistemic/polar dualism in epistemology and ontology, that is, that the mental is not an objective reality, but a subject–object and not an object–object relationship.[22] Therefore the mental is not an object we refer to from a third-person stance as a basic stance for understanding the mental. But there is a reciprocal relationship between the physical and the mental, because there is a cross-reference relation between them. The subject is not an object. The relation to reality is based on intentionality which is, like all mental states, immediately conscious as such (von Kutschera 2009, pp. 212–224). This, we think, is the insight in Sartre's early philosophy that is worth recalling.

Just a final comment. In this project on early Sartre, we were interested mostly in Sartre's philosophical writings before his turn to Marxism after the Second World War. Such a divide in the history of his work made sense to us, since the context of Sartre's philosophy was very much changed thereafter. Still, although what was at stake in the present project was the early

Sartre, and so mostly *The Transcendence of the Ego* (1957/1936), we are not arguing that there is no continuity in his philosophy.[23] One main feature to consider there would be the existential understanding of decision and freedom as the foundation of human existence and self-determination. Marxism itself as a political decision is obviously not implied in this foundation. Freedom is a primarily existential choice. That we have to think the *thought* of freedom, and not only freedom's *reality*, is something that was argued by Hegel and by the tradition which followed him. And looking at Sartre, we cannot fail to notice the looming importance of Hegelianism and Marxism in his work. But this was not the subject of the present project.

## Notes

1 On contemporary philosophy of mind, see S. Miguens and G. Preyer (2013, pp. 9–35) and C. M. Amoretti and G. Preyer (2013, pp. 9–28).
2 Such as, for example, U. Kriegel, T. Horgan, and K. Williford. F. Brentano's view, described as "self-representational," is often taken as a historical reference here.
3 In his early writings, Sartre also refers to Henry Bergson. It is worth pointing out that Sartre was not familiar with the late writings of Husserl. (On these late writings, see K. Held 1966.) Sartre has interpreted his "*cogito* préréflexif" as a deeper understanding of Husserl's "transcendental ego." Husserl himself did, in his later writings, take a step in this direction—see G. Seel (1971, pp. 97–98). On a systematic re-interpretation of Sartre's philosophy with reference to his philosophical context, see G. Seel (1971); see also, among the German philosophers, J. Möller's (1959) study on Sartre's ontology. In Portuguese, see P. Alves' Introduction to his 1994 translation of "The Transcendence of the Ego" (Observações sobre uma tese de Sartre).
4 This has nothing to do with Frege's logicism as a program for a reduction of mathematics to logic.
5 In French, there is a distinction between "réfléchir" and "refléter." Sartre's reading is: "Réfléchir" is the doing of reflection. Reflection means knowledge ("le savoir," "la connaisance"), and as such "implique distinction de l'objet et du sujet" ("implies [a] distinction of the object from the subject"): Sartre (1948, pp. 380–381). In contrast "refléter" means to reflect as a "mirroring." Within the *reflet–reflétant*, there is no contradiction of knowledge.
6 It should be mentioned that, for McGinn, Sartre's *pour-soi* is a negation. Such an interpretation is motivated by the fact that Sartre has not accepted something like the *noema* (as Husserl did). The *pour-soi* is not an object. Sartre is not an externalistic direct realist, because his account includes mental (epistemic) intermediaries. For an epistemic critique of these intermediaries of perceptual beliefs, see D. Davidson (2005, pp. 127–141). But Davidson's account does not work. Sartre's *reflet–reflétant* is an alternative, from an epistemological viewpoint. It is near to Husserl's *noema* and Frege's *Sinn*.
7 The "*en-soi block*" version of the *en-soi* requires a modification.
8 On the exchange between continental and American philosophers, particularly regarding the question of the impetus of D. Henrich, the so-called "Heidelberger School," see J. G. Hart (1999, pp. 17–31); on D. Henrich, see Preyer (2013, pp. 189–211).

9 On de *re, de dicto, de se*, see, for example, Frank (2013, pp. 171–187), N. Feit (2013, pp. 213–230); on R. Chisholm and H.-N. Castañeda, see Preyer (2015a).
10 Prominent representatives of the adverbial theory of awareness include C. J. Ducasse, R. M. Chisholm, W. Sellars, and J. Cornman. They present a description of the phenomenal content of experience without a reification of this content as a mental object.
11 Sartre (1948, p. 49).
12 Seel (1971, 1988, 1996, 2005a, b, 2010): on Husserl's philosophy of time, see A. B. Beils (1987).
13 See, for example, M. G. F. Martin (2004, 2005). For a critique on disjunctivism, see K. Farkas (2008, pp. 95–96, 123–124).
14 Sartre refers to the views of Descartes, Hume, and Leibniz as an identity of sorts between perceptual and imaginative experiences, the critique on the theory of association of conservative Catholicism (Bergson, Th. Ribot, H. Taine), and the experimental psychology of judgment (Husserl, Bühler). One could also mention here Brentano's critique of Hume.
15 For a new, detailed analysis, see Frank (2015), writing about Preyer (2015b).
16 Still, Brentano's concept of "inner perception" is misleading, since there is no subject–object relation in immediate consciousness.
17 On further studies about these questions, see Frank (2015), Preyer (2015b).
18 The question of higher-order thought theories is that they do not take into account the de se constraint of self-conscious self-reference in principle.
19 This is close to what N. Luhmann has called "inter-human interpenetration" (1984, pp. 304–309).
20 The "corridor" means that we do not cross the existential distinction between our body and our consciousness in the *ego–alter* relationship.
21 We have to take in also the quantum-physics turn which refers to the measurement instrument (the observer) as limit of all objective knowledge of classical physics. But the measurement (the observer) itself is constructed on the mesocosmical level. Both have the same dates. This is a note only with respect to the situation in natural sciences, which is not a unified domain of researches and theorizing in the meantime.
22 In contrast to Davidson's anomalous monism and his token identity theses, there are psycho-physical laws. This does not commit us to a naturalized (materialistic) epistemology.
23 Sartre, *Critique de la raison dialectique* précédé *de Questions de méthode. Tome 1: Théorie des ensembles pratiques*. Text established and annotated by Arlette Elkaïm-Sartre, Paris: Gallimard, 1960, is the end of his early philosophy. It goes along with a gradual abandonment of "existentialist ideology."

# References

Amoretti, C. M. and G. Preyer (2013). Introduction: Mind, Knowledge, and Communication in Triangular Externalism, pp. 9–28, in C. M. Amoretti and G. Preyer, Eds., *Triangulation: From an Epistemological Point of View*, 2nd ed., Berlin: De Gruyter.

Beils, A. B. (1987). *Transzendenz und Zeitbewusstsein. Zur Grenzproblematik des transzendental-phänomenologischen Idealismus*, Bonn: Bouvier Publisher.

Davidson, D. (2005). Seeing through Language, in D. Davidson, Ed., *Truth, Language, and History*, Oxford: Oxford University Press.

Farkas, K. (2008). *The Subject's Point of View*, Oxford: Oxford University Press.
Feit, N. (2013). Self-Ascription and Self-Awareness, pp. 213–230, in S. Miguens and G. Preyer, Eds., *Consciousness and Subjectivity*, Berlin: Ontos Publisher/De Gruyter.
Frank, M. (2012). Zeit und Selbst, pp. 191–261, in *Ansichten der Subjektivität*, Berlin: Suhrkamp Publisher.
Frank, M. (2013). *Ansichten der Subjektivität*, Berlin: Suhrkamp.
Frank, M. (2013). Varieties of Subjectivity, pp. 171–187, in S. Miguens and G. Preyer, Eds. *Consciousness and Subjectivity*, Berlin: Ontos Publisher/De Gruyter.
Frank, M. (2015). *Präreflexives Selbstbewusstsein. Vier Vorlesungen*, Stuttgart: Reclam.
Frege, G. (1918). Der Gedanke. Eine logische Untersuchung, pp. 58–77, in *Beiträge zur Philosophie des Deutschen idealismus*. Vol. I. Göttingen. Republished in: *Gottlob Frege Kleine Schriften*, 2nd ed. Herausgegeben und mit Nachbemerkungen zur Neuauflage versehen von Ignacio Angelelli, Hildesheim: Georg Olms Verlag 1990, pp. 342–362.
Hart, J. G. (1999). Castañeda: A Continental Philosophical Guise, pp. 17–31, in H.-N. Castañeda, J. G. Hard and T. Kapitan, Eds., *The Phenomeno-Logic of the I. Essays on Self-Consciousness*, Indiana: Indiana University Press.
Held, K. (1966). *Lebendige Gegenwart. Die Frage nach der Seinsweise des Transzendentalen Ich bei Husserl, Entwickelt am Leitfaden der Zeitproblematik*, The Hague: Martinus Nijhoff.
Husserl, E. (1966). *Vorlesungen zur Phänomenologie des inneren Zeitbewusstseins (1893–1917)*, Husserlina X, The Hague: Martinus Nijhoff.
Kant, I. (1996). *Critique of Pure Reason*, tr. W. S. Plurhar, Indianapolis, IN: Hackett.
Kierkegaard, S. A. (1845/1981). *The Concept of Anxiety: A Simple Psychologically Orienting Deliberation on the Dogmatic Issue of Hereditary Sin (Kierkegaard's Writings*, VIII), Princeton: Princeton University Press.
Kierkegaard, S. A. (1849/1983). *The Sickness Unto Death: A Christian Psychological Exposition for Upbuilding and Awakening (Kierkegaard's Writings*, XIX), Princeton, NJ: Princeton University Press.
Kriegel, U. (2009). *Subjective Consciousness. A Self-Represenational Theory*, Oxford, UK: Oxford University Press.
Luhmann, N. (1984). *Soziale Systeme. Grundriss einer allgemeinen Theorie*, Frankfurt a. M.: Suhrkamp Publisher.
Martin, M. G. F. (2004). The Limits of Self-Awareness. *Philosophical Studies* 120: pp. 3–89.
Martin, M. G. F. (2005). On Being Alienated, pp. 354–409, in T. Szabo Gendler and J. Hawthorne, Eds., *Perceptual Experience*, Oxford, UK: Oxford University Press 2005.
McGinn, C. (1989). *Mental Content*, Oxford, UK: Oxford University Press.
Miguens, S. and G. Preyer, Eds., (2013). *Consciousness and Subjectivity*, Berlin: De Gruyter.
Miguens, S. and G. Preyer (2013). Introduction: Are There Blindspots in Thinking about Consciousness and Subjectivity, pp. 9–35, in S. Miguens and G. Preyer, Eds., *Consciousness and Subjectivity*, Berlin: De Gruyter.
Möller, J. (1959). *Absurdes Sein? Eine Auseinandersetzung mit der Ontologie J. P. Sartres*, Stuttgart: Kohlhammer Publisher.
Peacocke, C. (1992). *A Study of Concepts*, Cambridge, MA: MIT Press.
Preyer, G. (2013). The Problem of Subjectivity: Dieter Henrich's Turn, pp. 189–211, in S. Miguens and G. Preyer, Eds., *Consciousness and Subjectivity*, Berlin: De Gruyter.

Preyer, G. (2015a). III What Is Self-Reference, in *Back to Cartesian Intuition: Internalism, Externalism, and the Mental*. Unpublished manuscript 2015a. Contents, I Overview on the Philosophy of Mind, *Academia.edu* under Gerhard Preyer, Unit "Consciousness, Mind."

Preyer, G. (2015b). *Subjektivität als präreflexives Bewusstsein. Jean-Paul Sartres "bleibende Einsicht."* On Manfred Frank, *Präreflexives Selbstbewusstsein. Vier Vorlesungen*, Stuttgart: Reclam.

Rosenthal, R. (2005). *Consciousness and Mind*, Oxford, UK: Oxford University Press.

Sartre, J.-P. (1936). *L'imagination*, Paris: F. Alcan.

Sartre, J.-P. (1936/1937). *The Transcendence of the Ego*. Translated by F. Williams and R. Kirkpatrick. New York: The Noonday Press. *La transcendance de l'ego*, Paris: Vrin.

Sartre, J.-P. (1940). *L'imaginaire*, Paris: Gallimard.

Sartre, J.-P. (1943). *L'Être et le néant*, Paris: Gallimard.

Sartre, J.-P. (1948). Conscience de soi et connaissance de soi, pp. 49–91, in *Bulletin de la Société Francaise Philosophie*, Bd. 42.

Sartre, J.-P. (1960). *Critique de la Raison Dialectic* (précédé *de Questions de Méthode*), I: Théorie des Ensembles Pratiques, Paris: Gallimard.

Sartre, J.-P. (1994). *A Transcendência do Ego (Seguido de Consciência de si e Conhecimento de si)*. Translated by P. M. S. Alves, Lisbon: Colibri.

Seel, G. (1971). *Sartres Dialektik: Zur Methode und Begründung seiner Philosophie unter besonderer Berücksichtigung de Subjekts-, Zeit- und Werttheorie*, Bonn: Bouvier Publisher

Seel, G. (1988). Wie hätte Sartres Moralphilosophie ausgesehen?, pp. 276–293, in T. König, Ed., *Sartre: Ein Kongreß*, Reinbek: Rowohlt Publisher.

Seel, G. (1996). La querelle de l'humanisme continue. A propos du livre d'Alain Renaut, Sartre: Le dernier philosophe, *Revue de Théologie et de Philosophie*, 128: pp. 161–172.

Seel, G. (2005a). Wie ist Bewusstsein von Zeitlichem möglich?, pp. 169–221, in Frank Hofmann, Catrin Misselhorn, Violetta L. Waible, and Véronique Zanetti, Eds., *Anatomie der Subjektivität, Bewusstsein, Selbstbewusstsein, Selbstgefühl*, Berlin: Suhrkamp Publisher.

Seel, G. (2005b). La morale de Sartre: Une reconstruction. *Le Portique* 16: Available online at: http://leportique.revues.org/737.

Seel, G. (2010). Husserls Probleme mit dem Zeitbewusstsein und warum er sie nicht löste, pp. 43–88, in Manfred Frank and Niels Weidtmann, Eds. *Husserl und die Philosophie des Geistes*, Berlin: Suhrkamp Publisher 2010.

von Kutschera, F. (2009). *Philosophie des Geistes*, Paderborn: Mentis Publisher.

Wider, K. (1997). *The Bodily Nature of Consciousness*, Cornell, NY: Cornell University Press.

Williford, K. (2006a). The Self-Representational Structure of Consciousness, pp. 276–293, in U. Kriegel and K. Williford, Eds. *Self-Representational Approaches to Consciousness*, Oxford, UK: Oxford University Press.

Williford, K. (2006b). Zahavi and Brentano: A Rejoinder, *Psyche* 12 (2): pp. 1–8.

Williford, K., D. Rudrauf and G. Landini (2013). The Paradoxes of Subjectivity and the Projective Structure of Consciousness, pp. 322–353, in S. Miguens and G. Preyer, Eds., *Consciousness and Subjectivity*, Berlin: De Gruyter.

# PART I
# Foundation of the mental

# 1 Why should we think that self-consciousness is non-reflective?

*Manfred Frank*

It was Sartre who introduced the expression "pre-reflective" (Sartre 1936/7, in: Sartre 1978)—even though commentators have wrongly attributed it to other authors such as Fichte, Novalis, Brentano, and even to Dieter Henrich and the Heidelberg School. Meanwhile, the term has also come to be quite commonly used in contemporary analytic and phenomenological philosophy (by authors such as Peter Goldie, Shaun Gallagher, Dan Zahavi, Ken Williford, and Dorothée Legrand). Yet, for many of these authors, the term "pre-reflective" does not have the meaning that Sartre meant to introduce; the following is guided by this original meaning.

First of all, the term was coined with a negative intention in mind. What it says is that there is a type of self-consciousness that is *not* the result of reflection, as many representatives of mainstream philosophy of mind—especially *higher-order* theorists—would take all forms of self-consciousness to be. Some critics accuse the proponents of pre-reflective self-consciousness of being stuck with a negative position and of not coming forward with a positive theory of consciousness. I will discuss this objection at the end.

In what follows, I will first remind readers of which philosophers have insisted on the reality of pre-reflective self-consciousness, and why they felt motivated to do so. Then, in the section on the failure of higher-order theories of consciousness, I will look at the differences between higher-level and one-level models of self-representation and defend the merits of the latter. However, the so-called *self-representationalists* I address here largely reject pre-reflective consciousness, as I understand it. They do this because they think, wrongly, that "representation" is the basic term—"the core necessary condition" (Kriegel 2009, pp. 107, 154ff.)—for any reasonable theory of consciousness. I attack this position in the section on an analogous failure of same-order theories, by showing, amongst other things, that self-representation founders on the *de se* constraint, which invites radical consequences that require us to adopt an understanding of pre-reflective self-consciousness that differs from what they can offer in their framework. In the section on why inner differentiation of "pre-reflective consciousness" doesn't prevent its transparency to the world, I seek to show, by way of a conclusion, that a common criticism of pre-reflectivity theory (as I shall refer to it) is ungrounded. According to this criticism, pre-reflectivity theories serve only as a negation of alternative models and, in particular, do not do justice to the internal differentiation that exists within the overall structure of subjective consciousness.

## The discovery of ubiquitous pre-reflective self-awareness

In 1966, Dieter Henrich published an essay with the unassuming title "Fichte's Original Insight" in the Festschrift for Wolfgang Cramer. Rarely has such a small seed sprouted into such rich food for thought—in this instance, concerning some special features of the structure of self-consciousness. The decisive point was presented negatively: self-consciousness cannot be understood to be the explicit turning-upon-itself of an (in itself and of itself) unconscious awareness. Since the times of Descartes and Leibniz, and in fact already with William of Ockham, the philosophical tradition had spoken of "reflection." That which can be grasped in the act of reflection *as* itself is that, and only that, which possesses, prior to all reflection, a criterion for knowing (in a non-conceptual sense) its own being and its own self-sameness. Thus: "What reflection finds *seems to already have been there*," as Novalis, in 1795—earlier than Fichte himself—had formulated the point (Novalis 1965, p. 112, Nr. 14).[1] Otherwise, reflection would not have discovered the phenomenon of consciousness, but rather created it: a case of something like brainwashing would have taken place.

Fichte's opinion was that his predecessors, even Kant, had misconstrued self-consciousness as reflection (Fichte 1798, p. 11; see Fichte 1797, pp. 18–19). With that they had involved themselves in a circle, the logic of which Henrich's article on Fichte put under the magnifying glass, and the overcoming of which Fichte took all the credit for. By "circle" here we understand the tacit use of a premise that is then simply reiterated in the conclusion. Nothing is thus explicated; all that happens is that the same opinion gets repeated. Yet those who think that there really is such a thing as self-consciousness should look for independent explication.

By "regress," we understand the infinite postponement of a justification. There can be non-harmful regresses. For instance, the repeated reiteration of the truth predicate (as in "The supposition that Gödel was right is true" and "It is true that the supposition that Gödel was right is true," etc.) is harmless. But some regresses are indeed vicious. For instance:

> Consciousness comes to be when an unconscious mental event becomes the object of a higher-order mental event. The higher-order mental event is itself unconscious and becomes conscious through the objectification by another mental event of yet higher order, which is itself unconscious. And so on.

Something similar is held nowadays by authors such as David Rosenthal, Peter Carruthers, and Rocco Gennaro. Yet Fichte had for the first time clearly shown (1) that those who take consciousness to exist cannot ground it by means of a regressive theory and (2) that consciousness must be unmediated, i.e., it must be awareness of itself from the start, so that no regress takes off. This was how Fichte justified his claim that consciousness presupposes immediate self-consciousness. This thesis is nowadays widely shared in *self-representationalist* circles, where one speaks of the *ubiquity of self-awareness*.

Fichte's achievement would of course have remained unnoticed if Henrich hadn't spelled it out in such a clear and impressive way and claimed that important things depend on it. Only thus could one call Henrich's rediscovery a discovery. The underlying doctrine was spelled out in rapid sucession by Henrich and some of his students[2] and with time, they came to be known as the "Heidelberg School"—maybe for the first time in Tugendhat's (1979) lectures on *Selbstbewußtsein und Selbstbestimmung* (*Self-awareness and Self-determination*).

Although Henrich's seminal idea was soon translated into English and although Henrich invited several leading proponents of analytic philosophy to Heidelberg or carried on discussions with them in the United States, his view had little influence in the then still young "Philosophy of Mind." Hector-Neri Castañeda (1966) and Sydney Shoemaker (1968) had, independently of one another and almost simultaneously, arrived at very similar insights. They had shown that one's self-consciousness does not reduce to the identification of an object, which then turns out to be "I, myself." While Henrich immediately noticed this convergence, and included both authors in the reader he organized for his seminars on self-consciousness (Frank 1991a, 1994 are nothing but extended and published versions of this original anthology), one cannot really speak of a corresponding reception by the Anglo-Americans. Henrich's difficult style, heavy with the influence of Kant and Idealism, was the first impediment; the second was the strong historical orientation of Henrich and his disciples, an orientation which in the anglophone world belongs not so much in philosophy but rather in the history of philosophy and in the literary disciplines. It is true that in 1987 Castañeda dedicated his contribution to the Henrich *Festschrift* to Henrich ("The Self and the I-Guises," in *Theorie der Subjektivität*, edited by Konrad Cramer et al.) thus: "Here is a mere prolegomenon to a general theory of self-consciousness—dedicated to Dieter Henrich with gratitude and with admiration for his illuminating contributions to our understanding of the nature of consciousness, selfhood, and self-consciousness" (Castañeda 1999, p. 180).[3] Nevertheless, one cannot really speak of the influence or of the dissemination of Henrich's arguments. Only James Hart and Tomis Kapitan, the editors of Castañeda's essays in *The Phenomeno-Logic of the I* (1999), brought to light, in their Introduction, what they had in common. Jim Hart, who had come across my views on such problems in a conference at Notre Dame, called my attention to the book Dan Zahavi had written in English on Husserl (Zahavi 1999), which is probably the most detailed and the most luminous representation of the basic idea of the Heidelberg School (and a defense of Husserl against their objections) and which has, as far as I can see, indeed had some influence on the anglophone scene and analytic circles.

Above all, it was cited in the circle of the young philosophers of consciousness who call themselves *self-representationalists*—and through Zahavi I too had the honour of being, at least indirectly, cited. And through Zahavi's mediation some knowledge of the Heidelberg School has percolated (for example, Kriegel and Williford 2006, p. 7 fn. 8; Williford 2006, p. 111f.).

## The failure of higher-order theories of consciousness

We know two varieties of subjective consciousness: impersonal and pre-conceptual self-consciousness and conceptual self-knowledge, with an I as owner or agent at the center.

"Separatists," such as Block in the 1990s, and Chalmers, hold that the first, only, is non-reducible from a functionalist viewpoint. "Anti-separatists" such as Horgan and Kriegel see in the *for-me* component, which is also present in phenomenal consciousness, the turning point from pre-conceptual into conceptual self-consciousness, i.e., into self-knowledge (Kriegel 2009, Ch. 4). This rather recent school in the "Philosophy of Mind" calls itself "self-representationalism." It sees phenomenal states as involving qualitative consciousness together with a *for-me* component, which they call "subjective consciousness." Consciousness, they think, is a case of "representation" (which can also naturally happen in the absence of awareness). At least, "representation" is the fundamental concept of the theory, which insists on dealing exclusively with conscious, i.e., with self-conscious states (for example, Kriegel 2009, pp. 101ff., esp. p. 105). This has a point: it commits the theory to dealing with self-consciousness at the same level as all other cases of representation.

With regard to qualitative consciousness, most self-representationalists are at first sight inclined to endorse hard representationalism's thesis that it is environment which determines the content of consciousness (Kriegel 2009, pp. 12f.; Ch. 3). They differ over the "for-itself aspect" of each consciousness (Kriegel 2009, pp. 71ff., Ch. 4), which the hard externalist would deny. Thus Kriegel matches purportedly mind-independent properties of objects against the disposition they have to cause in our minds, or rather, in our nervous systems, certain states, which he calls "response-dependent properties of the object." This is already an internalist maneuver that invokes a "subjective" aspect of experience; this aspect will be cashed out in terms of self-representing consciousness. This is in frank contrast to hard externalism. In order not to fall into the trap of the reflection model, it must be guaranteed that higher-order consciousness is not directed upon the representational (the outer) content, but on first-level consciousness as its sole content (Levine 2010, pp. 7 and 10).

(Authors like Harman, Dretske, and Tye do not take this subjective factor into account. According to them, consciousness is totally transparent or revelatory of the surfaces and properties of physical objects and does not in itself have access to any further intrinsic properties of consciousness which could appear in reflection. The inference which Dretske and Tye eventually recommend—that of a consciousness-*of* to a consciousness-*that*—seems to me clearly to involve a *petitio principii*. That which did not lie at all in the scope of consciousness before cannot suddenly come to be there through "displaced perception or 'secondary' seeing-that (seeing that P by seeing something not involved in the truth-conditions for the proposition that P)" (Tye 2002, p. 145). How could reflection make truth conditions accessible which are not, as it were, authenticated by the findings of primary consciousness?)

Also, unlike hard representationalists, self-representationalists defend the claim that each consciousness not only represents its environment but also represents itself, hence its for-me-ness character: "Thus, whatever else a conscious state represents, it always also represents itself, and it is in virtue of representing itself that it is a conscious state" (Kriegel 2009, pp. 13–14). So, whenever consciousness occurs, there are two things that the awareness is awareness *of*: something typically different from consciousness itself, and the consciousness itself. Kriegel calls this last aspect "subjective consciousness"—hence the title of his 2009 book.

The question that I have just hinted at is the following: Is self-representation a representation of the same kind as object representation? Or, to ask it again, more radically: Is self-consciousness a special case of object-consciousness? Clearly hetero-consciousness and self-consciousness differ in content. If the higher-order state not only renders the first-order state conscious, but even *self*-conscious, the first-order state must have already been aware of itself prior to the contribution bestowed upon it by representation. But represented content differs in principle from what represents it; so representation induces—by way of objectification—a kind of duality which undermines the pretended self-sameness of represented and representing. This is Levine's conclusion: "So what Kriegel does to solve his problem is to compromise a bit with the two-state view" (Levine 2010, p. 7).

Here is the fundamental question we should be asking: Is "representation"—as the "core necessary condition" for two-place models of consciousness—really the best choice for the basic concept around which to build a theory of consciousness? Representation is a case of relation which, as we have known since Hölderlin (1795), links relata, but which also separates. If a representation is cognitively directed at consciousness itself, one speaks, since Descartes and Leibniz, of "reflection." Still, this way of speaking is much less established in the anglophone world than it is in ours. Yet it is the way the term is generally used by the so-called *self-representationalists*,

34  *Manfred Frank*

as is clearly shown by the anthology edited by Kriegel and Williford in 2006 (*Self-Representational Approaches to Consciousness*). But this is the point: if one translates "self-representation" by "reflection," as these recent representatives of the "Philosophy of Mind" do, one makes the mistake all reflection theories of consciousness make. Fichte's original intuition consisted exactly in saying that one should attribute to self-consciousness a mode of consciousness different from that of hetero-consciousness, which is a mode of representation.

Not that the problem has not been acknowledged and analyzed, clearly and carefully, by Williford (2006, pp. 113–115). He distinguishes two types of regress: extensive and intensive.

The first postulates more and more extended rings of unconscious representations around an unconscious core of content; the second nests itself further and further in, so that the representation relation *has to represent itself ad infinitum* ("a represents a [aRa]" becomes aR[aRa], then becomes aR[aR[aRa]] and so on).

Yet the self-representationalists take the flaw inherent in the weave of the reflection model—circles and regresses—just to be a distinctive feature of the "higher-order theory" held by authors such as David Rosenthal, Peter Carruthers, or Rocco Gennaro. They do not see that they share the reflection model with the latter. Higher-order theorists think of self-consciousness according to the Act–Object model and thus make the mistake of separating numerically (and even temporally) the object and the subject sides of the self-apprehension (Rosenthal 1991, p. 465). Several higher-order theorists separate both acts also by type—thus Rosenthal defends the view that the higher-order act *constitutive* of consciousness is a *thought* that is itself unconscious, but that triggers a propositional attitude (Rosenthal 1991, pp. 465–466; against which, see Kriegel 2009, pp. 15, 18–20, 129–131).

Yet this is inadmissible, because the regresses and the circles against which the Heidelberg School warned occur again. This is something Rosenthal happily ignores (he finds nothing strange in the idea that the representation "on top" of the hierarchy of representations stapled one upon the other remains unconscious, see Rosenthal 1991, p. 466).

Thus, the self-representationalists propose to replace the multi-layer model with a *single-layer* (or *same-order*) model, a model in which one finds not one state directed to itself as to another, but one state exclusively concerned with itself *as* with itself. In addition, the reflecting (higher-order) consciousness is not, in the one-place model, unconscious but rather is explicitly conscious ("all conscious states are consciously represented; therefore: all conscious states are self-represented"; see Kriegel 2009, p. 129). In other words, the one-place model does not separate the primary state of consciousness and its reflection (its representation, as it puts it) into two (numerically different) acts, but rather has one and the same act represent itself. That is already implied in the expression "*self*-consciousness" which, according to the vocabulary of this school, should be translated as "self-representation."

Now, if we want to do away, in the easiest and most radical way, with the regresses that the multi-layer models produce, we should throw the two-layer models overboard, even those that masquerade as "same-order" models. Or so one would think. But that is not what Kriegel and Williford do, at least not explicitly. For the latter, such a proposal appears suspect in that it shrinks from honest conceptual toil and flees into the realm of mysticism (Williford 2006, pp. 112, 113, 115; also Levine 2006, p. 193). Kriegel considers non-relational self-consciousness as simply being a form of Husserlian madness, which he, employing a metaphor loved by Dennett, denounces as an "intrinsic-glow view," while trying to make rhyme or reason of something that seems nonsensical to him, based on his reading of Zahavi (1999) (and not, presumably, Husserl himself) (Kriegel 2009, pp. 101ff.). "Intrinsic glow" seems to mean: without the intervention of representation that is epistemically connected with a subject as its owner; consciousness is an inner light, "a quiet radiance from within," a unique, *sui generis* phenomenon. Something like that is supposedly simply impossible; each consciousness is intentional by being directed at something different from it (Kriegel 2009, p. 104; see p. 14). It came to his attention that Husserl postulated a non-objectual consciousness ("a *non-objectifying* awareness": p. 105); and thereabout he thinks that such a proposal is pure nonsense. It's true that Kriegel admits that what all this is about is "gaining clarity about the nature of that kind of consciousness, which alone constitutes the subjective character, the for-me-ness of self-consciousness" (Kriegel 2009, p. 106).

Kriegel's counterproposal and the consequences he draws are as questionable as his critique of the multi-layer models of self-consciousness is correct and reasonable. For if each consciousness-*of* is a consciousness excluding and distinguishing its object from itself, then it is not at all obvious that a one-place model can work without such exclusion and differentiation. Indeed, this is true entirely independently of the issue of whether the consciousness that *has* and the consciousness that *is had* are of the same kind.

## An analogous failure of same-order theories ("self-representationalism")

Now I would like to put forward a counter-critique of the self-representationalist model of self-consciousness and to draw from it some radical consequences for a pre-reflectivist theory of consciousness.

Two steps should be distinguished in the critique. The first (a) says that in self-consciousness content and consciousness of content are in principle identical; the second (b), the much more serious *de se* argument, claims that it is not sufficient that in cases of self-knowledge representing and represented coincide. It is in addition required that "both" members/relata of the identified dyad *know* themselves *as* being the same. Kriegel can integrate (a) with some difficulty in the self-representationalist model, but he definitely cannot cope with (b).

Regarding (a): The argument for the special status of consciousness says that consciousness, in addition to being directed at an object or state of affairs, must also know its existence and its mode in an unmediated way. Yet this knowledge could not at all be conceived of as representation, because representation introduces into consciousness an act–object, or subject–object, separation. We should not think of a relation at all, but rather of strict identity (with this I understand here with Williford and others not a relation but a sort of seamless unity). I demonstrate this need with a few quotes:

> There is a consciousness in which subjective and objective are not separated but are absolutely one and just the same. Such consciousness is what we are in need of in order to understand consciousness in general. [Es giebt ein Bewusstseyn, in welchem das Subjektive und Objektive gar nicht zu trennen, sondern absolut Eins und ebendasselbe sind. Ein solches Bewusstseyn sonach wäre es, dessen wir bedürfen, um das Bewusstseyn überhaupt zu erklären.]
>
> (Fichte 1797, p. 19)

> [I]l n'y a pas de distinction de sujet–objet dans cette conscience (Sartre 1947, p. 382—in contrast to self-knowledge, which implies such a difference: "le savoir [de soi] implique distinction de l'objet et du sujet."
>
> (Sartre 1947, p. 380)

> Someone can be in the same epistemic situation as he would be if there were heat, even in the absence of heat, simply by feeling the sensation of heat; and even in the presence of heat, he can have the same evidence as he would have in the absence of heat simply by lacking the sensation $S$. No such possibility exists in the case of pain and another mental phenomena. To be in the same epistemic situation that would obtain if one had pain *is* to have pain; to be in the same epistemic situation that could obtain in the absence of a pain *is* to have no pain. The apparent contingency of the connection between the mental state and the corresponding brain state thus cannot be explained by some sort of qualitative analogue as in the case of heat. [. . .] in the case of mental phenomena there is no "appearance" beyond the mental phenomenon itself.
>
> (Kripke 1980, pp. 152 and 154)

> [A]ll it *is* for something to be in pain is for it to feel like pain. There is no distinction between pain and painy stuff, in the way there is a distinction between water and watery stuff. One could have something that felt like water without it being water, but one could not have something that felt like pain without it being pain. Pain's feel is *essential* to it.
>
> (Chalmers 1996, p. 147; cf. p. 133 n.4, and p. 146)

[W]e can't make that sort of appearance–reality distinction for consciousness because consciousness consists in the appearances themselves. *Where appearance is concerned we cannot make the appearance–reality distinction because the appearance is reality.* [. . .] Consciousness is an exception to this pattern [of distinguishability between "objective physical reality," on the one hand, and mere "subjective appearance," on the other] for a trivial reason. The reason, to repeat, is that the reductions that leave out the epistemic bases, the appearances, cannot work for the epistemic bases themselves. In such cases, the appearance is the reality.
(Searle 1992, p. 121f)

[I]t is implausible that a conscious state is conscious in virtue of being represented by an *unconscious state*. But if it is conscious in virtue of being represented by a conscious state, the representing conscious state cannot be numerically distinct from the represented conscious state, on pain of vicious regress or disunity. It follows that *the representing and the represented conscious states are one and the same*—that is, that conscious states are self-representing.
(Kriegel 2009, p. 20; the last italics are mine; Kriegel's formulation raises the *de se* problem; also cf. Kriegel's awkward attempt to subdue, under categories of representation, the intimacy of the relation between represented and representing in inner consciousness: pp. 106ff)

Regarding (b): This sounds reasonable and acceptable. Yet the self-representationalists interpret the examples above as cases of self-representation. Thereby they overlook—and thus repeat the mistakes of higher-order models—that *a* self-*representation* only becomes a *self*-representation if the representing and the represented are not only numerically the same (and don't fall temporally asunder), but also *know* themselves to be the same, i.e., the identity of representing and represented must not only exist *de facto* (or, aptly, *de re*), but it must also exist *for itself* (*de se*)— without thereby engendering a new *relation* which threatens to split the identity into two. It doesn't matter whether the related members of the representation relation differ numerically, or by their contents, or only by type. Even in the latter case, this would lead to an unfortunate doubling of states in the theory. A "target state" becomes conscious when a higher-order representation is directed at it (Levine 2006, p. 175; also Kriegel (2009) himself (p. 107): "[F]or a mental state $M$ of a subject $S$ to have subjective character is [. . .] for $M$ to be the target of a representation of kind $K$ [= inner awareness]"). This is not enough, though, to result in consciousness. The sameness of the relata of the self-representation must also appear in the scope of the subject pole, i.e., the self-identification must recognize what is identified *as being itself.* This is what the following examples show:

If John Smith learns that John Horatio Auberon Smith has been bequeathed an inheritance, he does not have to know that in the testament of the bequether he was named with both his middle names, or that he is the heir.

(Anscombe 1981, pp. 22–23)

If the editor of *Soul* believes that the editor of *Soul* is a millionaire, he must think neither of the editor of *Soul* nor of himself that he is a millionaire. (The editorial board might have appointed him in an emergency meeting at night without his knowledge, and it was his predecessor who just died of heart failure who was a millionaire: freely from Castañeda 1966, in: Castañeda 1999, p. 38f.)

When Ernst Mach, entering a Vienna bus, thinks: "what a shabby-looking pedagogue is the guy who is just entering the bus" (ignoring the looking-glass fixed just opposite him), he does not have to be holding himself a shabby-looking pedagogue (Mach 1886, p. 3).

When the youngest high-school student-girl from Schriesheim believes that the youngest high-school student from Schriesheim will be elected the next Vineyard Queen, she does not have to be taking herself to be the youngest high-school student from Schriesheim or for the next Vineyard Queen.

All these examples perform conscious self-identifications, but not *as* self-identifications. Their structure is (as the last example exhibits it):

There is an $x$ such that $x$ is identical with the youngest student-girl (. . .) and with the future Vineyard Queen and $x$ is believed by $x$ to be the youngest student-girl (. . .) and the future Vineyard Queen.

Chisholm distinguished the two ways of identifying in 1981—looking back, it is a classical scholastic difference—as *de re* and *de se* (Chisholm 1981, Ch. 3). This is what he concludes: *De se* implies *de re*, but *de re* does not imply *de se*. Castañeda had expressed it the following way: Attitudes *de se* are "not analysable in terms of no matter which reference mechanisms," especially not "in terms of attitudes *de re*" (Castañeda 1999, pp. 15ff.). *Emphatic* epistemic self-reference (as Chisholm called it) is consequently not reducible to knowledge of objects (or to objectual knowledge). Because reflective self-knowledge consists in an outer-directed intention turned in upon itself, in other words, in a variety of objectual consciousness, it is ipso facto unsuitable to explain emphatic self-knowledge. Emphatic self-knowledge is not a case of objectual knowledge. It seems to be *sui generis*.

Besides Henrich (Chisholm 1981, fn. 12) and Castañeda (1999, pp. 18, 22, 35, 53 fn. 11), Chisholm rests essentially on David Lewis (1983, pp. 3, 32, 40). Two years earlier, Lewis had spoken of "attitudes *de se*," having in mind beliefs about oneself *as* oneself and—with some bellyaching—had accepted that they are not explainable by or reducible to objectual knowledge (by the way, with the same move of argumentation which rules out knowledge *de dicto* or propositional knowledge as substitute for knowledge *de se*): "[I]f it is possible to lack knowledge and not lack any propositional knowledge, then the lacked knowledge must not be propositional" (Lewis 1983, p. 139). "Some say [. . .] there is a kind of personal, subjective knowledge [. . .], and it is altogether different from the impersonal, objective knowledge that science and scholarship can provide. Alas, I must agree with these taunts" (Lewis 1983, p. 144).

Let me shortly sum up the arguments, which have taken us from the representationalist model, to a one-layer version of self-consciousness, and from there to abandoning the category of relation in the description of self-knowledge.

1  First step: the multi-layer model, according to which a higher-order consciousness unaware of itself is directed at a lower-order unconscious consciousness which is numerically and temporally different from it, fails as it leads to an infinite regress.

2  The same-order model which some self-representationalists advocate may avoid the vicious consequences, yet it insists that consciousness comes into being by a harmful doubling of states, namely by a target state being represented by an awareness of the same type. The danger of temporal shift or numerical difference is thus minimized even though Horgan and Kriegel have no qualms in characterizing the self-relation of the representation to be "roughly contemporaneous," endorsing the idea of immersion in a "specious present" (Horgan and Kriegel 2007, p. 127f.). Yet what is decisive is that same-order theory cannot explain how the representing consciousness can bend back upon the represented consciousness *as* upon *itself*. It falls at the feet of the *de se* constraint, defeated. (This holds also for the propositional theory of self-knowledge, represented by Tugendhat (1979). A speaker may in cognitively referring to a proposition which contains a proxy or a pronoun for the subject of the main clause not know that such discourse is about him- or herself.)

3  We must thus accept a non-objectual, non-propositional consciousness, which is appropriately labeled pre-reflective consciousness (or pre-reflective knowledge). Williford attributes this conclusion to Zahavi and rejects it as "unanalysable," and "mystical." He writes: "In the context at hand, we have the view of Dan Zahavi, according to which the ubiquitous pre-reflective self-consciousness is an irrelational, *sui generis*, feature at the foundation of all relational forms of self-consciousness" (Williford 2006, p. 115; cf. the citation at p. 111f.) This is in fact an unacknowledged quotation of Frank:

[I]t is necessary to differentiate *prereflective* self-awareness, which is an immediate, implicit, irrelational, non-objecticifying, non-conceptual, and non-propositional self-acquaintance, from *reflective* self-awareness, which is an explicit, relational, mediated, conceptual, and objectifying thematization of consciousness.

(Zahavi 1999, p. 33, referring to Frank 1991b, p. 7)

## Why inner differentiation of "pre-reflective consciousness" doesn't prevent its transparency to the world

Theories of pre-reflectivity—not only those of the Heidelberg School or of Sartre, but also those of Castañeda and his followers—have from the start been attacked not only because of the non-analyzability thesis, but also because of their bare negativity. That is, as the reproach goes, they say what self-consciousness is not—namely, it is not representation and it is not consciousness of an object (or objectual consciousness). Yet they contribute nothing positive regarding the internal structure of self-consciousness.

I do believe that a theory—to use the language of football—does a lot if it consistently keeps the ball on the opponent's side of the field. Indeed, the Heidelberg School didn't put "*pre-reflectivity*" into the game at the start, but only later brought it into the game as *ultima ratio*, after having thoroughly shown that in the case of self-consconsiousness nothing can fundamentally be done with the concept of object-consciousness. It is also the case that Henrich and his disciples worked with a historical depth of focus which is not available to their less cultured opponents. In addition, the diagnosis of pure negativity is not true either for Henrich or for Sartre. Both have paid attention to the internal structure of the allegedly purely non-relational self-consciousness. Henrich speaks of "an inner complexion, an inner manifold" of self-consciousness (Henrich 1986, p. 7). Sartre goes further: self-consciousness negates its own content and is not what it is, but rather it is what it is not. So he introduces a robust difference into the internal structure of consciousness.

It was Henrich himself who, in a paper from 1971, "Selfhood and Consciousness" ("Selbstsein und Bewußtsein," reprinted in Henrich 2007), took up the gauntlet and drew positive consequences from the predominantly negative findings of the previous essay "Self-consciousness: Critical Introduction to Theory" ("Selbstbewußtsein: Kritische Einleitung in eine Theorie") (1970). He has not only summarized the essence of the essay himself in a popular research report from the Ludwig-Maximilians-University of Munich (Henrich 1986, esp. p. 7f.), but also allowed me to summarize his main theses. I have done that in the penultimate chapter of my essay on *Zeitbewußtsein* ("time-consciousness") (Frank 1990).

Henrich proposes a fundamental separation between self-consciousness (which he terms *Bewusstsein*) and self-knowledge (which he terms *Selbstsein*). Self-consciousness should be thought of as an originary dimension of openness or an anonymous "field"; there is no I inhabiting it; no conceptual goings-on taking place there. Current "Philosophy of Mind" would speak of *self-awareness*. Self-knowledge (*Selbstsein*) has—as Kant's "I think"—an I as center; from there conceptual operations arise. A third element enters into the tripartite structure, which is a form component: the non-relational familiarity with oneself which Henrich also determines as a "self-registration mechanism" (Henrich 2007, pp. 12, 17), which our language cannot articulate otherwise than by reflexive phrases.[4] Self-consciousness and self-knowledge share this formal component.

I myself have thought before (following Sartre) that pre-reflective self-consciousness grounded reflective consciousness: "Seul le 'cogito' pré-réflexif fonde les droits du 'cogito' réflexif et de la réflexion" (Sartre 1947, p. 368, fourth thesis). But if we understand by "pre-reflective cogito" something pre-conceptual and under "reflective cogito" something conceptual—which in French ("réfléchir") gives rise to a possible equivocation, since there are two different meanings here: (1) to make our consciousness turn explicitly back upon itself, and (2) to think about things—then this thesis is surely false. I made it clear to myself about ten years ago, when I, under the influence of representationalism, discovered the same equivocation in the expression "Selbstbewusstsein." It can mean either states of what-is-it-likeness (qualitative, non-conceptual and not I-owned awareness; Block speaks of "consciousness without me-ishness": Block 1997, p. 389f.) or states of self-knowledge. Sartre draws this very distinction in the title "Conscience de soi et connaissance de soi". But he holds, as the quote shows, that self-knowledge is an explicitation of non-conceptual (and egoless) self-consciousness. If we take self-consciousness (*Selbstbewusstsein*) and self-knowledge (*Selbstwissen*) as varieties of subjectivity, then I now believe (and I do it with Henrich) the following: These varieties are not specifications of one common genus, although they do share some (or at least one) essential property, namely, the familiarity with oneself (*Selbstvertrautheit*). One should not deal either with self-consciousness or with self-knowledge, as Novalis said once, as "instances of one and the same concept" (Novalis 1977, pp. 328, 35). A somewhat weaker claim lies in the assumption that the latter might be derived from the former. This is what I had believed too for a long time. Thereby I fell into the trap set by the early Husserl and Sartre of wanting to derive the I- or self-knowledge ("connaissance de soi") from "conscience de soi" (Frank 1991a, p. 508, ch XIII, pp. 583ff.). Yet Fichte's reverse enterprise—deriving anonymous and preconceptual intentions and feelings from full-fledged self-knowledge—was similarly misoriented. There is no common generic basis for both varieties. They cooperate with necessity *a posteriori*, like parts of an organism do. The heart and the liver are not instances of one and the same organic "concept," yet the ruin of the one organ will certainly be followed by that of the other. In any case, the talk of a unity of subjectivity requires a theortical model which is yet to be developed.

In addition, Henrich had already, in 1971 (p. 17f.), pointed at the necessity for a theory of consciousness to be able to explain time-consciousness.

For time breaches and articulates (literally dissects) the supposedly jointless unity of consciousness and so gives an additional motivation for an inner structuring of the phenomenon. No theoretician of pre-reflectivity was as well aware of that as Sartre was. Yet doesn't the formula (taken from Hegel's determination of time), that consciousness is what it is not, and is not what it is (Hegel 1970b, vol. II at §258, p. 48; Sartre 1943, III *passim*; Sartre 1947, p. 368, second thesis; p. 387ff.) stand in blatant contradiction to the thesis of a complete subject–object indistinction in pre-reflective (self-)consciousness (Sartre 1947, p. 382)?

While Henrich wants to analyze the reflexive pronouns in our talk about self-knowledge away, Sartre takes their usage seriously, as simply irreducible. The very spirit of the French language directs him there, because the French must translate *Selbstbewusstsein* by a composite expression which is not commonly used, namely "conscience de soi." The reflexive pronoun *soi* points towards an indelible self-relation. In fact, and in spite of its firm unity, pre-reflective consciousness does not simply coincide with itself, in the way that a table is just identical to itself. Sartre has reserved the expression "identity" intentionally for talk about beings *en-soi* (Sartre 1943, p. 33). Self-consciousness, the quintessence of the type of being which Sartre has christened *être pour-soi*, entertains a split unity relation with itself that seems to make the rule "no entity without identity" come to a halt when it comes to consciousness, which is not what it is, but rather relates to itself (Sartre 1947, p. 381f.). It is a *sui generis* "type of being," says Sartre. But how may its structure be precisely characterized? On the one hand, there is no "présence d'un objet pour un sujet"; on the other hand there is the reference (or, rather, relation, Fr. *renvoi*) of something to something (pp. 382, 388). This relation or (self-)reference loosens the connection and allows for the distinction of a material moment from a formal one (Sartre 1943, p. 167, cf. p. 221). The former Sartre names the content, and the latter the act-moment of consciousness. He illustrates this with pleasure ("plaisir": this is the content), which discloses itself only through an awareness of pleasure ("conscience de plaisir")—the same way in which for Kripke and Chalmers pain implies a necessary co-presence of (or rather indistinction from) the *awareness* of pain. But differently from Kripke, Sartre also speaks of a distance to oneself ("distance à soi") (p. 385, second thesis; p. 388), also "absence de soi," "contestation" (p. 387), "interrogation ontologique du plaisir" (p. 385), "un léger décalage" (p. 388, cf. pp. 368, 386), "une esquisse de dualité" (p. 386), a "fissure" (breach) which leads to a loss of density ("décompression d'être") (p. 388f.; p. 394). "Like a maggot in a fruit," it robs the *pour-soi*, as he now calls the subject, of its *en-soi* identity, but it does not destroy its reflexive unity ("unity" is the expression that Sartre uses in the place of *en-soi* identity). To be for oneself implies "une séparation qui est en même temps unité" (p. 387). If I see it correctly, Levine flirts with a similar "trinitary," as he calls it, solution: "Somehow conscious awareness has a differentiable act–object structure but of a sort that involves genuine, not superficial, unity" (Levine 2010, p. 10).

By its capacity to differentiate between *refléter* and *réfléchir*, the French language allows for this intermediate placing of consciousness between identity and difference. Consciousness and its content would be definitely severed first in the dyad *réfléchissant–réfléchi*, i.e., in the case of explicit reflection that Sartre calls self-*knowledge* ("*connaissance* de soi") and which he denies to pre-reflective consciousness. Instead of "réfléchissant–réfléchi," he speaks of an interplay of "reflet–reflétant" (*jeu reflet–reflétant*) (Sartre 1947, 385ff.; Sartre 1943, pp. 118, 128). Why can he believe that this interplay doesn't endanger the pretended subject–object indistinction? Because and only while the (transparent) content, but not the (opaque) object represented by it enter the dyad *reflet–reflétant*: "Car le Pour-soi a l'existence d'une apparence couplée avec un témoin d'un reflet qui renvoie à un reflétant sans qu'il y ait aucun object dont le reflet serait reflet" (Sartre 1943, p. 167; cf. 221). The *reflet–reflétant* is a mirror mirroring itself, but nothing substantial or external to it. This empty (and therefore to its transparency not harmful) dyad is to be distinguished from the relation between an *en-soi* object and its apprehension through knowledge in that content doesn't exist independently from consciousness (pleasure depends on awareness of pleasure), whereas objects exist independently from our knowledge.[5] Definitely, Berkeley's *esse est percipi* does not hold for this latter relation, while it defines the former (375ff; Sartre 1943, pp. 16ff.).

For the same reasons, Sartre can be convinced that this does not contradict thereby his thesis of the transparancy of consciousness. In their interplay, reflex (*reflet*) and reflecting (*reflétant*)[6] remain empty as long as they do not "reflect" back an independently existing world-object. (A reflex neither *is* nor *is not* in a positive sense. Its ontological status is that of the Greek *mè ón* that is not exactly nothing-at-all (Greek *ouk ón*), but rather that which denies its own reality and that the French—in opposition to *rien*—call *néant*. It is that which "borrows" its quasi-existence like a parasite from the being-*en-soi*, to which it is intentionally directed and on which it depends ontologically: Schelling 1856/1861, p. 284; Schelling 1972, p. 385; and Sartre 1943, pp. 51, 65; 28 and 51, 58, 121—about this distinction see Frank 2002, p. 234ff.).)

But how then does one come to the actual complexity of the structure of consciousness, by which consciousness not only virtually but actually enters into a contradiction with itself? Through the encapsulation (*Einlagerung*) of an object, a piece of *en-soi*, that immediately makes the transparency of pre-reflective consciousness murky (opaque). There is, from now on, a real providing of data-supplies in the formerly sterile, solely self-mirroring, dyad that makes that consciousness able to grow. "It is not what it is" reveals itself now as a temporal property: it is *no longer* its past that presents itself as its inviolable *en-soi* identity; and "it is what it is not" in the mode of its *not-yet*—its future.

I cannot and should not go on here. The issue was to answer the question whether the thesis of pre-reflectivity of self-consciousness is compatible with that of its inner complexity. Sartre thought so. With that he sought to appease the grumblers accusing his theory of pure negativity. I have shown elsewhere that along this way one encounters the intuition that was at the origin of Hegel's dialectic: that what prima facie presents itself as simple lack of differentiation, can, in the course of further ongoing progressive conceptual determination be grasped as that what is differentiated in itself—and remains, in so being, in unity with itself (Hegel 1970a, p. 96). In other words, that which seems to lack inner structure opens a space for differentiation into phenomenal consciousness, time-consciousness, and self-knowledge. Still, in all of them, a non-relational dimension of pre-reflectivity persists. But in order to develop this idea further, another effort would be needed.

## Notes

1 Husserl said exactly the same in his lectures on *Internal Time-Consciousness* (Husserl 1966, p. 130, 14f.) and Sartre, quoting him, in his own lecture "Conscience de soi et connaissance de soi" (1947, pp. 63/381, said: "la caractéristique d'une [sic] *Erlebnis,* c'est-à-dire en somme d'une conscience vécue et réfléchie, c'est de se donner comme ayant déjà existé, comme étant déjà là").

2 First by myself in view of Novalis 1969 (reprinted in: Frank 2007, Text 1; and 1972, pp. 22ff., 130ff.), then in two lectures by Henrich himself (1970, 1971), finally by Ulrich Pothast (1971) and Konrad Cramer (1974) within the broader framework of the history of philosophy and with applications to Brentano, Husserl, and Neo-Kantianism.

3 Castañeda was certainly not stingy with such generous but unsubstantiated dedications. He wrote a dedication to me in the anthology of his ontology texts edited by Pape (Castañeda 1982): "To [. . .] Manfred Frank, with admiration for his firm defense of the role of self-consciousness in our lives and in our knowledge of the world." However, later on he substantiated this dedication by making two of my relevant papers available in translation and by commenting on them; his death and the change in the editorial office have prevented their appearance in print (in *Noûs*).

4 Some Indian and Buddhist philosophers have taught that one can reduce reflexive expressions to irreflexive ones (Beeh 2007) and thereby eliminate reflexive relations. If Beeh is correct about the import of this, it poses a challenge for the attempt (in Williford 2006) to model pre-reflective self-consciousness using non-well-founded sets (sets that are in their own membership chains or contain themselves as members). According to Beeh, one can also resolve some logical paradoxes by the elimination of reflexive relations.

5 "C'est qu'il suffit qu'il y ait conscience pour qu'il y ait être, à la différence de la connaissance. Car il ne suffit pas qu'il y ait conaissance pour qu'il y ait être" (Sartre 1947, p. 383).

6 Sartre seems to have borrowed his terms from the beginning of Hegel's *Logic of Reflection* where an interplay of *Schein* and *Widerschein* is being distinguished. Notoriously, Hegel also speaks of the "reflexion-in-itself" ("Reflexion an sich").

# Bibliography

Anscombe, Elizabeth M. (1975). The First Person, pp. 45–65, in S. Guttenplan, Ed., *Mind and Language: Wolfson College Lectures 1974*, Oxford: The Clarendon Press, reprinted in, and cited according to, *Collected Philosophical Papers* II [=*Metaphysics and the Philosophy of Mind*], Oxford: Oxford University Press, 1981, pp. 11–35.

Beeh, Volker (2007). Irreflexivität in Vasubandhus Abhidharma-Koo'sa, unpublished paper.

Block, Ned (1997). On a Confusion about a Function of Consciousness, pp. 377–415, in Ned Block, Owen Flanagan, and Güven Güzeldere, Eds., *The Nature of Consciousness*, Cambridge, MA: MIT Press.

Brentano, Franz (1874). Vom inneren Bewusstsein, pp. 131–160, in Frank (1991b).

Brentano, Franz (1928). Von der inneren Wahrnehmung im engeren und im weiterem Sinne und von den Täuschungsmöglichkeiten, pp. 161–168, in Manfred Frank (1971–1974)) *Psychologie vom empirischen Standpunkt*, Oskar Kraus (Ed.), 3 volumes, Hamburg: Meiner, vol. I 1973 (PhB 192), vol. II 1971 (PhB 193), and vol. III 1974 (PhB 207).

Castañeda, Hector-Neri (1966). "H3." A Study in the Logic of Self-Consciousness. *Ratio* 8, 130–157. Reprinted in Castañeda, Hector-Neri (1999), pp. 35–60.

Castañeda, Hector-Neri (1982). *Sprache und Erfahrung: Texte zu einer neuen Ontologie*, Frankfurt am Main: Suhrkamp.

Castañeda, Hector-Neri (1987). The Self and the I-Guises. Empirical and Transcendental, in: *Theorie der Subjektivität: Festschrift für Dieter Henrich zum 60. Geburtstag*. Frankfurt/Main: Suhrkamp, pp. 105–140. Reprinted in Castañeda, Hector-Neri (1999), pp. 180–203.

Castañeda, Hector-Neri (1999). *The Phenomeno-Logic of the I: Essays on Self-Consciousness*, James G. Hart and Tomis Kapitan, Eds., Bloomington: Indiana University Press.

Chalmers, David J. (1996). *The Conscious Mind: In Search of a Fundamental Theory*, New York: Oxford University Press.

Chisholm, Roderick (1981). *The First Person: An Essay on Reference and Intentionality*, Brighton: The Harvester Press.

Cramer, Konrad (1974). "Erlebnis." Thesen zu Hegels Theorie des Selbstbewußtseins mit Rücksicht auf die Aporien eines Grundbegriffs nachhegelscher Philosophie, pp. 537–603, in Hans-Georg Gadamer, Ed., *Stuttgarter Hegel-Tage 1970*, Bonn: Bouvier.

Fichte, Johann Gottlieb (1797). Versuch einer neuen Darstellung der Wissenschaftslehre, pp. 14–25, in Frank (1991b).

Fichte, Johann Gottlieb (1798). Auszug aus: *Wissenschaftslehre nova methodo*, pp. 9–13, in Frank (1991b).

Frank, Manfred (1972). *Das Problem "Zeit" in der deutschen Romantik: Zeitbewußtsein und Bewußtsein von Zeitlichkeit in der frühromantischen Philosophie und in Tiecks Dichtung*, Munich: Winkler.

Frank, Manfred (1990). *Zeitbewußtsein*, Pfullingen: Neske (Opuscula, Bd. 50).

Frank, Manfred (1991a, Ed.). *Selbstbewußtseinstheorien von Fichte bis Sartre*, Frankfurt a. M.: Suhrkamp (stw 964). From the same publisher: *Fragmente einer Geschichte der Selbstbewußtseins – Theorie von Kant bis Sartre*, l. c., pp. 413–599.

Frank, Manfred (1991b). *Selbstbewußtsein und Selbsterkenntnis: Essays zur analytischen Philosophie des Selbstbewußtseins*, Stuttgart: Reclam.

Frank, Manfred (1994, Ed.). *Analytische Theorien des Selbstbewußtseins,* Frankfurt a. M.: Suhrkamp (stw 1151).
Frank, Manfred (2002). *Selbstgefühl: Eine historisch-systematische Erkundung,* Frankfurt a. M.: Suhrkamp (stw 1611).
Frank, Manfred (2007). *Auswege aus dem deutschen Idealismus,* Frankfurt a. M.: Suhrkamp (stw 1851).
Hegel, Georg Friedrich Wilhelm (1970a). *Jenaer Schriften 1801–1807,* Theorie-Werkausgabe, Frankfurt a. M.: Suhrkamp.
Hegel, Georg Friedrich Wilhelm (1970b). *Enzyklopädie der philosophischen Wissenschaften,* Theorie-Werkausgabe, Frankfurt a. M.: Suhrkamp (3 vols.).
Henrich, Dieter (1967). *Fichtes ursprüngliche Einsicht,* Frankfurt a. M.: Klostermann (firstly, in *Subjektivität und Metaphysik.* Festschrift für Wolfgang Cramer, Eds., Dieter Henrich and Hans Wagner, Frankfurt a. M..: Klostermann (1966), pp. 188–233; appears in English as: — (1982). *Fichte's Original Insight,* in Darrel E. Christensen, Ed., *Contemporary German Philosophy,* Vol. 1, University Park, PA: The Pennsylvania State University Press, 1982, pp. 15–53).
Henrich, Dieter (1970). Selbstbewußtsein: Kritische Einleitung in eine Theorie, pp. 257–284, in Rüdiger Bubner, Konrad Cramer, and Rainer Wiehl, Eds., *Hermeneutik und Dialektik,* Tübingen: Mohr, vol. 1; appears in English as —(1971). Self-Consciousness: A Critical Introduction to a Theory, pp. 3–28, in *Man and World* IV.
Henrich, Dieter (1971). Selbstsein und Bewußtsein, unpublished essay (thereafter since made available with a new introduction. E-journal *Philosophie der Psychologie,* 2007, pp. 1–19 (available at: http://www.jp.philo.at/texte/HenrichD1.pdf).
Henrich, Dieter (1979). Zwei Theorien zur Verteidigung von Selbstbewußtsein. *Grazer Philosophische Studien,* VII: 77–99.
Henrich, Dieter (1982). Fichtes Ich, pp. 57–82, in *Selbstverhältnisse. Gedanken und Auslegungen zu den Grundlagen der klassischen deutschen Philosophie,* Stuttgart: Reclam (first published in French as: La découverte de Fichte. *Revue de métaphysique et de morale* (1967), 154–169).
Henrich, Dieter (1986). Selbstbewußtsein: ein Problemfeld mit offenen Grenzen, pp. 2–8, in Ludwig-Maximilians-Universität München Ed., *Berichte aus der Forschung,* 68.
Henrich, Dieter (2007). *Philosophie der Psychologie,* 1–19. Available online at: http://www.jp.philo.at/texte/HenrichD1.pdf.
Hölderlin, Friedrich (1795/1796). Urtheil und Seyn, in Frank (2002, p. 26). Horgan, Terence and Uriah Kriegel (2007). Phenomenal Epistemology: What is Consciousness That We May Know It So Well? *Philosophical Issues* 17, pp. 123–144.
Horgan, Terence and John Tienson (2002). The Intentionality of Phenomenology and the Phenomenology of Intentionality, pp. 520–531, in David Chalmers, Ed., *Philosophy of Mind,* Oxford: Oxford University Press.
Husserl, Edmund (1966). *Zur Phänomenologie des inneren Zeitbewußtseins (1993–1917).* Ed., Rudolf Boehm (= Husserliana Bd. X), The Hague; Martinus Nijhoff.
Husserl, Edmund (1980). *Logische Untersuchungen,* 2 vols, in 3 books, Tübingen: Max Niemeyer (= Unveränderter Nachdruck der 2., umgearbeiteten Auflage von 1913 [unaltered reproduction of the second, reworked edition of 1913]).
Husserl, Edmund (2001). *Die Bernauer Manuskripte über das Zeitbewußtsein (1917/18).* Eds., Rudolf Berner und Dieter Lohmar (= Husserliana Bd. XXXIII), The Hague: Martinus Nijhoff.

Kriegel, Uriah (2006). The Same-Order Monitoring Theory of Consciousness, pp. 143–170, in Kriegel and Williford (2006).
Kriegel, Uriah (2009). *Subjective Consciousness: A Self-Representational Theory*, Oxford: Oxford University Press.
Kriegel, Uriah and Kenneth Williford (Eds.) (2006). *Self-Representational Approaches to Consciousness*, Cambridge, MA: MIT Press.
Kripke, Saul (1980). *Naming and Necessity*, 2nd ed., Cambridge, MA: Harvard University Press
Levine, Joseph (2006). Conscious Awareness and Self-Representation, pp. 173–197, in Uriah Kriegel and Kenneth Williford, Eds., *Self-Representational Approaches to Consciousness*. Cambridge, MA: The MIT Press.
Levine, Joseph (2010). Review of Kriegel (2009). *Philosophical Reviews*, University of Notre Dame: pp. 1–11 (available at: http://ndpr.nd.edu/review.cfm?id=19227).
Lewis, David (1983). Attitudes *De Dicto* and *De Se*, pp. 156–159, in *Philosophical Papers*. Vol. I, New York: Oxford University Press.
Mach, Ernst (1886). *Beiträge zur Analyse der Empfindungen*, Jena: Gustav Fischer. (The 2nd [1900] and 3rd [1903] expanded editions bear the variant title, *Die Analyse der Empfindungen und das Verhältnis des Physischen zum Psychischen* 1903; more recently published in 2006 by VDM Verlag Dr. Müller).
Novalis (=Friedrich von Hardenberg) (1965 and 1968). *Schriften*. Zweiter und Dritter Band. Richard Samuel, Hans-Joachim Mähl and Gerhard Schulz, Eds., *Das philosophische Werk I und II*, Stuttgart: Kohlhammer.
Novalis (=Friedrich von Hardenberg) (1977). *Schriften*. I. Band: Das dichterische Werk, Paul Kluckhohn, Richard Samuel, and Gerhard Schulz, Eds., 2nd ed., Stuttgart: Kohlhammer.
Pothast, Ulrich (1971). *Über einige Fragen der Selbstbeziehung*, Frankfurt: Klostermann — (1987). Etwas über, Bewußtsein, pp. 15–43, in Konrad Cramer, H.F. Fulda, and R.P. Horstmann (Eds.), *Theorie der Subjektivität*, Frankfurt a. M.: Suhrkamp.
Pothast, Ulrich (1988). *Philosophisches Buch: Schrift unter der aus der Entfernung leitenden Frage, was es heißt, auf menschliche Weise lebendig zu sein*, Frankfurt a. M.: Suhrkamp.
Pothast, Ulrich (1998). *Lebendige Vernünftigkeit. Zur Vorbereitung eines menschenangemessenen Konzepts*, Frankfurt a. M.: Suhrkamp.
Rosenthal, David M. (1991). Two Concepts of Consciousness, pp. 462–477, in Rosenthal, David M. (Ed.), *The Nature of Mind*, Oxford: Oxford University Press.
Rosenthal, David M. (1993a). Higher-Order Thoughts and the Appendage Theory of Consciousness, *Philosophical Psychology*, pp. 155–166.
Rosenthal, David M. (1993b). Thinking That One Thinks, pp. 197–223, in Mertin Davies and Glyn W. Humphreys, Eds., *Consciousness: Psychological and Philosophical Essays*, Oxford: Blackwell.
Rosenthal, David M. (1997). A Theory of Consciousness, pp. 729–753, in N. Block, O. Flanagan, and G. Güzeldere (Eds.), *The Nature of Consciousness: Philosophical Debates*, Cambridge, MA: MIT Press.
Sartre, Jean-Paul (1943). *L'être et le néant: Essai d'ontologie phénoménologique*, Paris: Gallimard.
Sartre, Jean-Paul (1947). Conscience de soi et connaissance de soi. Lecture given on June 2, 1947, at the *Société française de philosophie*, in Frank (1991b): pp. 367–411 (first published (1948). *Bulletin de la Société Française Philosophie*, vol. 42, pp. 49–91. (In this article, the first page reference is to the first edition [1948], the second to the reprint [1991].)

Sartre, Jean-Paul (1978). *La Transcendance de l'Ego: Esquisse d'une description hénonménologique.* Introduction, notes et appendices par Sylvie Le Bon, Paris: Vrin. (First published 1936–1937, *Recherches philosophiques,* no. 6, pp. 85–123.)

Schelling, Friedrich Wilhelm Joseph (1856–1864, cited as: *SW*), in F. A. Schelling (Ed.), *Sämmtliche Werke,* 1st Partition [Abteilung] Vols. 1–10; 2nd Partition Vols. 1–4; Stuttgart: Cotta 1856–1864 (in citations, the numbers after the sigil *SW* refer to partition (Roman numerals), volume, and page (Arabic numerals), for example, I/6, 195).

Schelling, Friedrich Wilhelm Joseph (1972). *Grundlegung der positiven Philosophie,* Horst Fuhrmans, Ed., Münchner Vorlesung WS 1832/33 and SS 1833, Turin, Italy: Bottega d'Erasmo.

Schelling, Friedrich Wilhelm Joseph (1856–1861). *Sämmtliche Werke,* Ed., K. F. A. Schelling, Stuttgart: Cotta.

Searle, John R. (1992). *The Redisvovery of the Mind,* Cambridge, MA: MIT Press.

Seel, Gerhard (1971). *Sartres Dialektik: Zur Methode und Begründung seiner Philosophie unter besonderer Berücksichtigung der Subjekts-, Zeit- und Werttheorie,* Bonn: Bouvier.

Seel, Gerhard (2005). Wie ist Bewusstsein von Zeitlichem möglich? pp. 169–210, in Thomas Grundmann, Frank Hofmann, Catrin Misselhorb, Violetta L. Waibel, and Véronique Zanetti, Eds., Frankfurt am Main: Suhrkamp (= stw 1735), pp. 169–210.

Seel, Gerhard (2010). Husserls Problem mit dem Zeitbewusstsein und warum er es nicht löste, pp. 43–88, in Manfred Frank and Niels Weidtmann, Eds., *Husserl und die Philosophie des Geistes,* Frankfurt a. M.: Suhrkamp (stw 1980).

Shoemaker, Sydney (1968). Self-Reference and Self-Awareness. *The Journal of Philosophy,* 65, 19: 555–567; reprinted in Shoemaker, Sydney (1968). *Identity, Cause, and Mind: Philosophical Essays,* London: Cambridge University Press, pp. 6–18.

Shoemaker, Sydney (1984a). *Identity, Cause, and Mind: Philosophical Essays,* Cambridge: Cambridge University Press.

Shoemaker, Sydney (1984b). A Materialist's Account, pp. 67–132, in Sydney Shoemaker and Richard Swinburne (Eds.), *Personal Identity,* Reihe: Great Debates on Philosophy, Oxford: Blackwell.

Shoemaker, Sydney (1996). *The First-Person Perspective and Other Essays,* Cambridge: Cambridge University Press.

Shoemaker, Sydney and Richard Swinburne (1984). *Personal Identity,* Reihe: Great Debates on Philosophy, Oxford: Blackwell.

Tugendhat, Ernst (1979). *Selbstbewusstsein und Selbstbestimmung: Sprachanalytische Interpretationen,* Frankfurt a. M.: Suhrkamp (stw 221). (English translation: *Traditional and Analytical Philosophy: Lectures on the Philosophy of Language,* Cambridge: Cambridge University Press, 2010.)

Tye, Michael (2002). Representationalism and the Transparency of Experience. *Noûs,* vol. XXXVI, no. 1, pp. 137–151.

Williford, Kenneth (2006). The Self-Representational Structure of Consciousness, pp. 111–142, in Kriegel and Williford (2006).

Zahavi, Dan (1999). *Self-Awareness and Alterity: A Phenomenological Investigation,* Evanston, IL: Northwestern University Press.

# 2 Is subjectivity first-personal?

*Tomis Kapitan*

## Introduction

In the *Transcendence of the Ego*, Sartre distinguished reflective from non-reflective thinking and argued that the *I* and the *me* exist only in episodes of reflective thinking:

> there is no *I* on the unreflected level. When I run after a streetcar, when I look at the time, when I am absorbed in contemplating a portrait, there is no *I*. There is consciousness *of the streetcar-having-to-be-overtaken,* etc., and non-positional consciousness of consciousness. . . . but *me*, I have disappeared; I have annihilated myself. There is no place for *me* on this level.
>
> (Sartre 1957/1936, pp. 48–49)

There is an undeniably important datum here, for frequently, when absorbed in tasks that require intense concentration, we seem to harbor no *I* or *me* thoughts. Instead, as Sartre maintained, the *I* arises in consciousness only when a definite object, an *ego*, is reflectively posited or identified. Equally significant is Sartre's contention that every conscious state is non-positionally and non-reflectively directed upon itself. In *Being and Nothingness* (Sartre 1956/1943) he described consciousness as being *for-itself* (*pour-soi*) rather than merely *in-itself* (*en-soi*), and spoke of consciousness of consciousness as a form of pre-reflective or primitive self-consciousness.

A question immediately arises: if the *I* is confined to reflective thinking and not every conscious act involves first-person content, then in what sense is pre-reflective consciousness of consciousness a form of *self*-consciousness? An easy answer is that the term "self" is ambiguous between an egological meaning equivalent to first-person pronouns such as "I," "me," or "myself," and a purely reflexive meaning, expressing a status of whatever falls within a domain of a reflexive relation, as when we say that John accidentally locked himself in the room, that a vehicle is self-propelled, or that a number is equal to itself. Non-reflective, pre-reflective, or primitive self-consciousness, while reflexive and ubiquitous, is not egological. Instead, "self" here contributes no more than the pure reflexivity of "*x* is conscious of *x*," a formula that abstracts entirely from the character of *x*.

Unfortunately, this answer is inadequate. Pure reflexivity does not offer enough for understanding primitive self-consciousness either. Seeing oneself in the mirror is also a reflexive awareness, and, as illustrated by the famous example of Ernst Mach in the tram, it need not be first-personal. Such objectual consciousness of a human body, or an image thereof, even if it happens to be one's own, is no different from a sensory awareness of others. The latter is *external*, unlike the seemingly *internal* awareness of introspection, proprioception, and interoception. Catching a glimpse of oneself in a mirror, while reflexive, is not an instance of inner awareness characteristic of self-consciousness.

Sartre was sensitive to this problem. The pre-reflective self-consciousness he had in mind is not the kind of reflexive relation that numbers or manufactured vehicles might stand in, nor is it manifested in visual images. It is awareness of, and *only* of, what exhibits the for-itself (*pour-soi*) feature of intentional consciousness. For this reason, a richer characterization of its content is called for than what the mere reflexivity of "*x* is conscious of *x*" reveals, yet content that is independent of our conceptual activities. Sartre suggested that "we need not conclude that the *for-itself* is a pure and simple 'impersonal' contemplation," but, instead, is a consciousness of consciousness "in its fundamental *ipseity*" (Sartre 1956/1943, p. 103).

One might wonder whether anything is achieved by this language, since the Latin *ipse* exhibits the same ambiguity as the English "self." Yet, some commentators understand Sartre's "ipseity" to stand for what falls between bare reflexive awareness and first-person conceptualization, e.g., Dan Zahavi, who describes ipseity to be the quality of *mineness* or *first-personal giveness* and equates it with the *subjectivity of experience*. Subjectivity not only characterizes every experience, it is given *in* every experience, though, as Sartre emphasized, not as an *object* that we posit, identify, or refer to (Zahavi 2005, pp. 119–127). Others have expressed similar views, e.g., Flanagan (1992), Frank (1995), Bermudez (1998), Damasio (1999), and, more recently, Kriegel (2009), Gallagher (2012), and Grunbaum (2012).

> All the experiences are characterized by a quality of *mineness* or *for-me-ness*, the fact that it is *I* who am having these experiences. All the experiences are given (at least tacitly) as *my* experiences, as experiences *I* am undergoing or living through. All of this suggests that first-person experience presents me with an immediate and non-observational access to myself, and that consequently (phenomenal) consciousness consequently entails a (minimal) form of self-consciousness.
>
> (Gallagher and Zahavi 2010)

If this is correct, then a first-person element lingers, even though it falls short of the reflected-upon "object" expressed by "I" or "me," and Sartre's wholesale exclusion of the first-person from pre-reflective consciousness must be questioned (Zahavi 2005, p. 127).

In what follows I will resist this description of ipseity or subjectivity. I will not attempt an interpretation of what Sartre actually said about self-consciousness, still less a defense of his overall theory of consciousness. Instead, while agreeing that there is a ubiquitous primitive self-consciousness, I am suspicious that it is first-personal. As I understand them, first-person possessives like "my" and "mine" are mechanisms for representing what stands in unique physical, social, and normative relationships to oneself, since to view something as *mine* derives from a sense of how an item stands with respect to *me* (Evans 1982, ch. 7). Thus, "mine" is equivalent to "belongs to me," and, if so, then the concepts of *mineness* and *for-me-ness* are no more fundamental than those of *I* (*I-ness*) or *me* (*me-ness*). Insofar as Sartre was correct to confine the latter to reflective consciousness, then the same should be true of the former. I will motivate this conclusion by (i) arguing that the first-person, like all indexical phenomena, is essentially dependent upon our conceptualization, and (ii) offering a non-indexical account of the content of primitive self-consciousness.

## Modes of consciousness

Some preliminary distinctions are needed. The terms "conscious" and "consciousness" have many different senses, but I use them broadly to designate any type of awareness. We may be *directly* aware of content, say, of a certain bell-like sound, or *indirectly* aware, e.g., of the bell one thinks caused the sound. In every episode of consciousness there is always something of which we are directly aware, and insofar as it is also *about* content of which we are not immediately aware, it must be mediated by that of which we are.

The Sartrean division of reflective and unreflective consciousness is a contrast between *conceptual* and *non-conceptual* awareness of something with respect to a particular classification. For example, an infant might be aware of a pain, a round object, or its mother without having a concept of *pain, roundness,* or *mother,* and perhaps a dog can be aware of its owner or the sun without concepts of *ownership* or *the sun.* I have a conceptual awareness of this watch as a watch, though not, say, as something manufactured in Switzerland, but insofar as I am aware of it then I am aware of something manufactured in Switzerland. No doubt some sentient beings are aware of things they never conceptualize in any manner, e.g., their own heart beat, the force of gravity, or life. Since conceptualization typically follows upon felt contrasts and absences, we commonly fail to rise to the level of abstraction required for contrasting pervasive elements of experience.

There are also different degrees or levels of consciousness. One form of conceptual consciousness is *identifying* an item in order to predicate something of it, as when I refer to a person in saying "that man is coming over here." Identification requires distinguishing something through a unique mode of presentation and is perhaps the clearest example of what Sartre meant by *positional* consciousness. Identification of *x* is *direct* only if *x* is an item of direct awareness, otherwise it is indirect or *deferred*. Conceptual awareness extends beyond identification or reference; if I point to a dot on a map and think, *that's Paris*, then, while I refer to the city, the dot is also salient in my awareness, even though it is not the referent of "that." Watching a television interview with François Hollande, I notice that his tie is blue and think that he is French. I am aware of the color property *being blue* and of the sortal *being French* even though I do not attend to these properties as subjects of predication. They are both conceptualized and *salient*, but I am not referring to them via singular terms or thinking anything *about* them.

Something might be present in experience but not salient. As I read this chapter I am conscious of the individual words and the individual letters comprising those words. I am also aware of the shapes of the upper halves of each of the letters even though these shapes are not salient. I hear background noises as I compose this chapter, say, the sound of a fan, and I am aware of the chair I sit on, but, prior to thinking about that noise and that chair, I was not noticing them at all. I was *marginally* or *implicitly* aware of such items even though they were not salient to my consciousness. Consciousness is, thereby, stratified with respect to degrees of attentiveness. At one extreme is identificatory and referential consciousness, while at the other is marginal awareness folding into undifferentiated perception. Yet every conscious episode involves an integration of several stimuli into one unitary content. For example, in hearing the word "aluminum," the perceptions of individual phonemes are united into one auditory awareness of a word. The visual and tactile experiences of an aluminum pot blend together the activation of vast numbers of exteroceptors and the information they deliver. The single thought that *aluminum is a metal* results from a combination of conceptualizations.

## Indexical thought

Language is as much a means of thinking as it is communicating about the world, and indexical expressions are equally the vehicles of both, especially when purely qualitative discriminations are cumbersome or unavailable. We think indexically whenever we single out items as *this, that, these,* locate objects and events by means of *here, there, then, beyond,* and direct our thoughts upon people through *you, he, she, them,* etc. We identify objects and events in terms of complex demonstratives, e.g., *those apples, that book, this hideous war,* and we predicate indexically with phrases like *far away, in this direction,* and *over there*.

It is widely understood that indexical expressions do their work only through an interplay of their meanings and the contexts of utterance within which they occur. For example, given the meanings of the types "you" and "now," the referent of a "you" token designates the one addressed through its utterance, while a "now" token refers to an interval that includes the time of the utterance. This *utterance-reflexivity* of indexicals (Perry 1997, p. 597, and 2001, pp. 40–44) is as central to communication as it to the determination of truth conditions. For example, if you tell me,

(1)   I'll bring you a beer if you remain sitting there.

it is not enough that I grasp the meanings of the component expressions. I understand what you are saying only because I know who uttered the sentence, when and where it was uttered, and, perhaps, something about the utterer's gestures and bodily orientation. I work *from* my grasp of the meanings of your "I," "you," and "there," and my perception of relevant contextual parameters *to* the determination of your referents using, for example, the familiar semantic rule that a token of "I" refers to the producer of that token. You realize, in turn, that I am guided by such a rule. In this way, the mode of presentation—*being the speaker of (1)*—that guides my interpretation is itself utterance-reflexive, since to identify by its means I must grasp facts about your utterance, specifically, who its producer is.

While qualifications are needed to handle cases like that of answering-machine messages using indexicals (Kapitan 2006, p. 385), the general procedure for interpreting indexical tokens is this: (i) one perceives an utterance that mobilizes the meanings of the perceived indexical tokens; (ii) these meanings guide one's determination of relevant contextual information; and, thereby, (iii) one exploits that information in determining the values of, or what is expressed by, the tokens in question.

Indexical thinking is not confined to interpretation. We can identify in terms of *this* and *that*, *it* and *there*, have *now or never* sentiments, or regret what we did *yesterday* without saying or hearing anything at all. Utterances must be produced before they can be interpreted, and the thoughts that produced them are not exhausted by intentions to communicate, but also the antecedent conceptualizations from which these intentions derive. The meanings of "I," "you," and "there" in your uttering (1) might have been as instrumental in your picking out particular persons and a place as they were in mine. But you did not arrive at these identifications by doing what I did, that is, you did not first perceive your own tokens and then interpret them by recourse to the context of their utterance. These tokens were *inputs* of my interpretive process, but *outputs* of your executive process of indexical conceptualization. You did not identify through the utterance reflexive modes of *being a speaker* or *being an addressee*, nor did you begin with a thought that I am likely to have ended up with, e.g., one better expressed by,

(2)   He'll bring me a beer if I remain sitting here.

So, my identifying something by *interpreting* your utterance differs—in terms of cognitive procedure—from the executive thinking that caused you to produce that utterance.[1]

If both executive and interpretive thought processes are guided by indexical meaning, then there is a difference in the meanings associated with one and the same indexical type. To illustrate, suppose you listen to an audio tape you know was recorded on April 10, 2014, hear a voice saying, "It is raining today," and identify the day referred to by employing the rule:

*Take the referent of a "today" token to be the day on which its utterance is encoded.*

In so doing, you do not identify April 10, 2014 as *today* in the manner the speaker did, and, unlike you, the speaker did not pick out a duration as the day in which a particular "today" token occurred. If so, then for a given utterance U, the mode,

*being the day on which utterance U of "today" occurred*

that guides interpretation is not even similar to the concept, *being today*, that guides executive identification. I cannot think of a given day as being the day on which a certain utterance occurred without being aware of that utterance, but I can think, *What lousy luck we're having today*, without considering any utterance whatever. If the meaning that governed the production of a "today" token were identical to that guiding its interpretation, these differences could not be explained. Consequently, executive and interpretive meanings differ and *semantic duality* is a distinguishing mark of indexical expressions.[2]

Executive indexical thinking is also context-sensitive given its dependence upon the spatio-temporal standpoints or *perspectives* of thinkers. It is not perspectival because it occurs *from* a particular spatial or temporal standpoint(s)—all thought occurs from the thinker's unique standpoint—but because relations to this standpoint are constitutive of the way content is conceptualized.[3]

For example, if I utter,

(3)    You should take your umbrella; it may rain here today.

in addressing Jane in London in the afternoon of July 24, 2015, my words reveal my relations to a particular person, time, and place. I must be *in* London, *addressing* Jane, *on* July 24, 2015 and because of this I can think of Jane as *you*, of London as *here*, and July 24, 2015 as *today*. For this reason, too, my words are autobiographical, though biographical for my listeners. The same is not true of my utterance of,

(4)    Jane should take her umbrella; it may rain in London on July 24, 2015.

or,

(5)   She should take her umbrella; it may rain here then.

even though, in both cases, I might be identifying the very same person, place, and time.

Perspectival identification operates upon a spatial and/or a temporal array of content or *data* (objects, events, qualities, etc.) of which one is directly aware to varying degrees. Different modalities of consciousness, auditory, visual, tactile, imaginary, dreamlike, memory, proprioceptive, and so on, are associated with diverse arrays of data even when contemporaneous. For example, the spatial and temporal ordering of sounds one hears during a certain interval is an auditory array that might be simultaneous with a visual array of colored shapes. The data are ordered in terms of their spatial, temporal, or spatio-temporal *positions*, each of which is a particular volume, duration, or pair of such, of arbitrary extent, fixed by a distance, direction, and size of an immediate datum relative to a point of origin or, following Hintikka (1998, p. 208), a *locus*. The ordering of these data constitutes the *perspective* of that array, and the locus itself falls *within* the perspectival array.[4]

Given that the perspectival arrays of different modalities can be co-present within an interval of awareness, then distinct contemporaneous perspectives can be integrated into more comprehensive unities. Such integration is critical for behavior that relies upon cues from one or more sensory modality, so that an agent might rely on the fact that a visual *there*, say, converges with a tactile *there*. The maximally integrated perspective during any interval is the totality of immediate data co-presented in a single episode of awareness. How comprehensive it is depends on the extent of a subject's co-awarenesses through distinct modalities, but, on the content side, the unity of consciousness is a matter of membership in a single perspectival array. This maximal array *constitutes* an episode of consciousness, and, thus, while the episode is centered upon the zero point, its being extends throughout the array.

Each datum in an array is distinguished in terms of the position it occupies.[5] Sometimes, it is spatial position alone that distinguishes the items identified, as reflected by the use of "you" in,

(6)   You, you, you, and you can leave, but you stay!

or the demonstrative phrases in,

(7)   That ship [hearing a horn] is this ship [pointing through a window].

Sometimes, temporal factors play a more prominent role, as in anaphoric reference expressed through "the former," "the latter," "the previous one," or, when through a single window a person thinks the non-trivial,

(8)   This ship [observing the bow go by] is this ship [observing the stern go past].

Because an episode of consciousness is an event, and events are dynamic, it is more accurate to describe each datum as a *vector* because it involves transference of content *from* a position in an array *to* locus, more noticeable in auditory perception than in visual (Whitehead 1978/1929, pp. 55, 237–239). With (7), for instance, an auditory vector enables the initial demonstrative identification of a particular ship while a visual vector enables the latter.

These data vectors do not exist in isolation. Absorbed in a piano performance, none of the immediate data—the key here, this chord just played, that phrase soon to come—exists alone in the pianist's awareness. Each vector content is felt as embedded in a larger whole centered around a point of view, for there could be no noticed position unless there were at least one other position to contrast it with, and this is determined by an ordering of immediate data, viz., the perspective. There is no *over there* without what would qualify as a *here* or a different *there*, no *then* without a potential *now* or another *then*.

More formally, where $o$ is a position (spatial-temporal locale) occupied by an agent $Y$, and $m$ is a modality of consciousness (visual, auditory, etc.), then the triple $(o, Y, m)$ determines a perspectival array for $Y$ at $o$. The position $o$, the locus of the array, consists of either a pair $(t, v)$, that is, a time (duration) $t$ and a place (volume) $v$, or, when the agent and datum are in motion relative to each other, an ordering of such pairs $<(t,v), (t´,v´), \ldots>$. Letting $p$ be a schema for a representation of any locale within the array, then each datum $d(p)$ within the array $(o, Y, m)$ may be described as *d as located at p*, viz., *d-at-p*, or, to secure its vector character, *d-from-p*. (Note that the substituends of the $(o, Y, m)$ are third-person depictions of $Y$'s array at $o$, and should not be taken to represent $Y$'s conceptualization of that array.)[6]

Whenever a thinker $Y$ demonstratively identifies an item $X$ within an episode of consciousness whose array is $(o, Y, m)$, three factors are paramount:

(i)   an executive indexical concept $k$;
(ii)  a datum $d(p)$ within that array; and
(iii) a relation $R$ linking $X$ to $d(p)$.

For example, suppose I gaze at a dot on a map and think,

(9)   That city is north of Prague.

I am identifying a particular city, say, Berlin, but I am directly aware of the dot $d$ at position $p$, or, the vector image of that dot, $d(p)$. The latter is the *index* of my executive act, namely, an item of immediate awareness that I explicitly "latch on to" in the course of picking something out (Anscombe 1975, p. 92).[7] The relevant relation—the *orienting* relation—is that of representation, the executive concept is *being that city*, and the mode of presentation is a relational property, *being that city represented by d(p)*. Generalizing, whenever demonstrative identification of $X$ is deferred, $X$ is picked out by means of a relational property *R[d(p)]* that is fixed by an orienting relation

*Is subjectivity first-personal?* 57

*R* linking *X* to *d(p)* and a mode of presentation *k(R[d(p)])*. If the identification is direct, the orienting relation *R* is identity and the relevant mode can be represented equally well by *k([d(p)])*.

A few more examples further illustrate the pattern of analysis. Consider my use of the second-person pronoun in uttering:

(3)   You should take your umbrella; it may rain here today.

while talking on the phone to Jane. If the index is the sound of a voice coming from the phone's receiver at point *p*, viz. [sound at *p*], and the orienting relation is the property of *producing* the sound at *p*, and I employ the executive *you* concept, then my second-person individuating mode is,

*you* (producing [sound at *p*])

If, in speaking to Jane, I formed the thought:

(10)   She should take her umbrella; it may rain there tomorrow.

the identifying mode is,

*She* (producing [sound at *p*]).

Alternatively, if (3) reflects a *direct* second-person identification, say, if I am looking at Jane while addressing her so that Jane herself—from the position she occupies in my visual array—is the index, then my identifying mode would fit this schema:

*you* ([Jane at *p*])

The indexicals "now" and "here" require some adjustment. While they sometimes indicate the two parameters of a locus, they can also be used to demonstrate other locales. Where the locus of an array is $(t,v)$, "now" might identify a region that includes *t* as a proper part, or even a sub-interval of *t*. A demonstrative use of "here" occurs in (3), picking out a place that includes the locale of the locus. The mode of presentation is, perhaps,

*here* (being a city that includes [*v*])

while the mode associated with "today" might be

*today* (being a day that includes [*t*])

Similarly, the correlated mode of my "tomorrow" in (10) is

*tomorrow* (being the day immediately succeeding the day that includes [*t*])

If we balk at accepting volumes or durations in themselves as immediate data and insist that an additional qualitative element $d$ be included, say, a colored expanse, a sound, or an emotion, then the immediate data associated with my "today" can be depicted as $d(t)$, and the corresponding mode is,

*today* (being a day that includes $[d(t)]$).

Similar adjustments can be made for "here" and "tomorrow." These examples show how executive indexical identifications occur in virtue of an item's relation to a perspectival array, even though that array is not itself distinguished or conceptualized within that thought.

Three consequences of this account of executive indexical thought are worth noting. First, while indexical thinking is a matter of conceptualizing what is perspectivally presented, an act of conceptualizing does not itself create the perspectival array or its component data-vectors. The latter are *given* in an episode of consciousness, be it an auditory perception, visual imagination, olfactory memory, etc. Identifying is something we *do* in reaction to what is given (Levine 2010), and it is through such conceptualization that an item acquires an indexical status. There is no indexical conceptualization without perspective, but there can be perspective without indexicality.

Second, nothing is intrinsically a *you*, a *this*, a *here*, etc., since satisfying an indexical mode is invariably a property possessed only in relation to a thinker who distinguishes it as such. Unless someone addresses you, you do not have the status of *being you*. A sound is not a *this* unless noticed as such, a person is a not a *she* save through demonstrative identification, and a square kilometer of the Empty Quarter can exist without ever being *here*. An item acquires an indexical status only by satisfying an executive mode of presentation and, hence, only in relation to a thinker, more specifically, to a conceptualizing act. Indexical status is thereby relational rather than intrinsic, relative rather than absolute, ephemeral rather than permanent, and contingent rather than essential. Its *esse* is *percipi* (Castañeda 1989, pp. 69–71).

Third, each indexical concept imposes constraints upon what can be singled out by its means, e.g., only events or intervals can be *then*, and only a man can be a *that man*. Without observing these constraints, the concepts could not be applied to yield identifying modes. Constraints are vague for deictic uses of the pronouns like *he, she,* or *it* and the demonstratives *that, those, beyond,* etc. Perhaps nothing more than location distinct from the point of origin is imposed, though once *this/that, these/those,* and *here/then* are introduced then relative proximity is also a factor. Similarly, in non-demonstrative uses of *here and now*, what is identified is located at the locus of the perspective, while *I* carries (at least) the constraints that the identified is a conscious being identical to the identifier. The indexical *you*, on the other hand, restricts the temporal location of the identified item to times that are simultaneous with or subsequent to the identifier's temporal locus because what is picked out through *you* must be something that the user believes is susceptible to communicational influence. Thus, despite an executor's leeway as to which indexical concepts to use, once choices are made, anarchy is not the rule.

## The first person

First-person status is like that of any other indexical status. Just as nothing is intrinsically a *this* or a *you*, so too, nothing is intrinsically an *I*, and insofar as being a *self* is nothing more than to be identified qua a first-person concept, then there are no intrinsic or natural "selves." The *self*, just as much as the *I*, lives only within episodes of self-consciousness (Sartre 1957/1936, p. 45; Castañeda 1999, pp. 242, 270; Dreyfus 2007, p. 373).

To put this view on a firmer footing we need an account of first-person modes of presentation. Besides the first-person concept we must identify a datum that can qualify as an index and an orienting relation linking this index to what is identified, that is, to the *I* that is picked out. A content of exteroception, say a sensory content, will not suffice. Instead, the index must be sought in the inner awareness I have of myself and that no one else can share. I view the organism that I am "from the inside," through introspection, proprioception, or visceral interoception, and in so doing, I am *directly* aware of something *as* experiencing. If I conceptualize what I am aware of, as in first-person identification, I cannot help but think of that something as a *res cogitans*. Observing how you wrinkle your brow, lift your eyebrows, roll your eyes, I might also conclude that you too have an inner awareness. But this conclusion is drawn from my *indirect* external awareness of you as a consciously experiencing, feeling, and thinking being; it is neither an inner nor a direct awareness.

What is the index of an executive first-person identification? Suppose Jane thinks

(11)  I should take my umbrella; it may rain here today.

and thereby identifies the person or organism that she is. Is Jane herself— the person or organism—the index of her identification? If so, then her executive mode of presentation is

$I\,([\text{Jane at }(t,v)])$

and her first-person identification is direct, not deferred. But can the index be Jane herself? Is the single enduring organism with all its parts wholly present at a given time, or, taking a four-dimensionalist view, is the temporal sequence of person-stages itself ever presented? Either alternative seems an unlikely candidate as an index, for through what mode of inner awareness could one be aware of the whole persisting organism? Unless we are willing to describe both index and person as an enduring *soul* that is wholly present in a single conscious act, the hypothesis that the index is the whole person or organism is not very promising.

Here's a further proposal. The index is a perspectival array, moreover, the maximally integrated array constituting a given episode of awareness (cf., Castañeda 1999, pp. 244, 263). This array is always there at every episode of indexical awareness, however thick or thin it might be, for immediate data and the associated reactions exist only as part of a unified whole. Just as there is an awareness of individual data vectors, so too, there is an awareness of their perspectival assemblage, and while this awareness is typically marginal, it becomes salient in first-person thinking. It is the basis for thinking of the "me here and now" of which I, and I alone, am directly aware.

Accordingly, letting "$C(t,v)$" represent a maximal array centered on locus $(t,v)$, then a different candidate for Jane's executive *I*-mode is this:

$I([C(t,v)])$.

So understood, what Jane identified is identical to the index $C(t,v)$, and her first-person identification remains direct. This analysis works provided a maximal array—a "self" of relatively short duration—is an entity that can be identified and referred to with "I."[8] But if Jane thinks of herself as something that persists, as in,

(12)    I have been lecturing in Paris for 12 years.

or,

(13)    I am gradually losing weight,

then, on the assumption that what is identified is not an object of direct awareness, her identification is deferred rather than direct. The index is still the maximal array at the time, but since identification is deferred, the orientation differs. While the persisting *I* is not identical to the index, it can be thought to "have" or be "partly constituted by" the index, and the relevant mode of presentation is representable as,

$I$ (having $[C(t,v)]$)

where "having" expresses orienting relation, namely, a compositional tie between the maximal array and a persisting *I*.

With these proposals, we capture two ways of thinking of oneself in first-person terms; as a momentary self—the *me here now*—and as a persisting organism to which such momentary unities belong. The former is direct, the latter deferred, but in both cases the guiding concept is the executive *I-ness* concept and the index is a perspectival array.[9]

## Ipseity, subjectivity, and primitive self-consciousness

In supporting Sartre's restriction of the first person to reflective consciousness, I have argued that first-person expressions and concepts are no different from other indexicals, and that they apply only in virtue of conceptualizations. If correct, then primitive self-consciousness is *anonymous*, to use Manfred Frank's description, and its content, *ipseity*, or the *pour-soi* feature of conscious states is not to be described in first-person terms. Yet, as we observed at the outset, ipseity cannot be just anything; it must have some intrinsic feature(s) distinct from the status it acquires by being indexically identified. Ipseity is not a product of our thinking but, instead, something given "as a subtle background presence" (Zahavi 2005, p. 124).

Is a non-first-personal account of ipseity available? A description in terms of the "subjectivity of experience" (Zahavi 2005, p. 126) is appealing provided that we divorce the meaning of "subjectivity" from the decidedly first-personal "mineness" and "for me" locutions. The temptation to use these terms stems from the fact that subjectivity is that property of conscious states whereby they are privately, not publicly, accessible. Subjectivity exists because only *one* subject can ever be presented with a particular perspectival array and only *one* episode of consciousness can be centered upon that array. In fact, subjectivity is equivalent to the property of perspectivity or *being perspectival*, and the latter is the *pour-soi* aspect of consciousness. Yet, there is nothing first-personal about perspective as such; it exists wherever there are experiences, even those of the smallest and least reflective organisms. Similarly, there is nothing essentially first-personal about privileged access, as it is a property of all experiences. While the adjective "first-personal" can be used to modify thinking, thoughts, contents, concepts, statuses, identifications, and expressions, the phrase "first-person perspective" is, strictly speaking, undefined, though, if appropriate at all, it applies only when a thinker conceptualizes his or her perspective as *mine*.[10]

One might argue that a perspectival array is first-personal because its salience can *only* occasion a first-person identification. But this is not so. One can reflexively think of oneself through the second person, as with one who criticizes oneself with "you fool," or for modest people who are self-congratulatory in the second person, preferring

*You did wonderfully!*

to the hubris of

*I did wonderfully!*

That such an identification is a matter of inner awareness is evidence that the perspectival array can serve as the index of second-person thinking as well, and so, is not intrinsically bound to first-person presentation.

Once we distinguish subjectivity and first person, the door is open to identifying the content of primitive self-consciousness with a perspectival array. An integration of data vectors from a point of view is always present in our indexical experience even when this integration itself lacks salience. Because of its ubiquity, it often escapes our notice, but we are always marginally aware of it. It is not our invention, though how we conceptualize its embedded vectors is our contribution. At the personal level, it is mine, to be sure, and this is why my consciousness of it is reflexive, but in order to *be* mine I need not conceive it *as* mine.[11]

## Notes

1 The use of "executive" is borrowed from Castañeda (1989, ch. 4), though it also occurs in de Sausurre (1959, p. 13).
2 Frege hinted at the duality of "I" in his 1918 essay, "The Thought: A Logical Inquiry" (Frege 1956), as did Castañeda (1999, pp. 269–270). John McDowell, in addressing Frege's concerns, suggests that communication might occur through a *correspondence* of thoughts rather than *shared* thoughts (McDowell 1998, pp. 222–223).
3 Perspectival approaches to indexicals are found in several writers, including Russell (1948, part 2, ch. 4), Castañeda (1989, 1999), Evans (1982, ch. 6), Hintikka (1998), and Kapitan (2001). See also Lyons (1995, p. 311), which contrasts the "standard view" of deixis that dominates linguistics textbooks with an alternative view, one that takes the "egocentricity of the deictic context" as "rooted in the subjectivity of consciousness." Opponents of this approach generally acknowledge that indexicals play a unique role in our psychological economy, but are wary of the perspectivalist's acceptance of subjective, irreducibly perspectival features of the world (for example, Perry 2000, ch. 1, and Millikan 1993, ch. 13).
4 The phrase "point of origin" appears in Castañeda (1977, p. 305) and Evans (1982, p. 154), to designate the locale of the thinker within his or her own egocentric space, whereas Lyons speaks of the *zero point* of a locutionary act (Lyons 1995, p. 304).
5 The importance of spatial and temporal locale in describing indexicals was emphasized by William James, who wrote that the expressions "I," "here," and "this" are "primarily nouns of position" (James 1976/1904, p. 86). Castañeda spoke of demonstrative or indexical properties as properties that "fix" positions in spatio-temporal fields (1977, p. 320). See also Evans (1982, ch. 6).
6 Williford et al. (2013) describe lived experience (*Erlebnis*) in terms of what they call "projective space," but describe its directionality as going outward from a "subject" or "mind's eye" or "Cartesian spectator" or "subject-pole," writing that "three-dimensional conscious space seems to issue from a virtual origin that we spontaneously locate somewhere at the center of the head, at the egocenter" (p. 341). Such talk of "conscious space" issuing from "virtual origin" suggests that directionality is causally determined by some center of consciousness. But I do not think that this is the only way to view perspectival space. There is an alternative metaphysics—the Leibniz–Whitehead tradition—that takes perspectival arrays to be events (dynamic substances), where events are the spatio-temporal

physical realities that constitute persisting physical objects. The directionality of the perspectival array is in exactly the opposite direction, determined by the causal flow of data *toward* the locus rather than from it. This locus is not a spatial-temporal point, but an extended locale (a volume duration) into which the force vectors stream and are integrated.

7  The term "index" was introduced into philosophical discourse by C. S. Peirce, who used it to classify a sign that refers to an object in virtue of being "physically connected with" or "really affected by" that object (1998, pp. 5, 291). My usage follows Nunberg (1993), which distinguishes between a *deictic* component and a *classificatory* component of indexicals, both of which are distinct from the referent, and employs "index" to represent the "thing picked out by the deictic component of an indexical" (p. 19).

8  Compare Whitehead (1958/1938, p. 224): "My present experience is what I now am." William James was no doubt correct in that diachronic consciousness appears as a continuous "stream" even though there is a noticeable succession of individual states within it (James 1950/1890, ch. xi). Perhaps experience is ultimately granular, as Whitehead (1978/1929) contended, but nothing prevents us from focusing upon certain gross segments selected through our own focused self-awareness. Thus, the index of a first-person identification is a portion of the stream thick enough to be a unified content of marginal awareness.

9  Marcel (2003, pp. 50–51) also speak of self-awareness in the occurrent and the long-term sense of "self." Similarly, Strawson (2000) describes our experience of *I* as being sometimes of a momentary "subject of a unitary experience" and sometimes of a "persisting human." I have discussed the reciprocity between these two types of *I* identification (Kapitan 2006, section 5), and in it may lay the key to explaining the genesis of first-person thinking.

10  Intentional action involves desires, goals, and aversions together with proprioceptive information of a unique physical center of receptive feeling and reaction that is needed for their satisfaction. But the information needed need not be packaged in first-person terms; *it is sufficient for successful action that it be reflexive.* If *many* maximal arrays were co-presented, each differently centered, then one *would* need a way of distinguishing one of them as privileged, and this would open the door to a first-person reading of the representation. Otherwise, inner awareness of a *unique* center of reception and reaction is all that's required. There are, then, no grounds for concluding that intentional action requires non-conceptual first-person awareness.

11  In a sustained defense of the first-person reading of primitive self-consciousness, Thor Grunbaum writes that "all that is phenomenally present to me in a visual experience is the world as it is presented to me" (2013, p. 281) and goes on to argue against anonymity theories of self-consciousness on the grounds that they cannot explain first-personal thinking. While I lack the space here to do justice to all the nuances of his argumentation, I am unpersuaded by his two main reasons for concluding that perspectival explanations of the first person will not suffice. First, he thinks that perspectivity is a property of perceptual states only, and, thus, cannot account for non-perceptual first-person thinking. Second, the first-person reference that occurs at the reflective level presupposes an understanding that one is referring to *oneself* in a first-person way (2013, p. 284). As to the first, he is wrong to confine perspectivity to perception; it is equally there in other conscious states, e.g., in memory, imagination, dreams, and even in

theoretical thought as the presence of demonstratives in the expression of such thought reveals. As to the second, his premise requires far too much sophistication; little children can think first-person thoughts, but cannot reasonably be said to have the concept of *reference* that the attributed knowledge requires.

## Bibliography

Anscombe, G. E. M. (1975). The First Person, pp. 45–64, in S. Guttenplan, Ed. *Mind and Language*. Oxford: Clarendon Press.
Baker, L. R. (2012). From Consciousness to Self-Consciousness. *Grazer Philosophische Studien* 84: pp. 19–38.
Bermudez, J. (1998). *The Paradox of Self-Consciousness*. Cambridge, MA: MIT Press.
Castañeda, H-N. (1977). Perception, Belief, and the Structure of Physical Objects and Consciousness. *Synthese* 35: pp. 285–351.
Castañeda, H-N. (1989). *Thinking, Language and Experience*. Minneapolis: University of Minnesota Press.
Castañeda, H-N. (1999). I-Structures and the Reflexivity of Self-Consciousness, in J. G. Hart and T. Kapitan, Eds. *The Phenomeno-Logic of the I: Essays on Self-Consciousness*. Bloomington: Indiana University Press, pp. 251–292.
Damasio, A. (1999). *The Feeling of What Happens*. New York: Harcourt Brace.
De Sausurre, Ferdinand (1959/1915). *Course in General Linguistics*. New York: Philosophical Library.
Dreyfus, H. L. (2007). Response to McDowell. *Inquiry*, 50(4): pp. 371–377.
Evans, G. (1982). *The Varieties of Reference*. Oxford: Oxford University Press.
Flanagan, O. (1992). *Consciousness Reconsidered*. Cambridge, MA: MIT Press.
Frank, M. (1995). Mental Familiarity and Epistemic Self-Ascription. *Common Knowledge* (October): pp. 30–50.
Frege, G. (1956). The Thought: A Logical Inquiry. *Mind* 65: 289–311.
Gallagher, S. (2012). Multiple Aspects in the Sense of Agency. *New Ideas in Psychology* 30: 15–31.
Gallagher, S. and D. Zahavi (2010). Phenomenological Approaches to Self-Consciousness. *Stanford Encyclopedia of Philosophy*. Available online at: http://plato.stanford.edu/.
Grunbaum, T. (2013). First Person and Minimal Self-Consciousness, pp. 273–296, in S. Miguens and G. Preyer, Eds. *Consciousness and Subjectivity*. Berlin: De Gruyter.
Hintikka, J. (1998). Perspectival Identification, Demonstratives, and "Small Worlds." *Synthese*, 114: pp. 203–232.
James, W. (1950/1890). *The Principles of Psychology*. 2 vols. New York: Dover Publications.
James, W. (1976/1904). *Essays in Radical Empiricism*. Cambridge, MA: Harvard University Press.
Kapitan, T. (2001). Indexical Identification: A Perspectival Account. *Philosophical Psychology* 14:3: pp. 293–312.
Kapitan, T. (2006). Indexicality and Self-Awareness, pp. 379–408, in U. Kriegel and K. Williford, Eds. *Self-Representational Approaches to Consciousness*. Cambridge, MA: MIT Press.
Kriegel, U. (2009). *Subjective Consciousness: A Self-Representational Theory*. Oxford: Oxford University Press.

Levine, J. (2010). Demonstrative Thought. *Mind and Language* 25(2): pp. 169–195.
Lyons, J. (1995). *Linguistic Semantics.* Cambridge, UK: Cambridge University Press.
Marcel, A. (2003). The Sense of Agency, pp. 48–93, in J. Roessler and N. Eilan, Eds. *Agency and Self-awareness.* Oxford: Oxford University Press.
McDowell, J. (1998). *Meaning, Knowledge and Reality.* Cambridge, MA: Harvard University Press.
Miguens, S. and G. Preyer (Eds.) (2013). *Consciousness and Subjectivity.* Berlin: De Gruyter.
Millikan, R. (1993). *White Queen Psychology and Other Essays for Alice.* Cambridge, MA: MIT Press.
Nunberg, G. (1993). Indexicality and Deixis. *Linguistics and Philosophy,* 16: pp. 1–43.
Peirce, C. S. (1998). *The Essential Peirce.* The Peirce Edition Project. Bloomington, IN: Indiana University Press.
Perry, J. (1997). Indexicals and Demonstratives, in B. Hale and C. Wright, Eds. *A Companion to the Philosophy of Language.* Oxford: Blackwell, pp. 586–612.
Perry, J. (2000). *The Problem of the Essential Indexical and Other Essays.* Stanford, CA: CSLI Publications.
Perry, J. (2001). *Reference and Reflexivity.* Stanford, CA: CSLI Publications.
Russell. B. (1948). *Human Knowledge: Its Scope and Limits.* London: Allen and Unwin.
Sartre, J.-P. (1956/1943). *Being and Nothingness.* Translated by H. E. Barnes. New York: Philosophical Library. *L'être et le néant.* Paris: Gallimard.
Sartre, J.-P. (1957/1936). *The Transcendence of the Ego.* Translated by F. Williams and R. Kirkpatrick. New York: The Noonday Press. *La transcendance de l'ego.* Paris: Vrin.
Strawson, G. (2000). The Phenomenology and Ontology of the Self, in D. Zahavi, Ed. *Exploring the Self.* Amsterdam: John Benjamins, pp. 39–54.
Whitehead, A. N. (1958/1938). *Modes of Thought.* New York: Macmillan.
Whitehead, A. N. (1978/1929). *Process and Reality.* New York: Macmillan.
Williford, K., G. Landini, and D. Rudrauf (2013). The Paradoxes of Subjectivity and the Projective Structure of Consciousness, pp. 321–353, in S. Miguens and G. Preyer, Eds. *Consciousness and Subjectivity.* Berlin: De Gruyter.
Zahavi, D. (2005). *Subjectivity and Selfhood.* Cambridge, MA: MIT Press.

# 3 Degrees of self-presence
## Rehabilitating Sartre's accounts of pre-reflective self-consciousness and reflection

*Kenneth Williford*

**Introduction**

In *The Bodily Nature of Consciousness* (Wider 1997; see also Wider 1989, 1993), Kathleen Wider lucidly argues that Sartre's accounts of pre-reflective self-consciousness, and pure (vs. impure) reflection are fundamentally problematic. On the one hand, pre-reflective self-consciousness is supposed to be a "non-positional" (or "non-thetic") type of self-awareness essentially different from the objectifying and distancing consciousness involved in perception, imagination, emotion, and conceptual thought, which are all "positional" in that through them consciousness is present to (or presented with) transcendent objects (be they existent or not) that are given as *not* being the very consciousness taking up the position on them. (See, e.g., *The Transcendence of the Ego* (TE), pp. 8–13, *The Imagination* (IM), pp. 3–4, *The Emotions* (E), p. 52, *The Imaginary* (IPPI), pp. 12–13, *Being and Nothingness* (B&N), 1ff., pp. 73ff., and throughout, "Self-Consciousness and Self-Knowledge" (SC&SK), p. 116 and throughout.) On the other hand, in Chapter One of Part Two of B&N ("The Immediate Structures of the For-Itself"), Sartre argues that this sort of distancing applies at the level of pre-reflective self-consciousness as well, and thus that consciousness fails to coincide with itself or exists "at a distance" from itself (esp. B&N, p. 77).

He argues that this means that the "Law of Identity" (meaning here the universal reflexivity of identity) fails to apply to the for-itself: There exists a type of being, the *pour-soi*, that is not identical with itself. And the Law is "synthetic" or "regional," and not "analytic" (B&N, p. 74). In addition to making Sartre's account essentially dialetheic, this threatens to undermine his account of pre-reflective self-consciousness, making it not readily distinguishable from his account of positional consciousness of object other than consciousness. And this makes Sartre's account look like a "Reflection Theory" (see Frank 1997, p. 13).

Wider argues that it is the reintroduction of epistemic or cognitive elements into his account of pre-reflective self-consciousness that is Sartre's real undoing here (Wider 1997, pp. 86ff.). It is crucial to Sartre's enterprise in the Introduction to *Being and Nothingness* that pre-reflective self-consciousness *not* be understood as a matter of consciousness cognizing or knowing itself (B&N, pp. lii–liii). Yet, in the chapter on Bad Faith, Sartre seems to reintroduce cognitive elements into his account of pre-reflective self-consciousness to clinch the claim that, even at this most basic level, consciousness is distanced from itself (B&N, p. 69). This failure of self-coincidence is viewed by Sartre as a sort of ontological presupposition or foundation of the very possibility of Bad Faith, which is, he says, to believe and *not* to believe at one and the same time (he says this directly (B&N, p. 69): "To believe is not-to-believe," "Croire, c'est ne pas croire"). This foundational claim presupposed by and manifested in Bad Faith is, of course, of a piece with Sartre's central thesis that consciousness introduces negation and negativity into the world by being its own negation, by, in effect, being a concrete internal negation of itself—being what it is not (B&N, pp. 88–89 and throughout). Without this claim, the entire project of B&N seems to fall to the ground like a 700-page house of cards, something demonstrated quite clearly in Wider's second chapter.

To make matters worse, Wider argues, there is no reasonable account of pre-reflective self-consciousness and pure reflective self-consciousness that does not either collapse the two or collapse pure reflective self-consciousness into impure reflection (Wider 1997, pp. 75–85). In pure reflection, we are supposed to be able to attend to and make apodictic judgments about our ongoing consciousness without the deployment of the distorting psychological concepts characteristic of impure reflection. Yet, if pure reflection is merely a matter of consciousness being self-present without conceptualization, it does not look essentially different from pre-reflective self-consciousness. And if we claim that it is different from the latter because it involves the deployment of objectifying concepts, then, without some way of telling which concepts are legitimate and which not, it does not look like we can distinguish pure reflection from the impure variety.

In this chapter I take up Wider's formidable challenge and offer an interpretation of Sartre's distinctions that is textually and systematically plausible, if making a few decisive departures from the letter of Sartre's law. Here are the main counter-claims I will attempt to substantiate:

(1)   Pre-reflective self-consciousness is not cognitive or a matter of knowledge *in the sense of "knowledge" ("connaissance") Sartre has in mind.*

(2)   Pure reflection can be distinguished, in a principled and plausible way, from pre-reflective self-consciousness, on the one hand, and impure reflection, on the other.

(3)   We can find the "origin of negation" in the very being of consciousness without the radical claim that consciousness fails to coincide with itself; Sartre does not really need the idea that consciousness fails to coincide with itself to ground the project of B&N. Negation can still be drawn out from consciousness because the latter contains internal differentiation, not because it fails to be self-identical.

68  Kenneth Williford

I'll articulate these claims as an interpretation of Sartre and offer provisional defenses of them at the systematic level along the way. I will end by suggesting that pre-reflective self-consciousness, the shift to reflection, and the various "degrees of nothingness" separating consciousness from itself can be understood in terms of the non-contradictory notions of circular structure (in the form of non-well-foundedness) and projective structure (in the form of higher-dimensional projective geometry), though this will not be developed in detail here.

## Positional and non-positional consciousness

Putting the Sartrean view (onto)logically, given a positional consciousness $c$ of some transcendent object $o$, one can immediately infer that $c \neq o$. Putting it phenomenologically, transcendent objects of perception and imagination (etc.), are given as *not* being the very consciousness one has of them. I see the paper on the table. It is perceptually given *to* me, and it is given as *not being me* (IM, pp. 3–4). I imagine a centaur; this in no way threatens to make me think that a real centaur is in the room, or that I am perceiving one albeit faintly (IM, pp. 3–6; IPPI, pp. 4–7). The centaur is given to my imaginative consciousness as an irreal (and thereby also transcendent) being and, correlatively, as *not* being my consciousness of it—consciousness is very real indeed. Putting it in the jargon of B&N, consciousness "transcends itself" towards objects and in so doing "posits" the objects as *not being that very consciousness of them.*

Non-positional or non-thetic self-consciousness, by contrast, does not "posit" anything, itself included. In this context, this means that consciousness does not objectify itself; it does take itself to be a "transcendent" object. Here the relevant opposition is transcendence vs. immanence. And this is defined, in a way common to Husserl, Levinas, and many other phenomenologists, in terms of identity through variation of profiles (or manifold appearances). (See, e.g., TE, pp. 11–12; B&N, pp. xlv–xlvii; Levinas 1995, pp. 26ff.; Husserl 1982, §41.) As we walk around a perceived tree, we see *it* (putatively the very same "object") from a variety of angles and positions. *It* (the tree) is *transcendent* in that it has an identity that does not itself vary with the variation in each of my positions on it; it *transcends* all of those positions and variations. Moreover, its objectivity is manifested in the fact that we could multiply perspectives on the tree *ad infinitum* (or *ad nauseam* as the case may be). No single mind could take in *all* the possible perspectives on the tree. This means, effectively, that the tree's *esse* is not *percipi*. There is, as Sartre's puts it, a "transphenomenal" dimension to its being; it transcends all its appearances even though these are all the well-ordered appearances *of it* (B&N, pp. xlvii–xlviii). And since we never know what we might see on the other side of the tree, the transcendent object also has a certain quality of dubitability about it. It might surprise us. It could be made out of plastic. In fact, this is the standard account of perceptual error in the phenomenological literature on perception. And, so far as it goes, it is a good account.

By contrast, consciousness, without collapsing into instantaneity, is given to itself pre-reflectively at once and *without such profiles* (see, e.g., TE, pp. 22–24, 31–38). This is the mark of immanence. Fundamentally, it is not a transcendent object for itself, though it is self-present. It cannot walk around itself or turn itself over or otherwise multiply the angles it takes on itself (at least not without the mediating and sometimes distorting aid of conceptualization and memory). This means it does not "represent" itself. Consequently, it cannot, in the relevant sense, surprise itself or be wrong about itself. And if it morphs into a reflection while still retaining what's essential to its primary shape, we might simply take note of its character (as a perceiving, an imagining, etc.) without the danger of radical distortion (we'll return to this). But once the "specious present" morphs into a new "specious present," an episode of consciousness is forever gone, accessible only to reflection in memory or abstract thought. In this respect, it is quite unlike the tree, whose identity (rightly or wrongly from a metaphysical point of view) we take to remain stable for years—not merely for a second or less.

Whatever else non-positional self-consciousness is, it is a self-awareness without such profiles or facets. Though there are complications when we move from the objects of perception to those of imagination, emotion, and abstract thought, the mark of a transcendent object is that it gives itself having a certain capacity to be revealed over time via positions we can take on it and not to be exhaustively given in any one profile.

To say that pre-reflective self-consciousness is non-positional is also to say that in it one does not take up any particular "positing" attitude, as one does when one imagines, perceives, emotes, or thinks and judges. These positing attitudes are the noeses correlated with different types of transcendent objects or noemata. (The Sartrean "domains" of these noematic correlates are, respectively, the Irreal (Imaginary), the Real (Perceptual), the "Magical" or "Degraded" (Emotional), and relations and states of affairs or *Sachverhalte*, abstract or concrete (the conceptual part of knowledge and pure thought). That Sartre understands "positional" and "thetic" in basically this Husserlian sense is clear from IPPI, pp. 11–14 and p. 163 (*pace* Webber 2002, pp. 46–47. See, e.g., Husserl 1982, §§113–117, 122, 129).[1] What all forms of "positing" have in common is that they aim at transcendent objects to be given via profiles (even if it is an object of imagination that can only be "quasi-observed": IPPI, pp. 8–11). But different thetic or positing attitudes have different types of noematic correlates, and hence there are different ways in which the specific objectivities can be revealed. The way one must come to grips with a theorem one is trying to understand is quite different from the way one confronts an unpleasant and emotionally charged memory, and these are different again from the way one investigates the termites one has just discovered under the base boards. The positional characters of these acts are different in these cases but they all have in common that they aim at transcendent objects upon which one could, in one way or another, multiply profiles; and in many contexts, that is all that is important to Sartre. Clearly, the self-aware consciousness does not pre-reflectively imagine itself or hate or love itself, but more importantly given more recent discussions, it does not pre-reflectively perceive itself or think about or judge or thematize itself either. This is one reason, among many others, why it is quixotic at best to attempt to assimilate Sartre's account to a higher-order thought theory (see Gennaro 2002).

Consciousness also does not pre-reflectively attend to itself or focus on itself. This is why saying that pre-reflective self-consciousness is marginal, peripheral, lateral, or inattentive is not, strictly speaking, false. (But it is wrong, I now think, to say that it is or is like "empty" intending, as I did in Williford 2006, pp. 121–122.) It can, however, be quite a misleading thing to say (and has been: see Zahavi 1999, p. 61), because it is possible to have inattentive consciousness of an object that is also positional consciousness of it; the same goes for peripheral consciousness or the consciousness of backgrounds vs. figures. So one might think that Gurwitsch (1985, pp. 3ff.), Kriegel (2009, ch. 5), and myself (Williford 2006, pp. 123–126) have been saying that marginal, inattentive, or peripheral self-consciousness is *exactly like* inattentive (etc.) consciousness of transcendent objects.[2] And, of course, it is not. But this does not make it false that one can be inattentively (etc.) aware of something that is *not* a transcendent object. And, in point of fact, everyone who holds views in this ballpark would agree that in pre-reflective self-consciousness, it is *not* a matter of consciousness attending to or focusing on itself, something one only does during reflection. It is aware of itself, but it need not be attending to itself. Hence the description is not exactly *wrong*, but it does not cut deep enough, since there can be inattentive or marginal consciousness that is also positional (as is the case for all the background items I see on my desk behind my computer screen). Non-positional self-consciousness is indeed *not* a matter of attending to or focusing on oneself, though it is also present when one is doing these things. But simply to point out that it is not a matter of attention or focus is not to give a full account of it or to cut it at its joints. About that, the critics (Frank and Zahavi, in particular) are certainly right. And it is accordingly not strictly correct to reduce the positional/non-positional distinction to the attentive/marginal one, as Morris (1992, p. 107) and Wider (1997, p. 41) seem to. I now agree with Hatzimoysis (2011, pp. 24–27) that this is not the correct way to interpret Sartre or to draw the distinction.

So far we've characterized non-positional self-consciousness only negatively. It's *not* a matter of consciousness taking an attitude toward itself, judging, perceiving itself, let alone imagining, hating, or loving itself. It's *not* a matter of consciousness confronting a transcendent object via a multiplicity of profiles or facets. To put it in more common (and more ambiguous) language, it is thus *not* a matter of any sort of representation. And it's *not* a matter of attention or focus, as just noted. And, we should add, for the sake of explicitness, it's *not* a matter of conceptualization (cf. Webber 2002). To be present to oneself in this way is not to conceptualize oneself in any way, and this follows really from the denial that it is a matter of perception, imagination, thought, or judgment—the modalities of consciousness that can be most reasonably said to involve concepts at some level.

But one should not conclude from this denial that conceptualization is involved that it *is* a matter of *non-conceptual* representation, as that notion is currently used in anglophone philosophy of mind (again, see Webber 2002). Rather, it's not a matter of representation *at all*. Hence it's neither a matter of conceptual nor of non-conceptual representation. It follows from this, as Sartre emphasizes in the Introduction to B&N, that it is not a matter of *knowledge* (at least insofar as we define knowledge in such a way that it involves position taking on a transcendent object *and* adequate conceptualization; see below).

But is there a *positive* characterization of non-positional self-consciousness we can give? We can of course say that consciousness is "manifest to itself," that it is "present to itself," or even that it is "acquainted with itself," as I will say. But these formulations do not add very much beyond the datum itself. Recognizing the difficulty of giving a deeper characterization of non-positional self-consciousness, Sartre writes in *The Imaginary* (IPPI, p. 14), "it is a diffuse light consciousness emits for itself, or—to abandon comparisons—it is an indefinable quality that attaches itself to every consciousness."

Of course, the "quality attaching itself" locution should not be taken too literally here, supposing that Sartre's views on this issue did not change radically between 1940 and 1943, the dates of publication for IPPI and B&N, respectively. In B&N (pp. liv–lv), Sartre denies that "non-thetic consciousness is a *quality* of the positional consciousness"[3] and, taking the example of a conscious pleasurable experience, he denies both that pleasure is a quality of non-positional self-consciousness and that the latter is a quality of the former. Just prior to these denials he writes (B&N, p. liv, emphasis Sartre's):

> This self-consciousness [conscience (de) soi] we ought to consider not as a new consciousness, but as *the only mode of existence that is possible for a consciousness of something*. Just as an extended object is compelled to exist according to three dimensions, so an intention, a pleasure, a grief can only exist as immediate self-consciousness [conscience immédiate (d')eux-mêmes].

So we have it that it is *like* a "diffuse light" emitted by itself and that it is a bit *like* a dimension in that the various possible types of consciousness must all be pre-reflectively aware of themselves in something like the way that extended physical bodies, no matter their exact shape, must be three-dimensional. These are positive characterizations, but they are analogies. And Sartre does not develop them very much, perhaps because he realized that one must simply come to grips with the *phenomenon* itself and, as he says, "abandon comparisons."[4]

Sartre does, however, add something possibly helpful (but potentially puzzling) in the passage from IPPI. Here is the rest of the IPPI (p. 14) passage quoted above:

> The imaging consciousness of the object includes . . . a nonthetic consciousness of itself. This consciousness, which one could call transversal, has no object. It posits nothing, refers to nothing, is not knowledge [*connaissance*] . . . A perceptual consciousness appears to itself as passive. On the other hand, an imaging consciousness gives itself to itself as an imaging consciousness, which is to say as a spontaneity that produces and conserves the object as imaged. It is a kind of indefinable counterpart to the fact that the object gives itself as a nothingness. The consciousness appears to itself as creative, but without positing as object this creative character. It is thanks to this vague and fugitive quality that the image consciousness is not given as a piece of wood that floats on the sea, but as a wave among the waves. It feels itself to be consciousness through and through and homogeneous with the other consciousnesses that have preceded it and with which it is synthetically united.

Sartre borrows the term "transversal" from Husserl's account of inner time-consciousness (Sartre's *transversale* for Husserl's *quer*). In §39 of the 1905 lectures on time-consciousness, Husserl (1991/1928, pp. 84–88) distinguishes between the "longitudinal" or "horizontal" intentionality (*Längsintentionalität*) of the flow, which is, as Brough notes, "the retentional consciousness that intends the elapsed phases of the absolute consciousness," and "transverse" or "transversal" intentionality (*Querintentionalität*), which is the "consciousness of the elapsed phases of the immanent object . . . the act of perception, of memory, of judgment, and so on . . . [as well as] transcendent temporal object[s]" (in Husserl 1991, p. liii and pp. 84–88). (Put aside here any worries about the unfortunate use of the phrase "immanent objects" to designate acts of consciousness; it's just a bad terminological artifact in this context.) According to de Coorebyter, when Sartre writes "transversal," he actually means to be referring to horizontal intentionality, to *Längsintentionalität* (in Sartre 2003, p. 179, n15). I think that this is probably correct. But it actually does not matter that much since, for Husserl and surely for Sartre as well, horizontal and transversal intentionality are concretely inseparable: The flow always manifests itself in some immanent act or other (a perception, a fantasy, a dream) directed at some transcendent intentional object other, and all such acts only occur in the context of the flow of "absolute" consciousness and its "diasporic" awareness of itself as having just been thus-and-so and in the process of becoming such-and-such (IPPI, pp. 74–77; B&N, pp. 136, 157: "non-thetic consciousness (of) flow and . . . thetic consciousness of duration").

A very important point in this connection is that non-positional self-consciousness has, for Sartre, a status similar to that of protention, retention, and the resulting diachronic unity of consciousness (cf. TE, p. 7). These are generic, invariant and immanent structures of consciousness in one sense, but, in Sartre's radicalization of Husserl's play of protention and retention, they are also "diasporic" in that they really put us in touch with consciousness (non-thetically) presenting itself as in time—what consciousness has been but is not now; what it is becoming but is not yet (B&N, pp. 109, 122). But, even more important for our purposes, the flow of consciousness is manifest to itself immediately and without any need for cognitive or perceptual acts to constitute it.

It is true, of course, that to the extent that protention and retention enable us to relate to the temporal character of transcendent objects (Husserl's *Querintentionalität*), there is room for error (and hence one might say that "representation" is involved). I might think that tree in the lobby of the dentist's office is real, expect it to be hard, but find upon touching it that it is some sort of soft, nauseating plastic. This means I was wrong about the transcendent object and, correlatively, about the course of my future observational experience. But this does not mean that protention *per se* is erroneous or capable of misrepresenting anything. There is always a future for consciousness—a "what it is not yet but is becoming." And this is so even if that consciousness is unexpectedly cut short, since, in any case, its future is always a "not yet" and when that future does arrive it may well be an absolute nothingness. At this level, protention is infallible just because it is an internal relation consciousness bears to itself as already "reaching" into its future. This is at a level deeper than its projection of some *specific* future events. The anticipation of a specific future, that may or may not unfold in the way expected, is already a level or layer *above* the flow, though it presupposes the flow. The same goes, *mutatis mutandis*, for retention. There is always a past for consciousness, even if it is the nothingness preceding the sudden onset of consciousness. And consciousness bears an internal relation to its past as such. This deeper level of the flow is what enables us to retend specific past events understood as transcendent objectivities.

I may fantasize about fame and glory for a while and then think about getting lunch very briefly before being interrupted by a phone call, all the while looking out the window rather absently. I am aware that there was a sequence of contingent events here, that one sort of act lasted a certain time, that it was followed by another taking up less time, and then another. Reflection is not required for this sequence to be manifest. And had the sequence been of quite different events (e.g., hearing a buzz followed by seeing a bee, followed by a shock of fear of being stung, followed by ducking and swatting movements), this would only modify the underlying flow in terms of the transcendent objects constituted, not in terms of the flow *as such*. Moreover, there does not need to be a separate, second act (or second series of acts) for the flow to be manifest, and yet another, third act (or third series of acts) for the flow of the second series, which also must be flowing, to be manifest, and so on (cf. Husserl 1991, p. 88). The flow has no need of another flow, so to speak. In fact, the self-manifestation of the flow grounds any reflective judgment I may care to make about it, or report I may give should I be asked (cf. B&N, p. liii; Zahavi 1999, p. 57).

In identifying non-positional self-consciousness as belonging to "transversal intentionality," Sartre is reminding us, as he does in several other locations, that one major source for the very idea of pre-reflective self-consciousness was, for him, Husserl's lectures on time-consciousness (TE, pp. 6–7; SC&SK, p. 123). How does the investigation of time-consciousness lead to the conclusion that consciousness must be aware of itself in some non-representational way? With no space to go into the interesting and difficult details of Husserl's lectures, we'll have to content ourselves with this little sketch (cf. Zahavi 1999, ch. 5). A present episode of consciousness retends what just happened before *it* and protends what will happen after *it*. That is already a double self-reference (using "reference" here neutrally). On top of this basic flow, a specific transcendent objective chain of events may be protended to go a certain way (e.g., one protends that the ball will land *there*, and so readies one's swing accordingly). But suppose the ball does not land where one protended it would (or a familiar tune suddenly goes sideways). For one to be surprised, one must be retending one's prior protention at the moment the surprising turn occurs—when it becomes a *this-here-now* with its own protentions. Consciousness always has this tripartite self-referential structure: *what preceded this, this-here-right-now, what is already following this*. In each instance, the "this" refers to the very occurrent episode of consciousness itself. And since the episode necessarily contains this tripartite structure as an internal relation to its past and its future, in referring to itself, consciousness reaches beyond any instantaneously defined time. This is a more positive characterization of non-positional self-consciousness, but it is still only relational. This gives us an idea about how it is rooted in time-consciousness. But can we say more?

We can add that this passage from IPPI indicates clearly that for Sartre non-positional self-consciousness is on the noetic side of the noetico-noematic correlation (cf., e.g., B&N, pp. 204, 259, 263, and 322: "[Properties of things] . . . are correlates of non-thetic projects which we are, but they are revealed only as structures of the world"). To take an example from the domain of emotion, I perceive a horrific face in my window. The face appears as objectively horrible (cf. E, pp. 54, 59). It appears as "having-to-be-fled." But immediately after discovering that it is my son in a mask, I might say "*I* was terrified," attributing a certain reaction to myself (rather than a property to an object in the world). For Sartre, this spontaneous, reflective (but potentially distorting) way of reporting the event relies on the fact that during the moments of sheer terror, I was not solely aware of the fearsome face to-be-fled. My episode of consciousness was pre-reflectively given to itself as an emotive consciousness (which is to say, for him, in this case, suddenly on the quasi-magical plane where normal causal relations are suspended—though none of that is *conceptualized* (E, p. 52)). Similarly, in perception, I am non-positionally aware of my perceptual consciousness as passive; in imagination, I am non-positionally aware of it as active. And so on for other types of conscious awareness.

In fact, this sort of locution (non-thetically or non-positionally conscious of consciousness "as *X*") occurs all over B&N, and it marks what Sartre sometimes calls our "pre-ontological" or "pre-judicative" self-understanding and other times speaks of in terms of consciousness being "haunted" by its possibilities, values, the Other, one's "original project", etc. (B&N, pp. 35, 39, 49, 94–95, 104, 245, 273, 288, 289, 568–571). This "as *X*" locution has the tendency to make it appear as though non-positional consciousness *represents* positional consciousness as being a certain way. After all, how can one be aware of *Y as a P* without categorizing *Y* in some way, that is, without, at some level, conceptualizing it? But this would evidently be a complete misreading of Sartre.

One possibility, raised by Jonathan Webber (2002), is that Sartre has in mind something like *non-conceptual* representation as it is defined (more or less) in contemporary anglophone philosophy of mind.[5] On that reading, an episode of consciousness would represent itself as being, say, passive in the way we supposedly perceptually represent (non-conceptually experience) a ball as being phenomenally red, according to externalist "representationalist" theorists of sensory content like Harman (1990), Dretske (1995), Tye (1995, 2002), and Byrne (2001). On that view, the sensory qualities are (1) *objects* of representation (not contents in the sense of internal qualia or "mental paint"), and (2) *identical* with certain complicated, relational, physical structures. To see red is, on this view, just to represent a certain reflectance-absorption property (or disjunctive set thereof) non-conceptually, that is, without, at the level in question, deploying any concepts.[6]

Leaving aside the budget of problems raised by this type of theory as a theory of the consciousness of sensory qualities, let's just ask if it can be reasonably applied in the case of non-positional self-consciousness. This would mean that the conscious episode non-conceptually represents itself as having a certain character (e.g., being passive, being active, being degraded into the magical). This character would appear, given the theory, as a certain (only apparently) irreducible, non-relational quality of the episode of consciousness (the way red appears as an apparently irreducible, non-structural property of balls and shirts, etc.). How is it then that, upon reflection, it is so easy to say exactly what the relevant structures are? We say things like: "I kept watching and could not believe my eyes," reflectively registering the passive receptivity involved in perception; "I kept trying to picture what it would look like if I were upside down," reflectively registering the activity involved in imagination, and so on. This is rather unlike reflection on seeing something red. Such reflection does not yield up anything about wavelengths of light and reflectance and absorption profiles of the surfaces of physical objects.

Of course, one could just say this case is relevantly different. It is, perhaps, more like the perception of musical chords. One *can* listen to them in such a way that one does not *distinctly* hear the tones composing the chord. But one can also listen to them more attentively in such a way that one can hear the distinct tones in the chord as distinct tones.

But there is a deeper problem. If it is representation we are dealing with, there is the possibility of error, even radical error. This would mean I could pre-reflectively take my episode of perception to be an episode of imagination or thought or emotion. I could mix them all up, in fact. I could also take my episodes of smelling roses to be episodes of hearing bats. In other words, it's not just the act type (emotive, imaginal, etc.) that would have to be non-conceptually represented, it is also the "intentional content" (to speak in a non-Sartrean way) that would have to be so represented. Are we to imagine that there is specific, non-conceptual "cognitive phenomenology" present in the pre-reflective consciousness of every conceptual thought? A specific quality for the content of each type of thought? I am happy to grant that there is something it is like to think that $2 + 2 = 4$ and that that is different from what it is like to think that $3 + 3 = 6$, but it seems undesirable to postulate the non-conceptual (but pre-reflective) representation of "$2 + 2 = 4$" alongside the conceptual thought of it. Would such a non-conceptual representation of the propositional content "$2 + 2 = 4$" be somehow analogous to phenomenal red? Would it have a certain "feel"? It's hard to imagine, but maybe not completely inconceivable. Of course, once again the proponent of this interpretation could just say that in the case of conceptual "content," it is the vehicle (e.g., words, symbols, formalisms) that is non-conceptually represented at the pre-reflective level.[7]

One could, however, attempt to use something like the "phenomenal concepts" strategy here.[8] This would make pre-reflective self-consciousness conceptual again, but only in the sense of "phenomenal concepts." Phenomenal concepts, the story goes, are concepts that, in some way or other, include exemplars or instances of the very sort of things they are the concept of, but "in quotes," so to speak. So, for example, my (phenomenal) concept of red will, in some way or other (via memory or imagination or perhaps just causation or information transfer), involve an instance of phenomenal red. Applied to the present account, the idea would be that every episode of consciousness pre-reflectively represents itself by, to use the common metaphor, putting quotes around itself (or by employing something like "diagonalization"). This way, there's no need for *new* types of qualities to appear. The representation of the episode just rides piggyback on the episode itself. This would avoid both the possibility of the types of errors just enumerated as well as the need for *further* special qualities (construed as the *objects* of non-conceptual representations) or any further special stories about why these qualities do not so thoroughly conceal the internal structures of the properties they supposedly are. But the phenomenal concepts strategy applied here is actually very close to the account I think is more fitting.[9]

The more fitting notion here is something like the notion of direct acquaintance (made famous by Russell 1996/1914). And forget for the moment the merely terminological artifact that one normally speaks of "knowledge" by acquaintance, which might already seem to conflict with Sartre's insistence that non-positional self-consciousness is not a matter of knowledge. The idea here is rather something like this: A perceptual act, for example, is precisely an episode of consciousness in which something is passively given to awareness. But all perceptual acts, like all other conscious episodes, are, let us now say, directly *acquainted* with themselves. This is equivalent to the direct manifestation (to itself) of an act that is passive in just the specific perceptual way. This important structure of the perceptual act is self-given, on this proposal, given to the very act directly and without the mediation of representations or concepts. It is not that the act *represents itself* as being passive. Rather, the perceptual act *is* passive in the relevant sense, *and* is also acquainted with this very structure of itself.

However, this structure or fact *can be* conceptualized and thought about. That is, we do have terms and concepts for these structures, and so we *can* make judgments about them. This means, to speak in Husserlian jargon again, that we have a "pre-predicative" (or "antepredicative") grasp of the relevant concrete structures and relationships (see Husserl 1973; cf., e.g., IPPI, p. 121). It is this grasp that we merely "explicate" when we make a judgment. I am perceptually conscious of the "white wall" well before I can explicitly judge *that* the wall is white. Judging is just "making it explicit" (cf. Brandom 2000, p. 8). In perceptually confronting the white wall I am only implicitly aware "*that* the wall is white." But such explicit judgments are confirmed or falsified by recourse to pre-predicative experience. The latter is primary.

This means we can "go from" the one to the other. On this view, "explication" is just rendering the structures, similarities, and differences, and relations really inherent in the pre-predicatively experienced domain into concepts and words. Of course, such rendering comes to infect the very way such domains appear to us eventually, but there is a limit to the extent to which sedimented conceptual filtering can affect how things are given. And new experiences can evidently drive new conceptual development, something it could not do if perception, or self-acquaintance, to take the case at issue, were just straitjacketed in one's current conceptual repertoire (see Husserl 1973 and cf. Raftopoulos 2009). We can learn from pre-predicative experience, be it perceptual consciousness or be it pre-reflective self-acquaintance. It is thanks to this that we can *teach* the empirical sciences and practical disciplines (medicine, construction, auto-mechanics, etc.) on the one hand, and philosophy of mind and phenomenology, on the other. Students do not come to us with the *explicit* concepts of "what-it-is-like" or "retention and protention" or "intentionality," but they can surely learn them. And they learn the primary referents of these terms and concepts by reflecting on their experience again and again. This means they were, at some level, aware of the structures inherent in their experience *prior to* being asked to verify by reflection that, for example, their psychical processes are generally object-directed (intentional) or have a diachronic unity, etc. This is, in principle, not really different from a neuroanatomy student coming to be able to visually spot the difference between the fasciculus gracilis and the fasciculus cuneatus when looking at a section of spinal cord in anatomy lab. There is a process of learning to pay attention to differences one was aware of but did not think worthy of note and of relating these singled-out structures to other structures one may be more familiar with.

To sum up this section: Non-positional self-consciousness, I suggest, is best interpreted in terms of self-acquaintance. Accordingly, the claim that every episode of consciousness is non-positionally conscious of itself is just the claim that every episode of consciousness is acquainted with itself. Non-positional self-consciousness is also independent of attention and focus (and so, if one likes, can be described as inattentive and marginal or peripheral—though this can be misleading). It is not a matter of judgment, thought, perception, imagination, or emotion, or any other form of "representation" or positional consciousness, and is not a matter of the application of concepts (which is quite different from saying that it *is* a matter of non-conceptual representation). Non-positional self-consciousness is distinguished from positional consciousness of objects in that, in the latter case, specific objects are always given via profiles over time (and are hence always dubitable and only probable), whereas consciousness is given to itself without profiles or facets. Being given via profiles is the mark of transcendence (objecthood); being given without them is the mark of immanence (subjectivity, interiority). Being given via profiles also introduces a certain relativity into perception, since the profile through which an object is given is partly a function of the perceiver's (or thinker's) position in multiple spaces (not just in physical space, though that comes to mind first): From location *X*, I can see this side of the tree; from position *Y*, the other side, etc. By contrast, pre-reflective self-consciousness is *positionless, facetless*, and, as Sartre says many times, an *absolute* (e.g., TE, p. 8). Just as one way of indicating God as absolute is to say with Spinoza that God is *causa sui*, intending thereby that God does not depend for Its existence on anyone else, so consciousness is an "absolute" in the sense that its appearance does not depend on anything other than itself (at least phenomenologically speaking). It appears to itself, but this does not mean that there must be some *other* thing to which it appears. Just as God, by Its very nature, "causes" Itself to be without something else causing it. But consciousness is *conspectus sui* rather than *causa sui*.

We have also noted, following an indication of Sartre's, the important role pre-reflective self-consciousness has in time-consciousness. But we were searching for a genuinely *positive* characterization of non-positional self-consciousness. What can we say about it that is not a matter merely of saying what it is not, or saying what it relates to, or developing various analogies? Acquaintance is, unfortunately, also a notion that tends to be characterized negatively. It is *not* representation. It does *not* involve conceptual mediation. One positive thing that can be said about it is that, as classically conceived, it *does* entail the real existence of its relata, and this will be the one (onto)logical feature that we will make some use of in what follows.

We also added that, in being self-acquainted, consciousness is "pre-predicatively" aware of itself and (some of) its structures and inherent similarities and differences. Here we made an analogy with the Husserlian account of perception and perceptual judgment. And we borrowed a phrase, though not much theory, from Brandom. To make a perceptual judgment is just to explicate (encode into concepts and place into the "space of reasons") what one was aware of beforehand, prior to judging or thinking. And to confirm or disconfirm the perceptual judgments of others we always have recourse to the pre-predicative level of experience. We, as it were, decode the sentence and see if our pre-predicative experience corresponds to it. Something similar is true, on the interpretation here offered, of reflective judgment. Reflective judgments code up what one was pre-reflectively (and pre-predicatively) acquainted with. And to see if my experience is similar to yours, I must be able to decode the sentences in which you express your judgment to see if, *mutatis mutandis*, there is correspondence. This, of course, requires attention to experience and an attitude of interrogation that one may have generally lacked before the prompt of the other's judgment.

Relatedly, we made sense of Sartre's often-repeated claim that consciousness is non-thetically aware of itself *as P* (e.g., as passive, as transcending itself, as degraded) by arguing that in, for example, preception, consciousness is passive, is acquainted with itself, and thus is pre-perdicatively aware of *its own passivity*. Just as we go from *white tree* to *the tree is white* when we move from pre-predicative perceptual experience to predicative explication of and judgment based on the experience, we can move from *this passivity in regard to the appearance of X* to *I am perceiving X*, when we move from pre-reflective experience to reflective judgment.

This account does raise several issues for the Sartrean that we must address. Does it imply, contrary to what was said before, that consciousness *perceives* itself and thus treats itself as a transcendent object even at the pre-reflective level? Even if not, does it still run afoul of the supposed refutation of the "Myth of the Given"? Perhaps consciousness can no more be *given* to itself without the application of concepts than the physical world can than the physical world can be given to it without them. Does it imply, contrary to Sartre's contention in the Introduction of B&N, that consciousness *knows* itself prior to reflection? Does it really give us a way to distinguish impure and pure reflection without the latter just collapsing into pre-reflective self-consciousness? And if consciousness is self-acquainted in the way indicated, how does this affect Sartre's notorious claim that, because it is self-present, consciousness fails to coincide with itself? Is there a way to save the project of B&N, to recover the "origin of negation" without holding that consciousness is literally not itself? In what follows, I briefly treat each of these complex issues.

## Acquaintance, knowledge, and "the ontological proof"

The standard philosophical folklore examples of "knowing something by acquaintance" are things like experiencing the taste of coffee, the smell of roses, the sight of a red tomato, etc. However, for Sartre, such sensory qualities are transcendent objects for consciousness (they are "intentional objects" in *roughly* the way contemporary representationalism would suggest—in spite of the very un-Sartrean name). Acquaintance is usually contrasted with intentionality or representation. The relata of a real instance of an acquaintance relation definitely exist, while an intentional object need not exist. If I am acquainted with an instance of phenomenal redness, *there is* such a property instance. But if I merely represent the instance (even perceptually and non-conceptually), the instance need not exist. So far, so good, we might say, for our purpose (the purpose of claiming that non-positional self-consciousness can be interpreted as self-acquaintance). But the problem is that our relation to the *en soi* is, at a generic level, one of acquaintance. This comes out in the Introduction to B&N where Sartre, in a way somewhat reminiscent of G. E. Moore's "The Refutation of Idealism" (1903/1965), infers the existence of the *en soi* from, in effect, conscious perceptual intentionality (pp. lvii–lxii). Will this mean, unfortunately, that either Sartre's "ontological proof" fails (because we are not, after all, acquainted with the *en soi* and cannot infer its existence from its mere representation), or that, rather, the account of non-positional self-awareness in terms of self-acquaintance fails because it would entail that consciousness is, even at the pre-reflective level, a transcendent object for itself, contrary to one of Sartre's most central claims?

This dilemma actually rests on overlooking a very subtle difference between Sartre's account of perception and the accounts of contemporary representationalist theorists of perceptual consciousness. But we have to remind ourselves once again of the Husserlian background out of which Sartre's theory arose. Husserl drew a distinction between "hyletic" color or tone data and objective colors and tones. The idea was that we are, though he did not put it this way exactly, directly acquainted with hyletic data but only intentionally aim at objective colors through the flux of hyletic data, by "animating" them—basically, seeing them *as* profiles of such and such a transcendent object. Hyletic data were thought to be immanent and not transcendent objects of consciousness.[10] Sartre famously rejected Husserl's hyle as he famously rejected every other sort of "inhabitant" of consciousness

(B&N, p. lix). Nevertheless, there is still a similar sort of distinction to be drawn in Sartre's theory of perception.

Sartre's "ontological proof" in the Introduction to B&N is not a proof of the existence of any particular thing (tomatoes, chairs, hands, etc.). After all, he was well aware of the possibility of perceptual error, and the very account of perception via profiles, as recounted earlier, carries with it the implication that perceptual objects are always "dubitable," something Sartre well knew (see IPPI, p. 8). Rather, the proof is of the existence of the *en soi* at the generic level. It is a proof that *there exists* something other than consciousness to which consciousness is internally related in its very being, not anything about the specific character of this being (except that it is *other* than consciousness).

Since consciousness is, by essence, internally or intrinsically related to this "different" thing (different from consciousness itself), and consciousness necessarily involves the appearance to it of this *something-other-than-consciousness*, we can infer that *if* consciousness exists (and it obviously does), then something other than consciousness does too. Or rather, we can infer this if we assume that at some basic level consciousness necessarily *is* how it seems to be (even if it may also be ways that it does not necessarily seem to be: see Williford 2004, 2007). If we can assume this, then, indeed, containing an apparent difference, as consciousness evidently does, entails there being something different from consciousness, since this is an internal or essential, real and concretely instantiated relation. Consciousness involves real relata. And on the Sartrean view, which is not, in the end and despite the fanfare, all that different from Husserl's view, some of the relata are *other than* consciousness itself—and they are given that way.

The only real difference between Sartre and Husserl is that Husserl regards the hyletic data as serving as a sort of bridge between consciousness and the non-conscious (see Hintikka 1995; Williford 2013). Sartre finds this unintelligible, and kicks the hyle entirely out of consciousness (B&N, p. lix). But because consciousness is internally related to (or *acquainted with*) these bits of otherness and alterity, we can infer that they do indeed exist. Consciousness cannot exist without revealing something other than itself (along with itself). And this is prior to and presupposed by any intentional animation or constitution of the *en soi* as some particular transcendent objects or other (which, on the Sartrean view, will ultimately be a function of our facticity and our projects). What Husserl conceives of as a sort of bridge between consciousness and the non-conscious world, Sartre conceives of as something more like consciousness "glomming" on to something other than itself in its very being (B&N, p. lxi). I think these are just terminological variants of what is really essentially the same view: In its very being consciousness relates to (is acquainted with) something other than itself. It does not really matter if it relates to a part of itself that is different from the whole and different from the acquaintance relation as such, or if it relates, in exactly the same way, to something that is not literally a part of it but that it nonetheless ontologically depends on. The difference between the views seems to come down to whether we call the hyletic data (or the manifold manifestations of the *en soi*) immanent "parts" or properties of conscious wholes or not. Otherwise, consciousness is just as dependent on, revelatory of, and different from these bits of alterity and facticity on the one view as it is on the other.

In either case, for consciousness, on these views, to be is to appear to be in a world (i.e., related to something) not of its own making, to be penetrated with something alien, an alterity, a facticity; and this is, of course, what we do find. Once we see that for Sartre, the "ontological proof" is not a proof of the existence of any specific transcendent object (a table, a chair, etc.) but a proof of an alterity or non-conscious facticity that exists insofar as consciousness exists, then we can see immediately the error of assimilating his argument to an argument of the fallacious kind: $X$ (perceptually) represents $Y$, therefore $Y$ exists. It makes much more sense to treat the argument as an argument from acquaintance: $X$ is acquainted with $Y$, therefore $Y$ exists. This follows trivially from the understanding of acquaintance as a real relation (unlike representation). Again, one must always remind oneself that it would be erroneous to think that here one could be acquainted with dogs, chairs, etc. Such "transcendent objects" can only be revealed over time through profiles. For Husserl, such perceptual consciousness requires the intentional "animation" of the immanent sensory hyle; for Sartre it requires something quite similar to Husserl's "animation." However, what is animated is not the sensory hyle; it is the *en soi* which is already "transcendent" in the sense that it is *not* consciousness but not in the sense that it must be revealed over time via profiles as some specific object, though, of course, in any concrete case one will take it to be (a part or profile of) some specific sort of object. What is generic or "transcendental" in a quasi-Kantian sense is this difference from consciousness. This difference is a precondition or presupposition of all specific types of objectification or constitution (intentional animation).[11]

The view then is that in being acquainted with the *en soi* consciousness is also acquainted with itself and with its difference from the *en soi*—this latter is its non-positional self-consciousness of itself *as* not being the thing revealed to it (B&N, p. 88). This is a generic, universal structure of consciousness, presupposed by the consciousness of any specific transcendent objects. Moreover, in being thus self-conscious, consciousness is also directly acquainted with the fact that it is, say, an imagining of $X$, a perceiving of $Y$, an emoting about $Z$, etc. As Sartre would put it, it is non-thetically conscious of itself *as an imagining of Pierre, as a counting of cigarettes, as a sudden shrinking from the horrible face in the window*, etc. It is thus acquainted not only with itself, its existence, and the in-itself it reveals, it is also acquainted, in any concrete specific case, with the fact that it constitutes this in-itself as such-and-such a transcendent object (e.g., a tree) and the fact that it fears, loves, sees, feels, etc., the tree. (But it is not acquainted with the tree as such.) If we do not conceive of this as an acquaintance with the relevant consciousness-involving facts (where facts are conceived of as obtaining states of affairs with real constituents, not as "sentences that are true" or some other such linguistic philosophical construal), then we have to conceive of it as representation of some sort, which clearly Sartre would disavow, as should we.[12]

If one wants to call this consciousness's "knowledge by acquaintance" of the *en soi* and of itself, that is fine and does not at all undermine Sartre's claim in the Introduction to B&N and elsewhere that non-thetic self-consciousness is not a knowledge (*connaissance*); and this holds in spite of the fact that the *connaître/savoir* distinction in French is sometimes taken to mark the Russellian KBA/KBD distinction. It would be tempting to make this sort of claim especially since in B&N Sartre seems to reduce knowledge (ultimately) to intuitive knowledge (the direct confrontation with the object) and to downplay the role of conceptualization and inference in the sections in which he discusses knowledge (B&N, p. 172). But this is just because he has an essentially Husserlian model of knowledge and, like Russell's earlier models of knowledge, on the Husserlian conception, acquaintance (though not by that name) is the ultimate ground of all other, derived forms of knowledge. This does not, of course, mean that either Husserl or Sartre would deny the role of conceptualization in such knowledge. After all, one can handle a carburetor, say, without knowing very much about it; and one's knowledge of such an object is measured exactly by one's ability to relate perceptual intuitions of the carburetor to concepts of the functions of its parts.

In Part Two, Chapter Three of B&N ("Transcendence") Sartre is concerned with what we might call the scaffolding of knowledge, and the emergence of basic categories (quality, quantity, potentiality, etc.), the very differentiation of the world into *thises* and *thats*, and objective time, space, and motion. Sartre emphasizes that knowledge (*connaissance*) rests upon and includes "presence to ___" (B&N, p. 172) in these sections. And since non-thetic self-consciousness is also conceived of by Sartre as "presence to itself" and thus as "presence to ___", one might wonder if Sartre's claim that non-thetic self-consciousness is not a knowledge (*connaissance*) is simply not consistent. It is consistent, however, as long as we can find a natural and non-*ad hoc* difference between those instances of presence to ___ that count as knowledge and those that do not.

I think the easiest thing to do is to insist that knowledge involves conceptualization and constitution of the thing known in addition to presence to___, while presence to___, as such, does not, including *presence à soi*. Accordingly, it would be just as incorrect to say that consciousness "knows" itself, in the relevant sense of "know, as it would to say that it "perceives" itself, in so far as both perception and knowledge require some form of object constitution. In addition, knowledge requires conceptualization.

Given this, we can readily respond to Wider's criticism that Sartre illegitimately introduces cognitive or epistemic elements into his characterization of non-thetic self-consciousness in his discussion of Bad Faith (Wider 1989, 1997, pp. 86–90). There he seems to be saying that the believing (faith-filled) consciousness knows itself to be merely acting in faith, not knowledge, and thus undermines itself, making the overall state inconsistent, an act of faith that is simultaneously self-cancelling and thus an act of disbelief (B&N, p. 69). On the account offered here, the believing consciousness is acquainted with the fact that it is an act of faith but this does not, by itself, create a concrete, existing dialetheia.[13] Rather, it is upon reflection that one can be said to *know* that one merely has faith; and after such reflection all faith becomes "troubled," an eventuality expressed nicely in the book of faith itself: "I believe; help thou mine unbelief" (Mark 9:24).

This reflective knowledge that one believes something in the dramatic absence of sufficient evidence and, often, in the face of plenty of contrary evidence, is what brings one cognitive dissonance and leads to what we might call the "dialectic of faith and doubt." In the religious case, this often results in the self-application of all kinds of mind-stultifying and intellect-crucifying exercises—learning how to "doubt your doubt," as one fundamentalist preacher once liked to put it—in addition to techniques aimed at trying to achieve what might seem to be genuine perceptual intuitions of the object of faith (all-night prayer vigils, fasting, chanting, babbling in tongues, dancing erratically, taking *Datura*). But there are plenty of analogies in the non-religious sphere.

This construal of Bad Faith does indeed undermine Sartre's contention that the believing consciousness is ipso facto in contradiction with itself. And thus it does undermine one piece of evidence for his claim that consciousness fails to coincide with itself. So, in answering Wider, we seem to be undermining the claim that is the lynchpin of the project of B&N. We'll return to this issue after considering reflection.

## Reflection, pure and impure, and the (self-)given

Given the foregoing it is now fairly easy to characterize reflection, pure and impure.[14] What is common to both pure and impure reflection is that, at some level, one first *attends* to one's pre-reflective experience. This can be done "in memory," and it can be done while the experience continues to unfold. Following Husserl, Sartre writes of a modification or transformation that an experience undergoes when it comes to be reflected on while it still continues to unfold (B&N, p. 152; Husserl 1982, §§38, pp. 45, 77ff.). Indeed, there must be some sort of change, since one was not reflecting before but is doing so now. So what is this modification presumably common to pure and impure reflection?

Consider reflecting on something that continues to unfold while you are reflecting (for example, reflecting on how good the shower feels to you while it continues to feel that way). Consider just paying attention to the fact that this shower feels good.[15] I submit that one is not thereby necessarily judging or using concepts. One is merely attending to the *good-feeling shower*, rather than judging *that the shower feels good*. Attention to X seems to be situated somewhere between pre-predicative experience of X and explicit judgment about X. It is through attention that we single something out as of potential interest, but we may or may not issue a judgment about it (cf. IPPI, p. 43). And we may not even know what it is or how to categorize what we have singled out. Again, this is a common experience for students in the neuroanatomy lab.

Similarly, one can attend to the details of experience, whether or not one has concepts for all of the data one singles out. Indeed, initially, one will not have very good concepts, if any, as every experienced teacher of phenomenology and philosophy of mind will know. Just as one might attend to a configuration in the bushes and wonder what transcendent object it is the appearance of without knowing at all, so one can attend to some feature of consciousness and, without making it into a transcendent object—that is, while still *living it*, not know how to describe it or render an account of it. (If you don't believe me, just read the literature on psychedelic experiences.)

This means that there is a level at which conceptualization can be absent and at which one is just attending to a phenomenon as it appears. What does such reflection, this bare attention to the phenomenon, add to the experience that was not there before? I'm sorry, but it does more than just "turn up the volume" on the shower's feel on my skin. There is also the sense that this is happening right here, right now in this very awareness as it feels, and continues to feel, thus-and-so, just like *that*. One attends to the very fact that the feel of the shower is (has been and is continuing to be) present to one, right now. This should be a familiar for anyone addicted to phenomenological inquiries.

All that appears to be added is this shift of emphasis, as it were. A second ago one was abandoning oneself to the warmth of the shower's water on one's skin and thinking of as little as possible. Now one is, say, paying attention to just how awesome it feels, to the *fact* that it feels so awesome *right now* and just *keeps on going*. The enjoyment of the shower and the bare attending to the enjoyment of the shower as such (with or without an accompanying judgment or memory) only shifts the focus to what one was already aware of, but it is not just the amplification of the shower's feel. In some cases such introspection, on the contrary, *diminishes* the feel—take the case of reflecting during orgasm, or the case of certain meditative practices aimed at increasing one's pain threshold by precisely focusing on the specific character of the pain as such. This shift is a focusing on the very fact that one is having such-and-such an experience right now, that things are seeming to one just as they do right now.

If such a shift adds nothing to the experience over and above its already-existing elements, then we must accept that the appearance *of the appearance* of the shower's feel (or the *fact* that it was already appearing) appeared along with the appearance of the shower's feel. At root, reflection merely shifts attention to what was already there, as Husserl points out and Sartre reiterates in many places (e.g., B&N, p. 152). This sort of account, as has been noted by many others, makes easy sense of the shift from pre-reflective to reflective experience while the experience continues to unfold. If there is a "modification" that such reflection introduces, it is just, as Sartre says, a kind of "intrastructural" rearrangement of what is already there (B&N, p. 153). The experience is given as having already been there, and nothing material is added by such reflection.

Attention to some experience or aspect of experience or some sequence of experiences, past or ongoing, is what pure and impure reflection have in common. They differ in that one categorizes lived mental life in objectual, psychological terms, in terms, as Sartre says more than once, of the ego, and its states, actions, and qualities (dispositions and tendencies), while the other does not (B&N, p. 159ff.; TE, pp. 23–24). The former is impure reflection and is, as he says, something we have the tendency to do *first*, since we inherit a whole system of values and conceptualizations from others and, in any case, are accustomed to thinking of everything as being an object just like any other physical thing. In so doing, impure reflection goes way beyond the phenomenological evidence. If I am suddenly feeling a loathing for Pierre right now, this does not at all mean that I hate and shall always hate Pierre (TE, pp. 22–23). The latter would be an impure reflective judgment and would clearly fail to be apodictic. But we are not bound to remain stuck in impure reflection. We can, by practice, achieve, Sartre says, a sort of catharsis and break through to pure reflection (B&N, p. 155).

I suggest that pure reflection can be understood from two angles. On the one hand, if one merely reports what is currently unfolding in a rather minimally conceptual and neutral vocabulary, one is not necessarily involved in impure reflection. You seem to yourself to be reading right now and probably have so seemed for a while (only you know). Interpreted neutrally, this is not an impure reflective judgment. It is even apodictic (cf. B&N, p. 157). The concepts you possess that allowed you to encode the result of your reflection into words and communicate it to me rest upon your direct acquaintance with your own consciousness and the systems of similarities and differences we have found salient. Concepts like reading, seeming, but also, more generically, seeing, hearing, feeling, pain, pleasure, etc., that we apply to our experiences routinely and quite understandably. We absorbed the language used for naming and describing these gross contours of types of conscious experiences from infancy, and in manifold special contexts. (Can you tell me where it hurts? How intense is the pain? Is it a stabbing or a burning pain?) We long ago learned about the plexus of causal and behavioral relations associated with each type of experience and the set of analogies used to describe them, and the dynamic profile associated with them. (How long will this pain last?) Here the concepts applied in reflective judgment are so "close" to the given (they are like so-called phenomenal concepts) that there seems to be no possibility of error as long as the experience judged continues to unfold. As Sartre himself says about reflecting on perception, "for a reflecting consciousness directed at a perceptual consciousness, the perceptual nature of the consciousness reflected on is . . . an immediate and evident given" (IPPI, p. 163).

We have to begin from such "neutral" concepts when we attempt to think about, describe, and report our experiences. And, again, doing so is not necessarily engaging in impure reflection. However, transferring the habits of conceptualization that are pertinent to thinking about the world as revealed by sensory perception to consciousness is extremely misleading. One will think of consciousness in terms of Euclidean space and spatial relations and think of consciousness as containing little pictures and "representations" (the illusion of immanence: IPPI, pp. 5–6). One will imagine a strange mental alchemy going on sometimes behind the scenes in which feelings, drives, and motives mix and meld and produce new active compounds (B&N, pp. 167–170). One will imagine that knowing is like digesting, or reduce being in itself to a sequence of mental representations ("Idealism," IHP, p. 4; B&N, pp. 216–217). Or, conversely, one will imagine that consciousness is its own little sphere of being that at best bears external relations (causal or resemblance) to objects in space ("Realism," B&N, pp. 216–217). One will imagine that one real "ego" produces one's states, actions, and supports one's qualities via some irrational process of quasi-Neo-Platonic "emanation" (TE, pp. 34–35). More mundanely, if of more practical importance, one will take oneself to be something like a Humean billiard ball, one's mind to be a sequence of mental "states" that are in themselves passive and inert, reject one's own responsibility for one's actions, and *make excuses* for oneself (B&N, pp. 40–42). In short, one will misconceptualize the mind radically and in any number of ways. It is often forgotten in discussions of impure reflection that Sartre took it to be at the root of manifold ills, both theoretical and practical, and that the practice of phenomenology is what promises to be cathartic in that regard (cf. Zheng 2005, pp. 77–78).

The tendency to go beyond our rather neutral concepts for the garden-variety conscious experience types by incorporating conceptions that are not appropriate to experience and then tying these notions, often in Bad Faith, to moral, religious (and ultimately—or perhaps primarily—to economic and political) views is what should make us take the issue of impure reflection more seriously. Once we get beyond the bare attention to experience (that can be common to pure and impure reflection) and begin to conceptualize it, that is where the real potential for impurity, *and* for catharsis, resides. At the first level of conceptualization there is the relatively neutral vocabulary we learned from infancy. If its use articulating or making explicit what we are pre-predicatively aware of (acquainted with) does not automatically mean one is engaging in impure reflection, it is still not much beyond a starting point. We are merely applying the inherited concepts and reporting in the inherited vocabulary. By courtesy we can call this a type of pure reflection.

The other angle of approach is, so to say, "high-end" reflection, the post-cathartic kind. For this one must develop *appropriate* concepts and, by a process of consulting and re-consulting lived experience over years, become familiar with the contours and saliences, the patterns and flows, statics and dynamics, layers and ranges of types of experience. True enough, such habits of reflection can alter the very data one looks at to some extent. True enough, one can allow speculation, pure theory, and wishful thinking to creep in. But the field of one's own consciousness nevertheless constitutes a real domain of investigation. And given that consciousness is a real, natural phenomenon that has a similar basic structure in all its instances, there is no good reason to be perversely skeptical about the inter-subjective "validity" of phenomenology. "It looks that way to me; does it look that way to you?" Such a question, asked about some object observable with the eyes, is no more and no less a question about the Other's *experience* (of the world). Yet we take it as a matter of course.

Pure reflection, then, includes two things: (1) reflective conceptualization (and judgment) that uses the neutral, inherited experiential concepts just to report what continues to unfold before one's consciousness (and by extension, though this introduces dubitability, one's "reflections in memory"); and (2) reflective conceptualization that is on its way to or already past *catharsis*. The catharsis, again, is achieved by developing concepts that are appropriate to what is *really* given in experience.[16] And we can distinguish what is really given from what is not only by returning again and again to pay attention to lived experience. Since we experience our experience, there is no problem with the idea that we may learn from it, sharpen our concepts for its contours and patterns, expunge bad analogies and develop better ones, etc., just as we can do with any other domain of givenness. Almost paradoxically then, cathartic pure reflection, on this interpretation, involves much more of the bare attention to experience—holding concepts and thoughts in abeyance—that is at the ultimate ground of all reflective conceptualization and judgment. To learn more, one must first learn simply to watch and listen in silence.

On this interpretation of the distinction, pure and impure reflection are distinguished not by the degree of conceptualization, let alone the degree of nothingness separating consciousness from itself, but by the *quality* of the conceptualization and the degree of proper, receptive attention that conceptualization rests upon. This would make pure reflection a source of genuine knowledge on the one hand, and "quasi-knowledge" on the other (B&N, pp. 155, 162). In bare attention to consciousness as it is, consciousness becomes, as Sartre says, a "quasi-object" for itself. It is not objectified the way objects of perception are, but it, or an aspect of it, is singled out and focused on (cf. IPPI, p. 43). On this interpretation, attention is not automatically full objectification or the leaving of the sphere of immanence. This shift of attention is, again, just an intrastructural rearrangement of what is already present. And judgments in the neutral vocabulary can be thought of as expressing "quasi-knowledge." "Yes, I am in pain right at this moment." That may indeed be true and rest on reflective intuition but it is hardly worth getting worked up over. But to the extent that one has developed appropriate concepts for describing and thematizing conscious experience, one can have genuine reflective knowledge of consciousness and even make eidetic claims about its nature and structure the way Husserl and Sartre do on page after page.

If there is a way to capture Sartre's claim (B&N, p. 161) that in pure reflection the degree of nothingness separating consciousness from itself is greater than the degree of nothingness separating consciousness from itself pre-reflectively, it is this: Attention to one's ongoing experience (of the shower or the pain in one's back) does indeed set the experience up for conceptualization and judgment. When we attend to a broken electrical outlet, for example, we are suddenly engaged with it as an object of concern. We at once adopt an attitude that brings us closer to the outlet and makes it appear objective and, in that sense, more distant. We are suddenly "all about" the outlet and concerned with what it has to teach us about its properties. But precisely because we want to learn from it and don't want to deceive ourselves about it, we treat it as a subject matter for objective investigation and experimentation. Attention to our own experiences can have the same feel. On the one hand, we are suddenly "all about" the experience as such. On the other hand, it is as if we are ready to look at it with a telescope from another planet. It is as if to focus on it and let it teach us about itself, we must draw back and observe it from afar, meanwhile readying some attitudes (above all, the attitude of interrogation and questioning) and suppressing others (above all, the "who cares?" attitude and the "sit back and enjoy" attitude). Thus attention both draws the attended near and puts itself at a distance of sorts. Since we are talking about consciousness attending to itself, it does make some sense to think of consciousness as, in this sense, taking some (greater) distance from itself. On this interpretation, I hope Professor Wider will agree, Sartre's talk of reflective consciousness "deepening the nothingness" between itself and itself would not be "so enigmatic as to be useless" (Wider 1997, p. 91).

It remains to say a brief word about the "given" and the "apodictic." On the view presented here, consciousness is directly acquainted with itself and its structures (with the *fact* that it is such-and-such). This is at the pre-predicative and pre-reflective level. This is not a matter of applying concepts at all. To be non-positionally self-conscious of imagining, one need not be in possession of any concepts for imagination. Acquaintance is not a matter of applying concepts. However, the domain of acquaintance (i.e., what one is acquainted with) has a *conceptualizable* structure. Indeed, how else could it be? Direct contact with similarities and differences in the manifold of acquaintance is what ultimately gets encoded into our system of concepts. If this were not the case, we would not be able to decode them into verification-relevant perceptual expectations. You tell me there is orange juice in the fridge. I thereby know what I need to *see* (not think) in order to verify your claim. Sedimented concepts surely feed back into our experiences and modify how the world is given to us pre-reflectively, but this is no challenge here. There must be some acquaintance foundation if the feedback process is ever to begin in the first place and if it is to undergo revision or augmentation. And the results of the feedback process are themselves ultimately *given*, in a way that effaces the scaffolding and filtering that allowed them to emerge.

The given, then, has *conceptualizable* content, though it is not ultimately a matter of the deployment of concepts (see Fales 1996, ch. 4). Judgment, however, is a matter of deploying concepts. Moreover, apodicticity is a matter of thought or judgment and not solely a matter of the unconceptualized acquaintance with something. How are apodictic reflective judgments possible? Are they? Interpreting "apodictic judgment" to mean "a judgment that one cannot be mistaken in making," here is what we can say. A judgment like "I currently seem to be reading" can be apodictic as long as we take "I" to refer to the currently unfolding stream of consciousness one is directly acquainted with (and not to some more substantial ego notion), and one is indeed seeming to be reading while one thinks the thought. This is not very dramatic, of course. But how is this possible? Here one must say that one can be acquainted with one's own current awareness, know what one would have to be acquainted with in order to say if the judgment is true, and be acquainted with the fact that indeed the current awareness (seeming to be reading) corresponds to the propositional content of the judgment. This may seem crazy but it is no crazier than Russell and Husserl (or Fumerton (1985) and Fales (1996)).

## The failure of self-identity, circularity, and the real origin of negation

Even if I think Sartre's "deepening of the nothingness" talk is not *hopelessly* obscure, I do think that his view that consciousness does not coincide with itself, on which such talk is based, is, almost certainly, false. It's pretty clear that Sartre is willing to abandon the principle of non-contradiction in this connection and think that there are genuine dialetheias in the world. As he says, "to believe is not to believe" and consciousness "is what it is not" (B&N, pp. 67–70). Though there are technical ways to keep Sartre's claim about the failure of self-identity and avoid contradiction, he seems quite content to maintain that consciousness is a genuine ontological contradiction, a living dialetheia, so to speak. And there may be a way to reconstruct the Sartrean project here using the tools provided above all by Graham Priest, but we cannot enter into this interesting project here.[17]

I would like to suggest, rather, that Sartre does not need the failure of self-coincidence to carry out his project. All he needs is that consciousness is self-acquainted and simultaneously acquainted with something different from itself. This would be some sort of internal differentiation, no matter how we interpreted it. But, to keep it relatively simple, imagine that something like hyletic data exists. On this sort of view, consciousness is directly acquainted with the array of differentiated hyletic data as well as itself (including its own intentional animation of the data and its positing attitudes, but leave this aside for the moment). Insofar as it is acquainted with a range of hyletic data that differ from one another and from consciousness itself, it contains the acquaintance ground of the concept of difference. How does it know it's not one of these hyletic data? Doesn't it need to know itself somehow to be able to distinguish itself from the data? One can feel the Fichte–Shoemaker regress lurking here (see, e.g., Shoemaker 1968; Frank 2002, 2004, 2007). But the account proposed does not purport to offer an explanation of any of this, and certainly not the kind of pseudo-explanation that engenders the regress. In fact, it is right in line with Shoemaker's conclusion and the conclusions of Frank, Henrich, and Zahavi. That is to say, we are just postulating (on the basis of phenomenology, of course) that consciousness is directly acquainted with itself (and with alterity). It only "knows" itself in the sense of direct acquaintance. It does not "figure out" who it is on the basis of any sort of conceptualization or inference. It is immediately present to itself. And it does not matter if one takes this to be a self-*relation*. This does not generate a regress of any kind (see Williford 2006). And it is an elementary logical matter that there can be reflexive relations. It is simply false that "Every relation entails a distinction between two (or more) relata" (Zahavi 1998, p. 22). But this doesn't matter because the ground of consciousness's self-relation would have to be an intrinsic property in any case, something Frank, Henrich, and Zahavi should all be happy with. It is certainly *not* an external relation.

If consciousness in some way contains internal differentiation (even, say, multiple, integrated, but different parts), then why does it need to differ from itself for negation to be born? And as long as we have difference and negation within consciousness, there is no need for consciousness to *be* its own negation. We could imagine a recasting of the Sartrean project that would find the "origin of negation" in the internal differentiation that consciousness is acquainted with and not in its failure to coincide with itself. This would be a more sober project and could perhaps be carried out in a mere 400 pages rather than almost 700.

What about Sartre's claim that at the pre-reflective level an impalpable fissure slips in between consciousness and itself (B&N, p. 77)? Or that pre-reflective self-consciousness is "homologous with" reflective self-consciousness (B&N, p. 74)? Or that it contains an "outline" (*esquisse*) of duality (SC&SK, p. 126)? Or, less directly, that it is always "in question" for itself (B&N, p. 74)? Was this all just nonsense or wishful phenomenology?

Perhaps surprisingly, I do not think it was either. In fact, there are some salient phenomenological data that correspond to these claims that Sartre wants to cast as failures of self-identity, deepening of the nothingness between consciousness and itself, scissiparity, and so on.

Who hasn't felt suddenly and non-reflectively observed by oneself from time to time? The more extreme cases of depersonalization and derealization are of a similar character. And most strikingly, there are the bizarre cases of heautoscopy in which one does not know which of two mutually facing perspectives one occupies (Blanke and Dieguez 2009, pp. 304–308; Sacks 2012, pp. 265–270). And, of course, as noted above, mere attention to one's current unfolding experience has the odd effect of simultaneously bringing the experience closer while holding it "at arm's length," so to speak. How is any of this possible? Is it all best explained by a failure of self-identity?

I cannot argue this in detail here, but these phenomena of "self-distancing" can be accounted for by circularity and projective geometrical structure (see Khromov 2001; Williford 2006; Miranker and Zuckerman 2009; Williford et al., 2013; and Rudrauf et al. ms.). On the one hand, the circularity of consciousness grounds the capacity to attend to one's experience (and one's experience of one's experience, etc.) as a sort of "intrastructural modification." Assume that attention is a matter of ordering of some kind, as is not uncommon (see, e.g., Williford 2006 for this claim and more on this type of model). Add circularity. This will mean, for example, that an episode of consciousness looks something like this: $c = <a,b,c>$ (where $a$ and $b$ are, say, some hyletic data, animated or not). Being in its own membership chain (i.e., being non-well-founded) is what correlates with being non-positionally self-aware in this model (being self-acquainted). Now assume that reflection is just a matter of "pulling" $c$ up to the front of the ordering (focusing one's attention on $c$). Then the reflective consciousness $d$ of $c$ would look like this: $d = <c,d>$. Note that all it took to generate $d$ (which is not identical to but includes $c$, which may still be "ongoing" in the relevant sense) was to "move things around." Nothing is added in $d$ except a new structural arrangement. It is a reordering of what was already there. Of course, $d$ just *is* the result of this reordering. And since it is a consciousness as well, it appears to itself also. That is why it is also in its own ordering. But it is not a new, separable entity. It is just a repetition of the constant, self-manifesting structure of consciousness and an inclusion of the act of consciousness it is reflecting on. Now, if we assume that being first in the ordering correlates with the maximal degree of attention being devoted to what is in the first "slot," and if we consider attention as being this odd function of drawing closer while "holding at arm's length," then we can get some idea of how reflection could produce this weird sense of distancing by mere rearrangement.

We can also understand how one could easily generate layers and layers of reflection, something we can do to an extent but do have an attentional capacity limit for. I can reflect and then reflect on my reflection and maybe succeed in reflecting on my reflection of my reflection, but that is about it. This is just a contingent limit. But this is easily represented in the present framework: (1) $c = <a,b,c>$; (2) $d = <c,d>$; (3) $e = <d,e>$, and so on. (Remember that as one "ascends," the previous "sets" are still there in the later ones—$e$ has $d$ in its membership chain, $d$ has $c$, etc. And remember that $c$, $d$, and $e$ are all in their own chains because that is how we are modeling episodes of consciousness here! That is their self-acquaintance.) Circularity, here in the guise of non-well-founded sets or hypersets, gives us a powerful tool for thinking about pre-reflective and reflective self-consciousness just as it does for circular propositions and other circular structures (see Barwise and Moss 1996).

The other framework worth mentioning is that of higher dimensional projective geometry first developed in this connection by David Rudranf (see Williford et al. 2013, and Rudrauf et al. ms.). There are models in this domain that have as a consequence that the structure of consciousness is a bit like an odd tube that one looks through and sees not only what is "in front" but also oneself looking at what is in front, a bit like Magritte's *La réproduction interdite* (cf. B&N, pp. 298–299). This too is a sort of circular structure, and we do not have place to discuss how it may be related to models involving hypersets. Suffice it to say that such models can make some sense of how there can seem to be a "distance" between a point of view and itself, when, in fact, there is none.

So though I am inclined to reject Sartre's view that consciousness does not coincide with itself (in the sense of not being identical to itself), I think that the phenomenological data that made this description seem salient to him are important and should not be ignored, no more than should the phenomena connected with the "origin of negation." It seems we can capture the latter by recourse to the idea that consciousness is acquainted with itself as well as its internal differentiation. It seems that we may be able to capture the phenomenology of various kinds of "self-distancing" in terms of circularity and projective geometrical structure. If so, there'd be no need to reject the "Law of Identity," and we could preserve the spirit of the project of B&N without sticking to its letter.

## Conclusion: what is acquaintance? Why self-acquaintance?

I conclude by briefly considering these two questions. First, what is acquaintance? My answer: We know what it is as a phenomenon. We know some of its relations. We know what it enables. But we do not know what its internal nature is. Often philosophers are dissatisfied when another philosopher resorts to direct acquaintance. They don't like the buck to stop there and wonder what acquaintance could *be*. But in my view, the proponent of acquaintance should not just say "explanations must come to an end, and here I turn my spade." Though one has to say this at some point, we can in this case say something more interesting. We need not conceive of acquaintance as a magic relation holding between a magic being (the consciousness homunculus) and other things (the *en soi*, the sensory hyle, sense data, or whatever), which are only slightly less magical. Rather we take this description as, at first, phenomenology, a description of how it seems, and not automatically the presentation of an ontology. This means that we know what acquaintance is (and what self-acquaintance is) in the sense that we can attend to the relevant phenomena, that they seem to us to have certain relations to other phenomena (reflection, negation, time-consciousness, etc.), and that we can espy certain structures involving the relation. But this does not mean that we know what the relation is in the sense of its real, physical ontology. And here we definitely part company with Sartre.

For Sartre up through B&N, there is nothing hidden about consciousness. It could not contain hidden structures and properties. We have access to all its features and every feature of all its features. This idea, coupled with the fact that, contrary to what he thought, so much is indeed hidden from consciousness's view of itself, led Sartre to the view that consciousness is just the insubstantial revealed-revealing of objects other than itself (and thereby of itself, hence "revealed"). It has no intrinsic properties; it cannot be identified with anything substantial. It is a "nothingness." But once we see that Sartre's "phenomenological ontology" rests on the utterly unwarranted assumption[18] that consciousness has immediate access to everything essential about itself, we can say the following: Consciousness, acquaintance, etc., do have the structures they seem to have, but this does not mean that everything about their inner nature is revealed to us through phenomenology. In this latter sense, we do *not* know what consciousness is. It is almost certainly physical in a well-enough-defined sense. Indeed, I put my money on the idea that consciousness is a specific type of suitably circular computational process implemented in the neuronal hardware of the brain. This would mean that any further, non-phenomenological understanding of what acquaintance *is* would have to proceed by the development of an empirical theory (containing a non-trivial mathematical framework, of course). But this is how it should be, given that we cannot penetrate into the internal nature of consciousness by phenomenology or mere thought experiment. I would not expect Sartre to accept this sort of physicalism, of course. But it is Sartre as a *phenomenologist* I admire most, and not Sartre as an ontologist or metaphysician.

Finally, why believe that consciousness is self-acquainted? Forget about acquaintance as such, for the moment. Let's just ask why we should think that consciousness is non-positionally self-conscious, leaving open exactly how we interpret this. One cannot derive this claim from pure logic, definitions, or tendentious analogies (consciousness is like the candle flame, needing nothing other than itself to be illuminated) without begging the question. Likewise, one cannot refute it with regress arguments, different definitions, or equally tendentious analogies (consciousness is like a knife blade—it cuts other things but can't cut itself).

Though it can help to explain certain robust features of experience (reflecting on experience that continues to unfold while one reflects, reflecting in memory, time-consciousness, one's ability to answer immediately the question "What are you doing right now?", the dative of manifestation or subjective pole without homuncularism (see Williford 2011), keeping track of one's location in a multitude of spaces, and the sense that one's being is always "in question" for oneself), there are plenty of perverse ways to avoid the conclusion that any of these phenomena requires genuine, reflexive, self-presence. The back and forth can be interminable and is ultimately boring and unproductive. It is better to let the tribunal of empirical theory testing decide the issue. So, follow your phenomenological muse, build the model the muse inspires, test it empirically, and show that it leads to the verifiable identification of the neural correlates of consciousness. My money is on models that encode genuinely reflexive structure. If another model of consciousness that does not include that structure wins the race for the neural correlates, then I will concede that this very deep sense that you are intimately aware of this very experience you are having right now as you read this is just an illusion. Until then, however, I will operate on the assumption that it is not and build away.

## Notes

1 As Webber (2002) points out, to speak of something's "thetic" (*thetisch*) or "positing" character (*Setzungscharakter*) is, for Husserl, to speak of the same thing; see also Cairns (1973), pp. 103, 111.
2 It should be mentioned that Husserl himself makes this analogy (Husserl 1982/1913, §45).
3 This passage is presented by Gennaro (2002, p. 311) in such a way that he has Sartre saying precisely that it *is* a quality of the positional consciousness. Sartre is manifestly denying that in this passage.
4 Indian and Tibetan Buddhist philosophers have developed and argued about the "self-illuminating" light analogy (lamps, flames, etc.) at considerable length. See, e.g., Yao (2005), pp. 127ff., Williams (1998), pp. 19ff., Cabezón (1992), pp. 345ff., Shantarakshita and Mipham (2010), pp. 202–205. Zahavi has developed the "dimension" analogy to some extent. See Zahavi (2005), pp. 115ff.
5 For a good discussion of the "messy" anglophone literature on non-conceptual content, see Hopp (2011, ch. 5).
6 Some have seen Sartre as an ally to this sort of view with good reason. However, it would be quite a mistake to take Sartre's denial of internal sensory "content" (sense data or hyletic data) to be a wholesale denial of the sphere of immanence or an embrace of a completely radical version of the "transparency intuition" à la Tye; such an interpretation would make it very difficult to understand the centrality of non-thetic self-consciousness for Sartre. (See, e.g., Rowlands 2011.)

7 On the "cognitive phenomenology" debate, see the papers in Bayne and Montague (2011). For what is, in effect, Sartre's discussion of this issue, see IM, pp. 66ff.; and for his own sophisticated description of how thought oscillates between "empty intention" and imagination, see IPPI, pp. 57ff. and 112ff., esp. p. 122.
8 For discussion of the "phenomenal concepts" strategy see, e.g., Papineau (2002, ch. 4), Chalmers (2003), and Tye (2009, ch. 3). As far as I know the strategy, in essence, actually originated with Keith Lehrer's account of "Lucid Content" (Lehrer 1997, pp. 165–175; see also Lehrer 2006).
9 The connection between phenomenal concepts strategy and acquaintance is brought out in, e.g., Chalmers (2003) and Goff (forthcoming).
10 See Williford (2013) for an interpretation and defense of Husserl's account of perception. See IM, Chapter IV, for Sartre's fullest discussion of Husserl on perception and imagination.
11 Sartre would, of course, object that if we do not build transcendence into perception from the beginning and deny that the hyle are *in any sense* immanent in consciousness, we will lose his type of realism and lose the radical distinction between imagination (dream and hallucination) and perception (see the Introduction to B&N as well as IM, Chapter IV, and IPPI, Part I, Chapter I, and Part IV.) But there is no space to go into this here.
12 I do not here consider "modal" or "adverbial" construals of pre-reflective self-consciousness because I consider them to be generally unilluminating, at best terminological variants of representationalist views. I could, of course, be gravely mistaken. See, e.g., Rowlands (2011, pp. 179–180).
13 And this is more in line with what appears to be an account of pre-reflective consciousness (of) belief that is just not consistent with the account in B&N. See IPPI, p. 162, " . . . [I]f Pierre's friendship appears to me as the object of my belief, it is because my non-reflective consciousness of this friendship was non-thetic consciousness of itself as simple belief; but it is not necessary to conclude that the skepticism of the reflection [on its status as mere belief] was also a non-positional structure of the unreflective consciousness."
14 This account is in good resonance with much in Zheng (2005, ch. 5). But Zheng's account of non-positional self-consciousness in terms of "present-tense feelings" (see Zheng 2000, 2005, pp. 3–10) seems to be ambiguous. It can be assimilated to Webber's account in terms of non-conceptual representation (Webber 2002, penultimate paragraph) or to an acquaintance account. Zheng's (2005, p. 8) attempt to distance his account from an acquaintance account by claiming that acquaintances are instantaneous while feelings are continuous seems to me to rest on a specific understanding of the term "acquaintance" that is not at all obligatory.
15 This seems to be like Metzinger's "Introspection[3]" in Metzinger (2003, p. 36).
16 Cf. Wider's discussion of appropriate conceptualization in the reflective self-understanding aimed at in "existential psychoanalysis" (Wider 1997, pp. 83–85; B&N, pp. 568–571).
17 See Priest (2002, 2006), especially chapters 11 and 12 on change and motion. See also Kull (1997), who attempts to derive temporal oscillation from a structure like the Liar Paradox. These projects are very reminiscent of the "Temporality" and "Transcendence" chapters of B&N.
18 See Williford (2004, 2007).

# References

## Works by Jean-Paul Sartre

**B&N:** *Being and Nothingness: An Essay in Phenomenological Ontology*
Translated by Hazel E. Barnes. Edited by Arlette Elkaïm-Sartre. London: Routledge, 2003. Translation of *L'Être et le néant: Essai d'ontologie phenomenologique*, revised by Arlette Elkaïm-Sartre, Paris: Gallimard, 1994. First published by Gallimard in 1943.

**E:** *Sketch for a Theory of the Emotions*
Translated by Philip Mairet. Second edition. London: Routledge, 2002. Translation of *Esquisse d'une théorie des emotions*, Paris: Hermann, 1939.

**IHP:** "Intentionality: A Fundamental Idea of Husserl's Phenomenology"
Translated by Joseph P. Fell. *Journal of the British Society for Phenomenology* 1, no. 2 (1970): pp. 4–5. Translation of "Une idée fondamentale de la phénoménologie de Husserl l'intentionnalité," first published in *La Nouvelle Revue Française* 304 (janvier 1939), pp. 129–131, then collected in *Situations I: Critiques littéraires*, Paris: Gallimard, 1947.

**IM:** *The Imagination*
Translated by Kenneth Williford and David Rudrauf. Routledge, 2012. Translation of *L'Imagination*. Paris: Presses Universitaires de France, 1936.

**IPPI:** *The Imaginary: A Phenomenological Psychology of the Imagination*
Translated by Jonathan Webber. London: Routledge, 2004. Translation of *L'Imaginaire: Psychologie phénoménologique de l'imagination*, revised by Arlette Elkaïm-Sartre, Paris: Gallimard, 1986. First published by Gallimard in 1940.

**Sartre 2003**: *La transcendance de l'ego et autres textes phénoménologiques*. Textes introduits et annotés par Vincent de Coorebyter. Paris: J. Vrin. (I refer to some of de Coorebyter's notes in this edition.)

**SC&SK:** "Consciousness of Self and Knowledge of Self"
Translated by Mary Ellen and Nathaniel Lawrence. In *Readings in Existential Phenomenology*, edited by N. Lawrence and D. O'Connor, Englewood Cliffs, NJ: Prentice-Hall, 1967. Translation of "Conscience de soi et connaissance de soi," *Bulletin de la Société Française de Philosophie* 42, no. 3 (1948): pp. 49–91.

**TE:** *The Transcendence of the Ego: A Sketch for a Phenomenological Description*
Translated by Andrew Brown. London: Routledge, 2004. Translation of *La transcendance de l'ego: Esquisse d'une description phénomenologique*, Paris: Vrin, 1965. First published in *Recherches Philosophiques* 6 (1936–1937): pp. 85–123.

## Works by others

Barwise, J. and Moss, L. (1996). *Vicious Circles: On the Mathematics of Non-Wellfounded Phenomena*. Stanford, CA: CSLI Publications.

Bayne, T. and Montague, M. (Eds.) (2011). *Cognitive Phenomenology*. Oxford: Oxford University Press.

Blanke, O. and Dieguez, S. (2009). Leaving Body and Life Behind: Out-of-Body and Near-Death Experience, pp. 303–325. In S. Laureys and G. Tononi (Eds.) *The Neurology of Consciousness: Cognitive Neuroscience and Neuropathology*. Munich: Elsevier.

Brandom, R. (2000). *Articulating Reasons: An Introduction to Inferentialism*. Cambridge, MA: Harvard University Press.

Byrne, A. (2001). Intentionalism Defended. *Philosophical Review*, 110: pp. 199–240.

Cabezón, J. (Ed.) (1992). *A Dose of Emptiness: An Annotated Translation of the sTong thun chen mo of mKhas grub dGe legs dpal bzang* (Vol. 125). Albany, NY: SUNY Press.

Cairns, D. (1973). *Guide for Translating Husserl*. The Hague: Martinus Nijhoff.

Chalmers, D. J. (2003). The Content and Epistemology of Phenomenal Belief, pp. 220–272. In Smith, Q. and Jokić, A. (Eds.) *Consciousness: New Philosophical Perspectives*. Oxford: Oxford University Press.

De Coorebyter, V. (2000). *Sartre face à la phénoménologie: autour de l'Intentionnalité et de la Transcendance de l'Ego*. Brussels: Ousia.

Dretske, F. (1995). *Naturalizing the Mind*. Cambridge, MA: MIT.

Fales, E. (1996). *A Defense of the Given*. New York: Rowman and Littlefield.

Frank, M. (1997). Subjectivity and Individuality: Survey of a Problem, pp. 3–37, in Klemm, D. and Zöller, G. (Eds.) *Figuring the Self*. Albany: State University of New York Press.

Frank, M. (2002). Self-consciousness and Self-knowledge: On Some Difficulties with the Reduction of Subjectivity. *Constellations*, 9(3): pp. 390–408.

Frank, M. (2004). Fragments of a History of the Theory of Self-Consciousness from Kant to Kierkegaard. *Critical Horizons*, 5(1): pp. 53–136.

Frank, M. (2007). Non-Objectal Subjectivity. *Journal of Consciousness Studies*, 14(5–6): pp. 5–6.

Fumerton, Richard (1985). *Metaphysical and Epistemological Problems of Perception*. Lincoln: University of Nebraska Press.

Gennaro, R. (2002). Jean-Paul Sartre and the HOT Theory of Consciousness. *Canadian Journal of Philosophy*, 32(3): pp. 293–330.

Goff, P. Forthcoming. Real Acquaintance and Physicalism. In P. Coates and S. Coleman (Eds.) *Phenomenal Qualities: Sense, Perception, and Consciousness*. Oxford: Oxford University Press.

Gurwitsch, A. (1985). *Marginal Consciousness*. Athens, OH: Ohio University Press.

Harman, G. (1990). The Intrinsic Quality of Experience. *Philosophical Perspectives*, pp. 31–52.

Hatzimoysis, A. (2011). *The Philosophy of Sartre*. Montreal: McGill-Queen's Press.

Hintikka, Jaakko (1995). The Phenomenological Dimension. In B. Smith and D. W. Smith (Eds.) *The Cambridge Companion to Husserl*. Cambridge: Cambridge University Press.

Hopp, W. (2011). *Perception and Knowledge: A Phenomenological Account*. Cambridge: Cambridge University Press.

Husserl, E. (1973/1948). *Experience and Judgment*. J. S. Churchill and K. Ameriks, trans. Evanston, IL: Northwestern University Press.

Husserl, E. (1982/1913). *Ideas Pertaining to a Pure Phenomenology and to a Phenomenological Philosophy: First Book*. F. Kersten, trans. Dordrecht: Springer.

Husserl, E. (1991/1928). *On the Phenomenology of the Consciousness of Internal Time (1893–1917)*. J. B. Brough, trans. Kluwer: Dordrecht.

Khromov, A. (2001). Logical Self-Reference as a Model for Conscious Experience. *Journal of Mathematical Psychology*, 45: pp. 720–731.

Kriegel, U. (2009). *Subjective Consciousness: A Self-Representational Theory.* Oxford: Oxford University Press.

Kriegel, U. and Williford, K. (Eds.) (2006). *Self-Representational Approaches to Consciousness.* Cambridge, MA: MIT.

Kull, Andreas (1997). Self-reference and Time According to Spencer-Brown, pp. 71–79. In H. Atmanspacher and E. Ruhnau (Eds.) *Time, Temporality, Now.* Vienna: Springer.

Lehrer, K. (1997). *Self-Trust: A Study of Reason, Knowledge, and Autonomy.* Oxford: Oxford University Press.

Lehrer, K. (2006). Consciousness, Representation, and Knowledge, pp. 409–419, in U. Kriegel and K. Williford (eds.) *Self-Representational Approaches to Consciousness.* Cambridge, MA: MIT.

Levinas, E. (1995/1930). *The Theory of Intuition in Husserl's Phenomenology.* 2nd edn. A. Oriane, trans. Evanston, IL: Northwestern University Press.

Metzinger, T. (2003). *Being No One: The Self Model Theory of Subjectivity.* Cambridge, MA: MIT.

Miranker, W. and Zuckerman, G. (2009). Mathematical Foundations of Consciousness. *Journal of Applied Logic,* 7(4): pp. 421–440.

Moore, G. E. (1903/1965). The Refutation of Idealism, pp. 1–30. In *Philosophical Studies.* Totowa, NJ: Littlefield, Adams.

Morris, P. S. (1992). Sartre on the Self-Deceiver's Translucent Consciousness. *Journal of the British Society for Phenomenology,* 23(2): pp. 103–119.

Papineau, D. (2002). *Thinking about Consciousness.* Oxford: Oxford University Press.

Priest, G. (2002). *Beyond the Limits of Thought.* Oxford: Oxford University Press.

Priest, G. (2006). *In Contradiction.* 2nd edn. Oxford: Oxford University Press.

Raftopoulos, A. (2009). *Cognition and Perception: How Do Psychology and Neural Science Inform Philosophy?* Cambridge, MA: MIT.

Rowlands, M. (2011). Jean-Paul Sartre's *Being and Nothingness. Topoi,* 30(2): pp. 175–180.

Rudrauf, D., Bennequin, D., Landini, G., and Williford, K., unpublished ms. Phenomenal Consciousness Has the Form of a Projective 3-space under the Action of the General Projective Linear Group.

Russell, B. (1996/1914). On the Nature of Acquaintance, pp. 125–174, in *Logic and Knowledge Essays 1901–1950.* London: Routledge.

Sacks, O. (2012). *Hallucinations.* New York: Knopf.

Shantarakshita and Jamgon Mipham (2010). *The Adornment of the Middle Way.* Padmakara Translation Group, trans. Boston: Shambhala.

Shoemaker, S. (1968). Self-reference and Self-awareness. *Journal of Philosophy,* 65(19): pp. 555–567.

Tye, M. (1995). *Ten Problems of Consciousness: A Representational Theory of the Phenomenal Mind.* Cambridge, MA: MIT.

Tye, M. (2002). *Consciousness, Color, and Content.* Cambridge, MA: MIT.

Tye, M. (2009). *Consciousness Revisited: Materialism without Phenomenal Concepts.* Cambridge, MA: MIT.

Webber, J. (2002). Motivated Aversion: Non-Thetic Awareness in Bad Faith. *Sartre Studies International,* 8(1): pp. 45–57.

Wider, K. (1989). Through the Looking Glass: Sartre on Knowledge and the Prereflective Cogito. *Man and World,* 22(3): pp. 329–343.

Wider, K. (1993). The Failure of Self-consciousness in Sartre's *Being and Nothingness. Dialogue,* 32(4): pp. 737–756.

Wider, K. (1997). *The Bodily Nature of Consciousness: Sartre and Contemporary Philosophy of Mind*. Ithaca, NY: Cornell University Press.

Williams, P. (1998). *The Reflexive Nature of Awareness: A Tibetan Madhyamaka Defence*. London: Curzon Press.

Williford, K. (2004). Moore, the Diaphanousness of Consciousness, and Physicalism. *Metaphysica*, 5(2): pp. 133–153.

Williford, K. (2006). The Self-Representational Structure of Consciousness, pp. 111–142, in U. Kriegel, and K. Williford, (Eds.) *Self-Representational Approaches to Consciousness*. Cambridge, MA: MIT.

Williford, K. (2007). The Logic of Phenomenal Transparency. *Soochow Journal of Philosophy*, 16: pp. 181–195.

Williford, K. (2011). Pre-reflective Self-consciousness and the Autobiographical Ego. In J. Webber, (Ed.) *Reading Sartre*. Abingdon: Routledge.

Williford, K. (2013). Husserl's Hyletic Data and Phenomenal Consciousness. *Phenomenology and the Cognitive Sciences*, 12(3): pp. 501–519.

Williford, K., Rudrauf, D., and Landini, G. (2013). The Paradoxes of Subjectivity and the Projective Structure of Consciousness, pp. 321–353. In Sofia Miguens and Gerhard Preyer (Eds.) *Consciousness and Subjectivity*. Berlin: De Gruyter.

Yao, Z. (2005). *The Buddhist Theory of Self-Cognition*. Abingdon: Routledge.

Zahavi, D. (1998). The Fracture in Self-Awareness, pp. 21–40. In D. Zahavi (Ed.) *Self-awareness, Temporality, and Alterity*. Dordrecht: Springer.

Zahavi, D. (1999). *Self-awareness and Alterity: A Phenomenological Investigation*. Evanston, IL: Northwestern University Press.

Zahavi, D. (2005). *Subjectivity and Selfhood: Investigating the First-Person Perspective*. Cambridge, MA: MIT.

Zheng, Y. (2000). On Sartre's "Non-Positional Consciousness". *Southwest Philosophy Review*, 16(1): pp. 141–149.

Zheng, Y. (2005). *Ontology and Ethics in Sartre's Early Philosophy*. Lanham, MD: Lexington Books.

# 4 Sartre on pre-reflective consciousness

## The adverbial interpretation

*Mark Rowlands*

### Interpreting Sartre

The notion of pre-reflective consciousness plays a central role in Sartre's account of *being for-itself*. Sartre is adamant that "every positional consciousness of an object is at the same time a non-positional consciousness of itself."[1] I shall call this the *pre-reflective consciousness condition* (PRCC), for this "non-positional consciousness of itself" that is built into any act of positional consciousness is what Sartre means when he talks of pre-reflective consciousness. Sartre appears to regard PRCC as obvious, and so his argument for it is brief and, to anyone not already wedded to it, suggestive rather than compelling. Moreover, having established PRCC, to his satisfaction at least, he goes on to say very little about what sort of thing this "non-positional consciousness of itself" might be, characterizing it as an "immediate, non-cognitive relation of self to self."[2]

Perhaps the only thing that is clear from Sartre's discussion of the idea of pre-reflective consciousness is that he does not say enough about it to allow us to identify what this sort of consciousness is, certainly not with any sort of precision, by direct textual means alone. Instead, at least part of the interpretative endeavor must involve working out what pre-reflective consciousness must be for Sartre if it is (i) to play the role he requires of it in his overall account of consciousness and (ii) to be consistent with the many other—sometimes puzzling—things he says about consciousness. That is the strategy I shall pursue in this chapter. I shall argue for what I shall call an *adverbial* interpretation of Sartre's account of pre-reflective consciousness: pre-reflective consciousness is an adverbial modification of an act of positional consciousness.[3]

### The adverbial interpretation and what it is not

When an adverbial account of the mental is introduced, this is typically, at least in the context of anglophone philosophy of mind, done with a view to providing an account of the phenomenal content of mental states. A content of an experience that we might be tempted to render as "I see a red after-image," for example, is rendered as: "I am after-imaging redly."

The motivations for this view are well known. Whatever else is true of the after-image, it cannot, it is thought, really be red—on pain of rejecting its identity with a brain process on grounds of Leibniz's law. However, the problems that attend this attempt to reconstruct content adverbially are equally well known. It makes it impossible to accommodate certain inferences. We cannot, for example, construe the content "I have a red square after-image" as "I am after-imaging redly and squarely," because this is compatible with my having an after-image of two objects—one red and the other square.

These are difficult issues.[4] Happily, they are irrelevant to the topic of this chapter. An adverbial interpretation of pre-reflective consciousness is not at all the same thing as an adverbial interpretation of phenomenal content—for the simple reason that an account of pre-reflective consciousness is not the same thing as an account of phenomenal content. The former neither entails nor is entailed by the latter, and so each can be advanced logically independently of the other. While I shall exploit certain parallels between the (familiar) adverbial account of phenomenal content and the (less familiar) adverbial account of pre-reflective consciousness I shall develop, there is nothing in the latter that commits me to the former.

## The pre-reflective and the non-positional

Two preliminary distinctions are essential to proper framing of the interpretation. The first is between *positional* and *non-positional* consciousness. Sartre also employs the terms *thetic* and *non-thetic* consciousness. Positional consciousness is consciousness that "posits"—or, as we might put it today, in terms that are more familiar but ultimately no less metaphorical, "takes" or "has"—an object. In other words, an act of consciousness is positional when it is directed towards, or about, an object. This is the same thing as thetic consciousness: the object is the act's "thesis." A positional (thesis-positing) act of consciousness is intentional. A non-positional (non-thesis-positing) act of consciousness is, accordingly, non-intentional.

The second distinction is between *reflective* and *pre-reflective* varieties of consciousness. Reflective consciousness is a form of positional (thetic) consciousness that is directed, specifically, towards another act of consciousness. If I direct my attention to a thought, for example, perhaps focusing on some of its features (the thought is troubling, implausible, comforting, etc.), then the act of awareness in virtue of which my attention is thus directed is an instance of reflective consciousness. Pre-reflective consciousness, therefore, occupies a somewhat curious position in this framework. As we have seen, Sartre describes pre-reflective consciousness as "an immediate non-cognitive relation of self to self." As such it is a form of non-positional consciousness. However, while not "of" or about an act of positional consciousness, it is, Sartre tells us, nevertheless "(of)" this act of positional consciousness. Sartre tells us we should, when talking of the sense in which pre-reflective consciousness is consciousness of consciousness, put the "of" in parentheses to show that it satisfies merely a "grammatical requirement" (pp. 13–14). Understanding pre-reflective consciousness is, accordingly, a matter of understanding what the parenthesized "(of)" must mean for Sartre. The first step is to identify why Sartre thought that every act of positional consciousness must involve pre-reflective consciousness.

## The necessity of pre-reflective consciousness

Sartre argues that every act of positional consciousness involves non-positional consciousness of that act (PRCC). The argument for PRCC has two, logically distinct, strands. First, there is the argument that any act of consciousness must, in some sense, involve or require consciousness of that act. Second, there is the argument that this latter consciousness cannot be positional.

Consider the first strand. Any act of consciousness, Sartre argues, requires consciousness of that act:

> [T]he necessary and sufficient condition for a knowing consciousness to be knowledge of its object is that it be consciousness of itself as being that knowledge. This is a necessary condition, for if my consciousness were not consciousness of being consciousness of the table, it would then be consciousness of that table without consciousness of being so. In other words, it would be a consciousness ignorant of itself, an unconscious—which is absurd. This is a sufficient condition, for my being conscious of being conscious of that table suffices in fact for me to be conscious of it.
>
> (p. 11)

One may certainly put pressure on both the necessity and sufficiency claims, but the former is more germane to our purpose and so I shall focus on that.[5] It may not be immediately obvious to all why, precisely, the idea of a "consciousness ignorant of itself" is absurd. And so one might, here, and perhaps at more than a few other points in his discussion of consciousness, be tempted to think Sartre falls victim to an *argumentum ad lapidem*. However, in support of the PRCC, Sartre adds a further argument. He imagines a situation in which he is (absent-mindedly, as we might say), counting the cigarettes in his case:

> It is very possible that I have no positional consciousness of counting them ... [but] if anyone questioned me, indeed, if anyone should ask, "What are you doing", I should reply at once, "I am counting". This reply aims not only at the instantaneous consciousness which I can achieve by reflection but at those fleeting consciousnesses which have passed without being reflected-on in my immediate past. This

> reflection has no kind of primacy over the consciousness reflected-on. It is not reflection which reveals consciousness reflected-on to itself. Quite the contrary, it is the non-reflective consciousness which renders the reflection possible; there is a pre-reflective cogito which is the condition of the Cartesian cogito.
>
> (p. 13)

Sartre's argument seems to be this: the fact one is, in general, able to report on one's mental activity effortlessly shows that one must, on some level, be aware of it, even if this awareness is not, as we now tend to say, explicit. It is pre-reflective consciousness that allows one to do this. In reporting on my mental activity, I am in a state of reflective consciousness. But this ability to reflect on my mental processes cannot come from nowhere. It is the fact that I am always pre-reflectively aware of my mental activity that allows me to become reflectively aware of it. One can respond to the question immediately, only because one must have been—pre-reflectively—aware of what one was doing all along.

If one is not already wedded to the idea that consciousness requires self-consciousness, it is unclear how convincing one will find this argument. One might, for example, think that the ability to report on, through becoming reflectively conscious of, one's mental activity can be achieved through unconscious information-processing operations that, in certain eliciting circumstances, make this kind of reflective consciousness possible. Thus it is not immediately clear why these sorts of considerations necessitate appeal to another—novel and as yet poorly explained—form of consciousness. This is a complex and difficult issue, and this chapter is not the forum to attempt any sort of adjudication.[6] Therefore, I shall simply note that, to those not already wedded to the idea that consciousness requires self-consciousness, Sartre's arguments may be less than convincing.

Having established, to his satisfaction, that consciousness requires self-consciousness, Sartre then argues that this self-consciousness cannot be positional—and therefore that it is not reflective consciousness.[7] Here, I think, Sartre is on stronger ground:

> The reduction of consciousness to knowledge in fact involves our introducing into consciousness the subject–object dualism that is typical of knowledge. But if we accept the law of the knower–known dyad, then a third term will be necessary in order for the knower to become known in turn, and we will be faced with this dilemma: Either we stop at any one term of the series—the known, the knower known, the knower known by the knower, etc. In this case, the totality of the phenomenon falls into the unknown; that is we always bump up against a non-conscious reflection, and a final term. Or else we affirm the necessity of an infinite regress . . . which is absurd.
>
> (p. 12)

The argument takes the form of a dilemma. And, as any logician knows, a dilemma is only as good as its horns. The first horn seems reasonably compelling: no one wants to be committed to an infinite regress, at least if we assume the regress is vicious. It certainly does seem so in this case. If any act of positional consciousness requires an act of self-consciousness, and if this act of self-consciousness is itself positional, then we will need another act of self-consciousness—a third-order act—directed towards the original act of self-consciousness. But if that is also positional, then we will require a further act of self-consciousness—a fourth-order act—directed toward the third-order act, and so on. This is an unenviable logical position in which to find oneself.

The other horn of the dilemma, however, may be found less damaging. Once again, Sartre's proclivity for *argumenta ad lapides* asserts itself. Why, precisely, is it "absurd" to suppose that there is a final, non-conscious, act that halts the regress? There is, I think, a compelling argument that can be mounted in favor of Sartre's view. The claim Sartre wishes to attack is this: a second-order act of positional consciousness directed towards a first-order act of positional consciousness is required for the first-order act of consciousness to be conscious. This claim raises an obvious question: why? What reason could there be for this claim of necessity? If one wants to insist on the positional character of the higher-order act, then it seems only one answer suggests itself. Positional acts of consciousness make one aware of their objects. Thus, the higher-order positional consciousness is required for the consciousness of the first-order positional act because, and only because, it makes the subject aware of the first-order act.[8] But, if that is the case, there are compelling reasons for supposing that the higher-order act cannot be unconscious. Unconscious mental acts do not make their subjects aware of what they are about. Indeed, that is precisely the criterion of their being unconscious. My belief that Ouagadougou is the capital of Burkina Faso exists, most of the time, in unconscious—dispositional—form. In that form, it does not make me aware of its intentional object—the fact that Ouagadougou is the capital of Burkina Faso. This failure to make me aware of its intentional object is precisely what the unconscious character of the belief consists in.[9]

Therefore, if we accept that any act of positional consciousness requires another act of self-consciousness, there are, I think, good reasons for thinking that this latter act must not be positional. If this is correct, Sartre's denial that pre-reflective consciousness is positional is a reasonable one. Being committed to the idea that consciousness requires self-consciousness, Sartre therefore endorses the claim that self-consciousness is non-positional. Consciousness must be consciousness of itself without positing itself as an object. That is, any act of positional consciousness must involve non-positional consciousness of itself:

> We understand now why the first consciousness of consciousness is not positional; it is because it is one with the consciousness of which it is

consciousness. At one stroke, it determines itself as consciousness of perception and as perception. The necessity of syntax has compelled us hitherto to speak of the "non-positional consciousness of self". But we can no longer use this expression in which the "of self" still evokes the idea of knowledge. (Henceforth we shall put the "of" in parentheses to show that it merely satisfies a grammatical requirement.)

(pp. 13–14)

Consciousness must be non-positionally, or pre-reflectively, conscious of itself given that (i) consciousness must be conscious of itself, and (ii) this self-consciousness cannot take positional form. In other words, what we have so far are the following claims:

(1)  Any act of positional consciousness requires consciousness of that act.

This is a claim that will be found convincing by many, but if one is not antecedently of this many then it is not clear that one will be swayed by Sartre's argument. And:

(2)  Consciousness of an act of positional consciousness is non-positional.

If one accepts (1), then there are, I think, compelling reasons for accepting (2). This is a transcendental argument for PRCC: non-positional (pre-reflective) consciousness is a condition of possibility of any act of positional consciousness. But it does not, in any way, explain what non-positional consciousness is. At present, the idea is obscure, and this obscurity is in no way mitigated by the device of putting the "of" of non-positional consciousness—the sense in which a non-positional act of consciousness is (of) a positional act—in parentheses. Worse, there is another important facet of Sartre's view of consciousness that threatens to elevate the obscurity into an outright mystery. It is to this facet that we now turn.

## Consciousness as nothingness: the no-content thesis

There are two conjoined sentences to be found in section III of the Introduction to *Being and Nothingness*. The first is mundane. The second is rather startling. But even more startling is that Sartre seems to take the second to be an obvious implication of the first. Here are the sentences:

All consciousness, as Husserl has shown, is consciousness *of* something. This means that there is no consciousness that is not a positing of a transcendent object, or if you prefer, that consciousness has no "content".

(p. 11)

The first, mundane, claim is that all consciousness is intentional. The claim is, of course, not utterly mundane: it is far from clear that *all* consciousness is intentional. However, while doubted by some, it nevertheless provides the starting point for philosophy in the Brentanian—hence phenomenological—tradition, and is also widely accepted outside that tradition. For the purposes of this chapter, I shall assume this thesis—let us call it the *Intentionality Thesis* (IT)—is true. The second claim is far less mundane. Consciousness has no "content." Let us call this the *No-Content Thesis* (NCT). This claim does seem implausible. If consciousness has no content then, it seems, there is nothing in it. If this is correct then where, one might ask, are we to locate the familiar candidates for the contents of consciousness: thoughts, feelings, images, emotions, and so on? If they are not in consciousness, then where, exactly, are they? However, what is really striking about this short passage is that Sartre seems to regard NCT as a straightforward implication of IT. Indeed, so obvious does he think this entailment is that he seems to feel little need to support it with any (non-question-begging) argument. That NCT is an implication of IT is, Sartre appears to assume, too obvious to require supporting argument.

There is a tendency to relegate Sartre's claim that consciousness is nothingness to the domain of hyperbole. Sartre couldn't *really* have meant that consciousness is nothingness. I shall argue against this tendency. First, I shall argue that these two sentences are absolutely central to Sartre's arguments of *Being and Nothingness*. Indeed, it would not be too much of an exaggeration to say that *Being and Nothingness* is, in large part, an attempt to work out the implications of these sentences, and the assumed connection between them. Second, I shall argue that Sartre was correct. NCT is, in fact, a (relatively) straightforward implication of IT. If we assume that all consciousness is intentional, then consciousness is, indeed, a form of nothingness in Sartre's sense.

In this section, I shall identify, with a little more precision, the content of NCT. In the next section, I shall try to supply the thesis with (independent) supporting argument. The two tasks are not entirely independent of each other. Thus, for reasons that will not become fully clear until the supporting argument has been supplied, NCT should be understood as a thesis that applies to *objects* of consciousness. No object of consciousness—that is, no *intentional object* of experience—can be part of consciousness. That is:

(NCT) Necessarily, any intentional object is outside consciousness.

Sartre uses the term "transcendent" to refer to items that are outside consciousness. Thus, according to NCT, any intentional object is, necessarily, a *transcendent* thing.

To understand properly what NCT does and does not entail, we need, first, to observe the familiar distinction between acts and objects of consciousness. Acts of consciousness include things such as seeing (and perceiving more generally), thinking, remembering, desiring, imagining, emoting, anticipating, dreading, and so on. An object of consciousness—an intentional object—is that of which I am aware when I engage in an act of consciousness. Suppose I am thinking about an object: the bird that sits on the fence outside my office. That is, I am thinking that the bird is large and red. On the one hand there is the object of my thought: the bird. This is a transcendent object. But I am also thinking about the bird in a certain way, as falling under a given mode of presentation: as being large and red. Assuming my thought is true, the content of my thought—*that* the bird is large and red—is what we might regard as a fact. I can be aware of objects and aware of facts. Typically, a subject's awareness of objects is via his or her awareness of facts.[10] Both of these things—object and fact—are not part of my consciousness. They are, as Sartre puts it, transcendent items. This claim is unremarkable. Suppose now, however, that I close my eyes and mentally picture the bird. I attend to the mental image I have formed. This image is now an object of my consciousness—an object of the act of mentally imaging—and, if NCT is true, is therefore also a transcendent object, something that lies outside my consciousness. This claim is slightly less unremarkable.

The first scenario involved an act of thinking that took the bird (or a fact that had the bird as a constituent) as an object. The second involved an act of visualization that, supposedly, took the mental image of the bird as its object.[11] NCT is perfectly compatible with both the act of thinking and the act of visualization being parts of my consciousness. If I turn my attention from the bird to my thinking about it, and succeed in making the act of thinking into an object of thought, then, according to NCT, the erstwhile act of thinking now becomes a transcendent object. Likewise, if I attend not to the mental image of the bird but to my imaging of it, and succeed in turning the act of imaging into an object of my awareness—assuming this were possible—it too would become a transcendent object. According to NCT, all intentional objects of consciousness are transcendent, and this is true even when those objects were formerly conscious acts. The NCT is, therefore, compatible with the claim that consciousness is populated with conscious acts: of thinking, imagining, remembering, perceiving, and so on.

This may make NCT seem less remarkable than it originally appeared. I think that, to an extent, this is true. Nevertheless, it is still a surprising claim with some reasonably startling implications. One might think of NCT as supplying a challenge: try to point to the contents of consciousness. As you say "Here is one!"—mentally pointing to a thought, experience, feeling or sensation, for example—this becomes an object of your consciousness and so is, if NCT is correct, precisely not a part of your consciousness. To identify the contents of consciousness, we have to make them into objects of consciousness, and therefore, if Sartre is correct, this makes them transcendent objects—objects that exist outside consciousness. Conversely, if consciousness exists only as acts of consciousness, then it is a pure directedness towards the world, and nothing more:

> All consciousness is positional in that it transcends itself in order to reach an object, and it exhausts itself in this same positing. All that

there is of intention in my actual consciousness is directed toward the outside, toward the table; all my judgments or practical activities, all my present inclinations transcend themselves: they aim at the table and are absorbed in it.

(p. 11)

If we think of the world as a collection of actual or potential objects of consciousness, then, as Sartre puts it, the entire world is outside consciousness (p. 17). Consciousness is, in this sense, empty.

## Supporting NCT

Sartre supplies very little in the way of non-question-begging argument in favor of NCT, seeming to regard it as an obvious implication of IT. Others may not regard this as an obvious implication of IT at all. Indeed, given that IT is endorsed by so many and NCT by so few, the latter can scarcely be regarded as an *obvious* implication of the former. In this section, I shall argue that Sartre was right: even if it is not as obvious as Sartre seems to think, NCT is an implication of IT.

NCT, we should recall, is perfectly compatible with consciousness being populated by conscious acts: acts of thinking, imagining, remembering, and the like. NCT precludes only objects of consciousness—items of which a subject is aware when he or she engages in conscious acts—qualifying as contents of consciousness. Given NCT is supposed to be an implication of IT, the rejection of intentional objects as contents of consciousness must, it seems, be grounded in an argument of the following sort:

1 Consciousness is intentional.
2 No intentional object can be intentional.
3 Therefore, no intentional object can be part of consciousness.

For the argument to work, a little tidying up is required. First, we should distinguish between *derived* and *non-derived* or *original* intentionality. Derived intentionality is, roughly, intentionality that derives either from the minds or from the social conventions of intentional agents. Non-derived, or original, intentionality is intentionality that does not so derive. The Brentanian thesis, expressed as premise 1, is that consciousness is intentional in an original, or non-derived, sense. Moreover, the inclusion of derived intentionality would clearly make premise 2 false. We can, and often do, use symbols to stand in, or go proxy, for other things. Therefore, we should amend the argument to the following:

4 Consciousness is intentional in an original sense.
5 No intentional object can be intentional in an original sense.
6 Therefore, no object of consciousness can be part of consciousness.

Premise 4 is IT—which, for the purposes of this chapter, I have assumed is true. Claim 6 is NCT, which is where I want to get. It remains to defend premise 5.

When the object of consciousness is a non-mental one, it is pretty clear that premise 5 is on solid ground. Birds, rocks, clouds, trees, even bodies do not possess original intentionality. There are, of course, obvious circumstances in which we use one object of consciousness to stand in for another. To take the most obvious example, words are used to stand in for objects. But this intentionality is derived. The hard work in defending premise 5 begins when the object is a mental one. Consider, for example, something that, prima facie, seems a very good candidate for object of consciousness with original intentionality: a mental image. Suppose I stare at the aforementioned red bird. Then close my eyes and picture it, and so form a mental image of the bird. I am aware of this image. Therefore, it is an object of my consciousness. It is also about the bird. Therefore it certainly seems to have an original intentional status.

However, we can use an argument, generally associated with Wittgenstein rather than Sartre, to show why this is not, in fact, the case. The image is, logically, just a symbol. In itself, it can mean many things, perhaps anything. It might mean—stand in for, be about—this particular bird or about birds in general. It might mean "feathery thing," "thing with two wings," "thing with beak," "thing that stands on my fence," and so on. In itself, the image can mean many things. To have specific meaning—to be about one thing rather than other things—it must be interpreted. And this, on the Sartrean scheme, is what consciousness—as act—does. More accurately, it is what consciousness, as act, *is*. Consciousness, in this context, is the interpretation of the image as being about one thing rather than others—in the mode, as Sartre would say, of not being it. The expression "in the mode of not being it" signifies that it is not possible to assert that consciousness is interpreting activity. If the interpreting activity of my consciousness were, for example, to become an object of my consciousness, then it would no longer be part of my consciousness. The activity would be transcendent.

This conclusion might be thought peculiar to the choice of image as object of consciousness. But, as Wittgenstein has shown, essentially the same argument can be applied to any object of consciousness. We are tempted to suppose, for example, that we can understand the intentionality of content-bearing states such as thoughts and beliefs (or "signs," more generally) in terms of a set of rules that specify how they are to be applied. However, this approach is a victim of Wittgenstein's rule-following paradox: any course of action can be said to be in accord with a rule. So, there can be neither accord nor conflict here.

Wittgenstein's insight, in essence, was that any object of consciousness has the logical status of a symbol. Therefore, it does not possess original intentionality. This is not, by itself, to deny that thoughts, beliefs, mental images have original intentionality. When they occur as acts of consciousness directed towards the world, then clearly they possess all the original intentionality one could reasonably require: they are specific instances of intentional directedness. Rather, it is to claim that *when they occur as objects of consciousness* they do not have original intentionality. A thought, belief, image, etc. can be something *with* which I am aware, or something *of* which I am aware.[12] Typically, it functions in the first way: I am aware of the world in virtue of having thoughts, beliefs, images, etc. about it. However, I can also become aware of these thoughts, beliefs, and images. When I do so, Sartre's claim is that these are no longer parts of consciousness: they are now transcendent objects.

If this argument is correct, the prima facie surprising inference from IT to NCT has sound logical credentials. If this is correct, this has important implications, both with regard to understanding Sartre's views, and also with regard to wider issues in the philosophy of mind. The latter are beyond the scope of this chapter.[13] With regard to the former, there are two issues that are worthy of discussion. First, there is the peculiar centrality of NCT to those views. Secondly, and more importantly for our purposes, there is Sartre's attempt to reconcile NCT with another thesis that is, for him, non-negotiable: the claim that non-positional self-consciousness is essentially implicated in every act of positional consciousness (PRCC). Before moving on to this, I shall briefly examine the centrality of NCT to Sartre's view. This is necessary because NCT provides a crucial constraint on our understanding of PRCC in the sense that any viable account of PRCC needs to be able to accommodate NCT.

## The centrality of NCT to Sartre's views

Much of *Being and Nothingness* can plausibly be seen as an attempt to work out the implications of NCT. I shall focus on three prominent themes.

### *Being-for-itself and being-in-itself*

Sartre's basic distinction between two realms of being—*être pour-soi* (being for-itself) and *être en-soi* (being in-itself)—is not a distinction grounded in metaphysical intuition but, rather, is a straightforward consequence of the NCT. The distinction between the two types of being that an existent can possess is commonly glossed as a distinction between those things that are conscious and those that are not. Conscious things possess being for-itself. Non-conscious things possess being in-itself. This characterization is not incorrect. However, Sartre also believes that intentionality is the essence of consciousness. So, the distinction could equally be glossed as the distinction between those things that have (original) intentionality, and those that do not. More importantly, NCT underpins Sartre's account of the relation between these two kinds of being. The intentionality of consciousness, Sartre notes, has been understood in two ways:

> All consciousness is consciousness *of* something. This definition of consciousness can be taken in two very distinct senses: either we understand by this that consciousness is constitutive of the being of its object, or it means that consciousness in its inmost nature is a relation to a transcendent being. But the first interpretation destroys itself: to be conscious *of* something is to be confronted with a concrete and full presence which is *not* consciousness.
>
> (pp. 21–22)

The first interpretation "destroys itself" for the reasons ultimately grounded in NCT. No object of consciousness can be part of consciousness since consciousness is intentional (in an original sense) and no object of consciousness can be intentional (in an original sense). There is nothing in consciousness, and therefore there are no resources from which the being of transcendent objects could be constructed.[14] Therefore, Sartre concludes:

> Consciousness is consciousness of something. This means that transcendence is the constitutive structure of consciousness; that is, consciousness is born *supported* by a being which is not itself. This is what we call the ontological proof.
>
> (p. 23)

In Sartre's terminology: being for-itself requires and presupposes being in-itself. Being for-itself has no content. We might think of it as a hole in being in-itself. A hole cannot exist without its edges, but these edges are not part of the hole. The existence of a hole guarantees the existence of something outside it. In this sense, consciousness (the *pour-soi*) provides an ontological proof of being in-itself (the *en-soi*). The converse dependence does not hold. Being in-itself is complete and self-contained. NCT, therefore, in addition to entailing the basic distinction between being in-itself and being for-itself, also entails that idealism is false: "To say that consciousness is consciousness of something is to say that it must produce itself as a revealed-revelation of a being which is not it and which gives itself as already existing when consciousness reveals it" (p. 24). For this reason, Sartre characterizes his position as a "radical reversal of idealism."

### Nothingness and nihilation

Consciousness secretes little pockets of nothingness—*negatités*—into the world (i.e., being in-itself). This is a consequence of the fact that it exists only as acts directed towards the world. The term Sartre uses for this production of nothingness is *nihilation*. Our expectation, or hope, that Pierre will be in the café allows us, according to Sartre, to *perceive* his absence directly and not merely *infer* his absence from what we do experience. That is, we have what Sartre calls an *intuition* of Pierre's absence rather than merely *judging* that Pierre is absent (pp. 40ff.). Expectation, or hope, can produce this experience of absence only because it is itself empty—in the sense explained by NCT. Thus, Sartre argues:

> It follows therefore that there must exist a Being (this cannot be the In-itself) of which the property is to nihilate Nothingness, to support it in its being, to sustain it perpetually in its very existence, *a being by which nothingness comes to things*. It would be inconceivable that a Being which is full positivity should maintain and create outside itself a Nothingness ... The Being by which Nothingness arrives in the world is a being such that in its Being, the Nothingness of its Being is in question. *The Being by which Nothingness comes to the world must be its own Nothingness.*
> 
> (pp. 57–58, emphasis in original)

Something cannot come from nothing. Neither, Sartre thought, can nothing come from something. Nihilation—the ability to secrete *negatités*—is, therefore, a consequence of the fact that consciousness is empty.[15] This claim, I have argued, is best captured by way of NCT.

## Freedom and anguish

To the extent Sartre has been widely interpreted as a voluntarist, Sartre's conception of freedom has been widely misunderstood. Freedom, for Sartre, is freedom from motives or reasons, but this sort of freedom is of a quite specific and restricted sort. The reason we are free is that these motives or reasons—understood as items of which we are aware, as items that incline us to act in one way or another—cannot compel us. *Anguish* is the realization of the inefficacy of my motives. The question is: why should this be so? The answer is made clear in Sartre's discussion of a particular type of anguish: anguish in the face of the past.

> Anguish in the face of the past ... is that of the gambler who has freely and sincerely decided not to gamble anymore and who, when he approaches the gaming table, suddenly sees all his resolutions melt away ... what the gambler apprehends at this instant is again the permanent rupture in determinism; it is nothing which separates himself from himself.[16]

The "nothing" in question is consciousness conceived of simply as directedness towards objects that are outside—transcendent to—it.

> After having patiently built up barriers and walls, after enclosing myself in the magic circle of a resolution, I perceive with anguish that *nothing* prevents me from gambling. The anguish is *me* since by the very fact

of taking my position in existence as consciousness of being, I make myself *not to be* the past of good resolutions which *I am* . . . In short, as soon as we abandon the hypothesis of the contents of consciousness, we must recognize that there is never a motive *in* consciousness; motives are only *for* consciousness.

(pp. 70–71)

The gambler's resolution, as something *of* which the gambler is aware, is a transcendent object and therefore has no meaning in itself. It has the logical status of a symbol. It cannot compel the gambler because, and to the extent, it is a transcendent item. For the resolution to be about anything, and so possess efficacy *vis-à-vis* the gambler's future behavior, it must be continually interpreted anew by the animating consciousness. At any given time, consciousness is this interpreting activity—in the mode of not being it. Should the gambler interpret his resolution—the barriers and walls he has built up—as binding? Or are they merely the caprices of an earlier time that should now be discarded? Nothing can compel the gambler's interpretation of his resolution, and to this extent he is free. This, it should be clear, is far from the traditional voluntarist conception of freedom according to which (roughly) I assess options in the light of my preferences and freely decide on a course of action on this basis. Sartre's point is that if I were to do that, my decisions would always, and necessarily, fall short of compelling the action. Indeed, that is precisely why I am in anguish.

## The adverbial interpretation of pre-reflective consciousness

Nothing Sartre has said has removed the sense of obscurity surrounding the idea of pre-reflective consciousness. One might appreciate the arguments in favor of its existence. But this says nothing about what, precisely, pre-reflective consciousness is. This obscurity, however, is elevated to the level of mystery once we appreciate that an act of consciousness cannot become an object of consciousness without ceasing to be consciousness. If so, in what sense can pre-reflective consciousness be *of* or *about* an act of consciousness—or even (of) or (about) such an act? It now begins to look as if we are committed to the claim that consciousness does have content after all: this content consists in items (of) which consciousness is non-positionally aware. It is all very well to claim that this is a case of consciousness "(of)" rather than consciousness "of." But this still does not tell us how there can be consciousness "(of)" if there is nothing for it to be "(of)." Conversely, if there something for this consciousness to be "(of)," then how can we reconcile this with NCT?

The temptation to be avoided at all costs is one of thinking about pre-reflective consciousness on analogy with reflective consciousness. Reflective self-consciousness introduces what we might think of as a *gap* between the reflecting consciousness and the consciousness reflected upon, and this gap allows the former to be of the latter. If we thought of pre-reflective consciousness on analogy with this, we might be tempted to suppose that the gap it introduces between the pre-reflecting consciousness and the consciousness pre-reflected upon—or, rather, (upon)—is somewhat *smaller* than in the case of reflective consciousness. The consciousness pre-reflected (upon) is, somehow, less independent of the pre-reflecting consciousness than the consciousness reflected upon is independent of the reflecting consciousness. So, in understanding pre-reflective consciousness in this analogical way, we take the basic structure of reflective consciousness and modify it in certain ways.

This way of understanding pre-reflective consciousness simply returns us to the puzzle. How do we reconcile this interpretation with NCT, and Sartre's frequent characterizations of consciousness as "nothingness," "total emptiness"—as something with the "entire world outside it" (p. 15)? If the structure of pre-reflective consciousness is understood by analogical extension from reflective consciousness, then consciousness must be something for pre-reflective consciousness to be consciousness (of) it. If consciousness is really to be "nothingness," then pre-reflective consciousness must have an entirely different nature. The question, then, is precisely what this nature must be.

To be positionally conscious is to be aware of intentional objects, where the notion of "object" is sufficiently broad to include modes of presentation of ordinary objects. I can be aware of the bird, but also of the way in which it presented to me—its redness, its largeness, etc. Indeed often, perhaps typically, I am aware of objects (in the usual sense) in virtue of being aware of the way in which they are presented—that is, in virtue of being aware of their modes of presentation. When I am reflectively aware of what I am thinking, then my thought (and/or its properties) is an object of my awareness, and its experienced properties provide it with a mode of presentation. Of course, if Sartre is correct, this thought, these properties, are now transcendent of, rather than immanent to, my consciousness.

If this is what positional consciousness is, then what is it to be non-positionally aware of something? There is, it seems, only one option consistent with NCT—with the claim that consciousness has "no being outside of that precise obligation to be a revealing intuition of something—i.e. a transcendent being" (p. 23). To be non-positionally aware of an item is to be aware of that item in a certain *way*. But, crucially, *we must not equate this being conscious of an item in a certain way with being conscious of a mode of presentation of the item*. Non-positional consciousness is identical with a *mode* or *manner* of being conscious of consciousness. In other words, the expression "a way of being conscious of an object" must be understood to qualify the act of positional consciousness rather than supplying a description of that act. To understand pre-reflective consciousness, therefore, the key is to understand this idea of a *way* or *manner* of being conscious of my own mental states (understood as transcendent items), without reducing this to awareness of a mode of presentation of those states.

The only way to guarantee that "a way of being conscious of consciousness" qualifies the act rather than describes the object of the act is to go adverbial. Suppose I am positionally conscious of an object. This is, of course, itself an adverbial characterization. "Positionally" is an adverbial modifier that characterizes my relation to an object. That is, it modifies my consciousness of the object. There is nothing wrong with this, but it does cloud the adverbial function of non-positional consciousness. So, to make what is going on clearer, let us recast positional consciousness in non-adverbial terms: I have positional consciousness of an object. Then, the adverbial construal of pre-reflective consciousness becomes clear. I have positional consciousness of an object, and I have this positional consciousness non-positionally. "Non-positionally" is an adverbial modifier that qualifies my positional awareness.

This is horribly abstract. To make it more concrete, I am going to exploit some other cases of adverbial modifications. The point is not, necessarily, that all of these adverbial explanations are correct. Rather, they provide us with a way of illuminating and understanding the adverbial character of non-positional or pre-reflective consciousness. Let us begin with the classic form of the adverbial theory. The redness of my experience, as we might put it, need not be explained in terms of my introspective grasp of a property of redness (or even phenomenal redness, if this is understood in "mental paint" terms.). Rather, I experience *redly*. What does this experiencing redly amount to? It amounts to nothing more than the fact that in the having of the experience, the object of that experience is presented to me as red. This is true whatever the modality of the experience. The redness of my visual experience of a red bird, for example, is not a property of the experience toward which my introspection gaze might direct its gaze. Rather, it is a matter of the fact that, in my visual experience, the bird is presented to me as red.

The same is true when we switch from visual experience to mental imagery. If I, as we tend to say, "form a mental image" of the bird, there is no need to suppose that there is a mental image with introspectively graspable property of redness. Rather, the explanation proceeds in the same way as in the case of visual experience. The bird is presented to me as red, just that this time it is done so in the mode of imaging rather than in the mode of seeing. The object is always the same through the change of experiential modalities: it is the bird. And this object is always presented in the same way: as red. Thus, my experiencing is always an experiencing redly through the differing modes of experience (seeing, imaging, imagining, etc.). This experiencing redly is a function of the way the object of my positional act of consciousness is presented.

Now consider a case of adverbial modification that lies much closer in logical space to that of non-positional consciousness: what has become known as a *sense of ownership* of experiences. I suspect that this sense of ownership is at least part of what people have in mind when they talk of self-consciousness.

The experiences I have I take to be *mine*. Except, perhaps, in very unusual circumstances, it is not that a person first has experiences and then has to work out to whom they belong. My experiences, perhaps not necessarily but typically, present themselves to me as mine. If we tried to explain this on the act–object model supplied by reflective consciousness, we might look for an introspectively discernible feature of my experiences—the property of *mine-ness* or being mine—in virtue of which they present themselves to me in this way. I introspectively encounter the mine-ness of my experiences, and this is why I experience them as mine.

There is, however, another way of explaining this sense of ownership, one that does not appeal to introspective grasp of a peculiar sort of property. The same phenomenon can also be explained in adverbial terms. When I have experiences, I have them *minely*. Their mine-ness is an adverbial modification of the act rather than an introspectively grasped property of an object of that act. This adverbial modification is not a brute, unexplainable feature of the experiential act. Rather it stems from the nature of positional consciousness itself and, in particular, the way this sort of consciousness presents its objects. The adverbial modification results from the fact that the objects of my experiences—the intentional objects of my positional acts of consciousness—are presented, precisely, as things that are *for-me*. That is, they are presented as things I am experiencing. It is not as if I am, in experience, presented with objects and then must work out to whom the objects are being presented. It is part of the content of my experience that the objects with which I am presented are ones that are presented, precisely, to me. There is no need, in this explanation, to suppose that I am reflectively aware of a property of my experiential acts—a mine-ness that somehow clings to them and shows itself to my introspective gaze. Rather, the mine-ness—the sense of ownership—of my experience derives from the way the intentional objects of my experience (i.e., an act of positional consciousness) are presented to me in this experience.

This, I think, provides a useful template for thinking about non-positional consciousness. Just as the mine-ness of experience is an adverbial modification of positional acts of consciousness—a modification that derives from the way the intentional objects of those acts are presented—so too non-positional consciousness of positional acts of experience can be understood as an adverbial modification of those acts that derives from the way in which the intentional objects of positional acts of experience are presented. When I have positional consciousness of an object, I am non-positionally aware of this because, and precisely because, I experience the intentional object not simply as an object with various properties but, crucially, as something that is presented to me.[17] In other words, I am non-positionally aware of my positional acts of consciousness because of the way in which those acts present object to me.

The advantage of this adverbial construal of pre-reflective consciousness is that it preserves the central Sartrean insight of NCT—that consciousness

118  Mark Rowlands

is nothingness, a total emptiness with the entire world outside it. Non-positional consciousness modifies or qualifies my directedness to the world, but does nothing more than that. In particular, it carries no commitment to the idea—an idea that Sartre must reject—that when I am pre-reflectively aware, my consciousness is directed towards my consciousness in any more substantial sense. Pre-reflective consciousness characterizes my directedness to the world. It does not indicate a substantial form of directedness towards my own consciousness over and above modifying my directedness towards the world.

## Notes

1 Jean-Paul Sartre, *Being and Nothingness*, p. 11. Paris: Gallimard 1943, trans. Hazel Barnes, New York: Philosophical Library. All page numbers in text refer to the 1992, Washington Square edition.
2 See p. 11. Sartre writes: "rapport immédiat et non-cognitif de soi à soi." The notion of "rapport" is almost certainly richer than Barnes' translation as "relation."
3 I have defended an adverbial account of consciousness elsewhere, on grounds independent of Sartre's views. See, for example, Rowlands (2001a, 2001b, 2001c).
4 See Michael Tye (1984) for excellent discussion.
5 To safeguard the sufficiency claim, Sartre needs to understand pre-reflective consciousness in a peculiarly *factive* or success-oriented way. It cannot be, for example, that the table turns out to be something else—which merely looked like a table at the time. So, I must be pre-reflectively conscious of an act that is, in fact, the consciousness of a table in order to get sufficiency.
6 See Dan Zahavi (2008) for a robust defense of the claim that (positional) consciousness requires pre-reflective self-consciousness.
7 I say "having established." This succession, however, refers to the logical structure of Sartre's argument, rather than its presentation in *L'être et le néant*. In the text, this argument appears before the argument for the claim that consciousness requires self-consciousness.
8 This strategy is characteristic of *higher-order thought* (HOT) accounts of consciousness. I have pressed this kind of dilemma against such accounts in Rowlands (2001a, chapter 5, and 2001c).
9 For further development of this idea, see Rowlands (2012, pp. 171–178).
10 Some might reject this claim of dependency, but the claim is not important for my purposes.
11 I say "supposedly" because, given the interpretation of Sartre I shall eventually endorse, this is a bad way of thinking about what is going on when I visualize the tomato. It is, nevertheless, a common way.
12 See Dretske (1991) for the distinction between awareness of and awareness with.
13 See Rowlands (2010) for what is, essentially, a defense of a neo-Sartrean account of cognitive processes and application of this account to the issue of embodied and extended cognition.
14 This is a paraphrase of the rather tricky argument to be found in section IV of the Introduction, "The Being of the Percipi." While the overall argument is less than perspicuous, the claim being defended is: "Let us recognize first of all

that the being of the *percipi* cannot be reduced to that of the *percipiens*—i.e. to consciousness" (p. 18). Also relatively clear, at least in its general contours, is the argument Sartre uses to support this claim: "It is precisely because it is pure spontaneity, because nothing can get a grip on it, that consciousness cannot act on anything" (p. 20).
15 The secretion of *negatités*, Sartre thought, is essential to thinking and all other intentional acts. To think that there is a bottle on the table is to recognize that the bottle is not the table. *Negatités*, in other words, are essential to the individuation of objects in thought. See pp. 63ff.
16 *Being and Nothingness*, p. 69.
17 This "me" that is implicated in experience is not, of course the empirical ego that Sartre has consigned to being just another object in the world, like any other object. Rather, it is the transcendental me: the condition of the possibility of experience rather than an object of experience.

## References

Dretske, Fred (1991). *Explaining Behavior*. Cambridge, MA: MIT Press.
Rowlands, Mark (2001a). *The Nature of Consciousness*. Cambridge: Cambridge University Press.
Rowlands, Mark (2001b). Consciousness: The Transcendentalist Manifesto. *Phenomenology and the Cognitive Sciences* 2, 3: pp. 205–221.
Rowlands, Mark (2001c). Consciousness and Higher-order Thoughts. *Mind and Language* 16, 3: pp. 290–310.
Rowlands, Mark (2010). *The New Science of the Mind: From Extended Cognition to Embodied Phenomenology*. Cambridge, MA: MIT Press.
Rowlands, Mark (2012). *Can Animals Be Moral?* New York: Oxford University Press.
Sartre, Jean-Paul (1943). *Being and Nothingness*. Paris: Gallimard, trans. Hazel Barnes. New York: Philosophical Library, 1957/1992.
Tye, Michael (1984). The Adverbial Approach to Visual Experience. *The Philosophical Review* 93, 2: pp. 195–225.
Zahavi, Dan (2008). *Subjectivity and Selfhood: Investigating the First-Person Perspective*. Cambridge, MA: MIT Press.

# 5 Pre-reflective and reflective time-consciousness

## The shortcomings of Sartre and Husserl and a possible way out

*Gerhard Seel*

To emphasize the difficulties of any theory of time philosophers used to quote St. Augustine's famous remark in chapter 11 of the *Confessiones*: "Quid est ergo tempus? Si nemo ex me quaeret, scio, si quaerenti explicare velim, nescio." St. Augustine's question was metaphysical or ontological. We had to wait until Husserl's *Vorlesungen zum inneren Zeitbewusstsein* (1928, 1966) to understand that the question "How is time-consciousness possible?" is even more puzzling.

To explain time-consciousness one needs to presuppose a number of operations of the mind which are not conscious in a thetic way. What are these operations exactly? Most philosophers—contemporary philosophers included—have failed to resolve this problem or—what is worse—not even seen that there is a problem and what the problem is. (As an exception I should mention M. Frank 1990.) Among those who came close to seeing and resolving the problem, Sartre and Husserl occupy a prominent place. However, their theories are not satisfactory in many regards. In the following I shall first diagnose the shortcomings of Sartre and Husserl and then introduce my own solution to the problem.

### Sartre's achievements and shortcomings

Sartre's outstanding contribution to the ontology of the human being is well known. He made a big step forward in the explanation of consciousness and was the first to give a convincing explanation of the flowing of time. As we shall see, both problems are closely linked. Let us first have a look to Sartre's theory of time.[1]

It is important to see that Sartre distinguishes under the terms "statique temporelle" and "dynamique temporelle"[2] what we used to call—applying McTaggert's (1968) terminology—the "B-series" and the "A-series." However, Sartre's determination of static and dynamic time is not very precise. He sees that the first is based on the relation "before–after" and that this relation allows us to describe a temporal order "independent of change proper" (EN, p. 175, BN, p. 153), but he has not the analytical means that would allow him to determine the logical properties of these relations.

The only property he speaks of is "irreversibility." Furthermore he seems to discard the ontological question of what kind of entities stand in these relations.

In analytical philosophy one would first underline that the entities that stand in these relations are events. Furthermore one would attribute the following properties to these relations:[3]

| | |
|---|---|
| T1 Irreflexivity | $(x)$ $(\sim\!Fxx)$ |
| T2 Asymmetry | $(x)$ $(y)$ $(Fxy \rightarrow \sim\!Fyx)$ |
| T3 Transitivity | $(x)$ $(y)$ $(z)$ $((Fxy \cdot Fyz) \rightarrow Fxz)$ |
| T4' Orderedness | $(x)$ $(y)$ $[(x \neq y) \rightarrow (Fxy \vee Fyx \vee Sxy)]$ |

Sartre doesn't consider the possibility that two events stand in the relation of simultaneity. However, this possibility is evident. Unlike the relation "$x$ follows $y$ in time," the relation "$x$ is simultaneous to $y$" is symmetrical and reflexive. When Sartre speaks of the "irreversibility" of time order, he must mean that the relation "$x$ follows $y$ in time" is transitive.

Sartre is convinced that the static time order is founded on the dynamic time order. Therefore he pays much more attention to the latter. Here again current analytical philosophy has a different view. Given that modern physics doesn't need dynamic temporal determinations, one thinks rather that static time order is independent of dynamic time determinations. Sartre sees dynamic temporality as the fact of succession, "that is, the fact that a particular after becomes a before, that the Present *becomes* past and the future a former-future" (EN, p. 175, BN, p. 153). This is normally characterized with the metaphor of "flowing of time." Here again Sartre does not try to give a precise definition of the flowing of time.

While it is relatively simple to determine the logical properties of the relations that characterize the B-series, modern time logic has some difficulties in determining the flowing of time. However a first principle comes immediately to our minds:

T8 $(t')$ $(t' = N \vee t' \varepsilon P \vee t' \varepsilon F)$[4]

For all moments of time $t'$: $t'$ is either the present or a past or a future moment of time.

We can add a second principle which is evident as well:

T9 $(t')$ $(t'')$ $(t''')$ $[(t' = N . t'' < t' . t''' > t') \rightarrow (t'' \text{ e } P . t''' \text{ e } F)]$

For all moments of time $t'$, $t''$, $t'''$: If $t'$ is the present moment of time and $t''$ follows $t'$ and $t'''$ follows $t'$ in time, then $t''$ is a moment of the past and $t'''$ is a moment of the future.

However, these principles can express the flowing of time only if one already knows that the meaning of the expressions "$t'$ is the present moment," "$t$'s one of the future moments," and "$t'$ is one of the past moments" is token-dependent.

The explanation of dynamic temporality is one of the great achievements of Sartre's ontology of the subject.[5] He formulates this task right at the beginning of the chapter on dynamic temporality in the form of two questions: "Why does the For-itself undergo that modification of its being which makes it *become* Past? And why does a new For-itself arise *ex nihilo* to become the Present of this Past?"(EN, p. 188, BN, p. 165). However, if we look to his answer, we see that the questions were oddly put. For the For-itself does not become Past at all and there is no new For-itself that arises *ex nihilo* either. This odd formulation reflects the provisionary theory of the For-itself as it was developed before the chapter on temporality. According to the insights of this first step, the For-itself was determined as self-consciousness in the form of the pre-reflective *cogito* and consciousness of the object explained as negation of the In-itself. This structure did not imply any form of temporality. For the pre-reflective *cogito* determined as "reflection–reflecting" (*reflet–reflétant*) appeared to be completely intemporal. However, if the ontological structure of the For-itself did not go beyond this we wouldn't get any explanation of temporality and we would not understand either how the For-itself can be the foundation of its own nothingness. Sartre makes it clear that in this regard his first determination of the For-itself is not at all sufficient:

> A For-itself which did not endure would remain of course a negation of the transcendent In-itself and a nihilation of its own being in the form of the "reflection–reflecting." But this nihilation would become a *given*; that is, it would acquire the contingency of the In-itself, and the For-itself would cease to be the foundation of its own nothingness; it would no longer be as having to be, but in the nihilating unity of the dyad reflection-reflecting, it *would be*.
>
> (EN, p. 195, BN, p 172)

The only way out is determining the For-itself as the source of its own temporalization, or rather, showing that for the For-itself the nihilation of its own being must take the form of self-temporalization. The three dimensions of time are necessary moments of this self-temporalization. The past is the result of the negation of the being of the For-itself as In-itself. This negation is the act of the For-itself and this act creates the present and the past of the For-itself.

Sartre says: "Everything happens as if the Present were a perpetual hole in being—immediately filled up and perpetually reborn—as if the Present were a perpetual flight away from the snare of the In-itself" (EN. p. 193, BN, p. 170). The future, on the other hand, is the result of a negating act of the For-itself as well. It arises because the For-itself constitutes itself as an imperfect being, a being that projects its own perfection and necessarily pursues it in the form of its own future possibilities.

So, according to Sartre, there is no For-itself that passes away and no For-itself that arises *ex nihilo*; there is only one and the same For-itself that has to be its own past from which it separates itself by projecting itself as having to be itself as its own future (Seel 1995, pp. 172–193).

The For-itself is not only essentially a being that temporalizes itself in the way described above, but it is also essentially aware of this. Therefore the second great challenge for Sartre is the ontological explanation of this self-consciousness. Sartre's second great achievement is in fact the theory of self-consciousness (Frank 2002, pp. 247–264). His thesis is that thetic self-consciousness presupposes a non-thetic or pre-reflective self-consciousness and he describes the structure of the latter as "reflection–reflecting" (*reflet–reflétant*). Sartre's conception of the reflection–reflecting structure has to be seen as a great step forward in the theory of consciousness.[6]

However, if the For-itself is essentially self-temporalization, its self-consciousness must be consciousness of time or, more precisely, consciousness of the A-series. Therefore Sartre faces a second big challenge. He has to explain how time-consciousness is possible.

If thetic consciousness presupposes non-thetic consciousness, thetic time-consciousness should presuppose non-thetic time-consciousness as well. In fact, Sartre speaks of such a non-thetic consciousness of time. "The For-itself endures in the form of a non-thetic consciousness (of) enduring" (EN, p. 196, BN, p. 172), and he asks: "What relation can exist between original temporality and this psychic temporality which I encounter as soon as I apprehend myself 'in process of enduring'?" (EN, p. 196, BN, p. 173). Furthermore, Sartre sees that " the consciousness of duration is a consciousness of a consciousness which endures" (EN, p. 196, BN, p. 173). So, according to Sartre, thetic time-consciousness must ultimately be founded in a pre-reflective consciousness of time which has itself—ontologically speaking—duration. The problem is, however, that the "reflection–reflecting" structure will not do this job. For—as it was introduced in the first-place—it is completely lacking duration. In fact, Sartre describes it as follows:

> it is only a perpetual reference of self to self, of the reflection to the reflecting, of the reflecting to the reflection. This reference, however, does not provoke an infinite movement in the heart of the For-itself but is given within the unity of a single act.
> 
> (EN, p. 121, BN, p. 102)

In another passage Sartre speaks of the "instantaneity" of the reflection–reflecting. Consequently the reflection–reflecting is not consciousness (of) duration.

We have to acknowledge, though, that in passages that belong to the chapter on temporality, Sartre seems to shift away from his first position. As we have seen before, he now speaks of a non-thetic consciousness of duration and attributes duration to it. But his position is not very clear. In a later passage he says: "Thus reflection is consciousness of the three *ekstatic* dimensions. It is a non-thetic consciousness (of) flow and a thetic consciousness of duration"(EN, p. 204, BN, p. 180). So the reflection–reflecting cannot simply be instantaneous; it must have a kind of duration and be in a non-thetic manner conscious of this. It is curious that Sartre shifts also his terminology in this passage. While in a former passage he spoke of "consciousness (of) duration," he now uses the term "flow." That Sartre attributes to the For-itself a pre-reflective consciousness of time is also attested in the following passage: "On the unreflective plane, in fact, the For-itself is its own possibilities in the non-thetic mode" (EN, p. 210, BN, pp. 185–186). It is, however, difficult to understand how such a consciousness (of) flow or of one's possibilities as one's future is possible. Sartre offers no such explanation.

In any case, it is reflexion, i.e., thetic consciousness, that reveals to the For-itself its own temporality. Sartre distinguishes two modes of reflexion, pure and impure reflexion. Sartre's example for the latter is "this joy . . . that appears after a sadness and before that there was that humiliation which I experienced yesterday" (EN, p. 205, BN, p. 181). Sartre speaks of "succession of psychic facts." So impure reflection gives a wrong image of the For-itself as if it were a temporal In-itself. It is on this plane that the For-itself is conscious of itself in the form of "Ego." In fact, in the essay "La transcendence de l'Ego" (Sartre 1936–1937, pp. 85ff.), Sartre has argued against Husserl that the "Ego" is not the pole of constituting acts, but is rather itself an entity which is constituted. As having an "Ego" the For-itself is conscious of its past, present, and future in a thetic manner and the data of this consciousness are exterior of one another. Therefore this form of self-consciousness is not a consciousness of the essential temporal structure of the For-itself, that is, not a consciousness of the negation of one's past in the mode of having to be it and of the projection of one's future as what the For-itself is lacking.

These aspects of its temporal existence are revealed to the For-itself by what Sartre calls "pure reflection" (EN, p. 205, BN, pp. 180–181). While impure reflection reveals the three temporal dimensions as objects, pure reflection reveals them as quasi-objects (EN, p. 201, BN, p. 178). Sartre thinks that "pure reflection" can be reached from "impure reflection" by an act of catharsis.[7] But it remains unclear how this process of catharsis proceeds. The problem with pure reflection is that there seems to be no phenomenological evidence for it. One has the impression that it is a philosophical invention which Sartre needs to close the gap between what his ontology says about the For-itself and what impure reflection reveals to the For-itself about itself.

We can summarize our short overview of Sartre's theory of time-consciousness in the following critical points:

1   Though Sartre is aware that reflective time-consciousness presupposes a pre-reflective consciousness of time, he makes no effort to explain how the constitution of the former is made in the latter.
2   Instead of developing a theory of pre-reflective time-consciousness as foundation of reflective time-consciousness, Sartre introduces in the form of pure reflection a deeper level of reflection which cannot do the job of explaining time-consciousness either.
3   Sartre describes the data of reflective time-consciousness as ordered according to the A-series and he sees that pre-reflective consciousness must be consciousness of temporal flow as well. However, he does not see that the possibility of this consciousness is not evident at all and poses serious problems to the philosopher.

Sartre's blindness is the more astonishing as he perfectly knew Husserl's early theory of time-consciousness where these problems are clearly articulated. (See EN, p. 165, BN, p. 143; TE, pp. 6–7.[8] See also Chapter 3, by Kenneth Williford, in this volume.) We have in fact to go to Husserl in order to get a clear picture of these problems and a first step to their resolution. Actually Husserl was the first to try to explain how time-consciousness is possible[9] and he was the first to understand the point of the question.

## Husserl's achievements and shortcomings in the Vorlesungen

Like Sartre, Husserl developed a twofold theory of time. On the one hand he gave an ontological description of the subject (the transcendental Ego) as a being which is essentially in time. Here, as we have seen, Sartre's theory is much richer and more powerful in the explanation of the flowing of time. On the other hand, Husserl tries to explain the possibility of time-consciousness. Here, as we shall see, his theory is more powerful than Sartre's. However, in Husserl's theory the two aspects are interwoven and appear sometimes as one theory.

Husserl is convinced that our positional (thetic) consciousness of the succession of events, say our hearing of a melody, is based on a non-positional (non-thetic) consciousness of the very act of hearing. In positional consciousness the object of the consciousness is presented as existing; in non-positional consciousness this is not the case. As the acts of hearing succeed each other in time, this non-positional consciousness must be a kind of time-consciousness.[10] Like Sartre, Husserl calls the thetic form of self-consciousness "reflection." Consequently the non-thetic form of self-consciousness must be pre-reflective.[11]

Let us analyze the details of Husserl's theory of this pre-reflective time-consciousness. The starting point of his theory is the description of the pre-reflective consciousness of the act by which we are conscious of what happens right now. Husserl calls this act *Urimpression* (original impression). Husserl asks whether we are conscious of this act in an immediate way and his answer is positive (Husserliana X, Compl. IX, p. 119). However, we must be conscious of this act as present. How is this possible? If every present act is followed by a new present act and thus becomes a past act and if the subject were only conscious of the present act, she would not be able to determine this act as present. Husserl solves this problem by introducing a non-thetic consciousness of past acts of the subject. This consciousness is simultaneous with the awareness of the present act of consciousness. So, while hearing the present note Do and being conscious of this act of hearing, I am also conscious of my previous act of hearing a Fa. Husserl calls this non-thetic consciousness of my past acts of thetic consciousness "retention." He introduces also a non-thetic anticipation of future acts of consciousness—my future hearing of Re—and calls this "protention."

According to Husserl, the subject is conscious of all first-order acts of consciousness in a non-thetic manner. However, it is not conscious of the very acts by which this consciousness is established. These acts (second-order acts) are not objects of further acts of consciousness. Husserl says: "Subjective time is constituted in an absolute timeless consciousness, which is not an object."[12] This means that in this period Husserl adopts the conception that we call in our current debate "awareness-content-model" (Zahavi 2007, pp. 207, 459). According to Husserl, first-order acts of consciousness occur at the same moment as their correspondent second-order acts of consciousness. In this regard he agrees with Kant, who holds that the data of outer sense occupy the same moment of time as the correspondent data of inner sense. Both philosophers subscribe to the principle of presentational concurrence.[13]

How does Husserl describe the pole of consciousness ontologically? Like Sartre, he sees that it undergoes an uninterrupted temporal change. The subject which is conscious of an original impression is situated in the present instant, but this instant will necessarily become a past instant and thus be replaced by a new present instant, in which a new original impression is given. Unlike Sartre, Husserl doesn't offer any explanation of this flow of subjective time.

One would expect that he would at least offer an explanation of time-consciousness of which he gave such a precise description. But here again we are disappointed. Husserl sees that past acts of consciousness must be given—together with the act of the present original impression—to the subject in the present moment in the form of retentions and retentions of retentions. In this way they are ordered on a line and as such co-present to the subject in the present moment.[14] However, one must realize that the order in which the different acts of consciousness are given to the subject is a spatial order, a line, not a temporal order. Therefore the question arises how the subject can know which of the ordered data is earlier and which is later. To determine this, the subject must dispose of some criterion. Actually, Husserl thinks of such a criterion. He says that the qualia that are given in form of retentions are "conscious in a diminishing degree of clarity" (Husserl 1928, 1966, p. 26 "mit absteigender Klarheit bewusst"). He also uses characteristics like degrees of "weakness," "intensity," or "density" which remind us of Hume's approach (Husserl 1928, 1966, p. 63). However, he never says explicitly that the subject uses these criteria in order to establish the temporal order of first-order acts of consciousness. He even denies that the temporal position of the "Urdata" could be "established on the basis of reasons" (Husserl 1928, 1966, Beilage IX, 119 "aus Gründen erschlossen"). It seems that he has not really understood the difficulty of our problem. In fact, as long as the data are given in a one-dimensional spatial order, there is no way to determine by criteria in which temporal order they stand to each other. In order to do this the subject needs to be conscious in a non-thetic way of data given in an order that is at least two-dimensional.

## Husserl's achievements and shortcomings in the *Bernauer Manuscripte*

Husserl introduces for the first time such a two-dimensional order in the *Bernauer Manuscripte*, which he wrote in the years 1917–1918 and which were published in 2001 (Husserl 2001).[15] According to Husserl's new conception, the subject is conscious not only of the present original impression and the present retentions and protentions, but also of the former original impressions together with the corresponding former retentions and protentions (Figure 5.1). This makes it possible that the subject is conscious of the fact that former protentions are sometimes fulfilled and at other times disappointed. This difference will be decisive when it comes to determining the temporal order of the given data.

There is only one regard in which Figure 5.1 misrepresents Husserl's new conception. Actually, it shows the inner data of consciousness as discontinuous, while Husserl is convinced that these data form a continuum. We shall see later that this conception is utterly problematic and must be rejected.

Let me explain the diagram. The present situation of the subject is marked as the crossing of the bold vertical line with the horizontal line. This is the point of the absolute present. Above this point we find the present protentions; below are the present retentions. Husserl calls this bold vertical line $U(x)$. The decisive new insight is that we have to distinguish at the left of the bold line former original impressions with their respective former protentions and retentions and at the right of the bold line future original impressions with their respective protentions and retentions. This means that whenever the subject hears a melody she is conscious not only of hearing the present tone and the past hearing of the preceding tones together with an anticipation of the future deployment of the melody but also of its past anticipations of the melody. This makes it possible that the subject notices when such an anticipation was fulfilled and when it was

128  *Gerhard Seel*

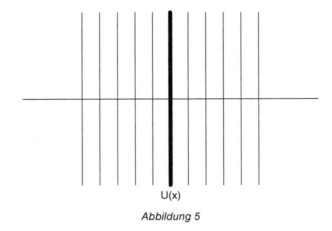

Abbildung 5

*Figure 5.1* Husserl's conception.

disappointed. Even if Husserl does not explicitly introduce the following distinctions, we are entitled to attribute them to him, i.e., the distinction of: (a) past future (the field left of and above the point of absolute present); (b) past past (the field left of and below this point); (c) past present (the points on the line left of this point); (d) present present (the absolute crossing point); (e) present future (the points above the absolute crossing point); (f) the present past (the points below this point); (g) future future (the field right of and above this point); (h) future present (the points right of the absolute point); and (i) future past (the field right of and below this point).

The problem is that these temporal determinations are introduced by the philosopher without explaining how the mind can make them. Husserl is not aware that this is simply a *petitio principii*. (Dainton 2000, pp. 155–161, criticizes Husserl in a similar way.) He makes no effort to explain how the human mind is able to produce them when it makes the experience of temporal flow. For, we must see that the data themselves do not contain any temporal connotation, even if they are organized in a two-dimensional order. They stand only in spatial relations and the subject is not aware of more than these spatial relations. So, Husserl has a problem here. But, if we carefully investigate his texts we come to the conclusion that he was not really aware of this problem. He believed that time-consciousness was the result of a process of self-affection in which reasoning had no role to play—in Kantian terms a product of sensibility without any implication of the understanding. Husserl even excludes explicitly that the temporal determinations of the original data given in the original consciousness are "deduced from reasons" (Husserl 1928, 1966; Beilage IX, p. 119, "aus Gründen erschlossen") In my view, the only way to solve the problem is to show that, and how these determinations are established by reasoning. But, before doing this we must first clarify what the problem is exactly.

## The problem and its solution

The starting point of our investigation is a principle that was first introduced by Kant. In our days it was reformulated by Dainton (2003, p. 17) and Zahavi (2007, p. 455), who called it the *principle of simultaneous awareness* (Dainton 2000, p. 133). According to this principle, we must experience the sequence of past acts of consciousness as given simultaneously in a single momentary act of consciousness. Dainton is right when he attributes this principle to Husserl (he doesn't mention Kant; Zahavi, 2007, p. 466 has some doubts about this). In Husserl's terms the series of retentions and protentions must be given as such in the present moment to the present consciousness. Therefore they are present as simultaneous. The reason why we have to postulate this principle is the following. If the different retentions and protentions were given in different acts of consciousness at different moments we would always experience just one such act of consciousness and never be aware of their sequence.

Zahavi (2007, p. 456) distinguishes two versions of the principle, i.e., temporal realism and temporal representational anti-realism. The first holds that in the present act of consciousness we are aware of the succession of the data with real temporal extension. The second holds that the data are given momentarily and only appear as temporarily extended. With reference to Dainton (2003, p. 8), he explains: "Thus, whereas we *seem* to be directly aware of temporally extended occurrences, we are in reality only aware of the *representations* of such occurrences" (Zahavi, 2007, p. 456). It seems to me that only the second version is sound. How can simultaneously given data have a real temporal extension? The only extension they may have is spatial. On the other hand, calling these data representations is problematic. They are representations of what? They simply are given contents of consciousness and not representations of former given contents.[16] So the denomination "representational anti-realism" is misleading.

Dainton presents the following objection to "representational anti-realism," which—according to him—is Husserl's position.[17] As according to this position we have no immediate or direct experience of change and succession, our mind needs to produce the consciousness of these out of simultaneously given data. However, the question is—as Zahavi (2007, p. 457) relates Dainton's point—how simultaneously given data can be present to the mind as successive ones. "How can they be both simultaneous and successive?"[18]

This is in fact the right question. I would only shape it a little differently, asking not how simultaneous data can be given as successive ones—of course they cannot—but rather how they can be transformed into successive data

130  *Gerhard Seel*

and experienced as such. In other words, how can a spatial order of data result in the experience of temporal succession?

In order to answer this question we must first of all introduce a further principle which is complementary to the principle of simultaneous awareness, namely the *principle of persistent givenness* of the simultaneous data. For, if the simultaneously given data would last just the short instant of present consciousness, the mind could not execute on them operations like comparing, identifying, and distinguishing. To do this the mind needs time and it needs the permanent presence of the same constellation of data. This is the profound reason why Husserl is right when he argues that consciousness of time needs its own time and that the structure of the latter must be different from the structure of the former. But what are the operations consciousness executes on the given constellation of data exactly? Before we answer this question we have to modify Husserl's two-dimensional diagram of the data of time-consciousness in some important points. We replace Husserl's diagrams by the diagram given in Figure 5.2.

As Figure 5.2 shows, my conception of the constellation of the data of time-consciousness differs from Husserl's in three important points:

1   As we have argued, Husserl's later diagrams show a two-dimensional order of discontinuous data. In Husserl's case, however, this is done for reasons of graphic representation only. In fact, as we have seen, Husserl considers the data of time-consciousness as continuous, whereas according to my conception they must be discontinuous in order to allow the

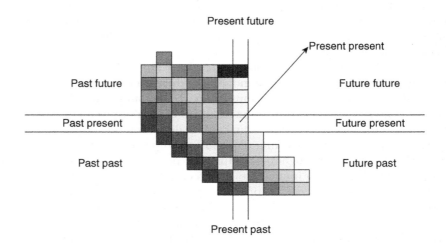

*Figure 5.2* The different shades of gray represent the data of consciousness, given as present protentions and retentions, past protentions and retentions, and future retentions.

mental operations I shall discuss later. As a first consequence of this conception my diagram shows crossing spaces filled with data—not crossing lines.

2  In Husserl's diagrams the contents of the protentions reappear below the horizontal line of the present. This is a consequence of what Husserl calls the "continuous sinking and lingering" of the data. Protentions are fulfilled in form of a primal impression and as such saved in form of retentions. In Figure 5.2, however, this is not always the case. Some protentions are fulfilled and some are not. In the latter case we have no correspondent primal impression and no correspondent retentions.

3  A further important difference concerns the field at the right of the vertical column of the present and below the horizontal row of the present. Husserl seems to believe that the lingering of the data takes place in this field as well. The truth is, however, that the subject cannot know in the absolute present whether the protentions of this moment will be fulfilled in the next moment or not. Therefore the little fields at the right of the column of the present remain progressively void in my diagram.

In Figure 5.2 the different fields have temporal denotations. We speak of present past, past present, and so forth. However, I should emphasize that these denominations are not justified so far. So, in order to make our task clear, we should abstract from them completely and consider the constellation of data as given in Figure 5.2 as a two-dimensional spatial order which is—according to the principle of permanent givenness—present to the subject over a short but extended period of time. During this period the subject must do the job of attributing temporal predicates to these data and thus experience them as temporally ordered. But how can this be done?

To answer this question I follow Kant's transcendental approach in explaining experience. As the temporal determinations of the data cannot be given as such, they must be the result of an operation of the understanding. They resemble Kant's categories, which are never given but are attributed to the given by the understanding as the result of a procedure Kant calls "transcendental schematism." As I have tried to show elsewhere, the schematism proceeds in two steps (Seel 1998, pp. 217–246; 1991, pp. 421–437). First the understanding produces judgments which determine certain characteristics of the sense data. For instance, the understanding finds that certain constellations of sense data do not change. Kant calls these kind of judgment "judgments of perception" (Kant 1783; 1903; 1968). In a second step the understanding brings the sense data under a category using a transcendental syllogism. This syllogism has as *premissa maior* the principle of the schematism of the category in question. In our example this would be the following principle:

> If a constellation of sense data does not change over a suitable period of time it has to be considered as a substance.

The understanding then adds as *premissa minor* a judgment of perception like the following:

> This constellation of sense data did not change over a suitable period of time.

The conclusion of the transcendental syllogism then is a judgment of experience, i.e.:

> This constellation of sense data is objectively a substance.

It is obvious that the schematism of the categories presupposes time-consciousness, as Kant himself underlines so many times. It is the more important to understand how time-consciousness itself is possible.

In my view, to get a grip on this problem we must suppose that also in this case a schematism is at work. What are the categories our understanding applies when producing time-consciousness? We have seen before that the flowing of time, the passing of the future into the present, and finally into the past, cannot be immediately given. The two principles we discussed earlier do not allow this. The only remaining possibility is that these properties must be something the understanding has at its disposal *a priori*. The three modes of time, that is, future, present, and past, and together with them the idea of the flowing of time, must be pure concepts *a priori*.

This is a revolutionary thesis. If one accepts it, an even more difficult question arises: How is the application of these concepts to the sense data possible? We have to find out what the principle of the schematism of time-consciousness has to be.

The crucial question will be how the understanding comes to know which of the given sense data lies in the absolute present. As this must be the sense datum situated in the crossing of the column of the present and the row of the present, the answer to this question presupposes that we can answer a further question, namely: "How can the understanding know which sense data lie in the row of the present and which lie on the column of the present?"

When the understanding compares the given data, it will observe that in the field under a certain row the sense data situated on this row reappear identically one row below and one column to the right. It will further observe that, in the field above this row, this rule doesn't apply. Here we have both identical reappearance of the same quality and replacement by a different quality. The first row to which the rule of reappearance applies must be the row of the present and consequently the principle of the schematism of the past present must be that the latter contains all and only those data that are unchanged in the field below, but do not regularly correspond to data situated at the left in the next row above. This corresponds to Husserl's insight that some of our past protentions have been deceived.

The column of the present contains our present protentions. We cannot tell yet which of these protentions will be deceived and which fulfilled. Therefore the column of the future present and past present must be the one which has no correspondent data on or above the row of the present. The principle of the schematism of the column of the present is exactly this. And as the absolute present lies on the crossing of the row and the column of the present we can never be in error about what tone we presently hear.

## The open future diagram

The constellation of the data of inner sense, as given in Figure 5.2, corresponds to phenomena like watching the passing of a train or listening to a well-known melody. But this is not the only kind of phenomena of time-consciousness. If, for instance, we watch a soccer game, it happens that we see a midfielder in a position where he could either pass the ball to the striker in front or try to shoot a goal directly. In this case our protentions are twofold. They contain alternative future data. To represent the openness of the future, philosophers have used the figure of a tree, as in Figure 5.3. Until the present and including the present, the succession of events forms a line, while into the future possible events are situated on widening branches.

Accordingly we have to modify Figure 5.2 in such a way that in the field at the right of the column of the present (including the latter) and above the row of the present we have above each datum two alternative data. Of course,

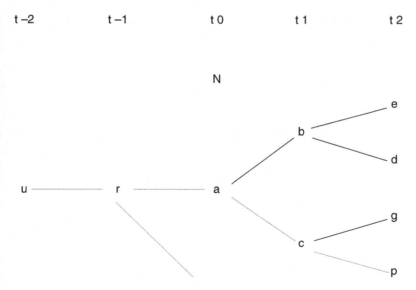

*Figure 5.3* The openness of the future.

only one of these reappears in the row of the present as the one which was finally realized. This modification of Figure 5.2 results in Figure 5.4.

Now it is even easier to determine the row of the present and the column of the present. The first is characterized by two salient features: (1) Its data reappear in the next row below in the next column at the right. (2) To each of its data correspond two data situated in the row above and in the column at the left. The column of the present is characterized by the feature that it is the last column that shows two alternative data in the row above the row of the present.

Having shown how the understanding is able to determine the relative time of each of the data of the inner sense, we must now explain how it comes to the experience of the flowing of time. Here again the understanding must interpret an aspect of the spatial order of the data in terms of temporal flux. It is again a transcendental schematism which allows the spatial succession of the columns to be read from left to right as a temporal succession. The understanding sees the data on and at the left of the column of the present as a "frozen flow" and has the expectation that this flow will go on.

The concepts of the three modes and of the flux of time are not the only concepts *a priori* that the understanding applies when it constitutes time-consciousness. It has also the concepts of the three modalities at its disposition. The transcendental judgment of the understanding comes to the conclusion that the row of the present contains data which once were only possible, then real, and in the future necessary for ever. In fact the understanding finds that once a datum appears in the row of the present it will remain in the field below this row, reappearing in each column at the left in the next row below. The understanding interprets this feature as the necessity of past events. On the other hand the alternative data above

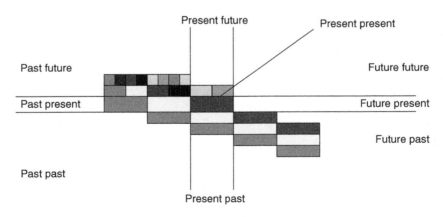

*Figure 5.4* Figure 5.4 differs from Figure 5.2 in only one aspect. In the field of former protentions, we have above each datum, instead of just one datum, two alternative data.

the row of the present are interpreted as purely contingent. They can, but must not, be realized. This corresponds to the phenomenon that we experience time as determined by the three modalities, contingency, reality, and necessity. Very early in the history of philosophy philosophers have seen the close connection between time and modalities and in modern logic the logic of time and the logic of modalities have to go together.

There is still a further concept *a priori* the understanding applies to the constellation of the data of inner sense. I mean the concept of the empirical self. Though Kant speaks of this concept, he doesn't consider it a category. He has two reasons for this. (1) It doesn't figure in the list of the categories he discovers through what he calls the "metaphysical deduction." (2) And, more importantly, he sees no possibility of having a schematism for the application of such a category. I think that, on the contrary, there is such a schematism. The data of inner sense given to the understanding in the form of Figure 5.2 or Figure 5.4 and then interpreted as temporal flux have to be considered as the objective life of the subject that has them. In fact, we consider immediately our past experiences when they are presented to us by memory as *our* experiences. This cannot be explained if we don't suppose a transcendental schematism at work which allows us to apply the concept of the empirical Ego to the data of inner sense. This occurs immediately. There is no need for a second turning-back of our intention as the higher-order thought (HOT) theorists hold. (See also Chapter 14, by Levine, in this volume.) The interpretation of the temporally ordered data of inner sense as my past, present, and future experiences goes along with an act of self-identification. For I know that the Ego who was the subject of my past experiences is the same being as the Ego of my present and future experiences.

My theory shows also that Sartre was perfectly right when he argued that the Ego is not the subject, but rather a transcendent product of subjectivity (in his TE). That is why it is misleading to speak of "self-ascription." The Ego doesn't ascribe mental acts to itself. It is the other way around. Pre-reflectively conscious mental acts are interpreted as making up the empirical content of an identical Ego. I should emphasize also that the whole mental process of constituting time-consciousness and the empirical Ego takes place on the basis of a background consciousness which has the Sartrean relected–reflecting structure. This distinguishes—among other minor points—my theory from HOT theories.[19] Such a background consciousness is considered by Husserl as well, when he tries to avoid infinite regression of the levels of consciousness. (See Husserl 2001, XXXIII, 277ff. See also Seel 2010, pp. 74–75.)

## Final remarks

The results of our investigation are revolutionary. They face, as transcendental philosophy in general, two obvious objections from the side of the phenomenologists. The latter argue that we are directly aware of the flow of time and that there is no phenomenological evidence for a transcendental schematism as we presuppose. We feel immediately the flowing of time; to experience this we need no judgment. Furthermore, how can a logical operation of the understanding result in the living experience of the flowing of time? The answer to these objections is that we are not thetically aware of the mental operations by which our mind constitutes the consciousness of time and the empirical Ego, as we are not thetically aware of the operations by which our mind constitutes the seeing of a tree. The application of pure concepts of the mind does not mean that the result of the operation is an abstract judgment. It is rather a concrete experience.

Our investigation has shown that time, if it really is, cannot be only a form of inner sense, as Kant held. To execute the operations we described above, the mind needs time. We have no consciousness of this time. Otherwise we would have to explain this consciousness as well and end up in an infinite regression. But this time is nevertheless real. This has also been shown by psychological tests. In fact, for each human individual there is a threshold—speed of the succession of sense data. Below this threshold the individual cannot tell any more which of the impressions was the earlier one and which the later.[20]

This gives me the opportunity to address some of the main issues of this volume from my point of view. The first question is whether there is a subject who does the complicated work of constituting time-consciousness. Of course there is one. Who is this subject? This is an ontological question. The answer must be that the subject is the being that later becomes self-conscious as an empirical Ego. There is only one such being. We should not double the number of subjects on the level of ontology.

The more interesting question is, however, whether this subject is conscious of itself as Ego during the constituting process. The answer is—*pace* Tepley, Chapter 12 in this volume—that it is not. The only possibility of such a self-consciousness would be by means of a Kantean transcendental Ego. But I see no necessity for this. Kant would have two arguments in defense of this hypothesis: (1) We need the "I think" in order to guarantee the unity of consciousness during the process. This argument doesn't convince me. (2) As in the application of categories, pure thinking is involved and the only subject of pure thinking is the transcendental Ego, the "I think" must be supposed to operate essentially in the constituting process. However, in the schematism I introduced, the concept of the transcendental Ego does not occur. Here functionalist accounts make a good point. In order to function correctly when constituting time-consciousness, the operations of the mind need not be controlled by a transcendental Ego. So, for reasons dear to Ockham, I think that we can avoid postulating the transcendental Ego.

The next question is whether the mind is conscious of the process of constituting time-consciousness during the process. The answer is that it is conscious of it in a non-thetic way and unconscious in a thetic way. Without the former we could not explain how reflective time-consciousness is possible. But as the latter is the product of the constituting process, it cannot be already present in it.

A further question debated in this volume is whether the consciousness involved in the constitution of time-consciousness is representational or self-representational. The answer is complicated. On the level of the "reflected–reflecting" structure, consciousness represents nothing. On the other hand retentions and protentions and the original impression could be seen as representing former, present, and future acts of consciousness. However, I have misgivings about this idea—as I have argued above. In any case, if we accept this position, these representations would not, strictly speaking, be self-representations. Only once the category of the empirical Ego is applied to them do they become self-representaions: I am conscious of myself as the identical subject of all the temporally ordered acts of consciousness, their necessity as past, their reality as present, and their contingency as future experiences. Therefore I disagree with Williford who—following Husserl and Sartre—thinks that non-positional self-consciousness is already time-consciousness, that "the flow of consciousness is manifest to itself immediately and without any need for cognitive or perceptual acts to constitute it" (Chapter 3, this volume).

From what I said before, it follows immediately that pre-reflective self-consciousness cannot be self-knowledge. However, the constituting process ends in self-knowledge. This means that errors can only occur when we reflect on our past experiences. However, they don't concern my past experiences, but what I experienced. I can think that I heard the note Fa, but it was a Do. But I cannot mistake my hearing of the Fa for a different act of hearing. Errors occur, of course, mostly in our memories of experiences situated in the far past.

A last question is whether we can reduce or naturalize consciousness. I think the philosopher should wait until neuroscience has made enough progress to give the answer.

## Notes

1 I use the translation of Hazel E. Barnes (2003). In some cases I feel however obliged to use my own translation for reasons of clarity. When quoting Sartre's text, "EN" refers to the French original (1943) and "BN" refers to the English translation.
2 See EN, p. 175, BN p. 153. The English translation "static temporal" and "dynamic temporal" imitates the French but sounds rather awkward.
3 The symbols $x$, $y$, and $z$ stand for event variables. The expression "$Fxy$" reads "$x$ follows $y$ in time." The expression "$Sxy$" reads "$x$ is simultaneous to $y$." The rest of the symbols are used in the usual way.
4 $N$ stands for the present moment of time; $P$ is the symbol for the set of all past moments of time; $F$ is the symbol for the set of all future moments of time; and $\varepsilon$ stands for "is an element of."

5 See Seel (1971). I quote from the enlarged and improved French version (Seel 1995).
6 This is recognized by most of the contributions to this volume as well. See especially M. Frank's contribution (Chapter 1 in this volume).
7 For a tentative explanation of Sartre's distinction, see Kenneth Williford (Chapter 3 in this volume).
8 "TE" refers to Sartre, J.-P. (1936–1937). La transcendance de l'ego. Esquisse d'une description phénoménologique. *Recherches philosophiques* 6.
9 Husserl criticized Brentano, saying that his theory of time was unable to answer the question: "How is time-consciousness possible and how can we understand it?" (1905, p. 19; my translation).
10 "It is evident that the observation of a time-object has itself temporality, that awareness of duration presupposes the duration of awareness, that the observation of whatever pattern of time has its own pattern of time" (Husserl 1928, 1966, p. 22; my translation).
11 M. Frank insists that the expression "pre-reflective" was introduced by Sartre, in his TE (1936–1937) (see Chapter 1 in this volume).
12 Husserl (1928, 1966, X, Beilage VI, p. 112). "Die subjective Zeit konstituiert sich im absoluten zeitlosen Bewusstsein, das nicht Objekt ist."
13 See Dainton (2000, p. 134). Zahavi (2007, p. 464) holds that "Husserl must be rejecting the Principle of Presentational Concurrence."
14 Husserl (1928, 1966, Beilage VI, p. 112). "Ich höre soeben einen langen Pfiff. Er ist wie eine ausgedehnte Linie . . . Der Blick dieses Moments umfasst eine ganze Linie, und das Linienbewusstsein wird als gleichzeitig gefasst mit dem Jetztpunkt des Pfiffs." (I hear a long whistle-blow right now. It is like an extended line . . . The consciousness of this moment embraces a whole line, and the consciousness of this line is taken as simultaneous with the present moment of the whistle-blow. My translation.)
15 Not all of the specialists have seen the revolutionary progress Husserl made in this period. Many think that he simply precised his old position. He also made considerable progress concerning the ontology of the subject. But we must leave aside this part of his theory. For a closer look on this, see Seel (2010, pp. 43–88).
16 See also Zahavi's (2007, p. 458) critique of Dainton's interpretation of Husserl's retentions as representations of past primal impressions.
17 Dainton presents two further objections to Husserl. He argues firstly that Husserl's thesis that protentions are lingering away has no phenomenological basis and secondly that the supposed continuity of retentions and protentions leads to a "clogging" of different contents (2000, p. 158). At least the second argument has to be taken seriously. I reject for similar reasons Husserl's continuity assumption.
18 See Zahavi (2007, p. 457). A similar point was made by Gallagher (2003, p. 2).
19 For a version of HOT theory see Chapter 13, by R. J. Gennaro, in this volume. For a critique, see Chapter 1, by M. Frank, and Chapter 14, by J. Levine, in this volume.
20 Dainton (2000, pp. 113, 171) holds as well that the extention of the lived present can be measured by a stop clock. This earns him sharp criticism from Zahavi (2007, p. 467).

# Bibliography

Barnes, Hazel E. (2003). *Being and Nothingness.* New York. Routledge Classics.
Dainton, B. (2000). *Stream of Consciousness: Unity and Continuity in Conscious Experience.* London: Routledge.
Dainton, B. (2003). Time in Experience: Reply to Gallagher. *Psyche* 9(10).
Frank, M. (1990). *Zeitbewusstsein.* Pfullingen: Neske.
Frank, M. (2002). Sartre's Vortrag *Conscience de soi et connaissance de soi,* Eine Argumentationsskizze, pp. 247–264, in H. Linneweber-Lammerskitten and Georg Mohr (Eds.), *Interpretation und Argument, Gerhard Seel zum 60. Geburtstag.* Würzburg: Königshausen and Neumann Publisher.
Gallagher, G. (2003). Sync-ing in the Stream of Experience: Time-Consciousness in Broad, Husserl and Dainton. *Psyche* 9(10).
Husserl, E. (1905). *Vorlesungen.* Hua X, p. 19. *Husserliana* XXXIII. The Hague: Nijhoff.
Husserl, E. (1928, 1966). *Vorlesungen zum inneren Zeitbewusstsein,* in Martin Heidegger *Jahrbuch für Philosophie und phänomenologische Forschung* IX, p. 367; new edition by R. Boehm as E. Husserl (1966). *Zur Phenomenologie des inneren Zeitbewusstseins (1893–1917). Husserliana* X. The Hague: Nijhoff.
Husserl, E. (2001). Die Bernauer Manuskripte über das Zeitbewusstsein (1917/18). R. Bernet and D. Lohmar (Eds.), *Husserliana* XXXIII. The Hague: Nijhoff.
Kant, I. (1783; 1903; 1968). *Prolegomena zu einer jeden künftigen Metaphysik, die als Wissenschaft wird auftreten können,* in *Kants Gesammelte Schriften* (Bände I–XXII). Herausgegebeen von der Preussischen Akademie der Wissenschaften (AA), Band IV. Berlin: Walter de Gruyter.
McTaggert, J. E. (1968). *The Nature of Existence.* Cambridge: Cambridge University Press, pp. 305ff.
Sartre, J.-P. (1936–1937). La transcendance de l'ego. Esquisse d'une description phénoménologique. *Recherches philosophiques* 6.
Sartre, J.-P. (1943, 1971). *L'Etre et le néant: Essai d'ontologie phénoménologique.* Paris: Gallimard. Translated as *Being and Nothingness: An Essay on Phenomenological Ontology,* trans. H. Barnes. New York: Philosophical Library, 1958.
Seel, G. (1971). *Sartres Dialektik. Zur Methode und Begründung seiner Philosophie unter besonderer Berücksichtigung der Subjekts-, Zeit-, und Werttheorie.* Bonn: Bouvier. French translation G. Seel (1995). *La dialectique de Sartre.* Lausanne: L'Age d' Homme.
Seel, G. (1991). Was sind und wozu braucht man <kategorien>?, pp. 421–437, in K. Borth and D. Koch (Eds.), *Kategorie und Kategorialität,* Festschrift für Klaus Hartmann. Würzburg: Königshausen and Neumann.
Seel, G. (1995) *La dialectique de Sartre.* Lausanne: L'Age d' Homme.
Seel, G. (1998). Die Einleitung in die Analytik der Grundsätze, der Schematismus und die obersten Grundsätze (A 130/B169–A 158/B 197), pp. 217–246, in G. Mohr and M. Willaschek (Eds.), *Immanuel Kant, Kritik der reinen Vernunft.* Berlin: De Gruyter.
Seel, G. (2010). Husserls Problem emit dem Zeitbewusstsein und warum er sie nicht löste, pp. 43–88, in Manfred Frank and Niels Weidtmann (Eds.), *Husserl und die Philosophie des Geistes.* Berlin: Suhrkamp Publisher.
Zahavi, D. (2007). Perception of Duration Presupposes Duration of Perception — or Does It? Husserl and Dainton on Time. *International Journal of Philosophical Studies,* 15(3): pp. 453–471.

# PART II
# I-knowledge, perception, and introspection

# 6 The zero point and I

*Terry Horgan and Shaun Nichols*

Der jeweilige Aspect hat seine notwendige Beziehung auf den Nullpunkt der Orientierung, auf das absolute "Hier"
(Edmund Husserl, *Ideen II*, p. 127)

## Introduction

One of the most influential ideas on subjectivity from the analytic tradition comes from Hector-Neri Castañeda and John Perry. The idea is that first-person pronouns are sometimes used in an important and distinctive way, viz., to play the role of the first-person "essential indexical." Perry memorably describes following a trail of sugar around a grocery store before realizing, "I was the shopper I was trying to catch" (Perry 1979, p. 3). Once Perry realized this, he fixed the leaky bag of sugar. He explains this new behavior by attributing to himself the new belief, "I am making a mess." This explanation wouldn't work, Perry argues, if the term "I" is replaced by a description or a proper name, including his own name. For Perry can have a belief that he would express by saying "Perry is making a mess" without having a belief he would express by saying "I am making a mess." A natural extension of this idea that "I" operates as an essential indexical—indeed, it is perhaps already implicit in Castañeda and Perry—is that there is a corresponding kind of mental representation which has this function in thought—perhaps a first-person indexical term in the "language of thought" (see, e.g., Rey 1997), perhaps a first-person, essentially indexical, imagistic or pictorial form of self-representation, or perhaps both. With a nod to Castañeda, we will use the notation I* (and me*) for such a first-person, essentially indexical, kind of mental representation.

A second important idea about subjectivity occurs in both the analytic and the continental traditions. In analytic philosophy of mind, it arises in connection with phenomenal consciousness. Phenomenally conscious mental states are typically described as those mental states such that there is *something that it is like, for the experiencer,* to undergo such a state. The "what it is like" aspect is often called *phenomenal character*, whereas the "for the experiencer" aspect is what we will here call *phenomenal subjectivity*. Phenomenal subjectivity, we take it, is essentially the same feature which, in the continental tradition, is sometimes called *pre-reflective self-consciousness*, or *pre-reflective self-awareness*.

A third significant idea, concerning certain perspectival aspects of conscious experience, is what Husserl called the experiential *zero point* (*der Nullpunkt*). A very similar idea sometimes surfaces in discussions of mental representation in the analytic tradition—for instance, the notion of "scenario content" advanced and deployed in Peacocke (1992, Ch. 3).

In an important respect, the second and third ideas both are sparser than the idea of I\*/me\* representations: viz., they both refer to aspects of subjectivity that are already present in each conscious experience whether or not that experience deploys any explicit self-representations.

We will focus here on two guiding questions. First: When, and why, are various cognitive tasks faced by humans accomplished in the sparser way, without the use of I\*/me\* mental representations? Second: When, and why, are certain cognitive tasks instead accomplished in the less sparse way, by deploying I\*/me\* representations?

We will address each of these questions in two complementary, mutually reinforcing, ways. On one hand we will resort to phenomenological description: giving attentive introspective characterizations of certain aspects of conscious experience, characterizations that we hope will resonate with you, the reader. On the other hand, we will also invoke pertinent aspects, both empirical and theoretical, of recent and contemporary cognitive science. Along the way we will have things to say about how we think these two kinds of inquiry are related to one another, and about other aspects of the two-pronged methodology we here employ.

## Phenomenal subjectivity, non-representational self-presence, and the zero point

### Preliminaries

In recent and contemporary philosophy of mind in the analytic tradition, there is growing advocacy for the contention that virtually every aspect of human mentality that is conscious-as-opposed-to-unconscious is also phenomenally conscious—and, moreover, has phenomenal character that is proprietary (i.e., is uniquely specific to the kind of attitude involved—e.g., belief, hope, desire), is distinctive (i.e., is uniquely specific to the particular intentional content, if any, of the given mental state), and is individuative (i.e., is that in virtue of which the given state counts as being the kind of state it is, and counts as having its particular intentional content, if any). There is also growing advocacy for the contention that virtually all types of phenomenal character are inherently intentional—and, moreover, that this phenomenal intentionality both (i) is the fundamental kind of mental intentionality, and (ii) is intrinsic to phenomenal character rather than being constitutively dependent on any historical or causal-covariational connections between one's phenomenally conscious mental states/processes and one's wider physical or social environment. (Externalistic elements might still combine constitutively with phenomenal intentionality to fix certain derivative aspects of mental intentionality—e.g., mental *reference* to individuals in one's environment, and/or mental reference to natural-kind properties instantiated in one's environment.) In slogan form, the position can be characterized this way: *Phenomenality is inherent to consciousness, and intentionality is virtually always inherent to phenomenality.*[1]

Although this package of views is still a minority position in analytic philosophy of mind, the position's popularity seems to be increasing rapidly. One of us (Horgan) has been among the philosophers championing such views in print (often collaboratively with John Tienson and/ or George Graham); others include Colin McGinn, David Pitt, Charles Siewert, and Galen Strawson.[2] For our purposes in the present chapter, we will assume henceforth that the position, as just sketched, is in essential respects correct. (The continental tradition, as we understand it (largely from secondhand sources), pretty much took the position for granted. Good for them, we say!)

In analytic philosophy of mind during the past 70 years or so, heavy emphasis often has been placed upon the *functional roles* played by various kinds of mental states/processes. Indeed, during much of this time period, orthodoxy had it that the only kinds of conscious mental states/processes that possess phenomenal character are *sensations*, such as tickles, smells, pains, and color-sensations. By contrast, the orthodox view of mental states like *conscious occurrent thoughts*, for example, was that the essential character of such a state, qua mental, consists of nothing more than its distinctive functional role in cognitive economy, vis-à-vis sensory "inputs," behavioral "outputs," and other mental states/processes (many of which likewise have an essence, qua mental, that is purely functional and not at all phenomenal). In Ned Block's highly influential terminology (Block 1995), mental states like conscious occurrent thoughts were said to be "access conscious" but not phenomenally conscious—where access consciousness is supposedly entirely a functional-role matter involving, for instance, availability of a mental state for accurate first-person characterization of oneself as currently instantiating that very state. (On more recent versions of this orthodoxy, the constitutive functional roles of states like occurrent conscious thoughts are allegedly "long-armed," extending outward into a creature's wider environment; thoughts about water, for instance, refer to $H_2O$ partly because $H_2O$ is the stuff in the wider environment that tends to trigger such thoughts.)

Our discussion in this chapter is predicated upon a thoroughgoing rejection of this long-prevalent orthodoxy in analytic philosophy of mind, and upon acceptance of the contention that phenomenality is inherent to consciousness and intentionality is virtually always inherent to phenomenality. Although this alternative orientation does not deny the importance of the functional roles played by various kinds of conscious mental states/processes, it casts these functional roles in a very different light than did the old orthodoxy. The basic new element is this: the inherent phenomenal character of a particular mental state or process is the *experiential categorical basis* of the pertinent functional-role aspects of that state/process. Consider, for instance, an occurrent conscious thought. Although part of the typical functional role of such a mental state, insofar as it is conscious-as-opposed-to-unconscious, is indeed that the state is *accessible*—which means, *inter alia*, that if one is queried about what one is currently thinking, one will easily be able to answer—the state has this functional-role feature *in virtue of its inherent, distinctive, phenomenal character*. The occurrent thought's distinctive phenomenal character, with its inherent intentional content, is immediately given to you experientially; this is what enables you to report accurately that you are now undergoing that very occurrent thought.

## *Phenomenal subjectivity as non-representational self-presence*

Phenomenal subjectivity, as we said in the first section, is the "for me" aspect of phenomenal consciousness; there can be no occurrent "what-it-is-likeness" apart from an experiential subject *for whom* there is something that a token phenomenal state is like. Moreover, in phenomenally conscious experience, the experiencing self is not just *instantiating* the pertinent phenomenal state/process. Rather, the experiencing self is *experientially present* within the state/process, and is present in a quite direct and intimate way. Such self-presence, via the fact that the experience's phenomenal character is its distinctive what-it-is-like-ness *for me*—is more direct and more intimate than would be the presence in consciousness of an overt *representation* of the self. It is also more direct and more intimate than the way that currently perceivable objects in one's ambient environment can be said to be "experientially present," since this latter form of experiential presence is still mediated via overt mental representations—ones that might aptly be called *presentational* representations.[3] Instead, such experiential self-presence is an *immediate*—i.e., *unmediated*—involvement of the self in consciousness, as opposed to mediated involvement via the conscious representation of self. Phenomenal subjectivity—the "for-me-ness" of phenomenal consciousness without which one could not instantiate states with phenomenal character (i.e., with "what-it's-like-ness"), is an experientially *direct* way in which the self is present in phenomenal consciousness.

As we understand it, phenomenal subjectivity, thus construed as a form of non-representational self-presence in phenomenal consciousness, is essentially the same feature that in the continental tradition is sometimes called "pre-reflective self-consciousness" or "pre-reflective self-awareness." The following passage from Shaun Gallagher and Dan Zahavi (2010) describes this latter notion in a way that explicitly connects it to phenomenality as typically described in analytic philosophy of mind:

> The notion of pre-reflective self-awareness is related to the idea that experiences have a subjective "feel" to them, a certain (phenomenal) quality of "what it is like" or what it "feels" like to have them. As it is usually expressed outside of phenomenological texts, to undergo a conscious experience necessarily means that there is something it is like for the subject to have that experience (Nagel 1974; Searle 1992). This is obviously true of bodily sensations like pain. But is also the case for perceptual experiences, experiences of desiring, feeling, and thinking. There is something it is like to taste chocolate, and this is different from what it is like to remember what it is like to taste chocolate, or to smell vanilla, or to run, to stand still, to feel envious, nervous, depressed or happy, or to entertain an abstract belief. Yet, at the same time, as I live through these differences, there is something experiential that is, in some sense, the same, namely their distinct first-personal character. All the experiences are characterized by a quality of *mineness* or *for-me-ness*, the fact that is *I* who am having these experiences. All the experiences are given (at least tacitly) as *my* experiences, as experiences *I* am undergoing or living through. All of this suggests that the first-person experience presents me with an immediate and non-observational access to myself, and that consequently (phenomenal) consciousness consequently entails a (minimal) form of self-consciousness. To put it differently, unless a mental process is self-conscious there will be nothing it is like to undergo the process, and therefore it cannot be a phenomenally conscious process ... It could consequently be claimed that anybody who denies the for-me-ness of experience simply fails to recognize an essential constitutive aspect of experiences.
>
> (Gallagher and Zahavi 2010, p. 3)

Although we find ourselves *largely* on board with the remarks in this passage, nonetheless we are unhappy with the resonances (in English, anyway) of expressions like "pre-reflective self-consciousness" and "pre-reflective self-awareness." These expressions seem problematic in two respects. First, locutions like "self-consciousness" and "self-awareness" strongly suggest the idea that the self is an *intentional object* of conscious awareness, and thus that the self is being *explicitly represented* in conscious awareness. (Presumably this is not intended, since the key idea is that the self is experientially present *without* being explicitly represented; but the resonances are there anyway.) Second, the modifier "pre-reflective" strongly suggests the idea that these states are to be contrasted with mental processes of *reflection*, such as deliberation or temporally extended discursive thought. (Presumably this too is not intended, since the intended contrast is with *explicit representation of self,* rather than with deliberation; but again, the resonances are there anyway.) So hereafter we will eschew expressions like "pre-reflective self-consciousness" and "pre-reflective self-awareness"; instead we will some-times deploy our own recommended replacement terminology—viz., "non-representational self-presence"—and we will some-times just deploy the expression "phenomenal subjectivity."

### Zero-point aspects of phenomenal subjectivity

An enormously fruitful idea we will draw upon from the continental tradition is the one expressed by Husserl's expression "*der Nullpunkt*" (the zero point). As we understand it, this expression denotes the experiential *perspectivalness* of much human conscious experience—including, in particular, sensory-perceptual consciousness. Visual experience, for instance, represents various objects in one's ambient environment as located relative to a specific vantage point—i.e., relative to a specific spatio-temporal "*absolute 'Hier'*." As we will emphasize shortly, consciousness exhibits a variety of different aspects of perspectivalness, what we will call zero-point aspects.

Concerning the zero point of visual-perceptual experience, the following question naturally arises. Is this zero point explicitly *represented* within such experience? The answer, which should be obvious introspectively, is no. Although the various objects that one now sees are each experienced as occupying specific locations—locations all positioned within a spatio-temporal frame of reference centered upon the "*absolute 'Hier'*" from which these objects are presentationally represented by one's current visual-perceptual experience—that perceptual vantage point is not *itself* being visually-perceptually represented. (Normally one can see parts of one's own body, of course; but one cannot see the portion of one's body, or the location, *from which* one sees the things that currently are presentationally represented visually.)

And so now the following further question naturally arises. Is the visual-perceptual zero point an aspect of phenomenal subjectivity? The answer, which should be obvious introspectively, is yes. The self that is present in consciousness directly and without the mediation of a self-representation—the me that is experientially present via the for-me-ness of consciousness—is directly present in experience *as spatio-temporally located* within the ambient environment. That is, the spatio-temporal location of the visual-perceptual zero point affects or *colors* the phenomenology. Although much of that ambient environment is indeed represented in one's current consciousness, and is represented via presentational representations of the visual-perceptual kind, one's own visual-perceptual zero point is present in the direct way—directly influencing the phenomenology—rather than being explicitly represented. One's visual-perceptual perspectival locus, then, is a zero-point aspect of phenomenal subjectivity. To see this with a concrete example, consider a sailor in a submarine looking down the length of the control room. Now consider the sailor putting the periscope in front of his eyes. This will cause an abrupt shift not just in the content of what he sees, but in the zero-point perspective from which he sees it. His phenomenology without the periscope is as of the perspective spatially inside the submarine; his phenomenology *with* the periscope is as of the perspective on top of the submarine. These different aspects of the visual-perspectival zero point will be phenomenologically salient, but not through any form of explicit representation.

In the subsequent subsections, we will maintain that attentive phenomenological introspection reveals a variety of zero-point aspects of phenomenal subjectivity, some of which involve features of consciousness other than sensory-perceptual.

*Sensory-perceptual experience*

The zero-point aspects of sensory-perceptual experience are rich, multifarious, and subtle. One dimension of subtlety is the way zero-point aspects combine with aspects of explicit sensory-perceptual representation. In tactile experience, for instance, it seems that various parts of one's body are themselves explicitly represented: one can feel them, and one can feel them as instantiating various properties both synchronic (e.g., pressure upon the bottoms of one's feet) and diachronic (e.g., the fingers of one's hand closing into a fist). On the other hand, one's tactile experiences often have externally directed intentional content as well (e.g., the shape and heft of the dumbbell one is now holding). Some aspects of external-world-representing tactile experience seem centered on one or several zero points that coincide with certain specific body parts that themselves are also explicitly represented tactilely; for instance, my tactile experience of the dumbbell's shape seems centered on my two hands, one of which feels (via gripping) the cylindrical shaft and the other of which feels the shape of one of the weight-plates to which the shaft is attached. Other aspects of external-world-representing tactile experience—for instance, my tactile experience of the dumbbell's heaviness, and my tactile experience of the balance of this heaviness on its two ends—seem centered upon a zero point that coincides with my entire body, which itself is also explicitly represented tactilely. And all these tactile intentional aspects of experience are experienced tactilely as *unified*, as all being aspects of current total tactile what-it-is-like-ness *for me*. The experiential zero point of this tactile dimension of the "unity of apperception" seems, once again, to coincide with my entire body—a body that also can be *explicitly* represented tactilely, via the ways I now tactilely perceive various of its parts.

Another dimension of subtlety is the way that zero-point aspects of sensory-perceptual experience arise multi-modally, often in combination with multi-modal aspects of explicit sensory-perceptual representation. For instance, the up/down axis of one's visual-presentational experience seems heavily dependent upon certain aspects of tactile and kinesthetic sensory-perceptual experience: roughly, down is the direction of the surface to which one's body at rest is attached, and toward which one's body moves when unattached to any surface. This up/down axis affects the explicit representational content of visual experience, which represents objects in the ambient environment as located within an implicit reference frame that includes the directions of up and down. The up/down axis also is a zero-point aspect of visual-perceptual experience: the experiential self is directly present in visual experience as visually located not only in the spatio-temporally "*absolute 'Hier'*" manner, but also in the (multi-modal) "up-vs-down" manner. (Husserl's mathematical metaphor already strongly suggests this, of course: mathematical "up" in a three-dimensional Cartesian coordinate system is the positive-number direction on the $y$-axis, and "down" is the negative-number direction on this axis.)

Much more could be said about such matters. But enough has been said for our purposes here. One main lesson is that sensory-perceptual experience is richly suffused with zero-point aspects—aspects that often are subtly multi-modal, and that often are subtly intertwined with explicit representation in sensory-perceptual experience. And, as emphasized in the section on phenomenal subjectivity as non-representational self-presence, above, zero-point aspects of consciousness—including zero-point aspects of sensory-perceptual experience—accrue to the direct presence in consciousness of the experiencing self, a self-presence not mediated by experiential representations of the self. One experiences *being* located at a specific sensory-perceptual zero point, rather than experiencing *representing oneself* as being thus located.[4]

### *Voluntary-action experience*

In this subsection we begin by describing some features of agentive phenomenology which, we submit, are readily ascertainable just on the basis of introspective attention to such phenomenology.[5] We then urge that these features are best characterized as zero-point aspects of phenomenal subjectivity, rather than as involving explicit self-representations.

What is behaving like phenomenologically, in cases where you experience your own behavior as action? Suppose that you deliberately do something—say, holding up your right hand and closing your fingers into a fist. What can you ascertain about the phenomenology of this item of behavior, on the basis of introspective attention to this phenomenology? To begin with, there are of course the purely bodily motion aspects of the phenomenology—the what-it's-like of being visually and kinesthetically presented with your own right hand rising and its fingers moving into clenched position. But there is more to it than that, of course, because you are experiencing this bodily motion *as your own action.*

In order to help bring into focus this specifically actional phenomenological dimension of the experience, it will be helpful to approach it in a negative/contrastive way, via some observations about what the experience is *not* like. For example, it is certainly not like this: first experiencing an occurrent wish for your right hand to rise and your fingers to move into clenched position, and then passively experiencing your hand and fingers moving in just that way. Such phenomenal character might be called *the phenomenology of fortuitously appropriate bodily motion.* It would be very strange indeed, and very alien.

Nor is the actional phenomenological character of the experience like this: first experiencing an occurrent wish for your right hand to rise and your fingers to move into clenched position, and then passively experiencing a causal process consisting of this wish's causing your hand to rise and your fingers to move into clenched position. Such phenomenal character might be called *the passive phenomenology of psychological state-causation of bodily motion.*[6] People often do passively experience causal processes *as* causal processes, of course: the experience of seeing the collision of a moving billiard ball with a motionless billiard ball is an experience as-of the collision causing the latter ball's subsequent motion; the experience of observing the impact of the leading edge of an avalanche with a tree in its path is an experience as-of the impact causing the tree to become uprooted; and so on. Sometimes people even experience their own bodily motions as state-caused by their own mental states—e.g., when one feels oneself shuddering and experiences this shuddering as caused by a state of fear. But it seems patently clear that one does not normally experience one's own actions in that way—as passively noticed, or passively introspected, causal processes consisting in the causal generation of bodily motion by occurrent mental states. That too would be a strange and alienating sort of experience.[7]

How, then, should one characterize the actional phenomenal dimension of the act of raising one's hand and clenching one's fingers, given that it is not the phenomenology of fortuitously appropriate bodily motion and it also is not the passive phenomenology of psychological state-causation of bodily motion? Well, it is the what-it's-like of *self as source* of the motion. You experience your arm, hand, and fingers as being moved *by you yourself*—rather than experiencing their motion either as fortuitously moving just as you want them to move, or passively experiencing them as being caused by your own mental states. You experience the bodily motion as generated by *yourself.*

The phenomenology of doing typically includes another aspect, which we will call *core optionality.* (More presently on the reason for the modifier "core.") Normally when you do something, you experience yourself as *freely* performing the action, in the sense that it is *up to you* whether or not to perform it. You experience yourself not only as generating the action, and not only as generating it purposively, but also as generating it in such a manner that you *could have done otherwise.* This palpable phenomenology of optionality has not gone unrecognized in the philosophical literature on freedom and determinism, although often in that literature it does not receive as much attention as it deserves. (Sometimes the most explicit attention is given to effort of will, although it takes only a moment's introspection to realize that the phenomenology of effortfully exerting one's will is really only one, quite special, case of the much more pervasive phenomenology of optionality.[8])

The core-optionality aspect of agentive phenomenology is intimately bound up with the aspect of self-as-source, in such a way that the former is an essential component of normal agentive self-source experience. In experiencing one's behavior as emanating from oneself as its source, one experiences oneself as being able to refrain from so behaving—or, at any rate, as being able to refrain from willfully producing such behavior. This is so even when one acts under extreme coercion or duress—e.g., handing over one's wallet or purse to a thief who is pointing a gun in one's face. It also is so even when one acts with an extreme phenomenological "imperativeness"— e.g., a mother's unhesitatingly leaping into the river to save her drowning child, Luther's acting out a sense of moral requirement (as expressed by his declaring "Here I stand, I can do no other"), or the compulsive handwasher's act of washing hands for the third time in ten minutes. The *core* phenomenology of optionality that is essential to ordinary agentive experience remains present in all such cases, even though there are further, superimposed, phenomenological aspects (duress, moral-obligation experience, intensely strong irrational desires, or the like) whose presence can render appropriate, in context, a judgment that the agent "could not have done otherwise," or "had no other option," or "did not act freely." (Such phenomenological aspects fall under a rubric we will call *superimposed non-optionality*.) Because the phenomenology of core optionality remains present even when the phenomenology of superimposed non-optionality is also present, it can be contextually appropriate to use "could" and "option" and "free" in a way that reflects this fact (rather than in a way that reflects the presence of one or another kind of superimposed non-optionality phenomenology). For instance, one might say this: "I could have refrained from giving the thief my wallet, and thus I gave it to him freely and with the option of refraining—even though refraining would have been quite stupidly irrational."

Agentive phenomenology is more closely akin to perceptual/kinesthetic experience than it is to discursive thought. (Many higher non-human animals, we take it, have some agentive phenomenology, even if they engage in little or no discursive thought.) Of course, we humans also wield *concepts* like agency, voluntariness, and the like (whereas it is questionable whether non-human animals do); but thoughts employing these concepts are not to be conflated with agentive phenomenology itself.

Our remarks thus far in this subsection are offered as the products of attentive phenomenological introspection. Pay attention to your own agentive phenomenology, we submit—perhaps while also contemplating intelligible-seeming contrast-cases, like the (imagined) phenomenology of fortuitously appropriate bodily motion and the (imagined) passive phenomenology of psychological state-causation of bodily motion—and you should find introspectively that your agentive experience has the features we have been describing.[9] The following question now arises. Are these features zero-point aspects of phenomenal subjectivity, or do they instead require, and deploy, an explicit self-representation?

An apt way to address this question is to recur to a consideration already emphasized above, viz., the fact that the experiential self is present in consciousness more intimately—more directly—via phenomenal subjectivity than it ever is—or ever can be—by being explicitly represented. With that in mind, ask yourself introspectively which of the following two descriptions better fits the fundamental character of your own agentive experience:

(A) My agentive experience is a matter of me myself being explicitly represented in consciousness, and moreover is a matter of me myself being explicitly represented as being the source of my action and as possessing core optionality in producing it.

(B) My agentive experience, rather than being a belief-like matter of explicitly representing myself, to myself, as the core-optionality possessing source of my action—and rather than being a matter of undergoing (via a presentational representation) an explicit, perceptual, or quasi-perceptual, *presentation* of myself, to myself, as the core-optionality possessing source of my action—instead is the direct experience of *being* the source of my action, and of *exercising* core optionality.

Description (B), we submit, is the better one. The intertwined experiential aspects of self-sourcehood and core optionality are, most fundamentally, aspects of the *directly* experienced presence of the self in consciousness—aspects of the *for-me-ness* of agentive experience. Thus, they are zero-point aspects. Although we humans also can undergo conscious states—e.g., beliefs or propositional entertainings—that deploy explicit self-representations and that explicitly attribute self-sourcehood and core optionality to this self, this is decidedly an "add-on," something over and above agentive experience itself. (And surely creatures like dogs cannot undergo mental states of that kind, even though it is plausible that dogs too undergo, to some extent at least, agentive phenomenology with its aspects of self-sourcehood and core optionality.)

What about presentational representations, of the kind deployed by sensory-perceptual experience? Well, what introspection seems to reveal is that the sensory-presentational aspects of agentive experience are all, and only, those that would also be possessed by experiences with the phenomenology of fortuitously appropriate bodily motion—viz., being perceptually presented (e.g., visually and kinesthetically) with various aspects of one's body's motion.[10] Self-sourcehood and core optionality are not *presented* in experience the way one's bodily motions are presented; rather, they are present more directly and intimately than that. They are zero-point aspects of phenomenal subjectivity.

## *Prospection and recollection*

Ordinary conscious experience typically is suffused with prospective elements. As one moves purposefully through one's ambient environment, for example, one constantly anticipates one's upcoming sensory-perceptual experience in the immediate and short-term future, and one constantly modulates the specifics of one's behavior in light of various prospective elements. Walking with proper balance, for instance, depends in part upon anticipated upcoming impact-cum-support experience *vis-à-vis* the leg and foot that one is now extending forward. Purposefully pushing one's grocery cart down specific aisles in the grocery store (while purposefully bypassing others), for instance, depends in part upon anticipated sensory-perceptual experiences of being visually perceptually presented with specific items that one intends to purchase, situated on a grocery shelf immediately in front of oneself and within reach. Such examples are legion.

Similar remarks apply to recollective elements of experience. Walking with proper balance depends in part upon recently experienced, recollected, impact-cum-support experience *vis-à-vis* the leg-cum-foot that just recently was supporting one's body and is now moving forward. Purposefully pushing one's grocery cart down specific aisles depends in part upon recently experienced, now recollected, experiences of seeing and removing certain specific items from certain shelves. Again, such examples are legion.[11]

The experiencing self is experientially present, in such prospective (or recollective) experiences, in a direct and immediate way: one is envisioning, or remembering, a certain what-it-is-likeness *for me*. Indeed, the experiencing self is directly and immediately present twice over, so to speak. The phenomenal character *for me now*, of my current prospective (or recollective) experience involves an envisioned (or recalled) phenomenal character *for me then*. Introspective attention to such prospective/recollective elements of experience thus reveals that these elements have temporally layered, or temporally superimposed, zero-point aspects: there is something it is like, *for me now*, to envision (or recollect) a something-it-will-be-like (or a something-it-was-like) *for me then*. And these are indeed zero-point aspects, rather than involving explicit conscious *representation* of oneself to oneself. For, to repeat, the experiencing self is *directly and immediately* present in such experiences, twice over.

## *Desire*

One's occurrent conscious desires frequently pertain to oneself: what one desires is some state of affairs involving onself—say (upon having just finished drinking the beer one has been holding), to be in the possession of another glass of beer, and to drink that beer. The following question now arises. In typical cases of undergoing such a self-directed, occurrent, desire (e.g., the desire to drink another beer), does one consciously and explicitly represent oneself, to oneself, as being in that desired situation, or does one rather experience a desire-attitude *vis-à-vis* an envisioned state of affairs with a prospective-zero-point aspect?

An apt way to address this question is to ask whether the prospective involvement of oneself, in the envisioned situation that one desires to come about, is experientially direct and immediate. Introspective attention to such desire-experiences reveals that the answer is yes. What one envisions, and envisions in the desiring-for way, is *to be drinking* another beer. One is envisioning occupying the sensory-perceptual zero point of a beer-drinking experience, and one is envisioning this (desire-ingly) while yet also occupying the zero point of a current sensory-perceptual experience that presents to oneself an empty glass in one's hand. Thus, occurrent conscious desires of this kind have the twice-over zero-point aspect we described in the section on prospection and recollection above. The experiential self is involved more immediately and directly in such experiences than it would be, or could be, through mediation via a conscious *representation* of oneself drinking beer.

This is not to deny that people can, and sometimes do, undergo occurrent, conscious, self-involving desires that do involve conscious self-representation. This can happen, for instance, when one's desire rests upon a distanced perspective upon oneself, such as a third-person perspective. Perhaps one actually does not desire *to drink* another beer (one feels beer-satiated); but one does desire to appear hip to others in the room, and one believes that drinking another beer will have this effect. One thereby forms a desire, *vis-à-vis* a state of affairs consisting of one's drinking another beer, in which this state of affairs is envisioned from a third-person perspective: one consciously, desire-ingly, represents oneself, to oneself, *as seen by others*, drinking beer and thereby looking hip to them. As one might express in words one's conative situation with respect to drinking another beer, "I don't desire *to drink* another beer, but I do desire *that I drink* another beer."[12]

Ordinary terminology for describing ordinary self-involving desires is suggestive and illuminating here, as is the locutionary awkwardness of describing such desires the way philosophers typically do when treating them as so-called "propositional" attitudes. The ordinary mode of speech is to use an infinitival construction, without any first-person pronoun—as in "I want *to drink* another beer." Philosophers are often tempted to think that a more philosophically revealing way to express one's desire would be propositionally, using an explicit first-person indexical term—as in the awkward, stilted-sounding, "I want *that I drink* another beer." Now, although one must certainly be cautious in seeking to extract philosophical morals from ordinary-language grammar, in the present case the facts of English grammar do seem to provide further support for what we are claiming (and we suspect that many other languages are similar in this respect). The ordinary locution seems especially apt as an expression of self-involving desires that have the twice-over zero-point aspect and are not explicitly self-representational. The awkward, stilted-sounding, locution does seem at least *somewhat* apt, however, as a device for expressing an explicitly self-representing desire involving a third-person perspective upon oneself.

### *Reasons*

Intention formations and actions normally are highly purposive, and normally exhibit practical rationality *vis-à-vis* the purposes that lie behind them. The paradigmatic structure of reasons-based intention formation and action is the familiar desire/belief structure: one has a certain desire (often a self-involving one) that is not overridden by conflicting desires, one has a belief to the effect that a specific available potential action would (probably) lead to the fulfillment of the desire, and straightaway one either performs such an action or forms an intention to do so later. Typically, the pertinent desire and the pertinent belief are each occurrent and conscious, although in some cases (e.g., performing highly routine actions like unlocking one's office door) they are not at the center of one's attention.

We will henceforth use the locution "voluntary act" to cover both actions (including mental actions, such as mental addition) and intention formations. We take it that in cases where one performs a specific voluntary act *because of* an occurrent, conscious desire/belief pair that together constitute a reason for such an act, the belief and desire jointly *state-cause* the act. On the other hand, as we emphasized in section 2.5, one normally does not experience one's act *as* being thus state-caused.[13] Rather, and again as we stressed in the section on voluntary-action experience, above, one's voluntary-act experience has the zero-point aspect of self-sourcehood. But, in addition, one's experience also has two further pertinent elements: first, one experiences such an act, considered prospectively, as *rationally favored* by the pertinent desire and belief; and second, in voluntarily performing the act, one experiences doing so *on the basis of* this favoring relation. And, once again, all this is not experienced, passively, as a state-causal process involving occurrent conscious mental states state-causing bodily motions or intention formations; rather, it is experienced actively and agentively. One experiences oneself as exerting voluntary agency, and as doing so rationally—i.e., as doing so on the basis of reasons that one experiences as favoring one's act. (Often, especially in performing routine acts like brushing one's teeth, the phenomenological features we are describing are outside the focus of attention; but they are present nonetheless.)

Wilfrid Sellars described in striking fashion a distinction of the kind we are now highlighting: the distinction between "the space of causes" and "the space of reasons." Phenomenologically, voluntary-agency experience involves occupying a specific locus in the space of reasons. That locus is determined by various aspects of one's own current experiential situation—in particular, one's present occurrent desires, and one's present occurrent beliefs concerning potential desire-implementing acts one might perform.[14]

The following question now arises. In ordinary cases where one exercises one's voluntary agency, does one consciously and explicitly *represent* oneself, to oneself, as occupying a specific locus in the space of reasons, or is it rather the case that being thus located is a zero-point aspect of consciousness? As with previous such questions addressed above, an apt way to address this question is to ask whether the reasons-appreciating, reasons-as-basis, elements of one's voluntary-agency are experienced in an *immediate* and *direct* way in one's voluntary-agency experience. The answer delivered by attentive phenomenological introspection is yes. One's experience is as-of *occupying* a specific locus in the space of practical reasons: (i) of immediately and directly having those reasons, (ii) of immediately and directly appreciating the favoring relation between those reasons and one's voluntary act, and (iii) of immediately and directly performing this act on the basis of those reasons.

This is not to deny that people can, and sometimes do, act voluntarily on the basis of reasons constituted by occurrent conscious states, some or all of which involve conscious, explicit, self-representation. Once again, however, voluntary acts of that kind typically rest upon a distanced perspective on oneself, such as a third-person perspective. Imagine someone, for instance, who has absolutely no desire to exercise at the local gym several days per week, but who does desire to lose weight. Although he immediately and directly believes that gym exercise is the most effective way to lose weight, and he immediately and directly desires to lose weight, his loathing of exercise is so intense that no immediate, direct, desire to exercise arises within him. Nonetheless, he is able to take a third-person perspective on himself, and to summon up a desire with respect to a state of affairs as envisioned in the explicitly self-representational way—a state of affairs envisioned via consciously deploying a self-representation, aptly expressible as "*I* go to the gym and exercise." Whenever it is gym time, he summons up this self-representing desire, perhaps by imagining seeing in the mirror a slimmer, trimmer, reflection than he actually still sees every day in the mirror. So, even though he has no desire whatever *to go* to the gym, he goes anyway because he is motivated by the self-representing desire *that I* go to the gym.

Thus far in this subsection we have been discussing the phenomenology of *voluntary* agency, and of the associated reasons-involving aspects of practical rationality. We have deployed the expression "voluntary act" broadly, to encompass voluntary intention formations as well as voluntary actions. But the space of reasons figures not only in the phenomenology of experiences involving practical rationality, but also in the phenomenology of experiences involving theoretical rationality. A central phenomenon in this domain is belief fixation—i.e., formation of, or maintenance of, beliefs. Most philosophers, ourselves included, maintain that belief fixation is not under voluntary control; one major reason to think so is that attentive introspection reveals it to be so. Nevertheless, there is the following, phenomenologically palpable, respect in which episodes of belief formation deserve to be classified as mental *acts*—albeit involuntary ones. One's experiences are as-of being a *rationally responsible epistemic agent*—an agent capable of appraising and evaluating one's available evidence, capable of appreciating the extent to which that evidence favors or disfavors various potential beliefs, and capable of forming beliefs on the basis of sufficiently strong evidential support. Such experiences are not passive, in the manner of sensory-perceptual experiences—even though they are not voluntary either. Rather, rational evidence assessment and rational belief formation are experienced as mental acts one consciously performs—acts consisting of exercising one's *rationality*.

So the following question now arises, similar to others raised above. In ordinary cases where one exercises one's epistemic agency, does one consciously and explicitly *represent* oneself, to oneself, as occupying a specific locus in the space of reasons, or is it rather the case that being thus located is a zero-point aspect of consciousness? Once again, an apt way to address this question is to ask whether the reasons-appreciating, reasons-as-basis, elements of one's (involuntary) exercises of epistemic agency are experienced in an *immediate* and *direct* way in one's evidence-appraising and belief-forming experience. The answer delivered by attentive phenomenological introspection is yes. One's experience is as-of *occupying* a specific locus in the space of epistemic reasons: (i) of immediately and directly having those reasons, (ii) of immediately and directly appreciating the favoring relation between those reasons and one's potential belief, and (iii) immediately and directly (albeit involuntarily) forming this belief on the basis of those reasons. Thus, the distinctive phenomenology of reasons-responsive exercises of epistemic agency constitutes yet another zero-point aspect of phenomenal subjectivity.

This is not to deny that people can, and sometimes do, rationally form (or maintain) beliefs only in a way that is non-immediate and non-direct, and that deploys an explicit conscious self-representation. Suppose, for example, that one remembers appreciating that the specific considerations $C_1, C_2, \ldots, C_n$ confer strong evidential support on proposition $P$, and one remembers forming the belief that $P$ on this basis, and yet at the present moment one is unable to generate an occurrent appreciation of why it is that $C_1, C_2, \ldots, C_n$ confer strong evidential support on $P$. (Perhaps this inability is the result of having recently consumed too much beer.) One can rightly say to oneself, "I believe that $C_1, C_2, \ldots, C_n$ confer strong evidential support on $P$," and one can legitimately persist, on this basis, in believing $P$. But this explicitly self-representational way of believing $P$ on the basis of $C_1, C_2, \ldots, C_n$ is a decidedly *indirect* way of being self-involved with respect to the reasons for $P$. Ordinary, full-fledged, evidence appraisal and evidence appreciation are *zero-point* aspects of experience, with the pertinent zero point being one's own present locus within the space of epistemic reasons.

## The phenomenal character of explicit self-representation

A general lesson that emerges from the preceding discussion is that explicit self-representations are apt to figure in conscious experience when one regards oneself from some kind of distanced perspective, such as a third-person perspective. Of course, the aspect of phenomenal subjectivity will still be present, since it is integral to all conscious experience: a conscious episode that includes explicit self-representation will still possess *for-me-ness*. Also, it seems entirely possible that some explicitly self-representational experiences will include yet another phenomenally subjective aspect: one's experience might represent some self-involving episode (with the self being experientially present in the immediate and direct way, non-representationally), while also incorporating a reflective, third-person, perspective toward oneself in that very episode.

Consider, for instance, experiences of regret. Phenomenological introspection suggests that often such an experience includes both elements lately mentioned. On one hand, one recollects being at the agentive zero point and the sensory-perceptual zero point of some specific past action. On the other hand, one also is taking a critical, distanced, perspective upon oneself—which involves explicitly representing oneself, to oneself, as having behaved badly in so acting.

It is to be expected, then, that instances of explicit self-representation will tend to arise when the cognitive task at hand calls for some kind of distanced perspective upon oneself. And it is also to be expected that sometimes such distanced, self-representing consciousness regarding some recollected (or prospective) self-involving episode will be experientially superimposed upon the direct, non-self-representing recollection (or prospection) of that very same episode.

Even if this is right, however, explicit self-representation also is apt to arise under various other kinds of circumstance too—in particular, when the cognitive task at hand can be more easily, more resource-efficiently, accomplished by deploying I*/me* representations. Indeed, and notwithstanding our remarks in the section on prospection and recollection, above, explicit self-representations often can enhance and streamline the cognitive-architectural operation of both episodic memory and planning—a theme we pursue below.

## Cognitive-architectural implementation: zero-point representations vs I* representations

### Preliminaries

As we said in the previous section on preliminaries, above, the inherent phenomenal character of a particular mental state or process is the experiential categorical basis of the pertinent functional-role aspects of that state/process—aspects that are appropriate to its intentional content. In the case of self-involving conscious states/processes—both those involving only zero-point aspects and those that also deploy self-representations—content-appropriateness of functional role normally will be relativistic: the functional role played by the given state/process, in the ongoing cognition-cum-behavior of the person experiencing that state/process will be content-appropriate *given* that the state/process is being experienced by that same person. Such experiencer-relativity of content-appropriateness will obtain not only for conscious states/processes in which the self is explicitly represented, but also for ones in which the self is present only immediately and directly via zero-point aspects.

Conscious states/processes are implemented—i.e., realized, or subserved—by states/processes that are characterizable in sub-phenomenological ways. Implementation, in turn, is a hierarchical matter: it involves various successive theoretical-descriptive levels, bottoming out at the level of subatomic physics. One implementational level, high up in the hierarchy and just below the level of conscious experience itself, is the level of what is sometimes called *cognitive architecture*. Much theorizing in cognitive science occurs at this level. Here the goal is to describe in a fairly abstract way nature's "engineering design" for cognitive agents, and for humans in particular. Theoretical hypotheses are put forward about abstract functional organization, involving notions like "central processing unit" and "belief box." Theoretical hypotheses are also put forward about the internal structure of the cognitive-architectural-level states/processes that implement conscious states/processes—for instance, the hypothesis that they all have digital, language-like structure and belong to a "language of thought," or the hypothesis that they all have analog, picture-like structure, or the hypothesis that some consciousness-implementing states/processes are language-like and others are picture-like.

Although the inherent phenomenal character of a given conscious state/process is indeed the *experiential* categorical basis of the pertinent functional role of that state/process, this functional role also will have successive *implementing* categorical bases as well—at the level of cognitive architecture, at the neural level, and ultimately at the subatomic level. Our concern in the remainder of this chapter is with cognitive-architectural implementation of various kinds of conscious states/processes. In particular, we are concerned with (i) when, and why, such implementation involves representations with an explicit I*/me* constituent, and (ii) when, and why, the implementing representations instead have zero-point structure.[15,16]

The deliverances of attentive phenomenological introspection, we take it, can be rightly treated as providing strong—albeit defeasible—evidence about this matter. Conscious states in which the experiencing self is present immediately and directly, and with various zero-point aspects, can be expected to be cognitive-architecturally implemented via representations with zero-point *structure*. And conscious states whose content is overtly self-representational can be expected to be cognitive-architecturally implemented via representations that include an explicit I*/me* constituent. The reason why the phenomenological evidence is defeasible is this: in principle, conscious states/processes might get cognitive-architecturally implemented via representations, some of whose structure is not reflected within consciousness itself. For instance, in principle the zero-point aspects of conscious experience could all be implemented by representations that deploy an I*/me* constituent subconsciously, even though these zero-point aspects do not involve *conscious* self-representation. But the theoretical burden of proof rests upon those who would make such claims; meanwhile, phenomenology can and should inform theorizing about the nature of the representations that cognitive-architecturally implement conscious states/processes. In addition, further evidence can be garnered from empirical data, and from pertinent extant theory, within cognitive science itself; some of this data and theory will be invoked below.

What might zero-point representational structure be like? Various possibilities suggest themselves. Picture-like analog representations, for instance, have built-in zero-point structure: they represent a scene from a point of view—a point of view that does not get represented itself. Language-like representations can deploy representational categories that presuppose an implicit frame of reference that is centered on oneself, and can do so without also deploying any I*/me* representational constituent—categories like "above and to the right." Also, some language-like representations might have a structure other than that of a declarative sentence, a structure that nonetheless is suitable for their self-involving functional role—e.g., representations that have the grammatical structure of commands. For instance, representations that have a command structure, and lack any language-of-thought analog of a grammatical subject, could contribute to intention formation by getting inserted into a cognitive-architectural "intention box." So there is certainly no in-principle obstacle to the possibility that certain representations can play self-involving roles in a creature's cognitive economy without containing an I*/me* representational constituent.

## Cognition without me*

### Judgment and decision making

In his textbook, Rey (1997) draws on the ideas of Perry and Castañeda to argue explicitly for a mental item in the language of thought (LOT) corresponding to the natural language term "I":

> Just as in English the speaker is supposed to use "I" only to refer to his or herself, in LOT the "system" uses a certain term to refer only to the receiver of present inputs, the instigator of outputs, and the subject of intervening mental states.
>
> (Rey 1997, p. 291)

Rey goes on to elaborate:

> Suppose the term were "i," and that the system uses "i" to record automatically that it had certain perceptions and judgments and preferences; and that *its behavior is crucially determined by just those attitudes that do have this "i" as their subject:* i.e. its actions are standardly caused by beliefs and preferences that are designated as belonging to "i." Merely my comp-judging the sentence "GR ought to get moving right now" won't be enough to get me moving; I've got to comp-judge "i had better get moving right now."
>
> (Rey 1997, p. 291; emphasis added)

Relatedly, Perry writes, "what is special about self-notions is that they are the normal repository of normally self-informative ways of perceiving, and the normal motivator of normally self-dependent ways of acting" (Perry 2002, p. 202).

These suggestions about the role of I* in action seem initially tempting. To be sure, Perry cases show how representing *SN ought to move right now* might not suffice to get SN moving where *I* ought to move* would suffice; similarly for TH. But it is a mistake to infer from this fact that the action of moving requires tokening the I* symbol, as in *I* ought to move right now*. It's perfectly coherent to have a decision-making architecture that effectively presupposes that perceptions are one's own and actions are one's own without having to represent I* explicitly.

Just to take one very prominent species of artificial intelligence models of decision making, consider production systems. Production systems are composed of conditional statements, where the consequent describes an action. If one of the antecedents is represented as satisfied (in a working-memory system), the program proceeds to carry out the act specified in the consequent. One simple example is provided by thermostats (e.g., Newell 1990). A thermostat might have the following production system:

> If temperature > 78 degrees and AC [air conditioning] is off, turn AC on
>
> If temperature < 77 degrees, and AC is on, turn AC off.

As in this example, typically, production systems do not including anything like the I* symbol. There is a hard-coded connection between the action indicated in the consequent and the requisite behavior. The thermostat doesn't need to specify "turn on my* AC." There is only one AC that is being controlled by the thermostat.

Let's consider now a perfectly reasonable (if very simple) production system for a familiar childhood winter activity—catching snowflakes on your tongue:

If there are snowflakes falling from directly above, then tilt head upwards, open mouth, stick out tongue.

Just as with the thermostat, this production rule has no I* symbol. But, one might ask, doesn't the system have to represent that snowflakes are falling above me*; that it's my* head, my* mouth, my* tongue? No. Just as the connection between the particular thermostat and the particular AC is hardwired into the system, so too the connections between the particular instance of the production rule and the particular head, mouth, etc. are hardwired into the system. In other words, the production rule only sends instructions to *my* head (it doesn't connect to other heads), so the rule doesn't need to include a further specification that it is my* head.

Unlike the thermostat, people can, of course, have a representation like *lift my\* head*. This is an important fact about us. One way in which it's important is that it allows us to convert ambiguous environmental information into self-relevant representations. All of Perry's examples work like this. I see a trail of sugar, and I seek someone under the description "guy spilling sugar" (Perry 1979). Or I see a frumpy guy in the mirror and I wonder who he is (Perry 2002). Or I am told that some individual is about to be attacked by a bear (Perry 1977). In each of these cases, in order to get the appropriate action, I have to realize that *I* am the guy. But in normal decision making, there isn't any question who the guy is.

While Perry's examples illuminate a key element in the human representational system, it's easy to exaggerate the role the I* plays in everyday cognition. We suspect that for most human problem solving and decision making, people do not token the I*.[17]

This is lent some support by concurrent protocol analysis, in which people report what is running through their mind as they are solving a problem. Although philosophers of psychology often emphasize ways in which introspection fails, a large tradition of unsung work shows that people are quite accurate, using the "think aloud" technique, at reporting how they solve problems. For instance, when people are asked to solve a simple arithmetic problem like 19×4 and "think aloud" while they do it, people are excellent at reporting the process. The accuracy of self-report is confirmed by independent measures (see Ericsson and Simon 1993). For example, those who report converting 19×4 to [(20×4) − 4] finish faster than those who report multiplying 4 by 9, carrying the 3, then multiplying 4 by 1, and adding the 3 to that.[18] Similarly, the accuracy of self-report is confirmed by the relation between the participant's solution and the reported process. This is especially clear in cases where participants make mistakes. For instance, if a participant says that 19×4 is 56, we can see how she went wrong if she reports an arithmetic error like 20×4 = 60. Thus, protocol analysis plausibly gives an accurate window into at least some critical aspects of cognitive phenomenology. When we turn to the issue at hand, the representation of the self in decision making, we find that when people think aloud during judgment and decision tasks, they rarely mention the self (except incidentally—"I guess," "I would say") For instance, in solving problems under uncertainty, here are some representative reports from subjects:

> He is most likely a nurse just because being well spoken and interested in politics and having lots of time has nothing to do with being a doctor, and he can be a very good nurse, and there are more nurses than there are doctors.
>
> He is a doctor because he is a male and not a lot of nurses are male, and he is well off and invests a lot of time in his career.
>
> I would say Paul is a doctor because he invests a lot of time in his career and that probably takes more time than being a nurse.
>                                            (De Neys and Glumicic 2008, p. 1288)

Or, for a mathematical example, here is the protocol from a participant asked to multiply 36 by 24:

> ok 36 times 24, um, 4 times 6 is 24, 4, carry the 2, 4 times 3 is 12, 14, 144, 0, 2 times 6 is 12, 2,carry the 1, 2 times 3 is 6, 7, 720, 720, 144 plus 720, so it would be 4, 6, 864.
>                                            (Ericsson and Moxley 2011, p. 94)

Here is a representative example from participants doing a logic problem:

> $A$ says $B$ is a knave, that's either true or false. Keeping that in mind, $B$ says that $A$ and $C$ are of the same type. So if $A$ is telling the truth, $C$ is also of $A$'s type, which is truth-telling—knights–$A$ and $C$ are both knights if $B$ is telling the truth. If $B$ is telling the truth and $A$ is telling the truth, well, something, neither, not both of them can be right, because either $A$ is correct about $B$'s being a knave, or . . . wait, this is getting confusing.
>                                            (Rips 1989, p. 89)

Here is an example from a decision concerning shopping:

> cucumbers are still too expensive / Bacon costs too much to get at all / I get the, the little tenderized ones [steaks], what are they called? These are the ones if they get below a dollar . . .
>                                            (Svenson 1979, p. 152)

And here is an example from that beloved technique in decision theory, gambling decisions:

> PL [probability of losing] is . . . is lower on $A$ / The $\$L$ [sum to be lost] is higher on $A$ than on $B$ / such a choice / Since $B$ has a much higher PW [probability of winning]/ I'll take that.
>                                            (Svenson 1979, p. 152)

Although "I" does appear in some of these concurrent reports, it doesn't seem to be integral to the problem-solving process in the examples (though it will be in other cases, as we'll see in the section on cognition that needs me*, below).

It's not that people are generally averse to mentioning themselves when engaged in reporting their thoughts. On the contrary, when people are asked to explain their thought process immediately after it occurs (using a "retrospective" rather than "concurrent" think-aloud method), people typically do include explicit self-reference:

> My first thought was I saw the 5600 dollars and I saw the 80 dollars but the 5600 dollars—there is still a chance for me to gain, it was really small (probability low), but you never know. That's why I chose B because 5600 dollars is a lot of money (value high).
>
> My first thought was with 20% chance of owing 900 dollars, that gives me 80% chance (recode probability) to not owe 900 dollars and I have pretty good chances (probability high).
>
> (Cokely and Kelley 2009, p. 28)[19]

Thus, for concurrent reports of thought processes, it is highly typical for subjects *not* to mention the self. Earlier we pointed out that sensible and efficient cognitive architectures don't need an I* representation for basic thought and action. These points fit together, of course. An efficient architecture for problem solving doesn't require the I*, and people don't mention the I when solving simple problems. We suspect that this is because the I* concept is simply not represented in these exercises. It is possible, of course, that people really are explicitly using the I* concept even in these reasoning exercises. But as far as we can tell, there is no reason to think this is the case. Rather, we maintain, the I* concept doesn't appear in the simple thought and actional processes that are ubiquitous in daily life.

*Phenomenology of agency*

We turn now to the agentive phenomenology vis-a-vis its cognitive-architectural implementation. One of the more interesting developments in explaining the phenomenology of agency comes from work on the *comparator* model (e.g., Gallagher 2000; Frith 2012). The basic idea is that in a normal case of acting, like raising one's hand in questions and answers when one forms the intention to raise one's hand, this sends two signals forward. One signal (of course) goes to the motor cortex to generate the appropriate muscular activity that eventuates in arm raising; the other signal is called an "efference copy" and it predicts a certain outcome—one that conforms to arm raising. This latter process is sometimes called a "forward" model because it's prior to the actual movement. So, we have a motor signal that should lead us to raise our arm and a predictive signal that anticipates certain activity associated with arm raising. A further mechanism, the *comparator*, evaluates whether the predicted activity actually occurs. Roughly, the comparator determines whether the arm has moved in the right way and at the right time given the prediction signal. If there is a match, then one will have the phenomenology of agency; otherwise one will not have that phenomenology.

The basic idea of the comparator model was developed earlier in animal models. Elephantfish are weakly electric fish that send out electrical discharges to gain information about their environment, including the location of other fish. But if they actually registered their own electric discharges, whenever the fish emitted a discharge, it would, as it were, think that it is right next to another fish. The fish need to discount their own electrical discharges to avoid all these false positives. The reigning model of how they do this is a comparator model. When the command to emit a discharge goes out to the electric organ, an efference copy also goes out to the comparator. When there is a match between the predicted discharge and the registered electricity, the electricity is discounted from the inferences about the environment (Gandevia 1996).

The comparator account thus has impressive precedents in animal models. In the present case, the comparator account of the phenomenology of agency helps to explain why one can't tickle oneself—the tickling phenomenology is defeated by the forward model which predicts the sensations. The account also explains why acting has a phenomenology different from being acted upon. If someone else pushes my hand up, the forward model isn't generated and so I don't have the comparator-generated phenomenology. The comparator account has also been invoked to explain clinical symptoms like anarchic hand, in which people generate finely tuned motor behavior but lack the normal phenomenology of action. Relatedly, the comparator account has been used to explain delusions of control and thought insertion in schizophrenia (e.g., Wolpert and Ghahramani 2000).

It's not clear how much of a reductionist one should be about all of this. But perhaps it's worth noting that neurons in motor areas have axon collaterals that get sent to the cerebellum. This means that, in addition to the main projection of the axon, it has an additional projection that goes somewhere else. The tempting inference in this case is that when an instruction is issued by the neurons in motor cortex, the axon collaterals of those very neurons send an efference copy to the cerebellum. And it's known that patients with a damaged cerebellum exhibit behavior indicating reduced predictions of their own movements (Haggard and Whitford 2004, p. 52).

Thus the comparator model gives us an account of why it feels different to act vs be acted on. But notice that nowhere in this discussion has there been need to make recourse to a self-representation. Researchers on electric fish do not posit an I* representation to explain how the fish discounts its own electrical activity. Similarly, in the comparator model of action, the entire process is run without invoking explicit self-representations. Of course, there is still a critical theoretical role for "self" in these theories. It is only because the motor instruction "raise hand" was issued by *me* that the forward model is generated. The same motor behavior forced on me by someone other than *me* would not produce the relevant phenomenology. But "I*" need not be tokened in order to generate that phenomenology (see also Prinz 2011).

## Cognition that needs me*

### Memory

Although we've argued that the bulk of human cognition can proceed perfectly well without representing the I*, we think that there are important exceptions. In recollecting a past event, we often need to represent *who* it happened to. I need to represent who the guy is that received the gift. That will determine whether I should express gratitude. Similarly, I need to represent who the guy is that was insulted. That will determine whether I should express hostility.

There are thus functional reasons for representing the self when we engage in recollecting episodes from our lives. It can be critical to determining the appropriate course of action. In addition, when we turn to descriptive psychology, we find that it's common ground that, in episodic recollection, the self is explicitly represented. The idea here goes back at least to William James, who wrote, "Memory requires more than the mere dating of a fact in the past. It must be dated in *my* past. In other words, I must think that I directly experienced its occurrence" (1890/1950, p. 650). This characterization of episodic memory continues to this day. In a recent piece on children's episodic memory, Harlene Hayne and Kana Imuta summarize the prevailing view that episodic recollection is "accompanied by conscious awareness that the event happened to 'me' or will happen to 'me' that does not accompany retrieval of other kinds of memories" (Hayne and Imuta 2011, p. 344).[20]

Indeed, there are cases of dissociations in which brain-injured patients lose the sense that their past experiences happened to *them*, and this is phenomenologically quite strange to the patient (e.g., Klein and Nichols 2012). One patient, RB, describes the phenomenon as follows:

> I could clearly recall a scene of me at the beach in New London with my family as a child. But the feeling was that the scene was not my memory. As if I was looking at a photo of someone else's vacation.

He described another example, this time from his university days:

> I can picture the scene perfectly clearly . . . studying with my friends in our study lounge. I can "relive" it in the sense of re-running the experience of being there. But it has the feeling of imagining, [as if]

re-running an experience that my parents described from their college days. It did not feel like it was something that really had been a part of my life. Intellectually I suppose I never doubted that it was a part of my life . . . But that in itself did not help change the feeling of ownership.

RB's lack of the felt sense that the past experience happened to *him* suggests that the normal course of episodic memory does indeed carry with it a distinct sense that the event happened to *me*.

There are two ways that the I* could get attached to episodic memories. One possibility is that the I* is actually encoded into each of the experience memories one has stored, e.g., in the hippocampus (and other regions critical to stored memories). Another possibility that we think more likely is that the I* is automatically attached to an experience memory as it is retrieved from the bank of experience memories. On this approach, what happens with RB is that he has the experience memories stored normally, but his retrieval process is defective and fails to attach the I* symbol normally. Of course, the functional reasons for having an I* attached to memory that we suggested earlier still apply. When I retrieve a memory from my store of experience memories, I need the representation of the experience to specify *who* the experience happened to. Moreover, this representation needs to be in a common language such that I can easily represent distinctions between the things that *I did*, the things that *Mark did*, and the things that *Mark and I both did*.

*Planning*[21]

In addition to its role in episodic memory, we maintain that the I* symbol plays a key role in efficient planning. Perhaps the most influential account of planning in recent philosophy and artificial intelligence is Bratman's "planning theory of intention" (e.g., Bratman 1987, 1999). Although it is not entirely explicit in Bratman's theory, there is reason to think that the symbol I* is essential to efficient planning.

Bratman's theory begins with the obvious fact that we are resource-limited creatures. We can't always be considering all the options before us. At any point, there are indefinitely many possible courses of action, and the world constantly changes in ways that bring about new courses of action, new consequences for old actions, and so forth. This makes ideal practical reasoning impossible for creatures like us. Bratman argues that one way that practical reasoning is eased for us is that we often *commit* to an intention and then stop deliberating *all things considered* about what to do. Once we commit to an intention, we no longer consider all the possible alternative courses of action, we just take things from the committed intention, and this commitment constrains and structures subsequent planning and decision making. A key part of Bratman's theory is that once you commit to a plan, you don't even consider options that are incompatible with the intentions that you've committed to—incompatible options are "filtered" out (Bratman et al. 1991). For instance, if I have committed to an intention to go to Germany on June 15th, then I don't even consider the option of hiking in the Sonoran desert on June 16th. A second key feature of the theory is that committing to an intention structures one's subsequent deliberations. Of particular importance is that once one commits to an intention, this will structure future deliberations about how best to execute the plan. So, once I'm committed to going to Germany, I generate the subplan that I must get my passport renewed. On Bratman's account, this kind of filtering and structuring is a much more efficient way to plan for creatures like us than to attempt a constant calculation of utility maximization.

Martha Pollack extends Bratman's model by exposing another way the decision making of a resource-bounded agent can be made more efficient—by "overloading" one's intentions (Pollack 1991, 1992). The idea is that, if an agent has a goal, she can try to search for whether that goal can be met in the course of executing some plan that has already been adopted. Suppose I realize that I need to get milk for breakfast tomorrow. I can then consider whether I already have a plan that will take me close to a grocery story. If I already planned to go to the hardware store to make a key, I can "overload" this prior plan to include a trip to the nearby grocery store.

What we want to suggest is that the I* symbol can play a critical role in these aspects of planning. If I plan to go to Germany on June 15th, then it's an asset to filtering that I represent that I* will be unable to hike in the Sonoran desert on the 16th. And unless I represent that I* am going to Germany, I won't know that I need to get my* passport renewed. Similarly, unless I represent that I* will be at the hardware store, it's difficult to see how I can overload that plan for something else that I will need to do. So, while simple action might not require an I* representation, efficient planning often does.[22]

As with memories, there are different ways that the I* could get attached to the representations of our intentions. The I* might be encoded directly into each intention in the "intention box." Another possibility is that the I* gets attached through the retrieval process. As with memory, we think this retrieval-based story is more plausible, partly because it strikes us as a more efficient cognitive architecture (and partly because we are sympathetic to the idea that the representations in the "intention box" are imperatival in form rather than declarative). Again, the functional reasons for thinking the I* symbol is important to efficient planning still apply on this retrieval-based story. I need to represent which things *I* intend to do, which things *my wife* intends to do, and which things *she and I* intend to do together. Representing these expected facts enables me to exclude various further paths of decision making and helps me to determine which plan should be overloaded—mine, hers, or ours.

## Conclusion

We have argued that phenomenal subjectivity—the direct, non-representational presence of the experiential self in consciousness as the *me for which* one's conscious experience has phenomenal character—is richly suffused with various, interpenetrating, zero-point aspects. These include the zero-point aspects of sensory-perceptual experience (in its several modalities), the zero-point aspects of voluntary-action experience (including self-sourcehood aspect and the core-optionality aspect), the temporally layered zero-point aspects that figure in at least some instances of prospection and recollection, the zero-point aspect of ordinary self-involving desires, and the zero-point aspect (within the space of reasons) of both practical and theoretical rationality.

We then took up the question of how self-involving conscious experiences of various kinds are cognitive-architecturally implemented. We argued that problem solving often proceeds without an I* symbol. In terms of cognitive architecture, it's easy to accommodate this for simple problems. Recall the example of production systems. The thermostat doesn't need to specify my* AC because the connection between the instruction and the control system (for the particular AC) is hardwired. There is no question, "which AC?" Something similar holds for simple problems and decisions. When I decide to lift my head, I don't need to have a my* representation, since the control structures are hardwired to my decisions. Again, there is no question about who the guy is who is being instructed to move his head. And when we look at think-aloud protocols, for simple problem solving, we find few invocations of the self. However, when we turn to planning and memory, we enter the domain of deeply diachronic processes. And it's plausible that often when we are engaged in processes that stretch back to the past or forward to the future—especially when such processes figure as components of fairly complex cognitive tasks like planning—it really is critical to keep track of the self via explicit I*/me* representations.

## Notes

1 The reason for the qualifier "virtually" is to leave open the possibility that some conscious mental states might have phenomenal character but lack any intentional content—for instance, perhaps, certain states of diffuse anxiety.
2 See, for instance, McGinn (1989), Strawson (1994, 2008), Siewert (1998), Horgan and Tienson (2002), Horgan et al. (2004), and Pitt (2004).
3 The notion of a presentational representation can be characterized, at least roughly and initially, as follows. An experience presentationally represents a putative object, and/or a putative state of affairs, just in case (i) it is a sensory-perceptual experience, and (ii) it represents such a putative object, and/or such a putative state of affairs, *as present* in the experiencer's ambient environment. We insert the word "putative" because it is possible in principle to undergo sensory-perceptual states that are radically non-veridical—e.g., hallucinations that

are phenomenologically indistinguishable from veridical sensory-perceptual experiences. Indeed, it is possible in principle for one's sensory-perceptual experience always to be radically non-veridical—e.g., by being a lifelong envatted brain whose sensory-perceptual states are phenomenologically indistinguishable from those of a normal human being.

4 Some philosophers maintain that sensory-perceptual experience does not involve representations at all, but instead has intentionality consisting of direct experiential acquaintance, unmediated by representations, with various objects in one's ambient environment and with instantiations by those objects of various properties and relations (e.g., Campbell 2002; Hellie 2007; Nudds 2009). In our opinion, however, the falsity of such "naïve realism" about sensory-perceptual experience should be virtually self-evident, among other reasons because advocates of the position are forced into wildly implausible "disjunctivism" about the intentionality of hallucinatory sensory-perceptual experience *vis-à-vis* the intentionality of phenomenologically indistinguishable sensory-perceptual experience that is veridical. The kernel of truth in so-called naïve realism is that objects in one's ambient environment are experientially *presented* in sensory-perceptual experience, when such experience is not illusory or hallucinatory; and being thus presented is a form of sensory-perceptual *acquaintance* with those objects (and with their perceived properties and relations). But the mistake is to construe sensory-perceptual acquaintance as non-representational. Rather, for objects to be presented by sensory-perceptual experience, and to be presented as instantiating various properties and relations, is, roughly, a matter of (i) one's current sensory-perceptual experience presentationally representing such putative objects, and presentationally representing such putative objects as instantiating those properties and relations, (ii) such objects' being now actually present in one's ambient environment, (iii) those objects' instantiating close enough (if not perfectly) the properties that one's current sensory-perceptual experience presentationally represents such putative objects as instantiating, and (iv) one's current sensory-perceptual experience, as-of such objects instantiating these properties and relations, being caused by those very objects' instantiating (close enough) those very properties and relations.

5 This first part of this subsection is adapted, with some modifications, from similar discussions in several other texts, including Horgan et al. (2003) and Horgan (forthcoming).

6 Phenomenologically speaking, exercises of one's agency are experienced as temporally located, and in that respect are experienced as "event-ish." Thus, the expression "state causation" works better than "event causation" as a way of expressing the way behaviors are *not* presented to oneself in agentive experience. (States can be short-lived, and often when they are, they also fall naturally under the rubric "event.") Although agentive experience is indeed "event-ish" in the sense that one experiences oneself as undertaking to perform actions *at specific moments in time,* one's behavior is not experienced as caused by *states* of oneself.

7 For discussion of a range of psychopathological disorders involving similar sorts of dissociative experience, see Stephens and Graham (2000).

8 This is not to deny, of course, that there is indeed a distinctive phenomenology of effort of will that *sometimes* is present in the phenomenology of doing. The point is just that this aspect is not always present.

9 Although it should be obvious to introspection that agentive experience has these features, this does not mean that it is obvious to introspection what constitute the *satisfaction conditions* of self-sourcehood and core optionality. For arguments in support of the claim that introspection alone cannot reliably ascertain these satisfaction conditions, see Horgan and Timmons (2011) and Horgan (2012, forthcoming).

10 Actually, kinesthetic experience sometimes presents parts of one's ambient environment through what might be called "extended touching"—e.g., feeling the leaves one is currently raking via how the rake feels, feeling the position of one's front wheels as one guides one's automobile through a turn. But this does not affect the point we are making in the text.

11 Extremely short-term cases of such prospection and recollection perhaps coincide with what Husserl called the retentive and protentive aspects of the "specious present." But presumably other cases do not, such as envisioning or recalling removing items from shelves that are located several aisles away from one's current location in the grocery store.

12 Our thanks to Mark Timmons for a conversation (over beer!) that prompted the present paragraph.

13 But note well: *not* experiencing one's voluntary act *as* state caused is different from, and weaker than, experiencing one's act *as not* state-caused. It is a vexed question whether or not the latter feature is an aspect of ordinary agentive experience, and it is also a vexed issue whether or not direct introspection can reliably ascertain the answer to this vexed question.

14 One's own current experiential situation might also have a phenomenal character that involves implicit appreciation of certain background desires and/or background beliefs—desires and beliefs that are not presently occurrent. For discussion of such "chromatic illumination" of conscious experience by such "morphological content," see Horgan and Potrč (2010).

15 Questions about how various kinds of phenomenally conscious states/processes are implemented, including questions about how they get *cognitive-architecturally* implemented, are themselves tractable, regardless of what one might think about the tractability or intractability of the so-called "explanatory gap" (Levine 1983) or "hard problem" of phenomenal consciousness (Chalmers 1996)—roughly, the question of why it should be that so-and-so physical or functional state/process should be a supervenience base for such-and-such phenomenal character, rather than instead either (i) being a supervenience base for some other phenomenal character, or (ii) occurring without any accompanying phenomenal character at all.

16 It is possible in principle, and may well be possible in practice, for there to be critters—say, certain kinds of robots—that (i) are correctly describable cognitive-architecturally as deploying both zero-point representations and I*/me* representations, but (ii) are "zombies" with no phenomenology at all (and hence with no zero-point aspects of phenomenology, and with no explicitly self-representational, essentially indexical, aspects of phenomenology). Much of what we say hereafter might well be applicable, *mutatis mutandis*, to such zombie critters, although none of our phenomenological discussion in the first section would apply to them.

17 Similarly, for most perceptions people have, we suspect that the I* isn't tokened. Perception delivers representations like "there is a shoe next to the bookshelf" free of any explicit I* representation.

18 The reaction time studies typically use "retrospective" techniques so that the result can't be attributed to the length of time it takes to utter the process. So, immediately after solving the problem, participants are asked to describe what went through their minds as they were solving the problem. People who report having gone through seven steps reliably took longer to solve the problem than those who report having gone through four steps.

19 Note that subjects were instructed to begin their retrospective reports with "my first thought was."

20 We acknowledge an apparent tension between this view and our remarks in the section on prospection and recollection as zero-point aspects of experience. Nonetheless, whereas we find it plausible that relatively short-term episodic-memory experiences normally are cognitive-architecturally implemented by zero-point representations, we also find it plausible that longer-term episodic-memory experiences instead need to be cognitive-architecturally implemented by I*-deploying representations. Roughly, the further in one's past is the recollected episode, the greater is the need for the cognitive-architectural implementation of the episodic memory to include an I*-constituent—thereby facilitating the functional role of a genuine self-involving *memory*, as opposed (for instance) to a mere self-involving imaginative episode.

21 Some of the following material is adapted from Nichols (2000).

22 The distinction between simple action and planning resolves an erstwhile apparent tension between what we have been saying in this section about planning and our earlier discussion of prospection in the section on prospection and recollection. Whereas the kind of prospection that is frequently involved in simple purposive action can plausibly be implemented by zero-point representations, the more complex one's planning task becomes, the greater are the cognitive-architectural advantages of implementation via I*-deploying representations.

# References

Block, N. (1995). On a Confusion about a Function of Consciousness. *Behavioral and Brain Sciences*, 18: pp. 227–287.

Bratman, M. (1987). *Intentions, Plans, and Practical Reason*. Cambridge, MA: Harvard University Press.

Bratman, M. (1999). *Faces of Intention*. Cambridge: Cambridge University Press.

Bratman, M., Israel, D., and Pollack, M. (1991). Plans and Resource-Bounded Practical Reasoning. In R. Cummins and J. Pollock (Eds.), *Philosophy and AI: Essays at the Interface*. Cambridge, MA: Bradford/MIT Press.

Campbell, J. (2002). *Reference and Consciousness*. Oxford, UK: Clarendon Press.

Chalmers, D. (1996). *The Conscious Mind*. Oxford, UK: Oxford University Press.

Cokely, E. T., and Kelley, C. M. (2009). Cognitive Abilities and Superior Decision Making Under Risk: A Protocol Analysis and Process Model Evaluation. *Judgment and Decision Making*, 4(1): pp. 20–33.

De Neys, W., and Glumicic, T. (2008). Conflict Monitoring in Dual Process Theories of Thinking. *Cognition*, 106(3): pp. 1248–1299.

Ericsson, K. A., and Moxley, J. (2011). Thinking Aloud Protocols. In Schulte-Mecklenbeck, M., Kühberger, A., and Ranyard, R. (Eds.). *A Handbook of Process Tracing Methods for Decision Research: A Critical Review and User's Guide*. New York: Psychology Press.

Ericsson, K. A., and Simon, H. A. (1993). *Protocol Analysis*. Cambridge, MA: MIT Press.

Frith, C. (2012). Explaining Delusions of Control: The Comparator Model 20 Years on. *Consciousness and Cognition*, 21(1): pp. 52–54.

Gallagher, S. (2000). Philosophical Conceptions of the Self: Implications for Cognitive Science. *Trends in Cognitive Sciences*, 4(1): pp. 14–21.

Gallagher, S., and Zahavi, D. (2010). Phenomenological Approaches to Self-Consciousness. *Stanford Encyclopedia of Philosophy*. Available online at: http://plato.stanford.edu/archives/spr2015/entries/self-consciousness-phenomenological/.

Gandevia, S. C. (1996). Kinesthesia: Roles for Afferent Signals and Motor Commands. *Comprehensive Physiology*, sec. 12: pp. 128–172.

Haggard, P., and Whitford, B. (2004). Supplementary Motor Area Provides an Efferent Signal for Sensory Suppression. *Cognitive Brain Research*, 19(1): pp. 52–58.

Hayne, H., and Imuta, K. (2011). Episodic Memory in 3- and 4-Year-Old Children. *Developmental Psychobiology*, 53(3): pp. 317–322.

Hellie, B. (2007). Factive Phenomenal Characters. In J. Hawthorne (Ed.), *Philosophical Perspectives 21: Philosophy of Mind* (pp. 259–306). Malden, MA: Blackwell.

Horgan, T. (2012). Introspection about Phenomenal Consciousness: Running the Gamut from Infallibility to Impotence. In D. Smithies and D. Stoljar (Eds.). *Introspection and Consciousness*. New York: Oxford University Press.

Horgan, T. (forthcoming). Injecting the Phenomenology of Agency into the Free Will Debate. In D. Shoemaker (Ed.). *Oxford Studies in Agency and Responsibility*, p. 2. Oxford: Oxford University Press.

Horgan, T., and Potrč, M. (2010). The Epistemic Relevance of Morphological Content. *Acta Analytica*, 25: pp. 155–173.

Horgan, T., and Tienson, J. (2002). The Intentionality of Phenomenology and the Phenomenology of Intentionality. In D. Chalmers (Ed.). *Philosophy of Mind: Classical and Contemporary Readings*. Oxford: Oxford University Press.

Horgan, T., and Timmons, M. (2011). Introspection and the Phenomenology of Free Will: Problems and Prospects. *Journal of Consciousness Studies*, 18: pp. 180–205.

Horgan, T., Tienson, J., and Graham, G. (2003). The Phenomenology of First-person Agency. In S. Walter and H. D. Heckman (Eds.). *Physicalism and Mental Causation: The Metaphysics of Mind and Action*. Exeter: Imprint Academic.

Horgan, T., Tienson, J., and Graham, G. (2004). Phenomenal Intentionality and the Brain in a Vat. In R. Schantz (Ed.). *The Externalist Challenge: New Studies in Cognition and Intentionality*. Amsterdam: de Gruyter.

Husserl, E. (1952). *Ideen zu einer reinen Phänomenologie und phänomenologischen Philosophie*. The Hague: M. Nijhoff.

James, W. (1890/1950). *The Principles of Psychology* (Vol. 1). New York: Dover.

Klein, S., and Nichols, S. (2012). Memory and the Sense of Personal Identity. *Mind*, 121: p. 483.

Levine, J. (1983). Materialism and Qualia: The Explanatory Gap. *Pacific Philosophical Quarterly*, 64: pp. 354–361.

McGinn, C. (1989). *Mental Content*. Oxford: Blackwell.

Nagel, T. (1974). What Is It Like to Be a Bat?, *Philosophical Review*, 83: pp. 435–450.

Newell, A. (1990). *Unified Theories of Cognition*. Cambridge, MA: Harvard University Press.

Nichols, S. (2000). The Mind's "I" and the Theory of Mind's "I": Introspection and Two Concepts of Self. *Philosophical Topics* 28(2): pp. 171–199.

Nudds, M. (2009). Recent Work in Perception: Naïve Realism and Its Opponents. *Analysis*, 69: pp. 334–346.

Peacocke, C. (1992). *A Study of Concepts.* Cambridge, MA: MIT Press.

Perry, J. (1977). Frege on Demonstratives. *The Philosophical Review* 86(4): pp. 474–497.

Perry, J. (1979). The Problem of the Essential Indexical. *Nous:* pp. 3–21.

Perry, J. (2002). *Identity, Personal Identity and the Self.* Indianapolis, IN: Hackett Publishing.

Pitt, D. (2004). The Phenomenology of Cognition; or *What Is It Like to Think that P?*, *Philosophy and Phenomenological Research* 69: pp. 1–36.

Pollack, M. (1991). Overloading Intentions for Efficient Practical Reasoning, *Nous* 25: pp. 513–536.

Pollack, M. (1992). The Uses of Plans. *Artificial Intelligence* 57: pp. 43–68.

Prinz, Jesse (2011). Wittgenstein and the Neuroscience of the Self. *American Philosophical Quarterly* 48(2): pp. 147–160.

Rey, G. (1997). *Contemporary Philosophy of Mind: A Contentiously Classical Approach.* Oxford: Blackwell.

Rips, L. J. (1989). The Psychology of Knights and Knaves. *Cognition*, 31(2): pp. 85–116.

Searle, J. (1992). *The Rediscovery of the Mind.* Cambridge, MA: MIT Press.

Sellars, W. (1956). Empiricism and the Philosophy of Mind. In H. Feigl and M. Scriven (Eds.). *Minnesota Studies in the Philosophy of Science, Foundations of Science and the Concepts of Psychology and Psychoanalysis* (pp. 253–329). Minneapolis: University of Minnesota Press.

Siewert, C. (1998). *The Significance of Consciousness.* Princeton, NJ: Princeton University Press.

Stephens, G. L., and Graham, G. (2000). *When Self-Consciousness Breaks: Alien Voices and Inserted Thoughts.* Cambridge, MA: MIT Press.

Strawson, G. (1994). *Mental Reality.* Cambridge, MA: MIT Press.

Strawson, G. (2008). Real Intentionality 3: Why Intentionality Entails Consciousness. In his *Real Materialism and Other Essays.* Oxford: Oxford University Press.

Svenson, O. (1979). Process Descriptions of Decision Making. *Organizational Behavior and Human Performance*, 23(1): pp. 86–112.

Wolpert, D. M., and Ghahramani, Z. (2000). Computational Principles of Movement Neuroscience. *Nature Neuroscience*, 3: pp. 1212–1217.

# 7 A sketch of Sartre's error theory of introspection

*Matthew C. Eshleman*

We must not make of reflection a mysterious and infallible power, or believe that everything that reflection attains is indubitable *because* it is attained by reflection.

(Sartre, 2004a, p. 21)

Only a pure reflective consciousness can discover the For-itself reflected-on in its reality.

(Sartre, 1956, p. 163)

While it was true in 1987 that "there [were] few extended studies of the topic of introspection" (D.S.M. 1987), the same cannot be said today. A growing body of monographs and peer-reviewed articles on all aspects of introspection (e.g., its function, epistemic warrant, ontological status, and the methodological role it might play in the study of consciousness) have burgeoned over the last 15 years or so in both philosophy (e.g., Gertler, 2001, 2003; Schwitzgebel, 2004, 2008; Byrne, 2005; Elshof, 2005; Gallagher and Sørensen, 2006; Hurlbert and Schwitzgebel, 2007; Kriegel and Horgan, 2007; Fernández, 2009, 2013; Reuter, 2010; Smithies and Stoljar, 2012; Butler, 2013; Kriegel, 2013) and psychology (e.g., Jack and Roepstorff, 2003, 2004; Hatfield, 2005; Price and Murat, 2005; Piccinini, 2009; Jäkel and Schreiber, 2013). This extraordinary revival of analysis and debate over introspection can, of course, be interpreted in numerous ways. As Matthew Boyle (2012) notes, "whether the story of this attraction is that of a doomed obsession from which self-respecting philosophers must break free, or of a comedy of errors that is bound to end in a happy reconciliation—this depends on who gets to tell the tale." These allegories of a "doomed obsession" and a "comedy of errors" parody two ends of a dialectical battlefield and potentially flatten a more complex spectrum of stories that one might tell. The following four interpretations of the introspection renaissance put a little flesh on these bare allegorical bones, and they help to measure the spectrum of positions that frame the aims of this chapter.

First, intransigent *local skeptics* with an exclusionary alliance to third-person method, e.g., behaviorists and logical behaviorists, may argue that cognitive science has reached a temporary impasse and that, for a momentary lack of any better ideas, doomed obsessions with introspection have, unfortunately, returned.[1] These local skeptics say: What we need is an absolutely non-introspective approach to cognitive science. Study the brain, study what people do—but don't take people's introspective reports about what they do, perceive, or "think" very seriously. Successful arguments that show such reports are too unreliable and unverifiable to assist in empirical research have been around for a long time: see, e.g., the now classic criticisms developed by Comte (1830) and the well-known contemporary case made by Nisbett and Wilson (1977). Alas, arguments do not easily cure doomed obsessions: perhaps only therapy will do. Short of that, wayward obsessions shall pass only after cognitive science emerges out of adolescence into maturity, and new generations of philosophers and scientists grow up in a new theoretical climate. One should, at most, enter the argumentative fray to put out smoldering fires. The sooner our doomed obsessions with introspection pass, the better off cognitive science will be.

Second, open-minded *general skeptics*, e.g., Eric Schwitzgebel (2008, 2011; Hurlbert and Schwitzgebel, 2007), may interpret the recent revived interest in introspection as highlighting an apparently insurmountable joint impasse.[2] "If there simply are no better methods, the scientific study of consciousness may prove wholly impossible in principle: vacuous without introspective report, intractably conflictual with it" (Hurlbert and Schwitzgebel, 2007, p. 5).[3] Of course, a lot rides on the perceived lack of any "better methods." A Pyrrhonist skeptic keeps an open mind and does not insist that no such better method shall ever be forthcoming, only that none has been discovered so far. After all, the general skeptic's attitude results from a non-skeptical commitment to the simultaneous unreliability and inescapability of introspection (Schwitzgebel, 2008, p. 246; 2011, p. 118). Consequently, such skeptics live parasitic lives that require optimistic hosts for sustenance. Is this relationship symbiotic? While these skeptics rehearse well-worn challenges to the reliability of introspection, their frequently corrective diagnoses entail that there is (or at least that they still believe there may be) an element of truth delivered by introspection (Schwitzgebel, 2002, 2004). This opens a door to optimism.

Third, *hesitant optimists* like Uriah Kriegel (2013) cautiously defend introspection and the role it should play in the study of consciousness. True, the current state of affairs is not, in some key areas, particularly satisfactory. Hesitant optimists, nonetheless, interpret the revived interest in introspection as indicating progress, or at least as an initial step in the right direction. While introspection was for a long time seen to be overly unreliable, the cautious optimist argues that we have asked too much of introspection. If we can work towards a "hesitant defense" of "introspective minimalism" (Kriegel 2013), we may be able to pave a way forward—one small step at a time. Cognitive science requires a provisional, practical acceptance of introspection: at least when it comes to certain aspects of our conscious experience, it remains entirely unclear how cognitive scientists could even begin to know what to study without first-person reports (Sartre 2012, p. 129; Overgaard 2006, p. 231). So understood, introspection can provide insights in the context of discovery; but we should leave questions of justification to science (Kriegel 2013). Perhaps the best approach to consciousness cautiously sorts through the comedy of errors for a few nuggets of "inner" truth, without which cognitive science cannot progress to its full potential.

Fourth, phenomenologists, i.e., contemporary philosophers nurtured in large measure on a diet of Husserlian thought, and who draw methodological sustenance from later figures in the tradition, sometimes inhabit a fourth category: that of *robust optimists* (e.g., Lawler, Zahavi, and Gallagher).[4] They are the least surprised by the current renaissance in studies of introspection: after all, it has been, *necessarily*, just a matter of time. Until cognitive science properly coordinates first-person and third-person methods in the study of consciousness, certain inherent limits shall remain unsurpassable. Unfortunately, mainstream cognitive science, as currently practiced, cannot explicitly recognize the transcendental dimension of conscious experience; hence, it fails to recognize its most distinctive aspect: subjectivity. However, unlike hesitant optimists who accept that descriptive phenomenology can play an important role in the context of discovery, robust optimists maintain that the transcendental structures of consciousness render experience possible; hence, first-person analyses of these structures shall always take logical priority over—and ground—every third-person approach.

Faced with these options, which should we choose? This chapter advocates for a version of robust optimism committed to the following two claims: first, the full advance of cognitive science requires coordination between first-person and third-person methods (Chalmers 2010); second, since that coordination is necessary, one's preferred phenomenological method should be compatible with non-reductive attempts to "naturalize" our understanding of pre-reflective conscious experience (Gallagher 2012b). With that said, this chapter makes its case indirectly. Since phenomenologists claim that we are all naturally bad at introspection, rather than meeting questions of epistemic reliability and operation head on, it sketches a topology of common errors that occur when we reflect upon our own conscious experience.[5] By systematically showing how introspection goes wrong, when attempting to discern the essential structures that make conscious experience possible, I hope to encourage pessimists and hesitant optimists alike that what Sartre calls "pure reflection" can reliably go right.

This would be an overly ambitious task, were it not for the following plausible hypothesis. Most, if not all, introspective errors share a common core: namely that, when we think about our own conscious experience, we frequently try to adopt the perspective of another person. In our efforts to gain objective purchase upon ourselves we attempt to view ourselves as others view us, as if we could adopt a third-person perspective upon our own personal experience. Doing so, however, requires standing outside one's own perspective, which is a little like pulling oneself up by one's own bootstraps. Sartre names this bootstrapping kind of effort "accessory" or "impure reflection," which "consists in an abortive effort on the part of the for-itself to be another while remaining itself" (1956, p. 161). Otherwise put, impure reflection amounts to the failed effort to stand outside of oneself and adopt a third-person perspective upon one's essentially first-person experience.

That impure reflection fails to achieve a genuinely third-person perspective upon itself should not be especially controversial in today's philosophical climate, at least not for those who accept that pre-reflective conscious experience involves an *essentially* first-person dimension. Even so, a puzzle remains. Those who recognize the impossibility of taking a third-person perspective on one's own first-person conscious experience, as one experiences it, are faced with the necessity of explaining the alternative: what can it mean to take a first-person perspective on one's own first-person perspective? In response to this question, I argue for two claims: first, that such a proposition doesn't mean anything coherent, since doing so is impossible; and, second, that the very attempt to take a "point of view" upon one's own conscious experience motivates many—if not most, or even all—errors made in our introspective efforts to understand consciousness better. To Kant's complaint that philosophers have for too long mixed empirical with transcendental claims, Sartre effectively adds that philosophers almost inevitably muddle the first-person vs third-person distinction when theorizing about (embodied) consciousness.

The rest of this chapter unfolds in five parts and a conclusion. The first part, Why Sartre? makes some general remarks that explain why Sartre motivates this project and it also serves as a programmatic introduction to Sartre's earliest philosophical works. The second part, Basic distinctions, provides a description of being absorbed in reading good fiction as a basis upon which to characterize several standard distinctions accepted by most phenomenologists. The third part, A topological sketch of introspective errors, sketches a general error theory that maps the central ways in which our thinking about thinking go wrong. The fourth part, The problem of purifying reflection, raises a challenge to Sartre's pivotal distinction between pure and impure reflection, necessary to showing how reflection can go right, and it offers a defense. The fifth part, An insuperable ambiguity, remarks on an insuperable ambiguity that is constitutive of self-awareness and that can, upon reflection, make self-awareness seem either paradoxical (Woodruff Smith, 1986) or mysterious (Kriegel, 2003).

## Why Sartre?

The choice of Sartre (instead of Husserl) as the subject of this chapter may seem unfortunate. Sartre rarely discusses methodology in any significant detail, his jargon can be impenetrable, and his views on consciousness appear to be highly revisionary and, hence, controversial. Consequently, looking to Sartre for resources to develop an error theory of introspection may seem like a dubious task that needs justification. Six points and an observation comprise this justification and will also serve as a programmatic introduction to Sartre's early philosophical writings.

First, Sartre's texts up to but not including *Being and Nothingness* read much more like rigorous academic philosophy, and they follow the spirit of Husserl's (1913) phenomenological method very closely. Sartre's incisive analyses based on astute descriptions shine through in these early works, and they sharply contrast his obscure language and hyperbolic claims that appear rather suddenly in *Being and Nothingness*. Thus, those sympathetic to careful applications of the spirit of Husserl's method, but who are understandably unwilling to suffer through the semantic jungle of *Being and Nothingness*, will find much more clarity in Sartre's earliest works. Of course, many of the contributions in this volume reinforce this point.

Second, Sartre read a great deal of research psychology from the nineteenth and early twentieth centuries (1936a, 1936b, 1939, 1940), and he was acutely aware of the debates over the epistemic reliability of introspection. He offers a rather weaker view of the epistemic reliability of claims derived from purifying reflection. On the one hand, while he holds that pure reflection can achieve apodictic certainty (2004a, pp. 10, 15; 1956, pp. 84, 156), the range of claims for which such certainty holds turns out to be very limited, namely, it holds only for claims about the stream-of-conscious experience (but not its objects) in the instantaneous moment. Yet such claims are sufficient to supply the evidentiary basis for situated, transcendental arguments from which to derive the basic structures of conscious human experience. On the other hand, he emphasizes that all claims about transcendent objects (i.e., any intentional object for consciousness that is not essentially part of the stream of consciousness itself, even with regard to how such an object merely seems) cannot be trusted. In fact, if he goes too far in any one direction, it could plausibly be in the direction of unreliability. He includes the empirical ego or psyche in the category of transcendent objects, and, consequently, he maintains that our observations about our own empirical ego—including claims about our character and explanations for our motives, etc.—are, more often than not, mistaken.

Third, whereas Husserl took many transcendental claims to be true in an absolute sense (i.e., necessarily true for any conscious activity whatsoever, whether that of God or a dog). Sartre, at least in his better moments, employs a weaker sense of situated transcendental claims. On the basis of phenomenological descriptions, e.g., of our ability to imagine non-existent future states of affairs, Sartre transcendentally deduces various ontological structures that must obtain, as a matter of factual necessity, given the truth of those descriptions (see, e.g., Sartre 2004b, pp. 179–188). Insofar as Sartre establishes merely factual necessities, this entails that, for a being which enjoys a categorically different kind of experience, its ontological structures, as transcendentally entailed by those experiences, would, presumably, differ. Needless to say, Sartre's weaker view of situated transcendental claims is more straightforwardly compatible with a non-reductive approach to cognitive science (Gallagher 2012b). In fact, some cognitive scientists have already begun to adopt a similar transcendental method.[6]

Fourth, even though Sartre is highly critical of psychology at the turn of the century, he accepts that a purely descriptive, first-person method needs to be supplemented by empirical research. This point comes out most clearly in the last two-thirds of *The Imaginary*, where Sartre abandons pure description and draws heavily, albeit critically, upon inductive inferences grounded in studies made by nineteenth- and early-twentieth-century psychologists like Galton, Binet, Messer, Flach, Tain, Leroy, and Spaier.[7] Sartre's appeal to such studies may be surprising, and while Sartre scholars can debate whether such sympathies were long-lasting, I think this appeal should come as a relief, for it helps to widen slightly the already open door to collaboration between phenomenology and cognitive science. In short, Sartre's early works make a better ally for those interested in a rapprochement between phenomenology and cognitive science than is generally supposed.

Fifth, all of Sartre's early philosophical works include sustained analyses of the various ways in which we go wrong when we reflect and report on our conscious experiences. As Jonathan Webber (2004) observes,

> throughout *The Imaginary*, Sartre is concerned not only to refute this [perception-based] view of the mind, but also to understand the pressures that have pushed theorists in its direction. The acceptability of [Sartre's] alternative model will, at least in part, be a function of how well it dissipates these pressures or can explain why they should be resisted.
>
> (p. xx)[8]

My efforts below aim to sketch what "dissipates these pressures" in a programmatic way that goes beyond *The Imaginary* but also draws upon Sartre's other early works up to and including *Being and Nothingness*.

Sixth, despite all of *Being and Nothingness'* liabilities, in that text Sartre offers several astute analyses of how philosophers frequently mix claims derived from first-person introspection with third-person or quasi-third-person perspectives. These analyses provide good explanations for why several classic philosophical problems arise and remain unresolved. To take one relevant example, Sartre argues that the "false problem" of understanding how mind and body interrelate is due to "the fact that people have wanted to link my consciousness of objects to the body of the Other" (1956, p. 305). Otherwise put, "I try to unite my consciousness not with my body but with the body of others" (1956, p. 303). Perhaps, in an analogous way, contemporary philosophers make a similar kind of mistake when discussing the so-called "mind–brain" and "body–body" problems. They try to unite their first-person conscious experience not with their own lived body, but with a brain that they've never directly experienced but have only studied via anatomy and neurophysiology (i.e., from a third-person perspective). These are two fundamentally different orders of description, or so it will be argued. If this criticism is correct, many discussions of the so-called mind–brain, mind–body, and body–body problems ride on a basic confusion between two irreducibly different orders of description.

A final observation: a complete account of Sartre's error theory of introspection would require taking into consideration both its existential and technical aspects. Whereas the existential aspects motivate errors, the technical aspects explain their theoretical shapes. These two dimensions of error can and should be kept separate; indeed, Sartre did not strongly press the motivational aspects of error until *Being and Nothingness*. Otherwise put, even though in *Being and Nothingness* Sartre maintains that discomfiting aspects of life motivate many, if not most, theoretical errors, the existential aspects of these errors are generally too controversial to meet any widely acceptable justificatory standard.[9] Thus, Sartre scholars will make better inroads into contemporary debates surrounding the philosophy of mind by emphasizing and explaining the technical aspects or shapes of Sartre's error theory as a propaedeutic to Sartre's account of embodied consciousness.

## Basic distinctions

Ordinarily we easily distinguish between explicitly self-directed experiences and lived experiences. Examples of engrossment, like reading good fiction, provide paradigmatic examples of the former. As one becomes imaginatively absorbed in the details of a captivating novel, every explicit sense of oneself as reading entirely disappears. One imagines the poplar trees, a blood-stained white coat, the axe grooves in the dirt; one feels trepidation and then horror at the tangled body, suddenly headless . . . and then empathy and sorrow for the parent's loss, as if the fictional victim were one's own child. When engrossed, the story becomes the focal aspect of experience, and, correlatively, the contours of one's body along the couch, the faint music from the other room, fade into an increasingly indeterminate, unattended background. Something similar, but not identical, happens to one's explicit sense of self during engrossment.[10]

In sharp contrast, if someone enters the room and asks, "What are you doing?" attention naturally shifts from the story to one's experience of reading it. Engrossed experience comes to an end and (in response to the question) reflection upon one's current conscious activity begins: "I am reading an amazing book about the South at the turn of the century, where a young white girl was raped and gruesomely murdered by an elderly white farmer. An innocent young black teenager was falsely accused and then lynched before the trial ended." Only upon reflection does one's sense of being a discrete agent of an activity, possessing an experience, become explicit. Only then can one make the following kinds of distinctions, organized here in five points.

First, most people, except the self-obsessed, spend considerably more time living life (pre-reflectively) than (reflectively) thinking about the life that one lives. This suggests that explicit self-awareness arises in specific contexts. Five common (but not comprehensive) cases motivate reflection: (1) When environmental anomalies interrupt implicit expectations, e.g., when something goes wrong (like the car won't start or there's no hot water in the shower), this can motivate reflective efforts to understand and integrate such anomalies into our lived experience. (2) When we learn new physical activities (e.g., dancing or sewing) we initially tend to reflect upon what to do *while trying to do it*, as opposed to spontaneously performing it. (3) When we feel like someone is watching us, we frequently experience explicit self-consciousness. (4) When we puzzle through major life decisions, this tends to motivate reflection over our motives and reasons for various possible choices. (5) Finally, most relevantly, when we theorize about consciousness we tend to reflect upon our pre-reflective conscious experience in our efforts to understand ourselves better.

Second, reflection *typically* does not discover anything *genuinely* new (Sartre, 1956, p. 155) about itself qua reflected upon. One does not have an anonymous pre-reflective experience, e.g., "someone is reading" and then infer from (or discover upon the basis of) that anonymous experience that it is me having it.[11] This suggests that reflection renders implicit aspects of pre-reflective experience explicit. Otherwise put, in reflection we recognize what we pre-reflectively already implicitly comprehend (Sartre, 1956, pp. 155–156), namely that we were enjoying a lived reading experience.[12] It follows, then, that reflective consciousness is not surprised by what it renders explicit (Sartre, 1956, pp. 155–156)—e.g., by the fact that I am reading. More strongly put, if reflection makes explicit what one already implicitly comprehends, reflection never discovers anything genuinely new or surprising about its pre-reflective experience.[13]

Third, prior to reflection, while engrossed, no explicit or *genuine* positing of oneself (qua agent) as distinct from one's activity (of reading) as distinct from the object (the story) takes place.[14] Insofar as these relations remain implicit, so too do various distinctions that one might make about them. This raises a thorny question about what happens in the process of making implicit aspects of conscious experience explicit (see below). The point here, however, is that one's implicit sense of self-awareness contrasts with explicit, reflective self-awareness in four ways. (A couple of these differences require justification that goes beyond description and must be stated here without argument.) Unlike explicit self-awareness that can operate as a kind of voluntary "self-observation," intrinsic self-awareness is (1) non-voluntary; (2) non-observational; (3) non-inferential; and (4) non-intentional. What follows amplifies each of these four points.

Implicit self-awareness is non-voluntary. It takes no effort. It's not something that we deliberately will, and it always seems to accompany our pre-reflective conscious experience. Second, it is non-observational. It does not require second-order, reflective acts to observe and, hence, constitute it. Rather, implicit self-awareness makes "self-observation" in the reflective sense possible (Sartre, 1956, p. lii). Thus, reflective acts do not cause or lead to self-awareness; they merely make implicit self-awareness explicit. Third, it's non-inferential, insofar as it is unmediated by secondary acts. We generally do not have anonymous experiences and then, on that basis, infer possession of them. Rather, we experience implicit self-awareness as inescapably built into our pre-reflective experience, not as added on. Finally, implicit self-awareness does not require doubling intentionality. Otherwise put, the best theoretical explanation for implicit self-awareness should not posit twofold intentional content, i.e., an inner representation of self and an outer representation of the world. (This last point requires amplification and justification, given below.)

Fourth, we can abstractly distinguish between two dependent parts (or moments) of pre-reflective conscious experience: (1) non-positional self-awareness—what I have been calling "implicit self-awareness," and (2) positional acquaintance with an intentional object. Unlike the non-positional dimension of self-awareness, our positional grasp of intentional objects frequently (not necessarily) includes predication. For example, we pre-reflectively know that the boy (the subject) in the story is falsely accused of murder (the predicate). In contrast, it will be argued below, our imaginary terror does not, at the pre-reflective level, form an object of experience at all. Rather, it's a constitutive feature of that which illuminates intentional objects as meaningful.

If correct, our account of "what it is like" to be acquainted with an object should sharply differ from the kind of account required by our description of the object with which we are acquainted. For example, it is one thing to describe the boy's response to the false accusations (in the novel) and wholly another to describe "what it is like" to live imaginatively through the boy's terror at the false accusations (and yet still another to give an account of actual lived terror, e.g., what it is actually like to be falsely accused in a racist context on pain of death). This suggests that we should not straightforwardly align pre-reflective consciousness with the first-person perspective. Rather, pre-reflective consciousness includes both a first-person dimension (implicit self-awareness of "what it is like" to experience an object), and a proto third-person dimension (acquaintance with the intentional object experienced).[15]

Fifth, locating the first- and third-person dimensions of perspectivity within pre-reflective consciousness indicates an insuperable ambiguity, to be further discussed in the conclusion. Whereas pre-reflective consciousness enjoys implicit self-awareness that does not explicitly posit itself as a subject of experience, in reflecting upon pre-reflective self-consciousness one can *simultaneously* feel like observer *and* observed, an "observer–observed," so to speak, and this constitutes a truly unique experience. We experience nothing in the world that is at all or in any way like this: nothing else gives rise to this peculiar observer–observed feel. Although the unusual character of this feel motivates philosophers to describe self-awareness as either paradoxical or mysterious, this chapter concludes that the peculiarity of implicit self-awareness made explicit is best characterized as ontologically (and not merely epistemically) ambiguous.

Finally, reflection modifies (but does not necessarily distort) pre-reflective experience. Two qualitative aspects *typically* characterize this modification: (1) an explicit sense of ownership that the recent and current experiences reflected upon are mine and (2) an explicit sense of agency that I am the source of my activity, e.g., reading.[16] Although reflection can involve the kind of doubling noted above, i.e., the simultaneous observer–observed feel, pure reflection is best characterized as amplifying that about which we are always already implicitly aware. Since that implicit awareness *never* includes being an object for ourselves, the peculiar observer–observed feel (noted above) amounts to a special kind of illusion (discussed below). Consequently, Sartre adds (3), that there are two kinds of reflection. On the one hand, impure reflection both modifies and distorts (by doubling) that upon which it reflects and, hence, it adds more than evidence serves. On the other hand, purifying reflection merely amplifies or makes explicit what is already implicitly comprehended (prior to reflection).

## A topological sketch of introspective errors

On the basis of these observations the following preliminary distinctions have been drawn: (1) pre-reflective conscious experience vs non-conscious objects of experience; (2) non-positional vs positional moments of pre-reflective conscious experience; (3) pre-reflective conscious experience vs reflective conscious experience; (4) implicit self-awareness vs explicit reflective self-awareness; and (5) impure vs pure reflection. These distinctions provide the basis for a nearly comprehensive list, as found in the work of Sartre, of all of the kinds of errors made when we reflect upon conscious experience:[17]

(1)  *The projection error.* Sometimes we illicitly project aspects of reflective consciousness on to pre-reflective consciousness. Sartre does not label this error as such, but he describes it in several places (2004b, pp. 52, 69; 2004a, pp. 10, 14, 17, 27).

(2) *The reification error*: Sometimes qualities of objects for consciousness are applied to conscious experience itself (1956, pp. 103, 163, 206; 1967, p. 127). Since the primary objects for conscious experience are most frequently material objects, this misleads us into attributing predicates suitable for material objects to our conscious experience. (Sartre most commonly calls this error bad faith.)

(3) *The illusion of immanence*: A subspecies of the reification error leads us mistakenly to attribute spatial qualities to consciousness, as if it were like a receptacle that contains ideas, representations, and psychic objects (2004b, pp. 5, 53, 87, 138).

(4) *The warping of thought*: Sometimes when we think we are describing some aspect of conscious experience we surreptitiously introduce claims based on subtle but misleading analogies; Sartre calls this the warping of thought (2004b, pp. 116–117).

(5) *The illusion of the primacy of knowledge*: Sometimes we confuse claims produced by positional observations for aspects of non-positional self-awareness (1956, p. liv). This leads us mistakenly to characterize pre-cognitive aspects of experience as cognitive (1956, p. x).

(6) *The standpoint error*: Most of the time when we reflect upon our conscious experience, in our effort to gain objective purchase upon ourselves, we try to "take a point of view" upon our viewpoint (1956, pp. 43, 155, 161). We attempt to adopt pseudo third-person perspective on our essentially first-person experience.

The projection error involves a confusion of "the essential structures of reflective acts with [those] of unreflective acts" (2004a, p. 17). Descartes' *cogito* offers the most famous instance of the projection error. In characterizing Descartes' mistake, Sartre follows Husserl and distinguishes pre-reflective doubt from reflective doubt. Whereas pre-reflective doubt occurs spontaneously (e.g., when one suddenly doubts that a coil of rope in the shadows is what it seems to be, namely a snake), reflective doubt occurs deliberately (e.g., in the application of a method of inquiry). Thus, pre-reflective doubt only concerns intentional objects—it cannot doubt its own existence due to its essential object orientation—whereas reflective doubt attempts, but necessarily fails, to doubt its existence. So understood, when Descartes arrives at his famous observation—every time I am thinking, I exist (1637, Discourse IV)—he does so via reflective doubt that renders implicit self-awareness explicit.[18]

In arriving at the *cogito*, Descartes makes two separate (but related) errors. Descartes mistakenly concludes (1) that the "I" resides at the level of pre-reflective consciousness (the projection error) and (2) that thinking is an attribute of a non-extended substance (a conceptual variation of the reification error). With regards to (2), Descartes hypostasizes self-awareness into an ego substance, qua source of thought, and then projects it into pre-reflective consciousness. In this way, Descartes confuses pre-reflective consciousness, which does the thinking, with the reflective level of consciousness, which constitutes the ego. Otherwise put, "the [reflective] consciousness that says 'I think' is precisely not the [pre-reflective] consciousness that thinks" (2004a, p. 10).[19]

This analysis motivates Sartre's observation that "the reason why Descartes moved from the *Cogito* to the idea of thinking substance is that he believed that the I and 'think' are on the same level" (2004a, p. 14/34). In projecting a reified ego into the heart of consciousness, Descartes characterizes thought as an attribute of a non-extended substance and, in so doing, unnecessarily multiplies theoretical entities. Sartre's parsimonious alternative shows why the introduction of any sort of thinker/thought, subject/object, or substance/attribute distinction into pre-reflective consciousness not only generates unnecessary theoretical complexity, but also that it tends to leave the structure of implicit self-awareness unexplained. Sartre reaches his minimalist view on both descriptive and argumentative grounds.

On descriptive grounds: when we reflect on pre-reflective consciousness, in a purifying way, we don't find anything in or behind conscious experience. Otherwise put, Sartre's account parallel's G. E. Moore's (1903) account of consciousness as diaphanous. As Kenneth Williford helpfully puts it,

> consciousness is phenomenologically diaphanous: one is aware of the objects and their qualities; there seems to be nothing literally in consciousness or behind it, and nothing between it and its objects. Still, it is distinguishable. The consciousness of an object is not (typically) the object of that consciousness.
> (Williford, 2004, p. 149)[20]

This way of putting matters suggests that Hume rightly saw that the kind of self putatively "discovered" and frequently posited to account for personal unity amounts to an illusion (based on reification). However, in pointing out this illusion, Hume was looking for the self "in the wrong place" (Woodruff Smith, 1986, p. 149). From the fact that Hume could not discover a self in introspection, Hume mistakenly supposed that the self must be part of the content of experience.[21] What Hume plausibly failed to appreciate is that self-awareness is built into pre-reflective conscious experience in such a way that it does not—even cannot—represent itself to itself. (An argument for this claim returns below.)

To be sure, reflection upon implicit self-awareness often generates a curious switching phenomenon. Like the well-known duck–rabbit optical illusion that sometimes looks like a duck and sometimes looks like a rabbit, yet cannot look simultaneously like both, a similar shifting can arise when we reflect upon conscious experience. When grasped reflectively, it can appear either diaphanously (and seem like nothing) or opaquely (and seem like something). This switching phenomenon forms two horns of a dilemma. On the one hand, like Descartes, in making itself into an observed object, consciousness arguably reifies itself into something that it is not. For in representing itself as an object, it cannot grasp itself as a subject. On the other hand, sometimes, like Hume, when you go looking for yourself, while you may never find yourself, you cannot escape the fact that conscious experience always ineluctably feels like it is your own. Call this Hume's dilemma. It returns in the conclusion.

The reification error includes a subspecies of error that Sartre labels "the illusion of immanence." This illusion results from "our habit of thinking in space and in terms of space" (2004b, p. 5), and this habit misleads us to "constitute the world of the mind from objects very similar to those of the external world and which, simply, obey different laws" (2004b, p. 6). Doing so motivates mistakenly locating ideas or thoughts inside of conscious activity (or, analogously, of locating consciousness inside of a body). There is, however, nothing literally inside of consciousness (and consciousness does not stand "inside" of its body).[22] If correct, the Latin roots of "introspection" mislead us into thinking that when we think about thought this literally involves looking inside of our minds. Words with spatial meanings, however, are, at best, misleading colloquial metaphors—more the province of philologists than phenomenologists.

Sartre gives a broad explanation for all three of these errors that characterizes how we arrive at *pensée spatialisée*. Sartre calls this "the warping of thought" and he claims that it "is one of the most frequent causes of error, particularly in psychology and philosophy" (2004b, p. 117). Warping occurs on the basis of illicitly introducing subtle analogical reasoning where one believes oneself to be giving a purely descriptive account. To put this matter in overly simplistic terms, the surreptitious analogy moves from either spatial qualities or quasi-spatial qualities, e.g., of imaginary objects or representations of spatial schema, and then attributes them to acts of consciousness themselves. In this way, via implicit analogical reasoning, one attributes spatial qualities to non-spatial thoughts and then to the activity of thinking itself.[23]

While the first four kinds of errors all relate to our natural proclivity to construe self-conscious experience in objectified, spatialized terms (a strategy Sartre adapts from Bergson), the illusion of the primacy of knowledge stands, on the surface, in a different category, and it is more difficult to unpack in its details. Most broadly put, this illusion results either when we construe our most basic relationships (to ourselves, the world, and others) in entirely cognitive terms (in the sense of being inherently conceptual, e.g., in the Kantian sense that all intelligible experience is already schematized) or, more broadly, when we suppose that epistemology should take theoretical primacy over ontology (as most modern philosophy does). The latter broader supposition cannot be fully discussed here for reasons of brevity.

Sartre addresses the narrower portion of this error in the context of making an argument that "the necessary and sufficient condition for a knowing consciousness to be knowledge of its object, is that it be consciousness of itself as being that knowledge" (1956, p. lii). Sartre proceeds by way of a two-pronged dilemma. On the one hand, if there were no self-consciousness of knowing X, then it would be a consciousness unconscious of itself, which, Sartre claims, is contradictory.[24] On the other, less controversial, hand, if one construes the relation constitutive of intrinsic self-awareness as involving a known–known dyad, an infinite regress results: the knower that knows needs another knower to know the first knower knowing . . . Sartre concludes that, in order to avoid this infinite regress, the transcendental ground for our knowing X requires "a non-cognitive relation of the self to itself" (1956, p. liii).[25]

This means, according to Sartre, that self-awareness does not posit itself as an intentional object. Consequently, no concepts can be attached to it, insofar as there is no subject to attach predicates (1956, p. 354). In this sense, its grasp of itself is non-cognitive or, perhaps better put, pre-conceptual. So understood, implicit self-awareness is necessary to know objects but it does not know itself knowing them.[26] Another way to come at the non-cognitive dimension of conscious experience is to note that many of its constitutive components are not intentional objects. Like intrinsic self-awareness that does not represent itself to itself qua intentional object; neither do any other of these non-positional aspects of conscious experience, and, thus, they function pre-predicatively.[27]

To help to clarify this matter, Sartre offers a few astute phenomenological descriptions: living through thirst (1956, pp. 82, 87), pain (1956, pp. 330–332), and fatigue (1956, pp. 453–459). Take the example of pain. When reading for a very long period of time the words may begin to tremble and quiver, as their meanings become increasingly difficult to comprehend (1956, pp. 332–333). At the pre-reflective level, it's the story that comprises the intentional correlate of painful reading, where pain is neither a thematic object represented in the content of experience nor something in addition to one's eyes. Rather, one's eyes exist in a painful way constitutive of the pre-reflective troubled-reading experience. We can, of course, turn our attention away from the story and reflect upon the pain and locate it in our eyes, but Sartre notes that doing so transforms pain into an object (1956, p. 355).

Although the act of objectification doesn't necessarily falsify pain, where it should be admitted that Sartre isn't especially clear on what distinguishes successful from unsuccessful objectifications, doing so requires introducing a third-person viewpoint and requires that we abandon our lived experience (see below). In reflecting upon pain in an objectifying way we adopt a position similar to how an ophthalmologist might examine and diagnose it. Thus, we shift the locus of experience away from the original intentional correlate (the increasingly unintelligible story) to an aspect constitutive of the experiential side, namely my painful eyes. In the process, we can overlook what lived pain is like in deference to objectified pain or mix claims about the two orders of description together.

That lived "pain is notoriously difficult to describe" (Gallagher and Nikolic, 2012, p. 139) does not result solely from the fact that painful experience is so specific to the individual, that our concepts are insufficiently fine-grained. Rather, pain is a constitutive feature of the non-cognitive dimension of our pre-reflective experience and comprises a pre-linguistic horizon that defies well-formed definitions. This explains why, in our best efforts to describe lived pain, we frequently employ metaphor, poetic allegory, and analogy. To think that one can give well-formed definitions is to succumb to the illusion of the primacy of knowledge.

This brings us to the crux of the matter. The reflective effort to take a position upon non-positional aspects of our conscious experience frequently involves the standpoint error. Due to its importance and complexity, this error will be approached in two stages. The first stage discusses embodiment, where it is easier to mark out the first/third-person distinction. The second stage addresses the issue of reflective consciousness, where the first/third-person distinction becomes murkier. The analogy from the case of embodiment to consciousness only goes so far, for reasons that should become clear below.

### Stage one

As seen above, Sartre argues that the "false problem" of understanding how the mind and body interrelate results from "the fact that people have wanted to link my consciousness of objects to the body of the Other" (1956, p. 305). It's easy to see how this can arise in the case of my body: I can straightforwardly look at my body as Others see it, e.g., by looking at it in a mirror. When I look at my body in a mirror, however, I'm not experiencing it qua lived. As Sartre puts it, "either [the body] is a thing among things, or else it is that by which things are revealed to me. But it cannot be both at the same time" (1956, p. 304).

Sartre reaches this asymmetry by way of a now familiar analogy tied to a transcendental argument. Here's the analogy: just as the eye cannot see itself qua seeing, we cannot know our body qua living it (1956, pp. 304–305, see also p. 316). Although I can look at my eyeball in a mirror, doing so does not capture the "what it's like" aspect of seeing; rather, it captures the eyeball as an object seen. So when we look our body in a mirror, qua third-person perspective, we abandon our first-person, lived perspective (1956, p. 318). Otherwise put, our inhabited viewpoint vanishes as soon as we try to take an exterior viewpoint upon it.

Thus, in a way similar to non-positional dimensions of conscious experience, Sartre argues that "the body is lived but not known" (1956, pp. 324, see especially pp. 354–355). Our lived body is not, first and foremost, an intentional object of experience; thus, it is not an object subject to predicates qua lived. For example, while absorbed in typing, I do not apprehend my hands. Rather, the words and sentences unfold on the screen as to-be-finished within an affective horizon of urgency: late again to meet a deadline. When understood in this lived way, my body isn't something in addition to or over and above my self-conscious experience of typing. So understood, my lived body is not a contingent feature added on to consciousness; rather, "it is the permanent structure of my being and the permanent condition for the possibility of my consciousness as consciousness of the world" (1956, p. 328, translation slightly altered). Qua lived, embodiment supplies a necessary condition for the possibility of having the kind of practical, spatially oriented experiences that we enjoy; hence, it conditions the range and meanings of our lived experience (1956, p. 328).

## Stage two

Unlike the case of our bodies, the case of pre-reflective consciousness turns out to be only roughly analogous. Sartre argues that we cannot ever take a genuinely third-person perspective upon it. We cannot look at our conscious experience, as we do our bodies, in a mirror, as it were. Although Sartre employs an array of optical terms, e.g., reflection, reflecting, reflected, that can make it seem like reflective consciousness can take some kind of perspective on itself, Sartre denies that any non-distorting reflection can take a perspective upon itself.

He puts the matter like this: Reflective consciousness cannot "detach itself completely from the reflected-on, and [hence] it cannot grasp the reflected-on 'from a point of view'" (1956, p. 155). Sartre's analysis continues as follows:

> Actually the consciousness reflected-on is not "presented" yet as something outside reflection, that is, as a being on which one can "take a point of view," in relation to which one can realize a withdrawal, increase or diminish the distance which separates one from it.
> (1956, p. 155)

Reflection and reflected being one and the same entails that reflection cannot stand outside of itself in order to take a viewpoint on itself. It would be something like standing outside of one's body in order to see it seeing, which is impossible, if not conceptually, then factually. Otherwise put, reflection cannot detach itself from itself (qua reflected upon) and take a position independent of itself. It is itself what it tries to grasp in the very activity of grasping. Now, what Sartre says next is very interesting:

> In order for the consciousness reflected-on to be "viewed from without" and in order for reflection to be able to orient itself in relation to it, it would be necessary that the reflective should not be the reflectedon in the mode of not being what it is not: this scissiparity will be realized only in existence for-others.
> (1956, p. 155)

In our failure to stand reflectively outside of ourselves, we resort to introducing the separation experienced with regard to others. This allows us to approximate a quasi-third-person perspective upon ourselves and leads us to reify consciousness and constitute it in terms of psychic objects. This is impure reflection, i.e., bad faith.

Here arises a serious problem. If we cannot reflectively take a perspective on our inhabited perspective, i.e., if we cannot grasp implicit self-awareness as an intentional object, without abandoning that perspective, then what does purifying reflection grasp in a non-distorting way? Kathleen Wider (1997) raises this worry and argues that Sartre has no satisfactory answer. It will be helpful, then, to answer this question by way of responding to Wider's worry.

## The problem of purifying reflection

Wider argues that Sartre fails to distinguish adequately pure reflection from pre-reflective consciousness "without at the same time destroying the distinction he draws between pure and impure reflection" (Wider, 1997, p. 80). Wider poses her worry as a twofold dilemma. On the one hand, if pure reflection grasps itself qua object, then pure reflection does not differ from impure reflection. On the other hand, if pure reflection does not grasp itself in as an object, then "it becomes indistinguishable from the actual self-consciousness of pre-reflective consciousness" (Wider, 1997, p. 81). Wider diagnoses this problem in epistemic terms. "[Sartre] fails to develop a theory of consciousness's non-cognitive presence to itself that allows him to distinguish when this self-presence is reflective from when it is not" (Wider, 1997, p. 92). The reason for this is that Sartre doesn't have a "clear enough notion of a knowledge that isn't a subject object relation" (Wider, 1997, p. 85). So, if purifying reflection cannot grasp itself in any non-object-like way, and if Sartre gives us no clear account of epistemic relations that do not invoke a subject/object form, then the explicit self-awareness of pure reflection seems to no different than implicit self-awareness. So in his effort to avoid the error of multiplying theoretical entities, he has multiplied empty conceptual distinctions.

Sartre's entire position hangs in the balance. If impure reflection necessarily distorts what it grasps, Sartre needs a clear account of a non-distorting kind of reflection that is tied to an epistemic framework that does not employ a subject–object form. Unfortunately, Sartre says very little about pure reflection; thus some of what follows must be reconstructive, if not somewhat speculative. To complicate matters, as Wider notes, Sartre equivocates in his epistemic language at a crucial juncture. In a context unspecified in terms of whether it's pure or impure reflection, Sartre claims that reflection achieves knowledge of itself qua reflected upon (1956, p. 151). Here the context concerns the certainty of my existence. A few pages later, however, he claims that reflection does not achieve knowledge but rather that it amounts to a form of recognition (1956, p. 156).

These two claims that seem to be at odds with one another can be straightforwardly reconciled. It would have helped had Sartre clarified his epistemic claims in the following way: reflection achieves apodictic knowledge *that* it exists but this knowledge does not extend to *what* it is. Indeed, the context of the second passage bears this out: it concerns reflection trying to understand its nature, as opposed to the mere fact of its existence. Once more, when Sartre claims that reflection achieves recognition, this makes good sense, since, as seen above, reflection merely makes explicit what it already implicitly grasps. Hence, it achieves some kind of re-cognition.

Putting matters this way is fine, so far as it goes, but Wider rightly wonders how this re-cognized form of self-awareness differs from implicit self-awareness. What does making self-awareness explicit amount to in epistemic terms? If it's not self-knowledge, then what is it? The spirit of Sartre's answer goes like this: the non-cognitive, non-positional dimension of experience should not be construed in terms of knowledge but in terms of (pre-judicative) comprehension (see, e.g., 1956, pp. 7, 17, 66, and 289). Thus, what pure reflection delivers must be an amplification that makes implicit, pre-judicative comprehension explicit, a point that returns below.

It is somewhat surprising that Wider, who reads texts very closely, misunderstands the centrality of Sartre's distinction between comprehension and knowledge, since comprehension employs the very epistemology that Wider finds lacking. After all, Sartre almost always employs the term pre-judicative comprehension (and comprehension *simpliciter*) in contexts that involve putatively objectless epistemic relations, e.g., when we enjoy lived experiences of nothingness (1956, p. 17), contingency (1956, p. 80), non-existent future possibilities (1956, p. 100), being for-itself (1956, p. 147), freedom (1956, p. 439), and, most relevantly, "being-myself" (1956, p. 289).[28] Since there is, strictly speaking, no extant "object" in any of these cases but only absences or non-beings, there is no positive thing or being to predicate straightforwardly and, hence, know. So what then does one comprehend when it comes to oneself?

In answer to this question Sartre's clearest example concerns the experience of shame, which

> encloses within it an implicit and non-thematized comprehension of being-able-to-be-an-object on the part of the subject for whom I am an object. This implicit comprehension is nothing other than the consciousness (of) my "being-myself"; that is, of my selfness reinforced.
> (1956, p. 289)

This passage does not describe an impure grasp of oneself as an object. Rather it describes an implicit comprehension of the possibility of my being objectified by Others.

This implicit recognition can, however, formally be made an explicit judgment via pure reflection. I can explicitly realize the ever-present possibility of social objectifications, e.g., pressures to conform to social roles that I must live but, ultimately, cannot know. Since this judgment concerns a possibility and possibilities do not, strictly speaking, exist in Sartre's technical sense, comprehension of this non-existent fact does not involve a subject–object relation. Sartre's point is not simply that I cannot know myself as others grasp me (1956, p. 242), but also that I cannot but live these objectifications by freely interiorizing them into my projects (1956, p. 467).

If correct, one thing pure reflection makes explicit concerns the ineliminable social dimension of my sense of "being myself." In fact, according to Sartre, it could not be otherwise, because "I cannot confer on myself any quality without mediation or an objectifying power which is not my own" (1956, p. 274). Consequently, the Other is "the necessary condition of all thought which I would attempt to form concerning myself" (1956, p. 271, see also p. 236). Unfortunately, it would take this discussion too far afield to develop the details that undergird Sartre's transcendental deduction for the social dimension of self-comprehension. Fortunately, this point conveniently sets up my initial thesis in a programmatic way: *all introspective errors involve attempts to take a third-person perspective upon oneself.* In short, because social relations necessarily mediate all thoughts that I form concerning myself, it's a natural, nearly inevitable fact that I try and take a third-person perspective upon myself—I try to see myself as I see others or as others see me.

So what then does pure reflection comprehend? It turns out not to be very much, where just a little makes a considerable difference (Sartre, 1956, p. 159). Pure reflection merely makes explicit or amplifies that which we already tacitly comprehend: the interminably fleeting temporal flux of our experience, our implicit self-awareness, intentionality, etc. Although when we impurely reflect upon ourselves we feel like we grasp ourselves qua observed, pure reflection cannot represent itself to itself qua observed. Thus, pure reflection merely amplifies our sense of the organized activity of being self-consciously engaged in the world. It does so without giving an accurate representation of ourselves qua observed: no such representation is possible (Sartre, 1956, pp. 241, 270). Introspection, then, should not be understood as self-observation but rather as an amplification of self-awareness and other non-positional aspects of our experience, without shifting them into the third-person position. On my reading, then, it is upon the basis of veridical descriptions of purified experience that we can, according to Sartre, transcendentally deduce the necessary ontological structures that make those experiences possible. It may not be much, but if implicit self-awareness makes reflection possible, without pure reflection the basic distinctions required by the philosophy of mind would be impossible.

## An insuperable ambiguity

Earlier it was claimed that implicit self-awareness simultaneously seems to be everywhere and somehow nowhere. We cannot escape self-awareness, we cannot representationally grasp it as an object, and we cannot discover it in the content of any experience. This truly puzzling phenomenon constitutes Hume's dilemma. It is this evanescence of self-awareness that arguably moors philosophers upon either the Charybdis of paradox (Rosenberg, 1981; Woodruff Smith, 1986) or the Scylla of mystery (Kriegel, 2003, p. 178). Self-awareness can seem paradoxical in the sense that when we try to grasp ourselves (qua observers) we seem to transform ourselves into something we are not (observed subjects). Thus, the very self-awareness that makes introspection of oneself possible also makes oneself simultaneously inapprehensible.

Alternatively, as Kriegel (2003) suggests, our account of self-awareness might require collapsing the gap between ourselves understood as subjects (observers) and objects (observed). For it can seem as if "the self is represented both as subject and object." Kriegel admits that "one may protest that this would make self-awareness quite mysterious, and will attribute to it a unique intentional structure. But then self-awareness is quite mysterious, isn't it, and its intentional structure is indeed unique" (Kriegel, 2003, p. 178). Kriegel effectively replaces the paradoxical experience of the self constantly slipping away from one's best effort to grasp it with a mysterious phenomenon: a self that represents itself as both subject (observer) and object (observed).

Sartre suggests how the simultaneous observer–observed feel is possible but illusory. It's a reification of the experience of being seen by Others that turns out to be a misrepresentation. To be sure, implicit self-awareness made explicit comprises a truly unique experience but, rather than claiming that it is either paradoxical or mysterious, Sartre argues that an insuperable ambiguity besets it. This ambiguity lies at the heart of self-conscious experience. Sartre's risky conceptual analysis goes like this. On the one hand, if we begin with a conceptually basic, ontologically simple object (in the sense of literally having no parts, abstract or otherwise), there would be no relations, and, hence, no possibility of self-awareness. On the other hand, every theoretical account that posits two extrinsically related, independent objects (mental states) fails to explain self-awareness. The reason for this parallels the infinite regress problem discussed above: the observer state that grasped a non-self-conscious observed state would itself need another observer to become aware of itself qua observer, and so on ad infinitum.

Sartre concludes that self-awareness is not simply implicit (a descriptive claim) but intrinsic, i.e., it necessarily structures consciousness (an ontological claim). Consciousness just is self-consciousness. This, however, requires an ambiguous duality built into a conceptual unity. It cannot be two, otherwise we end in regress. It cannot be one, otherwise no relations and, hence, no self-awareness would be possible. Sartre's proposed solution temporally distends one object (being in-itself) in order to arrive at the ambiguous, intrinsic relation that is temporally distended and constitutive of self-consciousness (being for-itself). Thus, self-awareness cannot be represented qua object, since doing so destroys the intrinsic relation that makes it possible. Neither should it be represented as a subject (that does the thinking), since this unnecessarily multiplies theoretical entities and threatens an infinite regress.

## Conclusion

If philosophers, for a long time, masqueraded about as if they could adopt a view from nowhere, when, as a matter of fact, they inevitably take a view from somewhere, then the problem of introspection inverts this game of charades. In our effort to gain an objective purchase on ourselves, we try to stand outside of the viewpoint we ineluctably inhabit. We find ourselves stranded in between two impossible positions: taking a view from nowhere and trying to adopt a view from somewhere other than our own. We try to adopt a third-person perspective on an essentially first-person phenomenon and in so doing we vitiate our inhabited perspectivity. Yet, we cannot take a first-person perspective upon ourselves. We can no more grasp ourselves from nowhere than we can from somewhere else. We can only amplify implicit features of our lived experience and make them explicit.

As David Chalmers once noted as a graduate student,

> perhaps the most important duality in the philosophy of mind is that between the first-person and third-person views of mental events. Some might say that the fundamental duality is that between mind and brain, or between subjective and objective—but all of these reduce to the first-person/third-person duality.[29]

The spirit of Chalmers' claim is well taken, insofar as my aim has been to show that muddling this most fundamental distinction constitutes the error of all introspective errors. Of course, if what I've said is correct, the letter of Chalmers' claim is mistaken: you cannot take a first-person perspective on your so-called mental states, since those mental states are constitutive of your first-person perspective. It's the very effort to adopt a first-person perspective on mental states that creates most, if not all, of our theoretical confusion about the structures of pre-reflective conscious experience.[30]

## Notes

1 It's not always entirely clear who, amongst philosophers, defends the possibility and efficacy of an absolutely non-introspective approach. Lowe (2004) follows tradition and includes logical behaviorists as belonging to this category, but, as Schwitzgebel (2008) points out, philosophers who deny the existence of

consciousness frequently accept something like "introspection" as a kind of inner sense perception; see, e.g., Churchland (1985, 1988).

2  In recent years Schwitzgebel comes across as highly skeptical (2007), and others like Hill (2011) label him a radical skeptic about introspection. However, Schwitzgebel doesn't sound, and hasn't always sounded, like a radical skeptic. He tentatively defended training people to improve introspection skills (2004). He explicitly criticizes "naive introspection" (2008), leaving the door open to sophisticated introspection, and he offers an especially interesting account of why we get things wrong when we introspect certain visual images (2002). Schwitzgebel's correcting tendencies suppose that an observer sometimes gets things right and, at least some of the time, he seems to do so because he carefully reflects upon his own experience, i.e., he strikes me as good at introspecting. Thus, Schwitzgebel frequently teeters towards tentative, non-egalitarian optimism, if one looks past all of the skeptical bluster.

3  The text from which this quote is taken is co-authored. Here is a similar claim made by Schwitzgebel, writing alone: "One must go surprisingly far afield to find major thinkers who unambiguously hold, as I do, that the introspection of current conscious experience is both (i) possible, important, necessary for a full life, and central to the development of a full scientific understanding of the mind, and (ii) highly untrustworthy" (2008, p. 246). Incidentally, one actually need not go so very far to find philosophers who hold (i) and (ii). Most phenomenologists fall into or come very close to falling into this category, especially, as argued below, the earliest Sartre.

4  Robust optimism need not be limited to philosophers trained as phenomenologists. David Chalmers arguably maintains a robustly optimistic view about the role introspection should play in consciousness studies, see, e.g., 2010, especially Chapter 2.

5  An early draft of this chapter spent considerable time distinguishing between two different non-egalitarian approaches to introspection, i.e., views that begin with the assumption that we are not all equally good at thinking about our conscious experience. It did so, in part, to show why what phenomenologists call "reflective analysis" differs from what nineteenth-century research psychologists called "introspection" and how these differences mitigate, in advance, a series of traditional skeptical challenges. This material interrupted the flow of the chapter and has now become an independent essay. Suffice it to say, the simplest way to capture the main difference is that, unlike early research psychologists, phenomenologists are not so much concerned with the particular content of experience, e.g., perceptual thresholds, as they are with the essential or universal structures that make conscious experience possible, e.g., intentionality, temporality, self-awareness. Otherwise put, whereas skeptics like Schwitzgebel spend a lot of time showing how introspective claims about the content of conscious experience are susceptible to error, e.g., whether a penny looks round or oval at arms-length, phenomenologists not only insist on this kind of susceptibility to error but they argue that it is an essential, i.e., inescapable, susceptibility.

6  Oizumi et al., for example, take "the phenomenology of consciousness as primary" in the effort to understand how neurological mechanisms allow consciousness to process information (Oizumi et al. 2014, p. 1). To be sure, Oizumi et al. admit that integrated information theory employs "the opposite of the approach usually taken in neuroscience," which typically starts with neural mechanisms

first "and [only then] asks under what conditions they give rise to consciousness" (Oizumi et al. 2014, p. 2). Oizumi et al. reverse the usual picture: they begin with phenomenological axioms and asks what neural mechanisms could possibly bring that kind of experience about. Needless to say, today such an approach is an outlier—but what about tomorrow?

7 For an exemplary and meticulous treatment of Sartre's relationship to psychology around the turn of the century, see Flajoliet (2008).

8 Anthony Hatzimoysis (2010) makes a similar case grounded in *The Transcendence of the Ego*.

9 For example, Sartre argues that reflective awareness of freedom and contingency leads to an overwhelming anxiety (in the former case) and to nausea (in the latter), both of which motivate bad faith: that is, a form of deceiving oneself with some awareness of the deception as it takes place, but in a way that, nonetheless, ameliorates the initial discomfit. Sartre gives the example of belief in psychological determinism as a paradigmatic example of bad faith, since the false belief that one lacks freedom mitigates the anxiety experienced due to freedom (BN, p. 40). Thus, Sartre implies that theoretical accounts of determinism are supported by an underlying existential motivation to believe that one is not free, or, as is practically almost always the case, to believe oneself less free than one really is (Eshleman, 2008). While it could be true that determinism finds its roots in a self-imposed illusion, this kind of claim immediately runs amok, since Sartre's account of bad faith is, at least on the surface, as controversial as determinism is speculative. The point here is that, even if Sartre were correct, no one outside of Sartre studies should find these putative existential motivations and self-deceptive efforts to conceal them initially illuminating. To argue that determinists are in bad faith would be like disagreeing with a Freudian on some theoretical issue and then being told you are resisting or exhibiting transference. In both cases, the objection stands within a theoretical system, and depends upon that system's validity for its meaning.

10 It's tempting to suppose that explicit self-awareness recedes into the background or periphery of conscious experience, as, e.g., Kriegel (2003, p. 177) claims. This requires a strong analogy between intrinsic self-awareness and extrinsic awareness of objects. Although one can shift attention from the contours of one's body on the couch to the background music to the story, etc. and one can switch between pre-reflective and reflective consciousness, the two "shifts" differ in at least one crucial way. When one attends to the story, the pressure of one's body on the couch recedes from explicit awareness; however, that pressure still exists—it's just unattended. The analogy does not *always* hold for explicit self-awareness. During engrossment, there simply is no explicit self-awareness. It's not lying obscurely on an indeterminate horizon; it comes into existence with the activity of reflection.

11 Bernecker (2011) gives the following case that might seem to suggest a counterexample to this claim that we don't have anonymous experiences that are then somehow personalized: "Consider, for example, the case of R.B., a 48 year old male who suffered a serious head injury in a car accident. Almost immediately following his accident, he was able to remember events from the past, yet his recollection of those events was compromised—he could not remember the events as having been personally experienced. His memory of these events was no different from what it would have been had they happened to someone else"

(pp. 111–112). As RB notes about his memories before the accident: "it was the same sort of knowledge I might have about how my parents met or the history of the Civil War or something like that" (ibid.). Clearly the accident causes RB to have an attenuated sense of personal identity. It's as if he takes a wholly third-person perspective on the content of his pre-accident memories. Notice, however, that RB does not fail to understand that he possesses the activity of remembering (i.e., experiences himself as an agent remembering), only that the content presents itself anonymously. So understood, this example amplifies a point made below, namely that one essential aspect of content susceptible to third-person claims is that they are about something or someone other than oneself, albeit with some necessary qualifications.

12 Here, a qualification is necessary: while impure reflection gives rise to "a new object" (TE, p. 9), namely the ego, Sartre argues that the ego is neither a part of consciousness nor is it something discovered. It's constituted on the basis of patterns of past actions and future anticipations, frequently with systematic distortions; consequently, it doesn't give rise to new information. To the contrary, at least in Sartre's view, the putative (reflective) exploration of one's psychic life tends not to be genuinely about self-discovery; rather, it's an activity of self-creation and most frequently an activity of self-concealment. Thanks to Joshua Tepley for motivating this footnote.

13 When performing a habituated, repetitive activity for a long period of time, like driving for many hours, one can suddenly experience a kind of surprise, namely that one has been driving while daydreaming. This kind of case might seem like an obvious counter-example to the claim that reflection is never surprised by its own pre-reflective activity. However, when one reflects upon the startling fact of driving while daydreaming, one does not discover being startled or surprised. Nor does one discover the fact that one was daydreaming. The surprise already happened pre-reflectively when you nearly drove off of the road. Why do they put vibration bumps on the side of highways? The sudden, surprising vibration bump experience motivates reflection. When things go smoothly (or habitually), one typically does not reflect. Incidentally, this kind of daydreaming while driving example has been employed to show that self-awareness does not accompany all conscious acts (Wider 1993). Although discussion of this worry would take matters too far afield, it might be noted here that the ubiquity thesis about self-awareness does not require an awareness of non-conscious aspects of, e.g., perception and habituated activity. The daydreaming driver might not be able to say what sign she just passed on the highway but she can tell you what she was daydreaming about while driving. After all, she does not discover her daydreaming via reflection, since she was implicitly aware of daydreaming all along. Needless to say, there are many autonomic and habituated activities that require no conscious attention. This obvious fact does not tell against the ubiquity thesis.

14 By "genuine" I mean, in part, the opposite of merely linguistic acts. For example, someone might utter the sentence "I am reading" while daydreaming or under hypnosis. These utterances would not count as genuine, since they are not accompanied by the *explicit* sense of self-possession distinctive to reflective acts. It is tempting to say that mere utterances are purely semantic (i.e., they have a sense but no genuine reference), and that they amount to what Husserl calls empty intentions. To be sure, the question of reference with regard to

first-person language turns out to be very complicated. See Thomas Kapitan (1999) for a clear account of the complexities surrounding first-person reference and a view very similar to Sartre's.
15 Zheng (2000, 2001) and Webber (2002) have been especially helpful in characterizing this hybrid account that maintains that pre-reflective consciousness enjoys both conceptual and pre-conceptual dimensions.
16 A skeptic might apply pressure to the qualification "typically." Shaun Gallagher (2012a) offers interesting analyses of cases where senses of agency and ownership seem to come apart. For example, a schizophrenic who experiences thought insertion may experience a sense of ownership, insofar as she comprehends it is she who hears voices; however, insofar as she does not recognize herself as the source of the inserted thoughts, the schizophrenic experiences an attenuated sense of agency. Gallagher also examines cases where we experience agency without clear ownership, e.g., Olaf Blanke's experiments where "you feel yourself several feet in front of your actual location" (p. 256). This kind of distorted self-ownership, as regards features of embodiment, does not undermine an underlying sense of embodied agency. Gallagher concludes that, although these kinds of examples require some qualifications to our implicit senses of agency and ownership that are characteristic of pre-reflective experience (and, thus, to what has come to be known as the principle of immunity to error through misidentification), some aspects of self-specific, first-person experience remain immune to such errors, e.g., the schizophrenic recognizes that she hears the inserted voice.
17 There is one prominent error found in Sartre's early works that is not listed below. The seventh error might be called the "reversal error." Sometimes we believe that the world causes aspects of our experience (or acts emanate from our egos) that actually result from the spontaneous, meaning-constituting activity of (embodied) consciousness. Sartre argues, e.g., that my example of the story about the falsely accused boy doesn't cause sadness; rather our sadness constitutes the lived meaning of the story. Unfortunately, there won't be time to discuss this error.
18 So understood, the *cogito* does not consist in a syllogistic argument with a suppressed premise. Rather, reflective doubt grasps what one already implicitly comprehends.
19 Sartre's account of the relationship between reflective and pre-reflective consciousness departs from *The Transcendence of the Ego* in *Being and Nothingness* in several ways. Most relevantly, in TE, Sartre frequently makes it sound as if pre-reflective consciousness and reflective consciousness are two separate and distinct acts of consciousness, as suggested by the quoted passage. Sartre rejects this heterogeneity view in B&N, where reflecting and reflected consciousness are construed as one and the same consciousness. Below we will see how heterogeneity kinds of views can motivate the standpoint error.
20 I take Williford's qualification that consciousness of an object is not "typically" an object for consciousness to mean that sometimes, perhaps under atypical conditions, the object for consciousness is consciousness itself. Although Husserl accepts putting matters this way, this kind of claim, in the case of Sartre, needs qualification. According to Sartre, consciousness as such can never straightforwardly be an "object" for itself, without falsification, in part, because it is not at all or in any way object-like (BN, p. 241). Needless to say, a great deal rides

on what we mean by "object." Husserl employs the term "object" in a broadly logical sense, namely as any subject susceptible of bearing true predicates; thus, insofar as one can make true claims about consciousness, it's an object in this most general, logical sense. In the case of Sartre, one can make two different sorts of interpretative moves. First, one can offer a deflationary reading of Sartre as employing "object" in a narrower sense than Husserl and allow that we can talk about consciousness qua object in a broadly logical sense, but not in a more narrowly construed ontological sense. Second, one can offer a robust reading and interpret Sartre as grounding logic in ontology. So understood, in a fashion akin to Aristotle, the rules of logic are what they are because reality is structured in the ways that it is. On this reading, the term object is, first and foremost, an ontological term that correlates to the mode of being in-itself. Since self-identity characterizes being in-itself, Sartre grounds the logical principle of identity (and, on that basis, the principles of excluded middle and non-contradiction) in this mode of being. In contrast, the mode of being-for-itself does not instantiate self-identity and, for this reason, it is not object-like. So understood, if the mode of being in-itself grounds traditional logic, since the mode of being for-itself is not object-like, it requires a non-traditional logic (Morris, 1976). If the robust reading is correct, then Husserl's broadly logical construal of "object" illicitly imports ontological implications that Sartre aims to resist. Consciousness is not the attribute of an underlying substance and, hence, it cannot, straightforwardly, be considered subject that bears predicates, at least not in a traditional logical sense.

21 An alternative account of Hume holds that, from the absence of a self in the content of experience, Hume denied that self-awareness exists (Kriegel, 2003, p. 178). This would be a truly unusual position that seems to be contradicted by nearly every one of our waking moments. My preference is for Woodruff Smith's interpretation given above, even if it leads to a dilemma, discussed below.

22 As noted above, Sartre maintains that the best descriptive evidence supports a diaphanous view of consciousness. This motivates (in my view) a qualified version of content externalism, namely that there is nothing literally inside of consciousness. See Rowlands (2003, 2011) for helpful exposition of Sartre's externalism, though see Zahavi (2008) for some well-placed, complicating considerations.

23 This is a rather attenuated account of Sartre's analysis, which isn't always easy to follow. Sartre discusses warping in the context of analyzing the relationship between thoughts, images and concepts (IPP, pp. 112–120/216–231). Sartre gives a nuanced three-stage account of concept formation, but the gist of it comes down to this. In our efforts to achieve purely formal concepts on the basis of imagination, we sometimes attribute quasi-spatial aspects of images to less than pure concepts. For example, in describing the spatial schema employed to explain spatial representations, early psychologists who were influenced by Kant sometimes attributed spatial qualities to the schema itself. Thus, they transferred the spatial qualities of the things represented by the spatial schema to the spatial schema itself, or so Sartre argues (IPP, p. 53). This roughly amounts to supposing that the concept "space" itself has spatial qualities.

24 Many contemporary philosophers of mind will reject this admittedly controversial claim. Sartre's rejection of unconscious mental states largely rides on his ubiquity thesis about self-awareness. All consciousness is intrinsically aware of itself as consciousness of the world. Sartre can easily admit that many things go

on, e.g., in our brains, about which we are not consciously aware. It's just that he won't call these mental states. My hunch is that debate over whether consciousness is essentially self-aware or whether there can be unconscious mental states is largely semantic, though this line cannot be pursued here for reasons of time.

25  Commentators have not all found Sartre's account of this aspect of non-positional self-awareness especially lucid (Wider, 1997); and others correctly note that Sartre leaves much unexplained (Webber, 2002). See Zheng (2000) for an inventory of the widely varying interpretations of Sartre's account of non-positional self-awareness. That there can be considerable disagreement about this aspect of Sartre's view results, in part, from the fact that much of his analysis of the non-positional aspects of consciousness is not descriptive. Rather he arrives at these kinds of claims via arguments and some admittedly obscure conceptual analysis (see below).

26  For this reason, the relation constitutive of ipseity does not, contra Kriegel (2003), enjoy both inner and outer intentional content. It is not a thinker that represents itself to itself, via an "internal" intentional object, in addition to "representing" an external intentional object. To think otherwise potentially commits the illusion of immanence and it also unnecessarily multiplies superfluous theoretical entities, as, for example, Descartes does when he posits a thinker (or subject) behind every thought. This multiplication of theoretical entities arguably results from a misleading analogy derived from reflective experience. In reflection, we explicitly grasp intentionality (i.e., the relational aspect of positional consciousness to its object); we then mistakenly project intentionality (a structure of the positional aspect of consciousness) on to the non-positional aspect of consciousness. To come at this point in another way, when Kriegel claims that explicit self-awareness recedes into the background or periphery of conscious experience (2003, p. 177) this forms too strong an analogy between self-awareness and perceptual objects. Sartre rejects this analogy between intrinsic self-awareness and objects of experience implied by Kriegel's claim. As pointed out in fn. # 9, it's not that explicit awareness recedes into the background in the way that perceptual objects do when they move from the figure to the ground of perception. Rather, self-awareness simply becomes implicit in a non-representational way. Perhaps Kriegel's model that holds self-awareness moves into the unattended horizon in an analogous similar manner to perceptual objects motivates his claims about twofold intentional content. If one thinks that explicit self-awareness is representational, then it can seem as if implicit self-awareness should also be representational. Needless to say, Sartre rejects self-representation at both levels.

27  Sartre builds desire, value, affectivity, and motivation all into the non-positional dimension of conscious experience. Time will not permit analysis of these aspects, so the below concrete example of pain will have to suffice.

28  Although Sartre's admission of absences, non-being, and negative facts into his broad-minded ontology may be controversial today (but see, e.g., McDaniel, 2010 and 2013), it's standard fare in the phenomenological tradition, as is the distinction between knowledge and comprehension. What follows does not, however, directly require invoking non-being as such. We can construe the non-cognitive dimension of self-awareness in non-object terms that shouldn't offend positivist sensibilities.

29  http://consc.net/notes/first-third.html.

30 A lot of people have made this chapter possible, though none of them is responsible for its many mistakes. I would like to thank the editors of this volume, Gerhard Preyer, Sophia Miguens, and Clara Bravo Morando for all of their work and supererogatory patience. An excerpted version of this chapter was presented at the *Thinking with Sartre Today* conference held at La Maison française d'Oxford on January 30th and 31st, 2015. I'd like to thank the audience members for their helpful questions, especially Sarah Richmond's incisive remarks. Thanks go to Joshua Tepley and Henryk Jaronowski for their comments on early drafts of this chapter, and Matthew Ally was especially helpful in offering a comprehensive commentary on the final draft. A special thank you also goes to Tom Flynn for all of our many conversations about Sartre.

## Bibliography

Barnes, H. (2005). Consciousness and Digestion: Sartre and Neuroscience. *Sartre Studies International* 11(1–2): pp. 117–132.
Bernecker, S. (2011). Further Thoughts on Memory: Replies to Schechtman, Adams, and Goldberg. *Philosophical Studies* 153: pp. 109–121.
Boring, E. (1953). A History of Introspection. *Psychological Bulletin* 50(3): pp. 169–189.
Boyle, M. (2012). Review of *Introspection and Consciousness*, D. Smithies and D. Stoljar (Eds.). *Notre Dame Philosophical Reviews*. Available online at: https://ndpr.nd.edu/news/38869-introspection-and-consciousness/.
Butler, J. (2013). *Rethinking Introspection: A Pluralist Approach to the First-Person Perspective*. Basingstoke: Palgrave Macmillan.
Byrne, A. (2005). Introspection. *Philosophical Topics* 33: pp. 79–104.
Carruthers, Peter (2011). Higher Order Theories of Consciousness. *Stanford Encyclopedia of Philosophy*. Available nline at: http://plato.stanford.edu/entries/consciousness-higher/.
Caudle, F. (1983). The Developing Technology of Apparatus of Psychology's Early Laboratories. *Annals of the New York Academy of Sciences* 412: pp. 19–55.
Cerbone, D. (2012). Phenomenological Method: Reflection, Introspection, and Skepticism. In: D. Zahavi (Ed.), *Oxford Handbook of Contemporary Phenomenology*. Oxford: Oxford University Press.
Chalmers, David (2010). *The Character of Consciousness*. Oxford: Oxford University Press.
Churchland, P. (1985). Reduction, Qualia, and the Direct Introspection of Brain States. *Journal of Philosophy* 82: pp. 8–28.
Churchland, Paul (1988). *Matter and Consciousness*. Cambridge, MA: MIT Press.
Comte, Auguste (1830). *Cours de philosophie positive*, Vol. 1. Paris: Bacheleier, Libraire pour les Mathématiques.
Costall, Allan (2006). 'Introspectionism' and the Mythical Origins of Scientific Psychology. *Consciousness and Cognition* 15: pp. 634–654.
Descartes, René (1637/1998). *Discourse on Method*. Trans. D. Cress. Indianapolis, IN: Hackett.
Dretske, F. (1995). *Naturalizing the Mind*. Cambridge, MA: Bradford Books/MIT Press.
D. S. M. (1987). Review of *The Disappearance of Introspection*, by W. Lyons. *American Journal of Psychology* 100(2): pp. 302–305.
Elshof, G. T. (2005). *Introspection Vindicated: An Essay on the Perceptual Model of Self-Knowledge Defended*. Hampshire: Ashgate.

Embree, L. (2011). *Reflective Analysis: A First Introduction into Phenomenological Investigation*, 2nd edn. Bucharest: Zeta Books.
Eshleman, M. (2008). The Misplaced Chapter on Bad Faith. *Sartre Studies International* 14(2): pp. 1–22.
Fernández, J. (2009). Introspection. In: J. Symons and P. Calvo (Eds.), *The Routledge Companion to Philosophy of Psychology*. London: Routledge.
Fernández, J. (2013). *Transparent Minds: A Study of Self-Knowledge*. Oxford: Oxford University Press.
Flajoliet, A. (2008). *La première philosophie de Sartre*. Paris: Honoré Champion.
Gallagher, S. (2007). Phenomenological Approaches to Consciousness. In: M. Velmans and S. Schneider (Eds.), *The Blackwell Companion to Consciousness*. Oxford: Blackwell.
Gallagher, S. (2012a). First-Person Perspective and Immunity to Error Through Misidentification. In: G. Preyer and S. Miguens (Eds.), *Consciousness and Subjectivity*. Frankfurt: Ontos Verlag.
Gallagher, S. (2012b). On the Possibility of Naturalizing Phenomenology. In: D. Zahavi (Ed.), *Oxford Handbook of Contemporary Phenomenology*. Oxford: Oxford University Press.
Gallagher, J. and Nikolic, S. (2012). Patients in Pain. In: M. Glynn, W. Drake (Eds.) *Hutchison's Clinical Methods*, 23rd edn. London: Saunders.
Gallagher, S. and Sørensen, J. B. (2006). Experimenting with phenomenology. *Consciousness and Cognition* 15: pp. 119–134.
Gennaro, Rocco (2002). Jean-Paul Sartre and the HOT Theory of Consciousness. *Canadian Journal of Philosophy* 32(2): pp. 293–330.
Gertler, B. (2001). Introspecting Phenomenal States. *Philosophy and Phenomenological Research* 63: pp. 305–328.
Gertler, B. (2003). How to Draw Ontological Conclusions from Introspective Data. In: B. Gertler (Ed.) *Privileged Access: Philosophical Accounts of Self-Knowledge*. Aldershot: Ashgate Publishing.
Hatfield, G. (2005). Introspective Evidence in Psychology. In: P. Achinstein (Ed.), *Scientific Evidence: Philosophical Theories and Applications*: pp. 259–286. Baltimore, MD: Johns Hopkins University Press.
Hatzimoysis, A. (2010). A Sartrean Critique of Introspection. In: J. Webber (Ed.), *Reading Sartre*: pp. 90–99. London: Routledge.
Hergenhahn, B. and Henley, T. (2014). *An Introduction to the History of Psychology*, 7th edn. Belmont: Wadsworth Publishing.
Hill, Christopher (2011). How to Study Introspection. *Journal of Consciousness Studies* 18(1): pp. 21–43.
Hurlbert, R. T. and Schwitzgebel, E. (2007). *Describing Inner Experience: Proponent Meets Skeptic*. Cambridge, MA: MIT Press.
Husserl, E. (1913/1976/1983a). *Allgemeine Einfuhrung in die reine Phänomenologie, Husserliana, Gesammelte Werke*, III/1, ed. K. Schumann. The Hague: Nijhoff, 1976. Translated as *Ideas Pertaining to a Pure Phenomenology and to a Phenomenological Philosophy*, First Book: *General Introduction to a Pure Phenomenology*, trans. F. Kersten. The Hague: Nijhoff, 1983.
Husserl, E. (1925/1962/1983b). *Phänomenologische Psychologie*, ed. by W. Biemel, Husserliana, Vol. IX (The Hague: Martinus Nijhoff, 1962). Translated as *Phenomenological Psychology: Lectures, Summer Semester, 1925*, trans. J. Scanlon. The Hague: Nijhoff, 1983.

Jack, A. I. (2013). Introspection: The Tipping Point. *Consciousness and Cognition* 22: pp. 670–671.
Jack, A. I. and Roepstorff, A. (2003). Trusting the Subject, Part I. *Journal of Consciousness Studies* 10: pp. 9–10.
Jack, A. I. and Roepstorff, A. (2004). Trusting the Subject II, special issue of *Journal of Consciousness Studies* 11: pp. 7–8.
Jäkel, F. and Schreiber, C. (2013). Introspection in Problem Solving. *Journal of Problem Solving* 6(1): pp. 20–33.
James, W. (1890). *Principles of Psychology*. New York: Dover.
Kapitan, T. (1999). The Ubiquity of Self-Awareness. *Grazer Philosophische Studien* 57: pp. 17–44.
Klein, S. B. (2011). The Two Selves: The Self of Conscious Experience and its Brain. In M. R. Leary (Ed.), *Handbook of Self and Identity* (2nd edn.), pp. 617–637. New York: Guilford Press.
Kriegel, U. (2003). Intrinsic Theory and the Content of Inner Awareness. *Journal of Mind and Behavior* 24(2): pp. 169–196.
Kriegel, U. (2013). A Hesitant Defense of Introspection. *Philosophical Studies* 165: pp. 1165–1176.
Kriegel, U. and Horgan, T. (2007). Phenomenal Epistemology: What is Consciousness That We May Know It so Well? *Philosophical Issues* 17: pp. 123–144.
Krueger, J. (2006). A Sartrean Critique of Functionalist Accounts of Mind. *Sartre Studies International* 12(2): pp. 44–60.
Lowe, E. J. (2004). *An Introduction to the Philosophy of Mind*. Cambridge: Cambridge University Press.
Lyons, W. (1986). *The Disappearance of Introspection*. Cambridge, MA: MIT Press.
McDaniel, Kris (2010). Being and Almost Nothingness. *Noûs* 44(4): pp. 628–649.
McDaniel, Kris (2013). Degrees of Being. *Philosophers' Imprint* 13(19): pp. 1–17.
Moore, G. E. (1903). The Refutation of Idealism. *Mind* 12: pp. 433–453.
Morris, Phyllis Sutton (1976). *Sartre's Concept of a Person: An Analytic Approach*. Amherst: University of Massachusetts Press.
Morris, Katherine (2008). *Sartre*. Oxford: Blackwell Publishing.
Nir, Y. and Tononi, G. (2009). Dreaming and the Brain: From Phenomenology to Neurophysiology. *Trends in Cognitive Science* 14(2): pp. 88–100.
Nisbett, R. E. and Wilson, T. D. (1977). Telling More Than We Can Know: Verbal Reports on Mental Processes. *Psychological Review* 84: pp. 231–259.
Oizumi, M., Albantakis, L. and Tononi, G. (2014). From the Phenomenology to the Mechanisms of Consciousness: Integrated Information Theory 3.0. *Computational Biology*, 10(5): pp. 1–25.
Overgaard, M. (2006). Editorial. *Consciousness and Cognition* 15: pp. 629–633.
Piccinini, G. (2009). First Person Data, Publicity and Measurement. *Philosophers Imprint*, 9(9): pp. 1–16.
Price, D. D. and Murat, A. (2005). The Experimental Use of Introspection in the Scientific Study of Pain and its Integration with Third-Person Methodologies: The Experiential-Phenomenological Approach. In: A. Murat (Ed.), *Pain: New Essays on the Nature of Pain and the Methodology of Its Study*: pp. 243–273. Cambridge, MA: MIT Press.
Reeder, H. (1986, 2010). *The Theory and Practice of Husserl's Phenomenology*, 2nd edn. Lanham, MD: University Press of America/Bucharest: Zetabooks.

Reuter, K. (2010). Is Imagination Introspective? *Philosophia* 39(1): pp. 31–38.
Rosenberg, Jay F. (1981). Apperception and Sartre's "Pre-Reflective Cogito." *American Philosophical Quarterly* 18(3): pp. 255–260.
Rowlands, Mark. (2001). *The Nature of Consciousness.* Cambridge: Cambridge University Press.
Rowlands, Mark. (2003). *Externalism: Putting Mind and World Back Together Again.* Montreal: McGill-Queen's University Press.
Rowlands, Mark. (2011). Untimely Review of Sartre's Being and Nothingness. *Topoi* 30(2): pp. 175–180.
Sartre, J.-P. (1936/2012). *L'imagination.* Paris: Librairie Felix Alcan. Translated as *The Imagination,* trans. K. Williford and D. Rudrauf. London: Routledge.
Sartre, J.-P. (1936/1992/2004a). *La Transcendance de l'égo. Les Recherches philosophiques* 6: pp. 85–123. Published as a separate book. Paris: Librairie philosophique J. Vrin. Translated as *The Transcendence of the Ego,* trans. A. Brown. London: Routledge.
Sartre, J.-P. (1939/1948). *Esquisse d'une théorie des emotions.* Paris: Hermann. Translated as *The Emotions: Outline of a Theory,* trans. B. Frechtman. New York: Citadel.
Sartre, J.-P. (1940/2004b). *L'Imaginaire: Psychologie phénoménologique de l'imagination.* Paris: Gallimard. Translated as *The Imaginary: A Phenomenological Psychology of the Imagination,* trans. J. Webber. London: Routledge.
Sartre, J.-P. (1943/1971/1956). *L'Etre et le néant: Essai d'ontologie phénoménologique.* Paris: Gallimard, 1971 [1943]. Translated as *Being and Nothingness: An Essay on Phenomenological Ontology,* trans. H. Barnes. New York: Philosophical Library.
Sartre, J.-P. (1948/1967). *Conscience de soi et connaissance de soi.* Translated as *Consciousness of Self and Knowledge of Self.* In N. Lawrence and D. O'Connor (Eds.), *Readings in Existential Phenomenology,* pp. 113–142. Upper Saddle River, NJ: Prentice Hall.
Schwitzgebel, E. (2002). How Well Do We Know Our Own Conscious Experience: The Case of Visual Imagery. *Journal of Consciousness Studies* 9(5–6): pp. 35–53.
Schwitzgebel, E. (2004). Introspective Training Apprehensively Defended: Reflection on Titchener's Lab Manual. *Journal of Consciousness Studies* 11(7–8): pp. 58–76.
Schwitzgebel, E. (2006). Do Things Look Flat? *Philosophy and Phenomenological Research* 72: pp. 589–599.
Schwitzgebel, E. (2008). The Unreliability of Naïve Introspection. *Philosophical Review* 117(2): pp. 245–273.
Schwitzgebel, E. (2011). *Perplexities of Consciousness.* Cambridge, MA: MIT Press.
Smithies, D. and Stoljar, D. (Eds.) (2012). *Introspection and Consciousness.* Oxford: Oxford University Press.
Terrace, H. and Metcalfe, J. (2005). *The Missing Link in Cognition: Origins of Self-Reflective Consciousness.* Oxford: Oxford University Press.
Webber, J. (2002). Motivated Aversion: Non-Thetic Awareness in Bad Faith. *Sartre Studies International* 8(1): pp. 45–57.
Webber, J. (2004). Philosophical Introduction: To Jean-Paul Sartre's *The Imaginary: A Phenomenological Psychology of the Imagination,* trans. J. Webber. London: Routledge.
Wider, Kathleen (1993). Sartre and the Long Distance Truck Driver: The Reflexivity of Consciousness. *Journal of the British Society for Phenomenology* 24(3): pp. 232–249.
Wider, Kathleen (1997). *The Bodily Nature of Consciousness: Sartre and Contemporary Philosophy of Mind.* Ithaca, NY: Cornell University Press.

Williford, Kenneth (2004). Moore, the Diaphanousness of Consciousness and Physicalism. *Metaphysica* 5(2): pp. 133–150.

Woodruff Smith, D. (1986). The Structure of (self-)consciousness. *Topoi* 5, pp. 149–156.

Zahavi, D. (2004). Phenomenology and the Project of Naturalization. *Phenomenology and the Cognitive Sciences*, 3(4): pp. 331–347.

Zahavi, D. (2006). Two Takes on a One Level Account of Consciousness. *Psyche* 12(2): pp. 1–9.

Zahavi, D. (2008). Internalism, Externalism, and Transcendental Idealism. *Syntheses* 160: pp. 355–374.

Zheng, Yiwei (2000). On Sartre's "Non-Positional Consciousness". *Southwest Philosophy Review*, 16(1): pp. 141–149.

Zheng, Yiwei (2001). On Pure Reflection in Sartre's Early Philosophy. *Sartre Studies International*, 7(1): pp. 19–42.

# 8 A pebble at the bottom of the water

## Sartre and Cavell on the opacity of self-knowledge

*Pierre-Jean Renaudie*

> En disant je nous affirmons bien plus que nous ne savons
> (Sartre, *La transcendance de l'Ego*[1])

Between 1900 and 1905, Claude Monet painted a series of paintings depicting the Palace of Westminster as he could see it from his window on the opposite banks of the Thames in London. However, one could hardly say that the Houses of Parliament constitute the topic of these paintings, since they are hardly perceptible, appearing in the distance as a rough and undefined shadow through a very thick fog typical of the London atmosphere. Monet attempts in these paintings to depict the remarkable and unique way the mist filters and retains the light, blurring the architecture of the Palace and making it hardly recognizable. This focus on the particularly striking visual impression produced by the effect of fog is even stronger in the series of paintings of Charing Cross Bridge, in which the opacity of the mist is such that it makes everything else vanish in the haze and prevents the spectator from seeing what was supposed to be the topic of these paintings.

In *Transcendence of the Ego*, Sartre uses this peculiar visual experience as a metaphor in order to describe the way we appear to ourselves and to stress the irreducible opacity of self-knowledge. Something is said to be opaque when we cannot see through it, as a perfectly transparent piece of flawless glass would allow us to. The opacity is the property of something that prevents one from seeing *further*; it stops one's look and obstructs the gaze, as does the London fog, preventing us from perceiving distinctly the contours of the Palace of Westminster. Likewise, according to Sartre, the *I* always appears through a mist that veils it and makes it similar to "a pebble at the bottom of the water" (Sartre 1960, pp. 51–52). The *I* always manifests itself as an opaque reality whose content is not immediately accessible to us and that cannot be distinctively perceived. Such claim about the opacity of the *I* seems to dismiss any conception of self-knowledge relying on the assumption that our mental states are transparent enough to provide us with an immediate and unquestionable knowledge of ourselves. Far from being grounded on our ability to have direct access to our states of mind, the process through which we get to know ourselves entails inevitably, according to Sartre's analysis, some irreducible opacity: by describing our mental states as *ours*, we make the *I* the source of consciousness and conceal to ourselves the transcendence of our own ego.

The purpose of this chapter is to measure the consequences of this account of the opacity of the Ego on self-knowledge. To be sure, Sartre's critical analysis of the status of subjectivity contributes to point out the limits of a strictly epistemic approach to self-knowledge, drawing on an "incorrigibly contemplative conception of knowledge," in the words of Anscombe, by which she means a conception which presupposes that knowledge must be something that is judged as such by being in accordance with prior facts or realities (Anscombe 2000, p. 57). However, does this criticism necessarily imply that the very quest for self-knowledge is illusive and that any kind of self-knowledge must be discarded?

To address this question, I will first try to show that Sartre's radical interpretation of the intentionality thesis allows him to keep separate two claims that are usually taken to stem from one another in philosophy of mind:

a) the claim according to which one enjoys some privileged first-personal access to one's own conscious states and

b) the idea that this privileged access grants one some kind of indisputable authority in self-ascribing such and such mental states.

This will lead me to highlight the paradox that arises from Sartre's theory, making the quest for self-knowledge both impossible and necessary. Finally, I will draw on Cavell's analysis of the use of first- and third-person narrators in literature in order to provide a more refined account of this paradox about the opacity of self-knowledge.

## The intentional translucence of conscious experience

Strongly influenced by Husserl's phenomenology and in particular by his *Logical Investigations*, Sartre develops in *Transcendence of the Ego* an analysis of consciousness that stresses the intentional dimension of conscious experiences and prioritizes the relation to an object over the link that allegedly ties the field of experience to a particular Ego. Experiences such as the perception of a bird in a tree, the feeling of the wind running through one's hair, the imaginative representation of a unicorn, the thought of the smallest prime number can all be characterized by their particular mode of relation to the object they are directed towards, and do not require an egological structure to establish this relation to an object. Knowing what kind of conscious experience we just had when we see a bird in a tree amounts to being able to tell what this experience is an experience *of*. The transitivity of conscious experiences constitutes the main feature, thanks to which experiences can be described. Following Husserl's analysis in the *Logical Investigations* (Husserl 1984b, pp. 353, 361), Sartre claims that consciousness' intentional orientation towards an object is all we need in order to be able to (a) identify and (b) describe conscious phenomena. To describe them is nothing but to set out their intentional structure, insofar as their specific way of intending or aiming at a peculiar object delivers the very meaning of conscious experiences.

This fundamental feature of conscious experience entails a second one, that Sartre calls the "translucence" of conscious phenomena (Sartre 1960, p. 42): the way the intentional object of an experience appears requires that the experience does not appear as such. In order for, say, a perceptual object to manifest itself within an act of perception, consciousness needs to be perfectly translucent and to let it appear as the object looked at, without hindering in any way the movement of the look pointing at the object. This translucence of consciousness implies that intentional experiences do not appear at all: by directing one's consciousness towards a particular object, intentionality withdraws, as it were, the experience itself from one's focus. This fundamental aspect of the intentionality thesis is familiar to whoever needs to wear glasses and does not keep them clean enough, or decided to buy colorful fancy frames. If some dust on the surface of the glass distracts us, or if our eyes are caught by the bright colors of our frames, we can no longer see what our glasses were supposed to let us look at; the glasses become an obstacle that jeopardizes visibility. In order to function properly—in order to let us see—glasses must not be *seen* as such but *looked through*. This example brings to more clarity the consequences of Sartre's analysis of intentionality: conscious experiences, insofar as they are intentional (and they all are, according to both Husserl and Sartre), are such that they establish a relation to an object through which the relation itself vanishes, so that the object can appear. The non-appearance of conscious experiences is required as a condition of possibility of the appearance of their object.

However, the translucence of intentional experiences and their exclusive orientation towards an object do not imply that experiences cannot be *present* to consciousness. They are definitely not *perceptible* in the same sense that the object of a perceptual experience is perceived, but they are nevertheless (and by definition) *conscious*. Seeing a bird in a tree certainly does not amount to seeing ourselves seeing a bird in a tree; these two experiences are essentially different and cannot be reduced to one another. Nonetheless, when we see a bird in a tree, this experience lets us be aware of the particular kind of experience we are having: the bird is precisely experienced as a perceptual object—the object of an act of perception, i.e., as a perceived rather than fantasized, recalled, or mentally depicted bird. We can misidentify the object we perceive when, for instance, we mistake a sparrow for a finch; we can be wrong about the *object* that appears to us, but we cannot be mistaken about the *way* this object appears to us, as if we were to take the thought of a sparrow for a perception. A perceptual experience is such that the object perceived is experienced *as* perceived. This is precisely what the adjective "conscious" is meant to encapsulate: an experience is conscious insofar as it lets us be aware of the peculiar relation to the object we are experiencing.

Accordingly, beside its intentional relation to an object, every conscious experience entails a form of non-intentional awareness of itself. Our intentional experience is always present to our consciousness, even though it does not appear as the transcendent object towards which our look is turned. Sartre expresses this idea by saying that consciousness is "non-positional consciousness of itself" (Sartre 1960, pp. 44–45), which means that we do not need to reflect on our experience in order for this experience to be present to our consciousness:

> A consciousness has no need at all of a reflecting consciousness in order to be conscious of itself. It simply does not posit itself as an object.
> (Sartre 1960, pp. 44–45)

Conscious experiences do not need to appear in order for us to be aware of them and to *know* (to be able to tell) the peculiar kind of experience we are having. The only thing that we need to be conscious of in order to be aware of our experience is the object towards which we are intentionally oriented:

> Consciousness is aware of itself *insofar as it is consciousness of a transcendent object*... Consciousness is purely and simply consciousness of being consciousness of that object. This is the law of its existence.
> (Sartre 1960, p. 40; emphasis in original)[2]

## Sartre's outer account of self-knowledge

So far, two major consequences regarding self-knowledge can be drawn from Sartre's account of the translucence of intentional consciousness. These two consequences can be presented, as it were, as the two sides—negative and positive—of one and the same point about the way one knows about whatever we are experiencing.

What makes our experience conscious and enables us to *know* something about it (to identify the peculiar kind of experience we are having):

a) is not primarily our capacity to perceive this experience inwardly or of reflecting on it *a posteriori*
b) is nothing but its intentional orientation towards a particular object.

The first consequence expresses a negative thesis concerning inner perception, while the second sets forth the primacy of the intentional object of conscious experience. Unlike intentional objects, conscious experiences do not need to appear positively and to be seen or perceived as such in order to come to our awareness. We do not know that we are having a perceptual experience of a bird in a tree by turning our look inwards and describing what we see: the *way* the bird appears to us is enough to make us aware of the experience we are having and to let us know that we are perceiving a bird and not fantasizing a unicorn, or whatever.[3] What makes an experience conscious is nothing but its intentional orientation towards an object that Sartre describes as *transcendent*, since it is posited by consciousness as something different to itself. In the quote mentioned above, one should emphasize that consciousness is aware of itself *only* "insofar as it is consciousness of a transcendent object" (Sartre 1960, p. 40). Prior to and independently of our ability to reflect on our conscious experiences or to perceive them inwardly, our knowledge about our experiences relies primordially on the identification of the intentional object we are oriented towards when "living" in a peculiar act of consciousness.

Consequently, Sartre's claim about the translucence of conscious experiences leads him to develop an outer account of self-knowledge, by which I mean a conception of our ability to know something about our conscious experiences that does not need to presuppose a substantial theory of the faculty which allows us to turn our look inwards in order to access our inner states. Far from entailing some inner knowledge of our internal states, the kind of transparency that self-knowledge requires is grounded on the intentional relation to a transcendent object that gives conscious experience its meaning. Our own experiences are transparent to us in that we do not need to reflect on them to know what we experience; we know it simply by looking "through" them directly to their objects. In that respect, Sartre's account of the translucence of consciousness can be understood as a way to apply to the description of intentional experiences the analysis of the structure of belief provided by Gareth Evans in a famous passage of *The Varieties of Reference*. Evans writes:

> [I]n making a self-ascription of belief, one's eyes are, so to speak, or occasionally literally, directed outward—upon the world. If someone asks me "Do you think there is going to be a third world war?," I must attend, in answering him, to precisely the same outward phenomena as I would attend to if I were answering the question "Will there be a third world war?"
>
> (Evans 1982, p. 225)

Evans' claim about the "transparency" of belief is very similar to what Husserl and Sartre have in mind when they describe the intentional structure of conscious phenomena: nothing but the way the world appears to us might tell us about the kind of experiences we have. To experience something, to be conscious of something, is to "live" within an intentional relation to the world or to any object so that the experiencing subject and all the subjective elements of this experience are completely absorbed in this relation.[4] Sartre describes, for example, the way we become absorbed in the contemplation of a landscape, captivated by the story we are reading or fascinated by the movie we are watching: "While I was reading, there was consciousness *of* the book, *of* the heroes of the novel, but the *I* was not inhabiting this consciousness" (Sartre 1960, pp. 46–47). The same conclusions that Evans draws about beliefs apply to conscious phenomena, if we follow Husserl's and Sartre's analysis of intentionality: the only aspect of conscious experiences that is relevant for phenomenological description is the object in its particular mode of manifestation, while the so-called mental objects or psychic events that occur whenever something is experienced are strictly irrelevant.[5]

## Sartre's version of the transparency thesis

Accordingly, Sartre's version of the transparency thesis can be summarized as follows: the description of a conscious phenomenon is always reducible to the description of the way its intentional object appears. The intentional structure of consciousness dissolves the egological features of conscious experience. Subjectivity vanishes as it is absorbed within the manifestation of the object. Take, for instance, the following statement:

(*S*1) I loathe Peter

This statement (*S*1) is supposed to express my feelings towards a specific object, namely Peter. (*S*1) looks like a statement that says something about myself rather than Peter: it provides an account of the way *I* feel and does not seem to disclose any information about Peter as such. (*S*1) describes nothing but my subjective attitude or disposition, so that the object towards which this attitude is oriented is not primarily and directly intended by the expression of my feelings. Peter is only *indirectly* or *obliquely* the object of (*S*1), which is primordially a statement about myself. This is the reason why (*S*1) is typically understood as a statement expressing the most common kind of self-knowledge, providing some information about our mental states that no one but us can have direct access to. (*S*1) sounds more personal than most beliefs, since beliefs, opinions, and knowledge can be shared and do not have this strictly private and subjective character that feelings seem to have. My feeling of hatred towards Peter seems to be much more significant and revealing, with respect to the kind of person I am, than my belief that it is going to rain tomorrow, which relies on the weather report and is shared by all those who read the same forecast and trusted it as well.

Yet, Sartre's interpretation of intentionality and his conception of the translucence of conscious experience urge us to reverse this analysis and come to the exact opposite conclusion. Far from revealing a strictly subjective aspect of one's conscious experience, (*S*1) is reducible to a statement (*S*2) that does not require the first-person pronoun and does not make any mention of the egological dimension of consciousness. (*S*1) can be paraphrased as follows:

(*S*2) Peter is loathsome

Of course, the validity of (*S*2) does not follow from the validity of (*S*1), and there are countless cases where (*S*2) is false although (*S*1) is true. My loathing of Peter does not make Peter loathsome, and Sartre certainly does not advocate so unreasonable a theory. However, Sartre holds that:

a) (*S*2) is always true *for me* when (*S*1) is true
b) (*S*2) does not appear as *true for me*, but simply as *true*

I would not loathe Peter if he did not appear to me that loathsome. In other words, I do not hate Peter because of the way I feel, but because of the way he appears to me. Sartre draws an intimate correlation between the two categories of statements to which (*S*1) and (*S*2) belong: our way of feeling about something always relates to how this thing towards which our conscious experience is directed appears to us. Now, the way Peter appears is nothing as far as I am concerned but the way he *is*. To me, being loathsome is not only the way Peter *looks*, but rather the way he *is*.[6] In virtue of consciousness' translucence, the intentional object towards which our conscious experience is directed does not need to appear as its intentional correlate. The hatred is so deeply embedded in Peter's way of appearing to me whenever I think of him or see him that my feeling of hatred cannot appear to me as something that qualifies *me*, but rather as something that qualifies *him*.

## The impersonality of consciousness

The description of the experience that (*S*1) and (*S*2) try to encapsulate in two diametrically opposed ways is therefore much more subtle and problematic than the so-called immediate expression of our feelings could let us assume. The interpretation of (*S*1) as a statement expressing our knowledge of our own feelings provides a very poor, partial, and misleading analysis of the phenomenon at issue, focusing exclusively on an aspect of conscious experiences that is inessential and "superfluous" (Sartre 1960, p. 49) to their description. I will call the category of statements to which (*S*1) belongs "Egological descriptions" (ED), whereas the second kind of statements (*S*2), can be called "Impersonal descriptions" (ID). Like (*S*1), all statements that look like they express a kind of self-knowledge allegedly grounded on our ability to enjoy some kind of direct and immediate access to ourselves (ED) can be paraphrased as statements of the second kind (ID), in which the first-person pronoun does not appear and which do not refer at all to the Ego.

Sartre does not claim that the Ego bears no relevance to the description of our experience whatsoever; he only wants to show that this kind of description does not need to presuppose the Ego as the *source* of the conscious experiences described and to make it the direct (as opposed to *oblique*) object of the kind of knowledge that such descriptions provide. Sartre denies that feelings and other subjective traits of one's experience must be counted as properties that need to be ascribed to an Ego. If we stick to the phenomenological description of conscious experience, we need to admit, according to him, that mental states are "not given as having formerly been in the *me*" (Sartre 1960, p. 77), but as features of the way the world manifests itself to someone. Our feelings are revealed to us within the appearance of the object towards which the intentional experience is directed, as shown in the example analyzed by Sartre:

> I pity Peter, and I go to his assistance. For my consciousness only one thing exists at that moment: Peter-having-to-be-helped. This quality of "having-to-be-helped" lies in Peter.
> (Sartre 1960, p. 56)

In this example, it is nothing but the way Peter appears to me that manifests what I take wrongly for an *inner* feeling of pity that qualifies me as compassionate. Far from expressing an immediate relation to myself upon which self-knowledge could be grounded, the experiencing of my feeling is nothing but an experiencing of the objective traits of the world:

> There is no me: I am in the presence of Peter's suffering just as I am in the presence of the color of this inkstand; there is an objective world of things and of actions, done or to be done, and the actions come to adhere as qualities to the things which call for them.
> (Sartre 1960, p. 56)

Consequently, if all conscious phenomena can be described without using the mark of the first person, then we must come to the conclusion that consciousness is impersonal and that its spontaneity does not need to be grounded on an Ego of any kind (Sartre 1960, p. 98: "transcendental consciousness is an impersonal spontaneity"). The Ego, Sartre writes, "has no *raison d'être*" and is "superfluous" (Sartre 1960, p. 40).

> When I run after a streetcar, when I look at the time, when I am absorbed in contemplating a portrait, there is no I. There is consciousness of the streetcar-having-to-be-overtaken, etc., and non-positional consciousness of consciousness. In fact, I am then plunged into the world of objects; it is they which constitute the unity of my consciousnesses; it is they which present themselves with values, with attractive and repellent qualities—but me, I have disappeared; I have annihilated myself. There

is no place for me on this level. And this is not a matter of chance, due to a momentary lapse of attention, but happens because of the very structure of consciousness.

(Sartre 1960, p. 49)[7]

## The coming back of the Ego through reflection

Egological descriptions of one's experience like (*S*1) are therefore misleading insofar as they misinterpret and overestimate the role of the Ego by positing it as the source of consciousness. Statements of this kind are less dangerous because of what they say than because of what they conceal. The use of the first-person pronoun in such descriptions is not only useless, but, as Sartre puts it, "a hindrance" (Sartre 1960, p. 49). Indeed, Egological Descriptions conceal to consciousness its own translucence and reverse covertly the order between consciousness and its objects: (*S*1) looks like the immediate expression of some feelings that are ascribed to one's I whereas the self-ascription of such states of mind is the result of a reflective process through which the I has been in fact constituted and posited as the source of consciousness. "Reflection," Sartre writes, "intends a relation which traverses time backwards and which gives the *me* as the source of the state" (Sartre 1960, p. 77). Then, coming back to the example of my compassionate feelings towards Peter's suffering, "it is no longer Peter who attracts me, it is my helpful consciousness which appears to me as having to be perpetuated" (Sartre 1960, p. 58). The so-called immediate self-knowledge that ED are supposed to express is in fact to be understood as a retroactive and mediated form of reflection that makes the Ego its direct and primary object, while the intentional object of the conscious experience is only considered the oblique and secondary object of the description. The Ego is nothing but the transcendent object of an act through which consciousness conceals its own spontaneity by positing the Ego as its origins:

> The ego is an object apprehended, but also an object constituted by reflective knowledge ... Consciousness constitutes it in a direction contrary to that actually taken by the production: really, consciousnesses are first; through these are constituted states; and then, through the latter, the ego is constituted. But, as the order is reversed by a consciousness which imprisons itself in the world in order to flee from itself, consciousnesses are given as emanating from states, and states as produced by the ego. It follows that consciousness projects its own spontaneity into the ego-object in order to confer on the ego the creative power which is absolutely necessary to it.
>
> (Sartre 1960, pp. 80–81; translation modified)

This reflective operation that reverses the relation between consciousness and the Ego is implicitly at work in the moral understanding of consciousness and underlies the feeling of guilt. I feel guilty when I take myself to be the origin and the cause not only of the actions I accomplish, but also of the thoughts, feelings, or desires that I experience. The I is always suspected to be the secret source of the conscious feelings one experiences, and should be made responsible for them for that reason. The theory of the self-love developed by French moralists like La Rochefoucauld pushes this reasoning to an extreme point, making the reference to oneself the essential structure of all moral emotions, even the most selfless and altruistic ones (Sartre 1960, p. 54). However, such analysis of the self is only made possible through reflection's reversal of the relation between consciousness and the Ego, preventing one from recognizing the impersonal structure and absolute spontaneity of consciousness. Therefore, that which one takes generally for the height of lucidity (for instance, the ability to discern self-love behind so-called moral feelings) in fact brings self-knowledge to the highest degree of confusion and opacity.

## The opacity of the Ego and the impossibility of self-knowledge

Not only does reflection reverse the intentional relation between consciousness and the Ego, it also conceals itself in such a way as to make ED look like the most obvious and immediate form of description of one's experience. By concealing its true nature, reflection prevents access to the unreflected level of conscious experience and introduces inevitably some opacity within consciousness.[8] Indeed, in opposition to consciousness' translucence, the Ego "is opaque like an object" (Sartre 1960, p. 78). Insofar as it has been posited by reflection, the Ego is primarily the intentional *object* (rather than the *subject*) of a peculiar act of consciousness that constitutes it (Sartre 1960, p. 80), an object that consciousness "*posits* and *grasps* . . . in the same act" (Sartre 1960, p. 41). Being the intentional object towards which reflective consciousness is oriented, the Ego is as transcendent and empirical an object as any other thing given in our experience of the world. The Ego, Sartre writes, "is outside, *in the world.* It is a being of the world, like the ego of another" (Sartre 1960, p. 31).[9] Therefore, far from being "a translucent quality of consciousness" (Sartre 1960, p. 41), the Ego is a transcendent object projected within consciousness as its "inhabitant" (Sartre 1960, p. 41), bringing with itself the opacity and the "indistinctness" (Sartre 1960, p. 85) that characterize the objects of perception. The Ego can be said to be "opaque" not only because of its ontological status as a transcendent object, but also (and maybe mostly) because it prevents consciousness from acknowledging its impersonal spontaneity. Reflection prevents us from seeing *further* than our Ego and lets impersonal consciousness "flee from itself" (Sartre 1960, p. 81).

Accordingly, Sartre's analysis of intentionality reveals the existence of a paradoxical relationship between translucence and opacity. The intentional translucence of conscious experience lets consciousness become fascinated by its own creation, introducing within itself the opacity of the object it constituted:

> Everything happens, therefore, as if consciousness constituted the ego as a false representation of itself, as if consciousness hypnotized itself before this ego which it has constituted, absorbing itself in the ego as if to make the ego its guardian and its law.
>
> (Sartre 1960, p. 101)

This reciprocity between translucence and opacity ruins the very possibility of self-knowledge. In virtue of its intentional structure, consciousness conceals from itself its true nature and confines itself to a "false representation of itself." Instead of letting us be aware of our impersonal spontaneity, the translucence of consciousness misleads our knowledge of ourselves by orienting us towards the wrong direction and making us focus on the Ego as the ultimate object that self-knowledge is about. This is why the notion of an ego is so profoundly "irrational," according to Sartre; it results from the paradoxical movement of a consciousness that introduces a contradiction within itself and becomes opaque to itself as consciousness posits its object as the source of its translucence (Sartre 1960, p. 81):

> Everything happens as though the ego were *of* consciousness, with only this particular and essential difference: that the ego is opaque to consciousness.
>
> (Sartre 1960, p. 85)

As a matter of consequence, the Ego is *both* transcendent and "given as intimate" (Sartre 1960, p. 85), which makes self-knowledge strictly impossible. Being a transcendent object, the ego to which the first-person pronoun refers in ED belongs as much to the world and to the outer experience as any other "ego." Therefore, we cannot pretend to have a privileged access to our own Ego that would provide self-knowledge a specific kind of certainty: "my 'I' is *no more certain for consciousness than the 'I' of other men*" (Sartre 1960, p. 104; emphasis in original). Knowing oneself should require the very same methods used in the case of objective knowledge: observation, approximation, anticipation, and experience. However, the intimacy that the Ego claims makes these methods inapplicable and irrelevant for self-knowledge.

> These procedures, which may be perfectly suited to any *non-intimate* transcendent, are not suitable here, because of the very intimacy of the *me*. It is too much present for one to succeed in taking a truly external viewpoint on it. If we step back for vantage, the *me* accompanies us in this withdrawal. It is infinitely near, and I cannot circle around it.
>
> (Sartre 1960, p. 86)

Instead of opening the way for self-knowledge, the so-called intimacy of the Ego prevents it and makes it illusory. "It would be useless," Sartre writes, "to address directly to the me, and try to benefit from its intimacy in order to know it" (Sartre 1960, pp. 86–87). Therefore, there is no ground upon which self-knowledge could be safely built: relying on the intimacy of the Ego in order to guarantee direct and immediate access to oneself is no less illusory than attempting to know oneself as a transcendent and non-intimate object. "Really to know oneself is inevitably to take toward oneself the point of view of others, that is to say, a point of view which is necessarily false" (Sartre 1960, p. 87). Both first- and third-person access to oneself are strictly unable to provide some solid grounds to self-knowledge. Those who identify with their transcendent Ego in order to ascribe to themselves some states of mind or psychological traits necessarily miss out on themselves.

Therefore, in spite of consciousness' transparency to itself, self-knowledge is necessarily a failure (in the best case) or an illusion (in the worst). Instead of providing us with some kind of privilege that only the "I" would enjoy, the translucence of consciousness, along with the discrete complicity of reflection, bars the way to our knowledge of ourselves. Sartre's analysis of consciousness keeps separated two theses that seem to be logically related and that are usually considered mutually dependent: although Sartre claims that we enjoy some privileged first-personal *access* to our own conscious states (thanks to the translucence of consciousness), he nevertheless stresses that we do not have indisputable *authority* in ascribing some mental states to ourselves, since we know ourselves through the very same procedures that we use to know other's egos. The kind of self-awareness that characterizes conscious states and makes them transparent is not likely to secure first-person authority in self-knowledge.

The conclusion must be drawn that nothing, even pure reflection, can provide sufficient grounds upon which the legitimacy of self-knowledge could be founded. It is true that Sartre holds in the second part of *Transcendence of the Ego* that a "pure" and "merely descriptive" form of reflection allows us to access our conscious experience without operating the fatal reversal of the relations between the Ego and consciousness (Sartre 1960, pp. 64–65)[10]. Sartre stresses that pure reflection is capable of revealing consciousness' absolute spontaneity and impersonal structure, as it "disarms the unreflected consciousness by granting its instantaneousness" (Sartre 1960, pp. 65, 101–102). However, pure reflection is of no help to self-knowledge, since its ability to disclose the unreflected spontaneity of consciousness prevents us from ascribing any kind of mental state to ourselves whatsoever, making any *positive* knowledge of ourselves illusory. Pure reflection can only lead to a strictly *negative* outcome: by putting forward the impersonal structure of consciousness, such reflection makes us aware of our absolute lack of determination as a result of the radical and "monstrous" spontaneity of our consciousness (Sartre 1960, pp. 99–100[11]).

Claiming some substantial and positive knowledge of ourselves would make us in "bad faith," in the sense established by Sartre in *Being and Nothingness*. "Bad faith" is described by Sartre as the "inauthentic mode of being" that characterizes our attempt to identify to our transcendent Ego, letting consciousness imprison itself into a "false representation" of itself (Sartre 1960, p. 101; 1993, p. 59). We might manage to know what we are not, but never what we are, insofar as we are not what we are and are what we are not (Sartre 1993, p. 58[12]).

## Self-knowledge and self-concealment: a Cavellian account

The quest for self-knowledge is therefore a *necessary* failure, both because such a quest is necessarily to fail, and because it is nevertheless unavoidable and bound to happen. At the very moment pure reflection discloses the impersonal spontaneity of one's consciousness, it seals the impossibility of self-knowledge and reveals its vanity. Self-knowledge seems to be both necessary and impossible; it remains an ideal, but an impracticable one. Knowing oneself is impossible if self-knowledge consists in ascribing certain experiences or psychological traits to an Ego that has been constituted through the very process that makes it the object of this quest. Then, self-knowledge is no less a way of *concealing* oneself than a way of *revealing* oneself, just as they fog both reveal the Palace of Westminster in Monet's painting. Unknown and by definition inaccessible, the self is bound to remain similar to a pebble at the bottom of the water—something that can be looked at but always in the distance, through murky and opaque waters, something that is seen, though never grasped, by a necessarily unhappy consciousness.

Such an analysis leaves very little hope concerning self-knowledge and seems to make the quest for this particular kind of knowledge pointless and absurd. In the final section of this chapter, I would like to sketch an approach to the opacity of self-knowledge that does not need to draw such desperate and dramatic conclusions from the acknowledgment of the close relationship between self-knowledge and self-concealment. Self-knowledge is impossible only as long as we consider that it is jeopardized and threatened by consciousness' inevitable (since grounded on its intentional structure) tendency to conceal itself and to flee away from itself. Sartre draws on such a conception of self-knowledge when he claims that knowing oneself amounts to taking toward oneself "a point of view which is necessarily false," namely "the point of view of others" (Sartre 1960, p. 87). By positing the self as an object, reflective consciousness conceals its true nature and turns the quest for self-knowledge into a form of self-deception.

> Even if I could see myself clearly and distinctly as an object, what I should see would not be the adequate representation of what I am in

myself and for myself . . . , but the apprehension of my being-outside-myself, for the Other; that is, the objective apprehension of my being-other, which is radically different from my being-for-myself, and which does not refer to myself at all.

(Sartre 1943, pp. 312–313; 1993, p. 273)

Understanding the third-person perspective on oneself as a "necessarily false" point of view presupposes that *another* kind of access to oneself should provide the truly authentic form of self-knowledge. Sartre occasionally betrays this aspect of his thought, for instance when he writes that "each of us exists in interiority and . . . a knowledge valid for interiority can be effected only in interiority" (Sartre 1943, p. 273; 1993, p. 234).

Sartre's approach to self-knowledge relies on the idea that a true knowledge of oneself requires the overcoming of consciousness' predisposition to conceal and "absorb" itself in a transcendent ego. Yet, this claim seems quite counter-intuitive if we distance ourselves a little bit from Sartre's analysis. If intentional consciousness is *by nature* involved in a self-concealing process through which it "hypnotises itself before this ego which it has constituted," it seems that this self-concealment is part of ourselves; it defines ourselves at least as much as, and maybe more intimately than, any other character that we could ascribe to ourselves. Should we not consider that self-concealment is precisely that which makes us the kind of person we are, rather than something that would characterize our existence as inauthentic? Coming back to Sartre's analysis of bad faith, it seems to me that the many so-called "inauthentic" roles we play all throughout our life (like the café waiter performing perfectly the expectations of any café waiter and identifying himself to his social function) disclose us to ourselves, precisely because we cannot be but actively engaged in this self-concealing process.

In a beautiful analysis of the function of the third- and first-person narrator in literature, Stanley Cavell provides a particularly interesting account of the relation between the act of concealment and the use of the first-person pronoun. In a novel, the third-person narrator does not participate in the story and is not involved in any way in the actions that he describes. The characteristic feature of the third-person narrator is both to be deprived of self-reference and to occupy a position that does not allow him to conceal anything. Cavell establishes a strong link between those two aspects of this narrative form: the logical space in which third-person narration takes place does not allow any space for any kind of concealment. The third-person narrator cannot lie, and the reader is expected to grant him absolute credibility.

> The third-person narrator, being deprived of self-reference, cannot conceal himself; that is to say, he has no self, and therefore nothing to conceal.
>
> (Cavell 2002, p. 336)

Cavell's insightful remark, as I understand it, attempts to wipe out a certain picture of the self that entails precisely the kind of presupposition upon which Sartre's conception of self-knowledge relies. There is a logical relation, according to Cavell, between having a self and having something to conceal. As the third-person narrator of a novel, one would not have a self at all out of this concealment process. The third-person narrator is deprived of self-reference because of his inability somehow to take part in the story he narrates; he "cannot make anything happen."

However, this is not the case in Shakespeare's *King Lear*, when Edgar pretends to interrupt the action to relate his father's death. Cavell stresses that Edgar's first-person narration of the events of the play is not an *interruption* but an *extension* of the action ; it does not introduce a break in the play. Unlike the omniscient third-person narrator of a novel, Edgar is still on stage and within the play. Then, as he relates the death of his father, narrating "is what he is doing, that has become what is now happening." This is precisely why, as Cavell notices, Edgar "remains concealed to himself throughout his revelations" (Cavell 2002, p. 336).

The existence of the self and the possibility of concealment are strictly coextensive. As Cavell puts it, "the man who has the word 'I' at his disposal has the quickest device for concealing himself" (Cavell 2002, p. 336). If self-concealment is not a contingent episode of one's existence but a fundamental aspect of what "having a self" means to us, then, rather than jeopardizing the possibility of self-knowledge and making it a vain pursuit, it gives meaning to such a quest and makes it legitimate. Therefore, self-knowledge must be understood as a way of dealing with one's concealment rather than an attempt to overcome it.

## Notes

1 Sartre (1936, p. 35; 1960, p. 51): "by saying *I* we affirm far more than we know."
2 For an in-depth analysis of the issues that these formulations raise, see Daniel Rodriguez Navas' chapter in this volume.
3 This point is made clear by Husserl's theory of adumbrations (*Abschattungen*) that Sartre knew and mentions in a different context in *Transcendence of the Ego*; see Husserl's *Ideas Pertaining to a Pure Phenomenology*, sections 41 to 44 (Husserl 1983, pp. 86–98; Sartre 1960, p. 49).
4 "If we simply 'live' in the act in question, become absorbed, for example in the perceptual 'taking in' of some event happening before us, in some play of fancy, in reading a story, in carrying out a mathematical proof, etc., the ego as relational centre of our performances becomes quite elusive" (Husserl 1984b, p. 217). For an analysis of the relationship between Sartre and Husserl's conceptions of intentionality, see my article: "Me, Myself and I: Sartre and Husserl on Elusiveness of the Self," *Continental Philosophy Review*, 46(1): 99–113, 2013. A broader study of Sartre's criticism of Husserl can be found in Stephen Priest (2000).

5 The source of such critique of the "mental" or "immanent" objects can be found in Husserl's fifth *Logical Investigation*, section 11 (2001).
6 Peter's way of appearing to me is a "phenomenon" in the sense "in which 'to be' and 'to appear' are one," according to Sartre's definition of this notion (Sartre 1960, p. 42).
7 Sartre follows here the conception Husserl advocates in his *Logical Investigations*, before abandoning it for a transcendental egology: "If we simply 'live' in the act in question, become absorbed, for example in the perceptual 'taking in' of some event happening before us, in some play of fancy, in reading a story, in carrying out a mathematical proof, etc., the ego as relational centre of our performances becomes quite elusive" (Husserl 1984b, p. 217).
8 Reflection "congeals" consciousness, it "darkens" it: "Consciousness is then no longer a spontaneity; it bears within itself the germ of opaqueness" (Sartre 1960, pp. 41–42).
9 Again, Sartre stays here very close to the analysis of the *Logical Investigations*, where Husserl writes: "We perceive the ego just as we perceive an external thing" (Husserl 1984b, pp. 204, 210).
10 On this particular question, see Raoul Moati's contribution to this volume (Chapter 20).
11 "Consciousness is frightened by its own spontaneity because it senses this spontaneity as beyond freedom." See Sartre's analysis of the case of the bride who did not want to be left alone in the same page.
12 "We have to deal with human reality as a being which is what it is not and which is not what it is."

## Bibliography

Anscombe, Gertrude Elizabeth Mary (2000). *Intention*. Cambridge, MA: Harvard University Press.
Cavell, Stanley (2002). *Must We Mean What We Say? A Book of Essays*. Cambridge: Cambridge University Press.
Evans, Gareth (1982). *The Varieties of Reference*. Oxford: Oxford University Press.
Husserl, Edmund (1983). *Ideas Pertaining to a Pure Phenomenology and to a Phenomenological Philosophy*, First book (translation F. Kersten). The Hague: Martinus Nijhoff.
Husserl, Edmund (1984a). Husserliana XIX/1, *Logische Untersuchungen*, Zweiter Band. *Untersuchungen zur Phänomenologie und Theorie der Erkenntnis*. The Hague: Martinus Nijhoff.
Husserl, Edmund (1984b). Husserliana XIX/2, *Logische Untersuchungen*, Dritter Band. Untersuchungen zur Phänomenologie und Theorie der Erkenntnis. The Hague: Martinus Nijhoff.
Husserl, Edmund (2001). *Logical Investigations* (translation J. N. Findlay). London: Routledge.
Jopling, David (2000). *Self-knowledge and the Self*. London: Routledge.
Priest, Stephen (2000). *The Subject in Question: Sartre's Critique of Husserl in Transcendence of the Ego*. New York: Routledge.
Renaudie, Pierre-Jean (2013) Me, Myself and I: Sarte and Husserl on Elusiveness of the Self. *Continent Philosophy Review*, 46(1), pp. 99–113.
Sartre, Jean-Paul (1936). *La transcendance de l'ego*. Paris: Vrin.

Sartre, Jean-Paul (1943). *L'être et le néant, essai d'ontologie phénoménologique.* Paris: Gallimard.

Sartre, Jean-Paul (1960). *Transcendence of the Ego* (translation F. Williams and R. Kirkpatrick). New York: Hill and Wang.

Sartre, Jean-Paul (1993). *Being and Nothingness* (translation H. Barnes). New York: Washington Square Press.

# 9 Does consciousness necessitate self-awareness?

## Consciousness and self-awareness in Sartre's *The Transcendence of the Ego*

*Daniel R. Rodríguez Navas*

**Introduction**

Sartre's *The Transcendence of the Ego* has been misunderstood. The misunderstanding turns on the thesis that consciousness necessarily involves at least some form of self-awareness. According to an increasingly standard, but in my view incorrect, reading, that is one of Sartre's central claims in the essay. Consider, for instance, the following passage of Zahavi's *Subjectivity and Selfhood*:

> Sartre, probably the best-known defender of a phenomenological theory of self-consciousness, considered consciousness to be essentially characterized by intentionality. He also claimed, however, that each intentional experience is characterized by self-consciousness [i.e., what I have called "self-awareness"]. Thus, Sartre took self-consciousness to constitute a necessary condition of being conscious of something.
> (Zahavi 2008, p. 12)

In this chapter I will present my reasons for thinking that the standard reading is wrong, and explain why this should matter to us.

As I just pointed out, the standard reading differs from mine over the thesis that consciousness necessarily involves at least some form of self-awareness. Let's begin by clarifying this thesis and its philosophical implications.

Consciousness is a familiar but notoriously difficult phenomenon to define. We can think of it as the capacity to have experiences; or as the capacity to be in states that there is something that it is like to be in, to be in states that "have a phenomenology"; or as the capacity to be in mental states that involve a perspective or a point of view; or as the capacity to be aware of things in general (regardless of what it is that one is aware of, or of the way in which one is aware of it).

Though these ways of thinking about consciousness do not quite capture "the nature of" this enigmatic phenomenon, they can work as ostensive definitions that enable us to identify the thing that we're talking about, and that suffices for present purposes.

In the same way we can think of consciousness as the capacity to be aware of things in general, we may think of self-awareness as the capacity that a conscious creature may have to be aware of itself as such. But what is it for a creature to be aware of itself as such? Here, again, we come before an infamously difficult question, the difficulty lying in unpacking the "as such," in giving an account of the capacity to have thoughts about the self or "the I."

Perhaps because of this difficulty, self-awareness is sometimes treated as a *sui generis* phenomenon, a phenomenon that is elusive, hard, perhaps even impossible to explain, but which is familiar to everyone because everyone knows what it is like to have thoughts about themselves.

However, as in the case of consciousness, identifying the phenomenon of self-awareness does not require that there be a priorly available account of "the nature of" self-awareness or of the concept of "self" at our disposal. It is that capacity, whatever it is, that makes it possible for you to use words like "I," "yo," "je," "ich," etc.; the capacity to be in first-personal states; the capacity to be in I* states (in Castañeda's sense). It is the capacity, in brief, that you have to be in mental states that are about yourself, and to understand all the while both that you are the subject (or bearer, or agent) of those states, and that those states are about you.

That thing, the self, whatever it may be, the thing that you associate with the "sense of ownership" or "feeling of mineness" that characterizes your mental life, the thing about which you think when you think of yourself, is the topic of Sartre's *The Transcendence of the Ego*, as well as the topic of this chapter.[1]

Let's now return to the thesis on which the standard reading and the one that I propose differ. The thesis bears on the relation between the capacity to be aware of anything at all, and the capacity to be aware of oneself *as oneself*.

According to the standard reading, Sartre argues that the ability to be aware of anything at all is intrinsically bound up with the ability to be aware of oneself as oneself, bound up in such a way that one cannot have the former without having the latter. According to the reading I propose, Sartre argues for the opposite point: the ability to be aware of things in general does not necessarily involve the ability to be aware of oneself as oneself; it is possible for an agent to be capable of being aware of a range of things, but altogether lack the ability to be aware of itself as itself.

Now, note that the thesis that consciousness necessarily involves at least some form of self-awareness is, so formulated, ambiguous. It admits of at least two readings, a weak and a strong one, depending on whether it is heard as a claim about types of conscious entities or as a claim about conscious states.

> Weak: All conscious entities are self-aware.
> Strong: All conscious states are states of self-awareness.

The reason I call them weak and strong is, as you might suspect, that while the latter implies the former, the converse does not hold. That all conscious states are states of self-awareness implies that all conscious creatures are self-aware. But since it is possible for a creature to be self-aware without always being in states of self-awareness, the converse does not hold.

In the passage from Zahavi's *Subjectivity and Selfhood* cited above, he attributes the strong version of the thesis to Sartre:

> Sartre . . . claimed, however, that each intentional experience is characterized by self-consciousness [i.e., what I am calling "self-awareness"]. Thus, Sartre took self-consciousness to constitute a necessary condition of being conscious of something.
>
> (Zahavi 2008, p. 12)

Yet I will not argue only against Zahavi's version of the standard reading. I will not only argue, that is, that Sartre rejects the strong version of the thesis. I will argue that he rejects even the weak version of the thesis. On my reading, in *The Transcendence of the Ego*, in addition to defending the view that conscious states are not necessarily states of self-awareness, Sartre maintains the possibility that there be conscious entities that completely lack the capacity to be aware of themselves as such. In other words, he argues that, at least in principle, it is possible that there be creatures that are at no point of their lives aware of themselves as such.

There is a further source of unclarity in the thesis, as I have formulated it. The thesis says that consciousness necessarily involves some form of self-awareness. The source of unclarity lies in the implied idea that there are various forms or types of self-awareness. The best way to clarify this point and its stakes is perhaps by describing the mental lives of four different types of hypothetical creatures capable of being in conscious states:

1. *Narcissus*, or the hyper-self-aware creature: Narcissus is a creature that is always actually thinking about itself. It's not just that the "I think" can accompany all its representations; it's that it in fact does. Narcissus does not think: "This croissant is delicious," but thinks "I am thinking that this croissant is delicious." Its occurrent mental life is crowded by its own presence. It's the kind of creature of which we might correctly say that it has an Ego that is almost the size of its entire universe.

2. *Tinnitus*, or the semi-hyper-self-aware creature: This is a creature that is always thinking about itself. All of its states are partly about itself. Yet most of the time, and this is what distinguishes it from Narcissus, Tinnitus' attention is not focused on itself, but on whatever else it happens to be thinking about. Thus when Tinnitus thinks about the delicious croissant that it is eating, it's almost entirely absorbed by the deliciousness of the croissant. It is still aware of itself as such. But only in a very minimal sense. It is merely peripherally aware of itself, you

might say. Or you may invoke the phenomenological idea of an intentional horizon, and say that Tinnitus is always there for itself in its intentional horizon, sort of waving at itself in the distance, rather than as a prominent object in the intentional field. Or you may also say, if you like this way of speaking, that Tinnitus is always tacitly, or implicitly, or primitively aware of itself. However you may like to think about it, what is distinctive about Tinnitus' mental life is that all its states are states of self-awareness (even if, to insist, most of them are states of self-awareness in a minimal sense). So Tinnitus is always aware of itself as such, it is permanently present to itself or has an ongoing sense of self, but its self-awareness is much like constant background noise, like the constant ringing noise that people who suffer from tinnitus hear all the time. Hence its name.[2]

3   *Marie Antoinette*, or the occasionally-self-aware creature: This is a creature that can sometimes think about herself as such, but is not always doing it. In fact, during much of her waking life Marie Antoinette is not thinking about herself as such, at all. Not even minimally. When she goes to the gym to play squash, she focuses on the game. When she watches movies she gets so absorbed in them that she literally forgets herself. When she's listening to her friends talk, she really is listening to them, and not thinking about herself at all. She can of course always think about herself. And she does it as often as whatever activity she is engaged in requires it. But the rest of the time she really is not present to herself at all.

In fact, her thoughts about herself are in this sense much like her thoughts about the back of her neck: they are able to, but do not, accompany all her representations. At any given time she can add, to any given occurrent thought, an awareness of the back of her neck. But that her awareness of herself and of the back of her neck are able to accompany all her representations does not imply that they in fact do, not even in the minimal sense in which Tinnitus' awareness of itself as such accompanies all its occurrent mental states. This is of course not to say that her awareness of herself as such plays a functionally analogous role in her mental life to the role therein played by her awareness of the back of her neck; it is not to say that the explanation of her ability to add back-of-the-neck awareness to any of her thoughts is the same as the explanation of her ability to add an "I think" to all her thoughts. It is just to point out that, much like Marie Antoinette is only aware of the back of her neck on particular occasions, when that is relevant, and just as the rest of the time she does not have a single thought about it, so it is with her awareness of herself as such.

4   *Trump*, or the never-ever-self-aware creature: Trump has never had a single thought about itself as such. It simply lacks the capacity for it. Every now and then it has the unpleasant experience of seeing an image of a creature in the mirror, a creature that, unbeknownst to it,

happens to be itself. But that "unnoticed reflectivity" is as close as it ever gets to self-awareness. Trump just lacks a conception of itself as such that it could identify anything to.

Note that one of the principles of differentiation between these four types of creatures is a distinction between minimal and higher forms of self-awareness. For the higher type, we can think of what would be the reference of phrases like "fully first-personal states," "states of explicit self-awareness," "states of maximal self-awareness," "fully reflective states," and so forth. These are all meant to refer to the kind of state that one is in when having the type of thought that could only be expressed by using the first-person pronoun as the grammatical subject. Evidently, the use of such phrases goes in hand with the idea that there are other, weaker forms of self-awareness. Thus we find in the literature the notions of implicit or tacit self-awareness, minimal self-awareness, peripheral self-awareness, and so forth. I shall henceforth refer to these two broad forms of self-awareness, respectively, as higher forms of self-awareness and minimal forms of self-awareness. In using them, I shall be thinking of them as umbrella terms that can replace the terms of any distinction between types of self-awareness involving the claim that one type is primitive, or basic, or minimal, etc., relative to the other one.

Bearing in mind this distinction, we may characterize our four creatures as follows: (1) Narcissus is always highly self-aware; (2) Tinnitus is always at least minimally self-aware (the question of whether it is ever "highly" self-aware is left open); (3) Marie Antoinette is at least sometimes not self-aware at all, though at other times she is self-aware (whether in these cases she is minimally or highly self-aware is left open); and (4) Trump is never self-aware, not even minimally.

The descriptions of these types of creatures have purely heuristic value: my argument does not require that these creatures actually exist, or even that their existence be a live possibility.

In addition to helping bring out the idea that one may (as many do) draw a contrast between two putative forms of self-awareness, minimal and high, the idea of these four types of creatures can also help illustrate some of the implications of the thesis that consciousness necessarily involves at least some form of self-awareness.

There were, you may remember, two versions of that thesis. According to the weak version, all conscious *entities* are self-aware; according to the strong version, all conscious *states* are states of self-awareness. The weak version rules out the existence of creatures like Trump, but allows for the possibility of the other three types of creatures. The strong version, which Zahavi attributes to Sartre, in ruling out the existence of any conscious state that is not a state of self-awareness, also rules out the existence of creatures like Trump and Marie Antoinette. Since on my reading Sartre denies even the weak version of the thesis, it is also part of my reading that he allows for the possibility that even creatures like Trump exist.

Leaving historical and exegetical concerns aside for a moment: What is the philosophical import of this thesis? What could a creature like Trump actually be like? Why might it matter whether creatures of that kind might in principle exist?

Whether or not you think that creatures like Trump can in principle exist, whether or not, in other words, you think that to be conscious is ipso facto to be aware of oneself as such, will determine the kind of constraints that you think an account of self-awareness must satisfy.

If, for instance, you think that consciousness necessarily involves at least a minimal form of self-awareness (if you think that all conscious creatures are at least like Tinnitus), then you may think that all that is required in order to explain fully the capacity to be aware of oneself as such is an explanation of how higher forms of self-awareness can be attained on the basis of minimal self-awareness. Depending on how you think of minimal self-awareness, the specific form of your account will vary. The key point for our purposes is that the idea that there is a minimal form of self-awareness necessitated by consciousness suggests that the task of accounting for higher forms of self-awareness is the task of addressing the question: What cognitive resources must be at work in order for a creature that has a capacity of being in states of minimal self-awareness to be in higher states of self-awareness? Or: How can higher forms of self-awareness be attained on the basis of minimal forms of self-awareness?

If, on the other hand, you do not think that consciousness necessarily involves even minimal forms of self-awareness, then you'll think that even minimal forms of self-awareness stand in need of explanation. And, for someone who does not think that consciousness necessarily involves self-awareness, pending such an explanation of minimal forms of self-awareness, an account of higher forms of self-awareness on the basis of minimal forms of self-awareness fails to fulfill its explanatory goal. It amounts to saying that creatures that are capable of higher forms of self-awareness are capable thereof because they're capable of minimal forms of self-awareness, without explaining how they're capable of minimal forms of self-awareness. And indeed, there is a tendency in the literature to model minimal self-awareness on perception (on the idea of a sense of self, of a background feeling of mineness, of a non-conceptual first-personal content), and to think that being in higher states of self-awareness consists in coming to grasp, in a more robust, or direct, or explicit, or thematic way, what was an essentially first-personal content that was in any case always already available in a minimal form.

To put it in yet a different way, if the question is: *How is self-awareness possible?* the family of answers that go in hand with the idea that consciousness necessarily involves some form of self-awareness often takes a form like the following one: being aware of anything at all involves being minimally aware of oneself as such, and being aware of oneself as such in the more robust sense that is our ultimate explanatory target just involves transforming that minimal form of self-awareness into a stronger form of self-awareness (by making explicit what was implicit or tacit, through the conceptual uptake of a non-conceptual first-personal content, by thematizing as the object of an intentional act something about which one was already minimally aware, by turning one's attention to what one was only peripherally aware of before). And yet, if self-awareness is not a necessary condition of consciousness, this answer is not a good one. For, while all the explanatory work is done by the notion of a minimal form of self-awareness, the latter is not one that is accounted for, but is merely postulated on the basis of the thesis that consciousness implies some form of self-awareness.

Thus, what lends interest to the exegetical controversy between the standard reading and the one that I propose is that, if the preceding argument is correct, and if the thesis that consciousness requires self-awareness is incorrect, the position that the standard reading attributes to Sartre is one that would commit him, and anyone who might endorse the view that he advocates in *The Transcendence of the Ego*, to a misconception of the form that an adequate explanation of self-awareness ought to take.

## Sartre's conception of the relationship between consciousness and self-awareness

In the previous section, I described the distinction between what I have been calling the standard reading of Sartre's *The Transcendence of the Ego* and an alternative. As we saw, that difference turns on the thesis that self-awareness is a necessary condition of consciousness: if the standard reading is correct, Sartre endorsed a strong version of that thesis, according to which all conscious states are ipso facto states of self-awareness. My main aim in this chapter is to show that that reading is incorrect, and to bring into view the philosophical importance of the matter.

The standard reading often relies on a passage in the first part of the essay, in the course of which Sartre makes claims that seem to provide unequivocal evidence in its favor, claims to the effect, for instance, that "*the type of existence of consciousness is to be consciousness of itself*" (Sartre 2003, p. 97 (23–24); emphasis added). The purpose of this section is to show that, in spite of what an initial reading of that passage may suggest, the standard reading is textually problematic. I will present three arguments for this claim. First, the standard reading renders Sartre's goal in *The Transcendence of the Ego* at worst unintelligible, and at best trivial. Second, there are passages of Sartre's text in which he seems explicitly to reject the thesis that the standard reading ascribes to him, namely that all conscious states are states of self-awareness. Third, while, as I just noted, there are statements in Sartre's text that might on a first approximation seem to work as conclusive evidence of the correctness of the standard reading, the interpretation that is required in order for those claims indeed to serve as evidence for the standard reading is ruled out by other claims that he makes in the context in which they occur. In addition, in the final part of the section, I will provide a positive reading of those claims, one that accounts for Sartre's motivation for making them while showing that, correctly understood, they do not lend support to the standard reading.

## *The Ego is "outside" consciousness: Sartre's goal in* The Transcendence of the Ego

Sartre announces his goal in the first paragraph of the essay:

> For the majority of philosophers the Ego is an "inhabitant" of consciousness. Some assert its formal presence within the "*Erlebnisse*" (the experiences), as an empty principle of unification. Others—for the most part psychologists—think they can identify its material presence, as a center of desires and acts, in each moment of our psychic life. We would like to show that the Ego is neither formally nor materially inside[3] consciousness: it is outside, in the world; it is a being of the world, like the Ego of others.
>
> (Sartre 2003, p. 93 (13))

What might it mean to say that the Ego is not inside consciousness, that it is outside, in the world? Within Sartre's conceptual framework, the notion of the Ego is the notion of the self; it is conceived as the agent of actions and as the bearer of states and qualities. He writes:

> The I is the Ego as the unity of actions. The Me is the Ego as the unity of states and qualities. The distinction that one establishes between these two aspects of a single reality appears to us purely functional, not to say grammatical.
>
> (Sartre 2003, p. 107 (44))

Now, in a footnote early on in the text, Sartre explains that he uses "consciousness" in the triple sense of the totality of consciousness, of monad, and of each single state or moment of consciousness (Sartre 2003, p. 95 (16)). Of these three senses of "consciousness," the one that is primarily at work in the goal-defining claim is the sense of consciousness as a single state or moment of consciousness. That this is the case can be seen from the fact that Sartre's arguments for the view that the Ego is outside consciousness are presented in the form of answers to the question whether the "I think" does in fact accompany all our representations (Sartre 2003, p. 94 (15)). In addressing this question, Sartre is addressing the question whether the Ego is in fact present, in some form or another, in each of our representations, in each of our conscious states.

Accordingly, Sartre's goal of showing that the Ego is outside consciousness is tantamount to showing that the Ego is not in fact part of all our conscious states. But insofar as the notion of the Ego is the notion of the self as the agent of actions and the bearer of states and qualities, the view that the Ego is not "inside" each of our conscious states amounts to the view that not all conscious states are states of self-awareness. Contrary to what the standard reading suggests, Sartre's goal in the essay is therefore to defend a claim whose immediate implication is that consciousness does not require self-awareness (i.e. that we are like neither Narcissus or Tinnitus).

In the face of this objection, it is open to the standard reader to suggest that "Egoless" is not the same as "lacking any form of self-awareness." The idea would be that, when Sartre talks about the Ego, what he has in mind are higher forms of self-awareness of the kind that you and I have when, say, we're deliberating about important, potentially life-changing decisions. Correspondingly, when Sartre raises the question of the relation between the Ego and consciousness, what he has in mind would be a question about the relationship between being conscious and being capable of such higher forms of self-awareness. Thus—the standard reader's story would go—Sartre's view would be that, although consciousness necessitates a minimal form of self-awareness, it does not necessitate a higher form of self-awareness, and what he announces in the opening paragraph of the essay as his goal would be the defense of the second part of that view: it would be just the idea that consciousness does not necessitate higher forms of self-awareness. In terms of the forms of consciousness described in the previous section, the standard reader's position would be that the goal announced by Sartre in the opening paragraph of his paper would be to show that our mental life is not like that of Narcissus, but it would also be part of Sartre's view that our mental lives is like the mental life of Tinnitus.[4]

But while this move is indeed open to the partisan of the standard reading, it does not much advance her cause. For it is problematic on two counts. First, the view that not all conscious states involve higher forms of self-awareness (the view that our mental lives and indeed the mental lives of any conscious creature is not like that of Narcissus) is uncontroversial, so this interpretive strategy renders Sartre's goal in *The Transcendence of the Ego* perfectly trivial. Second, on such an interpretive strategy, understanding Sartre's goal in the essay requires mobilizing a distinction between higher and minimal forms of self-awareness, a distinction that, as I shall endeavor to show, is absent from the whole essay.

Although these considerations do not conclusively show the incorrectness of the standard reading, they have at least the following upshot: since the standard reading generates a number of exegetical puzzles, we can begin to see that the textual evidence for the standard reading is not as conclusive as it may originally have seemed. Endorsing the standard reading comes at a high exegetical cost, and an alternative interpretation that does not impose such an exegetical burden would seem by default preferable.

### Consciousness does not require an I; furthermore, the I would be the death of consciousness: not all conscious states are states of self-awareness

As I mentioned in the previous section, in the first part of Sartre's essay, he argues that the Ego is "outside consciousness," and he does this by raising and addressing the question whether the "I think" does in fact accompany all of our representations.

By the end of section 1(A) of the essay, Sartre concludes that the "I think" does not in fact accompany all our representations:

> [T]he phenomenological conception of consciousness renders the unifying and individualizing role of the I (i.e. the active face of the Ego) totally useless. On the contrary it is consciousness that makes possible the unity and the personality of my I (i.e. Ego). The transcendental I (the pure Ego), therefore, has no reason for being.
> (Sartre 2003, p. 97 (23))

He then proceeds to argue that for the "I think" to accompany all our representations would be "the death of consciousness." Thus, by the end of section 1(A), he concludes:

> all the results of phenomenology are threatened by ruin if the I is not, in the same way that the world, a relative existent [i.e. a transcendent one], that is to say, an object for consciousness.
> (Sartre 2003, p. 99 (26))

Now, earlier in that first section, Sartre had listed the implications of those claims:

1. the transcendental field becomes impersonal, or, if one prefers, pre-personal, it is without I;
2. the I only appears on the level of humanity [of the person], and it is only a face of the Me, the active face [of the Me];
3. that the "I think" can accompany our representations because it appears on the surface of a unity toward the creation of which it has not contributed, and that it is on the contrary this prior unity that makes it possible;
4. that it is possible to wonder whether personality (even the abstract personality of an I) is a necessary accompaniment of a consciousness, or whether it is not possible to conceive of entirely impersonal consciousnesses.

(Sartre 2003, p. 96 (19))

These passages suggest that the standard reading is incorrect. For, as we saw, the standard reading is one that rules out the possibility of the existence of creatures like Trump, creatures who lack all forms of self-awareness and who consequently have only a purely impersonal form of consciousness. But, when Sartre writes about consciousness as a pre-personal or impersonal field, when he says that it is without I, when he suggests that we ought to wonder whether it is not possible to consider entirely impersonal consciousnesses, he is suggesting not only that consciousness does not necessarily involve self-awareness in the sense that not all conscious states are states of self-awareness; he is in fact making the stronger claim that nothing in the nature of consciousness rules out the possibility that there be Trump-like creatures.

Of course these passages do not conclusively establish the incorrectness of the standard reading. As I already mentioned in passing, and as we will see in more detail in the next section, there are passages in which Sartre seems to endorse the thesis directly that consciousness necessarily involves self-awareness. In light of this, the conclusion we're entitled to draw from this section is only that even the passages that lend support to the standard reading are, taken on their own, inconclusive. No local claim in *The Transcendence of the Ego* is sufficient, on its own, to establish the correctness or incorrectness of the standard reading.

## "*Consciousness is consciousness of itself...*"

As I just mentioned, Sartre argues for the view that the presence of the I inside consciousness would "be harmful." However, he makes a series of statements that seem to commit him to the view that consciousness essentially involves some form of self-awareness. Since this is the strongest textual evidence for the standard reading, it is worth considering them and the passage in which they occur in some detail:

(i) But, furthermore, this superfluous I is harmful. If it existed it would tear consciousness from itself, it would divide it, it would slide in every consciousness like an opaque blade. The transcendental I is the death of consciousness.

(ii) Indeed, the existence of consciousness is an absolute because consciousness is consciousness of itself. That is to say that the type of existence of consciousness is to be consciousness of itself. It has consciousness of itself insofar as it is consciousness of a transcendent object.

(iii) Everything is therefore clear and lucid in consciousness: the object is in front of it with its characteristic opacity, but consciousness, it is purely and simply consciousness of being consciousness of this object, that is the law of its existence.

(iv) One must add that this consciousness of consciousness—outside of the case of reflective consciousness, on which we'll insist later on—is not positional, that is to say that consciousness is not for itself its object. Its object is outside of it by nature and it is for this reason that in a single act it posits it and grasps it.

(v)   It does not know itself except as an absolute interiority. We will call such a consciousness: first degree consciousness or ir-reflective consciousness.
(vi)  We ask: is there a place for an I in this consciousness? The answer is clear: obviously not.
(vii) Indeed, this I is neither the object (since *ex hypothesi* it is interior [i.e. it would be in consciousness]), nor is it of consciousness, since it is something for consciousness, not a translucent quality of consciousness, but, in a certain sense, its inhabitant. Indeed, the I, with its personality, is, however formal, however abstract we take it to be, like a center of opacity [. . .].
(viii) Thus if one introduces this opacity inside consciousness, one thereby destroyed the very fertile definition [of consciousness] that we provided earlier, one fixes it, one obscures it, it is no longer a spontaneity, it carries within itself a germ of opacity.
(Sartre 2003, p. 98 (23–25))

What could Sartre mean by claims by (ii) and (iii), if not that the type of existence of consciousness, the law of its existence, is to require self-awareness? In the remainder of this section, I will provide three textual arguments and a positive reading of that claim in order to show that its intended meaning could not have been that consciousness requires self-awareness.

*Consciousness necessarily involves self-awareness . . . therefore, if the I were immanent it would be the death of consciousness?*

The first argument bears on the inconsistency between, on the one hand, the argumentative role of claims (ii) and (iii) to the effect that "consciousness is consciousness of itself" and, on the other hand, the standard reading, according to which they are to be read as the idea that consciousness necessarily involves some form of self-awareness.

The idea is simple: Sartre makes these claims as part of an argument whose conclusion is that the I cannot be inside of, or inherent to, part of, consciousness. Yet if we read the claim that consciousness is consciousness of itself as the claim that consciousness always involves self-awareness, we are saddled with the paradox that, in order to argue that the I is not inherent to consciousness, in order to argue that the I is not part of the content of every conscious state, Sartre would be relying on the claim that consciousness necessarily involves self-awareness, that the self is part of the content of every conscious state.

*Consciousness necessarily involves self-awareness . . . of a non-positional kind?*

On (iv), Sartre argues that consciousness is non-positionally consciousness of itself. He writes, once again:

[T]his consciousness of consciousness ... is not positional, that is to say that consciousness is not for itself its object. Its object is outside of it by nature and it is for this reason that in a single act it posits it and grasps it.

(Sartre 2003, p. 98 (24))

But note that, if the "consciousness of" in "consciousness of itself" is the "of" of "intentionality," then the idea of a non-positional consciousness, the idea of a consciousness of something that is not its object, is incoherent. This is not to deny that classical phenomenology contains the resources to accommodate the idea of peripheral forms of awareness, where an agent is simultaneously aware of various things at the same time, albeit of some more intensely or attentively than of some others. But in these cases, the objects of awareness are still, as such, *objects* of awareness; they are still within the intentional horizon of the relevant mental episodes. Furthermore, to the extent that they are objects of awareness, they are posited as objects. Indeed if, as Sartre says in the same statement, *positing* and *grasping* an object are a "single act," then where there is no positing of an object, there is no grasping it. Thus, that the "consciousness of itself" of which he is speaking is non-positional means that it is a "consciousness of itself" that does not "grasp itself." But a "consciousness of itself" that does not grasp itself is a "consciousness of itself" that is not aware of itself. Consequently, the claim that consciousness is non-positionally conscious of itself cannot be interpreted in the way that the standard reading requires, as the claim that consciousness necessarily involves self-awareness.

## *Ir-reflective . . . self-awareness?*

On (v), Sartre characterizes the type of consciousness of which he says that it is *consciousness of itself* as *ir-reflective*. Now, on the standard reading, the claim that consciousness is consciousness of itself is the claim that consciousness involves self-awareness. But a consciousness that involves self-awareness just is a reflective consciousness. So the standard reading renders Sartre's ir-reflectivity claim absurd.

To put it differently, the standard reading, which requires interpreting claims (ii) and (iii) as claims to the effect that consciousness necessarily involves some form of self-awareness, renders the ir-reflectivity claim (v) unintelligible. For the idea that consciousness necessarily involves even a minimal form of self-awareness is the idea that consciousness necessarily involves not only the minimal type of reflectivity that an agent can have when having a thought about itself without recognizing itself as such (e.g., the kind of reflectivity that animals that fail the mirror test have in seeing themselves in the mirror), but even the much more substantive kind of reflectivity at work in states that involves the recognition of oneself as such.

On the reading that I advocate, on the other hand, the ir-reflectivity claim can be easily accounted for. When Sartre writes about ir-reflective forms of consciousness, his point is exactly what it seems to be: that such states do not involve even a minimal form of self-awareness; they do not involve any form of reflectivity at all.[5]

*What does Sartre means when he says that consciousness is consciousness of itself?*

But how can we reconcile the claim that the type of existence of consciousness is to be conscious of itself with the idea that there are ir-reflective, non-positional conscious states? If the claim that the type of existence of consciousness is to be consciousness of itself does not mean that consciousness is necessarily aware of itself, then what does it mean?

Let's begin by trying to understand the argument that Sartre is sketching in that context. The upshot of the argument is meant to be that, if the I is "inside" consciousness, if it is part of consciousness in any way other than as its object, then it would be harmful. The argument itself is formulated in terms of the metaphor of light. Consciousness is conceived like light that shines on its intentional objects. It is thus described as essentially luminous or translucid, and its objects are described as opaque. The idea is that the I cannot be part of consciousness because "however formal, however abstract we may suppose it to be, in order for it to be a part of consciousness it would have to act like the center of opacity" (see (vii) above) and thus the light of consciousness would not be able to shine on to its objects: if being aware of transcendent objects required being aware of representations thereof and of ourselves as thinkers of those representations, we would not be able to reach "all the way out" to the objects themselves. The light would shine on our opaque representations of ourselves and the contents of our minds, and by the same token would fail to reach transcendent objects.

As an argument, this is of course too metaphorical to be particularly helpful. But it does give us an exegetical clue for understanding what Sartre means when he says that the type of existence of consciousness is to be conscious of itself. That and similar claims are meant by Sartre to be not only consistent with, but consequent upon, the fact that "everything is clear and lucid inside consciousness." They are meant to be, in contemporary terms, consequent upon the transparency of consciousness, understood as the view that consciousness is first and foremost world-directed, that mental content is not a primary object of consciousness, that being aware of the world and worldly things does not in any way require being aware of mental content as such. This works as an exegetical clue insofar as it sets constraints on the kind of interpretation that can be given to the claim that the type of existence of consciousness is to be consciousness of itself: it rules out any interpretation that would suggest that being conscious requires being aware of the contents of consciousness as such, or of the self as being aware of those contents.

A second clue to understanding Sartre's claim that the type of existence of consciousness is to be conscious of itself is the ambiguity of the term "consciousness." As we saw, there is a distinction to be drawn between consciousness in the sense of "conscious state or episode," in the sense of "conscious entity," and in the sense of "field of consciousness" (Sartre 2003, p. 94 (15)). As we have also seen, the interpretation according to which Sartre's idea is that any state of consciousness involves awareness of that state is ruled out (it contradicts the ir-reflectivity, the non-positionality, and the transparency claims). However, the interpretation according to which Sartre's idea is that conscious entities are in some sense conscious of "the field of consciousness" is not ruled out. The only constraint is that the sense in which it is conscious of the field of consciousness not be the sense in which they are conscious of the intentional, posited, objects of those states. What sense of consciousness is that?

It helps to bring in and develop the spatial metaphor. As I've been saying, we can think of consciousness as a field.[6] There's nothing peculiar in the idea of perceptual experiences in which one is not conscious of space as such, in which one is not actively, or explicitly, or thematically thinking about space, even though one is, in a very different sense, quite conscious or aware of space. Consider, for instance, the following situation. While you wait for the pedestrian light to signal that it is your turn to cross the street, you go over the list of things you need to buy at the grocery store. The light changes. You begin to cross, mindful of the environing traffic, mindful of the other pedestrians walking in your direction, careful to avoid stepping on the tiny little beast (is that a dog?) that someone's proudly walking on a leash. All the while you continue to go over your shopping list. All the while you are conscious of your environing space. And yet, at no point do you have a single thought about space as such, even about your environing space. You see things to be avoided, pathways to walk through, and so forth, but you don't have a single thought about space as such at all. In fact, even if you entirely lacked, as the little dog that you crossed paths with probably does, the capacity to think of space *as such*, it would still make sense to say of you, as it does of the little dog, that you were "conscious" or "aware of space." Although crucially, the sense in which you and the little dog could said to be "conscious of" space in such a situation is very different from the sense in which you can be said to be "conscious of," say, the taste of the coffee that you're actively savoring right now. The latter is the "of" of intentionality, of awareness of whatever object one is occurrently thinking about (in broad senses of "object" and "thinking"). The former isn't.

As it is with space in these cases, we may think, so it is with consciousness. In being conscious of an object, consciousness is conscious of what is within "its field." On these grounds it can be said, speaking very loosely, to be consciousness of itself: it is conscious of the objects present in the field of consciousness, and in that sense may be said to be "conscious" of "the field of consciousness." But it does not grasp itself; it is not conscious of itself thematically, or positionally, or as an object; it is not reflectively conscious of itself; the relevant conscious individual is not aware of itself.

On this way of hearing the claim that consciousness is consciousness of itself, the claim is not a very informative one. In the context of an argument for the transparency of consciousness, Sartre's point is merely that to be conscious is to be conscious of what is given "in" consciousness. The point is not that conscious creatures, insofar as they are conscious of things in the world, can be said to be conscious of what is "in" their minds, and thereby conscious "of their minds." To insist, in the context of an argument whose conclusion is that there is "no place for the I inside consciousness" that the presence of the I inside consciousness would be, as Sartre dramatically puts it, the death of consciousness, the emphasis is rather meant to be on the fact that conscious creatures are conscious, positionally conscious, of the things of which they are conscious, and that they can only be said to be conscious of themselves insofar as they are "conscious of" what is given "in" consciousness, in a sense of "conscious of" that is not, once again, that of intentionality, and which therefore does not warrant the idea that consciousness always involves self-awareness.

## Conclusion: Sartre on consciousness and self-awareness

In the last section, I provided a series of arguments against the view, characteristic of the standard reading, that it is part of Sartre's position in *The Transcendence of the Ego* that all conscious states involve at least a minimal form of self-awareness.

First, I argued that Sartre's project in that essay, the project of showing that the Ego is outside consciousness, is the project of showing that consciousness does not necessarily involve self-awareness. In the face of this fact, it is open to the standard reader to argue that there is a distinction between minimal (Egoless) and higher (Ego-involving) forms of self-awareness, and to argue that Sartre's explicit goal is only to defend the view that consciousness does not necessarily involve *higher* forms of self-awareness (that not all conscious creatures are like Narcissus), although it is also part of his view that consciousness essentially involves minimal forms thereof (that all conscious creatures are like Tinnitus). The problem with this way of reading Sartre's essay is twofold: first, since the view that consciousness essentially involves higher forms of self-awareness (the view that all conscious creatures are like Narcissus) is implausible, this way of reading Sartre renders his goal in the essay trivial; second, it involves drawing a distinction between higher and lower forms of self-awareness that is absent from Sartre's text.

The partisan of the standard reading might attempt to insist that, contrary to what I just suggested, this distinction is not absent from Sartre's text. Contrary to what I suggest, Sartre's idea of an Egoless consciousness would not be the idea of a consciousness that lacks self-awareness, but the idea of a consciousness that lacks a higher form of self-awareness. The reference to an ir-reflective consciousness whose "type of existence" is to be "*consciousness of itself being consciousness of an object*" would be precisely a reference to an Egoless form of consciousness that involves a minimal type of self-awareness (like the type of consciousness of Tinnitus). Yet this interpretation, I have argued, is also rendered implausible by the texts. The reason is, once again, twofold: first, in the course of arguing that the I is outside consciousness, Sartre explains that one of the implications of that claim is that one cannot rule out the possibility of purely impersonal forms of consciousness that do not even have the abstract personality of an I; second, considered in context, Sartre's claim that the type of existence of consciousness is to be consciousness of itself cannot be interpreted as the claim that consciousness involves self-awareness, even of a minimal kind, since Sartre uses that claim as a premise for an argument to the effect that the I, however formal, cannot be an intrinsic part of consciousness, and since he characterizes this most basic type of consciousness as both a non-positional consciousness of itself and as ir-reflective.

Finally, I have provided a positive interpretation of Sartre's claim to the effect that consciousness is consciousness of itself. In making that claim, Sartre merely means to be acknowledging the fact that being conscious of anything at all involves being conscious of what is given "in" consciousness, much like one can say of any conscious creature capable of perception and motion that it is conscious of the space it moves in. In neither case does the relevant sense of "being conscious of" imply that the relevant agent is conscious of what it is thus conscious of (consciousness/space) *as such*. Sartre's point, to insist, is not that consciousness necessarily involves some form of self-awareness.[7]

\*

In the first section, I suggested that Sartre's thesis, according to which consciousness does not necessarily involve self-awareness, has an important philosophical implication: self-awareness is a cognitive achievement. So long as the possibility for purely impersonal forms of consciousness (like the form of consciousness characteristic of Trump) is not ruled out, the starting point of an account of higher forms of self-awareness must be the capacity to be aware of objects in general, not the capacity to be in conscious states that involve minimal forms of self-awareness. The reason is that so long as such a possibility (i.e., of Trump-like creatures) is not ruled out, even minimal forms of self-awareness, if such there be, stand in just as much need of explanation as higher forms of self-awareness do. Consequently, their possession by conscious creatures cannot be presupposed or taken for granted within the context of an explanation of self-awareness. So long as the possibility of impersonal forms of consciousness is not ruled out, accounting for self-awareness in terms of more basic or minimal forms of self-awareness amounts to displacing rather than accomplishing the important explanatory task, the task of accounting for the first-personal or "self-involving" character of states of self-awareness.

\*

There are three important implications of the view that self-awareness is a cognitive achievement, implications that it would be the next major task to explore and develop. First, the idea that there is a minimal form of self-awareness that is intrinsic to consciousness can suggest a conception of self-awareness as a unitary phenomenon, a picture according to which for any conscious state to be a state of self-awareness is for it to involve awareness of a certain type of object, "a self," or for it to involve the actualization of a single, general capacity for self-awareness. On the contrary, the view that self-awareness is a cognitive achievement suggests a conception of self-awareness as a non-unitary phenomenon, a picture according to which there may be a range of distinct forms of self-awareness (e.g., proprioceptive self-awareness, "practical" self-awareness, psychological self-awareness), and which requires that, to the extent that it is possible, each of these forms of self-awareness be given an independent account.[8] A second implication, as Sartre himself notes in the conclusion of his essay, is the exclusion of a conception of our ability to represent minds that leads to solipsism (Sartre 2003, p. 130 (84–85)): the idea that consciousness necessarily involves at least a minimal form of self-awareness suggests that our awareness of other minded creatures as such has the form of the recognition that they are like us, the recognition that, in addition to having observable bodies, they also have unobservable minds. On the contrary, the idea that consciousness does not necessitate self-awareness leaves open the possibility that there be no priority between our self-understanding and our understanding of others as thinking creatures; it leaves open the possibility that the cognitive resources required to represent others as minded and to be aware of oneself as the subject of psychological states are the same. Thirdly, the view that self-awareness is a cognitive achievement also has important epistemological implications: it opens up the possibility that our awareness of much of our mental lives does not involve the type of immediacy and infallibility that a traditional, Cartesian conception of the mind would suggest, the possibility that, as Sartre himself suggests, our knowledge of ourselves is much more similar to our knowledge of others than has been traditionally accepted. These are not issues that can be pursued here, but further, in-depth work on Sartre's views about consciousness and self-awareness has the potential to illuminate them.

# Notes

1 Note, lastly, that I just switched from talking about our topic as a capacity, to talking about it as a "thing" of sorts; from the capacity that I have been calling "self-awareness," to the thing that I have been calling "self." Which one is our topic, properly speaking? I am partial to thinking primarily in terms of the capacities that certain organisms have, rather than to think of "selves" or "Egos." The latter, it seems to me, are not distinct types of things, but to borrow an expression from Castañeda, certain types of things regarded under a certain guise. The reason that I am partial to thinking in terms of capacities is that I think it can keep us clear of various metaphysical and philosophical pitfalls (think, for instance, of Anscombe's claim that "I" does not refer). Sartre, however, tends not to think in terms of capacities but in terms of entities, not in terms of self-awareness but in terms of the Ego (or the *cogito*, the I and the me, consciousness and the self); he writes of "things" or "entities." Since, accordingly, I cannot fully avoid this reifying way of speaking, I will continue to switch back and forth between talk of consciousness and self-awareness as capacities and to talk about them as things.

2 There are two ways in which we may conceive of the clinical condition called "tinnitus." Since which one of them we favor determines how we conceive this case, it is important to distinguish between them and to indicate which one should serve as the model here. We may think that people who suffer from tinnitus are always hearing the ringing in their ear, not just in the sense that whenever they pay attention to it they will be able to hear it, but also in the sense that it is impossible for them not to hear it, even if they choose not to pay attention to it. On the alternative model, the condition is such that people can hear it whenever they pay attention to it, but whenever they are sufficiently absorbed in any activity or whenever there are sufficiently strong competing aural stimuli, the ringing sound simply disappears completely from the person's field of consciousness. The way of thinking about the condition which is meant to serve as model for the type of creature in question is the former case, that is, the one in which the person is always conscious of a ringing sound.

3 The emphasis is Sartre's.

4 This revised version of the standard reading corresponds to the position defended (and attributed to Sartre) by Zahavi in *Self-Awareness and Alterity*, especially chapter 2 (Zahavi, 1999).

5 The partisan of the standard reading might be tempted to respond that the ir-reflectivity claim is about the question whether an *act* of reflection is involved in the type of consciousness that Sartre is discussing, rather than about the question whether such a type of consciousness has *the formal property* of reflectivity. In this case, there would be no incoherence in the idea of a form of consciousness that is reflective in the sense that it involves *self*-awareness, but ir-reflective in that it does not involve an *act* of reflection. The problem with this response is that it rests on the assumption that a state of consciousness can be reflective in the formal sense without involving an act of reflection. But, as we shall see in the next section, this is ruled out by Sartre's conception of consciousness, and more specifically by the thesis that consciousness is "translucid."

6 In the technical phenomenological sense, the concept of consciousness as a field is the concept of consciousness as the region of being that is the residuum of

the phenomenological reduction, and which constitutes the phenomenologist's field of investigation. See, for instance, Husserl (1982 §33, p. 66 [59] and §50, pp. 112–114 [93–95]).
7 A supplementary argument, but one whose exposition would require a paper of its own, is that the conception of consciousness that the standard reading attributes to Sartre can be shown to be much closer to Husserl's 1913s views than to his 1901 views in this regard. Since one of Sartre's goals is to defend the 1901 view against the 1913 view, this also suggests that the standard reading misrepresents Sartre's views about consciousness. See, in particular, Husserl (1982, §57).
8 Thus, for instance, in the second part of the essay, where Sartre describes the constitution of the Ego (i.e., how Ego-involving thoughts are possible), he provides relatively independent accounts of the kind of awareness that we have of our actions and thoughts on the one hand, and of our emotions and dispositions on the other.

## References

Husserl, E. (1982). *Ideas Pertaining to a Pure Phenomenology and to a Phenomenological Philosophy*, vol. I. (Kersten, E., trans.). Dordrecht: Kluwer.

Sartre, J.-P. (2003). *La Transcendance de l'ego*. Paris: VRIN.

Zahavi, D. (1999). *Self-Awareness and Alterity: A Phenomenological Investigation*. Evanston, IL: Northwestern University Press.

Zahavi, D. (2008). *Subjectivity and Selfhood: Investigating the First-person Perspective*. Cambridge, MA: MIT Press.

# 10 Perception and imagination
## A Sartrean account

*Uriah Kriegel*

**The perception/imagination distinction and Sartre**

Consider this very general question: What is the relationship between perception and imagination? When we consider this question, two facts pop out: (i) there is some commonality between the two, but (ii) there is a difference as well. Perception and imagination are alike in some respect(s), but also differ in some. The question is how to characterize the similarity and how to characterize the difference. Thus we may replace our single question with a pair: (Q1) What is the similarity between perception and imagination? (Q2) What is the dissimilarity between them?

These questions are still ambiguous, however, insofar as the terms "perception" and "imagination" are. The two nouns are most commonly used to denote putative *faculties* or *capacities*. These can be characterized in terms of the mental states they produce, or have the function of producing. Perception is the "faculty" that produces, or has the function of producing, perceptual states. Imagination is the faculty that produces, or has the function of producing, imaginative states. Thus Q1 and Q2 are best understood as ultimately about states (rather than faculties).

Imaginative states come in a several varieties.[1] One distinction is between imagining an object and imagining awareness of the object: I can imagine a dog or imagine seeing a dog.[2] Another distinction is between propositional and "objectual" imagining: I can imagine that Lena Dunham is elected president or I can imagine a purple dog. It is sometimes claimed that the relationship between objectual and propositional imagining is analogous to that between perceiving and believing (Currie and Ravenscroft 2002; McGinn 2004). But this is misleading. It is true that both the following are admissible reports of imaginative states:

(1)   *S* imagines *O*.
(2)   *S* imagines that *p*.

But a corresponding duality applies to perception reportage:

(1*)  *S* perceives *O*.
(2*)  *S* perceives that *p*.

The relationship between 1 and 2 is analogous to that between 1* and 2*. In both 2 and 2*, a propositional attitude is reported, but one which conceptually involves a sensuous dimension. By this I mean, it is part of the *concepts* of perceiving-that and imagining-that that some sensory experiences take place when a subject perceives-that or imagines-that.[3] One might hold that occurrent beliefs or judgments also involve sensory experiences, but if so it is not *part of the concept* of belief or judgment that such experiences must take place. In that respect, believing is more analogous to conceiving, a kind of purely intellectual exercise of an imagination-like capacity. When one conceives that some water is not $H_2O$, one may experience sensory images of a watery substance, but it is not part of the *concept* of conceiving that such imagery must occur. In sum, my claim is that belief is to perception what conception is to imagination, not what propositional imagination is to objectual imagination. If we add:

(3)  S conceives that *p*
(3*)  S believes that *p*

we may say that the two series 1–2–3 and 1*–2*–3* parallel each other in a relevant sense.

The above distinctions reveal some ambiguity in Q1 and Q2. Here my focus will be on objectual perceptual and imaginative states—as opposed to propositional states or faculties/capacities. A further ambiguity concerns the type of similarity and dissimilarity we are interested in. Arguably, the most important similarities and differences between mental states concern (i) those pertaining to phenomenal character, in this case the subjective experience of perceiving and imagining, and (ii) those pertaining to functional role, in this case the role of perceiving and imagining within the subject's overall cognitive architecture. Both are important, but my concern in the present chapter is specifically with *phenomenal* (dis)similarity. Thus, my topic is the following pair of questions: ($Q1_p$) What is the phenomenal similarity between perceiving *O* and imagining *O*? ($Q2_p$) What is the phenomenal dissimilarity between perceiving *O* and imagining *O*?[4]

☙ ❧

Approaches to this issue can be usefully divided into three groups.[5] One traditional approach, more often implicit than argued for, is that perceiving and imagining are forsooth phenomenally indistinguishable. The only difference is extrinsic to the phenomenology: in the perceptual case the phenomenal state is accompanied by a belief that endorses its content, whereas in the imaginative case it is not.[6] Another approach, associated with Hume, allows for phenomenal difference between perception and imagination, but only one of *degree*.[7] The difference may concern phenomenal intensity, or resolution, or determinacy, but perceptual and imaginative experiences have the same *kind* of phenomenology. That is, they instantiate all the same phenomenal determinables, but differ with respect to instantiating their determinates. A third, more daring approach insists on a categorical or qualitative difference between perceptual and imaginative experience: there is a certain phenomenal determinable present in the one that is entirely absent from the other. We may call these the "no-difference" view, the "degree-difference" view, and the "kind-difference" view:

> (ND) There is no phenomenal difference between perceiving $O$ and imagining $O$.
> (DD) There is a phenomenal difference-in-degree ("quantitative" difference) between perceiving $O$ and imagining $O$.
> (KD) There is a phenomenal difference-in-kind (qualitative difference) between perceiving $O$ and imagining $O$.[8]

Historically, ND and DD have dominated philosophical thinking about perception and imagination. Through a battery of phenomenological arguments, however, Sartre develops a formidable case against them. In what follows, I will use these arguments, or suitably strengthened versions, as a springboard for a broadly Sartrean answer to $Q1_p$ and $Q2_p$.

Sartre's interest in the imagination in fact predates all his later, better-known philosophical concerns. His 1926 thesis for an École Normale Supérieure diploma was about the imagination. His thesis director, one H. Delacroix, was a series editor at the publishing house Alcan, and asked Sartre for a book on the imagination (Contat and Rybalka 1970, pp. 50, 55). Of the book Sartre ended up writing, to be titled *The Image*, Alcan agreed to publish only the first half (see de Beauvoir 1960, pp. 168–171), under the title *The Imagination* (Sartre 1936). The second half was published four years later by the prestigious publisher Gallimard as *The Imaginary* (1940). Both books are organized around the question of the relationship between images and perceptions. The first presents a critical survey of failed accounts of imagination along the lines of ND and DD, with a diagnosis of their underlying error. The second develops a positive account of imagination in a KD vein.

It is worth noting that Sartre lumps together under the rubric of "the image" a great variety of phenomena. Three will concern me here: images we willingly and deliberately conjure up, as when I decide to form an image of a smiling octopus; images that pop up in our mind uninvited and fade out soon thereafter, as when an image of my mother's face appears to me suddenly; and images pertaining to episodic memory of individual objects or events, as when I suddenly remember the first giraffe I saw at a zoo.[9] Let us call the first *imaginative experiences*, the second *phantasmagoric experiences*, and the third *mnemonic experiences*.[10] In comparing the phenomenology of perception and imagination, my concern will be primarily with imaginative experiences, though phantasmagoric and mnemonic experiences will play a role later on.[11]

## Against the "classical conception"

Surveying historical accounts of imagination, Sartre isolates a fundamental strand he calls the "classical conception." He identifies two central tenets in this classical conception.[12] The first is a conception of the image as an *object* rather than *act* of consciousness, hence a "thing" among others; this is what Sartre (1936, p. 5/2012, p. 6) calls "thingism" (*chosisme*), which amounts essentially to a sense datum account of imaginative experience. The other, which will be our focus, is the assimilation of imagination to perception; this is ND:

> We begin again with the assertion that sensation and image are identical in nature. We assert once more that an *isolated* image does not distinguish itself from an *isolated* perception. But this time the discrimination will be the product of a judgment-act (*acte judicatif*) of the mind.
> (Sartre 1936, p. 101/2012, p. 91; my translation, italics original)[13]

On this pernicious view, there is no essential difference between perceptual experience and imaginative experience considered intrinsically ("in isolation"). The only difference between the mind of the perceiver and the mind of the imaginer is in their second-order judgments about their experiences ("I am seeing a dog" vs "I am visualizing a dog"). These judgments must have certain *grounds*: there is a *reason* why one judges that one's experience is perceptual in some cases and that it is imaginative in others. It is part of the view Sartre considers that these judgments are based on interrelations among experiences (and standing beliefs).[14] When one's experience coheres well with surrounding experiences and standing beliefs and expectations—when it is *orderly*, if you will—it is judged to be perceptual. When it is disorderly and incongruent, it is judged to be imaginative.

By my count, Sartre offers at least seven arguments against this "classical conception" of imagination. But the core of his case consists in a quartet of epistemological arguments of the following form: if perceptual and imaginative experiences were phenomenally indistinguishable, and distinguished only by accompanying judgments about their cohesion, our knowledge of whether we are perceiving or imagining would be very different from the way it really is.

First, if my knowledge that the dog presented by my current experience is perceived, rather than imaginary, were based on assessment of the experience's cohesion with other experiences, it would be a complex and somewhat impressive epistemic achievement. But this is false to the epistemology:

> Rather than the nature of the image as such [i.e., as being an image] being revealed to us by immediate intuition, we must finally make use of a system of infinite references in order to affirm of a content that it is an image or a perception ... Nobody will accept that recourse to a system of infinite references is needed to establish the discrimination between an image and a perception. Let everyone consult their internal experience.
>
> (Sartre 1936, p. 102/2012, p. 93)

Bracketing certain hyperboles (e.g., implicating infinity), the basic idea is this. I know that I am imagining a dog not by comparing my experience to indefinitely many other experiences, but *immediately*, that is, without the mediation of any cognitive process of experience comparison. Call this the *argument from immediacy*: (1) we have immediate knowledge of whether we are perceiving or imagining; (2) if ND were true, we could not have such knowledge; so, (3) ND is false.[15]

Secondly, knowledge of whether I am imagining or perceiving is characterized not only by immediacy but also by a warranted feeling of certainty. Compare the judgments that $2 + 2 = 4$ and that there is salad for lunch. The former features a characteristic absent from the latter: a *feel of certainty*. Moreover, the feeling is not misplaced—one is warranted in having it. Such a warranted feeling of certainty appears also to characterize my current belief that I am seeing (and not merely imagining) a dog. But it is hard to see how it could have that characteristic if it were based on assessment of cohesion among complex, temporally extended series of experiences:

> the discriminative judgment will only ever be *probable* ... We thus arrive at a paradoxical conclusion: far from the deep nature of the image being revealed to us by an immediate and certain knowledge, we will *never* be *sure* that such and such psychic contents on such and such a day and such and such an hour were really truly an image. Introspection is entirely deprived of its rights.
>
> (Sartre 1936, p. 102/2012, p. 93)

Call this the *argument from certainty*: (1) our knowledge of whether we are perceiving or imagining exhibits a warranted feeling of certainty; (2) if ND were true, it would not; so, (3) ND is false.

Clearly, Sartre's central line of argument depends on a certain epistemology of first-person knowledge, whereby such knowledge is distinguished by special epistemic and psychological properties. There are of course deflationary accounts of self-knowledge that reject such a conception. Obviously, Sartre's case against ND falls apart if we adopt one of them. This is not the place to defend Sartre's epistemology of first-person knowledge, which arguably is a prerequisite for the kind of phenomenological inquiry he is engaged in. However, it bears stressing that nothing about this mode of argumentation requires that first-person knowledge be infallible, incorrigible, or otherwise extraordinarily enviable. It only requires that such knowledge be *distinctive*, that is, exhibit certain epistemic features absent in other kinds of knowledge. Furthermore, the claim need not be that this distinctive knowledge is *always* present when we introspect our perceptual and imaginary experiences; merely that it is present in ordinary or typical circumstances.[16] This too is not beyond controversy (what is?), but it is much more innocuous to presuppose.[17]

A third epistemological argument, then, appeals to the *effortlessness* of first-person knowledge. If establishing that one is perceiving rather than imagining required sustained comparison with many other experiences and meticulous evaluation of their cohesion, it would be quite effortful. But, says Sartre, "Who has ever made so much effort to distinguish an image from a perception?" (1936, p. 104/2012, p. 94) Call this the *argument from effort*.[18]

A final epistemological argument may be called the *argument from incongruence*, as it rests on Sartre's phenomenological analysis of surprising, incongruent perceptual experiences:

> I believe my friend Pierre to be in America. There I catch sight of him at the corner of the street. Will I tell myself "it's an image"? Not at all. My first reaction is to seek to find out how it is possible that he has already come back.
> (Sartre 1936, p. 106/2012, p. 96)

Pierre's presence on a Paris street is unexpected (read: inconsistent with standing expectations). It is incongruent (coheres poorly with other experiences and beliefs). But this creates no tendency to classify one's experience as imaginative.[19] This suggests that the experience has an independent phenomenal feature which "marks" it as perceptual, and which one picks up on regardless of one's other experiences and expectations.

ܔܢ

Might this phenomenal feature simply be the enhanced intensity or resolution of perceptual experiences, as DD maintains? Sartre's main argument against this is again epistemological:[20]

> For a sensation to cross the threshold of consciousness, it must have a minimum intensity. If images are of the same nature, they will have to have at least this intensity. But then won't we confuse them with sensations of the same intensity? And why does the image of a cannon-blast noise not appear as a weak but real cracking?
> (Sartre 1936, p. 93/2012, p. 84; my translation)

Consider sensory perception of Hume's "minimal sensibilia," say hearing the faintest audible sound of a piece of furniture cracking; compare it to an imaginative experience of a deafeningly loud cannon blast a meter away. On the one hand, it is unclear in what sense the former may be said to be "more intense" than the latter. Certainly it is not *louder*: we could not even be *aware* of imaginary sounds, says Sartre, if they were less "loud" than minimal audibilia. (This remark is consistent both with the idea that imaginary noises have a loudness greater than minimal and with the idea—as it seems to me, more plausible—that they do not have a loudness at all, but only an imaginary-loudness.) On the other hand, DD cannot allow that imagining a deafeningly loud cannon is as phenomenally intense as perceiving minimally audible cracking, since it uses phenomenal intensity to separate the two categories to begin with. Either way, DD is unable to explain how we can tell by introspection alone whether we are perceiving or imagining when the phenomenal intensity is the same.

The same sort of argument would apply to other putative differences of degree between perception and imagination. Consider the view that perception is just an experience that uses a higher-resolution format than imagination. This is certainly the case with typical instances. But of course one can manually stretch the corners of one's eyes to blur one's visual experience increasingly, without at any point the experience changing status from vision to visualization.[21] More generally, as Byrne puts it,

> for any episode of visualizing or recalling [a strawberry], it should be in principle possible to create a physical picture of a strawberry such that viewing the picture in certain conditions exactly reproduces the felt quality of visualizing or recalling. And this is what seems wrong [in Hume's view]: any way of degrading the picture, such as blurring, desaturating, dimming, and so on, just yields another *perceptual* experience, plainly [introspectively] discernable from visualizing or recalling.
> (Byrne 2010, p. 17)

In other words, it is hard to see why the characteristic degradedness of an imaginative experience could not be matched by an intentional, willful degradation of a perceptual experience.

Another epistemological problem with DD is that it is unclear how it can allow for mixed episodes, as when I perceive the moon's front side, craters and all, and simultaneously imagine its back side, smooth and even-surfaced. DD seems to imply that my overall experience should be of a vivid cratered-moon image superimposed upon a faint smooth-moon image. But if that were the case, my introspection would surely suggest to me that I am having a perception of a craterish moon; but in fact it suggests to me that I am having simultaneous perceptual and imaginative experiences.[22]

It might be objected that first-person knowledge of perception and imagination is based not on the phenomenal character of the relevant experiences themselves, but on the processes by which they are formed. Compare and contrast: when my visual cortex computes a 15° angle between two edges and produces a visual experience accordingly, I have no introspective insight into the process by which my experience was formed; but when I calculate 15 percent of the bill and form a thought about the proper tip, I am introspectively aware of at least some aspects of the calculation process involved. Accordingly, the visual experience feels in some sense passive, while the thought feels active. This is the old contrast between receptivity and spontaneity in our mental life. The objector suggests that this contrast applies to perception and imagination: the former feels passive and receptive, the latter active and spontaneous (see Kind 2001, §3). Thus, when I *imagine* a dog I undergo an introspectively accessible personal-level process we might call the "creative exercise of imagination"; no such process takes place when I *see* a dog. On the objector's suggestion, I can tell by introspection whether my current experience is imaginative or perceptual by registering the presence or absence of this personal-level process. No difference need be assumed between the phenomenal characters of the perceiving and the imagining *themselves*.

This objection would be particularly embarrassing to Sartre, since he is explicitly committed to spontaneity as a distinguishing mark of imagination (Sartre 1940/2004, Ch. 1 §4).[23] The obvious problem with it, however, is that it does not extend to mental images formed through sub-personal processes—what I have called above phantasmagoric experiences. When an unbidden image of a smiling octopus pops up in my mind, the process producing it is introspectively inaccessible to me—the popping-up of the image is something that happens to me, not something that I do. I feel receptive and passive rather than spontaneous and active. And yet I am perfectly capable of telling whether my experience is perceptual or phantasmagoric. So there must be a deeper dimension along which these two differ, which we may then reasonably assume also distinguishes perception and imagination.

In general, the notion that perception and imagination differ only with respect to degree (of vivacity, resolution, or what not) seems based on two ideas: that what makes an intentional state phenomenal is the *format* of representation it uses, and that perceptual and imaginative experiences use the same format. But Sartre vehemently rejects the format conception of phenomenality. He contrasts, in this context, awareness of public and mental images:

> in the case [of public images], when the strictly imaging awareness had disappeared, there remained a sensible residue one could describe: it was the painted canvas or the spot on the wall . . . [But with mental images,] when the imaging awareness is annihilated, its transcendent content is annihilated with it; there remains no residue one could describe . . . We therefore cannot hope to grasp this content by introspection.
>
> (Sartre 1940, p. 76/2004, p. 53; my translation)[24]

This passage anticipates Harman's (1990) rejection of "mental paint," an intrinsic, non-intentional format property of experiences.[25] It makes clear why Sartre cannot accept any account of the perception/imagination distinction that implies a central role for representational format.

One objection to Sartre's argumentation is that there is a more plausible version of ND that he ignores. All versions of ND distinguish perception from imagination on the basis of accompanying beliefs. But while the version Sartre considers appeals to second-order beliefs about what experience the subject has, another version appeals to first-order beliefs about the ontological status of the experience's object. A perceptual experience is accompanied by the belief that its object is real, an imaginative experience by the belief that its object is unreal. On this version of ND, we know which experience we are having simply by knowing which first-order belief accompanies it; this neutralizes Sartre's epistemological arguments. Ignoring this version of ND remains a major lacuna in Sartre's critique, which we will have to address later on.

Bracketing this lacuna for now, the upshot of Sartre's argumentation is clear: there is a phenomenal difference between perceptual and imaginative experiences, and it is not merely a ("quantitative") difference in *degree* of intensity, resolution, or so on. It is a qualitative difference between two *kinds* of experience. It is "a difference of nature" (Sartre 1936, p. 91/2012, p. 83), "an intrinsic distinction" (Sartre 1936, p. 146/2012, p. 134), between two *sui generis* ways intentional objects appear to the subject (Sartre 1940, p. 24/2004, p. 13).

What is this categorical difference between perceptual and imaginative experience? In the final chapter of *The Imagination*, Sartre articulates an *initial view* whose inspiration he finds in Husserl's *Ideen* (Husserl 1913). However, in the final pages of *The Imagination* Sartre argues for a need to go beyond this initial view, and in the opening chapter of *The Imaginary* (published already as part of Sartre 1938), he articulates a *refined view* that goes beyond Husserl. I am much more attracted to the initial view, which I present and develop in the next section. In the section after that, I will turn to Sartre's argument for refining his initial view and offer reasons to resist it.

## Sartre's attitudinal account

The initial view is formulated by Sartre in terms of the *manner*, or *way*, or *mode* of intentional directedness at an object. Here is a representative passage:

> The image of my friend Pierre is not a vague phosphorescence, a wake left in my consciousness by the perception of Pierre. It is a form of organized consciousness that relates, *in its manner*, to my friend Pierre. It is

one of the possible *ways of aiming* at the thing, Pierre . . . [Accordingly,] image is only a name for a certain *way that consciousness aims at its object.*
(Sartre 1936, p. 144/2012, pp. 132–133; italics mine)[26]

This passage raises two questions. First: how are we to *understand* this talk of manners and ways? (It would be nice to be able to "translate" this talk into the terminology of contemporary philosophy of mind.) Second: how can we *characterize* the difference between perceptual and imaginative manners or ways? (It would be nice to be told not only *that* the manners are different, but also *how* they are different.)

Sartre's talk of "manners" and "ways" of intentionally relating to an object may be understood in current-day terminology in terms of the distinction between *attitude* and *content*. Believing that $p$ and desiring that $p$ have the same content—they both represent that $p$. If beliefs and desires have intensity at all, we may stipulate that $S$ believes that $p$ and desires that $p$ with the same intensity. Still, they are clearly very different mental states.[27] What they differ in is attitude: the specific relation they bear to $p$ is different. Consciously desiring that $p$ presents $p$ to the subject very differently from consciously believing that p. The two cast $p$ under very different lights. This attitudinal difference is clearly categorical: there is no continuum that leads us from a belief-end to a desire-end.[28]

According to Sartre, the difference between perceiving and imagining is of the same sort—it is an *attitudinal* difference. When I perceive my dog and when I imagine my dog, the dog presented in my experience is the same, and the intensity with which he is presented *can* be the same, but *how* it is presented is completely different—as different as how $p$ is represented in belief and in desire. Sartre writes:

> The word "image" thus designates but the relation (*rapport*) that consciousness has to the object; in other words, it is a certain way the object has of appearing to consciousness, or if we prefer, a certain way consciousness has of giving itself an object. In truth, the expression "mental image" invites confusion. It would be better to say . . . "imaging consciousness of Pierre."
> (Sartre 1940, p. 17/2004, p. 7; my translation)[29]

Speaking of a mental image of Pierre is ambiguous as between describing (i) an awareness of a Pierre-image and (ii) an image-awareness of Pierre. Only the latter is accurate. For in the latter, the image term modifies the intentional act, not the intentional object. It correctly casts the property of *being imagistic* as an attitudinal property of one's awareness. Call this the *attitudinal account* of the (phenomenal) difference between perception and imagination.

There is a traditional (and quite natural) view according to which seeing $O$ and hearing $O$ have the same content but differ in their mode or way of representing O. One uses a *visual* mode of representing O, the other uses an *auditory* mode; the difference is categorical. Within this framework, a proponent of the attitudinal account would insist that there is also a certain attitudinal *commonality* among all six perceptual modalities of representation, a commonality not shared by imagining O. Something about all six kinds of perceptual experience *makes* them perceptual, and whatever that is, it separates them from non-perceptual attitudes, including imaginings. Here too, the difference is one of kind, not degree: imagining O is as categorically different from perceiving O as seeing O is from hearing O.

How can we *characterize* attitudinal differences? For example, how can we characterize the difference between the belief-ish way of representing and the desire-ish way? There are familiar *functional* distinctions between the "belief box" and its inferential role and the "desire box" and its motivational role. But given our phenomenological concern, we are seeking a *phenomenal* distinction between the two. (I am assuming here, along with many others, that beliefs and desires do have phenomenal properties, including attitudinal ones.[30]) One promising suggestion is that conscious believing involves *feeling it true that p* whereas conscious desiring involves *feeling it good that p*. L. J. Cohen develops this idea:

> Feeling it true that *p* may thus be compared with feeling it good that *p*. All credal feelings, whether weak or strong, share the distinctive feature of constituting some kind of orientation on the "True or false?" issue in relation to their propositional objects, whereas affective mental feelings, like those of anger or desire, constitute some kind of orientation on the "Good or bad?" issue.
> 
> (Cohen 1992, p. 11)

The same view is developed a century earlier by Franz Brentano. In Chapters 5–9 of Book II of his *Psychology from an Empirical Standpoint*, Brentano develops a systematic classification of mental phenomena based entirely on "different ways of being conscious of an object" (Brentano 1874, p. 201). A key difference is between cognitive acts of "judgment" and conative acts of "interest":

> If something can become the content of a judgment in that it can be accepted as true or rejected as false, it can also become the object of [interest], in that it can be agreeable (in the broadest sense of the word) as something good, or disagreeable as something bad.
> 
> (Brentano 1874, p. 239)

The difference, then, is that cognitive states such as belief represent their contents *as true*, whereas conative states such as desire represent theirs *as good* (in some suitably general sense). This distinction is attitudinal, not content-based. Compare:

(B1) Belief *B* represents *p*-as-true.
(B2) Belief *B* represents-as-true *p*.

On the attitudinal view, B2 is the more accurate way of reporting the representational structure of belief; B1 is misleading. Similarly for desires:

(D1) Desire *D* represents *p*-as-good.
(D2) Desire *D* represents-as-good *p*.

Talk of manners/ways of representing should be understood as insisting that D2 is more accurate than D1.

If the belief/desire distinction comes down to a difference between representing-as-true and representing-as-good, what is the attitudinal distinction between perception and imagination? On this, Sartre's clearest passage is the following:

> Every awareness posits its object, but each in its own manner. Perception, for example, posits its object as existent . . . The intentional object of imaging awareness has this peculiarity that it is not there and it is posited as such, or that it does not exist and is posited as nonexistent, or that it is not posited at all.
> (Sartre 1940, pp. 24–25/2004, p. 13; my translation)

The verb "to posit" is unfamiliar in analytic philosophy of mind, but in the Husserlian tradition it is commonly used to describe precisely the kind of attitudinal feature of an intentional act whereby it presents its object in a specific way. In this terminology, we would say that belief "posits" its content as true while desire "posits" it as good—without truth and goodness needing to enter the actual content of belief and desire.

With this in mind, the above passage suggests a straightforward view of perception's distinctive attitudinal feature: it represents its object as existing. This should be interpreted along P2 rather than P1:

(P1) Perceptual experience *E* represents *O*-as-existent.
(P2) Perceptual experience *E* represents-as-existent *O*.

It is not part of the *content* of a perceptual experience that its object is real or existent. But the characteristic *way* perceptual experience represents its object is under the aspect of existence.

The view is more complicated when it comes to "imaging awareness" (*conscience imageante*), as the passage offers three different descriptors. The first casts the objects "as not there." In other passages, Sartre also speaks of acts that cast the object "as absent" and "as existing elsewhere."³¹ I propose that we formulate the canonical report of this kind of act as follows:

(I2.1) Imaging awareness $A$ represents-as-absent $O$.

Sartre's second descriptor more clearly calls for the following formulation:

(I2.2) Imaging awareness $A$ represents-as-nonexistent $O$.

The third is odder: Sartre speaks of an object that is not posited at all. This might invite all sorts of mysterian readings, if it were not for Sartre's repeated insistence that all consciousness is consciousness-of, that is, intentional consciousness. Given this insistence, I think the only open interpretation is that Sartre has in mind a sensory analog of entertaining that $p$, contemplating that $p$, apprehending $p$, and the like "atttidunally neutral" propositional attitudes. When you entertain or contemplate the proposition that there are more than eight provinces in Canada, you are in a state that presents the relevant proposition without commenting on its truth or goodness. Such states represent their propositional contents neither as true nor as good (nor otherwise). They represent them without commentary, so to speak. The objectual analog would be a mental state that represented $O$ while remaining neutral on $O$'s ontological status. This suggests the following canonical report:

(I2.3) Imaging awareness $A$ merely-represents $O$.

Here $A$ is said to represent without representing-as. That is an intentional act that does not posit its object, that is, an "attitudinally neutral" objectual attitude.³²

From the passage itself, it is unclear whether Sartre proposes I2.1–I2.3 as (i) three antecedently plausible options for construing a single attitudinal feature of all imagery, or as (ii) three distinct attitudinal features actually exhibited by three different varieties of imagery. Sartre is in fact never explicit on this, but the tenor of his subsequent discussion suggests (ii). He thus seems committed to a certain heterogeneity among images. And indeed, recall that Sartre's subject matter is wider than just imagination and covers three different varieties of imagery—what I called imaginative, phantasmagoric, and mnemonic experiences. It would be nice if these mapped neatly on to I2.1–I2.3. Sartre nowhere suggests that they do, but I want to argue that it is independently plausible.

Consider imaginative experiences. These were characterized as experiences involving deliberate conjuring up of images. Here we *exercise our imagination*, we are "creative" in producing an image without exogenous stimulation. If one is already committed to a categorical attitudinal difference between such experiences and perceptual experiences, it is quite plausible to suppose that the difference is simply this: perceptual experiences represent-as-existent whereas imaginative experiences represent-as-nonexistent. Thus, one difference between seeing my dog and visualizing a smiling octopus is that the former represents-as-existent the dog whereas the latter represents-as-nonexistent the octopus. It might be objected that we can also imagine things we know to exist, as when I visualize Barack Obama. But even here, it is plausible that my imaginative experience itself represents-as-nonexistent what it represents; it is just accompanied by an overriding belief that the imagined object in fact exists. Compare: looking down from an airplane I see tiny houses and cars, but the visual experience is accompanied by a belief that these are in fact much bigger. If we try to abstract away from the accompanying beliefs, we recognize that imagining Obama in itself represents-as-nonexistent that which is imagined. As I close my eyes and picture him, the Obama hovering just there on the other side of my desk is something I am aware of as unreal; the real Obama is in the White House talking to more important people.[33]

Consider next phantasmagoric experiences, where an image involuntarily pops up in one's mind. It is tempting to construe these as essentially continuous with imaginative experiences. On closer inspection, however, the fact that the imagination is not being consciously exercised, and the image is "spat out" by sub-personal processes, seems relevant. It makes it quite natural to propose that phantasms are in fact silent on the ontological status of their objects, presenting them "without commentary." If so, phantasmagoric experiences may well be attitudinally neutral in the above sense.

Finally, consider mnemonic experience, the imagery often implicated in episodic memory. When I sit alone in a hotel and picture my wife waving goodbye at the airport the day before, my experience is not at all in the business of denying my wife's existence. On the contrary, it casts my wife as real but not here, or as Sartre puts it, "as existing elsewhere." The reason I miss my wife even more when I picture her thus is precisely that the experience represents-as-absent something otherwise real.

If all this is right, then we can refine I2.1–I2.3 to target these three specific types of imagery. Thus:

(I2.1) Mnemonic experience $E$ represents-as-absent $O$.
(I2.2) Imaginative experience $E$ represents-as-nonexistent $O$.
(I2.3) Phantasmagoric experience $E$ merely-represents $O$.

Since our concern in this chapter is the relationship between perception and imagination, what matters for our purposes is the contrast between P2 and I2.2. The contrast is extremely straightforward on this Sartrean account: it is the contrast between representing-as-existent and representing-as-nonexistent. What is not straightforward is the notion that these are two *attitudinal* features that mark a *categorical* difference between the *phenomenology* of perception and imagination. These attitudinal features are moreover *constitutive* of perception and imagination—they are what makes a given experience perceptual or imaginative:

> These positional acts [captured in I2.1–I2.3]—this remark is of the first importance (*est capitale*)—are not superadded to the image once it is constituted: the positional act is constitutive of the image-awareness (*conscience d'image*).
> (Sartre 1940, p. 24/2004, p. 13; my translation)

Thus the overall view is that there is not only a functional but also a phenomenal difference between perceiving and imagining. Far from being a difference in degree, this is a difference in kind, as each presents what it does in its own *sui generis* way. These "ways of presenting" are felt attitudinal features: just as conscious belief that $p$ involves feeling it true that $p$ whereas conscious desire involves feeling it good that $p$, so perceiving $O$ involves feeling $O$ to be real, whereas imagining $O$ involves feeling $O$ to be unreal.

Observe that this view, like the version of ND that Sartre failed to address (the aforementioned lacuna in his argument), appeals crucially to the difference between reality and unreality in distinguishing perception and imagination. However, while that version of ND builds the reality/unreality difference into the content of accompanying beliefs, the present view builds it into the attitude employed by perception and imagination themselves. This seems to me to have at least two major advantages. First, it vindicates the intuition that there is some difference between the experiences of perception and imagination themselves, regardless of accompaniments. Secondly, it makes room for a perception/imagination distinction even in creatures completely lacking in the capacity for propositional thought—something that the appeal to *beliefs about* reality and unreality appears to rule out.

Sartre's initial account, thus understood, has a clear answer to $Q1_p$ and $Q2_p$. The phenomenal *similarity* between perceptual and imaginative experience is in content: *what* is represented in consciousness is the same. The phenomenal *dissimilarity* is in attitude: *how* it is represented is different. As we will see in the next section, however, Sartre's considered view is more complex than this.

※

I close this section with a historical note on the intellectual lineage of the attitudinal account from Brentano through Husserl to Sartre; readers uninterested in questions of historical development may skip directly to the next section.

Sartre heard of Husserl from his friend Raymond Aron, upon the latter's return from a year at the French Institute in Berlin. Sartre, 28 at the time, was immediately enthralled by the notion of "making philosophy out of real life" (that was the gist of Aron's presentation), and spent the following academic year (1933–34) at the Institute reading mostly Husserl, Scheler, Faulkner, and Kafka—and writing a brief note on intentionality as the fundamental notion in Husserl's philosophy (Sartre 1939; see Contat and Rybalka 1970, p. 71). Sartre credits Husserl with the attitudinal account of the perception/imagination distinction: the fourth and final chapter of *The Imagination* is titled simply "Husserl." And indeed, Husserl does develop such an account, though in his characteristically dense style (Husserl 1913, §§111–114). As noted above, however, the general approach of classifying mental states according to their attitudinal properties is central in Brentano's philosophy. Now, Husserl studied with Brentano in Vienna between 1884 and 1886, at the impressionable age of 25–27, and when Brentano's *Psychology* had already gained notoriety (indeed, had become a young orthodoxy in some quarters).[34] Furthermore, Brentano's attitudinal distinction between belief and desire, or more generally, his classification of mental states, is adopted virtually as-is by Husserl (1901, Investigation V, Chs. 4–5).[35] This raises the question of whether Husserl might have been influenced by Brentano in developing his attitudinal account.

It is highly plausible that Husserl was strongly influenced by Brentano's general way of thinking in terms of attitudinal differences and similarities. But might he have been influenced specifically with respect to the perception/imagination distinction?

In the *Psychology*, Brentano mentions the imagination about a dozen times in all, always in passing. In fact, in the entire Brentano corpus there is only one sustained discussion of the imagination. This is in the context of his lecture notes for a course on "Selected Questions from Psychology and Aesthetics" (published posthumously in Brentano 1959). Much of this course was dedicated to the concept of imagination or fancy (*Begriff der Phantasie*).[36] Brentano covers many issues related to this topic, and in a somewhat confusing way, but as Tănăsescu (2010) shows, "the fundamental idea of the [relevant] text is that perceptual representation and imaginative representation in the improper sense are different in their ... modality of representation" (Tănăsescu 2010, p. 58).[37] In other words, the difference is in the attitudinal features exhibited.

Interestingly, the course was offered at the University of Vienna in the academic year 1885–1886, so just during the window of time Husserl was there. There is every reason to believe that Husserl sat in on that course. If so, what he heard there may well have had a direct impact on what he wrote much later in the *Ideen* (Husserl 1913).[38] Now, there is no reason to suppose that Brentano's attitudinal distinction appeals to the presence or absence of representing-as-existent. Brentano speaks, somewhat opaquely, of perceptual representation being "intuitive" and imaginative representation being "conceptual with an intuitive core."[39] But then again, the distinction in terms of representing-as-existent and contrasting attitudinal features is not all that transparent in Husserl either. In truth it becomes clearly articulated only with Sartre.

What Sartre seems unaware of, however, is the deep influence Brentano's thought exercised on Husserl's. In this, he is representative of French phenomenology at large. There is no more awareness of Husserl's debt to Brentano in Levinas, Merleau-Ponty, de Beauvoir, and Ricœur. In general, Brentano's work has seen much less uptake in French philosophy than its German, Polish, and Italian counterparts.[40] The renowned medievalist Étienne Gilson discussed Brentano's interpretation of medieval philosophy in a 1939 piece (Gilson 1939), and his daughter Lucie Gilson offered the first systematic French-language exposition of Brentano only in the 1950s (Gilson 1955a, 1955b). Other than that, there is very little discussion of Brentano before the last quarter of the twentieth century. All the same, it is fair to say that Sartre's specific attitudinal account of the perception/imagination distinction is indirectly influenced by Brentano's attitudinal approach to mental classification and its public application to the perception/imagination distinction while Husserl studied with Brentano.[41]

## A refined account?

In the last 5–6 pages of *The Imagination*, Sartre argues that the attitudinal difference between perception and imagination, although central, cannot be the *whole* difference; there must be a difference in content as well (Sartre 1936, pp. 154–160/2012, pp. 137–142). My goal in this section is to argue that (i) Sartre's argument for this is uncompelling, but (ii) some plausible refinements of the last section's attitudinal account are nonetheless possible.

Sartre's argument is based on consideration of what happens, experientially and epistemologically, when we perform Husserl's "phenomenological reduction" on perception. In the phenomenological reduction, the subject "brackets" the reality of what she is aware of and considers only how it appears to her. Suppose I have a perceptual experience of my dog. To perform a phenomenological reduction on this experience is to bracket the reality of the dog and consider only how he appears to me in my experience: dog-shaped, mustard-colored, and so on. For Husserl, this means that the perceptual experience has undergone a "neutrality modification": the reality commitment built into its attitudinal character or mode of representing has been neutralized, canceled out. It is "a modification which, in a certain way, completely annuls, completely renders powerless every doxic modality to which it is related" (Husserl 1913, p. 257). Sartre observes that the possibility of neutrality modification of a perceptual experience raises a question: "how can one distinguish the centaur that I imagine from the blossoming tree that I perceive once the reduction is performed?" (Sartre 1936, p. 154/2012, p. 137). If the key difference between perception and imagination is the attitudinal feature of representing-as-existent involved in the former, then as soon as this representing-as-existent is neutralized through the reduction I should be unable to tell apart introspectively (thus bracketed) perception from imagination. Therefore:

> the distinction between mental image and perception could not come from [modes or kinds of] intentionality alone. It is necessary but not sufficient that the [kinds of] intentions differ; it must also be that the matters are dissimilar.
> (Sartre 1936, p. 159/2012, p. 141)

By "matters," Sartre clearly means something that contrasts with attitude or mode of representation—perhaps intentional content, but more likely what Husserl called the *hylē*: a proto-intentional aspect of experience that becomes intentional only by being "intentionally animated" (see Williford 2013 for recent clarification of this notion).[42] Either way, the introspective discriminability of imagination and neutralized/reduced perception implies some non-attitudinal difference between them.[43]

We might reconstruct Sartre's argument as another epistemological argument by elimination. It starts from an epistemological "datum" regarding what we can know in a characteristically first-personal way: namely, whether we are having an imaginative or neutralized-perceptual experience. The best explanation is then claimed to appeal to first-person knowledge of some non-attitudinal difference between the two. More precisely: (1) imaginative experience and neutralized perceptual experience are introspectively discriminable; so, (2) there must be a phenomenal difference between them; but, (3) there is no attitudinal difference between them; therefore, (4) there must be some non-attitudinal difference between imaginative experience and neutralized perceptual experience.[44]

I am not going to challenge premise 1, which seems to me antecedently plausible, nor the inference from 1 to 2, which is required for all the epistemological arguments Sartre employs, including those endorsed above. But premise 3 is eminently objectionable. When a perceptual experience undergoes the neutrality modification, it may no longer have the attitudinal feature of representing-as-existent. Its commitment to the reality of the perceived object has been bracketed. But this does not mean that it has now acquired a new commitment, to the *unreality* of the object. On the contrary, it is genuinely neutral on the object's ontological status. Husserl himself notes that the neutrality modification is "a modification in a totally different sense than that of negation" (Husserl 1913, p. 257).[45] In contrast, the characteristic attitudinal feature of imaginative experiences is representing-as-nonexistent, a kind of positive commitment to a specific ontological status of the object imagined. Thus there is still a clear attitudinal difference between imaginative experience and perceptual experience even after the neutrality modification.[46]

Sartre could overcome this specific objection by concentrating his argument on the contrast between neutralized perceptual experiences and neutralized phantasmagoric experiences. For, unlike imaginative experience, phantasmagoric experience does not involve representing-as-nonexistent but only what we called above "attitudinally neutral" mere-representing. Thus it might be suggested that neutralized perceptual and phantasmagoric experiences involve the same neutral(ized) attitude toward their represented object, and yet are introspectively discriminable. It would then be natural to suggest that their introspectively detectable difference must be non-attitudinal.[47]

The weak link in this revised argument is the notion that a neutralized representing-as-existent phenomenally feels the same as attitudinally neutral mere-representing. This conception of the phenomenological reduction casts it as genuinely altering one's commitments regarding reality and truth, if only for a moment. It is clear, however, that performing the phenomenological reduction involves no such thing. Instead, it involves an element of temporary *pretense*: one does not *really* change one's mind about how the world is, but assumes the position of someone who does. A phenomenologist standing on the train tracks and bracketing her perceptual experience of the coming train is fully alive to the approaching danger; she is thoroughly disposed to jump off the tracks in time to save her life. It is clear, then, that she continues to be attitudinally committed to the existence of the approaching train, even as she is engaged in her phenomenological exercises.

Compare: suppose $S$ believes that $p$, in fact has 97 percent credence that $p$, and on this basis decides to $\varphi$; and suppose that someone asks $S$ whether $\varphi$-ing would still be appropriate if $S$ only had 50 percent credence that $p$. In considering this, $S$ must perform a certain operation, but it is not part of the operation *really* to lower her credence by 47 percent (even for a time); it involves something subtler, which we may describe as *simulating* having 50 percent credence that $p$.[48] It would be most accurate to say that $S$ has a credence of 97 percent and a pretend-credence of 50 percent. Now, merely entertaining that $p$ is even more thoroughly neutral than having 50 percent credence that $p$: while the 50 percent credence does not present $p$ as true, it does present $p$ as an object of truth evaluation; it "brings up" the issue of truth in a way mere entertaining does not. So, a more radical exercise $S$ might be asked to perform is to consider whether she would $\varphi$ if she had no credence whatsoever in $p$ but merely entertained that $p$.[49] Again, to consider the matter, $S$ would need to perform a certain operation, but it is not part of this operation to stop having any commitment on the likely truth of $p$; it only involves pretending or simulating having no such commitment.

The analogy to the perception/phantasm case is clear. Just as belief involves the attitudinal feature of representing-as-true whereas entertaining is attitudinally neutral, so perceptual experience involves the attitudinal feature of representing-as-existent whereas phantasmagoric experience is attitudinally neutral. A subject who performs the phenomenological reduction on a perceptual experience of a coming train does not eliminate her commitment to the existence of the train any more than *S* stops being committed to the likely truth of *p*. It is a good question what *does* happen when one performs a phenomenological reduction on one's train perception.[50] But whatever it is, it cannot involve annihilation without trace of the original attitudinal features of the experience. So it is not true that there is no attitudinal difference between neutralized-perceptual and phantasmagoric experiences. The argument that there must also be a content difference therefore fails.

※※

Nonetheless, Sartre's attitudinal account could bear refinement. Perhaps its most notable phenomenological incongruence concerns the contrast between perception and the imagery involved in episodic memory. It is true that perception presents its object as present, "in the flesh" (to use Husserl's expression), whereas in episodic memory we are aware of the object as in some sense absent. But surely the deeper phenomenal difference between the two pertains to *time*. When I reminisce about meeting my dog for the first time, so little and fearful with his penetrating eyes, I have a mnemonic experience whose content may well be identical to that of the perceptual experience I underwent that day.[51] But the overall phenomenal character of the two experiences is certainly different, most perspicuously insofar as my current mnemonic experience presents the relevant scene as in the past, whereas my past perceptual experience presented the very same scene as in the present.[52] This phenomenal difference is not captured by the distinction between representing-as-existent and representing-as-absent, at least not in any direct or obvious way.

To account for this central phenomenal difference, the Sartrean should take another leaf from Brentano and introduce a second set of attitudinal features, pertaining specifically to time. The relevant distinction Brentano posits is between *modus praesens* and *modus passens*, as two manners or ways of representing objects:

> Above all we must designate temporal differences as modes of presentation. Anyone who considered past, present, and future as differences in objects would be just as mistaken as someone who looked upon existence and nonexistence as real attributes.
> (Brentano 1911, p. 279; see also Brentano 1928 Ch. 5, esp. §12)

For Brentano, just as existence and nonexistence are not really properties that some objects instantiate and others do not, so presentness and pastness (and futureness) are not really properties of objects. Rather, just as some objects are represented-as-existent and others are represented-as-nonexistent by categorically different mental states, so some objects are represented-as-present and others represented-as-past by categorically different mental states. In the first case, the relevant states are perceptual and imaginative; in the second, perceptual and mnemonic. Thus the deep phenomenal difference between mnemonic and perceptual experiences is best captured not by I2.1 and P2 but by:

(I2.1\*) Mnemonic experience *E* represents-as-past *O*.
(P2\*) Perceptual experience *E* represents-as-present *O*.

As for imaginative and phantasmagoric experiences, there are several ways to construe their characteristic attitudinal temporal tag, but perhaps the most natural is to suppose it is "attitudinally neutral," that is, that they represent their objects without any temporal orientation.[53] This would not rule out imagining or fantasizing something as in the past, in the present, or in the future; it would merely require building that temporal reference into the *content* of the relevant act.[54]

The key to this Brentanian refinement of Sartre's attitudinal account is the notion that not all attitudinal phenomenal differences must be accounted for in terms of a single set of attitudinal features. In addition to attitudinal features pertaining to the *ontological* status of the represented objects, Brentano posits also attitudinal features pertaining to their *temporal* and *modal* status.[55] (In the last case, Brentano's distinction is between apodictic and assertoric attitudes: the former represent-as-necessary *p*, the latter represent-as-contingent *p*—see Brentano 1889, p. 82 and Brentano 1933, p. 25.) For Brentano, the ultimate classification of mental states is determined by the various combinations of compossible attitudinal features exhibited by states. Thus perceptual experience not only represents-as-existent but also represents-as-present and represents-as-contingent. It contrasts with mnemonic experience insofar as the latter represents-as-past, but with imaginative experience insofar as the latter represents-as-nonexistent (and perhaps with intuitional experiences insofar as those represent-as-necessary).[56] Thus there need not be a single attitudinal dimension along which perception contrasts with all types of non-perceptual experience with potentially the same content as it.

It might be objected that there are no phenomenal differences between perception and imagery pertaining to time and modality, and any sense of such difference derives from accompanying beliefs: when I reminisce about meeting my dog for the first time, I *believe* that the scene I am aware of occurred in the past.[57] The experiential awareness itself, however, is silent on the scene's time.

This alternative account parallels, of course, what we called ND. But there is no reason to suppose it more plausible. In particular, it will be hard-pressed to account for the first-person knowledge we have of whether we are perceiving or episodically remembering. Thus, patients suffering from source amnesia have episodic memories of past events without knowing when or where they acquired those memories, nor when or where the remembered events took place. Nevertheless, they still do seem to themselves to be *remembering* the relevant scenes. That is, they experience their episodic memories *as memories*, and can introspectively recognize them as such. They are not inclined to mistake them for perceptions or imaginations. What source amnesiacs appear to lack is the ability to generate certain beliefs about the events they seem to themselves to remember. Nonetheless, they experience a phenomenology of pastness they can introspectively detect.[58]

## Conclusion

To summarize, contrary to a long Anglo-Saxon tradition, dating back at least to Hume, Sartre convincingly argues that there must be a *categorical* distinction between perception and imagination, a distinction in kind and not merely degree. This difference pertains to the *manner* in which the object perceived or imagined is represented in consciousness, that is, the *kind* of attitude consciousness bears to its content. The difference is that perception represents-as-existent its object, whereas imagination represents-as-nonexistent its. Sartre also flirts with the notion of a content difference between the perception and imagination, but this may be just another infelicitous Sartrean flirtation.

As noted, this account provides us with answers the two questions we started with: ($Q1_p$) What is the phenomenal similarity between perceiving $O$ and imagining $O$? ($Q2_p$) What is the phenomenal dissimilarity between perceiving $O$ and imagining $O$? The answer to $Q1_p$ is straightforward: perception and imagination are phenomenally similar in having the same kind of content. The answer to $Q2_p$ is also simple once we appreciate it: perception and imagination are phenomenally dissimilar in that they employ different kinds of attitude—the manner in which they represent what they do is categorically, qualitatively different. In a slogan: perception and imagination are similar in content, dissimilar in attitude.

This answer to our organizing question also sketches a phenomenological account of the nature of imagination—as well as of perception. It is perfectly possible that the deepest nature of imagination and perception is functional, that is, to be given by exhaustive specification their functional role within the cognitive architecture of the mind. But our concern here has been with the phenomenological approach to mental life. Phenomenologically, the nature of imagination is given by its distinctive attitude, its representing-as-nonexistent character. More fully, we may propose the following phenomenological existence and identity conditions for imaginative experiences:

For any imaginative experience *E*, *E* is the imaginative experience *it is* (rather than another imaginative experience) because it bears the content it does (and not another), and *E* is an imaginative experience *at all* (rather than a non-imaginative experience) because it employs the attitude it does (and not another).

For example, an imaginative experience as of a mustard-colored dog is the imaginative experience it is because it is *as of a mustard-colored dog* and is an imaginative experience at all because it *represents-as-nonexistent* that mustard-colored dog. The first half of this provides the (phenomenological) identity conditions of imaginative experiences, the second their (phenomenological) existence conditions. I leave the formulation of the parallel phenomenological existence and identity conditions of perceptual, phantasmagoric, and mnemonic experiences as an exercise for the reader.

Remarkably, the assumptions needed to establish this kind of attitudinal approach to imaginative phenomenology are rather innocuous. One assumption is that imaginative and perceptual experiences *can* have the same content; not that they always or even typically do, but just that they *can*.[59] The second assumption is that even when they do, the subject can have a *distinctively first-personal* knowledge of which state she is in; not infallible or otherwise privileged knowledge, but just *distinctive* knowledge. If these two assumptions are granted, it is hard to see how to avoid the attitudinal account of imaginative phenomenology. According to it, there is a categorical difference between imaginative and perceptual phenomenology.[60]

## Notes

1 In fact, there is not only a bewildering variety of imaginings, but also a considerable variety of axes along which they can be distinguished. Here I will distinguish them in terms of their intentional character, but there are other ways to distinguish very finely varieties of imagination (see, e.g., Stevenson 2003). Many have concluded that there is no hope of finding a commonality among all types of imagination (see Strawson 1970). A more sustained argument for the fundamental heterogeneity of imagination is provided by Kind (2013). This seems to me an overreaction, but I bracket the issue here.
2 When I imagine seeing a dog, there is a further distinction between imagining myself as part of the scene, with the imaginative state representing explicitly both the dog and me, and imagining the scene as seen from my viewpoint, construed as a sort of zero point of perceptual space.
3 It may turn out that this conceptual claim is too strong, and there are some conceptually possible propositional imaginings that involve no sensory imagery. Still, a softer claim in the same spirit (about typical or normal or paradigmatic instances, say) is surely right.
4 Byrne (2010) raises Q1 and Q2 (extended to cover episodic memory) as well, but cites functional (dis)similarities to answer them, which suggests that his concern is *not* with $Q1_p$ and $Q2_p$ but with their functional analogs.
5 Thanks to Margherita Arcangeli for helping me see this.

268  Uriah Kriegel

6   On this view, what it is like to have a perceptual experience of a dog and an imaginative experience of a dog (at the same distance, of the same shape and color, etc.) is strictly the same. The difference between them is entirely non-phenomenal: the former is, whereas the latter is not, accompanied by the belief that there really is such a dog before one. The view is discussed somewhat sympathetically by Russell (1921, Ch. 8), who nonetheless does not end up endorsing it, despite adopting an analogous view regarding the difference between perception and episodic memory (1921, Ch. 9).

7   Hume writes: "An idea assented to FEELS different from a fictitious idea, that the fancy alone presents to us: And this different feeling I endeavour to explain by calling it a superior force, or vivacity, or solidity, or FIRMNESS, or steadiness" (*Treatise*, I.iii.vii; emphasis original).

8   DD is intended to exclude KD, something that the present formulations leave to implicature. We can fix this by adding "mere" to DD, or else defining the second account of the relationship between perceptual and imaginative phenomenology in terms of DD&~KD. In all three theses, we probably have to add a qualifier such as "topically."

9   The notion of episodic memory comes from Tulving (1972), who contrasted it with "semantic memory," which concerns remembering certain impersonal facts (as when I remember that Pope Benedict IX was 11 years old when he was elected to the papacy). Tulving himself characterized episodic memory as concerned exclusively with "personally experienced events" (Tulving 2001: 1506), but, as Byrne (2010) shows, this is unduly restrictive. The distinguishing characteristic of episodic memory is that it is imagistic or sensory.

10  We may consider (non-lucid) dreams prolonged phantasma, given their production by subpersonal processes consciously uncontrollable by the person.

11  Throughout both books and without argument, Sartre assumes that for his purposes what I have called imaginative and phantasmagoric phenomena "belong together"; his stance toward episodic memory is a bit ambiguous. But the three appear on their face to share something rather essential. From the perspective of KD, ultimately one might say that there is a phenomenal determinable D that all three instantiate but perceptual experience (for example) does not, or more minimally that there is another phenomenal determinable D* that perceptual experience instantiates but none of these three does. (As I understand him, Sartre assumes the first, stronger claim. We will have occasion to revisit this assumption later on.) It is an open question, in any case, whether the distinctions drawn above with respect to imagination (propositional vs objectual imagining, etc.) apply to phantasm and episodic-memory imagery. It is highly plausible that they do, but I will not assume as much here.

12  The relationship between the two is not altogether clear in the text. In *The Imagination* (Sartre 1936), the fact that there are two prima facie independent (though clearly related) tenets is not transparent in the text. Only in *The Imaginary* (Sartre 1940) does it become explicit, and the classical conception is accused of a "double error" (1940, p. 14/2004, p. 5). This duality is entirely missed by Merleau-Ponty in his review of *The Imagination* (Merleau-Ponty 1936), which focuses entirely on the first tenet (admittedly more pronounced in the first three chapters of *The Imagination*).

13  I will often stick to the excellent English translations now available of Sartre's two books. Occasionally, however, I will offer my own translation, rarely very

different from the published ones. (There is only one significant translator's decision I have made—see note 24.) I will always indicate when I do. In any case, with quotes from Sartre I will always cite both the French original and the English edition; for quotes from other sources I will only cite the English edition. Quotes from the French original of Sartre (1936) will refer to the 1983 reprint by Presses Universitaires de France; those of Sartre (1940) refer to the first edition.

14 This is to be contrasted with any intrinsic features of the experiences considered in isolation; hence Sartre's emphasis in the quoted text.

15 If we wanted to formulate the argument with greater precision, we might offer: for some subject $S$ and any experience $E$, such that $S$ is a healthy human adult in normal circumstances and $E$ is either a perceptual experience or an imaginative experience, (1) $S$ knows whether $E$ is perceptual or imaginative immediately; (2) if ND, then $S$ would not know whether $E$ is perceptual or imaginative immediately; therefore, (3) ~ND.

16 To that extent, the claim is not undermined by the Perky experiment, where subjects asked to imagine bananas while staring at blank screen were shown (unbeknownst to them) increasingly clearer banana images on the screen but failed to realize they were now perceiving rather than (merely) imagining bananas (Perky 1910). As an alleged demonstration that we are unable introspectively to tell apart perception from imagination, the experiment suffers from a variety of difficulties (see Casey 2000, p. 149 for a notable one). But in any case, since the circumstances of the experiment are atypical and far from ordinary, they do nothing to undermine the claim Sartre needs for his argument.

17 For my part, I have argued for a relevant similar epistemology of first-person knowledge in Kriegel (2011, Ch. 1, 2013). In the latter, I present and defend a model of first-person knowledge as based on simple endorsement of introspective appearances: one knows that one is having perceptual experience $E$ by having an introspective appearance as of having $E$ and endorsing that appearance. If either introspection or endorsement malfunctions, one is liable to end up with a false first-person belief, or fail to form a true first-person belief. Thus neither infallibility nor self-intimation holds.

18 We may represent it as follows: (1) if ND were true, acquiring knowledge of whether one is perceiving or imagining would be considerably more effortful than it in fact is; therefore, (2) ND is false.

19 In sufficiently bizarre settings, I might be unsure whether I am perceiving Pierre or hallucinating him. But both perception and hallucination are perceptual experiences. Imaginative experiences are another thing still. In standard cases where I am unsure whether I am perceiving or hallucinating $O$, I am still certain that I am not imagining $O$.

20 Sartre appears to adduce two further arguments, but they are uncompelling.

21 Moreover, when we consider the lowest resolution a perceptual experience can have consistently with the laws of nature, it is hard to believe that no imaginative experience can match *that* level of accuracy.

22 Note: this argument does not require the claim that every perception of an opaque three-dimensional object involves imagining its invisible parts, the parts other than the directly visible surface (Nanay 2010). It only requires the claim that it is nomologically possible for us to perceive one part of such an object and imagine another simultaneously, and in such a way that the characteristics attributed to each part differ.

23 Thanks to Matthew Eshleman for helping me see more clearly the dialectical circumstance here.
24 In this passage (and others), I have translated *"conscience"* as *awareness* rather than consciousness. In French, the word *"conscience"* is much more elastic than in English. For example, it covers also conscience (e.g., political or moral). As part of this, it is noteworthy that there is no distinct word for awareness in French. When *"conscience"* occurs in a noun, or its cognate as an intransitive verb, it is natural to translate it as "consciousness"; but when it occurs as a transitive verb, it seems to me much more natural to translate it as "awareness." Although this is not a common practice in translation of French phenomenological text, in my opinion it should be.
25 Whether in doing so Sartre anticipates also "the transparency of experience" (Harman 1990), "representationalism" (Dretske 1995), or "intentionalism" (Byrne 2001) is a more delicate question. Sartre clear thinks that all introspectively accessible aspects of experience are intentional. However, as we will see in the section on Sartre's attitudinal account, he does *not* think that all introspectible aspects of an experience pertain to what is *presented* by the experience; some pertain to the *presenting* of whatever is presented. This would not qualify as transparency or representationalism/intentionalism by most contemporary standards. For a recent argument that Sartre *is* an early intentionalist, see Rowlands (2013).
26 Similar remarks are made in *The Imaginary*: "whether I perceive or imagine this chair, the object of my perception and that of my image are identical: it's this straw chair on which I sit. It is simply that consciousness *relates* to this same chair in two different ways. In both cases, I target the chair in its concrete individuality, in its corporeality. Only in one case, the chair is 'encountered' by consciousness: in the other, it is not" (1940, p. 7; my translation, italics original). The passage from *The Imagination* quoted in the main text is still the clearest and most explicit.
27 This is not Sartre's terminology—in fact, Sartre is quite hostile to describing conscious episodes as mental states. Here and in the remainder of the chapter, I use the expression as it is standardly used in contemporary analytic philosophy of mind—to denote more or less what Descartes called "thoughts."
28 Indeed, *S*'s belief that *p* and desire that *p* may be components of a single state, say her being glad that *p*. One might argue that in such a case the intensity of her belief and desire states is just the intensity of her gladness state, and therefore the same. (The assumption would be that a state such as gladness cannot vary in intensity across its different "components.")
29 The full sentence ending this passage is "It would be better to say 'consciousness of Pierre-as-imaged' or 'imaging consciousness of Pierre'." I excised the expression "consciousness of Pierre-as-imaged" because it seems to me to suggest, misleadingly, a content property of the relevant consciousness (or awareness). It might be claimed that it undermines my attitudinal interpretation of Sartre's account, but given the rest of the text, it rather seems like an instance of carelessness on Sartre's part. Or, perhaps more charitably: Sartre may have in mind here that imaged-Pierre is a sort of "formal object" of the image that must be distinguished from its intentional object. Consider being afraid of a dog. It is commonly claimed, and quite plausibly, that the formal object of fear is danger. But this is not to be understood as part of the intentional object/content of fear:

what one is afraid of, after all, is just the dog—not the dog's dangerousness. Talk of formal objects seems to be elliptical for something more fundamental. Arguably, this "something" is an attitudinal feature of mental states. Thus, it is an attitudinal feature of fear that it represents-as-dangerous what it does.

30 The notion that belief and desire have characteristic or proprietary phenomenal properties is often referred to as *cognitive phenomenology*—see Bayne and Montague (2011) for a recent collection pertaining to it.

31 In some places, Sartre takes the last two to be different, thus suggesting that there are in fact four types of image: "the imaginary object can be posited as nonexistent, or as absent, or as existing elsewhere, or not be posited as existent" (Sartre 1940, p. 232/2004, p. 183). I am going to ignore this wrinkle, nowhere motivated by Sartre, in my present discussion.

32 Interestingly, the existence of such attitudinally neutral mental states is recognized by Brentano, where they are claimed to constitute the third fundamental category of mental states, in addition to cognitive and conative attitudes. For Brentano, there are the categories of judgment and interest, but even more basic is the category of presentation (*Vorstellung*): while the latter is a component of all other attitudes, they are not components of it (see Brentano 1874, Book II, Chs. 6–7).

33 Some might also hold that we cannot imagine Obama *himself*, as opposed to just an Obama-like object. Imaginative reference might be claimed to be "descriptive" rather than singular, putting together a number of feature representations but lacking any tracking relation in virtue of which to represent particulars. If so, the imaginative experience proper represents-as-nonexistent an Obama-like object. This response to the objection strikes me as wrongheaded in a number of ways, but perhaps some readers would find it credible.

34 This was so especially in Vienna and Prague, then intellectual centers of the Austro-Hungarian Empire. In Vienna, Brentano himself wielded this influence, which extended beyond philosophy (for his place in the general cultural context, see Johnston (1972), esp. Ch. 20; for a fascinating analysis of his *direct* influence on Kafka, see Smith 1981). In Prague, it was Anton Marty, Brentano's student in Würzburg in 1868–1869, who presided over a philosophical scene centered on Brentanian philosophy (a scene which included the two chief organizers and propagators of the material from Brentano's literary estate, Alfred Kastil and Oskar Kraus). In those years, every Thursday a group of philosophers met at the Louvre café to debate the finest details of Brentano's thought.

35 As it was by many of Brentano's students, notably Marty (1908, Ch. 6). Interestingly, even Brentano's students who developed their own classifications of mental states did so by offering revisions to Brentano's classification, and while maintaining the attitudinal framework (see Meinong 1902, Ch. 1).

36 Under this heading Brentano enumerates a great variety of phenomena, including mere representations, feverish hallucinations, short-term episodic memories, dream representations, and more (see Brentano 1959, pp. 43–44, and for a systematic discussion, Tănăsescu 2010).

37 Part of what is confusing in Brentano's presentation is his distinction between representation in the proper and improper senses, which appears to do with this: in the improper sense representation is understood in terms of its object, what it represents; in the proper sense, it is understood in terms of that plus the mode or modality of representation, *how* it represents what it represents. In the

proper sense, suggests Brentano, there is no difference between perception and imagination/fancy—but in the proper sense there is (see Brentano 1959, p. 83). As Tănăsescu shows, the notion of content is used by Brentano for the wider (finer-grained) proper conception of representation. Not fully appreciating this distinction, the editor of these lecture notes, Franziska Mayer-Hillerbrand, casually replaces mentions of "content" (*Inhalt*) with "object" (*Gegenstand*) in key passages; but the original manuscripts in Prague show that Brentano's own talk here is of content (Tănăsescu 2010, fn 31).

38 This is certainly Tănăsescu's view—see the last four pages of Tănăsescu (2010).
39 This is stated explicitly in manuscript Ps 78/2c, B 19759, discussed in Tănăsescu (2010). According to Tănăsescu, this difference amounts to the difference between sensory and non-conceptual representation in the perceptual case and more abstract and conceptual representation, but with the undefined "intuitive core" in the imagination case.
40 This is so even as many French phenomenologists were cool to Husserl's "transcendental turn" and sought a much more realist phenomenology, of the sort arguably already developed by Brentano.
41 As we will see toward the end of the section, A refined account?, Brentano's attitudinal framework is more flexible and at the same time more systematic than Sartre's, positing at least three dimensions along which mental states can differ in their attitudinal features. At the same time, it is only in Sartre's work that this framework reaches its most plausible development with respect to the specific question of the perception/imagination distinction.
42 The disadvantage in postulating a hyletic difference between perception and imagination, as opposed to a content difference, is in the mysterious air surrounding the notion of *hylē*. The advantage is that it does not seem immediately implausible the way a content difference does. Yesterday I saw a plane flying above my house. It is exceedingly plausible that today I can in principle imagine *exactly* what I saw yesterday—not something very similar to what I saw, but exactly what I saw. This means that I can have an imaginative experience with the exact same content as yesterday's perceptual experience, not just a content very similar to it but differing in some details. Likewise, I can episodically remember or fantasize (in the technical sense of having a phantasmagoric experience) exactly what I perceived—just as I can entertain or believe exactly the same thing, not just very similar things.
43 Sartre is unclear on *what* that non-attitudinal (hyletic or content-related) difference might be. In one place, he tentatively floats the possibility that "spontaneity" might be involved (Sartre 1936, p. 159/2012, p. 141). But later Sartre tells us that its spontaneity is a matter of imagination taking a non-thetic position toward itself (Sartre 1940, p. 26/2004, p. 14); this makes it sound like an attitudinal feature after all. Another suggestion might flow from Sartre's claim that the imagined object is always exhausted by what the imagining subject knows about it, whereas the perceived object overflows what the perceiving subject knows (Sartre 1940, pp. 20–21/2004, pp. 10–11); this is what Sartre calls the "quasi-observational" character of images. It might be claimed this means that perception and imagination differ in terms of their contents' openness to interpretation: one can perceive a duck–rabbit figure without the perception settling which one it is, but if one imagines a duck–rabbit figure, it must be qua duck or qua rabbit (see, e.g., Pylyshyn 2003). However, this account cannot

explain ability to tell apart introspectively perception and imagination in cases not involving ambiguous figures.

44 Throughout this presentation of the argument, a perceptual experience that has undergone Husserl's neutrality modification is called a "neutralized perceptual experience."

45 Indeed, negation itself can undergo a neutrality modification, whereby "negating is no longer serious negating" (Husserl 1913, p. 258).

46 Furthermore, it is unclear what the argument's conclusion precisely shows. For there may be a non-attitudinal difference between imaginative experience and neutralized perceptual experience that does not pertain to their own phenomenal characters but to the processes leading up to them. Clearly, the process of performing a phenomenological reduction is a conscious, personal-level process. It is something that I do, not something that happens to me: a conscious, introspectively accessible process. The neutrality modification does not descend on my perceptual experience in the dark, without my awareness; it is the result of an operation that I myself consciously perform. Therefore, I should be able to tell by introspection not only that my neutralized perceptual experience has this content and that attitude, but also that it was formed by that particular conscious process which is the phenomenological reduction. Crucially, that process is absent in the formation of imaginative, phantasmagoric, and mnemonic experiences alike (and other introspectible processes are present at least in some of these). This could account for my first-person knowledge of which experience I am having.

47 The revamped argument would look like this: (1) neutralized phantasmagoric experience and neutralized perceptual experience are introspectively discriminable; so (2) there must be a phenomenal difference between neutralized phantasmagoric experience and neutralized perceptual experience; but (3) there is no attitudinal difference between neutralized phantasmagoric experience and neutralized perceptual experience; therefore (4) there must be some non-attitudinal difference between neutralized phantasmagoric experience and neutralized perceptual experience.

48 Presumably, the purpose of this is to consider what actions the latter recommends. In this respect, the operation is akin to supposing or hypothesizing that $p$ in the context of seeing what might follow from it. By the same token, the purpose of performing the phenomenological reduction is presumably to facilitate appreciation of the different appearances subtended by the object, in accordance with Husserl's method for phenomenological inquiry.

49 By "no credence whatsoever" I do not mean a credence of 0 percent, but rather lack of any assignment of credence.

50 One model might be that one simply adds a new experience to one's train perception, namely, a "pretend phantasm" of a train. Here there is not so much a neutrality *modification* as a neutrality *addition*. Another model is that one's perceptual experience is modified in such a way that it no longer exhibits representing-as-existent, but a subtler attitudinal feature we may call bracketed-representing-as-existent. Here there is a neutrality modification, but its result is not simple mere-representing that lacks any traces of the original, neutralized experience; on the contrary, every neutralized state exhibits its own special attitudinal feature (bracketed-representing-as-true for belief, bracketed-representing-as-good for desire, and so on).

51 It is of course possible that I am misremembering certain details of that encounter, or have an indeterminate mnemonic representation of a scene whose perceptual representation was fully determinate. But we can readily conceive of a pair of experiences, one perceptual and one mnemonic, for which the content really is identical.

52 This phenomenological claim, like any other, may be reasonably denied. I will consider the main objection to it at the end of this section. But a more minor objection can be addressed now: that unrecognized episodic memories and cases in which one is unsure whether one is remembering or imagining show that a feeling of pastness cannot be part of the very phenomenology of memory. Somewhat paradoxically, such objections falter on the assumption that phenomenology must always be self-intimating and introspection always infallible. Otherwise, we can suppose that unrecognized memories, and memories undistinguished from imaginations, have a phenomenology of pastness that introspection, being less than omnipotent, simply misses out on.

53 With this Brentano may disagree, however. He writes that "no presentation could fail to have a temporal mode" and "it is impossible to have a presentation of something with a general temporal mode, as though a thing might appear indeterminately as past, future [etc.]" (Brentano 1911, p. 280). However, I am unaware of any argument for this provided by Brentano.

54 Compare: desiring ice cream represents-as-good ice cream; believing that ice cream is good also represents ice cream as good, but it does so as part of the content believed, not as part of the mode of representing (that is, it represents-as-true that ice cream is good, which is structurally very different from representing-as-good ice cream).

55 A vague sense of plausibility attaches to this extension when we consider that existence, time, and modality have presented distinctive but often parallel challenges in metaphysics.

56 For example, when the occurrent intuition that identity is transitive dawns on one, it represents-as-necessary the transitivity of identity. It may also be held that, unlike perceptual experience, imaginative experience represents-as-possible. It is often thought that imagination represents possibilia (we cannot imagine a square circle, for example). If one held that it represents them *as possibilia*, one could also maintain that it is characteristic of imaginative experience of *O* that it represents-as-possible *O*; this would be a modal-attitudinal feature of imagination.

57 This is clearly Russell's view of memory: "Memory demands (*a*) an image, (*b*) a belief in past existence. The belief may be expressed in the words 'this existed'" (Russell 1921, p. 155).

58 Source amnesia has been known since the later 1950s (see Evans and Thorne 1966), and has been rigorously studied in experimental settings at least since the mid-1980s (see Schacter et al. 1984).

59 Thus we may concede that typically the content of perception presents a higher-resolution scene than that of imagination—as long as sometimes the resolution can be the same. Likewise, we may note that perceptual experience always presents its object as spatially located relative to the subject, whereas it is possible to imagine the same object in an entirely aspatial manner—as long as it is also possible to imagine the object as spatially located just the way a perceived object is spatially located.

60 This work was supported by the French National Research Agency grants ANR-11-0001-02 PSL* and ANR-10-LABX-0087. For comments on a previous draft, I am grateful to Margherita Arcangeli, David Chalmers, Matthew Eshleman, Jonathan Webber, and Kenneth Williford. For useful conversations, I would like to thank Margherita Arcangeli, Joëlle Proust, and Kenneth Williford.

## References

Bayne, T. and M. Montague 2011. *Cognitive Phenomenology*. Oxford: Oxford University Press.
De Beauvoir, S. 1960. *The Prime of Life*. Trans. P. Green. New York: Paragon, 1992.
Brentano, F.C. 1874. *Psychology from an Empirical Standpoint*. Trans. A.C. Rancurello, D.B. Terrell, and L.L. McAlister. London: Routledge and Kegan Paul, 1973.
Brentano, F.C. 1889. *The Origin of Our Knowledge of Right and Wrong*. Trans. R. Chisholm and E.H. Schneewind. London: Routledge and Kegan Paul, 1969.
Brentano, F.C. 1911. Appendix to the Classification of Mental Phenomena. In Brentano 1874.
Brentano, F.C. 1928. *Sensory and Noetic Consciousness*. Ed. O. Kraus, Trans. M. Schättle and L.L. McAlister. London: Routledge and Kegan Paul.
Brentano, F.C. 1933. *The Theory of Categories*. Ed. A. Kastil. Trans. R.M. Chisholm and N. Guterman. The Hague: Martinus Nijhoff, 1981.
Brentano, F.C. 1959. *Grundzuge der Ästhetik*. Ed. F. Mayer-Hillerbrand. Bern: Francke Verlag.
Byrne, A. 2001. Intentionalism Defended. *Philosophical Review* 110: 199–240.
Byrne, A. 2010. Recollection, Perception, Imagination. *Philosophical Studies* 148: 15–26.
Casey, E. 2000. *Imagining: A Phenomenological Study*, 2nd ed. Bloomington: Indiana University Press.
Cohen, L.J. 1992. *An Essay on Belief and Acceptance*. Oxford: Clarendon.
Contat, M. and M. Rybalka 1970. *Les Écrits de Sartre*. Paris: Gallimard.
Currie, G. and I. Ravenscroft 2002. *Recreative Minds: Imagination in Philosophy and Psychology*. Oxford: Oxford University Press.
De Beauvoir, S. 1960. *The Prime of Life*. Trans. P. Green. New York: Paragon, 1992.
Dretske, F.I. 1995. *Naturalizing the Mind*. Cambridge, MA: MIT Press.
Evans, F.J. and W.A. Thorn 1966. Two Types of Posthypnotic Amnesia: Recall Amnesia and Source Amnesia. *International Journal of Clinical and Experimental Hypnosis* 14: 162–179.
Gilson, E. 1939. Franz Brentano's Interpretation of Mediaeval Philosophy. *Mediaeval Studies* 1: 1–10.
Gilson, L. 1955a. *La psychologies descriptive selon Franz Brentano*. Paris: Vrin.
Gilson, L. 1955b. *Méthode et métaphysique selon Franz Brentano*. Paris: Vrin.
Harman, G. 1990. The Intrinsic Quality of Experience. *Philosophical Perspectives* 4: 31–52.
Hume, D. 1739. *A Treatise of Human Nature*. http://ebooks.adelaide.edu.au/h/hume/david/h92t/index.html
Husserl, E. 1901. *Logical Investigations*, Vol. II. Trans. D. Moran. London: Routledge, 1970.
Husserl, E. 1913. *Ideas Pertaining to a Pure Phenomenology and a Phenomenological Philosophy*, Vol. 1. Trans. F. Kersten. Dordrecht: Kluwer, 1982.
Johnston, W.M. 1972. *The Austrian Mind*. Berkeley, CA: California University Press.

Kind, A. 2001. Putting the Image Back in Imagination. *Philosophy and Phenomenological Research* 62: 85–109.
Kind, A. 2013. The Heterogeneity of the Imagination. *Erkenntnis* 78: 141–159.
Kriegel, U. 2011. *The Sources of Intentionality*. Oxford and New York: Oxford University Press.
Kriegel, U. 2013. A Hesitant Defense of Introspection. *Philosophical Studies* 165: 1165–1176.
McGinn, C. 2004. *Mindsight: Image, Dream, Meaning*. Cambridge, MA: Harvard University Press.
Marty, A. 1908. *Untersuchungen zur Grundlegung der allgemeinen Grammatik und Sprachphilosophie*. Halle: Max Niemeyer.
Meinong, A. 1902. *On Assumptions*. Trans. J. Heanue. Berkeley, CA: University of California Press, 1983.
Merleau-Ponty, M. 1936. L'imagination. *Journal de Psychologie Normale et Pathologique* 33: 756–761.
Nanay, B. 2010. Perception and Imagination: Amodal Perception as Mental Imagery. *Philosophical Studies* 150: 239–254.
Perky, C.W. An Experimental Study of Imagination. *American Journal of Psychology* 21: 422–452.
Pylyshyn, Z.W. 2003. *Seeing and Visualizing*. Cambridge, MA: MIT Press.
Rowlands, M. 2013. Sartre, Consciousness, and Intentionality. *Phenomenology and the Cognitive Sciences* 12: 521–536.
Russell, B. 1921. *The Analysis of Mind*. London: Routledge, 1995.
Sartre, J.-P. 1936. *L'imagination*. Paris: F. Alcan. Reprinted by PUF, 1983.
Sartre, J.-P. 1938. Structure intentionelle de l'image. *Revue de métaphysique et de morale* 45: 543–609.
Sartre, J.-P. 1939. Une idée fondamentale de la phénoménologie de Husserl: l'intentionalité. *Nouvelle Revue Française* 304: 129–131.
Sartre, J.-P. 1940. *L'imaginaire*. Paris: Gallimard.
Sartre, J.-P. 2004. *The Imaginary*. Trans. J.M. Webber. London: Routledge.
Sartre, J.-P. 2012. *The Imagination*. Trans. K.W. Williford and D. Rudrauf. London and New York: Routledge.
Schacter, D.L., J.L. Harbluk, and D.R. McLachlan 1984. Retrieval without Recollection: An Experimental Analysis of Source Amnesia. *Journal of Verbal Learning and Verbal Behavior* 23: 593–611.
Smith, B. 1981. Kafka and Brentano: A Study in Descriptive Psychology. In B. Smith (ed.), *Structure and Gestalt: Philosophy and Literature in Austria-Hungary and Her Successor States*. Amsterdam: John Benjamins.
Stevenson, L.F. 2003. Twelve Conceptions of Imagination. *British Journal of Aesthetics* 43: 238–259.
Strawson, P.F. 1970. Imagination and Perception. In L. Foster and J.W. Swanson (eds.), *Experience and Theory*. Amherst, MA: University of Massachusetts Press.
Tănăsescu, I. 2010. Le concept psychologique de la représentation de la fantaisie et sa réception chez Husserl. *Studia Phænomenologica* 10: 45–75.
Tulving, E. 1972. Episodic and Semantic Memory. In E. Tulving and W. Donaldson (eds.), *Organization of Memory*. New York: Academic Press.
Tulving, E. 2001. Episodic Memory and Common Sense: How Far Apart? *Philosophical Transactions: Biological Sciences* 356: 1505–1515.
Williford, K.W. 2013. Husserl's Hyletic Data and Phenomenal Consciousness. *Phenomenology and the Cognitive Sciences* 12: 501–520.

# PART III
# Pre-reflectivity disputed

# 11 Do we need pre-reflective self-consciousness?

About Sartre and Brentano

*Eric Trémault*

I want here to defend the idea that Sartre's conception of intentionality comes much closer to Brentano's than to Husserl's, even though Sartre almost never refers to Brentano, so that (even if Sartre knew of the influence Brentano had on Husserl's thought)[1] it is dubious that he ever read him. This easily explains why no study has ever been written on the links between Sartre and Brentano's thoughts, at least to my knowledge. However, it seems to me that Sartre's criticisms against Husserl have led him, whether he knew it or not, back to Brentano's initial notion of intentionality. This is most manifest in the fact that Sartre rejects Husserl's notion of *hylè* as an immanent and real element of consciousness because he claims that *hylè*, like any other being in-itself, can only appear as an intentional object. On this point, at least, he agrees with Brentano, according to whom "physical phenomena" (which include traditional empiricist sensations, and thus what Husserl would later conceptualize as "*hylè*") are intentional objects. Thus, all consciousness is for Sartre and Brentano intentional, whereas Husserl, when he admits the existence of *hylè*, is forced to acknowledge that it is somehow conscious without being an intentional object.

Another fundamental point on which Sartre and Brentano seem to agree is that all intentional consciousness (and hence all consciousness) is necessarily pre-reflectively conscious of itself: this idea is centrally developed by both authors through Brentano's concept of "inner perception" and Sartre's concept of "non-thetical self-consciousness." Note that this self-consciousness, for both authors, is not consciousness of an Ego that would transcend phenomenal time and support the intentional acts: it is consciousness only of the intentional acts themselves, which are perceived as selves because they are perceived by themselves. Sartre thus writes that: "The sure and certain content of the pseudo-'Cogito' is not 'I am conscious of this chair', but '*there is* consciousness of this chair'" (Sartre 2004, p. 9).

But I will leave the question of the Ego entirely aside, and focus only on the pre-reflective consciousness of the intentional acts by themselves, which is supposed by both authors to exist and to give its very meaning to the notion of consciousness itself.

Now, both points on which Sartre and Brentano agree at first sight seem to me wrong for reasons I shall try to explain in this chapter. One of them is that they seem to introduce unnecessary theoretical difficulties, such as understanding how self-consciousness can be non-reflective. So this led me to consider whether there might not be some fundamental reason for such a convergence on what appeared to me as similar mistakes. And I will try to show that this reason is precisely that Brentano and Sartre have a similar, though not identical, understanding of the Cartesian Cogito, as meaning that only intentional acts possess self-evidence. Such is not the way Husserl understands the Cogito, and I will end by trying to argue in favor of Husserl's interpretation on that matter.

## Descartes' Cogito according to Brentano

Let me start then by considering what the Cogito means for Brentano. I will then try to show that his notion of "inner perception," and the difficulties it involves, are the result of this interpretation he makes of the Cogito.

### *Inner perception*

In *Psychology From an Empirical Standpoint* (Brentano 1974), it is quite clear that Descartes' Cogito means for Brentano that mental phenomena appear with self-evidence, as contrasted with physical phenomena, which do not. Thus, he first defines "inner perception" by its object, as the presentation of mental phenomena, as opposed to "external perception," which is the presentation of physical phenomena. But he immediately adds that:

> Besides the fact that it has a special object, inner perception possesses another distinguishing characteristic: its immediate, infallible self-evidence. Of all the types of knowledge of the objects of experience, inner perception alone possesses this characteristic.
> (Brentano 1974, p. 70)

Now, what this self-evidence means is that inner perception is precisely a "perception," in the German sense of the word, "*Wahrnehmung,*" which literally means taking something to be true, or the grasping of the truth: therefore, inner perception "is really the only perception in the strict sense of the word" (Brentano 1974, p. 70), whereas "strictly speaking, so-called external perception is not perception" (Brentano 1974, p. 70). And that inner perception's objects are *true* objects means that they are *real* objects:

> of their existence we have that clear knowledge and complete certainty which is provided by immediate insight. Consequently, no one can really doubt that a mental state which he perceives in himself exists, and that it exists just as he perceives it.
> (Brentano 1974, p. 7)

They are true in themselves. As they appear to be, so they are in reality, a fact which is attested to by the evidence with which they are perceived.

(Brentano 1974, p. 15)

This is why Brentano grants "real existence" or "actual existence" only to mental phenomena, and not to physical phenomena:

> We said that mental phenomena are those phenomena which alone can be perceived in the strict sense of the word. We could just as well say that they are those phenomena which alone possess real existence as well as intentional existence. Knowledge, joy and desire really exist. Color, sound and warmth have only a phenomenal and intentional existence.
>
> (Brentano 1974, p. 70)

Mental phenomena

> alone, therefore, are perceived with immediate evidence. Indeed, in the strict sense of the word, they alone are perceived (*wahrgenommenen*). On this basis we proceeded to define them as the only phenomena which possess *actual existence* in addition to intentional existence.
>
> (Brentano 1974, p. 75)

It is important to note here that mental phenomena are intentional objects just as well as physical phenomena: inner perception is the (intentional) "presentation" of a mental phenomenon—for instance, the presentation of a presentation. So, mental phenomena's real or actual existence must not be opposed to intentional existence: it is "additional" to intentional existence. It must be opposed to deceptive existence (Brentano 1974, pp. 6–7).

## *Physical phenomena*

Now, what I think is not clearly justified by Brentano is the implicit assumption that deceptive existence must be *only* intentional, and cannot be real existence. One reason for this problem may be that Brentano does not clearly distinguish between real existence of the appearance and real existence of the thing signified by the appearance, which makes it difficult to know which one exactly is the intentional object. Another way to put it is to say that Brentano does not clearly distinguish between content and object, as has been often said and often discussed, since Husserl emphasized this problem in his *Logical Investigations* (Husserl 2001, Investigation VI, Appendix, pp. 335ff.; also Investigation V, Chapter 2, pp. 94ff.). But this is a complex debate, with which I cannot engage here. Brentano says that physical phenomena are the intentional objects of sensation, so it seems to me safe to say that they are the traditional empiricist contents of sensation, as is quite manifest through the examples Brentano gives, and the fact that he does not comment on them much: "Examples of physical phenomena ... are a color, a figure, a landscape which I see, a chord which I hear, warmth, cold, odor which I sense; as well as similar images which appear in the imagination" (Brentano 1974, p. 61).

Physical phenomena are not physical things but they are figures and secondary qualities of such things, and, as such, they are objects in their own right. Of course, Brentano also says that physical phenomena are objects of external perception, but he is very clear about the fact that this expression is "improper" (Brentano 1974, p. 76) and rests precisely on a confusion between physical phenomena and "the external causes of sensations" in which they occur (Brentano 1974, p. 76).

But then again, what Brentano does not clearly justify is the idea that the unreality of the thing, which the physical phenomenon signifies, implies the unreality of the physical phenomenon itself. As a matter of fact, Brentano has to argue (first against Bain and later against Aristotle himself) in favor of the *possibility* that physical phenomena might have absolute reality, despite the fact that they are intentional objects. For, as I said, mental phenomena are intentional objects too, and they do have absolute reality. So physical phenomena *could* also be absolute, however intentional they are. Brentano thus says against Bain:

> It is undoubtedly true that a color appears to us only when we have a presentation of it. We cannot conclude from this, however, that a color cannot exist without being presented. Only if the state of being presented were contained in the color as one of its elements, as a certain quality and intensity is contained in it, would a color which is not presented imply a contradiction, since a whole without one of its parts is indeed a contradiction. But this is obviously not the case ... The fallacy reveals itself quite clearly in the case of mental phenomena. If someone said, "I cannot think about a mental phenomenon without thinking about it; therefore I can only think about mental phenomena as thought by me; therefore no mental phenomenon exists outside my thinking," his method of reasoning would be identical to that of Bain. Nevertheless, even Bain will not deny that his individual mental life is not the only one which has actual existence.
> 
> (Brentano 1974, p. 71)

And he argues accordingly against Aristotle:

> The concept of sound is not a relative concept. If it were, the act of hearing would not be the secondary object of the mental act, but instead it would be the primary object along with the sound ... Likewise, we could not think of anything except certain relations to ourselves and our thoughts, and this is undoubtedly false.
> 
> (Brentano 1974, p. 101)

As I understand it, all this means that there is no necessary reason for physical phenomena to be relative, for their *essence* is not relative: in other words, they are not relational predicates of intentional presentations, but their concept is positive and absolute. Nevertheless, unlike mental phenomena, physical phenomena *are* relative in Brentano's view, if not in their essence, then probably in their existence, and *as a matter of fact*, as is clearly shown when, after this argumentation in favor of the absolute essence of physical phenomena, Brentano immediately adds: "We will nevertheless make no mistake if in general we deny to physical phenomena any existence other than intentional existence" (Brentano 1974, p. 72).

In my view, the only explanation one can find to this assertion by Brentano is precisely that the way he understands the Cogito excludes the existence of intentional objects and requires that only intentional acts exist. But before I justify my interpretation, the idea that physical phenomena might have *mere* intentional existence requires some more explanation. What this means is that they are only appearances of beings, not real beings: they only are insofar as their presentations are: "If mental phenomena did not exist in reality, neither physical nor mental phenomena would even exist as phenomena" (Brentano 1974, p. 133). And this remains true, even though those presentations present them as something other than them:

> Even if, in the act of hearing, nothing is perceived in the proper sense of the term but hearing itself, this does not make it any the less true that something else besides hearing itself is present within it as presented and constitutes its content.
> (Brentano 1974, p. 95)

But this appearance of something other than presentation is precisely an illusion. Thus, in dreams,

> that which these mental activities refer to as their content and which really does appear to be external is, in actuality, no more outside of us than in us. It is mere appearance, just as the physical phenomena which appear to us in waking life correspond to no reality.
> (Brentano 1974, p. 136)

Dreams and physical phenomena are "no more outside of us *than in us*": only the intentional acts of dreaming and sensing truly exist. I think the moment when Brentano is the most clear about how we should understand *mere* "intentional existence" is when he identifies the appearing of physical phenomena with their being presented, through the hypothesis he explicitly admits, and he believes is implicit in Weber and Fechner's laws, that the intensity of physical phenomena is equal to the intensity of the sensation that presents them:

284   Eric Trémault

> The intensity of the act of presentation is always equal to the intensity with which the object that is presented appears to us; in other words, it is equal to the intensity of the phenomenon which constitutes the content of the presentation.
>
> (Brentano 1974, p. 93)

The reason for this equality is, I think, that the intensity of the physical phenomenon is nothing else than the intensity of the act which presents it: "As we use the verb 'to present', 'to be presented' means the same as 'to appear'" (Brentano 1974, p. 62). "We speak of a presentation whenever something appears to us" (Brentano 1974, p. 153).

Thus, sensation is a more or less intense appearance of something that is not only this appearance. However, in the case of physical phenomena, there is nothing else than this appearance, even though there appears to be something else, and even though there might be physical things which are signified by this appearance, and some which might cause it.

### *Pre-reflective self-consciousness*

Let us now consider again the case of mental phenomena. We know now that they do not only appear, but are the only things that also really exist besides being intentional objects.

But it is impossible to prove their truth, Brentano argues, for this would require a comparison with a real thing which they resemble: but, unfortunately, to know this real thing would precisely require that it appears to us with self-evidence. So the evidence of the appearance's truth is the "ultimate foundation of cognition" of reality and:

> The truth of inner perception cannot be proved in any way. But it has something more than proof; it is immediately evident. If anyone were to mount a skeptical attack against this ultimate foundation of cognition, he would find no other foundation upon which to erect an edifice of knowledge. Thus, there is no need to justify our confidence in inner perception. What is clearly needed instead is a theory about the relation between such perception and its object, which is compatible with its immediate evidence.
>
> (Brentano 1974, p. 109)

This quote is crucial for my point in two ways. First, it explains why Brentano could not justify the unreality of physical phenomena: the falsity of external perception cannot be proven any more than the truth of inner perception, and for the same reasons. It is grounded on the evidence, or on the lack of evidence, of the perception concerned. This explains why Brentano's thesis concerning the existential relativity of physical phenomena seemed to lack justification: it can only be justified through evidence of the Cogito.

The second reason why this quote is crucial for my point is that it clearly presents Brentano's further developments regarding inner perception as means to understand the possibility of the evidence of the Cogito as Brentano understands it. In other words, Brentano's theory of inner perception as pre-reflective self-consciousness is a transcendental analysis of the conditions of possibility of the Cogito as Brentano understands it. Which means that if this understanding of the Cogito is wrong, the whole theory of inner perception as pre-reflective self-consciousness becomes pointless. Conversely, if the notion of a pre-reflective inner perception proves to be contradictory or excessively contrived, then we'll have good reason to suspect that Brentano's interpretation of the Cogito is wrong.

Let us start, then, with considering Brentano's notion of a pre-reflective inner perception, in order to justify that we later take a new look at his understanding of the Cogito.

If the inner perception of an intentional act (say, a presentation again, such as the hearing of a sound, even though it is well known that Brentano admits two other types of intentional acts, judgment and feeling or love) is another, higher-order or reflective presentation, then one has to admit, either that this higher-order presentation is unconscious, or that it is itself conscious through another higher-order presentation again, which would generate an infinite regress:

> If every mental phenomenon must be accompanied by consciousness, the presentation of hearing must also be accompanied by consciousness, just as the presentation of the sound is. Consequently, there must also be a presentation of it. In the hearer, therefore, there are three presentations: a presentation of sound, a presentation of the act of hearing, and a presentation of the presentation of this act. But this third presentation cannot be the last one. Since it too is conscious, it is present in the mind and in turn its presentation is also presented. In brief, the series will either be infinite or will terminate with an unconscious presentation.
>
> (Brentano 1974, pp. 93–94)

But Brentano refuses to admit that some intentional acts might be unconscious, and rather admits that inner perception is not a separate perception of the act by another act, but is an "incidental" (Brentano 1974, p. 22) presentation of the act by itself. Thus, every intentional presentation has two objects: "the sound is the *primary object* of the *act* of hearing, and . . . the act of hearing itself is the *secondary object*" (Brentano 1974, p. 98).

Brentano gives two main descriptive reasons for this thesis: first, if inner perception were a higher-order perception, then the intentional object of the presented presentation would have to "be presented twice. Yet this is not the case" (Brentano 1974, p. 98). But the most important reason is obviously that, if inner perception were a higher-order perception, then there would be no reason for inner perception to be more certain than external perception:

> If the cognition which accompanies a mental act were an act in its own right, a second act added on to the first one . . . how could it be certain in and of itself? Indeed, how could we even be sure of its infallibility at all?
>
> (Brentano 1974, p. 107)

Therefore, a pre-reflective consciousness of the presentation by itself is the only way to ground the possibility of a Cogito which is only a certainty of the intentional act, and not of the intentional object. If no intentional object can ever be certain, then inner perception can never be reflective. Brentano concludes:

> Whenever a mental act is the object of an accompanying inner cognition, it contains itself in its entirety as presented and known, in addition to its reference to a primary object. This alone makes possible the infallibility and immediate evidence of inner perception.
>
> (Brentano 1974, p. 107)

There seems to be here an implicit premise according to which it is always easier to know oneself than to know something else. But there is actually no need for such a dubious premise: the only premise is again Brentano's Cogito which excludes the certainty of the intentional object—so that it would simply be contradictory to this Cogito to admit that a reflective perception is certain.

Now, apart from the prima facie difficulty of admitting a self-awareness of the acts that is not reflective, there is another major problem in this pre-reflective self-consciousness theory as a consequence of the Brentanian Cogito: as Brentano himself emphasizes, we can pay attention only to the *primary* object of any presentation; to pay attention to the *secondary* object of the presentation would ipso facto turn it into a *primary* object and thus turn the presentation of that object into a reflective consciousness:

> The truth is that something which is only the *secondary object of an act* can undoubtedly be an object of consciousness in this act, but cannot be an object of observation in it. Observation requires that one turn his attention to an object as a primary object.
>
> (Brentano 1974, p. 99)

The evidence of the Cogito experience thus becomes a necessarily and permanently inattentive evidence. At first sight, it might seem an advantage to the Brentanian Cogito theory, since it makes it impossible to falsify: it becomes impossible to verify that we *do* have the Cogito experience that Brentano talks about. Thus, the Brentanian Cogito itself directly entails its own irrefutability. However, since Popper at least, the logical irrefutability of a hypothesis should not be seen as an advantage, but rather as itself a reason to reject it.

## Descartes' Cogito according to Sartre

### Pre-reflective self-consciousness as a transcendental condition for Descartes' Cogito

Let us now turn to Sartre and see whether he manages to overcome those difficulties with his own theory of pre-reflective self-consciousness.

At first sight, it seems that he does, since he admits that the Cartesian Cogito is actually reflective: the self-evident intentional act is not its own object, it is the intentional object of another intentional act: "My reflecting consciousness does not take itself for object when I carry out the Cogito. What it affirms concerns the reflected consciousness... Thus the consciousness that says 'I think' is precisely not the consciousness that thinks" (Sartre 2004, p. 6).

However, Sartre admits that such a reflective Cogito is evident nevertheless: "the certainty of the Cogito is absolute" (Sartre 2004, p. 6). Consequently, Sartre admits that evidence is achievable through reflection. Hence, it seems that he doesn't have to admit that the evidence of the Cogito is not attentive. Furthermore, pre-reflective self-awareness doesn't immediately seem to be a transcendental condition of the Cogito any more.

But, as we will now see, the transcendental conditions of the Cogito actually become much more complex in Sartre's thought than they already were in Brentano's.

First of all, pre-reflective self-consciousness actually remains an important condition of possibility of the reflective Cogito, though less directly than in Brentano's theory. Indeed, the reflective Cogito is an intentional act directed on another intentional act. Therefore, it has to obey the transcendental conditions of all intentionality. But Sartre's specificity is precisely to make pre-reflective self-consciousness the central condition of intentionality, for an intentional act must be consciousness of something as an object, an object being defined as that which faces and contrasts with consciousness by not being that consciousness: "to be conscious *of* something is to be confronted with a concrete and full presence, which *is not* consciousness" (Sartre 1994, p. lx).

That is why every thetical consciousness of an object implies a non-thetical self-consciousness: in order to be conscious of an object as not being oneself, it must be at the same time self-conscious as not being the object.

But Sartre also wants to radicalize the idea of "intentionality" whereby *every* consciousness is always, from the very beginning, the consciousness of an object.[2] Thus, if every consciousness is intentional, is the consciousness of an object, then: "each appearance . . . is already in itself alone a *transcendent being*, not a subjective material of impressions" (Sartre 1994, p. lxi).

Sartre thus matches Husserl, who explains in his *Ideen* that consciousness constitutes its objects from a *hylè*, a "subjective material of impressions," which itself is not intentionally conscious, but is "lived," which means it is not transcendent, therefore not an object, but is immanent. We would then have to admit a non-intentional form of consciousness inside the intentional consciousness itself. Whereas, if we are to radicalise the expression "all consciousness is consciousness of something," we have to say, as Sartre does, that:

> the odor, which I suddenly breathe in with my eyes closed, even before I have referred it to an odorous object, is already an odor-being and not a subjective impression. The light, which strikes my eyes in the morning through my closed eyelids, is already a light-being.
> (Sartre 1994, pp. 187–188)

Now, the whole problem is then to conceive the self in pre-reflective self-consciousness in such a way that self-consciousness remains nothing but a thetical consciousness of the *object* of the self. For all consciousness to be intentional, self-consciousness must remain a thetical consciousness of the object. As is known, the answer Sartre finds to that problem is to refuse to conceive of the self as an ego that would block the access of self-consciousness to the object, but to conceive of it as merely the pure and translucent negation of the object, which is possible, according to Sartre, if self-consciousness is consciousness of being a freedom, that is, a wrenching from being (and especially from its inward determinism) towards an imaginary end not yet in existence. This way, a non-thetical self-consciousness can only be the consciousness of a negation of the object, and therefore, strictly speaking, the very consciousness of the object itself. Sartre thus writes:

> the for-itself can be only in the mode of a reflection causing itself to be reflected as not being a certain being . . . The reflected causes itself to be qualified *outside* next to a certain being as *not being* that being. This is precisely what we mean by 'to be consciousness *of* something'.
> (Sartre 1994, p. 174)

And this is another reason for refusing *hylè*: if intentional consciousness is conscious of itself as not being the object, it must be conscious as translucent, and thus it cannot be conscious of itself as *hylè*: "the *hylè* in fact could not be consciousness, for it would disappear in translucency and could not offer that resisting basis of impressions which must be surpassed toward the object" (Sartre 1994, p. lix).

## The pre-reflective Cogito

Nevertheless, Sartre has to admit that this consciousness of self as freedom or pure nothingness constitutes another Cogito: "There is a pre-reflective Cogito which is the condition of the Cartesian Cogito" (Sartre 1994, p. 19).

And it is clear that this pre-reflective Cogito suffers from the same problems as the Brentanian Cogito: it is a non-reflective self-consciousness and it is inattentive, which makes it impossible to refute. Furthermore, this self-consciousness is consciousness of a pure negation of being in-itself: therefore, it is, as Sartre himself likes to say, the consciousness of *nothing else* than the being it posits as not itself. Surely it is quite vain in these conditions to try and verify the existence of such a non-reflective self-consciousness.

Indeed, this Sartrean pre-reflective Cogito is exactly the same as what I have called the Brentanian Cogito. The only difference between them is that Sartre manages to clarify the relationship between the primary and secondary objects of any intentional act. There is no such thing as a secondary object of the intentional act, which is to say that the intentional act is not its own intentional object: its only intentional object is the primary object. But it can only be intentionally conscious of this primary object through being non-intentionally conscious of itself as a negation of this primary object.

Therefore, by admitting that the Brentanian Cogito is not the same as the Cartesian Cogito, but that both Cogitos are evident nonetheless, Sartre only adds the difficulties of the reflective Cogito to those of the pre-reflective one. Let us now have a look at the reflective or higher-order Cogito, in order to measure those new difficulties.

## The reflective Cogito

How can the reflective Cogito be self-evident, based on these considerations about the nature of any intentional act? It has to be the intentional knowledge of an intentional act by another intentional act: therefore, it must be the obviously true thetical position of a non-thetically self-conscious act by another non-thetically self-conscious act. I won't go too far in analyzing Sartre's efforts to understand how the evidence of such a reflective act is theoretically possible. Those efforts expand notably in *Notebooks for an Ethics* (*Cahiers pour une morale*, Sartre, 1983), which Sartre never completed. But they spread from two main problems which are already set out in *Transcendence of the Ego* and *Being and Nothingness*, and I will limit myself to these two problems.

The first problem for understanding the certainty of the reflective Cogito is that, in the end, Sartre agrees with Brentano that evidence can only be achieved through self-consciousness. This is not surprising, since Sartre, like Brentano, always considers intentional objects as dubious, whereas the certainty of the Cogito is always the certainty of an intentional act, whether reflected or not. But this implies again that, even in reflection, the reflected intentional act must not become an intentional object: if "the certainty of the Cogito is absolute," then there must be "an indissoluble unity between the reflecting consciousness and the reflected consciousness (so much so that the reflecting consciousness cannot exist without reflected consciousness)" (Sartre 2004, p. 6); or again "the reflective cannot make itself wholly other than the reflected-on . . . It does not then detach itself completely from the reflected-on, and it cannot grasp the reflected-on 'from a point of view'" (Sartre 1994, 190). The conclusion is that the reflective and the reflected-on must have the same kind of unity and being as the pre-reflective self-consciousness, only this time this unity must occur, not between a negation and a self-consciousness of this negation, but between two pre-reflective self-consciousnesses:

> It is not the appearance of a new consciousness directed on the for-itself but an intra-structural modification which the for-itself realizes in itself; in a word it is the for-itself which makes itself exist in the mode reflective–reflected-on, instead of being simply in the mode of the dyad reflection–reflecting.
>
> (Sartre 1994, p. 153)[3]

The solution for the evidence of the reflective Cogito is thus the same as the solution for the evidence of the pre-reflective one, but its complexity is squared, so to say. If one has trouble admitting the first solution, then one will not be satisfied with the second either.

The second problem is that, as Husserl had already emphasized, the evidence of the Cogito can be indubitable only if it is an adequate evidence, which means that the reflected consciousness must appear entirely, and not, like any real spatio-temporal thing, through a stream of changing aspects:

> Husserl insists on the fact that the certainty of the reflective act stems from the way that in it, consciousness is grasped without facets, without profile, as a totality (without *Abschattungen*). So much is evident. On the contrary, the spatio-temporal object always yields itself via an infinity of aspects and it is basically nothing other than the ideal unity of this infinity.
>
> (Sartre 2004, p. 8)

But the risk here is precisely to transform the reflected consciousness into some kind of spatio-temporal thing, which would mask its purely negative being. This is what Sartre calls the "impure" or "complicit" reflection, which reflectively constitutes the stream of reflected consciousnesses into psychological facts. Pure reflection, on the contrary, must be able to grasp the reflected consciousnesses themselves, as the purely self-conscious negations which they are. It would be too long and too difficult to explain how this can be achieved according to Sartre, through "a sort of *katharsis*" (Sartre 1994, p. 155), or "conversion" (Sartre 1983, pp. 486ff.). But the important fact is that, whereas the Cartesian Cogito seemed rather simple to understand or experience, the "pure" reflective Cogito, by which Sartre is trying to understand the possibility of its evidence, is, as Sartre himself admits, "always possible *de jure*, but remains quite improbable or, at least, extremely rare in our human condition" (Sartre 2004, p. 24).

In the face of such complexities, it is inevitable to wonder whether we are not confronted with purely theoretical constructions which, though irrefutable, correspond to nothing in reality. After dealing with the perplexities of Sartre's transcendental reconstructions of the Cartesian Cogito, the difficulties we had detected in Brentano's theory of self-consciousness seem quite innocent in retrospect: namely, that it is precisely non-reflective and also inattentive. But those difficulties remain after examining Sartre, and are actually at the roots of all further difficulties we have found in Sartre's theory.

So it seems worth examining now whether the understanding of the Cartesian Cogito, from which both theories of pre-reflective self-consciousness are deduced, is justified. In the Cogito, are we only certain of the reality of the intentional acts, and nothing else? Did not all those constructions of the evidence of the Cogito lead us astray from this plain evidence itself?

## Descartes' Cogito according to Husserl

I will not engage in a full discussion of Descartes's *Meditations*, of course. Therefore, I will directly jump to the "Geometrical arrangement of the arguments" in the *Second Replies*, where Descartes concludes that at least the existence of thought is certain, because we are immediately conscious of its existence: "By the word 'thought' I include everything that is in us in such a way that we are immediately aware of it. Thus all the operations of the will, understanding, imagination, and senses are thoughts" (Descartes 1992, p. 285; 2006, p. 94).

This first seems quite in agreement with the Brentanian Cogito. Notably, Descartes is quite clear in his replies to the Seventh Objections about the fact that there is no need for a reflective act to achieve this immediate awareness of thought (Descartes 1992, p. 519). But what is thought exactly? Thought is only defined by Descartes as that which immediately appears to us through our consciousness. But whereas willing, understanding, and imagining can plausibly be said to appear to us in the form of operations such as intentional acts, is it really the case with sensing? In the case of seeing, for instance, what appears, and thus indubitably exists as thought, is only figures and qualities organized in space—and this is all that is required to be certain that some thought exists, even if I am dreaming. There is no consciousness of an intentional act of "presentation" here, and when we say that we are certain to see these things, we only mean that they exist in phenomenal space: we don't mean that we have a pre-reflective self-consciousness of an act of seeing them.

Such is the way Husserl understands the Cogito when he translates it into "I am, this life is, I am living: Cogito" (Husserl 1983, p. 100). The "I" in "I am" and "I am living" is referring to the Ego of attention and I will not discuss this point here, but "this life is" is clearly including the indubitability of *hylè*, or what Brentano calls physical phenomena, into the evidence of the Cogito. Certainly, Husserl explains that the Cogito supposes an inner or immanent perception, which is actually a reflection from the intentional object to the consciousness we have of this object (Husserl 1983, §46). But the consciousness which is reflected on is very different from Brentano's presentations, for it precisely includes the physical phenomena which Brentano treats as primary intentional objects and as uncertain. Husserl's intentional objects appear and are identified through the stream of Brentano's physical phenomena, while Brentano's intentional objects are those physical phenomena themselves, which only appear and exist through intentional presentations. This is impossible in Husserl's thought, for intentional acts precisely belong to the same stream as physical phenomena or sensation data do, even when they are reflective acts of immanent perception. Indeed, both are called *Erlebnis* by Husserl ("mental processes" in the English translation): both are components of the life which immediately appears as being in the Cogito. And this means that Brentano's mental and physical phenomena appear in the exact same way for Husserl. More precisely, they do not appear, but they simply *are* in such a way that they are conscious by essence (§45): "It is evident from the essence of cogitationes, from the essence of mental processes of any kind, that ... for an existent belonging to their region, ... anything like an 'appearing', a being presented, through adumbrations makes no sense whatever" (Husserl 1983, p. 91). To appear always means to appear through a stream of phenomena or "adumbrations" (*Abschattungen*) for Husserl, so phenomena themselves cannot appear:

> It is indeed evident ... that the adumbrative sensation-contents themselves, which really inherently belong to the mental process of perceiving a physical thing, function, more particularly, as adumbrations of something but are not themselves given in turn by adumbrations.
> (Husserl 1983, p. 97)

All that can be said is that they are "*perceptually given as something absolute, and not as something identical in modes of appearance by adumbration*" (Husserl 1983, pp. 95–96; emphasis in original). If we want to realize the absolute existence of those phenomena or "mental processes" in the broader sense, we need to pay attention to them, and that is what Husserl calls reflection. But it is clear when I thus reflect on a part of my stream of consciousness that "it becomes given as having just now *been* and, in so far as it was unregarded, precisely as having been unregarded, as not having been reflected on" (Husserl 1983, p. 175). So, the Cogito convinces me of the existence of those phenomena, but it is not through this reflection that they exist: they exist as beings in-themselves or absolute phenomena even before we pay attention to them.

## Sartre on "Cartesian freedom"

In his article on "Cartesian freedom," it is clear that Sartre is well aware of this meaning of the Cogito when he reproaches Descartes of having limited the possibility of the doubt only to false ideas, i.e., to ideas whose objects do not or might not exist. That is why Descartes identifies freedom with assent to evidence, rather than to an infinite capacity of negating being, which would be indifference freedom:

> If we are able to withhold our assent to the works of the Evil Spirit, it is not because they are, which means that, true or false, they have at least, insofar as they *are* our conceptions, a minimum of being, but because they are not, that is, insofar as they relate falsely to objects that do not exist.
> (Sartre 1962, p. 191; modified)

Here, Sartre refers to the Third Meditation, where Descartes says that: "Yet as imperfect a mode of being as this is by which a thing exists in the intellect objectively through an idea, nevertheless it is plainly not nothing; hence it cannot get its being from nothing" (Descartes 1992, p. 109; 2006, p. 23).

Therefore, the doubt stops in front of the evidence of the objective reality of ideas, however true or false those ideas may be. But Sartre wants the doubt to stop only in front of itself, as a pure power to suspend its judgment:

> At the very moment that he attains this unequalled independence, against the omnipotence of the Evil Spirit, and even against God, he discovers that he is pure nothingness. Confronted with the *being* that is placed, in its entirety, between parentheses, all that remains is a simple *no*, bodiless and without memories, without knowledge and without *anyone*.
> (Sartre 1962, p. 190)

Hence, we understand more profoundly the reason why Sartre wants to repudiate the immanence of hylè to consciousness: if hylè must be doubtful, then it has to be transcendent. It cannot remain as a residue from the epoche or the doubt, or it would limit the infinity of human freedom. Ultimately, Sartre's reasons for admitting the Brentanian Cogito rather than the Cartesian one are moral reasons rather than phenomenological ones: he wants to admit that human freedom is infinite and thus he cannot accept that indifference freedom can be limited by any truth or evidence other than its own negative being.

Indeed, as Sartre emphasizes against Descartes, if human freedom is really as infinite as God's will, as Descartes said, then it cannot be limited by truth, since Descartes admitted in his 1630 letters to Mersenne that God had created eternal truths and could not be limited by them (Descartes 2010, pp. 254ff.). Hence, even the existence of *hylè* has to be doubtful and put into brackets during the *epoche*. Sartre concludes:

> It took two centuries of crisis—a crisis of Faith and a crisis of Science—for man to regain the creative freedom that Descartes placed in God, and for anyone finally to suspect the following truth, which is an essential basis of humanism: man is the being as a result of whose appearance a world exists.
>
> (Sartre 1962, p. 196)

Now, we know from reading *Being and Nothingness* that this cannot mean that man is the creator of being-in-itself. Rather, Sartre tries to demonstrate through his own "ontological proof" that the transphenomenality and independence of being in-itself can be "derived . . . from the *pre-reflective* being of the percipiens" (Sartre 1994, p. lx). So, what Sartre means when he says that man is the being as a result of which a world exists is only that man is responsible for the *appearance of* being in-itself, because the "world" is precisely only this appearance of being-in-itself. The world appears as a situation when man totalizes present being in-itself through negating it towards a future end. And each "quality" then appears as in the world rather than as being in-itself, which means that it appears through an aspect which relates it to the end considered. That is why Sartre says that a phenomenon is a "relative-absolute": the being of the phenomenon is in-itself and absolute, but its appearance as phenomenon is relative to the human freedom to which it appears. As Sartre says: "While I cannot make this [tree bark] cease being green, it is I who am responsible for my apprehending it as a rough green or a green roughness" (Sartre 1994, p. 188). This is another central argument of Sartre against *hylè*.

> Although an *object* may disclose itself only through a single *Abschattung*, the sole fact of there being a subject implies the possibility of multiplying the points of view *on* that *Abschattung*. This suffices to multiply to infinity the *Abschattung* under consideration.
>
> (Sartre 1994, p. xlvii)

But this argument is actually rather weak. If Sartre only says that I am responsible for my knowledge *about* the tree bark, then he doesn't give any reason to admit that the appearance itself which is known in different ways should be relative. If, on the other hand, he admits that this knowledge about the appearance changes the appearance itself (that rough green is phenomenally different than green roughness, which is quite possible), then the changed appearance is now the *Abschattung* itself and not the appearance of a transcendent *Abschattung*, quite as much as the duck which I see in the duck–rabbit picture is now an absolute appearance in itself, and not the appearance of a duck–rabbit phenomenon.

## Conclusion

I think it is now possible to conclude that non-thetical self-consciousness is not required as a transcendental condition of the Cogito, because what actually appears in the Cogito, and thus resists doubt, is not only intentional acts or some actual negation of being in-itself, but also absolute phenomena such as colors and Gestalt qualities or figures, which are themselves beings in-themselves. If those phenomena are admitted as evident, then there is no reason to attribute their appearance to intentional acts: it must be attributed to them, for it is simply the way they are. To put it in a provocative way, it seems to me that the Cogito is the proof of the existence of sense data.

It might then seem possible to reply that, even if we grant that the Cogito thus directly reveals physical phenomena, it *also* reveals intentional acts, or mental phenomena, in Brentano's terms, and that non-reflective self-consciousness still seems very necessary in order to understand that such mental phenomena appear. But to say that physical phenomena immediately appear as the beings they are amounts to saying that no *presentation* act is required for them to appear. Hence, no presentation act is required for mental phenomena to appear either. More precisely, once we have gotten rid of the idea that presentation is a necessary condition for the appearance of anything in general, then neither physical nor mental phenomena need to be intentional objects in order to appear. All that is required is that they exist as the phenomena which they are. Of course, it remains quite possible, and indeed rather obvious, that operations such as will, understanding, imagination, and even perception, are intentional acts, and thus have intentional objects. But once sensations, or phenomena themselves, as sense data, are no longer intentional objects, then the problem of intentionality becomes much clearer: intentionality now only means that several distinct phenomena (successive acts of will, of understanding, of imagination, of perception) can be directed towards the same object. In perception, in particular, we do not only see a stream of successive colors and figures, but the successive figures which we see in phenomenal space can be numerically identified through all meaning the same thing in objective space. Such numerical identification of successive phenomena through the object they mean might be quite a difficult operation to conceive, but such an operation seems required in any theory of perception, and if we restrict our use of the word "intentionality" to this operation, it seems to me that we have a much more precise and limited problem to deal with under this name.

In addition, it now seems that non-thetical self-consciousness is no longer required for the perception of "self" either. If the consciousness which I am is made of absolute phenomena, then there is no question any more as to how this consciousness appears. The question of self-consciousness now only means the question of how certain phenomena among all others that fill myself as consciousness come to be selected as especially "me"—which is a very different question, namely the question of the appearance of an empirical self. To this question, many different answers seem possible: it may be for instance that the phenomenon of my body as a constant center of perspective, which Sartre calls "the body as for-itself" in *Being and Nothingness*, is all that is required for a self to appear in the phenomenal world, as opposed to all other phenomena whose position can be identified through their phenomenal distance to this center. The relation of the self to other phenomena would then only be a spatial relation, and in any case, no pre-reflective self-consciousness would be required for the appearance of this self or of the "external" phenomena which surround it.[4]

## Notes

1 The only reference by Sartre to Brentano I am aware of is in *Being and Nothingness* (Sartre 2004, p. 25), where Sartre talks about "the intentionality of Husserl and Brentano", without differenciation).
2 I developed this point in Trémault (2009).
3 "The dyad reflection–reflecting" translates Sartre's "reflet–reflétant" in French, which is the "game of mirrors" of pre-reflective self-awareness, between the negation and the consciousness of the negation, by which both exist. The "mode reflective–reflected-on" translates "le mode réflexif–réfléchi," by which Sartre designates the duality inside high-order self-awareness, between an intentional consciousness and the high-order consciousness of that consciousness.
4 A first version of this chapter was presented at Uriah Kriegel's PaCs seminar at the Institut Jean Nicod in Paris in March 2014. I want to thank Uriah Kriegel and the researchers present that day for their useful questions and comments. I also warmly thank Jonathan Webber for his valuable reading and comments on the resulting draft.

## Bibliography

Brentano, F. (1974). *Psychology from an Empirical Standpoint*, translated by A. C. Rancunello, D. B. Terrell and L. L. McAlister. London: Routledge.
Descartes, R. (1992). *Méditations métaphysiques, Objections et réponses*. Paris: GF-Flammarion.
Descartes, R. (2006). *Meditations, Objections, and Replies*, translated by R. Ariew and D. Cress. Indianapolis: Hackett.
Descartes, R. (2010). *Œuvres philosophiques, Tome I — 1618–1637*. Paris: Editions Classiques Garnier.

Husserl, E. (1983). *Ideas Pertaining to a Pure Phenomenology and to a Phenomenological Philosophy. First Book: General Introduction to a Pure Phenomenology*, translated by F. Kersten. The Hague: Martinus Nihoff.

Husserl, E. (2001). *Logical Investigations, Volume II*. Translated by J. N. Findlay. London: Routledge.

Sartre, J.-P. (1962). *Literary and Philosophical Essays*, translated by A. Michelson. New York: Collier Books.

Sartre, J.-P. (1983). *Cahiers pout une morale*. Paris: Gallimard.

Sartre, J.-P. (1994). *Being and Nothingness*, translated by Hazel E. Barnes. New York: Gramercy Books.

Sartre, J.-P. (2004). *The Transcendence of the Ego*, translated by Andrew Brown. London: Routledge.

Trémault, E. (2009). Sartre's 'alternative' conception of phenomena in *Being and Nothingness*. Sartre Studies International 15, 1: pp. 24–38.

# 12 Sartre's non-egological theory of consciousness

*Joshua Tepley*

### Introduction

The early Sartre's theory of consciousness is non-egological.[1] According to this theory, the ego is not the subject of consciousness.[2] As Sartre puts it, the ego is transcendent, not transcendental.[3] There are two ways of developing this theory: (1) there is no subject of consciousness, from which it follows that the ego is not the subject of consciousness; and (2) there is a subject of consciousness, but the ego and it are numerically distinct. As I read him, Sartre holds (1) in *The Transcendence of the Ego* and (2) in *Being and Nothingness*.[4] This chapter argues that both non-egological theories of consciousness, are untenable. *Pace* Sartre, there is a subject of consciousness, and it is the ego.

The body of this chapter has three parts: the first clarifies two key Sartrean terms (consciousness and the ego); the second focuses on Sartre's non-egological theory of consciousness in *TE*; and the third focuses on Sartre's non-egological theory of consciousness in *BN* with an emphasis on Phyllis Morris's interpretation of that work.[5] The chapter ends with a brief conclusion in which I identify some questions about Sartre's non-egological theory of consciousness that remain unanswered.

### Consciousness and the ego

Any discussion of Sartre's non-egological theory of consciousness needs to be clear on two key terms: consciousness and the ego. Consciousness is awareness.[6] Its defining feature, according to Sartre, is intentionality: consciousness is always awareness *of* something or other, what Sartre calls "objects of consciousness." Consciousness is usually directed at entities of kinds other than its own, such as trees and tables, but this is not always the case. A consciousness can be an awareness of another consciousness (e.g., a past consciousness), if the two consciousnesses are parts of the same stream. Sartre calls any consciousness directed at another consciousness "reflective" (or "reflecting"), and the consciousness at which it is directed "reflected." Consciousness that is not reflected Sartre calls "unreflected," and consciousness that is not reflective, i.e., not directed at another consciousness, he calls "non-reflective." According to Sartre, consciousness is most of the time non-reflective and unreflected.

The kinds of consciousness introduced in the last paragraph—reflective and non-reflective, reflected and unreflected—are examples of what Sartre calls "positional" (or "thetic") consciousness. Positional consciousness is consciousness directed at an object, whether it be another consciousness or an entity of some other kind (e.g., a tree or a table). Since all consciousness is directed at some object, according to Sartre, it follows that all consciousness is positional. But this is not the whole story. According to Sartre, every positional consciousness is also a "non-positional" ("non-thetic") consciousness of itself. A positional consciousness of a tree, for example, is simultaneously a non-positional consciousness of that very same consciousness.

This brief exposition of Sartre's concept of consciousness raises a number of questions. What is the difference between positional and non-positional consciousness? How can something be both a positional consciousness of an object and a non-positional consciousness of itself? Can a positional consciousness take itself as an object? How can a reflective consciousness take a past consciousness as its object if the latter no longer exists? In general, can the objects of positional consciousness be non-existent? What is a "stream" of consciousness, and what unifies and individuates such streams? These are interesting (if difficult) questions, and I will have the opportunity to address a few of them in what follows.

Setting these questions aside for now, let us turn our attention to Sartre's concept of the ego, which is even more obscure than his concept of consciousness. This obscurity notwithstanding, four things are certain.

First, according to Sartre, egos are the proper referents of first-person pronouns (e.g., "I" and "me"). When we say things like "I am hungry" and "she dislikes me," the words "I" and "me" refer to egos. The referents of first-person pronouns (and personal pronouns in general) are commonly known as "persons" or "selves," so we can also say that each ego is a person or a self.

Second, according to Sartre, the ego appears *always* in reflection. Reflective consciousness, i.e., consciousness directed at another consciousness, is always consciousness of, in addition to the reflected consciousness, an ego. As Sartre puts it:

> [E]ach time we apprehend our thought, whether by an immediate intuition or by an intuition based on memory, we apprehend an *I* which is the *I* of the apprehended thought.... If, for example, I want to remember a certain landscape perceived yesterday from the train, it is possible for me to bring back the memory of that landscape as such. But I can also recollect that *I* was seeing that landscape.... I can always perform any recollection whatsoever in the personal mode, and at once the *I* appears.
>
> (*TE*, pp. 43–44)

Third, according to Sartre, the ego appears *only* in reflection. This means two things: (1) The ego is never a positional object of non-reflective consciousness.[7] A positional consciousness of a landscape, for example, is never at the same time a positional consciousness of the ego. There is positional consciousness of the ego only in reflective consciousness, which is always, by definition, directed at another consciousness. And (2) no positional consciousness, whether reflective or non-reflective, is at the same time a non-positional consciousness of the ego. Of course, according to Sartre, every positional consciousness is also a non-positional consciousness of *itself* (a consciousness), but this is not to say that every positional consciousness is a non-positional consciousness of *the ego*. In Sartre's words: "while I was reading, there was consciousness *of* the book, *of* the heroes of the novel, but the *I* was not inhabiting this consciousness. It was only consciousness of the object and non-positional consciousness of itself" (*TE*, pp. 46–47).

Fourth, according to Sartre, the ego is in some sense a "unity" of what he calls "states" and "actions" (*TE*, p. 61).[8] Sartre's main example of a state is hatred, which he contrasts with the feeling of repugnance, the latter of which is not a state but a consciousness. Sartre highlights two differences between states (like anger) and consciousnesses (like repugnance): (1) States exist over time whereas consciousnesses are instantaneous (*TE*, p. 62). I may hate Peter for many years, but a feeling of repugnance for him lasts for only a moment.[9] And (2) states, unlike consciousnesses, can exist while there is no awareness of them (*TE*, p. 63). I may hate Peter without being aware of my hatred for him, but there cannot be an instantaneous feeling of repugnance for Peter without there being a (non-positional) awareness of this feeling. The only other example of a state given in *TE* is love, but I think we can plausibly assert that states include character traits such as cowardice, happiness, and jealousy, as well as relatively short-lived "passive" features like seeing a tree, feeling giddy, and having a headache (if these last for more than a single instant).

Sartre gives three examples of what he calls "actions": playing the piano, driving a car, and writing (*TE*, pp. 68–69). Actions, like states, exist over time. Can they also exist while there is no awareness of them? Sartre is not clear on this point, but presumably they can. It is doubtful that on my way to work, for example, there is an awareness of what I am doing (i.e., going to work) at every single moment of the trip. Of course, according to Sartre, there must be a non-positional awareness of any consciousness involved in such an action, and I can at any given moment, through reflection, come to realize what I am doing; but neither of these is to say that there is at any given moment of my journey either a positional or a non-positional awareness of this action as such.

If actions and states are alike in these two ways, then how do they differ from each other? According to Sartre, actions are unities of what he calls "active consciousnesses" (e.g., the consciousness involved in playing a single note on the piano) whereas states are unities of what he calls "passive consciousnesses" (e.g., a momentary feeling of repugnance). It is doubtful, however, that Sartre means by this that actions and states are unities of *only* active and passive consciousnesses, respectively. Surely playing the piano involves in addition to active consciousnesses (e.g., those involved in playing individual notes) also passive consciousnesses (e.g., those involved in reading sheet music). And surely hatred involves in addition to passive consciousnesses (e.g., momentary feelings of repugnance) also active consciousnesses (e.g., those involved in slamming a door). Moreover, it seems obvious that states and actions cannot be understood as unities of only active and passive consciousnesses if these are taken to exclude other such unities. The activity of driving a car, for example, involves a variety of "smaller" activities (e.g., pressing the clutch, shifting gears, etc.) and states (e.g., hearing the engine rev, watching the tachometer, etc.). What Sartre really means to say, I think, is that states are *ultimate* unities of *primarily* passive consciousnesses, and actions are *ultimate* unities of *primarily* active consciousnesses.

This discussion of Sartre's concept of the ego, like our discussion of consciousness, leaves a number of questions unanswered: In what sense is the ego a "unity" of states and actions? In what sense are states and actions "unities" of individual consciousnesses? Is this relation of unity transitive, so that the ego is also a unity of individual consciousnesses? If not, then how are egos and individual consciousnesses related? And how are egos related to streams of consciousness? Some of these questions will be answered in the following discussion.

## The transcendence of the ego

Having some idea of what Sartre means by "consciousness" and the "ego," let us turn our attention to the main subject of this chapter, Sartre's non-egological theory of consciousness, starting with his version of this theory as it appears in *TE*. In this short work, as I interpret it, Sartre maintains that there is consciousness of objects but no subject of consciousness. In other words, while there is consciousness of things, nothing (no thing, no entity) is conscious—not even consciousness itself. This position sounds paradoxical, but it is not self-contradictory. Sartre does not say that there is consciousness but nothing is consciousness. That would be a contradiction. Consciousness, for Sartre, is certainly *something* (some thing, some entity).[10] The apparent absurdity of the claim that there is consciousness but nothing is conscious results from our temptation to identify the properties *being conscious* and *being a consciousness*. As long as we keep these two properties distinct, we should all agree that Sartre's subject-less view of consciousness is not, at the very least, self-contradictory.[11]

Strictly speaking, Sartre's main thesis in *TE* is not that there is no subject of consciousness but that the ego is not the subject of consciousness. It is important not to confuse or conflate these two claims. It is also important to distinguish Sartre's "non-egological theory" from the "no-self theory," according to which there is no self. David Hume is perhaps the best-known advocate of the latter, which he derives from his radical empiricism, according to which a thing exists only if there is some experience of it. Since, according to Hume, there is no experience of the self, it follows that the self does not exist (Hume 1888, pp. 251–252). Hume makes no distinction, as Sartre does, between the self-as-subject-of-consciousness and the self-as-ego, and for this reason Sartre can be said both to agree and to disagree with Hume. If by "self" Hume means "subject of consciousness," then he and Sartre agree: there is no such thing, and we have no experience of it. If, on the other hand, "self" means what Sartre means by "ego," then Hume and Sartre disagree, for according to Sartre there *is* such an entity, and there is awareness of it *always* in reflection. Thus, while Sartre's non-egological theory of consciousness is closely related to the no-self theory (e.g., of Hume), the two are not identical.

As noted above, Sartre's main thesis in *TE* is that the ego is not the subject of consciousness. While Sartre gives a number of reasons in *TE* for this position, all of them, as I interpret this work, rely on the premise that there is no subject of consciousness. If there is no subject of consciousness, then the ego cannot be the subject of consciousness. The rest of this section focuses, therefore, not on Sartre's non-egological theory of consciousness per se, but on his view that there is no subject of consciousness.

Sartre offers, by my count, four arguments in *TE* for the view that there is no subject of consciousness. The first of these (call it the "argument from superfluity") is based on the claim that a subject of consciousness is needed neither to *unify* a given stream of consciousness (e.g., across time) nor to *individuate* such a stream as opposed to other such streams (*TE*, pp. 37–40). While a number of Sartre scholars have examined this premise in some detail, none of them thinks that anything significant follows from it if it is true. (See, for example, Scanlon 1971, pp. 334–337; Sukale 1976, pp. 69–71; Morris 1985, pp. 186–189; Priest 2000, pp. 34–36, 42–45.) In particular, it does not follow that there is no subject of consciousness, for a subject of consciousness may exist even if it is "superfluous" in these two ways.

Sartre's second argument in *TE* against the existence of a subject of consciousness is, in short, that a subject of consciousness, if it existed, would destroy consciousness. (For an alternative treatment of this argument, see Sukale 1976, pp. 72–73.) In his words: "this superfluous *I* would be a hindrance. If it existed it would tear consciousness from itself; it would divide consciousness; it would slide into every consciousness like an opaque blade. The transcendental *I* is the death of consciousness" (*TE*, p. 40). Why would a subject of consciousness destroy consciousness? As Sartre explains:

[T]he type of existence of consciousness is to be consciousness of itself. And consciousness is aware of itself *in so far as it is consciousness of a transcendent object.* All is therefore clear and lucid in consciousness: the object with its characteristic opacity is before consciousness, but consciousness is purely and simply consciousness of being consciousness of that object. This is the law of its existence.

(*TE*, p. 40)

Sartre's idea seems to be that there can be consciousness of a transcendent object (e.g., a tree or a table) only if that consciousness is a non-positional consciousness of itself *and of nothing else*. If there were a subject of consciousness, then every consciousness would be, in addition to a non-positional consciousness of itself, also a non-positional consciousness *of that subject*. It follows that there can be consciousness of transcendent objects only if there is sometimes no subject of consciousness. Since there *is* consciousness of transcendent objects, it follows that there is sometimes no subject of consciousness; and if there is sometimes no subject of consciousness, then it stands to reason that there is never a subject of consciousness.

Sartre's "argument from opacity," as I shall call it, raises two questions. First, if there were a subject of consciousness, then *would* every consciousness be, in addition to a non-positional consciousness of itself, also a non-positional consciousness of that subject? I think the answer is yes. If there were a subject of consciousness, then presumably it would relate to consciousness in whatever way a thing relates to one of its properties.[12] More specifically, since, according to Sartre, all consciousness is consciousness *of an object*, consciousness would be a relational property (relation) of the subject, in which case the subject of consciousness would relate to consciousness in whatever way a thing relates to one of its relational properties.[13] But there cannot be awareness of a thing's properties, including any of its relational ones, without an awareness of that thing itself. This is clearly so in the case of positional consciousness: positional awareness of the relational property *being on top of,* for example, the relata of which are, say, a cup and a table, requires simultaneous positional awareness of the cup and the table. I see no reason why things should be any different in the case of non-positional consciousness: non-positional awareness of a thing's properties, including any of its relational ones, entails non-positional awareness of the thing itself. And since, according to Sartre, all non-reflective consciousness (like all consciousness in general) involves non-positional consciousness of itself, it follows that there *would* be non-positional awareness of a subject of consciousness in non-reflective consciousness, if there were such a subject.

The second question raised by Sartre's argument from opacity is this: Why think that there can be consciousness of a transcendent object (e.g., a tree or a table) only if that consciousness is non-positional consciousness of itself *and of nothing else*? The only reason I can think of is based on the idea that non-positional consciousness of a subject of consciousness would have to involve an awareness of that subject's other properties in addition to its current consciousness.[14] If we assume that subjects of consciousness endure through time, for example, then they will have at any given time a vast number of properties, namely having had each and every one of their past consciousnesses (e.g., *having been conscious of a dog at $t_{-1}$, having been conscious of a house at $t_{-2}$, having been conscious of a sunset at $t_{-3}$*, etc.).[15] If non-positional consciousness of the subject of that consciousness requires, in addition to an awareness of that consciousness, also an awareness of these past consciousnesses, then it is easy to see why someone might think that positional consciousness would be impeded by such a subject. Consciousness would be so overwhelmed by being non-positional consciousness of these other properties that it would have a difficult, perhaps impossible, time being positional consciousness of any transcendent objects.

The problem with this line of reasoning is that there is no reason to think that non-positional consciousness of a subject would have to involve non-positional consciousness of *any* properties of that subject besides its current consciousness. It is arguably true that there can be awareness of a thing only if there is awareness of *at least one* of its properties. But why think that there can be awareness of a thing only if there is awareness of *more than one* of its properties? Suppose, for example, that I am looking with one eye through a narrow tube at a white wall in such a way that I do not see any of the wall's edges or corners. I am aware of the whiteness of the wall but not any of its other perceptible properties (e.g., size, shape, texture). Does it follow that I am unaware of the wall itself? Of course not. I am aware of the wall in virtue of being aware of its whiteness, and this is true in spite of the fact that I am unaware of any of its other perceptible properties. Likewise, I can be aware of the subject of consciousness, if there is one, in virtue of being aware of just one of its properties (its current consciousness) without being aware of any of its other properties (its past consciousnesses).

Sartre's third argument in *TE* for his subject-less view of consciousness is based on his belief that there is no non-positional awareness of a subject in non-reflective consciousness. (For alternative discussions of this argument, see Scanlon 1971, pp. 338–347; and Sukale 1976, pp. 73–78.) While there is consciousness of a sunset, for example, there is no non-positional awareness of a subject of that particular consciousness. As noted in our discussion of the previous argument, however, if there were a subject of consciousness, then there would be non-positional awareness of it in *every* consciousness, including every non-reflective consciousness. Together these two claims entail that there is no subject of non-reflective consciousness.[16] And if there is no subject of non-reflective consciousness, then it stands to reason that there is no subject of *any* consciousness. Call this the "argument from invisibility."

What makes Sartre so sure that there is no non-positional awareness of a subject of consciousness in non-reflective consciousness? In *TE*, he bases this claim on introspection (see *TE*, pp. 46–47). He must, therefore, believe that there is some phenomenologically introspectible difference between a non-positional awareness of a consciousness *alone*, on the one hand, and a non-positional awareness of a consciousness *and its subject*, on the other. But is there really such a difference? I don't think so. To start, there need not be a non-positional awareness of different properties in these two cases, for, as noted earlier, there is no reason to think that non-positional awareness of a subject of consciousness should involve an awareness of any properties of that subject besides its current consciousness. Accordingly, Sartre will have to insist that the mere presence of the subject itself, and not any of its properties, makes some phenomenologically introspectible difference to non-positional consciousness. I find this hard to believe. To see why, consider the following analogy: In contemporary analytic metaphysics, there is a debate over the metaphysical constitution of concrete particulars, like trees and tables. In particular, this debate concerns whether or not such things have, in addition to any material parts (e.g., bits of wood, molecules, electrons, etc.), also metaphysical parts (e.g., properties, substrata, etc.). Of the various positions one can take in this debate, two of them are: (1) *the bundle theory*, according to which concrete particulars *do* have metaphysical parts, and these parts are their properties (and only their properties); and (2) *the blob theory*, according to which concrete particulars do *not* have any metaphysical parts, although they may still have properties.[17] Assuming these two views are coherent, is there any way of deciding between them by means of perception alone?[18] Absolutely not. What makes this debate "metaphysical" is precisely that it cannot be decided by experience. You cannot look at a cup and determine, just from looking at it, whether or not its properties (if it has properties) are "parts" of it. The question of whether or not there is non-positional awareness of a subject of consciousness in non-reflective consciousness is, in my opinion, exactly the same in this respect. In asking whether there is, in addition to a putative property (i.e., a consciousness), also something which *has* this property (i.e., a subject), we are asking a highly abstract metaphysical question that cannot be decided by introspection alone. People are welcome, of course, to give theoretical (as opposed to purely phenomenological) reasons against the existence of such a subject, and these reasons may be based partly on the fruits of introspection (phenomenology). Indeed, Sartre's first two arguments in *TE* for this position are exactly of this kind. But I do not think that introspection (phenomenology) alone, without the aid of any theoretical considerations, will let us decide this question, any more than perception alone will let us decide between the bundle theory and the blob theory.

Sartre's final argument in *TE* against the existence of a subject of consciousness is the following:

> In addition, if the *I* is a part of consciousness, there would then be *two I*'s: the *I* of the reflective consciousness and the *I* of the reflected

consciousness.... For us, this problem is quite simply insoluble. For it is inadmissible that any communication could be established between the reflective *I* and the reflected *I* if they are real elements of consciousness; above all, it is inadmissible that they may finally achieve identity in one unique *I*.

(*TE*, p. 52)

If I understand it correctly, here is a paraphrase of Sartre's "two I's argument," as I shall call it: Reflective consciousness is, by definition, positional awareness of another consciousness. We know from introspection that any such consciousness is also a positional awareness of the ego, which is referred to by the word "I." If such a consciousness had a subject, then it could also be referred to by the word "I." But only one entity can be referred to by the word "I," and these two entities (i.e., the ego and the subject of consciousness) cannot be numerically identical. Therefore, there is no subject of consciousness.

One potential problem with the two I's argument is that Sartre gives us no reason to think that only one entity can be referred to by the word "I." Perhaps the word "I" is ambiguous.[19] For example, according to substance dualism, the word "I" sometimes refers to a mind ("I am thinking") and other times to a body ("I am six feet tall"). Perhaps the same is true of the ego and the subject of consciousness: sometimes "I" refers to the former, sometimes it refers to the latter. But even if the word "I" is ambiguous, it stands to reason that only one sense of the word is primary. Take substance dualism: the word "I" is ambiguous on this view, but only one sense of it refers to *me*—the *real* me—namely, the sense that refers to a mind. The other sense of "I," which refers to my body, is only a secondary or derivative sense of the word. In general, no matter how many legitimate meanings we are willing to attribute to the word "I," it seems that only one of them can be primary; only one of them can refer to the *real* me. And in that case, we can simply re-run the argument, replacing every instance of "referred to by the word 'I'" with "referred to by the word 'I' in its primary sense."

There is certainly room for debate over whether or not the ego and the subject of consciousness (if there is one) can both be referred to by "I" in its primary sense. I want to set this issue aside, however, and turn our attention to what I take to be the weakest link in the argument, namely Sartre's claim that the ego and the subject of consciousness cannot be numerically identical. Why think this is true?

I think that Sartre's unexpressed reasoning for this claim is as follows: The ego is an object of reflective consciousness. If there is a subject of consciousness, and it is numerically identical to the ego, then it follows that the subject of consciousness is sometimes an object for itself. This is impossible; the subject of consciousness *cannot* be an object for itself. Therefore, the subject of consciousness cannot be numerically identical to the ego.

The key premise of this argument is that the subject of consciousness cannot be an object for itself. I am aware of only two reasons for thinking this is true.

First, one could argue that this is true by definition. If the subject of consciousness were an object for itself, then it would be both a subject and an object, which is impossible. By definition, no subject can be an object. The problem with this argument is that it is simply false that "no subject is an object" is true by definition. It is true by definition that "no subject is a non-subject" and "no object is a non-object," but there is nothing in the concepts "subject" and "object" which prevents them from applying to the very same thing. This is especially clear when we take a closer look at what "subject" and "object" mean in this context: the subject of consciousness is a "subject" in the sense that it is a "conscious thing"; the ego is an "object" in the sense that it is a "thing of which there is consciousness." There is nothing in these two concepts that prohibits something from falling under both of them at the same time.

Second, one could argue that the subject of consciousness cannot be an object for itself based on the following analogy: If there is a subject of human consciousness, then it is visually aware of objects by using, among other things, a pair of human eyes. No subject of consciousness, however, can see its own eyes directly, i.e., without the aid of mirrors, photographs, etc. This limitation is not a mere contingent fact of human biology; we cannot even imagine a world in which a subject of consciousness sees directly the eyes with which it sees.[20] As it is with the subject of consciousness and its own eyes, so it is with the subject of consciousness and itself. Just as the subject of consciousness cannot be directly aware of its own eyes, so it cannot be positionally aware of itself. And like the subject and its eyes, this limitation is not contingent; it is an essential and unavoidable feature of subjects of consciousness, if they exist.

There are two problems with this argument. First, arguments from analogy are supposed to proceed by first identifying features that are common between two different things and then, on the basis of this, inferring that a feature known to be possessed by one of these things is also possessed by the other thing. In the previous paragraph, however, the first step is completely missing. No features common to the two cases (i.e., the subject of consciousness and its eyes, and the subject of consciousness and itself) are identified. This is no accident, for it is not at all clear what features these could be. The second problem with this argument arises when we try to explain why a subject of consciousness cannot see its own eyes. Two ideas come to mind: first, a subject of consciousness *uses* its eyes in order to see things, and in general a thing used to do something to something cannot be used to do that thing to itself (e.g., a pair of pliers, used for gripping things, cannot be used to grip itself); second, in order for a subject of consciousness to see its own eyes, each of its eyes would have to be in two places at once, which is impossible.[21] The problem is that neither of these reasons is relevant to the case of a subject being aware of itself. Regarding the first, a subject of consciousness does not *use* itself in order to be positionally aware of things; it *is* itself. Regarding the second, even if the subject of consciousness turns out to be a spatially located material thing (e.g., a body), there is no reason to think that it would have to be, *per impossibile*, in two places at once in order to be aware of itself. For these two reasons, this argument from analogy fails. The fact that a subject of consciousness cannot see directly its own eyes might be used to *illustrate* the idea that such a subject cannot be positionally aware of itself, but the former cannot be used as the basis of an *argument* for the latter.

So much for Sartre's "two I's" argument. Before moving on to consider some arguments *against* Sartre's subject-less view of consciousness, let us discuss one final argument for this view, although Sartre does not give such an argument in *TE*. According to this argument, if there were a subject of consciousness, then there would be for each of us *two* conscious things at any given time: consciousness and the subject of that consciousness. This is one conscious thing too many. Without consciousness there cannot be a subject of consciousness, so if only one of these two things exist, then it must be consciousness, not the subject of consciousness. Therefore, there is no subject of consciousness. The problem with this argument is obvious: there is no reason to think that, if there were a subject of consciousness, then there would be for each of us *two* conscious things at any given time. As noted earlier, consciousness is not itself conscious. If there is a subject of consciousness, then there is for each of us just *one* conscious thing—namely, that subject.

\*\*\*

So far I have argued in this section that Sartre's reasons in *TE* for holding that there is no subject of consciousness, which grounds his position that consciousness is non-egological, are not convincing. I have not argued that Sartre's subject-less theory of consciousness is false. Are there any reasons to think that there *is* a subject of consciousness? Here are three:[22]

First, the claim that *there is consciousness but nothing is conscious* is puzzling, to say the least. This sounds like saying that something is being pushed but nothing is pushing it, or that something is being scratched but nothing is doing the scratching. Consciousness seems to be a relational property, like pushing and scratching, and this implies that its instantiation requires two relata: a subject of consciousness and an object of consciousness.[23]

Second, as some readers will have noticed, Sartre actually admits in *TE* that reflective consciousness reveals the ego *as the subject of consciousness*. As quoted earlier: "[E]ach time we apprehend our thought, whether by an immediate intuition or by an intuition based on memory, we apprehend an *I* which is the *I* of the apprehended thought" (*TE*, p. 43). Since, according to Sartre in *TE*, there is no subject of consciousness, this must be an illusion. The ego appears in reflective consciousness to be the subject of the reflected consciousness, but in reality it is not. The problem is that Sartre can justify this claim only if he can independently motivate his view that there is no subject of consciousness. The fact that the ego appears in reflection to be the subject of consciousness gives us prima facie evidence that there is a subject of consciousness (and, moreover, that it is the ego), and this evidence can be discounted only if we have a good reason to think that the ego is not the subject of consciousness. At this point, we have no such reason.

Third, a subject-less theory of consciousness makes no sense of certain kinds of consciousness, such as fear, guilt, and regret. These kinds of consciousness take as their objects things that have already happened or will (possibly) happen to other consciousnesses.[24] Fearing consciousness, for example, may be directed at a harm that is expected to befall some future consciousness. If there is a subject of consciousness, then this makes sense: the subject is afraid of what might happen to *it* in the future. But if there is no subject of consciousness, then why should this be? Why should there be a fearing consciousness directed at something that will (or might) happen to some future consciousness? The fearing consciousness and the future consciousness are numerically distinct, so whatever happens to the latter does not happen to the former. One might point out that these two consciousnesses belong to the same ego, but unless the ego is the subject of these consciousnesses I do not see how this is going to help. The same is true if one points to the fact that these two consciousnesses belong to the same stream of consciousness. Unless a stream of consciousness is the subject of these consciousnesses I do not see how this is going to help either. As a last resort, one could argue that consciousnesses like fear and regret are inherently irrational. While there is often fear about what will (or might) happen to a future consciousness, for example, this fear is always misplaced. The problem is that the existence of these types of consciousness provides prima facie evidence for the existence of a subject of consciousness, and Sartre can ask us to disregard this evidence only if he gives us a good reason to think that there is no such subject, which he has failed to do.

## Being and nothingness

Although the main topic of this chapter is Sartre's claim that the ego is not the subject of consciousness, the previous section focused on the claim that there is no subject of consciousness. This is because Sartre's reasons for holding a non-egological theory of consciousness in *TE* are grounded in his position in that work that there is no subject of consciousness. All of these reasons, as well as my reasons to the contrary, go by the board if Sartre admits after publishing *TE* that there is a subject of consciousness and endorses a non-egological theory of consciousness by distinguishing this subject from the ego. According to Phyllis Morris (1976), whose interpretation of Sartre will be the focus of this section, this is precisely what

Sartre does in *BN*.[25] According to Morris, Sartre admits in *BN* that there is a subject of consciousness, namely the body (which Morris calls the "body-subject"),[26] but Sartre refuses to identify this entity with the ego. Thus, according to Morris, Sartre's theory of consciousness in *BN*, like in *TE*, is non-egological, but the details of this theory are different, and presumably so are his reasons for holding it.[27]

If, according to Sartre in *BN*, there is a subject of consciousness, then why not simply identify it with the ego? Why insist that the ego and the subject of consciousness are numerically distinct? We already examined one reason for thinking this, based on the idea that the subject of consciousness, if it existed, could not be aware of itself, and found it wanting. To find another argument, we will have to deepen our understanding of what the ego is. I mentioned earlier that the ego is the "unity" of what Sartre calls "states" and "actions," but I left it open what exactly this "unity" amounts to. We now have to address this issue.

According to Morris, another word for "ego," as Sartre uses the term, is "character," and character, Morris says, is just a "pattern" of past actions.[28] She gives the following example to illustrate her idea: "[I]n Sartre's view, 'I am a coward' might be translated, with no remainder, into some such series as this: 'I ran from a lion at $t_1$,' 'I ran from a dog at $t_2$,' 'I ran from the war at $t_3$,' ... " (Morris 1976, p. 88). Based on this example, I think we can infer that by "pattern" Morris means "conjunction": the character trait *cowardice* is just the conjunction of properties such as *running from a lion at $t_1$, running from a dog at $t_2$, running from the war at $t_3$*, etc. Of course, a person's character consists of more than just a single character trait, but the "unity" of such traits would seem to be no different in kind: a person's character is simply a conjunction of his or her character traits.[29] If I have understood her correctly, then, Morris understands the sense of "unity" involved in the ego as conjunction. The ego, on this view, is therefore a property—a conjunctive property, to be more exact, the conjuncts of which are at one level character traits, and at another level past actions.[30]

If my interpretation of Morris's interpretation of Sartre is correct, then it is certainly true that the ego and the body-subject are numerically distinct, for the body-subject is a substance, not a property.[31] Has Sartre's non-egological theory of consciousness been vindicated? I don't think so. One defining feature of the ego, is that it is a proper referent of the word "I." This makes no sense if the ego is identified with character. I have character, but I am not identical to that character. Morris herself runs into trouble on this point. She claims that "We use 'I' [in the sense that refers to the ego] when we want to speak of certain characteristic patterns of action, as in 'I am a thief' or 'I am an irascible person'" (Morris 1976, p. 91). But in these two examples, the word "I" clearly refers, not to certain patterns of actions, but to the *subject* of these patterns. In the sentence "I am a thief," the predicate "$x$ is a thief" may refer to a pattern of past actions (e.g., $x$ stole something at $t_1$, $x$ stole something at $t_2$, $x$ stole something at $t_3$, etc.), but the word "I" refers to that of which this predicate is predicated (i.e., that which stole something at $t_1$, stole something at $t_2$, stole something at $t_3$, etc.). In short, Morris cannot coherently maintain both that the ego is identified with character and that the ego is the proper referent of the word "I."

Suppose that in order to avoid this objection we modify Morris's view. Perhaps the ego is closely related to a pattern of past actions (character) without being that pattern. Perhaps the ego is best understood, not as character, but as that which has character. In that case, it makes sense to refer to this entity with the word "I." The problem is that in order to attribute this view to Sartre, who clearly maintains a non-egological view of consciousness in *BN* (pp. 102–103), we have to insist that this entity is not identical to the subject of consciousness, which is going to be difficult to do. Not only have we lost our reason for thinking that the ego and the subject of consciousness are numerically distinct (the former is a property, the latter is a substance), but we have actually gained a reason to think that the two are identical. Recall that character is a unity of character traits in the sense that the former is a conjunctive property of which the latter are conjuncts, and that character traits are unities of past actions in the sense that the former are conjunctive properties of which the latter are conjuncts. One point we have hitherto overlooked is that, according to Sartre, actions are also "unities"; more specifically, they are unities of individual consciousnesses. If the kind of unity involved in character and character traits is conjunction, then it stands to reason that this is also the kind of unity involved in actions. In other words, actions are just conjunctive properties of which individual consciousnesses are conjuncts. But whatever instantiates a conjunctive property also instantiates its conjuncts. Thus, if the ego instantiates character, then it also instantiates (1) the character traits which are conjuncts of its character; (2) the actions which are conjuncts of its character traits; and (3) the individual consciousnesses which are conjuncts of its actions. And whatever instantiates individual consciousnesses is the *subject* of those consciousnesses. In short, if the ego is that which has character, character is a conjunction of character traits, character traits are conjunctions of actions, and actions are conjunctions of individual consciousnesses, then the ego is the subject of consciousness.

One might argue that this conclusion can be avoided if we understand the "unity" involved in the constitution of character in some way other than conjunction. Perhaps character is *not* just a conjunction of character traits, past actions, and (ultimately) individual consciousnesses. Perhaps the kind of unity involved here is what Sartre calls "magical," which is just to say, I take it, that it cannot be identified with some other, better-known relation (e.g., conjunction).[32] Will this save Sartre's non-egological theory of consciousness? I don't think so. As long as we understand character, character traits, actions, and individual consciousnesses as things that other things can "have" (e.g., instantiate), Sartre cannot avoid the view that whatever has the first of these (character) must also have each of the other three, regardless of how he understands the relation of "unity" which binds them together. For, whatever has character must have character traits; whatever has character traits must perform actions; and whatever performs actions must have conscious states. This makes clear what should have been obvious to us from the start: it makes sense to attribute character to a thing only if that thing has conscious states, i.e., that thing is a subject of consciousness. Therefore, no matter how we understand the "unity" involved in the constitution of character, either as conjunction or as some "magical bond," if the ego is that which has character, then it must be the subject of consciousness.

In this section I have argued for two things: First, Sartre cannot identify the ego with character itself, for the former but not the latter is properly referred to with the word "I." Second, if Sartre identifies the ego with that which has character, then this entity must be the subject of consciousness. Since these are, as far as I can tell, Sartre's only options, I conclude that Sartre's non-egological theory of consciousness in *BN*, like his non-ecological theory in *TE*, is false.

## Conclusion

In closing, let me just mention three sets of questions that are left unanswered by this chapter: (1) How central to Sartre's philosophy in *BN* is his non-egological theory of consciousness? If this theory is untenable, as I have argued, then which other, if any, theses in *BN* come under threat? (2) Does Sartre continue holding a non-egological theory of consciousness after *BN*? If so, does this theory change in such a way that it avoids any of the criticisms offered in this chapter? (3) To what extent do the arguments given in this chapter cut ice only against Sartre's non-egological theory of consciousness in particular as opposed to non-egological theories of consciousness in general? Can someone without Sartre's particular theoretical commitments sidestep any of these arguments? These are interesting questions, each of them worth pursing in its own right. Unfortunately, I cannot pursue any of them here.[33]

## Notes

1 By "the early Sartre" I mean the pre-war Sartre, whose philosophical writings include *The Transcendence of the Ego* and *Being and Nothingness*. Classic discussions of the early Sartre's non-egological theory of consciousness include Aron Gurwitsch (1941), John D. Scanlon (1971), and Phyllis Sutton Morris (1985). For a recent introduction to this theory, especially as it appears in *The Transcendence of the Ego*, see David Detmer (2008).
2 According to an *egological* theory of consciousness, by contrast, the ego *is* the subject of consciousness.

3 For a discussion of Sartre's uses of "transcendent" and "transcendental," see Morris (1985, pp. 182–184).
4 Jean-Paul Sartre (1937, 1943). Hereafter, these works will be abbreviated as *TE* and *BN*, and references to them will be cited parenthetically in the text. All Sartre scholars agree that Sartre holds a non-egological theory of consciousness in *TE*; most of them agree that he does so in *BN*. For a dissenting opinion regarding the latter, see Matthew Eshleman (2002).
5 Phyllis Sutton Morris (1976, 1985).
6 Throughout this chapter, I will use "consciousness" and "awareness" as synonyms. I will use these terms sometimes as mass nouns (as I do here) and other times as count nouns. Of these, the latter use is preferred, for consciousness/awareness is best understood as a *thing* (in the most general sense of the word), not as a *stuff*. Sentences using the mass nouns can be rephrased using the count nouns. For example, "consciousness is awareness" can be rephrased as "every consciousness is an awareness." For a recent introduction to Sartre's concept of consciousness, see Katherine J. Morris (2008, pp. 59–75).
7 A "positional object" is an object of a positional consciousness.
8 Strictly speaking, this unity may also include what Sartre calls "qualities" (*TE*, pp. 61, 70–71). To keep things simple, I will ignore this possibility in this chapter.
9 Must a feeling of repugnance last for only a moment? Cannot such a feeling last for a few seconds, if not much longer? I think Sartre would say that feelings such as this, i.e., feelings that last for more than an instant, are states, not consciousnesses. It is important to keep in mind, however, that such states, like all states, are unities of individual consciousnesses, e.g., instantaneous feelings of repugnance.
10 Doesn't Sartre say in *BN* that consciousness (being-for-itself) is nothingness? No, he doesn't. According to *BN*, consciousness (being-for-itself) and nothingness are closely related (e.g., there is nothingness only if there is consciousness), but Sartre never identifies the two in that work.
11 This is not to say that Sartre's subject-less view of consciousness is true or even conceptually coherent. As I use the term, a sentence is "self-contradictory" if and only if it formally entails (e.g., using the inference rules of first-order logic) both *P* and not-*P*, for some instance of *P*. Thus, the sentence "Bob resembles Tom, but Tom does not resemble Bob" is not self-contradictory; but it is, I would say, conceptually incoherent.
12 Here and in what follows I treat properties as particulars (tropes), not as universals. This has two consequences relevant for our discussion: first, properties are unique to the individuals that have them (e.g., only this particular piece of paper has, or even could have, its particular whiteness); and second, some properties are perceptible/introspectible (e.g., I am perceptually aware of, in addition to this piece of paper, its whiteness).
13 Morris (1976, pp. 15, 30), who interprets Sartre in *BN* as countenancing a subject of consciousness, understands consciousness as a relation. In defense of her view, she cites *BN*, (pp. 216, 306, 362).
14 Do I mean *some* or *all* of that subject's other properties? It does not matter, for I shall argue in the next paragraph that non-positional consciousness of a subject of consciousness requires an awareness of *none* of its other properties besides its current consciousness.
15 Hereafter, I will refer to the properties of having had past consciousnesses as "past consciousnesses."

16 Note that both claims are needed for this inference to be valid.
17 To my knowledge, the term "blob theory" was introduced by D. M. Armstrong (1989). While Armstrong uses this term to refer to any theory according to which concrete particulars have no *properties*, I use it to refer to any theory according to which concrete particulars have no *metaphysical parts* (e.g., properties, substrata, etc.). For a precedent in using this term in the latter sense, see Peter van Inwagen (2011).
18 Because these are not the only theories one can hold in the debate over the metaphysical constitution of concrete particulars, by "deciding between [these theories]" I do *not* mean "deciding which one of these theories is true." Rather, I mean "deciding whether one of these theories is true or one of them is false."
19 For a discussion of the possible ambiguity of the word "I," see Morris (1976, pp. 89–92).
20 Sartre writes that "nothing prevents me from imagining an arrangement of the sense organs such that a living being could see one of his eyes while the eye which was seen was directing its glance upon the world" (*BN*, p. 304). Imagining this, however, is not the same thing as imagining a world in which a subject of consciousness sees all of its eyes using all of its eyes.
21 I owe the second of these explanations to Keith Gunderson (1970, p. 290).
22 The first and third of these reasons, if good, show only that there is a subject of consciousness, not that consciousness is egological. For reasons to think the latter given the former, see the following section.
23 This is not to say, of course, that these two relata cannot be numerically identical.
24 Of course, things cannot literally "happen" to consciousnesses, for happenings (events) require change, and consciousnesses, as instantaneous, cannot change. Nevertheless, for stylistic reasons, I will allow myself the liberty of using this expression in what follows.
25 I will not take a stand in this chapter on whether or not this interpretation of *BN* is correct. If it is not correct, and Sartre does not admit in *BN* that there is a subject of consciousness, then his theory of consciousness in *BN* faces all of the objections I raised against his theory of consciousness in *TE*.
26 Morris (1976, p. 30) cites *BN* (pp. 305, 316) in defense of her reading of Sartre, according to which he identifies the subject of consciousness with the body-subject. Why does Morris refer to the subject of consciousness as the "body-subject" rather than just the "body"? Because, according to Morris, the word "body" is ambiguous: it can mean either "body *qua* subject" or "body *qua* object," and the subject of consciousness, for Sartre, is the body *qua* subject, not the body *qua* object (Morris 1976, pp. 54, 90). This puzzles me. Is the body *qua* subject numerically identical to the body *qua* object? If so, then how can something be the body *qua* subject but not the body *qua* object? On the other hand, if the body *qua* subject is not numerically identical to the body *qua* object, then how are they related?
27 If Sartre changes his non-egological theory of consciousness in *BN* and thereby avoids the objections I raised against this theory as it appears in *TE*, then why did I devote so much attention (indeed, an entire section) to the latter theory in this chapter? Because doing so forestalls any attempt to save Sartre's non-egological theory of consciousness in *BN* from the criticisms to follow by insisting, contra Morris, that Sartre does *not* countenance a subject of consciousness in *BN*.

28 Morris (1976, pp. 41, 85). I take it that by "actions" Morris denotes a certain subset of what Sartre refers to as "states and actions." Hereafter, I shall use "actions" in Morris's sense, not Sartre's.
29 Since *conjunction* is a transitive relation, it follows that character (the ego) is also a conjunction of past actions.
30 I assume that actions are properties of some kind or other.
31 Morris offers a different argument for the view that the ego and the body-subject are numerically distinct, though she puts it in terms of different uses of the word "I," one of which refers to the ego (character) and the other of which refers to the body-subject. Her argument, in brief, is that the body-subject exists before the ego (character) exists; therefore, ego is not the body-subject (Morris 1976, pp. 91–92). Since I will presently argue that Morris's identification of the ego with character is mistaken, I will not evaluate her argument here.
32 Sartre suggests this is true of the unity involved between an action (in his terms, "state") and individual consciousnesses: "We readily acknowledge that the relation of hatred to the particular *Erlebnis* of repugnance is not logical. It is a magical bond, assuredly" (*TE*, p. 68).
33 Many thanks to Matthew Eshleman for helpful comments on an earlier version of this chapter.

## References

Armstrong, D. M. (1989). *Universals: An Opinionated Introduction*. Boulder, CO: Westview Press.
Detmer, David (2008). *Sartre Explained: from Bad Faith to Authenticity*. Chicago, IL: Open Court.
Eshleman, Matthew. (2002). Two Dogmas of Sartrean Existentialism. *Philosophy Today* 46: pp. 68–74.
Gunderson, Keith (1970). Asymmetries and Mind-Body Perplexities, in *Minnesota Studies in the Philosophy of Science*, IV, edited by Michael Radner and Stephen Winokur, pp. 273–309. Minneapolis: University of Minnesota Press.
Gurwitsch, Aron (1941). A Non-Egological Conception of Consciousness. *Philosophy and Phenomenological Research* 1: pp. 325–338.
Hume, David (1888). *A Treatise of Human Nature*. Edited by L. A. Selby-Bigge. Oxford: Clarendon Press.
Morris, Phyllis Sutton (1976). *Sartre's Concept of a Person: An Analytic Approach*. Amherst: University of Massachusetts Press.
Morris, Phyllis Sutton (1985). Sartre on the Transcendence of the Ego. *Philosophy and Phenomenological Research* 46: pp. 179–198.
Morris, Katherine J. (2008). *Sartre*. Oxford: Blackwell Publishing.
Priest, Stephen (2000). *The Subject in Question: Sartre's Critique of Husserl in* The Transcendence of the Ego. London: Routledge.
Sartre, Jean-Paul (1943). *Being and Nothingness: An Essay on Phenomenological Ontology*. Translated by Hazel E. Barnes. New York: Philosophical Library, 1958. Translation of *L'Être et le néant: Essai d'ontologie phénoménologique*. Paris: Gallimard.
Sartre, Jean-Paul (1937). *The Transcendence of the Ego: An Existentialist Theory of Consciousness*. Translated by Forrest Williams and Robert Kirkpatrick. New York:

Noonday Press, (1960). Translation of "La Transcendance de L'Ego: Esquisse d'une Description Phénoménologique." *Recherches Philosophiques* 6 (1936–1937).

Scanlon, John D. (1971). Consciousness, the Streetcar, and the Ego: *Pro* Husserl, *Contra* Sartre. *Philosophical Forum* 2: 332–354.

Sukale, Michael (1976). Sartre and the Cartesian Ego. In *Comparative Studies in Phenomenology*, pp. 68–79. The Hague: Martinus Nijhoff.

Van Inwagen, Peter (2011). Relational vs. Constituent Ontologies. *Philosophical Perspectives*, 25, edited by John Hawthorne and Jason Turner, pp. 389–405. New York: Wiley-Blackwell.

# 13 The "of" of intentionality and the "of" of acquaintance

*Rocco J. Gennaro*

## Introduction and terminology

The term "consciousness" is of course notoriously ambiguous. One key distinction is between *state* and *creature* consciousness (Rosenthal 1993, 2005). We sometimes speak of an individual mental state, such as a pain or perception, as conscious. On the other hand, we also often speak of organisms or creatures as conscious, such as when we say that dogs are conscious. Creature consciousness is also simply meant to refer to the fact that an organism is awake, as opposed to sleeping or in a coma. Most contemporary theories of consciousness are aimed at explaining state consciousness, that is, explaining what makes a mental *state* a conscious mental state. Perhaps the most fundamental and commonly used notion of "conscious" among philosophers is captured by Thomas Nagel's famous "what it is like" sense (Nagel 1974). When I am in a conscious mental state, there is "something it is like" for me to be in that state from the first-person point of view. When I am, for example, smelling a rose or having a conscious visual experience, there is something it "seems" or "feels" like from my perspective. There is also something it is like to be a conscious creature, whereas there is nothing it is like to be a table or tree.[1]

In Gennaro (2002), I argued that Sartre's theory of consciousness and his belief that consciousness entails self-consciousness can be fruitfully understood against the background of the so-called "higher-order thought (HOT) theory of consciousness," which, in turn, sheds light on the structure of conscious mental states and Sartre's theory of (self-)consciousness. Another goal of that paper was, following Wider (1997), to show how Sartre's view can be understood from a contemporary analytic perspective. The HOT theory of consciousness says that what makes a mental state conscious is the presence of a HOT directed at the mental state. These HOTs are typically themselves unconscious unless one is engaged in "reflection" or "introspection," in which case the HOT is itself conscious and accompanied by another HOT (Rosenthal 2005; Gennaro 2012). So, when a conscious mental state is a first-order world-directed state, the HOT is *not* itself conscious; otherwise, circularity and an infinite regress would follow. When the HOT is itself conscious, there is a yet higher-order (or third-order) thought directed at the second-order state. In this case, we have *introspection*, which involves a *conscious* HOT directed at a mental state. When one introspects, one's attention is directed back into one's mind.

Following Husserl, Sartre urges that "all consciousness . . . is consciousness of something" (1956, pp. 11, 23). The key point here is the essentially intentional aspect of consciousness. But Sartre also distinguishes between *positional* (or thetic) consciousness and *non-positional* (or non-thetic) consciousness. According to Sartre, an act of consciousness is "positional" when it asserts the existence of its object. Obviously related to the intentional nature of consciousness, the idea is that when one's conscious attention is focused on something else, one "posits" the existence of an intentional object. On the other hand, one merely has "non-positional" consciousness of "anything that falls within one's field of awareness but to which one is not now paying attention" (Wider 1997, p. 41). It is a kind of ubiquitous background "self-awareness." Every act of consciousness, Sartre argues, has both a positional and non-positional aspect. It is the latter which is more important for and relevant to this chapter. Further, Sartre distinguishes between *reflective* and *pre-reflective* consciousness. The former is the positional consciousness of consciousness, such as when one introspects a mental state, whereas the latter is the non-positional consciousness of consciousness.

It is also worth first noting here that my 2002 paper pre-dated much of the more fruitful and recent work by Uriah Kriegel (2003, 2006, 2009), who has defended a related "self-representational theory of consciousness," and other relevant work by Rowlands (2001, 2003, 2013), Zahavi (2004, 2005), Thomas (2003), Thomasson (2000) and others which have affinities to the theories found in Sartre (1956, 1957) and Brentano (1874/1973). The purpose of this chapter is to elaborate further on these matters and especially to delve more deeply into the Sartrean notion of "pre-reflective consciousness" in light of recent work on theories of consciousness. Overall, I will argue that it is still best to construe the non-positional and pre-reflective "self-awareness" as representational and unconscious, as opposed to some weaker form of "intentionality" or some kind of "acquaintance." For the purposes of this chapter, I'll treat "intentional" as interchangeable with "representational."

In the remainder of this chapter, I first provide some further background on Sartre's theory of consciousness and pre-reflective self-awareness, especially with respect to how it might be favorably compared to my own version of HOT theory. Then, I critically examine a few initial attempts to understand the "acquaintance" relation and to link it with Sartre's notion of pre-reflective self-awareness. Then, I briefly address a related problem often raised against HOT theory, namely, the problem of misrepresentation. Following this, I critique several further attempts to explain the acquaintance relation and argue that they are inadequate.

Next, I critically evaluate Hellie's (2007) argument favoring acquaintance theory over higher-order theories. Then, I argue that the move to "adverbialism" fails to save acquaintance theory and should also be rejected on other grounds. Lastly, I offer some brief concluding remarks. Overall, I argue that many of the properties associated with pre-reflective non-positional consciousness or self-awareness can be best accommodated by a version of HOT theory.

## Sartre, HOT theory, and pre-reflective (non-positional) self-awareness

In Gennaro (2002), I argued in great detail that Sartre's theory of consciousness could be helpfully understood as a version of HOT theory, especially one which is closer to my own. Unlike Rosenthal, who holds that the (unconscious) HOT is *entirely distinct* from its target, I had previously argued that first-order conscious states are better construed as complex states with two parts: a mental state part directed at the world (M) and an unconscious "metapsychological thought" (MET) part directed at M. This is what I have called the "wide intrinsicality view" (WIV), such that consciousness is indeed an intrinsic aspect of conscious states, and thus such states should be individuated widely (Gennaro 1996, 2006, 2012). It is, we might say, an intrinsic version of HOT theory. Nonetheless, during "reflection" or "introspection," there is a *conscious* HOT (or MET) directed at a mental state. In this case, there is a greater "gap" between the MET and its object. The conscious MET is entirely distinct from its target mental state.

With regard to Sartre, it is worth noting first that he, much like HOT theorists and others, noticed a potentially troubling infinite regress problem. However, instead of responding in like manner by holding that the "self-awareness" in question is normally unconscious, he says the following:

> All reflecting consciousness is, indeed, in itself unreflected, and a new act of the third degree is necessary in order to posit it. Moreover, there is no infinite regress here, since a consciousness has no need at all of a reflecting consciousness in order to be conscious of itself. It simply does not posit itself as an object.
>
> (Sartre 1957, p. 45)

Sartre also puts it as follows:

> Either we stop at any one term of the series—the known, the knower known, the knower known by the knower, etc. In this case the totality of the phenomenon falls into the unknown; that is, we always bump up against a non-conscious reflection and a final term. Or else we affirm the necessity of an infinite regress (*idea ideae ideae*, etc.), which is

absurd ... Are we obliged after all to introduce the law of this [knower–known] dyad into consciousness? Consciousness of self is not dual. If we wish to avoid an infinite regress, there must be an immediate, non-cognitive relation of the self to itself.

(Sartre 1956, p. 12)

What are we to make of these passages? First, we must keep in mind that Sartre is often taken as rejecting unconscious mental states, though some commentators have questioned the notion that Sartre denied the existence of *all* unconscious mentality (see Gennaro 2002, pp. 299–305, for some discussion). Thus, we might suppose that the option open to the HOT theorist to avoid an infinite regress, i.e., by invoking *unconscious* self-awareness, is not open to Sartre. But Sartre seems to think that, by treating conscious states as including non-positional self-awareness, an infinite regress can still be avoided. I am not convinced by this but won't quibble with it here (but see Gennaro 2002, pp. 305–308). Sartre is of course correct that if one were to suppose that conscious states required *reflective* (positional) conscious states directed at first-order conscious states, then an infinite regress would certainly follow. But neither Sartre nor HOT theory is committed to such a claim. In any case, it is also worth noting up front that Sartre obviously did not share the reductionist motivations found in many current representationalists (including myself).[2]

Second, we can see that Sartre is recognizing that when there is "reflecting" (i.e., introspective) consciousness, there must be "a new act of the third degree." This is reminiscent of the HOT theorist's contention that a third-order state is necessary for introspection. But there is no infinite regress because "a consciousness has no need of a reflecting consciousness in order to be conscious of itself," which can be taken as meaning "conscious mental states need not have a reflective (or introspective) state directed at it in order to be self-conscious." The idea that a conscious mental state need not be accompanied by introspection is, once again, certainly the view of any HOT theorist. One can, for example, have an outer-directed conscious mental state of a table without being introspectively conscious of one's own perception. After all, one's conscious attention cannot be directed both at the table and at one's own mental state at the same time (though we may often switch back and forth).

But Sartre must still also account for the non-positional self-awareness in pre-reflective consciousness. He holds that "every positional consciousness of an object is at the same time a non-positional consciousness of itself" (Sartre 1956, p. 13). In the first passage quoted above, Sartre is making the point that such non-positional consciousness of itself "does not posit itself as an object." "This [non-positional] self-consciousness we ought to consider not as a new consciousness ... [it is] a quality of the positional consciousness" (Sartre 1956, p. 14). Sartre says "Consciousness (of) pleasure is *constitutive* of the pleasure as the very mode of its own existence" (Sartre

1956, p. 14; emphasis added). So Sartre is recognizing, as he did in attempting to avoid the infinite regress, that non-positional self-consciousness is really part of a first-order conscious state. It is "constitutive" of the first-order conscious state. "We understand now why the first consciousness of consciousness is not positional; it is because it is one with the consciousness of which it is consciousness" (Sartre 1956, pp. 13–14).

I argued in Gennaro (2002) that this is tantamount to holding the WIV (or something very close to it in structure) such that non-positional self-awareness is part of the conscious mental state. This self-awareness is not entirely separate from the mental state it is directed at, and this is why Sartre says that it "does not posit an object." So, despite Sartre's claim that all consciousness is consciousness of something, he is apparently saying that, when it comes to such non-positional self-consciousness, it does not really posit an object, or at least not a *distinct* object. This is also why Sartre feels the need to explain that he uses the "of" [*de*] in parentheses merely out of "grammatical necessity" when speaking of non-positional self-consciousness (of) self. Sartre tells us that

> when I am aware of a chair, I am non-reflectively conscious of my awareness. But when I deliberately think of my awareness, this is a totally new consciousness; and here only am I explicitly positing my awareness or myself as an object of reflection. The pre-reflective cogito is a non-positional self-consciousness.
> (Sartre 1956, p. xi)

But why not just call such meta-psychological implicit awareness an "unconscious thought (or self-awareness)"? Sartre's reluctance to call the "non-positional awareness" in pre-reflective consciousness an "unconscious thought" is perhaps again partly due to his apparent rejection of the first-order unconscious. However, I suggested that we could interpret (or reasonably modify) Sartre's view as being committed to the existence of unconscious METs. As we shall see, it is difficult to understand it any other way.

Reflection or introspection is, however, "an operation of the second degree ... performed by a[n act of] consciousness directed upon consciousness, a consciousness which takes consciousness as an object" (Sartre 1957, p. 44). Thus, the higher-order (i.e., second-order) reflecting consciousness "posits" a lower-order consciousness. In these cases, we might call the higher-order state "the reflecting consciousness" and the lower-order state "the reflected-on." And so reflection, for both Sartre and the WIV, involves a reflecting consciousness directed at an inner reflected-on object (i.e., mental state). So "the reflecting consciousness posits the consciousness reflected-on, as its object" (Sartre 1956, pp. 12–13).[3]

Thus, to summarize, it is clear that Sartre views "non-positional self-awareness" as a form of self-consciousness, since he believed that first-order outer-directed conscious states are also self-conscious states. Like

322  *Rocco J. Gennaro*

a HOT theorist, however, he also recognized a yet higher-order form of self-consciousness, which he called "reflection" (instead of "introspection"). So when one is in a first-order conscious mental state, one has a (complex) state such that one is positionally aware of an outer object but also non-positionally aware of that awareness. When one is in a second-order reflective state, one has a (complex) higher-order conscious "reflecting" state directed at (or positionally aware of) a first-order "reflected-on" state of consciousness (Figure 13.1).

The main differences between my view and Sartre's are (1) to the extent that Sartre rejects *all* unconscious mental states (and can somehow still avoid an infinite regress), his non-positional self-awareness could obviously not be *un*conscious; and (2) assuming that Sartre or others can make

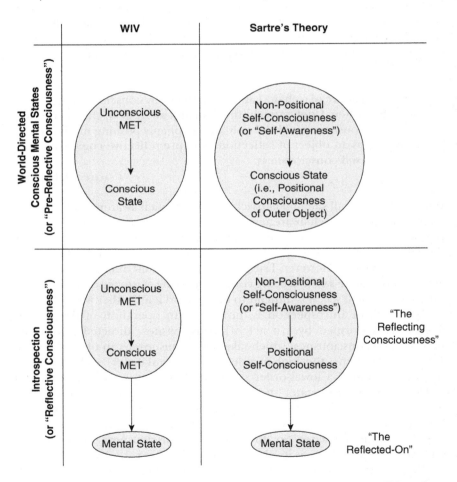

*Figure 13.1* A side-by-side comparison of the wide intrinsicality view (WIV) and Sartre's theory. MET meta-psychological thought.

sense of some kind of "acquaintance" relation between such self-awareness and conscious states, that would differ from my view that it can best be understood to be a more robust intentional or representational relation.

## Pre-reflective self-awareness and acquaintance: a first pass

Now the notion that such pre-reflective self-awareness (i.e., pre-reflective awareness *of* conscious states) can be fruitfully explained in terms of some kind of "acquaintance" relation to our conscious states has been suggested by some authors, perhaps even as an alternative to a standard higher-order representational view (Hellie 2007). So a key question is: does the "of" of acquaintance fare better than the "of" of intentionality or representation in trying to understand pre-reflective self-awareness? For all of us who do believe that some kind of self-awareness accompanies all first-order conscious states, it is crucial to address this issue.

But there are numerous problems with this approach. It is worth emphasizing at the outset that the notion of "acquaintance" at work cannot be the same notion that Russell (1910/1929, 1912/1997) famously employed, for several reasons. This can help to limit the potential for confusion. First, much of Russell's concern was about knowledge of *outer* objects or features of the world, not self-awareness in any sense. He was primarily concerned to distinguish knowledge by acquaintance from knowledge by description (Russell 1910/1929), where the former is a kind of immediate (or direct) experience of objects or things and the latter is knowledge *that* something is the case (or some kind of factual knowledge). One feature of acquaintance with $X$ is that we are directly aware of $X$ without any intermediary process of inference. Second, even if one turned knowledge by acquaintance inward to one's own mental states, it wouldn't appear to be at the right level, i.e., at the pre-reflective level. Rather, it would seem to enter at the level of "introspection" or "reflection," as opposed to a more intimate self-awareness of first-order conscious states. That is, when I consciously turn my attention to my own mental states, I might be said to be acquainted with my conscious states, but then they are very clearly objects of my higher-order conscious thoughts. As we have seen, even Sartre concedes that we can have reflective consciousness which is "positional," that is, which posits a distinct object.

Third, and perhaps most importantly, to the extent that one wishes to invoke acquaintance with our conscious states as having some sort of special epistemic status or even implying infallible knowledge of our mental states, this seems mistaken both as a matter of fact and as the proper interpretation of Russell's view (Wishon 2012). Gertler (2011, especially Ch. 4) discusses this so-called "acquaintance theory of self-knowledge" as involving introspection of events in our minds. But she clearly recognizes that "acquaintance theorists are not generally committed to infallibility or omniscience," though introspection "can be more epistemically secure than other empirical judgments" (Gertler 2011, p. 96). "The core of any acquaintance theory is the idea that some introspective knowledge involves acquaintance" (Gertler 2011, p. 96), as opposed, for example, to "inner-sense" accounts of introspective self-knowledge. HOT and other theorists might of course allow for some notion of "acquaintance" with our conscious states even with regard to introspection, but just because the relation seems direct (i.e., without inference), it doesn't follow that it really is the way it appears or that it is infallible. Once again, the discussion at hand is clearly taking place at the introspective or reflective level, not at the pre-reflective level. The issue remains as to how we should characterize the pre-reflective self-awareness that accompanies conscious states.[4]

In any case, it still remains the case that "acquaintance" is often described is a kind of *relation*, e.g., a relation between a subject and a conscious state and/or a relation between self-awareness (not introspective) and a conscious state. If it is not meant to be relational at all, then the onus is on the acquaintance theorist to explain it. As I briefly sketched in the previous section, my own way of explaining the pre-reflective awareness in question is that it is unconscious representational self-awareness (the "ubiquitous self-awareness") that accompanies all conscious states, along the lines suggested by HOT theory. However, I also hold, unlike Rosenthal and others, that it is best to construe such awareness as part of an overall complex conscious state. So, according to my WIV, we have two parts of a single conscious state with one part *directed at* ("aware of") the other. In short, we have a complex conscious mental state with an *inner intrinsic relation between parts*. There is thus a kind of "self-referential" or "self-representational" or "self-reflexive" element to conscious states. But given that there is still a relational aspect, it is best to treat it also as intentional and representational.

Some have tried to cash out the notion of pre-reflective self-awareness in terms of a ubiquitous (conscious) "peripheral" self-awareness which accompanies all of our first-order focal conscious states (Kriegel 2003, 2006, 2009). Not all conscious "directedness" is attentive, and so perhaps I have mistakenly restricted conscious directedness to that which we are consciously focused on. If this is right, then a first-order conscious state can be both attentively outer-directed and inattentively inner-directed. I argue against this view at length (Gennaro 2008, Gennaro 2012, Ch. 5). For example, although it is surely true that there are degrees of conscious attention, it seems to me that the clearest examples of genuine "inattentive" consciousness are outer-directed awareness in one's peripheral visual field. But this obviously does not show that any such inattentional consciousness is *self-directed* when there is outer-directed consciousness, let alone at the very same time. Also, what is the evidence for such self-directed inattentional consciousness? It is presumably based on phenomenological considerations, but I confess that I do not find such ubiquitous inattentive self-directed "consciousness" in my experience, which should presumably show up in a clear Nagelian sense if it is based on phenomenological observation. Except when I am introspecting, conscious experience is so completely outer-directed that I deny we have such peripheral self-directed consciousness when in first-order conscious states. It does not seem to me that I am consciously aware (in any sense) of my own *experience* when I am, say, consciously attending a movie or to the task of building a bookcase. Even some who are otherwise very sympathetic to Sartre's overall view and a generally phenomenological approach also find it difficult to believe that pre-reflective (inattentional) self-awareness accompanies conscious states (Siewart 1998; Zahavi 2004) or at least that *all* conscious states involve such self-awareness (Smith 2004). And none of these authors are otherwise sympathetic to HOT theory or reductionist approaches to consciousness.

Interestingly, there has also been a noticeable shift in emphasis to talk of parts and wholes in Kriegel's later work (e.g., Kriegel 2006, 2009). He had even previously said, for example, that "the mental state yielded by that integration may not actually represent itself . . . . At most, we can say that one part of it represents another part" (Kriegel 2005, p. 48). But Kriegel later explicitly explains that only an *indirect self-representation* is applicable to conscious states (2009, pp. 215–226). This comes in the context of Kriegel's attempt to make sense of a self-representational view within a naturalistic framework, but it is also much more like the WIV in structure, the main difference being that he thinks that pre-reflective self-awareness is itself (peripherally) conscious. As we shall see later, Kriegel also rejects the notion that the relation between his peripheral inattentive self-directed consciousness and conscious states is best understood in terms of "acquaintance."

## An aside on misrepresentation

One related difficulty that arises in this context for any HOT theorist (and any acquaintance view, for that matter) is what to say about the possibility of misrepresentation between a conscious mental state (M) and an unconscious HOT. For example, there might seem to be a more immediate epistemic relation between them even in HOT theory, especially in light of the implicit "self-reference" in the HOT. This element of self-reference might then seem to rule out the kind of *misrepresentation* that is frequently raised as an objection to HOT theory. But how can one have a representational relation without the possibility of misrepresentation? The main example of misrepresentation used in Gennaro (2012) comes from the following hypothetical case from Levine (2001):

> Suppose I am looking at my red diskette case, and therefore my visual system is in state $R$. According to HO, this is not sufficient for my having a conscious experience of red. It's also necessary that I occupy a

326   Rocco J. Gennaro

> higher-order state, say HR, which represents my being in state R, and thus constitutes my being aware of having the reddish visual experience.... Suppose because of some neural misfiring (or whatever), I go into higher-order state HG, rather than HR. HG is the state whose representation content is that I'm having a greenish experience, what I normally have when in state G. The question is, what is the nature of my conscious experience in this case? My visual system is in state $R$, the normal response to red, but my higher-order state is HG, the normal response to being in state $G$, itself the normal response to green. Is my consciousness of the reddish or greenish variety?
>
> (Levine 2001, p. 108)

So the question is: In such a hypothetical case, what "is it like for the subject"? The higher-order content is green whereas the first-order content is red. Levine initially points out that we should reject the following two possible answers:

> Option 1: The resulting conscious experience is of a *greenish* sort.
> Option 2: The resulting conscious experience is of a *reddish* sort.

I agree with Levine on these two options. The main problem is that one wonders what is the point of having both states, on HOT theory, if only one of them determines the (color of the) conscious experience. Rosenthal, however, continues to favor option 1, which I think is much more problematic. Somehow the higher-order representation alone is what matters. But doesn't this defeat the purpose of HOT theory, which is supposed to explain state consciousness in terms of the relation between two states? This problem reappears in so-called "targetless" or "empty HOT" cases where there is no lower-order state at all (Gennaro 2012, pp. 59–70). But how could a lone *unconscious* thought result in a conscious state?

So instead I favor a third option and argue that the self-reference and complexity of conscious states in the WIV rule out this kind of misrepresentation such that neither color experience would result in such a case. If there isn't a "match" (that is, an accurate representation) between a HOT concept and the content of a lower-order state, then it seems perfectly appropriate for the HOT theorist to hold that something like this third option is a legitimate possibility. After all, this is an abnormal case where applying the HOT theory could not be expected to result in a normal conscious state. If specific brain lesions are involved, perhaps the subject would experience a loss of color vision (achromatopsia) with respect to the diskette case perception. On the WIV, if the proper interconnectedness between M and MET is absent, then there will be no resulting conscious state. If a MET is misrepresenting M (or if there is no M at all), then what would otherwise be the entire complex conscious state does not exist and thus cannot be conscious.

On the neural level, much the same seems reasonable, since, for example, there may be some overlapping parts of feedforward and feedback loops that extend from M to MET or vice versa. Edelman and others have argued that feedback loops (or re-entrant pathways) in the neural circuitry of the brain are essential for conscious awareness (Edelman and Tononi 2000a, 2000b). It is well known that forward-projecting neurons are matched by an equal or greater number of back-projecting neurons. The brain structures involved in these loops seem to resemble the structure of at least some form of HOT theory such that lower-order and higher-order states are combining to produce conscious states. More specifically, such evidence seems to support the WIV because of the intimate and essential interrelationship between the "higher" and "lower" areas of the brain involved. There is mutual interaction between the relevant neuronal levels (see Gennaro (2012), Chs. 4 and 9 for more on the neural realization of my theory).

So am I saying that misrepresentations cannot occur or that there is some kind of infallibility at work between MET and M? In one sense, yes, but I also point out how the following two claims are really two sides of the same coin (Gennaro 2012, p. 64):

(1)   There is no resulting conscious state when a misrepresentation does occur.
(2)   Misrepresentations cannot occur.

I am unsure which is preferable, but either one seems plausible to me, especially if we think of (2) as:

(2') Misrepresentations cannot occur between M and MET *and still result in a conscious state.*

Once again, we must be careful not to conflate any kind of infallibility in outer-directed conscious states with allegedly infallible introspective knowledge. In the WIV, it is possible to separate the higher-order (complex) conscious state from its target mental state in cases of *introspection*. This is as it should be and does indeed allow for the possibility of error and misrepresentation. Thus, for example, I may mistakenly consciously think that I am angry when I am really jealous, I may be wrong about why I am sad, and so on. The WIV properly accommodates the anti-Cartesian view that one can be mistaken about what mental state one is in, at least in the sense that when one *introspects* a mental state one may be mistaken about what state one is really in. There is more of a "gap" in this case. However, this is very different from holding that the relationship between M and MET within an outer-directed conscious state is similarly fallible. There is indeed a kind of infallibility *between M and MET* according to the WIV, but this is not a problem. The impossibility of error in this case is merely *within* the complex conscious state and is certainly not one that holds between one's conscious state and an outer object.[5]

## More on acquaintance and pre-reflective self-awareness

Let us return to the problem of trying to make sense of acquaintance. First, one might suppose that there must be a causal connection between a conscious state and any kind of ubiquitous self-awareness. But, as Kriegel rightly points out, the causal relation is antireflexive, and so we can, at best, make sense of such a relation only by invoking talk of one part of a complex state directed at another part. The WIV can clearly accommodate the notion of a causal relation between M and MET combining to produce a conscious mental state (as described above in neural terms, perhaps). Notice, however, that there is still no "pure self-reference," that is, no conscious (brain) state (or state part) that is literally directed at itself. This kind of self-reference is ruled out if we take the requisite notion of "self-reflexive" conscious states too literally.[6]

But now if we suppose that the self-awareness or self-reflexivity in question involves a causal relation, then we are faced with a different potential problem. It is made vivid by Buras (2009), who argues that if some mental states are reflexive, then "it spells trouble for causal theories of mental content" (p. 117), which hold that mental states acquire their content by standing in appropriate causal relations to objects and properties in the world (see Gennaro 2012, pp. 33–36). That is, if we allow for truly reflexive intentional content as in some literal "pure self-reference," then causal theories of mental content must be wrong because causal relations are "irreflexive." But Buras has at most shown that intentional reflexivity is inconsistent with causal theories of mental content. Even if we grant this, I suggest that we ought to reject the notion that a mental state can literally be directed at itself, which is not really the case for the WIV or Kriegel's view. Buras does mention that an alternative strategy would be to allow for some sort of non-representational awareness (or "acquaintance") between M and MET, as opposed to a standard representational relation. Such acquaintance relations would presumably be understood as somehow "closer" than the representational relation and thus can also help to avoid the problem of misrepresentation (and perhaps other problems). But Buras does not really in the end wish to argue for or offer a theory of acquaintance.

Janzen (2008), on the other hand, takes Kriegel to task for mischaracterizing some authors in the phenomenological tradition, such as Husserl and Sartre, by insinuating that they would not agree with Kriegel's way of describing the relation between M and MET (Janzen 2008, p. 116 n30). But I agree with Kriegel (2009, pp. 106–113, 205–208) and Buras (2009, pp. 119–121) that this strategy is at best trading one difficult problem for an even deeper puzzle, namely, just how to understand the allegedly intimate and non-representational "awareness of" relation between MET and M. Finally, it is even more difficult to understand such "acquaintance relations" within the context of a reductionist approach. So I agree with Kriegel in opposition to any "acquaintance" alternative. I am still not sure what to make of this "*sui generis*" alternative. Indeed, acquaintance is often taken to be unanalyzable and simple, in which case it is difficult to see how it could usefully explain *anything*, let alone the nature of conscious states.[7]

Shear (2009) challenges Zahavi's (2005) arguments for the view that all conscious experience involves self-consciousness, that is, a kind of "for-me-ness" or "mineness" internal to conscious experience. I won't evaluate his entire critique of Zahavi's arguments, but Shear rightly points out that "when it comes time to offer a *positive* description of this consciousness, we are told, for example, that it is a 'subtle background presence'" (Shear 2009, p. 103; emphasis added). I have also argued that, for example, Kriegel uses a number of vague and mysterious characterizations of "peripheral self-awareness," such as "subtle awareness of having M," "implicit awareness of M," "dim self-awareness . . . humming in the background of our stream of consciousness," and "minimal self-awareness" (Kriegel 2003, pp. 104–105). It is still not clear to me that Kriegel's peripheral self-awareness is conscious in any phenomenological sense. So I suggest that the difficulties faced by those who hold that pre-reflective self-awareness is conscious (in any sense) can easily be avoided by thinking of such self-awareness as unconscious HOTs (or METs). Nonetheless, much of what Zahavi says could be acceptable to Shear if he recognized the alternative WIV. That is, Zahavi's arguments for the ubiquity of self-awareness can be accommodated by unconscious METs in a way that can avoid the worries raised by Shear.

In other work discussing Henrich and Frank, Zahavi (2007) also recognizes how unsatisfying invoking "acquaintance" can be. Zahavi explains that they acknowledge that pre-reflective, irrelational self-awareness is characterized by internal differentiation and complexity, but they

> never offer a more detailed analysis of this complex structure. That is, when it comes to a positive description of the structure of original pre-reflective self-awareness they are remarkably silent, either claiming in turn that it is unanalysable, or that the unity of its complex structure is incomprehensible. This is hardly satisfactory.
> 
> (Zahavi 2007, p. 281)[8]

Preyer (2013) also discusses "what Heinrich has called subjectivity is . . . the *primary self-consciousness* we are acquainted with immediately" (p. 196) but it is also not "higher-order" in the sense of being a distinct state or extrinsic to the first-order conscious state (p. 196). To this extent, I agree with Preyer against standard HOT theories. However, I disagree that it is better to think of such acquaintance as somehow not representational. Partly for this reason, I think of the WIV as a modified version of HOT theory. The other reason, again, is that I think it is best to construe the self-awareness in question as unconscious.

Strawson (2013) nicely illustrates, in a very upfront and honest way, just what a struggle it can be to offer a positive account of the notion that all conscious awareness (A) involves awareness of A. Strawson, no friend of HOT theory, ultimately concedes that we should not give up the relationality claim in describing pre-reflective self-awareness or "acquaintance." He doesn't see how genuine "reflexivity" or "self-reference" cannot involve genuine "relationality." So he is willing to allow, contra Sartre, that the "of" in non-positional self-awareness is metaphysically correct and not merely some unhappy grammatical obligation. I agree. Like Zahavi and others, Strawson also seems willing to concede that non-positional self-awareness does not show up in the phenomenology.[9]

## Hellie's argument

With the above analysis in place, I will now turn to examine Hellie's (2007) paper in more depth. He thinks the "correct view . . . is that consciousness consists of a bearing a nonintentional relation of awareness [NIRA] to a *diversity* of mental features, some intentional, some not" (p. 290). He thinks that his view has a "trio of advantages over Higher-Order Intentionalism" (p. 299), such as HOT theory, but I am very puzzled as to why he thinks so.

The first alleged "advantage" is supposed to be that there is "a reason for reductively minded naturalists to prefer Acquaintance Theory [AT] to Higher-Order Intentionalism [HOI]" in the sense that "the latter involves intentional relations and the former doesn't. Maybe intentional relations can be reduced, maybe they can't; but introducing them into the mix raises a prima facie difficulty for reductivism" (Hellie 2007, p. 299).

But surely representationalists and reductionists, such as HOT theorists, believe and argue at length for the view that intentional relations can be reduced and that consciousness can be reduced to intentionality. Indeed, this is the overall strategy for virtually all representationalists. One need not even be a representationalist on consciousness to recognize how much work has been done to give a naturalistic account of intentionality. Hellie may not be satisfied with them or extant HOI theories of consciousness, but how is introducing intentional relations a difficulty for reductivism *especially in comparison with* the rather mysterious "nonintentional acquaintance relation," discussed earlier? If Hellie is merely stating that he thinks all such HOI attempts don't (or can't) work, then that is a different argument, but it is somewhat question begging as it stands. Further, how could AT possibly be "preferred" by "reductively minded naturalists"? Indeed, as we have seen, there is normally a clear non-reductivist strain in AT, not to mention that some acquaintance theorists describe the acquaintance relation as unanalyzable. So, introducing NIRA into a theory of consciousness is surely at least as problematic as introducing intentional relations of awareness (IRA). Very little seems understood about the former. Much like some of the other authors mentioned earlier, Hellie offers little by way of a positive account of the acquaintance relation.

Second, Hellie thinks that:

> Acquaintance Theory arguably is the view of common sense ... To have pain and to feel pain are one and the same ... More generally, it seems an article of common sense that no mental state can have phenomenal character $K$ unless the subject is somehow aware of (or "feels") its instance of $K$; and that if a subject is aware of, in the relevant way, an instance of $K$, the subject's mental state has $K$ as its phenomenal character—there cannot be phenomenal illusions of the sort Higher-Order Intentionalism predicts.
>
> (Hellie 2007, p. 299)

There are several responses one might offer here: (a) As was discussed earlier, if Hellie has in mind the introspective or reflective level, then he is off the mark in terms of what we are concerned with here, namely, the prereflective level. Recall that even Russellian acquaintance was never meant to imply infallibility. Moreover, if we are at the introspective level, virtually all HOI theorists have argued that one could be mistaken about being in pain. (b) Hellie's claim that it is "an article of common sense that no mental state can have phenomenal character K unless the subject is somehow aware of (or 'feels') its instance of K" is not a problem for HOI as such. Indeed, it sounds very much like the "transitivity principle" often used by HOT theorists, namely, that a conscious state is a state whose subject is, in some way, aware of being in it (Rosenthal 2005). I agree that this is "common sense." (More below.) (c) Hellie is mistaken that it then follows that "there cannot be phenomenal illusions of the sort Higher-Order Intentionalism predicts." If we are again at the introspective level, then there is enough of a gap to allow for the possibility of being mistaken about the object of introspection. Now if Hellie does have in mind the pre-reflective level, then he may have more of a point. I agree that the problem of misrepresentation is an important one facing intentionalists and HOT theorists. However, as I explained in the section "an aside on misrepresentation," it is possible for an HOI theorist to accommodate the notion that misrepresentations (and illusions) cannot occur at this level. Once again, I differ with Rosenthal on this matter.

Hellie's "third advantage" mainly says that

> a number of concerns about the view that consciousness-of is a form of awareness either misfire unless it is an IRA, or are much more easily rebutted if it is a NIRA. To the extent that one finds the view attractive but the concerns worrisome, one has reason to endorse the Acquaintance Theory.
>
> (Hellie 2007, p. 299)

But this is more of a conclusion than a third separate argument or alleged "advantage" for AT. If I am right about the above two alleged advantages, then he should withdraw this one as well.

Hellie then addresses a number of arguments in favor of HOI and argues that they are "powerless" to discriminate between HOI and AT (pp. 302–306), such as two of Rosenthal's arguments (pp. 303–304). One involves his rationale for favoring HOT theory to higher-order perception (HOP) theory and the other has to do with why positing HOTs can explain how it is that we can report our mental states.

I am willing to concede at least for the sake of argument that those arguments don't automatically force one to conclude that AT has been ruled out and thus that one must opt for HOI, but the onus is surely still on AT to offer a much more positive alternative account. As we have seen, this is no easy task. Rosenthal's arguments are also not necessarily intended to argue against *all* other alternative views. Again, he seems to have HOP theory in mind when he rejects the notion that we somehow "sense" the mental states that we are aware of being in. He is there mainly concerned with showing that HOT theory is superior to HOP theory.[10] Further, there are other arguments that might be used to make the case for HOI (more on this in the next section). Indeed, some other arguments for HOI may not rule out all other theories (Lycan 2001), such as a self-representationalist alternative. That is why a HOT theorist ought to argue against this view more specifically and directly, as I have done briefly in the section on "pre-reflective self-awareness and acquaintance: a first pass" above, and at length in Gennaro (2012, Ch. 5). No argument or two is likely to be able to eliminate all other competing theories.

Finally, Hellie says he will then:

> assess arguments powerful enough to make the needed discriminations. First, an explanation argument due to the Intentionalists Byrne (2001) and Thau (2002) which collapse into an argument from illusions of phenomenal character. This second argument cuts both ways: if there can be such illusions, the Higher-Order Intentionalist wins; if not, the Acquaintance Theorist wins. Given the difficulty in assessing the prima facie case for or against such illusions, I turn to a third argument from explanatory priority, which makes a very strong case for Acquaintance Theory.
>
> (Hellie 2007, p. 306)

I won't enter into a detailed discussion of his first two arguments, especially since Hellie himself basically reduces them in the end to the problem of "illusions" (or, we might say, "misrepresentation"). Assuming he is right about that, we already have the readymade reply from earlier: if we are at the introspective level, virtually all HOI theorists will acknowledge that we can be mistaken about our introspective states. But this is not very controversial, and recall that even those who invoke Russellian acquaintance do not take it to be infallible. On the other hand, if Hellie does have in mind the pre-reflective level, then he may have a stronger argument. However,

*The "of" of intentionality and acquaintance* 333

as I explained in the section "more on acquaintance and pre-reflective self-awareness," it is possible for an HOI theorist to accommodate the notion that misrepresentations (and illusions) cannot occur at this level. Further, it is not necessarily the case that "if there can be such illusions, the Higher-Order Intentionalist wins; if not, the Acquaintance Theorist wins." My reply with the problem of misrepresentation allows for HOI to win *and* that there are no such illusions ("misrepresentations") at the pre-reflective level (that is, between MET and M). This is very different from the possibility of illusions both at the introspective level and between any conscious state and the outer world.

Hellie explains that "according to the Acquaintance Theorist, consciousness-of is acquaintance, a NIRA. Since acquaintance is nonintentional, if one's experience has phenomenal character F, it is F. There cannot be illusions in acquaintance, according to the Acquaintance Theorist" (Hellie 2007, p. 310). But, once again, we have no positive account of this allegedly more intimate acquaintance relation which, according to Hellie, cannot result in illusions. Interestingly, he actually says that "whether there can be illusions in acquaintance is the subject of considerable debate. I am on the side of those who refuse to accept such a possibility" (Hellie 2007, p. 310). But it seems to me that he still has in mind some sort of introspective level. For example, he mentions the interesting phenomenon of "dental fear" to support his view:

> when the dentist informs the nervous patient he hadn't started drilling yet and the patient says "ah, so I didn't feel pain after all," this reveals in my view either that there is more to pain than a phenomenal character or that dentistry patients are easily shamed into behaving solicitously.
> (Hellie 2007, p. 310)

But surely a good part of this process involves introspection and even some reporting on the patient's own mental state. Even prior to when the patient initially reports the dental pain, there is a significant period of anticipation accompanied by introspective thoughts about being in pain. Intense and fearful introspection might even *cause* a patient to confuse fear with pain or represent oneself as being in pain when there is no pain. Introspection can even *create* a lower-order conscious state. I can surely, via introspection, cause myself to have a strong desire for lasagne if I think about the taste for long enough.[11]

Hellie's third argument for AT is called the "argument from explanatory priority" (Hellie 2007, p. 310). He examines two strategies for explaining the following "necessary truths" (Hellie 2007, pp. 310–311):

1 NIRA ↔ PC: Bearing a NIRA to an F is always accompanied by (but might, for certain NIRAs, not always accompany) a certain characteristic phenomenal character (PC).

2. IRA ↔ PC: Bearing an IRA to an F always accompanies, and is accompanied by, the PC characteristic of bearing its broadening to an F.

> An IRA-first strategy takes the IRA and its characteristic features as primitive, and declares its broadening to be that IRA *plus* . . . NIRA-first strategy takes the NIRA and its characteristic features as primitive, and declares its narrowing to be a functionally-defined state: to be in the narrowing of a NIRA is to be in some "realizer" state which is from the subject's perspective like being in the NIRA.
> (Hellie 2007, p. 311)

I do not see why he thinks that the NIRA-first strategy is better off than the IRA-first strategy with respect to explanatory priority. What is the "primitive" on the NIRA view? Well, it almost seems just to *be* phenomenal character: "to be acquainted with an instance of Kness *is just to be* in some state with the phenomenal character K. That is, if the NIRA-first strategy is correct, phenomenal character *explains* acquaintance" (Hellie 2007, p. 312). Hellie concedes that "no fact can explain itself" but there seems to me to be a sense in which this is precisely what the NIRA account offers, that is, some form of consciousness (phenomenal character) explaining (state) consciousness. Granted that NIRA is still supposed to be a *relation* (mysterious as it is), we don't quite have an absurd form of self-explanation, but we still apparently have phenomenal character explaining acquaintance with our mental states. This order of priority is problematic regardless of one's views about the possibility of explaining consciousness, but it is obviously even more problematic if one wishes to offer a reductionist account via IRA.

On the other hand, the IRA strategy holds out promise for explaining state consciousness (and phenomenal character) in terms of IRAs between (unconscious) mental states. To be sure, there is much that needs to be spelled out for any representationalist, but it is clearly mistaken to say that "we have no idea what the *plus* is for any broadening of any IRA" (Hellie 2007, pp. 311–312). Numerous efforts have been made by representationalists to fill out the "plus," including many of the authors that Hellie cites. Once again, Rosenthal (2005) and myself (Gennaro 2012) have gone into great depth as to how to explain state consciousness in terms of HOTs or METs. Intentionality or representation is indeed primitive in explaining state consciousness and phenomenal character. For the above reasons, then, I disagree with Hellie when he says that "rather than facts about phenomenal character being explained by facts about a certain sort of intentionality . . . the truth of the matter is that facts about this sort of intentionality [IRA] are rather explained by facts about phenomenal character" (Hellie 2007, p. 313). Further, Hellie does little to advance the issue regarding the *structure* of conscious states along the lines discussed earlier in this chapter. If Sartre's "pre-reflective" consciousness is just a kind of (conscious) NIRA, then we just revert back to the problems described in previous sections.

Hellie does not properly recognize representational theories of consciousness (first-order, higher-order, whatever). He seems baffled as to how a representationalist might even *attempt* to explain how certain kinds of intentionality could give rise to consciousness when others don't. Instead he concludes:

> Intentionalism promised to leave us with one unsolved problem in the philosophy of mind where there were previously two. It doesn't do this. Intentionality is all over the place in the world, including: the intentionality of organismal processes, as when an acorn is growing into a mighty oak, ... the intentionality of dynamical processes, which proceed so as to minimize the use of energy ... The Intentionalist is thus left with the problem of explaining why certain varieties of intentionality give rise to consciousness when others don't. A healthy pessimism about the prospects of such an approach leaves one suspicious that the Intentionalist can only explain consciousness in terms of conscious intentionality.
> (Hellie 2007, p. 315)

Perhaps this shows that one's prior view about the prospects for a reductionistic explanation of consciousness is really what drives authors on both sides. Moreover, one might think that "representation" or "intentionality" is all over the place in the world but that "intentionality" (understood as something *mental*) is clearly not everywhere. Most of us think there are important differences between a *mental* representation (= intentionality) and any other kind of representation, such as in tree rings and photographs. In order to possess genuine (mental) intentionality, one option is to hold that a creature or object in question must have complex-enough behavior such that simple mechanistic explanations are not sufficient to explain its behavior. More positively, we might demand that creatures display a significant degree of inferential integration (or "promiscuity") among their intentional states (Stich 1978). The contents of, say, beliefs and desires are interconnected in various ways and acquire their content within a web or network of mental states. Absurd implications can also be blocked by recognizing that, for example, stomachs and rivers do not meet the criterion above, namely, that there is no significant degree of inferential connections among its states and that attributing intentionality to stomachs or rivers or tree rings does not add any explanatory value to a purely mechanistic account.[12] In any case, Hellie has unfairly ignored numerous detailed attempts to give a representationalist theory of consciousness.

## Adverbialism to the rescue?

Finally, some authors have sought refuge in "adverbialism" as a way of understanding the acquaintance relation or, better, as a way to avoid commitment to *distinct objects* of such self-awareness (Rowlands 2001, 2003,

2013; Thomas 2003, unpublished). This was also a strategy used by some to avoid ontological commitment to troublesome non-physical "sense data." Rowlands explains that "when I have experiences, I have them *minely*. Their mine-ness is an adverbial modification of the act [of consciousness] rather than a property of an object of that act" (Rowlands 2013, p. 535). Thomas (2003, unpublished) similarly holds that we should give priority to the whole person when trying to explain consciousness. Consciousness is mainly a feature of organisms rather than mental states. So, for example, to experience green is not to have a mental *act of awareness* that takes a green *object* as its target, but it is rather a way of "experiencing greenly" or "being appeared to greenly." The central idea, then, seems to be that creature or person-level consciousness is somehow ontologically prior to state consciousness. The acquaintance relation, if there is one, is between a person and a conscious state.

But, first, any theory of consciousness should still be able to answer the question: What makes a mental *state* a conscious mental state? A HOT theorist presents a theory of state consciousness and a way to explain the difference between unconscious and conscious mental states. If pushed further, this is also where the HOT theorist typically relies on the intuitive claim that has come to be known as the transitivity principle (TP). One motivation for HOT theory is the desire to explain precisely what differentiates conscious and unconscious mental states:

(TP) A conscious state is a state whose subject is, in some way, aware of being in it (Rosenthal 2005).

Thus, when one has a conscious state, one is aware of being in that state. For example, if I am having a conscious desire, I am aware of having that desire. Conversely, the idea that I could be having a conscious state while totally unaware of being in that state seems very odd. A mental state of which the subject is completely unaware is clearly an unconscious state. For example, I would not be aware of having a subliminal perception, and thus it is an unconscious perception. I view TP primarily as an *a priori* or conceptual truth about the nature of conscious states (see Gennaro 2012, pp. 28–29 for some discussion).

Adverbialism, as far as I can see, does nothing to explain (or even try to explain) state consciousness. It passes the buck to creature consciousness without really offering an account of that either. What then makes a *creature* conscious? Perhaps it is simply that conscious creatures have conscious states but this is more of a definition than an explanation of state or creature consciousness. At least HOT theory also offers a positive and fairly detailed theory about state consciousness. I suppose that one might reasonably argue that even TP mentions (or presupposes) a "subject" in explaining state consciousness. It is not clear to me that TP assumes the existence of conscious subjects, but again it may just be true that state and creature consciousness normally go hand in hand such that any conscious mental state is possessed by a conscious creature.

However, it does seem possible to be state-conscious and not creature-conscious. For example, if one supposes (reasonably, I think) that vivid dreams are conscious mental states then we would seem to have a case of state consciousness without creature consciousness. Perhaps the same might be said of some hypnotic states. On the other hand, if we suppose that sleepwalkers do not have conscious mental states, perhaps they can be rightly described as creature-conscious but not state-conscious. The same might be said about the philosopher's hypothetical zombie. In any case, it remains unclear to me what adverbialism *explains* that HOT theory or related representational theories of consciousness cannot explain, especially with respect to state consciousness and the nature of pre-reflective self-awareness.

Let me close by mentioning another related and compelling rationale for HOT theory and the TP (based on Rosenthal 2004, p. 24). We might reason as follows: Even a non-HOT theorist might still agree with HOT theory as an account of introspection or reflection, namely, that it involves a conscious thought about a mental state. This seems to be a fairly common-sense definition of introspection. It also seems reasonable for anyone to hold that when a mental state is unconscious, there is no HOT at all. But then it stands to reason that there should be something "in between" those two cases, that is, when one has a first-order conscious state. So what is in between no HOT at all and a conscious HOT? The clear answer is an unconscious HOT, which is precisely what HOT theory says. Moreover, this explains what happens when there is a transition from a first-order conscious state to an introspective state, that is, an unconscious HOT becomes conscious. Indeed, perhaps this transition can also be understood in evolutionary terms and, in particular, the evolution of the brain and mental capacity.

Finally, it cannot be emphasized enough just how interconnected some views are on both sides of this issue. Sartre and Brentano did not apparently even think there were unconscious mental states and neither desired to offer a reductionist account of conscious states. It is no surprise that many today in that phenomenological tradition, such as Zahavi, Siewart, Hellie, Janzen, and Smith, also tend to be anti-reductionist. Since HOT theory is reductionist at least in mentalistic terms, it should be no surprise that they also reject HOT theory and any reductionist representationalist view. On the other hand, those of us who desire to provide a reductionist account of state consciousness are naturally more likely to find representationalist approaches more attractive. I think there are good methodological reasons to aim for a reductionist theory of consciousness (Gennaro 2012, Ch. 2), but it would be silly to pretend that these views aren't mutually supporting and interconnected. Those who are anti-reductionist will then be more likely to embrace some notion of "acquaintance" in accounting for conscious states. I hope I have shown, however, that one can usefully bring together Sartre's theory and a reductionist version of HOT theory in an effort to make sense of ubiquitous pre-reflective self-awareness.

## Conclusion

Thus, on my view, many of the properties associated with pre-reflective non-positional consciousness or self-awareness can be accommodated by a version of HOT theory. According to the WIV, for example, conscious states are intrinsic, relational, self-referential, analyzable, and complex. There is also a very immediate and intimate relationship between METs and Ms (conscious mental states). However, the key difference from standard interpretations of Sartre's theory is that METs are unconscious and representational and so are not states of "acquaintance," as normally defined. Attempts to characterize the "acquaintance" relation in a positive way are rare; instead, we are usually told what it is *not*, such as non-representational, non-positional, and so on. Thus, pre-reflective non-positional self-awareness is best understood as representational and unconscious. Overall, though, Sartre's theory of consciousness and the structure of conscious states on the WIV have much in common (recall Figure 13.1).

## Notes

1 There are also a cluster of other expressions and terms related to Nagel's sense, for example, philosophers sometimes refer to conscious states as "phenomenal states" having qualitative properties called "qualia," which are perhaps best understood as the felt properties or qualities of conscious states. I'll avoid these terms for the most part.
2 I argue independently for these motives in Gennaro (2012, Ch. 2), but won't defend them here. It seems at least *more difficult* to avoid an infinite regress if one thinks that the pre-reflective (non-positional) awareness is itself conscious in some sense.
3 In Gennaro (2002), I bolster this line of comparison with additional references to major secondary sources on Sartre's theory, such as Catalano (1974), Morris (1975), and Busch (1990).
4 See also Gertler (2012) for a nice related discussion on this topic. Chalmers (2010, especially pp. 285–294) also utilizes a notion of "acquaintance" in an effort to account for a rather special and intimate epistemic relation between a subject and a phenomenal property—such as an instance of phenomenal greenness—though he also stops short of claiming that the resulting phenomenal beliefs are thereby infallibly justified by a subject's acquaintance with that phenomenal property. "What is central is . . . that whenever a subject has a phenomenal property, the subject is acquainted with that phenomenal property" (Chalmers 2010, p. 287). See also Hasan and Fumerton (2014) for additional background in Russell's initial distinction and for more on the pros and cons regarding the notion of "acquaintance," especially in more recent work in epistemology.
5 There is much more on misrepresentation and related matters in Gennaro (2012, especially pp. 59–70, 96–100, 158–160, and 179–180). See also Gennaro (2013) in response to commentaries by Van Gulick, Weisberg, and Seager as part of a *Journal of Consciousness Studies* book symposium on Gennaro (2012).
6 For more on my critique of what I called "pure self-referentialism," see Gennaro (2012, pp. 104–116). This view is probably closest to Brentano's actual position

but he is also committed to rejecting the existence of unconscious mental states. Kriegel seems to have held this view in some of his earlier work.
7 Another important and difficult issue arises when some put forward the idea that "acquaintance" is non-conceptual. Recall that Sartre even calls it "non-cognitive," by which he does not seem to mean "non-mental." Sartre says that there must be "an immediate, *non-cognitive* relation of the self to itself" (Sartre 1956, p. 12; emphasis added). I also disagree with Sartre here because I defend conceptualism and because HOTs are composed of concepts. See Gennaro (2012, especially Ch. 6).
8 The same might be said of Montague (2013), who thinks that "conscious awareness always involves—constitutively involves—some sort of awareness of that very awareness" (p. 76). But what exactly is "some sort of awareness of that very awareness"? We are really never told. Moreover, if it is itself also conscious, then the infinite regress (and circularity) rears its ugly head. If it is not conscious, then how does the view differ from HOT theory or, especially, the WIV.
9 So now how exactly does the relationship between two unconscious state parts result in a conscious state? My answer to this and a related "hard problem" objection can be found in Gennaro (2012, Ch. 4). The key lies in the way that concepts are applied in HOTs. But, again, anyone who doesn't wish to pursue a reductionist strategy will likely never think that the hard problem can be solved in any way.
10 See also Lycan (2004), Rosenthal (2004), and Gennaro (2012, pp. 49–53) for much more on this family squabble.
11 For more on my take on this dental fear and pain case, see Gennaro (2012, pp. 68–70).
12 For more on the relationship between consciousness and intentionality, see Gennaro (2012, pp. 21–27).

# References

Brentano, F. (1874/1973). *Psychology from an Empirical Standpoint.* New York: Humanities.
Buras, T. (2009). An Argument Against Causal Theories of Mental Content. *American Philosophical Quarterly* 46: pp. 117–129.
Busch, T. (1990). *The Power of Consciousness and the Force of Circumstances in Sartre's Philosophy.* Bloomington: Indiana University Press.
Byrne, A. (2001). Intentionalism Defended. *Philosophical Review* 110: pp. 199–240.
Catalano, J. (1974). *A Commentary on Jean-Paul Sartre's* Being and Nothingness. Chicago, IL: University of Chicago Press.
Chalmers, D. (2010). *The Character of Consciousness.* New York: Oxford University Press.
Edelman, G., and G. Tononi. (2000a). Reentry and the Dynamic Core: Neural Correlates of Conscious Experience. In T. Metzinger, Ed. *Neural Correlates of Consciousness: Empirical and Conceptual Questions.* Cambridge, MA: MIT Press.
Edelman, G., and G. Tononi. (2000b). *A Universe of Consciousness.* New York: Basic Books.
Gennaro, R. (1996). *Consciousness and Self-Consciousness.* Amsterdam: John Benjamins Publishers.
Gennaro, R. (2002). Jean-Paul Sartre and the HOT Theory of Consciousness. *Canadian Journal of Philosophy* 32: pp. 293–330.

Gennaro, R. (2006). Between Pure Self-referentialism and the (Extrinsic) HOT Theory of Consciousness. In U. Kriegel and K. Williford, Eds. *Self-Representational Approaches to Consciousness*. Cambridge, MA: MIT Press.

Gennaro, R. (2008). Representationalism, Peripheral Awareness, and the Transparency of Experience. *Philosophical Studies* 139: pp. 39–56.

Gennaro, R. (2012). *The Consciousness Paradox: Consciousness, Concepts, and Higher-Order Thoughts*. Cambridge, MA: MIT Press.

Gennaro, R. (2013). Defending HOT Theory and the Wide Intrinsicality View: A Reply to Weisberg, Van Gulick, and Seager. *Journal of Consciousness Studies* 20 (11–12): pp. 82–100.

Gertler, B. (2011). *Self-Knowledge*. New York: Routledge.

Gertler, B. (2012). Renewed Acquaintance. In D. Smithies and D. Stoljar, Eds. *Introspection and Consciousness*. New York: Oxford University Press.

Hasan, Ali and Fumerton, Richard (2014). Knowledge by Acquaintance vs. Description. *The Stanford Encyclopedia of Philosophy* (Spring 2014), Edward N. Zalta (Ed.). Available online at: http://plato.stanford.edu/archives/spr2014/entries/knowledge-acquaindescrip/.

Hellie, B. (2007). Higher-order Intentionality and Higher-order Acquaintance. *Philosophical Studies* 134: pp. 289–324.

Janzen, G. (2008). *The Reflexive Nature of Consciousness*. Amsterdam: John Benjamins.

Kriegel, U. (2003). Consciousness as Intransitive Self-consciousness: Two Views and an Argument. *Canadian Journal of Philosophy* 33: pp. 103–132.

Kriegel, U. (2005). Naturalizing Subjective Character. *Philosophy and Phenomenological Research* 71: pp. 23–56.

Kriegel, U. (2006). The Same Order Monitoring Theory of Consciousness. In U. Kriegel and K. Williford, Eds. *Self-Representational Approaches to Consciousness*. Cambridge, MA: MIT Press.

Kriegel, U. (2009). *Subjective Consciousness*. New York: Oxford University Press.

Levine, J. (2001). *Purple Haze*. New York: Oxford University Press.

Lycan, W. (2001). A Simple Argument for a Higher-order Representation Theory of Consciousness. *Analysis* 61: pp. 3–4.

Lycan, W. (2004). The Superiority of HOP to HOT. In R. Gennaro, Ed. *Higher-Order Theories of Consciousness: An Anthology*. Amsterdam: John Benjamins.

Montague, M. (2013). The Content, Intentionality, and Phenomenology of Experience. In S. Miguens and G. Preyer, Eds. *Consciousness and Subjectivity*. Berlin: De Gruyter.

Morris, P. (1975). *Sartre's Concept of a Person: An Analytic Approach*. Amherst: University of Massachusetts Press.

Nagel, T. (1974). What Is It Like to Be a Bat? *Philosophical Review* 83: pp. 435–456.

Preyer, G. (2013). The Problem of Subjectivity: Dieter Henrich's Turn. In S. Miguens and G. Preyer, Eds. *Consciousness and Subjectivity*. Berlin: De Gruyter.

Rosenthal, D. (1993). State Consciousness and Transitive Consciousness. *Consciousness and Cognition* 2: pp. 355–363.

Rosenthal, D. (2004). Varieties of Higher-order Theory. In R. Gennaro, Ed. *Higher-Order Theories of Consciousness: An Anthology*. Amsterdam: John Benjamins.

Rosenthal, D. (2005). *Consciousness and Mind*. New York: Oxford University Press.

Rowlands, M. (2001). *The Nature of Consciousness*. Cambridge, UK: Cambridge University Press.

Rowlands, M. (2003). The Transcendentalist Manifesto. *Phenomenology and the Cognitive Sciences* 2: pp. 205–221.

Rowlands, M. (2013). Sartre, Consciousness, and Intentionality. *Phenomenology and the Cognitive Sciences* 12: pp. 521–536.
Russell, B. (1910/1929). Knowledge by Acquaintance and Knowledge by Description. In *Mysticism and Logic*. New York: W. W. Norton.
Russell, B. (1912/1997). *The Problems of Philosophy*. New York: Oxford University Press.
Sartre, J.-P. (1956). *Being and Nothingness*, trans. Hazel E. Barnes. New York: Philosophical Library.
Sartre, J.-P. (1957). *The Transcendence of the Ego*, trans. Forrest Williams and Robert Kirkpatrick. New York: Hill and Wang.
Shear, J. (2009). Experience and Self-consciousness. *Philosophical Studies* 144: pp. 95–105.
Siewart, C. (1998). *The Significance of Consciousness*. Princeton, NJ: Princeton University Press.
Smith, D. W. (2004). *Mind World: Essays in Phenomenology and Ontology*. Cambridge, MA: Cambridge University Press.
Stich, S. (1978). Beliefs and Subdoxastic States. *Philosophy of Science* 45: pp. 499–518.
Strawson, G. (2013). Self-intimation. *Phenomenology and the Cognitive Sciences* 13: pp. 44–73.
Thau, M. (2002). *Consciousness and Cognition*. New York: Oxford University Press.
Thomas, A. (2003). An Adverbial Theory of Consciousness. *Phenomenology and the Cognitive Sciences* 2: pp. 161–185.
Thomas, A. (unpublished) Reconciling Conscious Absorption and the Ubiquity of Self-awareness.
Thomasson, A. (2000). After Brentano: A One-level Theory of Consciousness. *European Journal of Philosophy* 8: pp. 190–209.
Wider, K. (1997). *The Bodily Nature of Consciousness: Sartre and Contemporary Philosophy of Mind*. Ithaca, NY: Cornell University Press.
Wishon, D. (2012). *Russellian Acquaintance and Phenomenal Concepts*. Ph.D. dissertation. Stanford University.
Zahavi, D. (2004). Back to Brentano? *Journal of Consciousness Studies* 11 (10–11): pp. 66–87.
Zahavi, D. (2005). *Subjectivity and Selfhood*. Cambridge, MA: MIT Press.
Zahavi, D. (2007). The Heidelberg School and the Limits of Reflection. In S. Heinämaa, V. Lähteenmäki, and P. Remes, Eds. *Consciousness: From Perception to Reflection in the History of Philosophy*. Dordrecht: Springer.

# 14 A "quasi-Sartrean" theory of subjective awareness

*Joseph Levine*

## Introduction

First, a disclaimer. This chapter is not intended to be a scholarly investigation of Sartre's theory of consciousness. Rather, I want to explore a certain problem in the treatment of conscious experience over the last several decades in the analytic tradition, and suggest that certain basic ideas that have their source, at least for me, in Sartre's account of consciousness in *Being and Nothingness* might point the way toward a solution. Let me begin by laying out the problem.

Perhaps the easiest way to introduce my topic is to ask the simple question: what distinguishes a conscious state, an experience, from an unconscious mental state? In Thomas Nagel's (1974) famous "bat paper" he gave the following answer: conscious states are those for which there is something it is like for the subject having them. He argued there, and elsewhere, that conscious experiences were essentially "subjective," involving a particular "point of view" on the world. It was this essential subjectivity of conscious experience, he believed, that made it so difficult to incorporate into the natural, physical world.

The "what-it's-like-for" formulation of conscious experience directly expresses the two aspects of conscious experience that have bedeviled attempts to naturalize it: phenomenal properties, or qualia, the features of experiences that determine *what* it's like for the subject; and subjectivity, an experience's being like something *for* the subject. It is the second aspect that is constitutively tied to the idea of a point of view, and is what I want to explore in this chapter.

While Nagel argued that the subjectivity of conscious experience would make it extremely difficult to naturalize, many philosophers have responded with attempts to show that subjectivity is not the obstacle to naturalization that Nagel thought it was. But even before addressing the question of naturalizability, or reducibility, it's important to clarify just what it is for a mental state to be subjective in this way, to embody a point of view. Over the last several decades there have been many different theories of consciousness, and each one has had something to say about what subjectivity is. It seems to me that, when you abstract from many of the differences in detail, one can see two basic approaches: what I will call the "secondary awareness" approach and the "access" approach. Interestingly, this division cross-cuts the division between reductivists (materialists) and non-reductivists (who are often anti-materialists, though not always). What I will argue is that neither approach is successful in the end. What's needed is a third approach, the one that is inspired by aspects of Sartre's account in *Being and Nothingness*. I'll call it the "for-itself" approach.

## Access approach

Ned Block (1995) has famously distinguished between two notions of consciousness: "access consciousness" and "phenomenal consciousness." By calling a mental state "access conscious" Block means that the state in question is available to higher-level processes of reasoning, action planning, speech, and the like. "Phenomenal consciousness" is supposed to capture the Nagelian "what it's like" feature of conscious experiences, or what is also called an experience's "qualitative character." On Block's view, the phenomenal, or qualitative, character of a mental state is an intrinsic feature, the one that presents such a problem for materialist reduction, the source of the explanatory gap. Block insists that phenomenality is quite distinct from access, arguing that one can find cases, both hypothetical and actual, of mutual disassociation between the two.

While Block resists the idea that access is essential to any form of consciousness, many theorists see it as the key to understanding the subjectivity of conscious experience, what it is for a state to be *for* a subject. For example, Michael Tye's (1995 and 2000) "first-order representationalist" account of phenomenal consciousness, his so-called PANIC theory, makes access an essential feature of the account. "PANIC" stands for poised abstract non-conceptual intentional content. On the PANIC theory, what determines *what* it is like for a subject to have an experience is the intentional content of the mental representation that constitutes her having the experience. That the content in question is non-conceptual is meant to capture the apparent difference in format between paradigmatically phenomenal states like perceptual experiences and cognitive states like thoughts and beliefs, for which there is no phenomenal character (according to Tye). But since there could easily be unconscious representational states that have the same non-conceptual contents as their corresponding conscious states—as in subliminal perception—we still need to know what distinguishes conscious states from unconscious ones. This is the work that the "poised" in PANIC is supposed to do. When a state is poised to affect reasoning, deliberation, etc. in the right way—in other words, when it is *access*-conscious—that is what makes it conscious. Subliminal perceptions are unconscious precisely because they are not poised to affect higher-level cognitive processes in the right way (though they do have noticeable effects, which is why psychologists believe they exist).

While first-order representationalist theories are explicitly reductive, it seems to me that there are non-reductive versions of access theory as well. For instance, among those who do not claim to reduce phenomenal character to anything else there is a debate concerning whether a state of conscious awareness must contain some reflexive conscious awareness as an essential component. In the phenomenological tradition, this idea of a secondary awareness is often associated with Brentano.[1] But a number of contemporary philosophers of mind who have no reductive ambitions still eschew the commitment to a reflexive component within a conscious experience. On their view, what makes a mental state phenomenally conscious is just its having this special mental feature, phenomenal character. While some, like Siewert (1998), argue that phenomenal character is essentially intentional—it presents how things look, sound, feel, etc.—they do not think any self-directed intentionality is an essential part.

Even though their analysis of phenomenal consciousness appeals to the looks and feels of experiences and not to any explicitly self-directed, or reflexive, components, it seems to me that something of the sort enters the account nevertheless. Where does it come in? Well, it comes in by way of introspection. That is, one way of distinguishing *conscious* mental states from the unconscious ones is to say that the conscious ones are the ones to which we have introspective access, and this accessibility is essential to them. Unlike the reductive first-order representationalists, the non-reductive intentionalists do not attempt to provide a functional account of access. Still, the idea that a kind of subjective accessibility is essential to what it is to be a conscious state seems to be crucial to what distinguishes the conscious from the unconscious. It is the way such a view can capture the "for the subject" in "what it is like for the subject."

So what is wrong with the access approach? When it comes to the reductive versions there are, of course, all the explanatory gap problems associated with the reduction of qualitative character to either a functional or a physical property. But that isn't a problem with the access move itself, and it certainly doesn't apply to the non-reductive versions of the approach. Rather, it seems to me that the problem is that access—or, better, accessibility—is a dispositional feature, and subjectivity, what it is for a state to be *for* a subject, isn't adequately captured by a dispositional account of it.

I don't have a lot to say to support this claim, other than what I think is strong intuitive backing. As I look at my computer screen right now as I type these words it seems very clear to me that I embody a point of view on it, not just in the sense that I see it from a certain spatial perspective, but in the sense that the experience is *for* me; and its being *for* me is essential to what makes it a *conscious* experience.[2] But if this is right, than what it is that makes it for me must be something happening right now, in the moment, and thus an occurrent feature of the experience. That is, it isn't by virtue of the mere dispositional fact that I could, if I so desired, turn my conscious light on my own experience, that makes it conscious. Rather, it is by virtue of something it has right now that it is consciously experienced—as I keep repeating, it is *for* me. To my mind, as I just said, this means that the subjectivity of the experience is something occurrent, and not captured by any notion of accessibility, whether reductive or not.

## Secondary awareness approach

Perhaps the most straightforward way to capture the idea of an occurrently subjective feature of conscious experience is to posit a secondary awareness as intimately tied to the primary awareness involved in any conscious experience. After all, isn't it my being *aware* of the experience what its being *for* me consists in? This basic idea motivates both reductive and non-reductive versions of the secondary awareness approach.

The reductive version of this approach is represented by the so-called "higher-order theory" of consciousness. David Rosenthal (1997), its most prominent proponent, presents the foundation for the theory this way. He says, expressing the point just made above, that conscious mental states are those mental states we are *conscious of*. For him this is a truism; it's just what we mean by calling a mental state "conscious." Certainly there is something deeply intuitive about this. If asked to say what distinguishes paradigm conscious mental states, such as the visual experiences I am now having of the computer screen in front of me, from paradigm unconscious mental states, such as the Freudian repressed desires I now battle, or the Chomskian states of my language device, a natural thing to say is that I am aware of, conscious of, the former, whereas I am unaware of, not conscious of, the latter. Rosenthal introduces the distinction between "transitive consciousness" and "intransitive consciousness," where the former is a matter of being conscious of some mental state, whereas the latter is a mental state's having the property of being conscious. He argues, on several grounds, that the right way to approach a theory of consciousness is to take transitive consciousness as basic and intransitive consciousness as derivative. That is, a mental state is intransitively conscious just in case one is transitively conscious of it.

Rosenthal's particular version of higher-order theory is "higher-order thought" theory, which is distinguished from other versions like "higher-order perception" theory, as defended by Lycan (1997). The distinction turns on whether the awareness of one's mental state is in the form of a thought, a cognitive state, or something more like a perception. I think there are pros and cons to each of these choices, but for present purposes the difference won't matter. What both versions share is the idea that being aware of, conscious of, one's mental state is in what its being conscious consists.

Higher-order theory is unabashedly reductive. The first step in its reduction of consciousness to something else more tractable is to identify awareness, this transitive relation, with mental representation, as it is understood in cognitive science. Mental representations, on this view, are like other representations—natural language sentences, pictures, maps, etc.—in the sense that they are physically realized tokens that have both an intrinsic structure and a semantic relation to entities external to them. Just like the sentence "David Rosenthal is a prominent philosopher of mind" has intrinsic physical features and a meaning—it is about a particular man, and ascribes a property to him—so too mental representations have physical features—presumably neural properties—and also are about objects and their properties. While the analogy between the physical features that individuate sentences and those of mental representations seems straightforward enough, problems arise when comparing their semantic, or intentional, features. The problem is that if we ask what it is about a sentence of English, like the one above, by virtue of which it is about a man and a property being ascribed to him, the most plausible answer is that it derives ultimately from the mental states of users of the language. It seems uncontroversial that if humans had never lived but the wind caused a shape to form in the sand on a beach of the same form as our sentence above, it wouldn't be about anything; it would be meaningless. But on pain of infinite regress (or appeal to God—and then, what makes His states meaningful?) something similar can't be said about our mental representations.

This problem, that the intentional "buck," as it were, stops at our minds, with their mental representations, has given rise to the "naturalizing intentionality" industry.[3] It is notorious that, after all the ink that has been spilled on this topic, no consensus has been reached on how to naturalize intentionality. To my mind, the most promising approach is the "informational," or "nomic-covariation," approach. On this view, a physical token of a certain type in the brain is about an object/property by virtue of a causal law that correlates instances of the object/property in question with tokens of the type in question. Of course lots of bells and whistles need to be added to this basic formulation in order to overcome problems about the possibility of misrepresentation, and other, related problems. As far as I know, no account of these bells and whistles has been shown to be counter-example-free. Nevertheless, if a genuine reduction of conscious awareness to mental representation, as envisioned by higher-order theory, is to occur, some such account of intentionality must be found.

I will set aside the problem of naturalizing intentionality and just assume some solution along the lines of informational semantics can be found. The fundamental idea, then, is that the intentionality of a mental state derives from the intentionality, or semantics, of the relevant mental representation. Therefore, on higher-order theory, the consciousness of a mental state has to be cashed out as the mental representation of that state (together with certain added conditions on the nature of that representation). The dispute between higher-order thought theory and higher-order perception theory is thus very much about the format of the relevant higher-order representation.

One of the added conditions on the higher-order mental representation that Rosenthal emphasizes is that it should have the form of a self-ascription:

that it should say something like "I am now perceiving a computer screen," rather than merely "there is a perception of a computer screen going on in such-and-such a location." One reason for insisting on the self-ascriptive format is precisely to capture the essential subjectivity of conscious experience, that it involves there being something it is like *for the subject*. Representing *oneself* (with a mental "essential indexical") as undergoing a certain perceptual state, say, is what captures that idea of being "for the subject."

We now have the principal elements of higher-order theory before us, or at least those that will concern the topic of this chapter. So what are the problems? To begin with, a standard objection to higher-order theory is that it leads to a regress problem. If a first-order state, such as a perceptual state, is conscious by virtue of another state, the higher-order one, constituting consciousness of it, then the higher-order state must be conscious as well. But now we need to say what makes the higher-order state conscious. Clearly, appealing at this point to an even higher-order state leads to an infinite regress of states. As stated, however, this isn't a real problem for higher-order theory, since its advocates are quite clear that they do not claim that the higher-order state by virtue of which the lower-order state is conscious is itself conscious. Quite the contrary. It is by virtue of the higher-order state's representing oneself as occupying the lower-order state that the *latter* is conscious. It's crucial for the view that one is *not* conscious of the higher-order state. In fact, introspection alone reveals that; after all, as I currently am enjoying a conscious visual experience of the computer screen in front of me I am not aware of any higher-order thought or perception. If the higher-order state had to be conscious this would make the theory quite implausible from a phenomenological point of view, in addition to leading to an infinite regress.

There are two counter-replies that critics of higher-order theory make at this point. First, some wonder how it is that by having one unconscious mental state represent oneself as being in another (previously) unconscious state one comes to be in a conscious state. Put another way, how can an unconscious mental representation make an unconscious state into a conscious one? To this challenge higher-order theorists respond that the objection reveals a serious misunderstanding of the view. It isn't that the higher-order state makes the lower-order state conscious, as if this were a causal process. That indeed would be mysterious. Rather, the two states, standing in the relevant representation relation, together *constitute* the conscious experience in question. This is a reductive theory, so one can't expect to find consciousness itself appealed to in the explanans. On the contrary, argues Rosenthal, it's only by analytically breaking the allegedly monadic property of being-conscious into these non-conscious components—a representation relation holding between two unconscious states—that one can even hope to *explain* consciousness. As Fodor famously quipped about intentionality—"if it's real, then it must really be something else"—so too for consciousness.

The second reply is similar in spirit, but doesn't confuse the constitutive nature of the higher-order account with a causal one. Siewert (2013) puts the point this way. The original intuition—indeed, alleged truism—that supported higher-order theory was the principle that conscious states are those mental states we are conscious of. This is what motivates the principal idea that intransitive consciousness must be analyzed in terms of transitive consciousness. But notice that in this formulation the phrase "conscious of" appears, not "represented by." If we're to honor the alleged truism, then our relation to the target state must be one of being *conscious* of it, and thus the higher-order advocate is faced with a dilemma: either honor the fundamental principle on which the theory is based, but then face the regress problem, or avoid the regress problem, but lose the support claimed from the fundamental principle, the alleged truism. The first horn is clearly unacceptable. While the second horn does not lead to any outright refutation, it does, so the argument goes, undermine that initial intuitive support claimed by advocates of the theory.

A plausible rejoinder to this argument is basically the same as to the previous one: higher-order theory is attempting to *explain* consciousness, which clearly cannot be done by taking it as primitive. Therefore, no analysis of what it is for a mental state to be conscious can rest with the idea that it is a state we are, literally, *conscious* of.[4] The point of appealing to the truism is just to show that what many theories take to be a monadic property of mental states is really a relation between the subject and the state in question. It is just another way of capturing the "for the subject" in the characterization of conscious experience in terms of "what it is like for the subject."

Here is one way to see what's at stake here. Two opposing reductivist programs are higher-order theory and first-order representationalism. On the latter view, conscious states are first-order representational states—paradigmatic cases are perceptual states—that meet certain further conditions. While Rosenthal, the standard bearer for higher-order theory, battles under the slogan "conscious states are states we are conscious *of*," Dretske (1997), one of the standard bearers for first-order representationalism, captures the view with the slogan, "conscious states are those we are conscious *with*." Neither Rosenthal nor Dretske intends to leave the "conscious" in "conscious of/with" as a primitive. Both want to analyze it as a matter of mental representation, a notion that too requires some analysis, but one that seems much closer to having a realization theory than an unreduced notion of consciousness does. So in their dispute what matters most is the preposition following the term "conscious," not the term "conscious" itself.

As I stated at the start of the chapter, I don't think higher-order theory does adequately capture subjectivity in the end. Part of the problem is that I don't think any reductivist account of conscious experience works, neither for subjectivity nor for qualitative character. But the objection I want to press here against higher-order theory isn't a general worry about reduction; it's quite specific to the way it tries to reconstruct subjectivity, a state's being *for* the subject. I want to introduce the problem I see by drawing an analogy with another issue, one that exercised philosophers some decades ago when appeal to mental representation became popular in the context of cognitive science.

When it first became fashionable to appeal to mental representations (again) to explain behavior, a challenge that was often pressed against this sort of explanation went like this: Genuine representations are representations *for* someone. To represent *X* is to represent *X* to or for some subject who utilizes the representation in some way. But, went the objection, this would entail positing some sort of homunculus to interpret and use the representation, to be the subject *for whom* the representation represents what it does.[5]

The standard computationalist response to this objection was to say that mental representations are, at least ultimately,[6] self-interpreting, or self-understanding, so one doesn't need a subject for whom it represents and who must count as understanding the representation. But how do they then cash out the "self" in "self-understanding"? Basically they functionalize it. Mental representations are for the subject possessing them when they play the appropriate role in the cognitive economy that constitutes the subject. So in a sense they are happening in the subject, they are not something the subject explicitly takes an attitude toward, except in the somewhat deflationary sense in which playing the functional role in question realizes the relation of taking an attitude toward the relevant representations.

With respect to the project of legitimating appeal to mental representation in cognitive science, I think this response to the challenge is fully adequate. But notice what this does to the higher-order theory. We start by asking: what is it that makes a perceptual state conscious? We then immediately analyze what it is for a state to be conscious in terms of its subjectivity, its being like something *for* the subject. But of course we still need an account of this notion itself, and higher-order theory responds by positing an extra representation, one over and above the state to which we want to ascribe consciousness. But the question can still be asked: what makes this representation itself, the higher-order one, for the subject? The answer, in the end, is just the same as the one we found for the access approach: it's a matter of its functional role, and thus its dispositional profile.

My point is that insofar as we are trying to capture the idea of an occurrent *for* the subject, higher-order theory doesn't do much better than first-order theory. The reason is that we still primarily get the effect of the "forness" through functional role, which makes this a kind of access approach. If we were unhappy with the access account in the first place because it doesn't adequately reconstruct the relation of being for the subject, making it dispositional, rather than occurrent, my claim is that the same problem attends the higher-order theory.[7]

One reaction to the criticism I've mounted of higher-order theory is to say that the fundamental problem stems from its reductive ambitions. Indeed,

I am quite sympathetic to the idea that no reductive theory can reconstruct the full-blooded notion of subjectivity. (Reductivists would agree, on the whole, though they'd claim that that's because there is something either incoherent, or just fictional, about the full-blooded notion. Their claim is that their theories can capture what in reality there is to capture. But this isn't the place to play out that battle.) So let's turn now to a non-reductive version of the secondary awareness approach, and see whether it can properly account for the subjectivity of experience.

The kind of approach I have in mind here has been attributed to Brentano (see Thomasson 2000, for instance) in a number of recent discussions of consciousness. The idea is that each conscious experience contains within itself a primary intentional object—whatever it is we are consciously aware of at the time—and a secondary intentional object, the conscious experience itself. So, for example, suppose I am visually perceiving a ripe tomato sitting on my kitchen counter. Let's assume there is nothing funny going on and the experience is fully conscious, though I am not especially reflecting on it, or engaging in any kind of introspection. I simply see it, fully aware of its presence and its properties (such as being round and red).

On the theory under consideration, my conscious experience contains two objects: the ripe tomato on the counter and my visual experience of the ripe tomato itself. However, the two objects do not have equal billing in my current theater of consciousness. The tomato is the *primary* object, whereas the experience itself is merely the *secondary* object. But how should we understand this distinction? What work does it do? Also, how do we understand the two awareness relations posited here, the awareness of the tomato and the awareness of the experience? Are these relations substantially of the same kind, just with different objects—indeed, with objects of different grades—or are the relations quite different in character, which would explain the difference in the kinds of objects they take (one taking primary objects and the other secondary ones)?

Let's begin with the relation. In common with its reductive sibling, higher-order theory, the non-reductive secondary awareness approach begins from the alleged truism that conscious states are states we are conscious of, or aware of. If this is right—if we're going to reconstruct being *for* the subject in terms of awareness of the state by the subject—then it's hard to see how the awareness involved in secondary awareness can be different in kind from the awareness involved in primary awareness. This echoes Siewert's earlier challenge to higher-order theory, though now there need be no explicit commitment to the effect that secondary awareness isn't itself a kind of conscious awareness.

However, if the awareness in secondary awareness really is of the same sort as that involved in primary awareness, then we are faced immediately with the regress problem again. After all, there is no attempt here to reduce the consciousness of a single state to a naturalistic representation relation between two non-conscious states, as with higher-order theory. Thus we can't escape the requirement that the secondary awareness be itself susceptible to the analysis that attends the original conscious experience as a whole. If so, then it seems in order for the secondary awareness to be a kind of conscious awareness that it must be attended by a "tertiary" awareness of it, and then we're off and running into the depths of infinite regress.

One way of making the primary–secondary distinction actually reinforces the regress problem. If asked, in what does the secondary awareness's being *secondary* consist, a natural answer appeals to differences in attentional focus across the objects of consciousness. When I'm absorbed with seeing the tomato—say, as I stare at it while deciding whether or not to include it in the salad I'm making—my attention is fixed on the tomato, not on my own experience. Just as we know that visual attention selects out certain among the items visually perceived for increased processing, yet without totally losing the perception of objects not within the current scope of attention, so too, on this view, one maintains the awareness of one's own experience while attention is focused on its primary object.

On this model what distinguishes primary from secondary awareness is whether or not the object of awareness lies within the focal area of attention. But this really makes the two forms of awareness seem very much alike, especially since, as one might expect from such a model, it is possible to switch attentional focus so that the secondary object becomes primary; this is one model of introspection. But if this is the case, if the awareness relation itself is pretty much the same for both primary and secondary awareness, then it does seem that the regress problem becomes all the more pressing.

While I think there really is a regress threat against the secondary awareness view, there are ways to counter it. For one thing, Brentano's view is often described as a "self-representational" view, though the "representational" part is a modern, reductive add-on. The idea is to beat back any regress problems by treating a conscious state as not a combination of two conscious states, but rather as a single state that has two intentional contents: the primary object and the state itself. Given there is only one state involved, which itself possesses all the conditions (including "self-representation") necessary for being a conscious state, there is no way to get the dreaded regress going.[8]

Now, as developed in a reductive manner by Kriegel and others, I don't think this move works. As I have argued elsewhere, the kind of mereological view that underlies reductive self-representational accounts can't really support a substantive distinction between higher-order theory and so-called "same-order" theory. So long as the self-representation function is reserved for a constituent of the entire state, I don't see that one can lean much on the alleged unity of the entire state to avoid the problems that attend the explicitly two-state higher-order theory. But these consequences largely follow from demands brought on by the reductive enterprise of analyzing awareness as representation, naturalistically construed. If we leave awareness unanalyzed, then it may be easier to avoid the regress problem.

The idea is this. My conscious visual experience of the ripe tomato indeed constitutes a single mental state. On this non-reductive version of the view, the state itself does not decompose into parts, each of which stands in its own awareness relation to its object—whether primary or secondary, a move required by the reductive analysis in terms of physically realized mental representations. Rather, this one state involves the subject's simultaneously standing in two awareness relations, one to the primary object and the other to the state itself.

I think it's just possible this view can avoid regress, but only by taking on board some very implausible features. The basic problem is this. Regress gets off the ground once one analyzes consciousness in terms of the conscious-of relation. If you want to say what makes my visual experience of the ripe tomato *conscious* is that I am conscious of it, then one faces a dilemma: either by "conscious of" one is using "conscious" to mean the same thing one means in "is conscious" or one isn't. If they do mean the same,[9] then it's hard to see how to avoid the regress. If being aware of a state is what it takes for it to be conscious, then you have to say the same thing about the consciousness of the state itself. If, on the other hand, one doesn't mean the same thing, then one is engaged in a reductive project after all, though it needn't be reduction to a naturalistic, or physically realizable, relation.

To elaborate on this second horn of the dilemma, consider again our example of my visual experience of the ripe tomato. This experience is a single conscious state, embodying two instances of the awareness relation. However, whereas we can freely characterize my overall visual experience of the tomato as my being *conscious of* the tomato, when we now break down that consciousness of the tomato into its component relations, primary awareness of the tomato and secondary awareness of the state of being primarily aware of the tomato, we cannot appropriately characterize either of these awareness relations as "conscious of" relations. There has to be something about the awareness that figures in my basic relation (i.e., basic with respect to the non-basic consciousness relation) to both the tomato and to my experience that doesn't quite qualify as full-blooded consciousness.

The non-naturalistic yet reductive theory would then look like this. Consciousness is a relation one stands in with respect to an object when one stands in a more basic awareness relation to the object *and* simultaneously to the state of being aware of the object. But what is this awareness relation? It's not the representation relation holding between a token mental representation and its object. It's not what we normally identify as consciousness. Is there such a thing as awareness of this kind? I find it mysterious and phenomenologically implausible. To me, it's precisely my awareness of the tomato that bears all the marks of consciousness. I find I can't discern a kind of awareness that isn't consciousness itself. This isn't a knock-down objection, but it does make the view harder to accept.

To my mind, when I have a visual experience of an object—say, the ripe tomato—it is that very awareness of the tomato that is the instance of consciousness at issue here, and this includes the feature of subjectivity. That is, I want to say that the awareness of the tomato is a form of *conscious* awareness (at least in part) by virtue of the fact that it—that very awareness of the tomato, not some other awareness stuck on top of it—is a subjective taking of a point of view on the tomato, which, to me, is another way of saying that my awareness of the tomato is for me. In other words, I don't know what awareness is if it isn't full-blooded *conscious* awareness, and taking this line seems to preclude the secondary awareness approach to analyzing consciousness.

## For-itself approach

As I stated at the beginning of the chapter, this is not intended to be a scholarly interpretation of Sartre's theory. Furthermore, there are elements of (what I take to be) his view that I do not endorse and will not incorporate into the approach I want to outline here. Still, I think enough of what I have to say is legitimately to be found in Sartre's work that it is appropriate to call this a Sartrean approach—or, as in the title, a "quasi-Sartrean" approach—to the question of subjectivity.

The fundamental distinction in the Sartrean framework that defines the For-Itself approach is that between the "in-itself" and the "for-itself" (or, between "being" and "nothingness"). The subjectivity of a conscious experience, its constituting a point of view on its content, or there being something it's like *for* the subject, is a matter of the holding of a primitive consciousness relation between the subject and the object. The subjectivity of the relation is an essential feature of the relation, not a constituent of the relation. That is the crux of the approach. Let me now elaborate on the distinctions involved (including between being a feature and being a constituent), show how they are brought together to explain subjectivity, and then delineate how this approach both incorporates features of the other two approaches while avoiding their problems. (Of course this doesn't mean it has no problems of its own.)

For Sartre, as I understand him, the distinction between the in-itself and the for-itself is intended to mark a fundamental ontological cleavage in reality. I do not endorse all of the features of this distinction that play crucial roles in Sartre's philosophy (especially his account of human freedom), but I do want to take on board the idea that the for-itself, consciousness, is a basic phenomenon in nature, not reducible to the in-itself. So what is the distinction, as I employ it? There are two features of the in-itself that distinguish it from the for-itself: the in-itself encompasses all of the objects and properties that constitute concrete, material reality—the universe, with all that composes it, and all that is subject to its fundamental and derived laws of nature; and also, it provides the contents for the conscious awareness that is the for-itself.[10] The for-itself, on the other hand, is just the pure relation of conscious awareness itself, with no substantial reality in its own right, but ontologically exhausted by its content—*what* it is aware of—and the relation of being aware of it.

The insubstantiality of the for-itself, the conscious subject, is what suggests the appellation of "nothingness." Whether there is a more fundamental ontological base underlying the structural relations between the for-itself and the in-itself, one that constitutes both the subject and object of a conscious experience, is not an issue on which I currently take a position; clearly Sartre thought there was not. What matters for me, however, is the fact that this pure relational, point-of-view-ness of the for-itself is all that is revealed within the (Cartesian?) theater of conscious experience.

The idea that consciousness is fundamentally a relation, and a fundamental relation at that, explains a number of features that many philosophers, of various persuasions, have emphasized. So, for instance, Hume (2012, Book 1, Part 4, section 6) famously denied that we have any impression of the self. Mental states, according to Hume, consisted of the having of impressions and ideas, faint copies of impressions. Impressions are always of something, whether it be colors, shapes, sounds, or bodily sensations. In each of these cases there is a content that the impression delivers to the conscious mind, and the consciousness of this content exhausts the mental state in question. Since ideas—the Humean stand-in for concepts, the material of thought—derive their contents from the impressions of which they are copies, there would need to be an impression of the self if we were to have a substantial idea of the self. But try mightily as he did, Hume, as he surveyed the contents of his conscious experience, could find no impression of self. Well, if consciousness, the for-itself, is a kind of "nothingness," then this isn't surprising. In other words, if all there is to the subject of experience is its being the point of view on the contents of the experience, and nothing more, then there couldn't be an impression of it, as there really isn't anything there to constitute the content of the impression.

As I said above, though for Sartre the ontologically special status of the for-itself as nothingness is clearly of prime importance, my point doesn't rely on this. What matters is not so much whether or not there actually is something in the world (e.g., the brain), in the realm of the in-itself, that can be identified with the subject of experience. Maybe there is; indeed, it seems likely. But two points need emphasis. First, I doubt whatever object we might find to count as the subject will support the heavy-duty intuitions of personal identity that we seem to have. Second, more important for our discussion, within the relation of conscious awareness the subject does not figure as content, as element of which we are aware, but rather as the implicit audience member, as it were, for the point of view *on* the contents that constitute the experience.

A point related to Hume's is expressed in contemporary discussions of the so-called "transparency" of experience. The idea that phenomenally conscious states are transparent is principally associated with reductive representationalists. Following Harman (1990), they argue that the allegedly queer features of phenomenal experience—the phenomenal properties, or qualia—are in fact the everyday features of the external objects we experience. Where anti-materialists claim to find the queer property of a reddish qualitative character as a feature of our visual experience, Harman and his followers claim to find only the redness we see in the ripe tomato. They argue that if you reflect clearly on your experience, you'll see that you can find no special features of the experience over and above the features of the objects that your experience presents to you. Thus phenomenal, or qualitative, character, on this view, is identified with the intentional content of the relevant perceptual representation. Once you add a naturalized theory of mental representation, you have the ingredients for a fully reductive theory of conscious experience.

While I do not buy the reductive theory being sold here, I have always thought there is something right about the transparency intuition itself. For one thing, it supports the idea that conscious experiences are essentially intentional—that phenomenal character is a kind of intentional content, and that much I do buy. But more than that, what seems right here is that it isn't one's state of awareness itself that one is aware of, or any special features of it, but rather the objects of which one is directly conscious—that ripe tomato on the kitchen counter. The idea is that there is nothing that can be made an object of awareness within a state of awareness over and above the original object of awareness itself. Nothing to see here but the tomato and its features.

Interestingly, I think the Sartrean theory of the for-itself does a better job of explaining transparency than does reductive representationalism. After all, if the visual experience of the ripe tomato is constituted by the physical tokening of a mental representation, then there is no reason in principle why introspection couldn't detect features of the representation itself, over and above its content; and therefore no reason one couldn't identify the phenomenal redness one experiences when looking at the ripe tomato (as opposed to the redness of the tomato itself) with features of the representation itself—the "mental paint" dismissed by Harman and others. But if conscious awareness is insubstantial, nothing more than a point of view, a pure awareness, of whatever is its object, its content, then the metaphor of "seeing through" the experience to what the experience is of seems perfectly natural, indeed the only way it could be.

There are two features of the for-itself that are crucial for our discussion: first, that it is insubstantial, and therefore ineligible for being an object of awareness itself, constituting a pure point of view on genuine objects, in-themselves; and second, that it is in fact *for itself*. By this I mean that the awareness relation that constitutes the for-itself is intentionally directed on its object, but inherent in this form of intentional directedness is the awareness's being *for* the subject. But what does for-ness come to for Sartre?

Gennaro (2002) argues that subjectivity for Sartre is captured by a kind of secondary awareness. There are certainly many passages that Gennaro quotes that seem to support his interpretation. For instance, the following seems especially clear on this point:

> the necessary and sufficient condition for a knowing consciousness to be knowledge of its object is that it be consciousness of itself as being that knowledge. That is a necessary condition, for if my consciousness were not consciousness of being consciousness of the table, it would then be consciousness of the table without consciousness of being so. In other words, it would be consciousness ignorant of itself, an unconscious—which is absurd.
> (Sartre 1956, p. 11)

While I grant the import of this quote (and others Gennaro cites), it seems to me that there is a way to capture the subjectivity Sartre is after here, using his idea of the primitive relation that the for-itself brings to the world, without positing a secondary awareness. Let me explain.

First let me introduce another couple of Sartrean distinctions of relevance for this discussion: that between "pre-reflective consciousness" and "reflective consciousness" and between "positional" and "non-positional" consciousness. Pre-reflective consciousness is essentially the outer-directed form of awareness we've been discussing, as when I visually experience that ripe tomato on the kitchen counter. Reflective consciousness, on the other hand, is achieved when one trains one's awareness on oneself, or one's experience, thus a form of introspection. Positional consciousness is a matter of the focal object of one's awareness, and involves "positing" an object as the content of awareness. "Non-positional" consciousness refers to what surrounds, as it were, one's focal awareness, and does not involve treating its contents as objects. So, Sartre claims at one point, speaking of pre-reflective consciousness, "every positional consciousness of an object is at the same time a non-positional consciousness of itself" (Sartre 1956, p. 13). This too provides support for Gennaro's interpretation.

Clearly what exercises Sartre in the first passage quoted is that a pre-reflective conscious experience that isn't somehow "taken up" by, or of significance to—that is, is *for*—the subject, just isn't a conscious experience. But must one posit a secondary awareness relation in order to capture this? I don't think so, unless, of course, one takes one's analysis of conscious experience to be part of a reductive project. If that's the case, then I think there is good reason to go that route. That is, if one only has natural causal relations out of which to construct the consciousness relation, then perhaps the only way to capture subjectivity is via an analysis of consciousness into constituent representation relations, one of which is outer-directed and the other inner-directed. This is how Gennaro does it (and is the basis of higher-order theory). But, I now want to argue, if you take the consciousness relation as a primitive, not analyzable or constructible out of naturalized representation relations, then another option presents itself.

On the secondary awareness approach, whether of the reductive or non-reductive variety, the overall conscious experience is decomposed into two constituent relations: awareness of the object, and awareness of itself. When these two relations hold, then one's state constitutes a conscious experience. On the reductive approach, given that awareness is cashed out as physically realized mental representation, the only way to get subjectivity into the state is to posit this secondary awareness—a second mental representation. There is no way literally to build the subjectivity into the primary awareness relation, given its status as an unconscious mental representation. So you build it into the conscious state by treating the overall conscious state as a mereological sum of two constituent representation relations.[11]

But if one is a non-reductivist, then there is another way to build subjectivity into the primary, "pre-reflective" awareness: make it a *feature* of the primary awareness relation itself, rather than a constituent, or component awareness relation. That is, for-ness isn't a matter of a second awareness accompanying the primary one, but rather being for the subject is part of what it is to be aware of something. Awareness that isn't *for* anything (or anyone) just isn't awareness.

Earlier I compared the question of what makes awareness for a subject to the question facing cognitive science of what makes representation for the subject in whom the token representation resides. I said that what legitimates appeal to mental representation in cognitive science is treating representation-for as constituted by the mental token's realizing the relevant functional role(s). I also argued that the functional account of being-for didn't seem appropriate for the way in which conscious experience is for the subject. As we saw with higher-order theory, merely adding on another layer of awareness—or representation—doesn't solve the problem since the question of what makes that added layer for the subject just recurs. As far as I can see the for-ness of experience is not something that can be analyzed. Rather, it's just inherently part of what it is to be a conscious awareness of something that that awareness be *for* the subject. Again, that's all there is, on this view, to being a subject: being that for which/whom the awareness exists, for whom it has significance. Hence the appropriateness of saying that the conscious subject is entirely captured by calling it a "for-itself."

Above I objected to the non-reductive secondary awareness approach that it had even more of a regress problem than did its reductive cousin. Sartre, in passages like the following, clearly worried about this: "Consciousness of self is not dual. If we wish to avoid an infinite regress, there must be an immediate, non-cognitive relation of the self to itself" (Sartre 1956, p. 12).

Gennaro interprets Sartre here as blocking the regress by appealing to a kind of secondary awareness that is joined within the same conscious state as the primary awareness of the external object. This is the constituent analysis. The "non-cognitive" is understood to mean "non-positional," not positing the self as an object when the primary object of one's "positional" consciousness is something external.

But I think one gets a better position if one takes Sartre to be hinting at the view of subjectivity as a *feature* of the original consciousness relation to the object, this feature of being for-the-subject as a necessary condition of a cognitive relation constituting a state of consciousness at all.[12] Now, there is clearly something awareness-like about the notion of for-ness. The idea is most easily characterized as being of significance, being somehow "taken up," by the subject, as mentioned above, and this certainly is intuitively related to being aware of it. Given that conscious awareness is intrinsically subjective, we can't really aptly characterize the subjectivity as itself a kind of awareness, or we start down the path of regress, as we saw earlier. What's more, this means that awareness doesn't take itself as its own object, but rather counts as awareness of its proper object precisely because it makes *that object* (not the awareness of it) as of significance *for* the subject. One can think of this on the model of adverbial approaches. Subjectivity is not a separate element within awareness, but rather a *way* of being aware of an object. Only being subjectively aware is a kind of being consciously aware.

One might object to this alternative to the secondary awareness approach as follows.[13] When we do introspect—engage in what Sartre calls "reflective consciousness"—we find that there is a kind of epistemic immediacy to our encounter with our own conscious experience that is distinctive of the first-person perspective. If the original, pre-reflective conscious state didn't itself contain awareness of itself, how would the explicitly reflective, introspective attitude be capable of, as it were, "finding" the experience? How is it we so easily and immediately know what we are experiencing if it isn't by virtue of some self-awareness already embodied in pre-reflective conscious experience?

Indeed, Sartre himself explicitly links the non-positional consciousness of self with the ability to reflect positionally on one's conscious experience when he says, "it is the non-reflective consciousness which renders the reflection possible" (Sartre 1956, p. 13). I must admit that I don't have a worked-out view of introspection, so I can only speculate here. What I'm inclined to say is this. Surely, if there is some kind of epistemic distinctiveness to introspection, it must have something to do with the epistemic immediacy, or acquaintance, embodied in first-order, pre-reflective conscious experience itself. But it isn't clear to me that whatever it is about pre-reflective conscious experience that enables taking a first-person perspective on it—positionally, as it were—requires that it already contain a form of secondary awareness within it as a constituent relation. It could very well be that the for-ness feature of the pre-reflective consciousness relation plays the requisite role. At any rate, I don't see why it couldn't.

## Conclusion

Conscious experiences are not merely instantiations of phenomenal properties, but rather inherently intentional and subjective relations of a particular, ontologically fundamental kind. Philosophers have wrestled with integrating the subjectivity of the experience with its content, and traditional views tend to take either the secondary awareness approach or the access approach. I have argued that neither of these approaches achieves the kind of integration necessary to capture the subjective nature of a conscious experience of a typical object like a ripe tomato. Rather, the only way to integrate the two is to do just that—make them inseparable—as is found in the "quasi-Sartrean" approach presented here.[14]

## Notes

1  See especially Thomasson (2000), who explicitly rejects the reflexive view.
2  I can hear Brie Gertler asking, "Is this a conceptual truth?" I don't know how to answer this. I certainly don't think of it as an analytic truth, just an analysis of what is meant by "conscious." Rather, it seems to me something revealed by reflection on our experience, to which we have first-person, intimate access. But what sort of truth is this? Is it straightforwardly empirical? If pushed I guess I'd say so, but I find the taxonomy of "empirical or conceptual" not quite adequate for philosophy. This is of course a large topic in itself.
3  Some of the seminal work in this area is Millikan (1989), Fodor (1990), and Dretske (1995).
4  Siewert supports his criticism by appeal to a principle he calls "IC" (for "is conscious") that reads as follows: "Every state of being conscious of something is a conscious state" (Siewert 2013, p. 244). He argues that IC is every bit as intuitive as CO (for "conscious-of"), Siewert's name for the principle appealed to by Rosenthal to the effect that a conscious state is one we are conscious of. As I see it, IC is sustainable, even by the higher-order theorist, so long as we modify CO so that the "conscious of" isn't taken literally, for reasons argued in the text. That way, we can still maintain, in keeping with IC, that if we are literally *conscious* of something, our being so involves our being in a conscious state.
5  A version of this objection can be seen in Ryle's (1949) attack on the "intellectualist legend."
6  I say "ultimately" because there may indeed be homunculi of a sort for certain cognitive systems communicating with others.
7  So, in a sense, I'm adopting a version of Siewert's regress argument. That is, rather than IC, I have IF: Any state by which an object is "for the subject" is itself "for the subject."
8  See Kriegel (2009), and also Gennaro (1996) for a defense of a version of self-representationalism he calls "WIV," for "wide intrinsicality view," and also Gennaro (2002), in which he attributes an analogous view to Sartre. More on this below.
9  As in Siewert's (2013) IC principle. See note 4 above.
10 Actually, on my own view of the consciousness relation, which I dub the "AA relation" (for acquaintance/appearance), the objects of consciousness are not

found within the realm of objective concrete reality, but rather have the status of "virtual objects" (see Levine 2010). But this difference won't matter for present purposes.
11 As Gennaro (2002, p. 307) puts it: "What else is a 'non-positional self-awareness' except some kind of non-conscious meta-psychological mental state? I cannot understand it any other way." I think within the reductive program this is exactly right.
12 Some support for this reading of Sartre's intentions comes from this passage: "This [non-positional] self-consciousness we ought to consider not as a new consciousness ... [it is] a *quality* of the positional consciousness" (Sartre 1956, p. 14). Gennaro quotes this passage to support his self-representational interpretation, taking the point to be about there being a single state of which this non-positional self-consciousness is an integral part. But one can read the "quality" here in the feature, or adverbial sense I am advocating.
13 I am grateful to Tom McClelland for pressing a version of this objection.
14 An earlier version of this chapter was presented to a workshop on *The Subjective Structure of Consciousness*, at the University of Manchester, June 22, 2014. I would like to thank the participants in that workshop for their very helpful comments during discussion. In particular, I want to thank Aaron Henry, Tom McClelland, Donnchadh O'Conaill, and Sebastian Wazl for discussion on the topic of this chapter.

## References

Block, N. (1995). On a Confusion about a Function of Consciousness. *Behavioral and Brain Sciences*, 18: p. 2.
Dretske, F. (1995). *Naturalizing the Mind*. Cambridge, MA: Bradford Books/MIT Press.
Dretske, F. (1997). Conscious Experience. In Block, N., Flanagan, O., and Guzeldere, G., Eds. *The Nature of Consciousness*. Cambridge, MA: MIT Press Bradford.
Fodor, J.A. (1990). *A Theory of Content and Other Essays*. Cambridge, MA: Bradford Books/MIT Press.
Gennaro, R. (1996). *Consciousness and Self-Consciousness: A Defense of the Higher-Order Thought Theory of Consciousness*. Amsterdam: John Benjamins Publisher.
Gennaro, R. (2002). Jean-Paul Sartre and the HOT Theory of Consciousness. *Canadian Journal of Philosophy*, 32:3: pp. 293–330.
Harman, G. (1990). The Intrinsic Quality of Experience. In J. Tomberlin, Ed. *Philosophical Perspectives, 4, Action Theory and Philosophy of Mind*. Atascadero, CA: Ridgeview Publishing, pp. 31–52.
Hume, D. (2012). *A Treatise of Human Nature*. Mineola, NY: Dover; originally published in London, 1739–1740.
Kriegel, U. (2009). *Subjective Consciousness: A Self-Representational Theory*. Oxford: Oxford University Press.
Levine, J. (2010). Phenomenal Experience: A Cartesian Theater Revival. *Philosophical Issues*, 20, *Philosophy of Mind*.
Lycan, W.G. (1997). Consciousness as Internal Monitoring. In N. Block, O. Flanagan, and G. Guzeldere, Eds. *The Nature of Consciousness: Philosophical Debates*. Cambridge, MA: MIT Press.
Millikan, R. (1989). Biosemantics. *The Journal of Philosophy*, 86:6: pp. 281–297.

Nagel, T. (1974). What Is It Like to Be a Bat? *The Philosophical Review*, 82: pp. 435–450.
Rosenthal, D. (1997). A Theory of Consciousness. In Block, N., Flanagan, O., and Güzeldere, G. Eds. *The Nature of Consciousness: Philosophical Debates*. Cambridge: MIT Press, pp. 729–753.
Ryle, G. (1949). *The Concept of Mind*. London: Hutchinson.
Sartre, J.-P. (1956). *Being and Nothingness*, Hazel E. Barnes, translator. New York: Philosophical Library.
Siewert, C. (1998). *The Significance of Consciousness*. Princeton, NJ: Princeton University Press.
Siewert, C. (2013). Phenomenality and Self-Consciousness. In Kriegel, U., Ed. *Phenomenal Intentionality*. Oxford: Oxford University Press.
Thomasson, A. (2000). After Brentano: A One-Level Theory of Consciousness. *European Journal of Philosophy*, 8:2: pp. 190–209.
Tye, M. (1995). *Ten Problems of Consciousness: A Representational Theory of the Phenomenal Mind*. Cambridge, MA: Bradford Books/MIT Press.
Tye, M. (2000). *Consciousness, Color, and Content*. Cambridge, MA: Bradford Books/MIT Press.

PART IV

# Body as a whole, the other, and disorder of the mental

# 15 Pain

## Sartre and Anglo-American philosophy of mind

*Katherine J. Morris*

This chapter is an attempt to bring Sartre into dialogue with Anglo-American philosophers of mind on the topic of pain.[1]

One complication should be noted straight away. There is a rough tripartite distinction to be made between acute, long-lasting, and chronic pain, and the Anglo-American focus is almost exclusively on the first, whereas Sartre's focus is largely on the second.[2] (Neither has anything to say about chronic pain as I shall be defining this.) By "acute" pain, I mean pain which is intense, sudden in onset, and of short duration (usually because easily treatable, or whose source does not require treatment). "Long-lasting" pain, by definition, lasts for days, weeks, or months; it may or may not have been intense and sudden in onset; it typically ebbs and flows over its course; and it has a "biomedical" explanation: a physiologically identifiable source (e.g., an ulcer, a broken bone) which is, however, difficult or time-consuming to treat. "Chronic" pain is identical to long-lasting pain in respect of the first three points; but, crucially, it is pain that lacks biomedical explanation, since the pain persists in the absence of, or after the removal of, identifiable disease or tissue damage.[3] The distinction between them isn't rigid—e.g., what begins as an acute pain (due to a laceration on the foot, say) may develop into a long-lasting pain if the wound becomes infected; long-lasting and chronic pain are typically characterized by episodes of acute pain; chronic pain may become long-lasting pain through a new biomedical diagnosis, and so on—but I will treat them separately, since they raise interestingly different issues.

The most direct evidence that Anglo-American accounts focus on acute pain is that they tend to take as their paradigm cases instances such as "a sharp pain in the back of my right hand" (Aydede 2009, p. 2), although the types of theories of pain offered (see section on Anglo-American philosophers of mind on pain, below) might lead us to the same conclusion. That Sartre's focus in *BN* is on long-lasting pain also emerges from his examples: his cases seem to be of pain that allows one to concentrate on something else, and that ebbs and flows (these characteristics tend to rule out acute pain); they also have biomedical diagnoses (which rules out chronic pain as I have defined this).[4]

The first part of this chapter sets out some of the essentials of the philosophical framework for Sartre's discussion of pain, then explores what Sartre said about long-lasting pain, and finally considers some issues that might arise for him about the other types of pain. The second part does something similar for Anglo-American accounts of pain, though beginning with acute pain. Some conclusions are drawn at the end.

## Sartre on pain

### Background: Sartre's framework

Some basics: Sartre's ontology is phenomenological (subtitle of *BN*). He draws a basic distinction (Introduction to *BN*) between being-for-itself and being-in-itself (the mode of being of conscious and non-conscious beings respectively). Being-for-itself is characterized by various internally related dualities, e.g., facticity and transcendence, being-for-myself and being-for-others, and being-in-the-world and being-in-the-midst-of-the-world (*BN*, pp. 57–58). Consciousness is intentional, which for him implies that through consciousness the world is present to me unmediated by representations (*BN*, p. xxvii). Consciousness of something in the world is also "non-positional" or "non-thetic" *self*-consciousness, which may be made positional or thetic through reflection (*BN*, p. xxviiiff.).

Sartre's most sustained discussion of pain takes place—notably—in his chapter on the body (*BN*, Part III, ch. 2). His discussion must be understood against a background which contains complexities along several axes: the dimensions of the body; the "*ekstases*" of the for-itself; and the figure-ground structure which shapes both the world and the body (as least in the first *ekstasis*).

The chapter on the body officially distinguishes between three "dimensions" of the body, three ways in which human bodies figure in our experience (the body-for-itself, the body of the other, and the lived body-for-others).[5] Although he explicitly claims that these three dimensions have "exhausted the question of the body's modes of being" (*BN*, p. 351), he adds an "aberrant type of appearance" (*BN*, p. 357); moreover, within his section on the body-for-itself he introduces the body "on a new plane of existence," what he calls the "psychic body" (*BN*, p. 337), which is both one's own body as revealed in impure reflection and what is perceived by others (likewise, what we perceive when we perceive others).[6] The body-for-itself and the lived body-for-others are aspects of one's *own* body as opposed to that of the other; Sartre discusses pain only in connection with one's own body, though what he has to say about pain in connection with the body of the other is implicit in what he says about pain in the lived body-for-others.

These dimensions of the body are interwoven with the three *ekstases* of the for-itself (cf. *BN*, p. 298). The first *ekstasis* is the experience of the subject unreflectively engaged in the world; the second *ekstasis* involves reflection on the first; the third focuses on how that experience is altered by the presence of the other. In the present context, the first *ekstasis* is linked to the body-for-itself, the second to the psychic body, and the third with the lived body-for-others.[7]

*The body-for-itself*

"For human reality, to be is to-be-there; that is, 'there in that chair', 'there at that table'. . . " (*BN*, p. 308); the body-for-itself is the contingent "thereness" of the for-itself, its facticity. Bearing in mind that facticity is what the for-itself *is* (*BN*, p. 79), we can say that "the body is what this consciousness is" (*BN*, p. 330); however, the for-itself "is not what it is," i.e., transcends its facticity (*BN*, p. 58), so that "[t]he for-itself forever surpasses this contingency toward its own possibilities" (*BN*, p. 309). The body-for-itself as it is lived in everyday unreflective dealings with the world (hence in the first *ekstasis*) is the unperceived center of the field of perception and the unutilizable center of the field of action (it is "the tool which we cannot *utilize* . . . for we *are it*": *BN*, p. 324). "[T]he body is present in every action although invisible, for the act reveals the hammer and the nails, the brake and the change of speed, not the foot which brakes or the hand which hammers" (*BN*, p. 324). My body is my "point of view" on the world, but it is also "the point of view on which I can no longer take a point of view" (*BN*, p. 329). Thus the body-for-itself "is the *neglected*, the '*passed by in silence*'." (In Leder's (1990) terminology, it "disappears.") It is one of "the structures of the non-thetic self-consciousness" (*BN*, p. 330); and "consciousness *exists* its body[-for-itself]" (*BN*, p. 329; italics added). ("Exists" as a transitive verb is contrasted with "knows": the body-for-itself is not an *object* of consciousness.)

Sartre's description introduces a further set of complexities through its central use of a radicalized version of the Gestalt psychologists' notion of figure and ground: an object, e.g., the book that I am reading, "appears on the ground of the world" (*BN*, p. 316); the "world as ground" as "mundane totality" "indicates" my body-for-itself as a "corporal totality" (*BN*, p. 334). This "corporal totality" itself serves, in a sense, as a ground upon which parts of the body may become figures. ("In a sense" because in the context of the first *ekstasis*, this corporal totality is still "the '*passed by in silence.*'"). When for example I am reading, the eyes "appear as a figure on the ground of a corporeal totality"; they are "the very contexture of my [non-thetic] consciousness of seeing" (*BN*, p. 334).[8] A part of the body not currently in explicit play, say my finger or back while I am reading, "disappears in the ground of corporeality" (*BN*, p. 334). (Leder (1990, p. 26) marks this distinction with the terms "focal disappearance" and "background disappearance." He adds a third type, what he calls "depth disappearance," about which Sartre says nothing; this refers to the phenomenological status of visceral processes, which "ordinarily . . . recede from the arc of personal involvement as a whole, neither subject nor object of direct engagement" (Leder 1990, p. 54).)

*The psychic body*

In what Sartre calls "impure" or "accessory" reflection in the second *ekstasis*, we apprehend what he terms "psychic objects" ("the shadow cast by the For-itself reflected-on": *BN*, p. 164);[9] of particular relevance for our purposes are those psychic objects he calls "states" (as opposed to actions and qualities). A state (his paradigm in *TE* is hatred) is a "transcendent [i.e. transphenomenal] object," in this sense like an inkwell, such that "Each *Erlebnis* reveals it as a whole, but at the same time each *Erlebnis* is a profile" (*TE*, p. 63). The psychic "appears as constituted by the synthesis of a Past, a Present and a Future" (*BN*, p. 165), so that "[h]atred is credit for an infinity of angry or repulsed consciousnesses in the past and in the future" (*TE*, p. 63).[10] The individual, "instantaneous" consciousness (e.g., my present consciousness of anger) "appears to reflection as a spontaneous emanation from hatred" (*TE*, p. 66), where "emanation" is neither causal nor logical but "magical" (*TE*, p. 67, cf. *BN*, p. 169).[11] In *TE*, a state is said to be "real" (*TE*, p. 61), although its existence is "relative to reflective consciousness" (*TE*, p. 66). In *BN*, a psychic object is said to be "virtual" (*BN*, p. 163), a "quasi-object" (*BN*, p. 354), and "an unreal" (*BN*, p. 354), though still—at least at times—characterized as "a reality" (*BN*, p. 335). Evidently the word "real" is being used in two different senses: psychic objects are real in the sense that an absence is real (although an absence is relative, not to reflective consciousness, but to an expectation or project: cf. *BN*, p. 10); but they are unreal in the sense that they are essentially unknowable by me via reflection alone: it takes the look of the other to "realize," i.e., make real, the virtual psychic object revealed by impure reflection (*BN*, p. 170).[12] Thus we may "think of impure reflection as an attempt to constitute an object that cannot properly be constituted without the experience of the Look" (Reisman 2007, p. 68).

The second *ekstasis* also reveals the psychic body, which "provides the implicit matter of all the phenomena of the psyche [i.e. all psychic objects]" (*BN*, p. 337); it is "a sort of implicit space supporting the melodic duration of the psychic" (*BN*, p. 338).

*The lived body-for-others*

The psychic body (as "the implicit matter" of states, acts, and qualities) revealed by impure reflection is also what I (normally) see when I look at another, and what another (normally) sees when he looks at me. ("Normally," because there is also a kind of "medical gaze" for which the body of the other, or my body for him, is "in the midst of the world" [as opposed to in-the-world], "a certain living object composed of a nervous system, a brain, glands, ... " (*BN*, p. 303). As has often been noted, Sartre creates trouble for himself by using the same terminology of "object" and of "the body of the other" both for the object of this "medical gaze" and for the psychic body.) "The [psychic] body is the psychic object *par excellence*," and "the perception of it cannot *by nature* be of the same type as that of inanimate objects" (*BN*, p. 347). Sartre's descriptions of perceiving another's psychic body are well known (e.g., the differences between seeing the man in the park as a *man* as opposed to a mere spatio-temporal thing: *BN*, pp. 254ff.); the other's psychic body is, for me, a "transcendence transcended" (e.g., *BN*, p. 347), as is mine for him. Just as my body is the unperceived and unutilizable center of the fields of perception and action, so too is the other's body: encountering another brings it about that "instead of a grouping *toward me* of the objects, there is now an orientation *which flees from me*" (*BN*, p. 254). In perceiving another's body we perceive his consciousness, albeit (since we *perceive* it) in a "degraded" form: "These frowns, this redness, this stammering, this slight trembling of the hands, these downcast looks which seem at once timid and threatening—these do not *express* anger, they *are* the anger" (*BN*, p. 346).

By making use of language (by which the other communicates any knowledge he has of my body) to qualify my psychic body, we can surpass this "quasi-object" "toward characters of being which on principle cannot be given to me and which are simply signified . . . It is by means of the other's concepts that I *know* [rather than live] my body" (*BN*, pp. 354–355). How then does such knowledge transform the ways in which one *lives* one's own psychic body? Again, Sartre's general descriptions of the transformations undergone via awareness of the look of another are well known (the voyeur caught looking through the keyhole: *BN*, pp. 259ff.). In the present context, through "the contingent, absolute fact of the Other's existence," my "lived experience" is "extended outside in a dimension of flight which escapes me"; "at the very moment when I live my senses as this inner point of view on which I can take no point of view, their being-for-others haunts me"; likewise, through the other, "this instrument which I am is made-present to me as an instrument submerged in an infinite instrumental series" (*BN*, p. 352). Thus "[m]y body is designated as alienated." Affective structures such as shyness exemplify the experience of alienation, and the shy man may try "to suppress his body-for-the-other . . . he longs 'not to have a body [-for-the-other] anymore', to be 'invisible'" (*BN*, p. 353).

## Sartre on long-lasting pain

### *First ekstasis of pain: unreflective engagement in the world*

Pain participates in the figure-ground structure of the body-for-itself: indeed, much of what Sartre says about pain in the first *ekstasis* directly *echoes* what he says about the body-for-itself (e.g., pain in the eyes while reading is "the translucent matter of consciousness, its *being-there*, its attachment to the world, in short the peculiar contingency of the act of reading": *BN*, p. 333). Why? Because pain (say, "in the eyes") is not "in the eyes" due to some "local sign" or other "criterion"; rather, "*is precisely the eyes* insofar as consciousness 'exists them'" (*BN*, p. 332: emphasis in original; cf. *BN*, p. 355).

Sartre (*BN*, pp. 333–334) makes a distinction (corresponding to the distinction between focal and depth disappearance) between "pain in a functioning organ" (e.g., "pain in the eye while it is looking, in the hand while it is grasping") and pain in a part of the body not currently in play (e.g., a pain in my finger while I am reading).

Pain in a functioning organ is, while we are unreflectively engaged in the world, "*indicated* by the objects of the world"—just as the body-for-itself is; the difference between reading while the eyes are pain-free and while they are painful is that the world of painful eyes becomes *difficult*: "[i]t is with more difficulty that the words are detached from the undifferentiated ground which they constitute; they may tremble, quiver; their meaning may be derived only with effort" (*BN*, p. 332).[13] This "vision-as-pain" "is not distinguished" from the trembling and quivering of the words (*BN*, pp. 332–333). Thus pain in the eyes (like the body-for-itself) is "the very contingency of my 'act of reading'" (*BN*, p. 334). There is, moreover, a "non-thetic project" "given" via the world's difficulty (wherein "the whole universe is pierced with *anxiety*"): namely, "a project toward a further consciousness which would be empty of all pain" (*BN*, p. 333). The difficulty of the painful world and the project to be rid of the pain are strictly correlative.

In the case of pain in an organ not currently in play, I "exist the pain in such a way that it disappears in the ground of corporeality" (*BN*, p. 334), until such time as I bring that part of the body into play by turning the page, when the pain (like the finger, since, again, the pain *is* the finger insofar as consciousness "exists it") "will pass to the rank of existed contingency as a figure on a new organisation of the body as the total ground of contingency" (*BN*, p. 336).

This description might be extended in a couple of directions (I only gesture at them here). First, long-lasting and chronic pain (as we will see in more detail in a moment) ebbs and flows; how does the *anticipation* or *expectation* that use of the relevant part of the body will "awaken" the pain affect the structure of the body-for-itself?[14] Secondly, what of parts of the body (e.g., the stomach) whose normal mode of existence is, in Leder's terms, "depth disappearance"? Sartre does develop the example of pain in the stomach later (in connection with the third *ekstasis*), where he suggests that in this first *ekstasis* "pain 'in the stomach' is the stomach itself as painfully lived" (*BN*, p. 355), but how, if at all, does this differ from pain in a functioning organ?

*Second ekstasis of pain: (accessory) reflection*

We have described already how accessory reflection apprehends psychic objects.[15] In the case of accessory reflection on pain, the psychic object apprehended is termed by Sartre "illness" (*mal* as opposed to *douleur*: *BN*, p. 335).[16] Illness is a state in the sense defined earlier (*BN*, p. 162). Thus it "is a reality which has its own duration since it . . . possesses a past and a future" (*BN*, p. 335). It, like all states, is a transcendent object:

> A pain which is given in twinges followed by lulls is not apprehended by reflection as the pure alteration of painful and non-painful consciousnesses . . . the brief respites *are a part* of the illness just as silences are a part of a melody.

At the same time, "each concrete pain is like a note in a melody: it is at once the whole melody and a 'moment' in the melody" (*BN*, pp. 335–336), and (although he does not use this word here) each concrete pain is given as magically "emanating" from the illness.

We have seen already how the body-for-itself figures in pain at the unreflective level: "for the unreflective consciousness pain *was* the body[-for-itself]." The relationship between the psychic body and states such as illness in some ways parallels the relationship between the body-for-itself and consciousnesses such as pain, so that somewhat as the body-for-itself "was existed by each consciousness as its own contingency, so the psychic body is *suffered* as the contingency" of states, acts, and qualities (*BN*, p. 337).[17,18]

## Third ekstasis of pain: being-for-others

The specific case to be considered here is how the experience of illness is transformed by awareness of the look of the other. First, as we might expect, the other provides concepts through which I can know (as oppose to live or suffer) my body; such

> [o]bjectivating empirical knowledge . . . surpasses the Illness suffered toward the stomach named . . . I know that it has the shape of a bagpipe . . . that it produces juices, and enzymes . . . that the stomach has an ulcer . . . I can imagine it as a redness, a slight internal putrescence.
> (*BN*, pp. 355–356)

This initiates the third *ekstasis*, whereby the psychic object "illness" is "surpassed" toward what Sartre calls "disease" (*maladie* as opposed to *mal*).[19] The disease is "objectively discernible for Others" (for medics, by whatever symptoms and criteria they use to diagnose diseases, for others, "by the 'twinges' of pain, by the 'crises' of my Illness": *BN*, p. 356); for me, like all aspects of my being-for-others, it is "an object which on principle is out of reach, for which others are the depositories" (*BN*, p. 356).

The disease, like the illness, is a psychic object, with its own characteristics of "magical spontaneity," "destructive finality," "evil potentiality," and so on (*BN*, p. 356). Whereas the psychic body "was the support of the Illness, it is ... the substance of the disease, that which is destroyed by the disease" (*BN*, p. 356). Somewhat as being seen by the other as a voyeur is lived in shame, being seen by the other as having a diseased body is non-thetically lived in "disgust with my too-white flesh, with my too-grim expression, etc.," or rather, I live my awareness of my body-for-others' shape, bearing, and physiognomy, and my so living this awareness is "nausea," extended, through knowledge, "toward that which it is for others" (*BN*, p. 357).

This may seem phenomenologically objectionable: surely at least some others, in perceiving the body of another who has a disease, perceive his *suffering* (and thus, perhaps, respond with sympathy and compassion). If so, might not the other's gaze make me "feel secure, important and desirable, and not in spite of, but because of, my body" (Svenaeus 2009, p. 59)? Sartre needn't deny this; but it is entirely compatible with nausea. "Nausea," in Sartre's usage, like "shame," is ambiguous: shame is sometimes an empirical notion, where it refers to the *unpleasant* awareness of oneself as an object which arouses disapproval in another, and sometimes an ontological one, where it is "only the original feeling of having my being outside" (*BN*, p. 288). In like manner, "nausea" is sometimes a "concrete and empirical" notion referring to an unpleasant feeling of disgust ("caused by spoiled meat, fresh blood, excrement etc.": *BN*, pp. 338–339), and sometimes an ontological notion referring simply to the awareness of the body as *flesh* (cf. "the nauseous character of all flesh": *BN*, p. 357). The compassion felt for another on account of a diseased body—unlike the compassion felt for someone who has lost his job, say—cannot but be grounded in an awareness of *his* body as flesh, as "that which is destroyed by the disease"; and this is more fundamental than compassion *per se*, since not all others will respond to my diseased body with compassion, but all will be aware of my body as flesh. Thus my lived diseased-body-for-others may appropriately be described in terms of nausea, and this is compatible with being made to "feel secure, important and desirable."[20]

## Sartre on chronic pain

Sartre's paradigms of pain do not include chronic pain, which, as we noted at the outset, is pain that, unlike long-lasting pain as I have defined it, lacks biomedical explanation. This difference, it seems to me, affects only the third *ekstasis*, but the difference might be argued to be of considerable phenomenological importance. The illness described in the previous section became a disease via the other-mediated third *ekstasis*, via "objectivating concepts" such as "stomach" and "ulcer"; and the lived diseased body-for-others was "nausea," extended through knowledge "toward that which it is for others."

In chronic pain, however, precisely because there is no biomedically identifiable injury or disease process, there is, it seems, no "flesh" being "destroyed by the disease." Thus, it seems, others' awareness of the body of the chronic pain sufferer need not include awareness of his body as flesh. On the face of it, then, others' compassion for the chronic pain sufferer will be more like the compassion felt for someone who has lost his job than that felt for someone on account of a diseased body, i.e., it won't have an underlay of flesh-as-nausea.

However, if there can be a "cultural phenomenology" (Singer 1994, p. 457), this difference entails another within the cultural phenomenology of the chronically painful body-for-others in modern Western culture. Critical medical anthropologists note that the "deep cultural logic" of biomedicine involves a dualistic fragmentation of experience into "[p]hysiological, psychological; body, soul . . . subjective, objective; real, unreal" (Kleinman et al. 1994, p. 8). To the extent that the cultural logic of biomedicine is deeply embedded in modern Western culture, members of that culture are inclined to accept both this dichotomy into "mental" or "physical" and this equation of "real" with "physical, i.e. (when it comes to pain) possessing a biomedical explanation." "No organic cause" is taken to mean that nothing is wrong (Garro 1994, p. 109). "If there is a single experience shared by virtually all chronic pain patients it is that at some point those around them . . . come to question the authenticity of the patient's experience of pain" (Kleinman 1988, 57); cf. the title of Jackson (1994): "After a While No One Believes You." Thus in modern Western biomedicalized culture, chronic pain, unlike long-lasting pain, is not viewed as *calling* for compassion or sympathy, and this in part precisely *because* there is no identifiable disease, no flesh being destroyed by that disease, this being taken to imply that *there is no pain*: the pain is "all in the mind," or the individual is malingering or "just seeking attention."

Not surprisingly, chronic pain patients pursue diagnoses relentlessly, not just because they hope for a cure but because they hope for a validation of their pain as "real": the one good result of Howie's back surgeries is that they have "created icons of his travail, scars that he can show people" to convince them that his pain is genuine (Kleinman 1988, p. 68; cf. Jackson 1994, p. 142). For further investigation: how might a chronic pain patient live the awareness that others view him as not in pain, but as a malingerer or attention-seeker or suffering from a mental disorder?

## *Sartre on acute pain*

Some commentators have argued that Sartre needs to add to his phenomenology of the body in order to accommodate acute pain. We noted earlier that Leder (1990) distinguishes between three modes of the "disappearance" of the body-for-itself (focal, background, and depth). He then argues that a sudden acute pain breaks through those modes of disappearance so that the body, in his terms, "dys-appears." (Dys-appearance is at core "a heightening of body-focus at times of suffering or disruption":

Leder 1990, p. 92.) Thus, for example, he asks us to imagine a man engaged in playing tennis who feels a sudden pain in his chest. First, "he is called back from ecstatic engagement [in the world] to a focus on the state of his own body"; secondly, a "background region, the chest, is now thematized" (this region of the body "suddenly speaks up"); and thirdly, "a once tacit viscerality now floods through perception and cries out for action" (Leder 1990, p. 71).

This illuminates what may be called the "attention-grabbing" nature of acute pain. Can Sartre allow such dys-appearance via pain? Leder, amongst others, argues not:[21] "Corporeal alienation does not come to be solely through the social confrontation [as, he suggests, Sartre believes] but from within the body-for-me" (Leder 1990, p. 93). Now, it would be wrong to read Sartre as claiming that it is *only* through the look of the other that I can experience my body as an object: my own body (in what he calls an "aberrant appearance" of the body) *can* be something which I myself perceive or use as I would an instrument.[22] This, however, does not seem to help us here; in any case, it seems to me that the point about acute pain is not simply that the body becomes an "object," a focus of attention, without the intervention of the other, but that it *demands* that attention: an acutely painful body "exerts upon us a *telic demand*" (Leder 1990, p. 73), both for "a search for interpretation and understanding" and for the "pragmatic goal" of getting rid of the pain (Leder 1990, p. 74).

What Leder thinks Sartre needs is something like Zaner's "body uncanny," and in particular the idea that the body "is essentially an *alien-presence*... Whatever I want, wish or plan for, I irrevocably 'grow older', 'become tired', 'feel ill'," and I must "see to it that my bodily functions and needs are 'looked after' . . . on which I must at times 'wait' in order to go about my affairs" (Zaner 1981, p. 54). How radical a modification of Sartre's phenomenology would be required in order to accommodate the "body uncanny"? The difficulty for him is that it seems that the body uncanny has a telos *of its own*. Correlatively, pain effects an "intentional disruption" (Leder 1990, p. 73); the tennis player's game comes to a stop. "The highly affective and significant call of pain renders unimportant projects that previously seemed crucial" (Leder 1990, p. 74). To be sure, Sartre does recognize a "non-thetic project" "toward a further consciousness which would be empty of all pain" (*BN*, p. 333); but there is no suggestion that this is a project of *the body*, and no recognition that it *disrupts* consciously chosen projects (even if we can—on occasion and up to a point—choose to ignore the body's telic demand and continue with our own consciously chosen projects). And it is difficult to see how to fit this notion with Sartre's view of the body as facticity: how can facticity have *projects*, much less projects which disrupt "our own" projects? Thus we may tentatively conclude that, complex and nuanced as Sartre's phenomenology of the body is, it is importantly incomplete.

## Anglo-American philosophers of mind on pain

### Background: Anglo-American philosophy's framework

Some basics: Anglo-American philosophers tend to presuppose *naturalism*; this is understood as both an ontological and a methodological outlook, according to which "reality is exhausted by nature, containing nothing 'supernatural', and that scientific method should be used to investigate all areas of reality, including the 'human spirit'" (Papineau 2007, p. 1). From ontological naturalism, together with "causal closure" ("according to which all physical effects can be accounted for by basic physical causes"), may be inferred *physicalism* ("any state that has physical effects must itself be physical": Papineau 2007, p. 4), although there a great many species of physicalism, some more reductive than others. (When it comes to Anglo-American philosophy of mind in particular—and it is noteworthy that Anglo-American philosophers see investigations of pain as part of the philosophy of *mind*— ontological naturalism takes for granted that "mental processes can causally influence non-mental processes" and sees this as a reason for adopting ontological naturalism, and thus some version of physicalism, in the mental realm: Papineau 2007, p. 2.) Methodological naturalism sees "philosophy and science as engaged in essentially the same enterprise, pursuing similar ends and using similar methods" (Papineau 2007, p. 13). Philosophy's distinctive contribution may be understood as analyzing ordinary concepts, understood as "folk theories," which science can then confirm or disconfirm; or articulating our "intuitions," which science can then adjudicate, and so on. (When it comes to Anglo-American philosophy of mind in particular, methodological naturalists can also happily embrace introspection, understood as "ordinary cognitive mechanisms by which mental states reliably, but not infallibly, give rise to subjects' knowledge of those states": Papineau 2007, p. 19, and even a kind of *verstehen*, grounded in "some relatively innate capacity for thinking about others' mental states," perhaps consisting in "our ability to simulate the mental processes of differently situated individuals": Papineau 2007, p. 20.)

Many Anglo-American philosophers of mind consider mental states and processes (including, in their view, pain) to be identical to, or a function of, or "realized in," the *brain*. A consequence of this is that Anglo-American philosophy of mind tends toward a type of "internalism," understood in this context as "the idea that cognitive phenomena can be accounted for locally, and that elements beyond the boundaries of the skull are of interest only insofar as they provide sensory input and allow behavioural output" (Foglia 2011, p. 9).[23] From this perspective, the body (apart from the brain) is treated as part of the "extramental environment" (Aydede 2009, p. 13). The body itself "is from the start posited as a certain *thing* having its own laws and capable of being defined from outside" (*BN*, p. 303). That is, it is understood as science understands it: as an anatomical/physiological object, what the phenomenologists call *Körper* (the body-thing), by contrast with *Leib* (the lived body). Thus, as has often been said, much Anglo-American philosophy of mind is committed to "brain/body dualism," a kind of naturalized Cartesian dualism.

### Anglo-American philosophers on acute pain

Anglo-American accounts of acute pain often begin from what they see as a kind of paradox: pain on the one hand is "typically attributed to a bodily location," and on the other is "often thought to be logically private, subjective, self-intimating, and the source of incorrigible knowledge for those who have them" (Aydede 2009, p. 1). Most Anglo-American accounts of pain consist in responses to this "paradox" (and to objections to other responses).

On one view, pain is a kind of *sense-datum*: it is a "mental particular" with "phenomenal qualities" "whose existence depends on their being sensed or felt." Some see no difficulty in allowing such a "mental particular" to have "literally, a spatial location" (e.g., in the hand) (Aydede 2009, p. 7; cf. Jackson 1976);[24] however, many Anglo-American philosophers find it difficult to make the first idea plausible ("does this mean that one's mind spatially extends or overlaps with one's body?": Aydede 2009, p. 8), and anyway sense-datum theory is intrinsically objectionable to physicalists, since "there seem to be no sense-data to be found in the physical world" (Aydede 2009, p. 9). Others offer *perceptual* models. According to these, "when one feels, say, a sharp pain in the back of one's hand, one perceives some physical feature or condition of one's hand" (Aydede 2009, p. 9), say, tissue damage. (See, e.g., Armstrong 1962, Pitcher 1970.) The perception of tissue damage, like all perception, is an experience; in the case of pain, it is an "experience as of tissue damage" (i.e., it "represents" tissue damage). However, unlike the perception of, say, a red apple, our primary interest in the case of pain is in "the perceptual experience we are having," not "the object of this experience" (Aydede 2009, p. 11), and this explains why we take ourselves to be incorrigible about pain but not about other types of perception: while our experience may misrepresent the state of the world (there may not actually be any tissue damage), we are incorrigible about our "occurrent experiences" (Aydede 2009, p. 12). On this view, we may say that the pain is "located" in the body (the damaged hand, say), but this does not mean that the *experience* is in the hand (after all, "[e]xperiences are in the head, if they are anywhere": Aydede 2009, p. 5); location here is "intentional location": we say that the pain is "in the hand" because the experience *represents* tissue damage as occurring in the hand (Aydede 2009, p. 13). And yet other Anglo-American philosophers of mind adopt "*representationalism*" about pain, according to which "the entire phenomenology of a pain experience is strictly identical to its representational or intentional content" (Aydede 2009, p. 17).[25] Pain experiences still represent tissue damage, but "[t]he way they represent these conditions is analogous to the way our visual system represents colours," i.e., they do so non-conceptually, and via phenomenal rather than objective features (Aydede 2009, p. 18).[26] Thus, for example, "a twinge of pain represents a mild, brief case of damage. A throbbing pain represents a rapidly pulsing disorder. Aches represent regions of damage inside the body rather than on the surface," etc. (Tye 1997, p. 133). The issue of pain location is dealt with in a manner parallel to the way in which perceptual theories dealt with it.

A general objection to all of these accounts, made from within Anglo-American philosophy, is that they are addressed only to one of two "dimensions" of "pain phenomenology": the "sensory-discriminative" dimension; but there is also an "affective-emotional" (or motivational, evaluative, etc.) dimension (Aydede 2009, p. 22). And in order to account for this, we might be better off with psychofunctionalism, since the notions of perception and representation seems tailor-made only for the sensory-discriminative dimension. (Functionalism in Anglo-American philosophy of mind in general asserts that what makes a mental state the state that it is "depends not on its internal constitution, but solely on its function, or the role that it plays, in the cognitive system of which it is a part": Levin 2013, p. 2. Psychofunctionalism sees these roles as those specified by latest scientific theory in cognitive psychology: Levin 2013, p. 7.) Here the suggestion might be that "feeling pain involves perception although perception doesn't exhaust its nature: feeling pain is also an affective/emotional experience that can be explained in terms of the functional role of pain's sensory/representational content" (Aydede 2009, p. 24; cf. e.g., Lycan 1987, pp. 60–61).

What, if anything, might phenomenologists take from this? We may note that the "paradox" from which many Anglo-American accounts of pain take their rise is only a paradox on the supposition that the body is a *Körper*. Thus phenomenologists have no motive to seek accounts which resolve the "paradox."

### Anglo-American philosophers on long-lasting pain

Sartre's account of long-lasting pain brings out features that may present interesting challenges for Anglo-American philosophers of mind.

Sartre's discussion of the first *ekstasis* suggests that Anglo-American philosophers will need to find ways of making sense of a pain which is not the current object of attention, and of the idea that this account may differ according as the pain is in a functioning organ or in an organ not currently in play. (Are such pains still "perceived"? Do they still "represent"? Does the "representational content" still have the same "functional role"?) Sartre's discussion of the second *ekstasis* presents a different challenge: as he noted, "A pain which is given in twinges followed by lulls is not apprehended by reflection as the pure alteration of painful and non-painful consciousnesses." How might Anglo-American philosophers of mind make sense of the unity between the "twinges," stretching across the "lulls"? Sartre's discussion of the third *ekstasis*, minimally, suggests that the experience of pain alters when mediated through concepts; how might Anglo-American philosophers of mind accommodate this?

*Anglo-American philosophers on chronic pain*

We argued earlier that the experience of chronic pain, at least within the third *ekstasis*, is affected by culture. But that same argument also suggests that the very *concept* of pain may undergo changes when the pain is chronic and when the culture is biomedicalized, as ours is: Anglo-American philosophers are wont to say that certain concepts, e.g., paradigmatically, the concept of pain, exhibit "first/third-person asymmetry": that is, whereas first-person ascriptions of pain are supposed to be incorrigible, indubitable, and made on some basis other than one's own behavior (this links with the idea that pain is supposed to be "logically private, subjective, self-intimating, and the source of incorrigible knowledge for those who have them" (Aydede 2009, p. 1), ascription of pain to others is neither incorrigible nor indubitable and is made on the basis of their (verbal and non-verbal) behavior. Such behavior is taken as "criterial" for the other's being in pain, such that in the absence of reason for doubting the other's sincerity, if he exhibits pain behaviour we can say that he is in pain. (See Morris 1996.) Yet it seems that, for cultural reasons, others may refuse to acknowledge my pain behaviour as manifesting pain, with the *only* "reason" for this refusal being that my pain lacks a biomedical diagnosis; there is something to explore here about the concept of pain.

## Concluding remarks

The major obstacle to dialogue between Sartre and Anglo-American philosophers of mind lies in their respective starting points. Anglo-American philosophy of mind, as we noted, tends to presuppose naturalism; phenomenologists set themselves against naturalism from the beginning. (Husserl understood naturalism as the view that "[w]hatever *is* is either itself physical, belonging to the unified totality of physical matter, or it is in fact psychical, but then merely as a variable dependent on the physical" (1965, p. 79), which is close to ontological naturalism; Merleau-Ponty was critical of a turn of thought close to methodological naturalism: "It is not a matter of denying or limiting the extent of scientific knowledge, but rather of establishing whether it is entitled to deny or rule out as illusory all forms of enquiry that do not start out from measurements and comparisons" (2008, pp. 34–35].) They rejected naturalism, not because they embraced the "supernatural," but because they believed that it got the order of ontological and methodological priority wrong: "The whole universe of science is built upon the world as directly experienced ... we must begin by reawakening the basic experience of the world of which science is the second-order expression" (Merleau-Ponty 2002, p. ix). The fundamental ontology is phenomenological, not scientific, and the methods for investigating scientific realities may be inappropriate for phenomena.

From this fundamental difference in outlook come others. We have noted already that the body for Anglo-American philosophy of mind is *Körper*, whereas for phenomenology it is in the first instance *Leib*. We also noted that, whereas for Anglo-American philosophers, pain as a topic is firmly to be dealt with within philosophy of mind, for the phenomenologists, including Sartre, it is to be dealt with within a discussion of the body (but qua *Leib*, not qua *Körper*); indeed, the phenomenologists almost never use the word "mind," arguably for the very reason that it contains a history of association with some kind of Cartesian dualism.

Moreover, the phenomenologists' central conception of human beings is as being-in-the-world is at odds with the internalism from which, as we also observed, much Anglo-American philosophy of mind begins. To be sure, internalism has recently come under attack within Anglo-American philosophy of mind, via notions like "embodied cognition." Proponents of embodied cognition and its kin have yet to explore pain; more importantly for present purposes, however, is that embodied cognition remains within the overarching framework of naturalism: "Cognition is embodied when it is deeply dependent on features of the physical body of an agent, that is, when aspects of the agent's body beyond the brain play a significant causal or physically constitutive role in cognitive processing" (Foglia 2011, p. 1). It retains naturalism's commitment to seeing the body as *Körper* rather than *Leib*, as well as its commitment to seeing all relations as external.

We have seen that Sartre and Anglo-American philosophy may be able to converse around the periphery in ways that don't depend on resolving these fundamental differences in philosophical outlook. But, I submit, those fundamental differences in philosophical outlook make it unlikely that the dialogue can go any deeper.

## Notes

1 Earlier versions of this chapter were presented before the Oxford Phenomenology Network (May 7, 2014) and at a workshop on "The body in modern philosophy," University of York (June 25–26, 2014). I am grateful for the comments received on these occasions.
2 There are passages in *BN* that have been taken to be relevant to acute pain. In particular, Ireland (2005) has so taken Sartre's discussion of sensation (*BN*, p. 311),

presumably on the grounds that we tend to speak of acute pain as a sensation, but this seems wrong. Sartre is here critiquing the empiricist psychologists who analyse *sense perception* in terms of sensation. Also of relevance, although I will not discuss it here (Ireland does), are Sartre's comments on torture, e.g., in What Is Literature? (Sartre 1988).

3 See, e.g., the widely cited International Association for the Study of Pain (IASP 1994). *Pain* is defined by IASP as "an unpleasant sensory and emotional experience associated with actual or potential tissue damage, or described in terms of such damage," adding the note that "[m]any people report pain in the absence of tissue damage or any likely pathological cause." The distinction between long-lasting and chronic pain is not always drawn as I have drawn it here; moreover, sometimes chronic pain as I have defined it is called "chronic pain syndrome" and given a *psychiatric* classification. See Morris (2014).

4 For present purposes I focus on *BN*, in particular on Sartre's extended discussion of pain in his chapter on the body. There is no one Anglo-American author whose account of pain is universally accepted; for my purposes I will mainly rely on the article on pain in the *Stanford Encyclopedia of Philosophy* (*SEP*) (Aydede 2009), which reviews the major Anglo-American literature; the *SEP* has a certain status as an authoritative source for Anglo-American philosophical thought, and I make use of it on other occasions in this chapter.

5 The last is also sometimes called the body-for-itself-for-others: Sartre simply calls it "the third dimension of the body." In fact he calls the second dimension "the body-for-others," but his focus there is not on our experience of our own body-for-others (that is the third dimension) but on our experience of others' bodies.

6 As Moran rightly points out, "Sartre's three-fold ontological distinction is awkward since the ontological categories appear to overlap" (2011, p. 274).

7 Curiously, Svenaeus (2009) interprets Sartre's three *ekstases* of pain as stages of falling ill.

8 "Contexture" is another Gestalt psychology notion which comes from Gurwitsch and has been highlighted by Zaner, who defines it as the "system of mutually interdependent and interdetermined constituents" of a whole (Zaner 1981, p. 80; italicized in original).

9 His best-known description of psychic objects comes in *TE;* he returns to the topic in his section on reflection in *BN* (Part Two, Ch. 2.iii).

10 In *BN* this point is developed in connection with yet another triumvirate of *ekstases*, the temporal *ekstases* of past, present, and future (*BN* p. 165f.).

11 See Richmond (2011) for a discussion of the ambiguous status of "magic" in Sartre. Impure reflection is in bad faith (*BN* 161) and thus psychic objects (*qua* the counterpart of impure reflection) are the product and the instrument of bad faith; they too have an ambiguous status.

12 Some Anglo-American philosophers may find puzzling this apparent switch from epistemology to ontology: within phenomenology, epistemology and ontology are inseparable. This is an important source of potential misunderstanding between the two traditions, but cannot be pursued here.

13 Although Sartre does not develop this point about the difficulty of the pain-full world, it has in effect been considerably elaborated both by other phenomenologists and by medical anthropologists writing phenomenologically about chronic pain (what they say here applies equally to long-lasting pain): such pain, they claim, brings about a wholesale "disruption of the taken-for-granted world of

everyday life" (Garro 1994, p. 104). "Space loses its normal directionality as the world ceases to be the locus of purposeful action" (Leder 1990, p. 75; cf. Toombs 1988, p. 211). Objects formerly presented as utilizable "are now obstacles 'to be circumvented,' 'avoided,' or even 'feared'" (Toombs 1988, p. 208), etc.

14 In chronic and long-lasting pain "[t]he ordinary sense of free and spontaneous movement is now replaced by calculated effort; one does not want to take chances" (Leder 1990, p. 81). For a patient with chronic back pain, "[r]eaching for something in the kitchen, bending over to pick up a small garbage bag, twisting to lift up the receiver of the telephone, . . . all can trigger a flash of pain" (Kleinman 1988, pp. 63–64), so he must be "hypervigilant" (cf. Kleinman 1988, p. 61; cf. Garro 1994, p. 105).

15 Sartre makes a distinction between "pure" and "impure" or "accessory" reflection (*BN*, p. 155f.); his description of the second *ekstasis* of pain is explicitly confined to accessory reflection (*BN*, p. 335).

16 It is not quite clear what motivates this choice of words: not everything we ordinarily call an illness involves *pain*; we must think of his use of the word "illness" as a technical use. The same is true of his later use of the word "disease."

17 The modalities "existing," "suffering," and "knowing" correspond to the three *ekstases* of the For-itself.

18 Somewhat confusingly, he also says that in illness the stomach ("this suffered figure") is "raised on the ground of the body-existed" (*BN*, p. 355); one might expect him to say "the body-suffered," i.e., the psychic body; in fact, he says rather little about figure-ground structures in the psychic body.

19 The distinction which Sartre draws here between illness and disease is distinct from, though bears some parallels to, a distinction which medical anthropologists used to draw; for them, disease was a biomedical category, illness a cultural one. (Most medical anthropologists now reject this distinction, as it seems to suggest that biomedicine is acultural.)

20 Nonetheless these reflections suggest yet a further ambiguity: in Sartre's use of "psychic body." As we saw earlier, the medical gaze is directed, not on the psychic body but on the body as in-the-midst-of-the-world. But the look of the other directed on the *psychic* body is sometimes the correlate of (ontological) shame, and sometimes the correlate of (ontological) nausea. Reisman, who has one of the few sustained discussions in the literature of the psychic body in Sartre, calls the body of the other "the psychophysical body" (e.g., 2007, p. 108); this seems more appropriate for the first than for the second.

21 Leder here cites Zaner (1981, ch. 3) and van den Berg (1952, p. 175, although I don't read van den Berg's "fourth dimension" as Zaner's body as "alien presence"; his point is rather to do with the ways in which illness and aging influence our "primary appreciation" of our own bodies (see note 22); see also Svenaeus (2009, pp. 57–59). Peckitt's (2010) critique of Sartre on pain takes a very different route but arrives at the same conclusion.

22 van den Berg also argues that there is a "primary appreciation" of the body "which is decidedly not constituted by the supposed or real glance of the other . . . An invalid may cherish an immediate, unwarrantable sympathy for his maimed arm, which in the company of others appears a complete deprivation" (1952, p. 175).

23 A recent trend in Anglo-American philosophy of mind, so-called "situated cognition" (which includes variants such as "embodied cognition," "embedded

cognition," and "the extended mind hypothesis"), resists such internalism; it is noteworthy that some versions of this claim influence from phenomenology (see, e.g., Varela et al. 1991 and Gallagher 2005). I will say more about this in the final section; the crucial point at present is that such thinkers have not, to my knowledge, turned their attention to pain.

24  An interesting variant is Hyman (2003), who sees pains as "modes" of the body. Hyman begins his discussion by noting, correctly, that most Anglo-American accounts of pain have trouble accommodating the idea that pains are in bodies (2003, p. 5), so that most responses to the alleged paradox end up denying or at least reinterpreting the idea that pains are ever where we say they are, e.g., that a pain "in my foot" is actually *in my foot*.

25  Note that what Anglo-American philosophers mean by "phenomenology" has little to do with what phenomenologists mean, and many such philosophers are moving away from the term "phenomenology" to the term "phenomenality."

26  Representationalism, like perceptual accounts but unlike sense-datum theory, is to be understood as a form of direct realism. Sartre's account of consciousness of course rejects representations (*BN*, p. xxvii), but arguably his objections would be fewer, or anyway different, if these representations are not understood as part of indirect realism.

## Bibliography

Abbreviations used in this chapter:

*BN*: Sartre, J.-P. (1986; original French Publication 1943). *Being and Nothingness*. Tr. H. E. Barnes. London: Routledge.
*TE*: Sartre, J.-P. (1957; original French publication 1936). *The Transcendence of the Ego*. Tr. F. Williams and R. Kirkpatrick. New York: Noonday/Farrar, Straus & Giroux.
Armstrong, D.M. (1962). *Bodily Sensations*. London: Routledge & Kegan Paul.
Aydede, M. (2009). Pain. *Stanford Encyclopedia of Philosophy*. Available online at: http://plato.stanford.edu/entries/pain/.
DelVecchio Good, M.-J., P.E. Brodwin, B.J. Good, and A. Kleinman, Eds. (1994). *Pain as Human Experience: An Anthropological Perspective*. Berkeley: University of California Press (paperback edition).
Foglia, L. (2011). Embodied Cognition. *Stanford Encyclopedia of Philosophy*. http://plato.stanford.edu/entries/embodied-cognition/.
Gallagher, S. (2005). *How the Body Shapes the Mind*. Oxford: Oxford University Press.
Garro, L.C. (1994). Chronic Illness and the Construction of Narratives. In M.-J. DelVecchio Good, P.E. Brodwin, B.J. Good, and A. Kleinman, Eds. *Pain as Human Experience: An Anthropological Perspective*. Berkeley: University of California Press, pp. 100–137.
Husserl, E. (1965). Philosophy as a Rigorous Science. In E. Husserl, Ed. *Phenomenology and the Crisis of Philosophy*. Tr. Q. Lauer. New York: Harper Torchbooks, pp. 71–147. (Original German publication 1911.)
Hyman, J. (2003). Pains and Places. *Philosophy*, 78: pp. 1, 5–24.
IASP (1994). Available online at: http://www.iasp-pain.org/Taxonomy.
Ireland, J. (2005). Sartre and Scarry: Bodies and Phantom Pain. *Revue Internationale de Philosophie* 231: pp. 1, 85–106.

Jackson, F. (1976). The Existence of Mental Objects. *American Philosophical Quarterly* 13: pp. 33–40.

Jackson, J.E. (1994). "After a While No One Believes You": Real and Unreal Pain. In M.-J. DelVecchio Good, P.E. Brodwin, B.J. Good, and A. Kleinman, Eds. *Pain as Human Experience: An Anthropological Perspective*. Berkeley: University of California Press, pp. 138–168.

Kleinman, A. (1988). *The Illness Narratives: Suffering, Healing, and the Human Condition*. New York: Basic Books.

Kleinman, A., P.E. Brodwin, B.J. Good, and M.-J. DelVecchio Good (1994). Pain as Human Experience: An Introduction. In M.-J. DelVecchio Good, P.E. Brodwin, B.J. Good, and A. Kleinman, Eds. *Pain as Human Experience: An Anthropological Perspective*. Berkeley: University of California Press, pp. 1–28.

Leder, D. (1990). *The Absent Body*. Chicago: University of Chicago Press.

Levin, J. (2013). Functionalism. *Stanford Encyclopedia of Philosophy*. Available online at: http://plato.stanford.edu/entries/functionalism/.

Lycan, W.G. (1987). *Consciousness*. Cambridge, MA: MIT Press.

Merleau-Ponty, M. (2002). *Phenomenology of Perception*. Tr. C. Smith. London: Routledge (Routledge Classics). (Original French publication: 1945.)

Merleau-Ponty, M. (2008). *The World of Perception*. Tr. O. Davis. London: Routledge (Routledge Classics). (Original French publication 1948.)

Moran, D. (2011). Revisiting Sartre's Ontology of Embodiment in *Being and Nothingness*. In V. Petrov, Ed. *Ontological Landscapes: Recent Thought on Conceptual Interfaces between Science and Philosophy*. Frankfurt: Ontos-Verlag/Vrin, pp. 263–293.

Morris, K.J. (1996). Pain, Injury and First/Third-person Asymmetry. *Philosophy and Phenomenological Research* 56: pp. 1, 125–136.

Morris, K.J. (2014). Chronic Pain in Phenomenological-Anthropological Perspective. In R.T. Jensen and D. Moran, Eds. *The Phenomenology of Embodied Subjectivity*. Heidelberg: Springer.

Papineau, D. (2007). Naturalism. *Stanford Encyclopedia of Philosophy*. Available online at: http://plato.stanford.edu/entries/naturalism/.

Peckitt, M. (2010). Resisting Sartrean Pain: Henry, Sartre and Biranism. In K.J. Morris, Ed. *Sartre and the Body*. Basingstoke: Palgrave Macmillan, pp. 120–129.

Pitcher, G. (1970). Pain Perception. *The Philosophical Review* 79: pp. 3, 368–393.

Reisman, D. (2007). *Sartre's Phenomenology*. Continuum Studies in Continental Philosophy. London: Continuum.

Richmond, S. (2011). Magic in Sartre's Early Philosophy. In J. Webber, Ed. *Reading Sartre*. London: Routledge, pp. 145–160.

Sartre, J.-P. (1988). What Is Literature? In *What Is Literature and Other Essays*, various translators. Cambridge, MA: Harvard University Press.

Singer, M. (1994). Review of DelVecchio Good et al., Eds. *Applied Anthropology* 96, pp. 457–458.

Svenaeus, F. (2009). The Phenomenology of Falling Ill: An Explication, Critique and Improvement of Sartre's Theory of Embodiment and Alienation. *Human Studies* 32: pp. 1, 53–66.

Toombs, S.K. (1988). Illness and the Paradigm of Lived Body. *Theoretical Medicine* 9, pp. 201–226.

Tye, M. (1997). A Representational Theory of Pains and Their Phenomenal Character. In N. Block, O. Flanagan and G. Güzeldere, Eds. *The Nature of Consciousness: Philosophical Debates*. Cambridge, MA: MIT Press.

van den Berg, J.H. (1952). The Human Body and the Significance of Human Movement: A Phenomenological Study. *Philosophy and Phenomenological Research* 13: pp. 2, 159–183.

Varela, F., E. Thompson, and E. Roach (1991). *The Embodied Mind: Cognitive Science and Human Experience.* Cambridge, MA: MIT Press.

Zaner, R.M. (1981). *The Context of Self: A Phenomenological Inquiry Using Medicine as a Clue.* Athens, OH: Ohio University Press.

# 16 Sartre, enactivism, and the bodily nature of pre-reflective consciousness

*Kathleen Wider*

The Sartre of *Being and Nothingness* would have been encouraged by the rather recent move among some philosophers of mind away from a brain-based model of mind, as extended-mind theorist Andy Clark calls it, to a notion of mind that takes into account the rest of the body and its interactions with the world. Clark argued in *Being There: Putting Brain, Body, and World Together Again* that "In place of the intellectual engine cogitating in a realm of detailed inner models, we confront the embodied, embedded agent, acting as equal partner in adaptive responses which draw on the resources of mind, body, and world" (Clark 1997, p. 47).[1] However, Sartre would have rejected the representational and computational elements that remain in theories such as Clark's. He would be much more sympathetic to another recent movement in philosophy of mind, enactivism, with its roots deeply based in phenomenology, and with its rejection of indirect realism and representationalist theories of mind. Francisco J. Varela, Evan Thompson, and Eleanor Rosch first coined the term "enactive" in *The Embodied Mind* and used it "to emphasize the growing conviction that cognition is not the representation of a pregiven world by a pregiven mind but is rather the enactment of a world and a mind on the basis of a history of the variety of actions that a being in the world performs" (Varela et al. 1991, p. 9). They speak of the "structural coupling" of organism and environment and emphasize the close relation between perception and action. Varela emphasizes the anti-representationalism in enactivism once again in his later essay on neurophenomenology:

> Practically since its inception cognitive science has been committed to a very explicit set of key ideas and metaphors which can be called *representationalism*, for which the inside–outside distinction is the centerpiece: an outside (a feature-full world) represented inside through the action of complex perceptual devices. In recent years there has been a slow but sure change toward an alternative orientation [which treats] mind and world as mutually overlapping, hence the qualifying terms *embodied,* situated, or *enactive* cognitive science.
> 
> (Varela 1996, p. 345: emphasis in original)

One can hear, as I shall show, echoes of Sartre's analysis of consciousness in *Being and Nothingness* in ideas such as Evan Thompson's in the Preface to his *Mind in Life*, his further development of the ideas of enactivism. There he says that "mental life is also bodily life and is situated in the world" (Thompson 2007, p. vxi). Alva Noë is another enactivist philosopher who rejects the widespread view "that perception is a process *in the brain* whereby the perceptual system constructs an *internal representation* of the world" (Noë 2004, p. 2; emphasis in original). He argues explicitly against those who defend the "consciousness is in the head" thesis (Noë 2004, p. 213). Indeed, his 2009 book is entitled *Out of Our Heads,* and in it he argues that "the locus of consciousness is the dynamic life of the whole, environmentally plugged-in person or animal" (Noë 2009, p. xiii). Sartre would support Noë's bringing perception and action together even more closely than Varela et al. did in *The Embodied Mind.* For Noë "perceiving is a way of acting" (Noë 2004, p. 1). Sartre anticipated as well the enactivists' rejection of representationalism. In the introduction to *Being and Nothingness*, Sartre makes clear his view:

> consciousness has no "content".... A table is not *in* consciousness—not even in the capacity of a representation.... The first procedure of a philosophy ought to be to expel things from consciousness and to reestablish its true connection with the world.
> (Sartre 1956, p. li)

For Sartre consciousness is not a substance and so "it" certainly won't be found *in* the brain. Consciousness is a relation to the world and as such the subject of consciousness must be in the world and hence bodily. "The body is nothing other than the for-itself.... The very nature of the for-itself demands that it be body; that is, that its nihilating escape from being should be made in the form of an engagement in the world" (Sartre 1956, p. 309). Consciousness involves a relation between the body and the world.

But the enactivists rarely mention Sartre as a predecessor and they even at times reject him as such. They see their view of mind as inspired by the work of Merleau-Ponty. Critics of Sartre and no doubt some of the enactivists may well have been led astray by Merleau-Ponty's remark that "the analytic of *Being and Nothingness* is the seer who forgets he has a body" (Merleau-Ponty 1968, p. 77). In the first part of this chapter, I will argue that this is a mistaken view of *Being and Nothingness* and that if one has a proper understanding of Sartre's work on the body and its relation to pre-reflective consciousness, he can be seen as another predecessor to the current enactivists. To offer further evidence of Sartre's predecessor status, I have next chosen to focus on the work of one particular enactivist philosopher, Noë, examining his key ideas side by side with Sartre's. In doing so the similarities between Sartre's and Noë's analysis of perceptual consciousness, including the centrality of the role of the body in consciousness, will be brought to light. Finally I will show, at least briefly, how Sartre's analysis of consciousness could enrich and deepen the enactivist account. Enactivists would do well to re-examine Sartre's rich phenomenology in his exploration of the body as the subject of consciousness and consciousness as a relation between the self and the world.

## Pre-reflective consciousness and the body

To see why the Sartrean analysis of consciousness was overlooked by the enactivists in favor of Merleau-Ponty's work in *Phenomenology of Perception* and elsewhere, one must understand the intertwined nature of Sartre's discussion in the early part of *Being and Nothingness* of being-for-itself, the being which is aware of itself in being aware of the world, and his discussion of the body, which doesn't appear until the middle of the book. Its appearing so late may make it seem buried and unimportant in terms of Sartre's analysis of human consciousness and its most primary form: pre-reflective consciousness. But it would be a mistake to interpret Sartre's ideas about the body as unimportant in his early philosophy. As Dermot Moran notes: "[T]he chapter titled 'The Body' in *Being and Nothingness* offers a groundbreaking if somewhat neglected philosophical analysis of embodiment" (Moran 2010, p. 135). Moran goes on to say that "in fact the body pervades the whole of *Being and Nothingness*" (Moran 2010, n. 2, p. 139). A few years later a collection of essays on the importance of the body in *Being and Nothingness* appeared, entitled *Sartre on the Body* (Morris 2010). Most often, however, the Sartrean analysis of the body is seen in terms of the body as it exists as an object for the other rather than the body as it exists for itself as a subject of consciousness.[2] But it is the person's body as it exists for that person, as a lived reality, that is central to Sartre's notion of pre-reflective consciousness and ties his analysis of consciousness to enactivism. Joseph S. Catalano, in his essay "The Body and the Book: Reading *Being and Nothingness*," delineates the reasons Merleau-Ponty's work was so readily picked up as an inspiration for the later theories of the embodied nature of consciousness and why Sartre's work was overlooked. He argues—rightly, I believe—that Merleau-Ponty's *Phenomenology of Perception*, although a difficult work, is direct in making the position he will be defending clear from the beginning. Any reader of the work will readily see his emphasis on the body and its role in perceptual consciousness.[3] Since, as Catalano points out, Sartre does not even begin to treat the role of the body in his analysis of consciousness until Part Three of his work, a reader may be forgiven perhaps for failing to see how essential the body is to Sartre's account of consciousness, including his account of pre-reflective consciousness. Catalano argues for a reading of *Being and Nothingness* that makes sense of Sartre's delaying his discussion of the body until the latter half of the book, despite its crucial role in his philosophy. Sartre does not foreground the body as Merleau-Ponty does, because for Sartre in a phenomenological account of consciousness, the body is revealed as that which is neglected and passed over in silence (Sartre 1956, p. 330). As Catalano notes, *Being and Nothingness* is an "attempt to disclose how we pass through the body in our engaged activities" (Catalano 1998, p. 158). In our experience of consciousness, in particular on the pre-reflective level, consciousness is directed toward the world and not the body, although it is the body which is the subject of consciousness. It is a point of view upon which I cannot take a point of view, Sartre argues. Yet it is "a permanent structure of my being and the permanent condition of possibility for my consciousness as consciousness *of* the world and as a transcendent project toward my future" (Sartre 1956, p. 328). At the pre-reflective level the body as it exists for oneself is a necessary condition for consciousness. Catalano quotes Sartre as saying:

> Perhaps some may be surprised that we have treated the problem of knowing without raising the question of the body and the senses or even once referring to it. It is not my purpose to misunderstand or to ignore the role of the body. But what is important above all else, in ontology as elsewhere, is to observe strict order in the discussion. Now the body, whatever may be its function, appears first as the *known*.
> (Sartre 1956, p. 218, as quoted in Catalano 1998, p. 163)

For Sartre, the body is *always* present to itself in being aware of the world. "To be conscious is always to be conscious of the world, and the world and body are always present to my consciousness although in different ways" (Sartre 1956, p. 334). However, Sartre rejects those who claim that it is my body as it is for others (my body as object) which is present in pre-reflective consciousness. No, it is the body as subject of consciousness which is pre-reflectively aware of itself as a relation to the world, but it is present in its presence to the world first as a kind of absence. Although the body, he says, is everywhere in the world (Sartre 1956, p. 318), it is inapprehensible as an *object* of consciousness for the subject of consciousness whose body it is and in that sense it is absent.[4] That is why it only first *appears* in the world when it becomes known, that is, when it becomes objectified.[5] Hence, the appearance of the body as a known object comes later, phenomenologically speaking, than its presence as a necessary condition for consciousness and as "spread across all things" (Sartre 1956, p. 318). As Moran points out, "For Sartre, traditional philosophy has misunderstood the body because the orders of *knowing* and *being* have been conflated or inverted" (Moran 2010, p. 135). Sartre puts them in what he considers their proper order. Since an analysis of being comes first, the body doesn't *appear* until late in the analysis of the relation between the two kinds of being Sartre identifies in the introduction to *Being and Nothingness*: the for-itself and the in-itself. Being-for-itself is human being, a being which in being conscious of the world is conscious of itself. Being-in-itself is the world and the object of which the for-itself is conscious. The body remains absent until the discussion focuses on our being-for-others in the third part of *Being and Nothingness*. But there

Sartre identifies the body *as it exists for itself* with consciousness and his earlier characterization of consciousness as a relation to the world. He characterizes consciousness as a relation to the in-itself and he characterizes the body as subject in the same way because consciousness and the body are, in a sense, identical since they are both the person as a presence to the world. This identification of the body-for-itself with pre-reflective consciousness is complicated since the body is what is the neglected and that which is passed over in silence, but in the end "the body is what this consciousness *is*; it is not even anything except body" (Sartre 1956, p. 330). I shall return to his analysis of the body in its existence for itself and examine it in much more detail as I take up an exploration of the kinship and differences between Sartre and Noë on the nature of consciousness.

## Sartre and Noë

### Anti-representationalism

In *Action in Perception*, Noë discusses the sources in philosophy, psychology, and cognitive science upon which the enactive view of perception draws. He mentions several philosophers by name, including Husserl and Merleau-Ponty, but there is no mention of Sartre (Noë 2004, p. 17). However, an examination of Noë's and Sartre's analyses of perceptual consciousness reveals many similarities between them. The most obvious similarity, already mentioned in the introduction to this chapter, is their rejection of indirect realism and the anti-representationalism that accompanies it. For the indirect realist, whether of the Cartesian sort or the more current materialist sort, one is not directly conscious of the world. Rather one is conscious of the world indirectly by means of mental ideas or representations in the brain. In this section I will explore the reasons why Sartre rejects this kind of view. For Sartre, our relation to the world as a conscious body is direct and immediate. Early in *Action in Perception*, Noë points out that an "implication of the enactive approach is that we ought to reject the idea—widespread in both philosophy and science—that perception is a process *in the brain* whereby the perceptual system constructs an *internal representation* of the world" (Noë 2004, p. 2). In dealing with vision in Chapter 2 of the same work, he argues that there is no need to think of vision as producing a rich and detailed picture or representation in the brain. He reiterates this view in his later works as well.[6]

The anti-representational stance of both Sartre and Noë is evident in their discussions of perceptual consciousness.[7] Both reject the existence of sensations as private, inner states by means of which one encounters the world. For both, perception is relational and the relational properties of objects (properties which appear given a certain orientation of an observer to an object) are perfectly real and objective properties of those objects. In spelling out the relational nature of perception, each philosopher makes clear that there is an intimate connection, if not identity, between perception and action and that the body plays a central role in perception.

It is in Part Three of *Being and Nothingness*, within Sartre's discussion of the body as it exists for oneself, that he begins his discussion of sensations with reference to his experiences as a subject in various research work of physiologists and psychologists.

> From time to time the experimenter asked me if the screen appeared to me more or less illuminated, if the pressure exerted on my hand seemed to me stronger or weaker, and I replied; that is, I gave *objective* information concerning things which appeared in the midst of my world.
>
> (Sartre 1956, p. 311; emphasis mine)

When Sartre responded, for example, that the screen appeared less illuminated in his opinion, he says he was not talking about some private sensations, but rather he was referring to "the objectivity of the world-for-me" as opposed to "a stricter objectivity which is the result of experimental measures and of the agreement of minds with each other" (Sartre 1956, p. 311). For example, if I were to say a room felt warm to me and another person said the room felt cold to her, although we both agree that the thermostat says 68 °F, I am not, on the Sartrean view, contrasting an objective fact with subjective sensations. Rather there are three objective facts here: (1) the room is 68 °F; (2) given the facts of my standing and lecturing and moving my arms about combined with my current physiological state, I feel warm; and (3) given the fact that the other person is sitting, etc., she feels cool. Since perception is a relation between myself as a bodily subject of consciousness and the world, it is an objective fact about that relation that I feel warm. Sartre gives the example of plunging his heated hand into warm water. It is an objective fact about the world that my hand is cold. The temperature of the water given by the thermometer is also an objective fact, he says. If I choose the one over the other and choose to call the second "true objectivity" and the other "subjectivity," I'm simply giving the second designation to the objectivity I have not chosen (Sartre 1956, p. 311). I am in the world. The water is in the world. Both the temperature of the water as read by the thermometer and the temperature as felt by me are objective facts. Again, the fact about me is a fact about the relation between myself as a bodily subject of consciousness—as a body which exists for itself, that is, that is aware of itself at the pre-reflective level—and the world. He rejects the so-called "relativity of sensations" which forms the basis of one of the standard arguments against direct realism. Sartre claims that, on the mistaken view of the indirect realist, "this objective relation of the stimulant to the sense organ is itself surpassed toward a relation of the *objective* (stimulant-sense organ) to the subjective (pure sensation)" (Sartre 1956, p. 312). This view sees a sense organ as just an intermediary between the stimulant (in the world) and subjective sensation. Now the problem with this view, according to Sartre, is that this creates the need to posit somewhere for this sensation to exist as a passive in-itself. Thus the idea of the mind or consciousness as a closed box arises. But this is a mistaken move and it happens because a holder of this view starts with the consciousness of the other, that is, consciousness as an object. Then, because the view must be universal, "I posit that the consciousness thus conceived must be also *my* consciousness, not *for the other* but *in itself*" (Sartre 1956, p. 313; emphasis in original). This is how I come to believe in some inner space in which sensations are formed when certain external stimulations are present. "Since this space is pure passivity, I declare that it *suffers* its sensations" (Sartre 1956, p. 313). Then the mind becomes a closed box with sensations inside of it. Sartre rejects this analysis. This idea of sensations is a pure fiction, he contends. It does not fit with one's experience.

Noë, like Sartre, refuses to think of perception as of private sensations or sense data hidden in the dark recesses of mind or brain.

> Perception may be a mode of encountering how things are by encountering how they appear. But this encounter with how they appear is itself an encounter with the world. For how things appear is a matter of how things are in the world. What is encountered (or "given") in perception is not sensational qualities or sense data, but rather the world.
> (Noë 2004, p. 85)

Like Sartre, in denying sensations as purely subjective and private entities in a mind or brain, Noë does not deny the existence of what he calls perspectival properties or P-properties. The perspectival size of a tree, for example, will change as the perceiver moves closer or further away from it, although the actual size of the tree does not change. However, Noë argues, these facts do not support indirect realism. Just as Sartre maintained, Noë also maintains that both the actual size of the tree and the size of the tree as it appears from a certain point occupied by a perceiver are *objective* properties of the world. P-properties are relational properties. "P-properties depend on relations between the perceiver's body and the perceived object (and also on conditions of illumination). P-properties are, in effect, relations between objects and their environment" (Noë 2004, p. 83). One need not posit the existence of sensations or feelings, Noë contends, to explain these properties. Just as Sartre maintains that the idea of sensation he rejects does not fit with our experience, Noë mentions important criticisms raised by earlier philosophers against the sense-datum theory. One of these was Strawson's point that, when we take experience at face value, we find that what we experience is not a round, red sense datum, for example, but a solid item of fruit on the table (Noë 2004, p. 85). The phenomenology of perceptual experience goes against the indirect realist view. Noë explains how this can be the case by arguing, like Sartre does, that perception is active not passive. "Perceiving is a kind of skillful bodily activity" (Noë 2004, p. 2). He reiterates this view in *Out of Our Heads:* "Consciousness is not something that happens to us. It is something we do or make" (Noë 2009, p. xii). For both Sartre and Noë, perception is an active relation between a bodily perceiver and the world. This brings perception and action into an intimacy that borders on identity. For both, perception is tied to, and in some ways defined by, a set of possible actions.

*Perception and action*

For Sartre the actions to which perceptual consciousness is tied are determined by the perceiver's ends or goals. "It is impossible to distinguish 'sensation' from 'action'" (Sartre 1956, p. 320). Objects are always given in a place and this place is not defined by pure spatial co-ordinates, but rather in relation to the perceiver and her possible future actions. Sartre offers the following examples. If the glass is *on* the coffee table, what this means is that if I want to move the table, I have to be careful not to move it in such a way that the glass falls over. If the tobacco for my pipe is *on* the mantle, this means I have to cross three meters to get it, avoiding bumping into end tables and footstool, etc. that are between me and the mantle. I *see* this furniture as obstacles around which I must move to get to the tobacco. I *see* the glass as something fragile which I may damage in moving the table. "Perception is naturally surpassed toward action; better yet, it can be revealed only in and through projects of action" (Sartre 1956, p. 322). What is made manifest to me in perception is hodological space, which Sartre defines as space that is

> furrowed with paths and highways; it is instrumental and it is the *location* of tools. Thus the world from the moment of the upsurge of my For-itself is revealed as the indication of acts to be performed; these acts refer to other acts and those to others, and so on. It is to be noted however that if from this point of view perception and action are indistinguishable, action is nevertheless presented as a future efficacy which surpasses and transcends the pure and simple perceived.
> (Sartre 1956, p. 322)[8]

As Adrian Mirvish points out in his article, "Sartre, Hodological Space, and the Existence of Others," hodological space involves no fixed set of co-ordinates independent of any particular subject. There is, rather, a constantly varying field of force of the experiencing subject. This field of force is space structured relative to the subject's body and to her goals. Thus Sartre's view of perception and its connection to action brings into central focus the role of the body in perception.[9]

For Noë perception is also connected to possible actions and, in explicating what he means by this, the central role of the body in perception becomes clear. Noë argues that a certain kind of knowledge is needed in order to have meaningful perceptual experience. It is not a propositional knowledge but rather a practical knowledge of how sensory stimulation would change as the subject moves (Noë 2004, p. 8). For Noë *"what we perceive* is determined by *what we do* (or what we know how to do); it is determined by what we are *ready* to do" (Noë 2004, p. 1; emphasis in original). He gives several examples in *Action in Perception* to support his view about the necessary connection between perception and action. His first set of examples is of post-cataract surgery patients. He reviews three such cases as described by the neurologist who treated each patient. Noë points out that the descriptions given by three neurologists of their patient immediately after the cataracts were removed fit the result that enactivism would predict.[10] When the cataracts which were the cause of the patient's congenital blindness were removed, they began receiving visual data; but they did not actually see at first, Noë contends, because, initially this data made no sense to them. He quotes from various descriptions of the initial experience of such patients when the bandages were removed after surgery. One such description quoted is Oliver Sacks' report that his patient Virgil told him later "that in this first moment he had no idea what he was seeing. There was light, there was movement, there was color, all mixed up, all meaningless, a blur" (Noë 2004, p. 5, quoting Sacks 1995). Noë calls their state one of "experiential blindness." Why this is the case, on Noë's view, is because the patients lacked the knowledge of how the visual sensations would change as they moved. They lacked the sensorimotor or skill knowledge that Noë argues is necessary for perception.

His second example is a set of experiments in which the subjects were given left–right inverting spectacles to wear. The lenses caused light coming from objects on the subjects' left side to enter the eye the way light coming from objects on the subjects' right side would have entered without the glasses being worn. As Noë points out, one would expect the subjects to see objects on their left as being on their right side. But that was not what happened initially. At first the subjects experienced "experiential blindness." That is, their visual world was chaotic—at least in terms of spatial content—although they were receiving normal visual stimulation in the sense that the light was focused properly when it reached their eyes and it bore the usual amount of information. Noë argues that enactivism would predict this result because "the patterns of dependence between movement and stimulation are altered" by the lenses (Noë 2004, p. 8). The subjects went through various stages of adaptation and, if they were allowed or required to move about in their environment and engage with it, their experience returned to normal and, while still wearing the glasses, objects to the left looked once again as though they were on the left and such was also the case with objects on the right.

Noë's contention is that it is the subjects' activity which allowed them to gain the sensorimotor knowledge, the knowledge necessary for perception, that is, knowledge of how their movements changed the sensory stimulation received from objects around them. Action is required to gain this practical knowledge.[11] It is the actions of a bodily subject of consciousness which provides the "sense" to the sensory stimulation that the subjects failed to understand when they first donned the inverting glasses. When the glasses were removed, their sensations of space and the arrangement of objects in it were again chaotic and senseless until they once again moved around and acted within their environment and so regained the sensorimotor knowledge needed to perceive the world as it now appeared *sans* glasses.

To support his enactivist stand further, Noë reviews the experiment with kittens that Varela et al. also appealed to in order to support their version of enactivism. Two kittens born with normal visual apparatus are placed by a carousel. One walks around it and the other goes around it but while suspended from the air. As a consequence, both go round in a circle, but only the walking kitten develops normal depth perception and eye–paw coordination. Noë takes this to show that not only movement but *self-activated* movement is necessary for perception (Noë 2004, p. 13; Varela et al. 1991, pp. 174–175). Noë goes on to diffuse a counter-example offer by his critics, the case of a quadriplegic. Such severe paralysis does not make a person blind, the critics contend. Noë agrees because, he points out, the quadriplegic can still move her eyes and hand and she can move her body as well, although moving it requires the use of a wheelchair. So engagement with the environment is still possible and thus the person can acquire the sensorimotor skills needed for perception (Noë 2004, pp. 12–13). Perceptual experience, Noë claims, gains content because of our having and using "practical bodily knowledge" (Noë 2004, p. 34). This knowledge involves knowledge of possible actions.

## *Body's role in perception*

I would like to examine more carefully how the relational nature of perception brings the body's role in consciousness into focus for both Sartre and Noë. Let's look first at why this is the case in Sartre's analysis of perception. From the beginning of *Being and Nothingness*, Sartre has argued that consciousness is a relation to the world. "Consciousness in its inmost nature is a relation to a transcendent being" (Sartre 1956, p. lx). Consciousness, the for-itself as Sartre calls it, a human consciousness which exists conscious of itself in being conscious of the world, exists as presence to being. As such, it is dependent on the world (the in-itself) for its existence. It is intentional in nature and so, in its very nature, it requires an object toward which it is directed. But the relation between consciousness and its objects is two-way. Consciousness requires the in-itself to exist, but the in-itself which, on Sartre's view is in-itself a flat realm of being, requires consciousness for it to arise as this or that. Consciousness confers meaning on the in-itself and makes it into a world. The entire *Being and Nothingness* is devoted to spelling out the relation between the two forms of being Sartre identifies in the Introduction to the work: being-for-itself and being-in-itself. The discussion of the body as it exists for itself, as pre-reflective consciousness, is part of this exploration of the relation between the two regions of being. Indeed, he gives a presentiment of his identification of pre-reflective consciousness with the body (as subject) fairly early in *Being and Nothingness* when he says that "[t]he consciousness of man *in action* is non-reflective consciousness" (Sartre 1956, p. 36) and "our being is immediately 'in situation'; that is, it arises in enterprises" (Sartre 1956, p. 39). How could that be if consciousness were not bodily? How else could it engage with the world? We can see similarities between the general points he makes about consciousness at the beginning of *Being and Nothingness* and the points he makes about the body as subject later in the work. The for-itself, Sartre argues in the early sections of the work, is present to both the in-itself and to itself. Consciousness is always self-conscious.[12] At the pre-reflective level, consciousness is aware of itself in being aware of the world. Indeed, it is aware of itself *as* an awareness of the world. Likewise the body as pre-reflective consciousness is aware both of itself and the world.[13] Indeed, it is aware of itself in being aware of the world and, in a sense, *as* an awareness of the world.

Sartre also argues in his earlier discussion of consciousness that consciousness' awareness of itself at the pre-reflective level is its awareness of itself as nothingness, that is, as not being an object in-itself, a thing, but rather being a presence to objects without, however, being identical to any particular object of which it is conscious since it may become conscious of other objects. So too the body's presence is experienced as a kind of absence—a kind of nothingness—in perception. In the chapter entitled "Transcendence" which comes just before his discussion of the body in *Being and Nothingness,* Sartre said, "For human reality, being-in-the-world means radically to lose oneself in the world through the very revelation which causes there to be a world" (Sartre 1956, p. 200). And even earlier in the work he described the for-itself as "a nihilated in-itself" (Sartre 1956, p. 82). The for-itself is "the in-itself losing itself as an in-itself in order to found itself as consciousness" (Sartre 1956, p. 82). He makes these same kinds of claims in his analysis of the body as subject of consciousness. All things in the world (from my perspective) indicate me—my body; yet it is the one thing which cannot be given to me as an object of perception.

> The object which the things of the world indicate and which they include in their radius is for itself and on principle a non-object. But the upsurge of my being, by unfolding distances *in terms of a center,* by the very act of this unfolding determines an object which is itself in so far as it causes itself to be indicated by the world; and I could have no intuition of it as object because I am it, I who am presence to myself as the being which is its own nothingness.
> 
> (Sartre 1956, p. 318)

He repeats again in this section on the body as subject what he said earlier in his chapter on transcendence. "It is necessary that I lose myself in the world in order for the world to exist and for me to be able to transcend it" (Sartre 1956, p. 318). What does this mean in terms of the body? Sartre identifies the body as subject with the structures of pre-reflective consciousness. But he also wants to modify this claim or at least complicate it. This is because "consciousness (of) the body is lateral and retrospective; the body is the *neglected*, the '*passed by in silence*'" (Sartre 1956, p. 330; emphasis in original).

Consciousness of the body is like consciousness of a sign, according to Sartre. You must be conscious of the sign for its meaning to exist, but you must surpass the sign toward its meaning. To apprehend the meaning of a sign, one must not pay attention to the sign and its properties for their own sake. If you get so caught up in the shape of a stop sign and the construction of the letters upon the red background, you may miss the order to stop which is the meaning of the sign. Likewise, Sartre contends, the body is that through which we are aware of the world. Indeed it *is*, as for-itself, consciousness of the world. But it functions in the background. By keeping the body's presence to itself at the pre-reflective level, the body is able to perceive the world. The body's presence to itself must also be a kind of absence. In an analogous way, I must be conscious of the sign to understand the meaning it conveys. Yet the sign must be present as a kind of absence. Sartre says that "absence is a structure of *being-there*" (Sartre 1956, p. 342; emphasis in original).[14] Although my body is experienced as an absence,

> my body is everywhere in the world; it is over there in the fact that the lamp-post hides the bush which grows along the path, as well as in the fact that the roof up there is above the windows of the sixth floor or in the fact that a passing car swerves from the right to left behind the truck or that the woman who is crossing the street appears smaller than the man who is sitting on the sidewalk in front of the café. My body is co-extensive with the world, spread across all things, and at the same time it is condensed into this single point which all things indicate and which I am without being able to know it.
>
> (Sartre 1956, p. 318)

This single point which all things indicate is the body as a point of view on the world, as the center of reference and action. As we saw above in Sartre's characterization of the relation between perception and action, objects are revealed to me "at the heart of a complex of instrumentality in which they occupy a determined *place*" (Sartre 1956, p. 321). This place is not defined by geometric co-ordinates, but rather in terms of goals and desires, as instruments by which to achieve my ends. Hence hodological space is instrumental and the location of tools. That is why perception is tied to action. I see the world in terms of my possible actions and the things in the world as objects to be used or overcome or avoided or moved around in order to achieve my goals. The "instrumental things," as Sartre calls them, that I perceive in perceiving the world indicate other instruments and objective ways to use them. He gives as an example of this point the fact that the hammer indicates the nail and that indicates objective ways to use the hammer to pound in the nail (Sartre 1956, p. 322). But the key to all these instruments, the point of reference which the world indicates, is my body for me, given though inapprehensible (Sartre 1956, p. 323).[15] I do not apprehend my hand as just another tool to be used, for I *am* my hand, Sartre says. In the act of writing "my hand has vanished. It is lost in the complex of instrumentality in order that this system may exist. It is simply the meaning and orientation of the system" (Sartre 1956, p. 323). He repeats once again that because of this the body is everywhere since everything within the complex which constitutes my world points to me as its center (Sartre 1956, p. 325). It is the point of view upon which no point of view can be taken. I can step back and take a point of view on the scenic overlook which is my point of view on the valley and the mountains beyond. I can step back and take a point of view on the telescope which is my point of view on the stars. But I cannot step back from my own body as lived subject of experience. I cannot make myself as a bodily subject of consciousness—as the center and reference of the world I perceive—an object for me within that world.

We have seen how a careful examination of the relational nature of perception for Sartre brings into focus the central role the body plays in consciousness. The same is true on a more extensive analysis of Noë's view of the relational nature of perception. "The environment is the physical world *as it is inhabited by the animal.* The perceptual world (the environment) is not a separate place or world; it is the world thought of from our standpoint (or any animal's standpoint). It is our world" (Noë 2004, p. 155; emphasis in original). For Noë the world shows up and with it we ourselves show up. That is because the world's showing up (in perception) is only possible given "our mastery and exercise of skills of access" (Noë 2012, p. 12). The world shows up because we show up as actors in the world. Perception depends on sensorimotor skills—skills of the body which indicate possible (or actual) actions. The world and the bodily self are co-present in perception as they are for Sartre. "Insofar as we achieve access to the world, we also achieve ourselves" (Noë 2012, p. 12). But for Noë as it is for Sartre, in perception, as an engagement with the world, the body remains in the background. Like Sartre, Noë believes we have "the power to bring the world forth. It is our nature to do this" (Noë 2012, p. 14). We do this by being bodily persons exploring our world. This exploration which just is perceptual consciousness requires the bodily skills so necessary for perception. Let's look more closely at the nature of these bodily skills and the knowledge and mastery of them one must have to perceive the world successfully.

For Noë our sensory relation to the world has two dimensions, one provided by the perceiver and the other by the perceived. It is dependent on both the movement of the perceiver and on the object perceived. A change in either one produces a different sensory experience for the perceiver. He concentrates on the movement of the perceiver since his primary concern is with the sensorimotor skills needed for perception. What these skills come to is made clear in his discussion of how it is we see a whole object *in* seeing a part of it. On his view both are present to the perceiver. How can we see the front of a tomato while *at the same time* the rest of the tomato is present to us as well?[16] The sensorimotor skills necessary for perception are central to his answer. Phenomenologically speaking we experience objects, such as a tomato, as a whole. We do not think or judge that the tomato has a back. We actually have a visual sense of the entirety of the tomato, Noë argues (Noë 2012, p. 16). What constitutes that sense of the tomato's wholeness is "our implicit understanding (our expectation) that movements of our body . . . will bring further bits of the tomato into view" (Noë 2004, p. 63). It comes into play when, for example, I stand looking out at the world. It is not as though I am in the presence of a detailed scene before me because vision consists in the taking of a series of snapshots of all the details in the scene with which the brain then constructs a rich, full-colored, detailed *representation* of the entire scene. He spends all of Chapter 2 in *Action in Perception* arguing against this "pictures in the mind" conception of vision. The reason I feel as though I am seeing the entire scene in all its details is because all of the scene and its details are present, but only *virtually* present. They are not present as a detailed picture in the brain. What Noë means by the detailed scene being virtually present is that the perceiver understands she can move her eyes and head and whole body in such a way that she can access the various details and aspects of the environment of which she is now sensing a portion. The details of her current environment to which she is not paying explicit attention are there virtually or, using the language of some psychologists as Noë does, they are *amodally* "present as absent" (Noë 2004, p. 61). They are present without being actually perceived. However, although not currently perceived, they are accessible to her. They are accessible to her by means of her mastery of certain sensorimotor skills. That is, she knows what actions would be necessary to bring the other details of the scene out of virtual presence and into actual presence.[17] This may require, for example, simply turning her head if she wishes to look at the refrigerator which is to her left just out of view or walking around the couch if she is considering buying it. The details of the environment in which she is situated are accessible to her not because there is a representation of it in her brain but because the world is right there, available for her to access in all its richness by means of bodily actions. These actions may be as minor as lifting up her head to see the color of the ceiling or pivoting her body to face in a different direction. To see a circular plate from an angle, for example, is "to see something with an elliptical P-shape, and it is to understand how that perspectival shape would vary as a function of one's (possible or actual) movements with respect to the perceived object" (Noë 2004, p. 84).[18] It is not that I see the elliptical shape and then infer the circular one. Noë contends that I see the circularity of the plate *in* seeing that from where I'm viewing it, it appears elliptical. How things appear combined with the sensorimotor knowledge Noë describes gives a perceiver things as they are, he argues. It is because how a thing appears is part of how a thing is. Thus an exploration of the world, experiencing various ways objects within it appear, is "a process of meeting the world."[19] This exploration is a bodily exploration. We move our bodies (in part or as a whole) or understand how to do so to bring various aspects of the world into focus. In doing so, we come to know the world. As bodily perceivers we are not separate from the world; we are a part of it.[20]

## Sartre's enrichment of enactivists' accounts of consciousness

I repeat once again that the enactivists' failure to see Sartre as one of their ancestors and as someone they could mine for inspiration as much as Merleau-Ponty arises from a misunderstanding of the role of the body in Sartre's analysis of consciousness which derives from his identification of pre-reflective consciousness with the body as subject. It is because of Sartre's view of pre-reflective consciousness as body that there exist so many similarities between Noë's enactivist account of consciousness and Sartre's account of it. Both see the body as essential in any such account. Noë sees his work as a development of Merleau-Ponty's on the sensorimotor body and its role in perception. We have seen how he utilizes that work to explain how perception is of the world and not of sensations and how this can be the case even though there can be disparities between an object's apparent shape and its actual shape.[21] However, I believe Sartre's work in *Being and Nothingness* can enrich in important ways Noë's and others' enactivist accounts of consciousness.[22] It can do so because Sartre offers a much richer phenomenological account of the point of view that humans as *bodily* subjects of consciousness bring to the world. His account also highlights how deeply individual our perceptual worlds are although we live in a shared world.

Noë, in defending his rejection of sensations as mental representations, concentrates on the body as a sensorimotor organism that moves and acts in the world as the most primary level of the body as a subject of perception. His account of perceptual consciousness excels at exploring the spatial aspects of a person's point of view and how that point of view, given an understanding of sensorimotor skills, encompasses both her current point of view in space and other possible points of view in space. That, however, is a limited analysis of the human point of view and its relation to perception. Sartre offers a much more full-bodied analysis of the human point of view and its affect on perception than Noë does while still keeping the body in its central role in perceptual consciousness. He offers not only an analysis of how humans in general as bodily subjects of consciousness constitute the world and themselves as consciousness in and of the world, but also how each *individual* human constitutes the world for herself. Given that both philosophers contend that it is the whole person that is the conscious subject of perception, I think Sartre gives a much fuller phenomenological account of this than Noë does. This is because he examines various aspects of a perceiver's point of view, not simply the spatial one. Noë of course recognizes that perception is affected by more than one's spatial point of view. He acknowledges that

> how things look depends [in a sense] on what you are interested in, or on what you ask, or on how you probe. There is a sense in which there is no thought or interest-neutral fact of the matter about how things look. It's relative.
>
> (Noë 2004, p. 165)

However, his interest is in exploring the spatial aspect in order to explain how we can see the plate, for example, as circular while it appears elliptical to us. Although Noë's development of his theory to account for this phenomenon is couched within a general concern for the perceiver's relationship to the world, Sartre explores this relationship much more fully in *Being and Nothingness* and in doing so he brings out the multifaceted nature of the role of the body in perceptual consciousness.

At the beginning of the first section of Chapter 1 of Part Four of *Being and Nothingness*, Sartre says that he does not want to end his work "without giving a broad outline for the study of action in general" (Sartre 1956, p. 431). As he did earlier in *Being and Nothingness*, he once again draws a close connection between perception and action in this last section of the work. In doing so he offers a more expansive view of what constitutes a person's point of view in perceiving the world. Although one's position in space is part of one's point of view, as we saw with the examples from Sartre that I gave at the beginning of the section on Perception and action, one's point of view is defined by much more than that. His discussion of action as a projection toward an end brings this out. In this last major part of *Being and Nothingness*, he gives several examples to support his point that a necessary condition for action is the perception of a lack in the present situation and the positing of an end toward which the action is directed. One of his examples is the emperor Constantine, who sees the need for a city to counterbalance the weight of pagan Rome because he sees that such a Christian city is missing. So he acts to create Constantinople as the needed counterweight to Rome (Sartre 1956, pp. 433–434). Until a worker sees his condition as unbearable, Sartre claims, he will not act to revolt against it (Sartre 1956, p. 435). He must withdraw from what is the case in order to see what is not, what is missing. In the worker's case, he might see just wages, for example, as missing in his situation. It is in perceiving this lack that the goal of achieving just wages through revolt creates action. How the goal or end toward which a person projects herself as action affects one's perception is spelled out in greater detail in the second section of Chapter 1 of Part Four, entitled Freedom and Facticity: the Situation. Although he does not use the term hodological space, the discussion of *situation* in this section is a development and expansion of his earlier discussion of hodological space, space as *human* space configured in terms of one's needs and interests. Sartre's discussion of the relation between freedom and facticity in this section is a continuation of his examination of the relation between the for-itself and the in-itself, between a person and the world. "Freedom [that is the for-itself as a free choice of action] is originally a *relation to the given*" (Sartre 1956, p. 486; emphasis in original).

It is in his discussion of a person's situation that we can see that it is a person as a bodily subject of consciousness that is a relation to the world. This relation is a richly layered one. The given, the in-itself, is "the plenitude of being" which the for-itself "*colors* with insufficiency ... *illuminating* it with the light of an end which does not exist" (Sartre 1956, p. 487; emphasis mine). A specific given never appears to freedom, that is, to the for-itself, as simply a brute existent, Sartre argues. It is given "as *already* illuminated by the end which freedom chooses" (Sartre 1956, p. 487; emphasis in original). This constitutes the situation of a person. The situation is a product of the in-itself and the for-itself, although Sartre believes that the contribution of each to the situation cannot be distinguished.

To illustrate how the situation is co-created by a person and the world, he uses an example of hikers who come across a steep crag. The crag appears in light of each hiker's end or goal in the hike. For the climber the rock may appear as something to be scaled, although whether it is one that can be scaled or not is in part determined by the rock. However, it does not appear to be either able to be scaled or not by a hiker who is only interested in appreciating aesthetic beauty. For that person the rock appears as beautiful or ugly. Her situation is a different one than the climber, although they may be hiking along the same trail. For Sartre, Noë's P-properties exist or not for a perceiver depending on her situation which is constituted by both her choice of ends and the being of the rock. The rock for that matter may be seen as an aid for someone hiding out from pursuers or as resistance for someone trying to climb over it. On Sartre's analysis, how the rock is perceived, what the person actually sees, is determined by her ends as well as by the object in the world. "Man encounters an obstacle only within the field of his freedom.... What is an obstacle for me may not be so for another" (Sartre 1956, p. 488). For example, the rock is not an obstacle if my goal is to get to the top of the mountain no matter what. But it is an obstacle if my desired goal is to climb only as far as I can without endangering my life. Whether or not and in what way I view an object as, using Sartre's terminology, a "coefficient of adversity" depends on the ends I choose.

Sartre maintains that I can never know if my situation with its coefficients of adversity is giving me information about myself or about the world. It manifests both since it is a co-creation of the for-itself and the in-itself. Like Noë in perception we access both ourselves and the world.

In this co-creation the body is central. In fact, Sartre says,

> the body is not distinct from the *situation* of the for-itself since for the for-itself, to exist and to be situated are one and the same; on the other hand the body is identified with the whole world inasmuch as the world is the total situation of the for-itself and the measure of its existence.
> (Sartre 1956, p. 309)

We can see, in his discussion of the rock, how the body of the perceiver appears in her situation and constitutes it as well. Sartre says that for two people, both of whom want to climb the rock, doing so will reveal each one's body as weak or strong. This is the case because of each one's choice of climbing. However, the body is often in the background in one's situation. For the lawyer in the city who is arguing a case and whose body is hidden beneath his robes, the rock, Sartre says, is neither difficult nor easy to climb. It never emerges as a figure on the ground of the world for him and so neither does his body. I choose my body as weak or strong only by choosing to engage in strenuous physical endeavors. He goes on to say that for a person who is active solely in business or intellectual pursuits, the body *from this point of view* has no quality at all, although it is still there, as I noted in the section on Body's role in perception, above. Having given an overview of how a person's situation is created by both the world and the self, he goes on to consider various structures of the situation: my place, my past, my environment, my fellowman, and my death. Sartre's detailed phenomenological analysis of all these various aspects of one's situation which manifest one's point of view in its relation to the world provides a richly layered phenomenology of our relation as bodies to the world.

To give a flavor of the richness of Sartre's analysis of these structures that create the world I inhabit, I will examine one of them in particular, my place. As I do so, keep in mind that for Sartre it is all the structures he discusses that *together* create my situation and the point of view it embodies. As a bodily being I am born and must be born one place or another. I do not choose the place of my birth. It is also true that I must always be one place or another. However, that is not all there is to it. A human being is an interplay between freedom and facticity. One cannot characterize a person's place by stating as a bald fact, "John is at home." No, one's place is determined by one's ends as well as by the world. I am my place in the sense of not being it, Sartre says. What that means is that I transcend it by a projection of myself into the future. That is what it means to see one's place in terms of one's chosen ends. If I wish to see Pierre, Sartre says, my place (where I am) is a 20-minute, very hot bike ride away from Pierre. If I wish to see Annie, it is an overnight train ride away from her. If I wish a cup of tea, I am a few steps from the teapot. For a soldier, where he is is 120 days from discharge. If I am fleeing from a group of men or from public opinion, my place is a week away from being discovered hiding out in this small village (see Sartre 1956, p. 493, for these examples). The perception of my place is co-created, like all the other structures that create my situation, by both myself and the world. "A particular city situated twenty miles from my village and connected to it by a streetcar is much nearer to me than a rocky peak situated four miles away but at an altitude of two thousand eight hundred meters" (Sartre 1956, p. 494). These examples and the others he gives in his discussion of place offer a very rich phenomenology of place and reveal the body's role in creating situation. But it is not my body as an object among others, situated next to the lamp the way the couch is. My body is the body of a human being as a subject of consciousness that is able to go beyond what is to what is not but could be. Human beings as conscious subjects of experience, points of view on the world, are a very complex relation to the world. Sartre explores this complexity in detail.

Another strength of Sartre's analysis of this relation is that it shows how deeply individual the perceptual world that each person inhabits is. This is an aspect of consciousness as a relation between a body and the world that the enactivists too often overlook. Of course Sartre recognizes that the existence of others means I am engaged in a world with instrumental complexes that have been created and given meaning by others. There are many examples of meanings independent of my choices. In a city, for example, Sartre notes streets, houses, shops, streetcars, warning signs, etc. The world I perceive and within which I act is not revealed solely in terms of my ends. A person comes to consciousness "in a world which is given to him as *already looked at*, furrowed, explored, worked over in all its meanings, and whose very contexture is already defined by these investigations" (Sartre 1956, p. 520). In addition, there are other factors of my situation which I did not choose: my gender, the social class I was born into, the place of my birth, for example. However, Sartre argues, in our interactions with this world we make sense of these in light of our own free choices of goals and ends. Consequently, although there are limits to the freedom of the for-itself, a person never encounters those limits as such because they are always seen through the lens of the ends and desires of the person whose limits they are. I perceive the world in terms of ends toward which I propel myself in action, in the action of a bodily subject of consciousness which exists for itself as pre-reflective consciousness even when it is fully engaged with the world, or perhaps it is more accurate to say *as* an engagement with the world. The fact that we occupy a perceptual world constituted in part by our individual ends does not mean each person exists isolated within his or her own private perceptual world. Because of the relation Sartre argues holds between perception and action and how one's situation brings together perception, action, and ends, I can understand how it is you perceive the world because

I have access to your actions. As embodied subjects of consciousness we are individual but not alone.

The enrichment Sartre can add to the enactivist program of seeing consciousness in terms of a relation between a bodily person and the world can be appreciated if one is willing to abandon a mistaken reading of *Being and Nothingness* and comes to see the role the body as pre-reflective consciousness plays in Sartre's investigation into the nature of consciousness. Sartre did not neglect the body but wove it into his discussion of the relation between the for-itself and the in-itself in complicated and multi-layered ways.[23]

# Notes

1 See also Clark (2008) for a further development of his extended mind theory. It's there that he contrasts what he calls the BRAINBOUND model of cognition with his EXTENDED model of mind (p. xxvii; caps are his). Both these books are developments of the ideas put forth by Clark and Chalmers (1998).
2 Sartre distinguishes three dimensions of our bodily existence: my body as it is for me, my body as it exists for the other, and my body for me as it exists for the other.
3 In addition, since enactivists often focus explicitly and sometimes exclusively on perceptual consciousness, a work entitled *Phenomenology of Perception* would appear immediately relevant to their work.
4 There is one exception and that is when, caught by the look of the Other, the self appears to itself at the pre-reflective level as an object for the other.
5 For Sartre knowledge always objectifies.
6 See Noë (2004, 2009), where he once again argues that, although "many philosophers and thinkers take for granted that presence is . . . re-presence; we make the world present by re-presenting it," that view is a mistake which gives rise to many problems, including the challenge of understanding how we or our brain are able to do this (Noë 2012, pp. 30–31).
7 Sartre's is evident throughout his analysis of consciousness, but I will focus here on his rejection of sensations and the alternate view he gives of perception.
8 Sartre took this notion of hodological space from the psychologist Kurt Lewin.
9 I will return to a discussion of hodological space when I address the added dimension I claim Sartre brings to the enactivist analysis of perceptual consciousness.
10 For a discussion of these cases, see Noë (2004, pp. 4–6).
11 It is not my intention to evaluate Noë's enactivist claims. I'm simply trying to show similarities between Sartre's view of perceptual consciousness and Noë's enactivist account.
12 See Wider (1997) where I explore this claim in detail.
13 Noë thinks Sartre (among others) has argued that the self only appears in reflection and that at the pre-reflective level "I myself am absent from the story." It is true that for Sartre in pre-reflective consciousness there is no self in the sense of a Cartesian ego. But the self is indeed present in perception and at the pre-reflective level. It is present in just the activity Noë points to as what phenomenology should turn its attention to: "our engaged activity" (Noë 2012, p. 130).

Indeed that is where we find the self in its bodily existence in the world and this self is aware of itself.
14 For an extended discussion of the presence/absence structure of the body as pre-reflective consciousness, see Wider (1997, pp. 115–119).
15 In my lived experience of my body as it is known by others, my body is also inapprehensible but for very different reasons (Sartre 1956, p. 353).
16 Sartre (1956, p. 317) also says we see a whole object while of necessity viewing it from a particular point of view or orientation. "An object *must always appear to me all at once* . . . but . . . this appearance always takes place in a particular perspective which expresses its relations to the ground of the world and to other *thises*." This point is connected, I think, to his discussion of appearances in the Introduction to *Being and Nothingness* where he says that, although an object only discloses itself through one appearance to a perceiver at a given time, that appearance points to an infinite number of other possible appearances of the object. "What appears in fact is only an *aspect* of the object, and the object is altogether *in* that aspect and altogether outside of it" (Sartre 1956, p. xlvii).
17 He argues for this same view in *Varieties of Presence* and in that work, in order to emphasize the crucial role of bodily actions in perception, he calls his view "actionism" (Noë 2012, p. 23).
18 Noë responds to various critics of his view in Noë (2012).
19 Noë (2004, p. 164). In our exploration of the world, Noë says, we create trails and habits of locomotion and action. In creating such trails we also alter our environment and the possible actions within it. This is akin in some ways to Sartre's idea of hodological space with its paths and highways.
20 Despite the body playing such an essential role in consciousness on both Sartre's and Noë's account, both express a negative view of the body. Even though they both realize the necessity of the body for experiencing the world, they resent it in a way as though there still resides within them some hidden longing for the old Cartesian immaterial (non-animal) self. For Noë we are "saddled" with an animal body (Noë 2012, pp. 12 and 13) and for Sartre the taste of one's body is the taste of nausea (Sartre 1956, p. 338).
21 Noë focuses on an aspect of the body Sartre has frequently been accused of neglecting and Merleau-Ponty has been praised for exploring. I criticized Sartre in a similar way in Wider (1997). However, my reflection here on the body as pre-reflective consciousness has made me aware that perhaps my criticism of Sartre was too harsh there. I took Sartre's analysis of consciousness as a withdrawal from being, a nihilation of being, as undermining his claim that it is the body which is the subject of consciousness. (In Wider (1997, p. 173) I discuss an ambiguity in Sartre's discussion of this claim which could lead to such a criticism.) But I now see how the body could be both a being-in-the-world and absent from the world at the same time. The body as pre-reflective consciousness, as subject of consciousness, is *nothing* in the sense of not being an object in the world for oneself. The body disappears into the background as objects of perception arise as figures on the ground of the world. I also think many come to think he ignored the sensorimotor body because he explores it in all its complexity as a *human* sensorimotor body acting in the world.
22 There is not space here to discuss his view specifically in relation to Varela's and others' views.

23 One might object to Sartre as a predecessor to the enactivists because nowhere does he discuss the brain and its role in the relation between the self and the world. But that is not because he thought that understanding the body as object had nothing to contribute to our understanding of consciousness. In a 1975 interview when asked about the relation between consciousness and the brain, he gave this response: "This is a problem I studied for several years at the time of *L'Être et le Néant* and afterward. I tried to deal with it, but I did not finish it. . . . I first wanted to define consciousness. . . . I wanted to posit a definite object which others would then have to try to explain within the materialist system, that is, to study its relation to the brain" (Gruenheck et al. 1981, p. 40).

## Bibliography

Catalano, J. S. (1998). The Body and the Book. In Jon Stewart, Ed., *The Debate between Sartre and Merleau-Ponty*, pp. 154–171. Evanston, IL: Northwestern University Press.

Clark, A. (1997). *Being There: Putting Brain, Body, and World Together Again*. Cambridge, MA: MIT Press.

Clark, A. (2008). *Supersizing the Mind: Embodiment, Action, and Cognitive Extension*. New York: Oxford University Press.

Clark, A., and D. Chalmers (1998). The Extended Mind. *Analysis* 58: pp. 10–23.

Gruenheck, S., O. F. Pucciani, and M. Rybalka (1981). An Interview with Jean-Paul Sartre. In P. A. Schilpp, Ed., *The Philosophy of Jean-Paul Sartre*, pp. 1–51. LaSalle, IL: Open Court.

Merleau-Ponty, Maurice (1968). *The Visible and the Invisible* [*Le visible et l'invisible*, 1964], trans. Alphonso Lingis. Evanston, IL: Northwestern University Press.

Mirvish, Adrian. (1984). Sartre, Hodological Space, and the Existence of Others. *Research in Phenomenology* 14: pp. 149–173.

Moran, Dermot. (2010). Sartre on Embodiment, Touch, and the "Double Sensation." *Philosophy Today* 54: pp. 135–141.

Morris, K. J. (2008). *Sartre*. Malden, MA: Blackwell Publishing.

Morris, K. J., Ed., (2010). *Sartre on the Body*. New York: Palgrave Macmillan.

Noë, A. (2004). *Action in Perception*. Cambridge, MA: MIT Press.

Noë, A. (2009). *Out of Our Heads*. New York: Hill and Wang.

Noë, A. (2012). *Varieties of Presence*. Cambridge, MA: Harvard University Press.

Sacks, O. (1995). *An Anthropologist on Mars: Seven Paradoxical Tales*. New York: Knopf.

Sartre, J.-P. (1956). *Being and Nothingness* [*L'Etre et le Néant*, 1943], trans. H. E. Barnes. New York: Philosophical Library.

Thompson, E. (2007). *Mind in Life*. Cambridge, MA: Harvard University Press.

Varela, F. J. (1996). Neurophenomenology. *Journal of Consciousness Studies* 3(4): pp. 330–349.

Varela, F. J., E. Thompson, and E. Rosch (1991). *The Embodied Mind*. Cambridge: MA: MIT Press.

Wider, K.V. (1997). *The Bodily Nature of Consciousness: Sartre and Contemporary Philosophy of Mind*. Ithaca, NY: Cornell University Press.

# 17 The body is structured like a language
## Reading Sartre's *Being and Nothingness*

*Dorothée Legrand*

## Reading

My aim here is very modest: read one sentence written by Sartre, and read it in its own context of enunciation. My approach will thus not be comparative—I will compare Sartre neither to himself nor to others, as one would do in order to detect some (in)consistencies and (dis)agreements between one "Sartre" and another and/or between Sartre and other authors. Rather, my approach here may be said to be "myopic," in the sense that it aims at seeing more clearly by looking more closely. If this approach seems to be "short-sighted" and to lack ambition and relevance, by missing "the big picture," this impression will be reinforced by the fact that, here, I will not even circulate around *all* the concepts the chosen sentence contains. I will leave aside notions which are crucial for Sartre, like the notion of freedom—not only for the sake of space, but more importantly because "freedom" is not the question I wish to ask Sartre here, as will soon appear. By reading Sartre in this way, by leaving aside an analysis of freedom as conceived of in this work, for example, I am extracting from his writing "less" than it contains. But I am also extracting "more" than it contains—in the sense that I don't necessarily expect that Sartre himself would have agreed with the way of reading his text that I will propose here. Beyond his posthumous agreement, however, I am seeking to reach the text itself, in a way that is at least coherent, at best fruitful.

The target sentence I will explore has first been published in 1953, in *Being and Nothingness*, as Sartre considers one's *Being-for-Others* (Part 3) through the investigation of one's "Concrete Relations with Others" (Chapter 3). In this context, one can read: "By the sole fact that, whatever I may do, my acts freely conceived and executed, my projects launched toward my possibilities have outside a meaning which escapes me and which I feel, I *am* language" (p. 372[1]). The prism through which I will read Sartre here is the working hypothesis following which this sentence contains the idea that *the body is structured like a language*. This is what I will work on here. To do so, and to orient my reading, three "steps" impose themselves: language, others, and the body. These "steps," however, are hardly dissociable from each other (that's precisely the working hypothesis); it is only artificially that they will be distinguished from each other in distinct sections.

## Language

"I *am* language," and for Sartre, language is not one: there is "language— in so far as it is I who employ it for the Other" and language "when the Other hears it" (p. 374). As spoken, language is, *for the listener*, magical; and as listened to, language is, *for the speaker*, sacred. Language is *magical* for the listener in the sense that my "attitudes, expressions, and words" are manifested to the other and have an effect on him, even though "my transcendence," as the one who speaks, remains inaccessible (p. 374). Language is *sacred*, as spoken and listened to, in the sense that, as I speak, I "point" to an other who transcends me and my world: "Language reveals to me . . . the transcendence . . . of the one who listens to me in silence" (p. 374). Importantly, this distinction, between language for me and language for the other, is not merely a distinction between language as *spoken*, and language as *listened to*. Rather, because it is spoken by me as listened to by the other, because it is listened to by the other as spoken by me, language is *structurally twofold*. It is twofold because it does not only involve speaking, but also and necessarily, it involves listening: listening is constitutive of language; or more precisely, the act of listening of one is constitutive of the act of speaking of the other. In other terms, one does not speak *alone*; and this is not a contingency; rather, this is the very structure of language. In Sartre's terms: "Language is not a phenomenon added on to being-for-others. It is originally being-for-others" (p. 372); "Language is therefore not distinct from the recognition of the Other's existence" (p. 373). It is because one does not speak alone, i.e. it is insofar as speech is *structurally* listened to by another, that language is a mode of being that happens *between* oneself and others.

To insist that language is a mode of being-for-others is not a contingency, tied to the presence of another concrete person tuning her ears to the sounds coming out of my mouth. Rather, and by analogy with the analysis of the gaze Sartre develops in *Being and Nothingness*, we can understand that my speech is addressed to the other even if no one is here. About the look, Sartre underlines that "the fact of being-looked-at cannot . . . depend on the object which manifests the look" (p. 276); "it is never eyes which look at us; it is the Other-as-subject" (p. 277). Just like my bodily acts are shaped by a pervasive "onlooker," even if I am factually alone, language as it is spoken by me is shaped by a pervasive "listener." The facticity of my body prevents any possibility of acting in the world without being visible by someone else; likewise, the facticity of language prevents any possibility of speaking alone.

Now, not only one does not speak alone but, moreover, language does not speak "all by itself" (p. 516). Here again, language is defined as structurally twofold, as it involves the differentiation and thereby the joining of two irreducible dimensions: language as meaningfully articulated by the speaker and language as following laws which "are not for the one who speaks, [but] for the one who listens" (p. 517).

On the one hand, it is only because someone speaks that the laws of language are incarnated, thereby being not only manifested but rather enacted. What is at stake here is the *necessary* incarnation of language into an act of speech. Incarnation does not make of language a "natural event" (p. 517). On the contrary, Sartre positions himself against the idea that "speech is a Nature" which the human being must obey, against the idea that there could be "a sort of living order of words, of the dynamic laws of speech, an impersonal life of the logos," against the conception of speech as "dead," i.e. as "already spoken." The speaking being is not reducible to "a pilot employing the determined forces of winds, waves, and tides in order to direct a ship" (p. 516). Rather, speaking enacts the laws of language which do *not* pre-exist the concrete act of speaking but "exist always only incarnated" (p. 519): "there can be no laws of speaking before one speaks" (p. 518), no language before speech in the sense that "the sentence is the order of words which become *these words* only by means of their very order" (p. 519). Speaking is thus a performance by which is operated an "assumption" of the "not yet existing" laws of language (p. 518). By speaking, the speaker operates a "synthetic unity" (a sentence made of words which enter in relation one with another), and without this "synthetic unity," "the block which is called 'speech' disintegrates; each word returns to its solitude and at the same time loses its unity, being parceled out among various incommunicable meanings" (p. 517). Speaking, thereby, "is the only possible foundation of the laws of language" (p. 517).

On the other hand, it is only because someone listens when someone else speaks that the laws of language are detected without ever being reduced to natural laws, but rather by always being received as the multi-vociferation of speech. On this point, Sartre is precise and concrete:

> if we discover that two (or several) words hold between them not *one* but several defined relations and that there results from this a multiplicity of meanings . . . , this can be only under the two following conditions: (1) the words must have been assembled and presented by a meaningful rapprochement; (2) this synthesis must be seen *from outside*—i.e., by *The Other* and in the course of a hypothetical deciphering of the possible meanings of this rapprochement. . . . the rapprochement will be *multivocal.*
>
> (p. 517; emphasis in original)

The one who speaks cannot capture by himself anything else than the significance which he himself puts into the words he pronounces: by himself, he "apprehends the order of the words only insofar as he makes it. The only relations which he will grasp within this organized complex [of words making a meaningful sentence] are specifically those which he has established" (p. 517). It is the one who listens who can hear the equivocation of this speech, and can reflect it back to the speaker, thereby allowing the latter "to adopt with respect to the sentence the point of view of the Other" (p. 517, note 18), which in turn may lead him to learn his own thought from his speech as listened to by the other, i.e., as multivocal. Notice that what occurs here has nothing to do with agreeing—or not—with some interpretation the listener might have on the meaning of the speaker's speech; rather, what is at stake is that, *by the very fact of being listened to,* the speaker can hold multiple perspectives on his own speech, thereby opening the "multivocal" structure of language—over and above any confrontation of interpretations.

Thus, hearing one's own speech as irreducibly multivocal depends upon someone else listening to one's speech as the enaction of the laws of language according to which words do not mean anything in and of themselves, and thus always hold multiple meanings depending on the relation they entertain with other words in and beyond the sentence they are participating in, a sentence which is thus always multivocal in that it never incarnates only the meaning purposefully chosen and articulated by the speaker but the series of meanings enacted by the chain of words entering in relation with one another, equivocal meanings which exist only when words are joined to one another within and beyond a spoken sentence, a sentence which is spoken only insofar as it is listened to, addressed to another even if no ears are factually around.

In short, language is structurally listened to, and it is also structurally spoken—this two-sidedness may be precisely one sense in which language is structured as an address. As an address, a sentence passes between one and another. It thus cannot be fixed into any univocal chain of words, whose meaning could be decided by one alone, before speaking, or interpreted by another alone, after the utterance has occurred. As speech is an address, it occurs between oneself and another; and as it occurs between oneself and another, speech is structurally multivocal and thus equivocal. In that sense, "language is not an instinct of the constituted human creature, nor is it an invention of our subjectivity" (p. 373); rather, language is incarnated in an act occurring between oneself and another.

Moreover, and primordially, the language I speak is always already a gift or a graft from the other. The laws of the language I incarnate in the speech I address to the other, I got them from the other (p. 519). The laws of language do not exist outside of the act of speaking, but the language I do employ, "I have learned it from others . . . My speech is then subordinated to the speech of others" (p. 519). Sartre "should not think of denying this fact" (p. 519): it is an "undeniable fact" that one "is not the origin" of the meanings one "can choose itself" (p. 520) to incarnate in one's speech but precisely, for Sartre, one is singularized "beyond" the given structure imposed on him, and "this 'beyond' is enough to assure [one's] total independence in relation to the structures which [one] surpasses" (p. 520). Surpassing, however, is not effacing; rather, Sartre insists:

> the meaning of the world is alien to [oneself]. This means simply that each man finds himself in the presence of meanings which do not come into the world through him. He arises in a world which is given to him as already looked-at, furrowed, explored, worked over in all its meanings, and whose very contexture is already defined by these investigations.
> (p. 520)

It is worth quoting Sartre at length on this point, as he deploys explicitly the idea that my expressions, i.e. my speech, like

> my gestures and attitudes ... will always be taken up and founded by [another subject who] will surpass them and ... they can have a meaning only if this [other subject] confers one on them. Thus the "meaning" of my expressions always escapes me; I never know exactly if I signify what I want to signify nor even if I *am* significant; at this precise instant, it would be necessary that I read in the Other, which is, on principle, inconceivable. And, for lack of knowing what I actually express, for the Other, I constitute my language as an incomplete phenomenon of flight outside myself. As soon as I express myself, I can only speculate about the meaning of what I express, that is, in short, the meaning of what I am, since, in this perspective, to express and to be are one. The Other is always there, present and experienced as the one who gives to language [p. 374] its meaning. Each expression, each gesture, each word is on my side a concrete proof of the alienating reality of the Other.
> (translation modified, pp. 373–374)

In this sense, through the language I address to the other, I am alienated to the other as to "a transcendence which is not mine" (p. 270)—an "alienation" to the other which makes of language a sacred speech.

Now, we can return to our target sentence. After unfolding Sartre's considerations on language, we shall be in a better position to start understanding in which way "I *am* language," a language which has "outside a meaning which escapes me."

## Others

My speech incarnates my equivocal modes of being with another and, for Sartre, "being-for-others is a constant fact of my human reality" (p. 280). But what is this "reality"? Who is the other "present to me everywhere" (p. 280)? "*For me* the Other is first the being *for whom* I am an *object*; that is, the being *from whom* I *gain* my objectness" (translation modified: I emphasize "for me," "for whom," "object," and "gain." Sartre emphasizes "from whom": "par qui," p. 270). This sentence summarizes several points which are crucial to understand how one is tied to another, according to Sartre.

First, my being-an-object-for-others is a "gain" for me. It would be a mistake, therefore, to think that Sartre conceives of one's being-for-others as involving only a *loss*. Loss, alienation, slavery, fall, disintegration, hemorrhage—such terms abound in Sartre's writing, but it should be kept in mind that it is not being for others but being only for myself (if it were possible at all) which would be a "degraded" mode of being myself (p. 273). Even more radically, "if [Me] could coincide with myself in a pure selfness, I should refuse it as mine" (translation modified, p. 285).

Second, being for others, "*I* gain *my* objectness" (my emphasis) This ties being for others to *self*-consciousness but does not reduce the former to the latter. Indeed, on the one hand, the other as onlooker is apprehended by me as I apprehend *myself* being looked at, and in this sense, being for others is a mode of being oneself—oneself as an object, an object which necessarily is for others as "I cannot be an object for myself" (p. 270). But on the other hand, it is just as much the case that the "certainty" of being-looked-at "reveals to me . . . the *other*-as-subject, a transcending presence to the world" (my emphasis, p. 276), and in this sense, being for others is a mode of apprehending others, and not only a mode of being oneself—or, more precisely, being for others is a mode of being oneself by apprehending others.

Third, being for others is apprehending the other as "the being *for whom* I am an object" (my emphasis). Indeed, "the Other does not constitute me as an object for myself but *for him*. In other words he does not serve as a regulative or constitutive concept for the pieces of knowledge which I may have of myself" (p. 275). Even when language reveals to me explicitly how I am for the other, as the other may describe how he sees me, I shall only feel "my alienation," an alienated me which "I shall feel that I am," but about which I have no "concrete intuition": "I apprehend nothing but an escape from myself toward . . . " (p. 275). In this sense, being for others "is radically different from my being-for-my-self, and . . . does not refer to the latter at all" (translation modified, p. 273). Simply: being for others is not being for me.

Fourth, the other is "the being *from whom* I gain my objectness" and to understand this, it may not be vain to state explicitly what is obvious throughout *Being and Nothingness*: the way for me to be for the other is nothing like the way a gift is for the other. For me to be for the other is not to be in such a way that the other "gains" anything from me; by being *for* the other, I am not giving anything of myself *to* the other; rather, I am given *by* the other. Being for the other is being what the other makes me be: an object for him, from his point of view, the object his gaze points at. Thus, to be *for* the other is to be *from* the other.

Fifth, the other is "the being for whom *I am an object*" (my emphasis). What must be clarified is that, if what one is given from others is one's being-as-object, "it is precisely as Me-escaping-myself that I [am] this Me-as-object.

This Me-as-object is the Me which I am to the exact extent that it escapes me" (p. 285). Being for the other, i.e., being an object, is being "conscious of myself as escaping myself" (p. 260). If I am an object, it is primordially in the sense that "I am not the foundation of my being" (p. 308) and what I "gain" from the other is precisely "my foundation outside myself" (p. 260). Not only is "the Other's look . . . the necessary condition of my objectivity" (p. 269), but also, and by the same token, "the Other as a look is only . . . my transcendence transcended" (p. 263). It thus appears that my objectivity is exactly that: my transcendence transcended, the existence for me of a transcending subject who founds my being, but a subject who I am not, who I cannot be. In other terms, the apprehension of my being an object for the other is "the objective apprehension of my being-other" (p. 273), other than my own foundation as subject, as well as the apprehension that I remain irreducibly separated from the other subject "by accepting a limit to my subjectivity" (translation modified; this sentence is omitted in the published translation, p. 6). "The nature of my Self-as-object" is precisely "the limit between two consciousnesses," a limit between oneself and another which "can neither come from me nor be thought by me, for I cannot limit myself; otherwise I should be a finite totality" (p. 286). In short, being *for* the other, I am an object, which means: I am irreducibly separated *by* the other *from* the other.

Sixth, "*for me* the Other is first the being *for whom* I am an object" (I emphasize "for me"). If the other founds who I am outside myself, I myself found the other as who I am not: "If in general there is an Other, it is necessary above all that I be the one who is not the Other; and it is in this very negation effected by me upon myself that I make myself be and that the Other arises as the Other" (p. 83). If being for/from the other involves the other's negation of myself as being for/from myself, it is just as much the case that apprehending the other involves my own negation of myself as being the other: the other is the subject who I myself refuse to be. But precisely, it is *as subject* that the other is refused, i.e., it is in as much as he himself refuses to be the subject I am that I refuse to be the subject he is. Refusing to be the other, maintaining the separation between me and the other, avoiding any fusion with the other, involves recognizing the other as a subject who recognizes that I am a subject who he refuses to be. And recognizing the other as subject in such a way involves recognizing my own being for this other, i.e., recognizing that, as subject, he alienates me by founding my being outside myself. To recognize the other as subject is thus both at once to refuse being the subject he is, and "to assume and recognize as mine [the] alienated Me" (p. 285) who I am for him and who he refuses to be. "Thus this Me which has been alienated and refused [by the Other] is simultaneously my bond with the Other and the symbol of our absolute separation" (p. 285).

Now, we can read again the whole sentence we've just analyzed: "*For me* the Other is first the being *for whom* I am an *object*; that is, the being *from whom* I *gain* my objectness" (translation modified: I emphasize "for me," "for whom," "object," and "gain"; Sartre emphasizes "from whom" ("par qui"), p. 270). As it has been analyzed above, we can now see how to put it all back together again. The Other is first manifested to me "as a subject beyond my limit, as the one who limits me," as the one who "strips me of my transcendence," a negation of myself "which does not come to me through myself" (p. 287). But my own "apprehension of this negation" by myself is just as much the "affirmation" of myself as a subject who "is responsible for a negation of the Other, [negation] which proceeds from me to the Other" (p. 287). These two "negations" are inseparable from each other: if there is an other for me, it is in the sense that there is a subject (the other) who negates me as the subject he is himself, i.e., there is a subject (the other) for who I am an object, i.e., there is a subject who I am not and who founds the subject I am, i.e., there is a subject I am and who is founded by a subject I am not, i.e., there is a subject (myself) for who the subject I am not is an object, i.e., there is a subject (myself) who negates the other as the subject I am . . . , etc.

As these two negations intertwine, I am both at once, and inseparably, "responsible for a negation of the Other" (p. 287) and "responsible for the existence of the Other" (p. 287): negating the other is negating that the other is the subject I am; negating the other, therefore, is maintaining the other as irreducibly other. Likewise, the other's negation of me maintains me as irreducibly myself. Thus being-for-others "*is the fact that my negation that I am the Other is not sufficient for the Other to exist, but that the Other must himself negate that he is me simultaneously with my Own negation.* This is *the facticity* of being-for-others" (translation modified, p. 301; emphasis in original). But as "I cannot realize both negations at once" (p. 287), one negation always "masks" the other, and while "these two negations are equally indispensable to being-for-others" and are "simultaneous" one with another, "they cannot be reunited by any synthesis" (p. 300).

These considerations of my being-for-others now allow us to return to our target sentence, to unfold it a little more. "I *am* language": my speech incarnates my equivocal modes of being with an other who founds the subject I am as I found him as the subject I am not. "I *am* language": whoever I may be, "whatever I may do," any of "my acts freely conceived and executed," any of "my projects launched toward my possibilities" have their foundation in a subject who I am not, "have outside a meaning which escapes me and which I feel," precisely as what escapes myself.

## The body

What shall now be considered more closely is the way in which "whatever I may do . . . I *am* language": not only articulated speech but *any of my acts* "have outside a meaning which escapes me and which I feel." "Of course by language [Sartre] mean[s] all the phenomena of expression and not [only] the articulated word" (p. 373), but despite the apparent obviousness of this claim, what remains to be clarified is the way in which the body is structured like a language, i.e., the way in which, like my speech, my bodily acts "have outside a meaning which escapes me and which I feel." Language is a vehicle of others' knowledge of my body: "it is by means of the Other's concepts that I know my body" (p. 355). However, that's not all there is to language: language does not only lead one to know but to experience (p. 373). What is thus this experience which one is led to through language, i.e., through "all the phenomena of expression" (p. 373)? What is this experience which makes me feel my equivocal modes of being with an other who founds the subject I am as I found him as the subject I am not? This experience, Sartre argues, is tied to "whatever I may do," to any of "my acts freely conceived and executed," to any of "my projects launched toward my possibilities." Thus, this experience is bodily. But again, what remains to be clarified is the manner in which my body escapes myself, the manner in which the body incarnates my equivocal modes of being with an other.

The "Other's omnipresence" (p. 352) reveals to me my "objectivity," i.e. a "dimension of my facticity" which "surreptitiously flees me": "my body escapes me on all sides" (p. 352). But for Sartre, our "body-for-the-Other is the body-for-us," the same body, "but inapprehensible and alienated" (p. 353), hence the "constant uneasiness" which comes with "the apprehension of my body's alienation" which is just as "irremediable" (p. 353) as the other is "omnipresent" (p. 352). Thus, my body for others is not only the body I know through others' language. Rather, my body for others is also the body I experience as inapprehensible and alienated, a body which has "outside a meaning which escapes me and which I feel" (p. 372).

In and of itself, however, this is insufficient to conclude that, as bodily "I *am* language" (p. 372). Indeed, if language has "outside a meaning which escapes me and which I feel" (p. 372), it is in the sense that my speech incarnates my equivocal modes of being with an other who founds the subject I am as I found him as the subject I am not. Language is a relation between separated and inseparable terms: the speaker and the listener. The question that remains open, therefore, is how the body is not only alienated but *related* to an other. This bodily relation between oneself and another, it seems that Sartre describes it nowhere else more clearly than when he describes desire. Desire is one of the "fundamental structures of being-for-others" (p. 383). Nonetheless, desire reveals a mode of being for others "of an entirely original type" (p. 386). What, then, is desire? Sartre unfolds this question in several steps.

First, "desire *of what*" (p. 384)? Desire is defined "by its transcendent object" (p. 385). Through a "fundamental sexuality" (p. 383), "I desire a human being, . . . and I desire him (or her) . . . as he is an Other for me and as I am an Other for him" (p. 384).

Second, what, in the transcendent other, is the object of my desire? "Shall we say that desire is the desire of a body? . . . this can not be denied ... it is the body which troubles us, [the body apprehended] on the ground of the presence of the whole body as an organic totality" (translation modified, p. 385): a living body incarnating subjectivity, "such is the object to which desire *addresses* itself" (translation modified, p. 386; emphasis in original).

Third, "what does desire wish from this object?" (p. 386). Sexual desire, and its enaction in the caress of the other's body, is "my original attempt to get hold of the Other's ... subjectivity through his objectivity-for-me" (382). Desire is "an attempt to incarnate the Other's body," "an attempt to strip the body of its movements as of its clothing and to make it exist as pure flesh" (p. 389), a flesh for me, an exorbitant materiality in touch with my own flesh.

Fourth, how does desire proceed? "The ensemble of those rituals which incarnate the Other" into his flesh is the caress. Caressing is "shaping" the other's body, to cause it "to be born as flesh for me and for herself" (p. 390). "In the caress it is not my body as a synthetic form in action which caresses the Other: but it is my body as flesh which causes the Other's flesh to be born. The caress is designed to cause through pleasure the Other's body to be born for the Other and for myself as a *touched* passivity insofar as my body is made flesh in order to touch the Other's body with its own passivity; that is, by caressing itself with the Other's body rather than by caressing her" (translation modified, p. 390). To caress is not to act upon the other's body but to lean one's own body against the other's body.

Thus, the subsequent question arises: "who is the one who desires?" Myself? My body? "The answer is clear. I am the one who desires, and desire is a singular mode of my subjectivity" (translation modified, p. 386). What is then this "singular" mode of being myself in desiring another? Desiring the other is not a form of "cognitive consciousness" (p. 386), not only because its object would not be an object to be known, but also because of the particular mode in which "the man who desires exists his body" (p. 387). To exist my body for myself is escaping myself "in the form of an engagement in the world" (p. 309). My body for me is what I depart from, it is "a point of departure which I am and which at the same time I surpass toward what I have to be" by engaging myself in a worldly situation (p. 326). As such, the body is not a local object to be found in the world and to be known; rather "it is there everywhere as the surpassed" (p. 309), surpassed by the world which I project myself toward. For example, according to Sartre, a man who experiences hunger experiences its facticity and "immediately flees it ... toward a certain state of satisfied-hunger" (p. 387). Hunger is thus "a pure surpassing of corporal facticity" (p. 387). But in this respect, "an abyss separates sexual desire from other appetites" (translation modified, p. 387). Indeed, far from fleeing from facticity, desiring is nothing else than falling entirely "into complicity with the body" (p. 388): "one is invaded by facticity, ... one ceases to flee it and ... one slides toward a passive consent to the desire" (p. 388). Hunger would be elicited as a lack for myself which I flee from and surpass toward a satisfied hunger, i.e., toward a possible, even if temporary, fulfillment (p. 87). Hunger, as a need, is an escape from itself toward the needed object, food, thanks to which the lack is surpassed (p. 88). Desire, in contrast, does not arise from a lack for myself, but surges from the assumption of my own flesh. "*Desire is consent to Desire*" (p. 388). Desiring is surrendering and subordinating oneself to one's facticity, rather than resisting and fleeing it: the subject lets himself "be[ing] swallowed up in the body."

If one's desire is one's assumption of one's facticity, one's desire is also, as we saw above, desire of the other's body as transcendent. Both at once, therefore, desire is "the revelation of my own body" (translation modified) and "the unveiling of the Other's body" (p. 388). "In desire I make myself flesh in the presence of the Other in order to appropriate the Other's flesh" (p. 389).

> In desire and in the caress which expresses desire, I incarnate myself in order to realize the incarnation of the Other; and the caress, by *realizing* the Other's incarnation, reveals to me my own incarnation; that is, I make myself flesh in order to impel the Other to realize *for herself* and *for me* her own flesh, and my caresses cause my flesh to be born for me insofar as it is, for the Other, *flesh causing her to be born as flesh.* I make her taste my flesh through her flesh in order to compel her to feel herself flesh. And in this manner . . . appears . . . a double reciprocal incarnation.
> (translation modified, p. 391; emphasis in original)

This "chiasm" leads us back to our working hypothesis: the body is structured like a language. This structure is chiasmatic. Like language, the body, as a flesh incarnating subjectivity, incarnates my equivocal modes of being with an other who founds the subject I am as I found him as the subject I am not. Like speech, the language of desire, the caress is a relation between separated and inseparable terms: the speaker and the listener, the caressed and the caressing.

As we emphasized above, desire is one of the "fundamental structures of being-for-others" (p. 383), "of an entirely original type" (p. 386). And indeed, we can now see that the language of desire is bewitching (p. 396),

> desire is an attitude aiming at bewitchment. Since I can capture the Other only in his objective facticity, the problem is to glue his [subjectivity] within this facticity. . . . by touching this body I should finally touch the Other's . . . subjectivity. . . . Such is the impossible ideal of desire: to possess the Other's transcendence as pure transcendence and at the same time as body.
> (translation modified, p. 394)

Importantly, the caress, as the enchanting language of desire, does not aim at fascinating the other, i.e., it does not aim "at constituting myself as a fullness of being and at making myself recognized as such" by the other who is thereby exposed to "the consciousness of his state of nothingness as he confronts the seductive object" (p. 372). Whereas "in fascination there is nothing more than a gigantic object in a desert world" (p. 177), desire is less like a desert than like water when troubled "by an inapprehensible presence . . . , changed by the presence of an invisible something. If the desiring consciousness is troubled, it is because it is analogous to the troubled water" (p. 387): in desire, the other is not fascinated by me in a world deserted of any other object; in desire, the other and myself inhabit a "world of desire," a world which surges from the destruction of my willful projections and actions in situations, "a destructured world, which has lost its meaning, and where things stand out like fragments of pure matter, like brute qualities," a world where I project myself toward "a new possibility: that of being "absorbed by my body as ink is by blotting paper" (translation modified, p. 395).

## A world without desire

A world with language is a world where separated terms are inseparable: oneself and another, speaker and listener, irreducible to each other, and as such jointly constituting speech as what occurs between them. The caress is the language of desire, strictly speaking, in the sense that the caress occurs between separated terms which are thus made inseparable from each other. In this sense, the body is structured like a language.

A world without desire would be a world where separated terms, oneself and another, remain separated. Sartre untiringly describes such a world. Admittedly, "as soon as 'there is' the body and as soon as 'there is' an Other, we react by desire, by Love, and by . . . derived attitudes" (p. 406). And yet, "desire is itself doomed to failure" (p. 396) and Sartre describes several ways in which *non-contingently* "desire stands at the origin of its own failure" (p. 398). Each of these ways amounts to being forgetful of the other as incarnating "the double property of the human being, who is at once a facticity and a transcendence" (p. 56).

Self-fulfillment and self-consciousness brought by the pleasure of satisfying one's desire, "is the death and the failure of desire" (p. 397). Indeed, its fulfillment is "its limit and its end" because "it motivates the appearance of a reflective consciousness of pleasure, . . . attention to [one's own] incarnation . . . and by the same token it is forgetful of the Other's incarnation" (p. 397).

Willingness to appropriate the other also "brings about the rupture of the reciprocity of incarnation which was precisely the proper goal of desire" (translation modified, p. 398), as my body thereby "ceases to be flesh and becomes again the synthetic instrument which I am. And by the same token the Other ceases to be an incarnation" (p. 398). The other becomes an object under my sight and by my action, as much as I thereby become an isolated subject exercising the power of touching the other without being myself touched.

Self-closure of the flesh reveals its "nauseous character" (p. 357) and isolates it from desire. The "pure intuition of the flesh... is the affective apprehension of an absolute contingency, and this apprehension is a particular type of *nausea*" (p. 344). While apprehending flesh as the incarnation of the other's transcendence "refers to my [own] facticity" (p. 344), apprehending the other as *pure* flesh reveals its acquaintance with the corpse, its closure upon itself, its severing from myself and from himself as "the center of reference in a situation which is synthetically organized around [him]" (p. 344). Pure flesh "falls to the level of the corpse if it ceases to be simultaneously revealed and hidden by the transcendence-transcended" (p. 348). Flesh reduced to a corpse finds no escapes from itself, no openness toward the other, no other flesh to encounter through the language of desire.

Obscenity prevails when the body is entirely cut away from the world of desire and cannot excite desire, i.e. when the body is stripped of its acts, thereby exhibiting "the inertia of its flesh" whose movements occur as "a pure obedience to the laws of weight" (p. 401). Such body is not engaged and justified by the situation it participates in. This "unjustifiable facticity" is thus "isolated in the body" and has the "passivity of a thing" (p. 401). Severed from its situatedness into the world and from its openness to the other, the flesh is obscene: a facticity which is "super-abundant relative to the effective presence which the situation demands" (translation modified, p. 402), and which obstructs one's engagement in the world, including one's surrendering to the world of desire where to encounter an other.

If encountering the other is bound to fail, one may abandon any attempt "to realize any union with the Other" (p. 410). This implies a "fundamental resignation" (p. 410) which may manifest itself as a hate of the other, a project of the death of the other. Again, that failure of desire is not contingent:

> what I hate in the Other is not this appearance, this fault, this particular action. What I hate is his existence in general as a transcendence-transcended.... hate is the hate of all Others in one Other. What I want to attain symbolically by pursuing the death of a particular Other is the general principle of the existence of others.
>
> (p. 411)

Hate of the other is abhorrence of oneself, a wish "to get rid of [one's] own inapprehensible being-as-object-for-the-Other and to abolish [one's] dimension of alienation. This is equivalent to projecting the realization of a world in which the Other does not exist" (p. 410). What starts to appear here is that it is only in the chiasmatic encounter with another that one can inhabit a world of desire which gives hospitality to the other and which departs from obscenity, nausea, control, murder. In other terms, it is by making separated terms inseparable that one is a responsible being. Not only is the other "on principle inapprehensible" (p. 408) but also encountering the other through language—including through the caress as the language of desire—is my responsibility. Sartre insists on my own responsibility for myself: my facticity is "totally unjustifiable" but I am "totally responsible" (p. 309) for it. "In particular I feel myself touched by the Other in my factual existence; it is my being-there-for-others for which I am responsible. This being-there is precisely the body" (p. 351). But the other does not only annihilate the supremacy of my subjectivity by taking me as an object paralyzed at the tip of his gaze. Rather, being responsible for myself, i.e., being responsible for my being for others, is being responsible for the others' being as the incarnation of the "double property of the human being, who is at once a facticity and a transcendence" (p. 56). Through the investigation of the manner in which the body is structured like a language, it appears here that to incarnate one's own transcendence, without corrupting it, is to surrender to one's flesh, through the desire of others' flesh; it is to desire the other as flesh, incarnation of his transcendence; it is to desire the other as a subject in the assumption of the incarnation of his own transcendence, a transcendence bound to remain "omnipresent and inapprehensible" (p. 270). One's responsibility for others, therefore, is tied to the very structure of the body as a structure of language.

**Unfaithfulness**

Any reader of Sartre will have recognized that the reading I am proposing here is not entirely faithful. The very idea that the body is structured like a language, and the manner in which I have chosen to unfold it here, is not a thesis Sartre himself has defended explicitly. The view that I've worked on here ends up partly agreeing with other authors with whom Sartre would have disagreed. And yet, this reading is also faithful to Sartre, at least because it abundantly relies on his text itself. The very idea that the body is structured like a language is in full agreement with his own consideration that "I do not know my language any more than I know my body for the Other. . . . The problem of language is exactly parallel to the problem of bodies, and the description which is valid in one case is valid in the other" (p. 374). Granted, extracting quotes, even numerous and lengthy quotes, can never give any proof of faithfulness. My faithfulness to Sartre's own words is in and on itself unfaithful at least because different aspects of his philosophy are highlighted differently in his own writing and here. But this way of reading a philosopher may be nothing else than the enaction of the structural multi-vociferation of language by which it unceasingly escapes any *one*.

## Note

1 Tr. modified. "Du seul fait que, quoi que je fasse, mes actes librement conçus et exécutés, mes projets vers mes possibilités ont dehors un sens qui m'échappe et que j'éprouve, je *suis* langage" (p. 413). All references in this text are from Sartre, J.-P. *Being and Nothingness: An Essay on Phenomenological Ontology.* Tr. Hazel E. Barnes. London: Routledge (1969).

# 18 Basic forms of pre-reflective self-consciousness

A developmental perspective

*Anna Ciaunica*

**Introduction**

The notion of pre-reflective self-consciousness is usually characterized both in terms of (i) subjective "feel," i.e., the idea that experiences have a certain phenomenological quality or "what it is like for the subject" to have them; and (ii) "mineness" or "for-me-ness" (Zahavi 2005; Kriegel 2009), i.e., the idea that all the experiences are implicitly given as my experiences. According to a longstanding phenomenological tradition (Husserl, Sartre, Merleau-Ponty, Henry) our experiences are not given to us neutrally, in the sense that they can be anyone's experiences. Whenever we consciously perceive something or feel an emotion, these perceptions and feelings are somehow given to us as our own. This immediate and first-personal givenness of experiential phenomena is accounted for in terms of a pre-reflective self-consciousness. In what follows, I am mainly concerned with the notion of "mineness" or "for-me-ness" that characterizes pre-reflective awareness, namely the idea that it is *I* who is having these experiences. Most accounts describe "for-me-ness" in terms of first-person givenness of experience that is subsumed under the notion of "minimal self-consciousness" or "minimal self." Recently, a growing number of authors (Gallagher 2000; Sass and Parnas 2003; Metzinger 2004; Zahavi 2005; Cermolacce et al. 2007; Hohwy 2007; Mishara 2007; Blanke and Metzinger 2009) defended several versions of the "for-me-ness" thesis, i.e., the idea that our everyday phenomenology is characterized by a pre-reflective sense of self, referred to as the "minimal" or the "core" self.[1] Despite significant disagreements, these authors share the important assumption that pre-reflective self-consciousness is an on-going and more primitive self-consciousness. Yet, it is not clear whether this "on-going" dynamic aspect refers exclusively to a self-centered continuity or encompasses self–other relatedness as well. Here I defend the idea that, at the most primitive level, pre-reflective self-awareness might be experienced as other-relatedness rather than self-centered or first-personal "for-*me*-ness."

This chapter is set up as follows. In the first section I give a brief overview of current attempts to define the notion of "pre-reflective self-consciousness" in terms of "for-me-ness" and suggest that it is preferable to place the investigation of pre-reflective forms of self-awareness at the outset of development. The next section highlights the crucial role of *bodily* self-awareness and bodily actions in constituting the pre-reflective foundations of self-awareness and argues that implicit self-awareness in infancy is rooted in intermodal perception and action (Rochat and Striano 2000). Then I introduce the notion of *bodily coupling* in early social interactions and review empirical studies supporting the idea that, before developing self-reflecting abilities, infants rely on basic sensorimotor, perceptual, and affective capacities which allow them to become interactively (i.e., relationally) involved with and not only neutral onlookers of others' behavior. In the final section I summon recent empirical work on the distinction between visual versus social perspective taking (Moll and Kadipasaoglu 2013) in order to argue that self-apprehension through others' eyes (based on a visuo-spatial model of perspective taking) is *not* the most primitive form of self–other relatedness. Prior to developing a reflective mode on oneself (around 18 months), infants are pre-reflectively aware of being the focus of someone's attention, although not as an object of others' visual awareness, but rather as co-subject of a co-attended experience, or co-awareness (Rochat 2004).

## What is pre-reflective self-consciousness?

Philosophers usually start with the intuitive idea of reflecting upon our inner experiences: for example, I can introspect what I am experiencing right now while drinking my coffee. I can also recognize myself in a mirror and reflect aloud "this face is mine." Hence, one convenient way of defining the notion of *pre-reflective* self-consciousness is by contrasting it with *reflective* self-consciousness, which occurs, for instance, whenever one reflectively introspects one's on-going experiences or during explicit self-recognition of one's face in the mirror. In contrast, pre-reflective self-consciousness does not involve any form of high-order self-consciousness, or self-monitoring. Pre-reflective self-consciousness is pre-reflective in the sense that:

> (1) it is an awareness we have before we do any reflecting on our experience; (2) it is an implicit and first-order awareness rather than an explicit or higher-order form of self-consciousness. Indeed, an explicit reflective self-consciousness is possible only because there is a pre-reflective self-awareness that is an on-going and more primary self-consciousness.
> (Zahavi and Gallagher 2010)

Importantly, as Sartre put the point, pre-reflective self-consciousness should not be regarded as an extra layer added to the on-going experience; rather it ontologically constitutes the very mode of being of the experience: "This self-consciousness we ought to consider not as a new consciousness, but as the only mode of existence which is possible for a consciousness of something" (Sartre 1943, p. 20 [1956, p. liv]).

Despite important disagreement on crucial questions about whether there is an ego or self, phenomenologists are in close agreement about the idea that the experiential dimension always involves this kind of implicit, pre-reflective self-awareness. One can get a bearing on the phenomenological notion of pre-reflective self-consciousness by contrasting it with the notion defended by Brentano. According to Brentano (1874/1973), when I perceive a cat, I am aware that I am perceiving a cat. Importantly, he acknowledges that I do not have here two distinct mental states, but one single mental phenomenon: my consciousness of the cat is one and the same as my awareness of perceiving it. But by means of this unified mental state, I have an awareness of two objects: the cat and my perceptual experience. Now, Sartre famously disagreed on this point, as did Husserl, Heidegger, and, more recently, Zahavi (2005). In their view, my awareness of my experience is not an awareness of it as an object, in the sense that I cannot endorse the perspective of an external observer or spectator. In pre-reflective self-awareness, experience is given not as an object, but as a fundamentally *first-personal* subjective experience.

Another point of contention in the contemporary philosophy of mind concerns the understanding of the intransitive use of the term "conscious." Indeed, one can distinguish between the transitive and the intransitive use of the term "conscious." For example, one can speak of our being conscious *of* something. Or we can speak of our being conscious *simpliciter* (rather than non-conscious). For the past three decades, a highly influential view in analytical philosophy of mind and cognitive sciences was to account for the intransitive use of the term "conscious" by means of some kind of higher-order theory (Carruthers 1996; Rosenthal 1997). For these authors, the presence/absence of a relevant meta-mental state was supposed to serve as a criterion in distinguishing conscious/unconscious mental states. Phenomenologists disagree and explicitly deny that self-consciousness that is present while experiencing something is a kind of higher-order self-monitoring. As Sartre wrote, "a consciousness has no need at all of a reflecting [higher-order] consciousness in order to be conscious of itself. It simply does not posit itself as an object" (Sartre 1936, p. 29 [1957, p. 45]). In other words, pre-reflective consciousness is an intrinsic feature of the primary experience and does not stand in a transitive relation to the state of which it is aware. To give a full and detailed account of his views on this topic would require a substantial digression. For present purposes, it is sufficient to note that those philosophers who are inclined to claim that one attains self-consciousness only if one can conceive of oneself (i.e., has the linguistic ability to use the first-person pronoun "I" to refer to oneself) are also committed to the idea that infants are not capable of self-consciousness (Dennett 1976; Carruthers 1996).

However, as will become clear throughout this chapter, evidence from developmental studies challenges these views and supports the idea that self-consciousness does not depend on the acquisition of concepts and language. Rather, there is a basic proprioceptive form of self-consciousness already in place from birth. This primitive self-awareness may serve as a basis for more sophisticated and demanding types of self-consciousness (Butterworth 1995; Gibson 1966; Stern 1985; Neisser 1988; Meltzoff 1990). Importantly, these empirical findings are consistent with the phenomenological views according to which "it is the non-reflective consciousness which renders the reflection possible" (Sartre 1943, p. 20 [1956, p. liii]). Now, it is not my intention here to develop the phenomenological approach in detail. In this chapter I will simply assume that phenomenologists are right in stressing the primacy of pre-reflective forms of self-awareness. However, as I shall argue, while phenomenologists typically explore pre-reflective self-consciousness from an individualistic perspective, this chapter aims to highlight instead its irreducibly relational nature. Before I delve deeper into my argumentation, some methodological clarification is in order.

First, this chapter builds on the idea that if one wants to get a clear grasp of the notion of "for-me-ness" or "minimal self" at the basic pre-reflective level, a good place to start looking would be the developmental perspective. Examining the notion of pre-reflective self-consciousness from a developmental angle proves instructive for at least two reasons. First, doing so usefully helps us to address this phenomenon within a truly dynamic perspective. Indeed, clarifying what really lies at the primitive basic level of pre-reflective self-awareness in young children might be useful in examining how the full-blown reflective self-consciousness arises from more basic forms of self-awareness. Second, and more importantly, assessing infants' understanding of their own self-awareness provides not only a snapshot of the developing self-consciousness of the child, but also a panorama of the very nature of consciousness itself.

Second, the standard procedure of defining pre-reflective self-conscious ness by contrasting it with the reflective, more sophisticated forms of self-consciousness might be misleading since it fails to capture the dynamic nature of the more basic forms of pre-reflective self-awareness. It is widely agreed that pre-reflective self-consciousness is an on-going and more primitive self-consciousness. Yet, it is not clear whether this "on-going" dynamic aspect refers exclusively to a self-centered continuity or encompasses self–other relatedness as well. The overarching aim here is to argue that privileging a visual-based perspective in examining the self–other relatedness might have unexpected and misleading consequences in understanding basic forms of pre-reflective self-awareness. Indeed, prior to developing a reflective-mode on oneself (around 18 months), infants are pre-reflectively aware of being the focus of someone's attention, although not as an object of others' visual awareness, but rather as co-subject of a co-attended experience, or co-awareness (Rochat 2004). With these terminological clarifications and introductory elements in our pocket, let us now turn to our main concern here, namely the investigation of primitive or basic forms of pre-reflective self-awareness from a developmental perspective.

## The pre-reflective bodily foundations of for-me-ness

As I mentioned in the introductory section, it is customary to define the notion of pre-reflective self-consciousness by contrasting it with its reflective, more elaborated forms. However, taking the "reflective" component as a criterion in defining more primitive forms of self-awareness tacitly endorses an overly mentalistic perspective and might fail to capture the role of *bodily awareness* in constituting pre-reflective self-consciousness. Indeed, the "how it feels of experience" does not occur in a vacuum. "For-me-ness" is embodied. Embodiment refers to the fact that the experiences I am living through are given to me through my body, an organism situated in a particular space–time context. It could consequently be claimed that anybody who denies the embodied aspect of "for-me-ness" of experience simply fails to recognize an essential, constitutive aspect of human experience. Crucially, bodily self-awareness is not an awareness of the body in passive isolation from the world. It is the awareness of an *active* body exploring the environment. Indeed, both Husserl and Merleau-Ponty insisted on the idea that pre-reflective self-awareness is both embodied and embedded in the world. Consequently, recent years have seen a flood of research into self-consciousness with increased interest in its bodily foundations (Bermúdez et al. 1995; Gallagher 2005). The main challenge consists in understanding the pre-reflective bodily foundations of minimal phenomenal selfhood, i.e., all those components which are independent of explicit cognition and linguistic abilities, and which give rise to the subjective experience of being a self. These pre-reflective bodily foundations can function as an enabling condition for a reflection-based first-person perspective and sophisticated high-level social cognition (Baker 1998; Bermúdez 1998; Metzinger 2004).

For example, research focusing on minimal forms of phenomenal selfhood (Blanke and Metzinger 2009) insisted on the idea that minimal phenomenal self-consciousness is not a static internal snapshot of some mysterious substance called the "self," but only on-going processes of tracking and controlling bodily properties as a whole. There is wide agreement on the idea that bodily awareness contributes to the development of a pre-reflective sense of self and self-awareness. However, it has been argued (Smith 2010) that one cannot give a clear account of the unified space of egocentric perception or "for-me-ness" without taking seriously into consideration the role of bodily *movements* in spatial perception. In other words, the best way to understand an egocentric perceptual field is in terms of the perceiver's dispositions for bodily *actions*. Crucially, the action possibilities in a perceiver's environment are specified *relationally*, that is, both by particular features of the environment and things in it, as well as the repertoire of sensorimotor capacities the perceiver employs to detect and respond to these structural features. According to this relational way of thinking, there is mutuality between perceiver and environment. Perception and action are fundamentally interwoven (Gibson 1979). The important claim is that, even at the most basic level of minimal forms of phenomenal selfhood, subjective experience involves more than passive embodiment. All of this, however, serves as introductory remarks. Let me now turn to the discussion of whether the minimal "for-me-ness" which constitutes pre-reflective self-awareness is already relational as well.

In the next section I review empirical studies supporting the idea that, before developing reflective abilities, infants rely on basic bodily sensorimotor capacities that allow them to enter into genuinely *relational engagements* with caregivers. It is crucial for my argumentation to make clear the idea that this set of sensorimotor, perceptual, and affective capacities allows infants to become *interactively* (i.e., relationally) involved with, and not just externally (i.e., *visually*) *observers* of, others. The section on Bodily coupling in early social interactions is thus designed to prepare the ground carefully for the introduction, in the section on Seeing onself through the eyes of others, of the important distinction between visual versus social perspective taking. The overall aim is to provide evidence supporting the idea that (i) at the most primitive level pre-reflective self-awareness might be characterized as other-relatedness rather than self-centered "for-*me*-ness"; and that (ii) self-alienation through others (Sartre 1943) is developmentally preceded by self-realization through others (de Haan 2010).

## Bodily coupling in early social interactions

As I previously mentioned, the standard way to cash out the notion of pre-reflective self-awareness is in terms of first-person perspective, or as I suggested here, "embodied for-me-ness." In what follows I shall argue that, if one wants to get a clear grasp of the notion of "minimal self" or minimal "embodied for-me-ness," a good place to start investigating is the developmental approach. Indeed, what could be more "minimal" than infants' pre-reflective self-awareness? There are at least two good and inseparable reasons to place the investigation of pre-reflective self-consciousness at the outset of development, that is long before the emergence of language and explicit self-consciousness. First, recent evidence has been mounting to suggest that infants have much more sophisticated social-cognitive skills than previously suspected. A sizeable literature has illustrated that, before their first birthday, preverbal human infants not only understand what goals others have (Gergely et al. 1995; Carpenter et al. 1998) and what preferences others have (Repacholi and Gopnik 1997); they also track what others know, in the sense of what they have and have not *experienced* in the immediate past (Moll and Tomasello 2007). Moreover, several studies have illustrated that infants already discriminate between objects and agents (Ellsworth et al. 1993). Importantly, infants' understanding of others is more robust within *interactive* contexts (Moll et al. 2008; Királ y 2009). In other words, the more engaged the infant/agent interactions are, the more robust the infants' understanding of others becomes. Furthermore, goal-relatedness is differently perceived by infants in social versus physical event configurations (Woodward et al. 2001; Sommerville and Woodward 2010). As we shall see in the next section, these findings are closely related to recent studies suggesting the primacy of social versus visual perspective taking.

Second, from birth infants are not merely *passive* receptors of internal/external stimulation, but *actors* in a meaningful environment (Rochat 1998; Rochat and Striano 2000). For example, a classic debate within developmental literature strived to elucidate whether infants are initially more sensitive to *internal* or to *external* stimuli. In other words, the main concern was: how does an infant develop awareness of and come to represent the cues of sets of internal states? On the one hand, it has been hypothesized the infants' initial state is characterized by direct introspective access to *proprioceptive* feelings, and that they have conscious access to their basic internal emotion states from the beginning of life (Mahler et al. 1975). On the other hand, theorists such as Gergely and Watson (1999) argued that at the beginning of life "the perceptual system is set with a bias to attend to and explore the external world and builds representations primarily on the basis of *exteroceptive* stimuli" (Gergely and Watson 1999, p. 110; emphasis added). These disputes have been abundantly discussed in the literature and the details will not be pursued here. For the moment, suffice it to note that these debates insisted on the role of bodily receptive stimulation (internal versus external) and overlooked the role of the active, relational engagement between infant and caregivers. Indeed, as Gibson (1979) pointed out, perceiving and acting in the environment consist in co-perceiving oneself as perceiver and actor. This means that information about the self accompanies information about the environment. Put otherwise, proprioception accompanies exteroception like the other side of a coin.

Within the past three decades, the previously dominant paradigm of the "radically egocentric" and "solipsistic" newborn (Piaget 1954; Mahler et al. 1975) has been vigorously challenged on the basis of empirical findings suggesting that infants possess an innate *social* competence. Indeed, since the work by C. Trevarthen (1979), much emphasis has been placed on the notion of "primary intersubjectivity," i.e., a set of emotional, perceptual, and sensorimotor capacities that allow the infant to interact meaningfully with others via pre-linguistic bodily mediated "protoconversations" (Trevarthen 1993; Hobson 2002; Meltzoff and Brooks 2007; Reddy 2008). These early intersubjective skills are rooted in pre-reflective matching of movements, gestures, and facial expressions (Merleau-Ponty 1945/1962; Meltzoff and Moore 1977), i.e., capacities that ontogenetically predate more sophisticated theory-of-mind reflective abilities (Premack and Woodruff 1978).

Indeed, long before infants develop the linguistic and representational abilities needed to explain/predict the mental states of another, neonates comprehend another's gestures, facial expressions, emotions, and intentions as *socially salient* (Hobson 2002). As Trevarthen (1979) insightfully argued, human babies are born with the ability to generate shifting states of self-awareness, to show them to others, and to provoke interest and affectionate response from them. Research on affect attunement (Stern 1985), neonate imitation (Meltzoff and Moore 1977), and gaze following (Senju and Csibra 2008) supports the idea of a strong *bodily coupling*[2] between infant/caregiver. The basic claim is that the infant perceptually gears on to synchronous *coupled interactions* with the caregiver (Krueger 2011; Varga and Krueger 2013). To put it in a slogan: "the developmental power is in the coupling" (Sheya and Smith 2010, p. 125).

An example might help us to see this point more clearly. In a well-known experiment, Murray and Trevarthen (1985) proposed an experimental set-up in which a baby and a mother interact via video. In the test condition, the live video of the mother that the baby sees is replaced by a video of the mother from an earlier sequence in the interaction. The researchers found that this upsets the baby just as much as if the mother's face suddenly went blank i.e., the "still face" condition (Tronick et al. 1978), and no longer expressing anything. As Krueger and Michael (2012) rightly point out, this suggests that the baby is interested not just in the mother's expressiveness, but in being *coupled* with her, that is, in mutually exchanging with and influencing her reactions, which in turn shape the baby's own responses, and so on and so forth.

This sensorimotor synchronization of bodily coupling between infant/caregiver supports the formation of interpersonal bonds. Indeed, from the start, infants process a rudimentary sensorimotor understanding of how modulations of bodily movements and attentional focusing affect sensory change. Sensorimotor understanding is the implicit, pre-reflective understanding that we, as embodied agents, possess the sensorimotor skills needed to secure experiential access to different relevant features of the world, by using our bodily movements in appropriate ways. Babies are highly skilled perceivers in this sense. Especially significant are the *emotion-expressing bodily movements*, i.e., smiles, frowns, pouts, intent or "interested" focusing of seeing (Oster 2005), with shifting of seeing and hearing by turns of the head, and hand and feet movements carefully modulated by attention to experiences of holding and touching (Trevarthen 1986; Adamson-Macedo 2004). It is crucial for my argumentation here to point out that such bodily movements are not only tailored to sustain the flow of an emerging self-awareness, but may demonstrate self-regulations of movement "publicly," anticipating others' response. Newborns, in addition to very remarkable bodily expressive capacities, show (i) a predisposition for face-related stimuli (Mondloch et al. 1999; Bushnell 2001) and (ii) preferences for responding to many forms of human signal: certain tastes and odors; felt, heard, or seen cadences of movement; forms, colors, or sounds that identify persons, especially a responsive and sympathetic caregiver (Zeifman et al. 1996; Blass 1999). With this in mind, let us now return to our discussion of basic forms of pre-reflective self-consciousness.

Up to this point, I have argued that the standard way to cash out the notion of pre-reflective self-awareness is in terms of first-person perspective, or as I have suggested here, "embodied for-me-ness." I then defended the idea that even at the most basic level of minimal forms of phenomenal selfhood, subjective experience involves more than passive embodiment, but encompasses also dispositions for bodily *actions*. Indeed, we are responsively attuned to different action possibilities in our immediate environment. I have also claimed that, if we want to get a clear grasp of the notion of "minimal self" or "embodied for-me-ness," a good place to start looking is the developmental approach, by investigating the crucial role of bodily coupling in early infant/caregiver dyadic interactions. I provided evidence illustrating that, when we engage with others, there is a pre-reflective layer of implicit bodily coupling at work involving involuntarily synchronizing by the mimicking of the gestures, facial and bodily expressions of others. This automatic motor mimicry acts as an implicit, pre-reflective kind of "social glue" (Chartrand and Bargh 1999). Now, the important question is: how are these developmental findings supposed to help us in understanding pre-reflective forms of self-consciousness? In what follows I argue that if Trevarthen (1979) is right in emphasizing the fact that human babies are born to generate shifting states of self-awareness and to show them to other persons in order to *relate* to others, then an obvious philosophical question to ask is whether the standard understanding of pre-reflective self-awareness in terms of minimal self or for-me-ness doesn't leave a lacuna. In other words, are there pre-reflective, basic forms of sociality or relatedness constitutive of the formation and the development of selfhood?

The next section addresses these questions and suggests that, before developing an awareness of self and other as being two *objects* of each other's *visual* perception, infants rely on a different type of awareness, namely *co-awareness* (Rochat 2004)—one in which the self and other are experienced as co-subjects of a shared experiential scenario. The aim is to argue that, at the most primitive level, pre-reflective self-awareness is best characterized as other-relatedness rather than self-centered or first-personal "for-*me*-ness." I turn to this discussion now.

## Seeing oneself through the eyes of others: visual versus social perspective taking

It is widely agreed that taking an outside stance towards oneself is an important developmental milestone. It is also common to claim that explicit self-consciousness is only present from the moment the child is capable of recognizing herself in the mirror (Lewis and Ramsey 2004), that is, around 18 months of age, when a child engages in self-directed behavior and manifests embarrassment when confronted with her mirror image. This hypothesis rests on the basic idea that the view others have of us functions as a social "mirror" through which the child becomes aware of herself. However, as we shall shortly see, the usual expression—to *see* oneself through the *eyes* of others—is highly misleading when examining more primitive forms of pre-reflective self-awareness, since at the basic level, the self–other relatedness is not experienced in this visual perspective-taking fashion.

Take, for example, Sartre's famous analysis of shame, in which he points out that, in experiencing shame, I am revealed to myself as existing for and *visible* to others. My being-for-others is characterized as an external dimension of being and he speaks of the existential alienation provoked by my encounter with the other (Sartre 1943, p. 287). Importantly, in Sartre's account, to apprehend myself from the perspective of the other is to apprehend myself as an object among other things with features that are independent of my will. The primary experience of the other is not that I perceive her as some kind of object in which I must find a person. Rather I perceive the other as subject who perceives *me* as an *object*. My experience of the other is an experience that involves my own self-consciousness, that is, a self-consciousness in which I am pre-reflectively aware that I am an *object* for another. In what follows, I question this idea of one's "visibility" through others' perceptual awareness and argue that this type of self-apprehension through others' eyes (based on a visuo-spatial model of perspective taking) is *not* the most primitive form of self–other relatedness. Indeed, long before infants start to become aware of others' attention, they promptly engage in complex interactions in which they act not as *objects* of others' visual attention or evaluation, but rather as *co-subjects* of a shared or co-attended experiential scenario. Of course, this is not to deny the importance of adopting the perspective of the other and thereby gaining sufficient self-distance to allow a critical self-questioning. This performance occurs rather late in development, however, and is highly dependent on more primitive forms of self–other relatedness. Since so much of my argumentation hangs on the distinction between visual versus social perspective taking, it is worth going over familiar ground carefully in preparation for my argument.

It is generally taken for granted that perceptual perspective taking precedes and serves as a basis for the more complex or "deeper" forms of social perspective taking (Kessler and Thomson 2010). Social perspective taking is a set of manifold abilities which help infants to establish reference against the background of prior social interactions. Importantly, most discussions of perceptual experience take *vision* as the paradigm case of perceiving. Recently, this view has been challenged by a number of empirical studies illustrating that visual perspective taking does not ontogenetically precede but follows *social* perspective taking. In a recent paper, Moll and

Kadipasaoglu (2013) convincingly argued in favor of the developmental primacy of social over visual perspective taking. These theorists argue that knowledge of visual perspective taking is a relatively late cognitive achievement that is derivative of social perspective taking. In their view, children first learn to take perspective in situations that are *not* defined by differences in how self and other perceive agents and objects *visually*, but by differences in their *experiential* backgrounds, i.e., in what they did, witnessed, or heard. Indeed, before children can develop an "awareness of what exactly is seen or how an object appears from a particular *viewpoint*, they must learn to share attention and build common *experiential* ground (Moll and Kadipasaoglu 2013, p. 1; emphasis added).

An example might help us to make this point clear. Moll and colleagues (2010) compared 2-year-olds' ability to detect an adult's ignorance due to absence versus impeded vision. They found that when the adult disengaged entirely from her interaction with the child by leaving after having shared two toys with her, the children later knew that the adult was unfamiliar with a third object that they were presented with. But when the adult remained co-present, with her visual access to the third object blocked by a barrier as the child explored it, the children later acted as if the adult was familiar with this object. They failed to recognize the effect of the barrier. These robust findings suggest that infants readily note and update "experiential records" (Perner and Roessler 2012). They have a "general bias to point out what is mutually familiar and *unifies self and other* in prior bouts of shared experiences" (Moll and Kadipasaoglu 2013, p. 2; emphasis added). It is crucial for my argumentation here to insist on the idea that learning about others' as well as one's own "snapshot" perspectives in a literal, i.e., *optical*, sense of the term, is a secondary step in development. In order to discern or establish reference, infants rely on prior joint perceptual experiences at least 1 year before they take into account others' visuo-spatial relations to the things around them. This is consistent with the idea that, before developing an awareness of self and other as being two objects of each other's perceptual awareness (i.e., in a visuo-spatial perspective-taking fashion), infants rely on a different type of awareness, i.e., *co-awareness* (Rochat 2004), one in which the self and other are experiencing their mutual engagement as second-personal co-subjectivity rather than as a self-centered first-personal subjectivity. Co-awareness refers to the ability to be co-aware of the attitudes and experiences of others as directed toward a shared world (Hobson 2002). A shared co-subjective, i.e., second-personal, experience would be one in which the understanding that each has of the other is not of the form $<X$ perceives that $<Y$ perceives that $p>>$ and $<Y$ perceives that $<X$ perceives that $p>>$, but rather of the form $<X$ and $Y$ jointly perceive that $p>$ (Wilby 2012). Hence the participants' relation to each other is as co-subjects, not as objects of each other's attention (Wilby 2010). Indeed, the synchronous infant/adult micro-regulatory dynamics in early dyadic interactions allows both members of the interactive duo to enter into dyadic states of consciousness, that is, a state in which both infants and caregivers experience an expansion of their own state of consciousness and together form a new, shared state (Tronick et al. 1998; Tronick 2005).

We now have the tools we need to reconsider the term "pre-reflective self-consciousness" from a non-individualistic perspective. Indeed, recall that the notion of "for-me-ness" or "minimal self" (Zahavi 2005) is supposed to secure the idea that experiencing is inherently subjective (i.e., first-personal) in its very structure. However, as I have argued here, the experiencing only gets established in the doing, that is, in an embodied and socially embedded context. Our presence in the world is not individual, solipsistic, or solitary, but a fundamentally shared experience. When we engage with others, there is a pre-reflective layer of implicit bodily coupling at work through involuntarily synchronizing with the mimicking of the gestures, facial and bodily expressions of others. It is only subsequently, through repeated socially coupled interactions, that infants become capable of endorsing a detached perspective (visuo-spatial perspective taking-inspired) on their own subjective inner life. If Rochat (2004) is right in saying that, at the primitive, developmental level, self-awareness is fundamentally experienced as co-awareness, then one important corollary would be that, at the basic level, my being-for-others is *not* experienced as an external dimension of being or as an existential "alienation" provoked by my encounter with the other (Sartre 1943).

## Conclusion

I have argued here that the standard way to cash out the notion of pre-reflective self-consciousness by contrasting it with its reflective, more elaborated forms fails to capture the role of *bodily awareness* and *bodily coupling* in constituting basic forms of pre-reflective self-awareness in early infancy. I have summoned recent developmental findings on the primacy of social versus visual perspective taking to support the idea that, at the basic level, pre-reflective self-awareness is experienced first and foremost as other-relatedness rather than self-centered or first-personal "for-*me*-ness." Indeed, infants rely on basic bodily sensorimotor capacities that allow them to become *interactively* (i.e., relationally) involved with, and not just neutrally (i.e., *visually*) *observers* of others. This suggests, against Sartre (1943), that my-being-for-others is *not* primarily experienced as an external dimension of being or as an existential "alienation" or as an experience in which I am pre-reflectively aware that I am a *visible object* for another. Rather than two distinct objects of each other's visual awareness, my-being-for-others is primarily experienced as *co-awareness*, i.e., an essentially shared dimension of being (Rochat 2004). Hence, privileging a visuo-spatial perspective in examining the self–other relatedness might have unexpected and misleading consequences in understanding basic forms of pre-reflective self-awareness.

## Notes

1 There is much debate over the appropriate understanding of the notion of self. This is not the place to undertake a comprehensive review of the literature (see Gallagher 2013 for a recent analysis).
2 The notion of "coupling" draws upon dynamical system theory and stipulates that two systems can be said to be coupled when "the conduct of each is a function of the conduct of the other" (Thompson 2007, p. 45; see also Spivey 2007).

## Bibliography

Adamson-Macedo, E. N. (2004). Neo-haptic Touch. In R. L. Gregory, Ed. *Oxford Companion to the Mind*, 2nd ed. (pp. 637–639). Oxford: Oxford University Press.

Baker, L. R. (1998). The First-person Perspective: A Test for Naturalism. *American Philosophical Quarterly* 35: pp. 327–346.

Bermúdez, J. L. (1998). *The Paradox of Self-Consciousness*. Cambridge, MA: MIT Press.

Bermúdez, J., Marcel, A., and Eilan, N., Eds. (1995). *The Body and the Self*. Cambridge, MA: MIT/Bradford Press.

Blanke, O., and Metzinger, T. (2009). Full-body Illusions and Minimal Phenomenal Selfhood. *Trends in Cognitive Sciences* 13(1): pp. 7–13.

Blass, E. M. (1999). The Ontogeny of Human Face Recognition: Orogustatory, Visual and Social Influences. In P. Rochat, Ed. *Early Social Cognition: Understanding Others in the First Months of Life* (pp. 35–65). Mahwah, NJ: Erlbaum.

Brentano, F. (1874). *Psychologie vom empirischen Standpunkt* I. Hamburg: Felix Meiner. English translation: L. L. McAlister. *Psychology from an Empirical Standpoint*. London: Routledge (1973).

Bushnell, I. W. R. (2001). Mother's Face Recognition in Newborn Infants: Learning and Memory. *Infant Child Development* 10: pp. 67–74.

Butterworth, G. (1995). An Ecological Perspective on the Origins of Self. In J. Bermúdez, A. Marcel, and N. Eilan, Eds. *The Body and the Self* (pp. 87–107). Cambridge, MA: MIT/Bradford Press.

Carpenter, M., Nagell, K., and Tomasello, M. (1998). Social Cognition, Joint Attention, and Communicative Competence from 9 to 15 months of age. *Monographs of the Society for Research in Child Development* (4, serial no. 176): p. 63.

Carruthers, P. (1996). *Language, Thoughts and Consciousness: An Essay in Philosophical Psychology*. Cambridge: Cambridge University Press.

Cermolacce, M., Naudin, J., and Parnas, J. (2007). The "Minimal Self" in Psychopathology: Re-examining the Self-disorders in the Schizophrenia Spectrum. *Consciousness and Cognition* 16(3): pp. 703–714.

Chartrand, T. L., and Bargh, J. A. (1999). The Chameleon Effect: The Perception–Behaviour Link and Social Interaction. *Journal of Personality and Social Psychology* 76: pp. 893–910.

De Haan, S. (2010). Comment: The Minimal Self Is a Social Self. In Th. Fuchs, H. Sattel, and P. Henningsen, Eds. *The Embodied Self*. Stuttgart: Schattauer.

Dennett, D. (1976). Conditions of Personhood. In A. Rorty, Ed. *The Identities of Persons* (pp. 175–196). Berkeley: University of California Press.

Ellsworth, C. P., Muir, D.W., and Hains, S. M. J. (1993). Social Competence and Person–Object Differentiation: An Analysis of the Still-face Effect. *Developmental Psychology* 29: pp. 63–73.

Gallagher, S. (2000). Philosophical Conceptions of the Self: Implications for Cognitive Science. *Trends in Cognitive Sciences* 4(1): pp. 14–21.
Gallagher, S. (2005). *How the Body Shapes the Mind.* New York: Oxford University Press.
Gallagher, S. (2013). A Pattern Theory of Self. *Frontiers in Human Neuroscience* 7 (443): pp. 1–7.
Gergely, G., and Watson, J. (1999). Early Social-emotional Development: Contingency Perception and the Social Biofeedback Model. In P. Rochat, Ed. *Early Social Cognition: Understanding Others in the First Months of Life* (pp. 101–137). Hillsdale, NJ: Erlbaum.
Gergely, G., Nadasdy, Z., Csibra, G., and Bıró, S. (1995). Taking the Intentional Stance at 12 Months of Age. *Cognition* 56: pp. 165–193.
Gibson, J.J. (1966). *The Senses Considered as Perceptual Systems.* Westport, CT: Greenwood Press.
Gibson, J.J. (1979/1986). *The Ecological Approach to Visual Perception.* Hillsdale, NJ: LEA.
Hobson, R.P. (2002). *The Cradle of Thought: Exploring the Origins of Thinking.* London: Macmillan.
Hohwy, J. (2007). The Sense of Self in the Phenomenology of Agency and Perception. *Psyche* 13(1): pp. 1–20.
Kessler, K., and Thomson, L.A. (2010). The Embodied Nature of Spatial Perspective Taking: Embodied Transformation versus Sensorimotor Interference. *Cognition* 114: pp. 72–88.
Király, I. (2009). Memories for Events in Infants: Goal-relevant Action Coding. In T. Striano and V. Reid, Eds. *Social Cognition: Development, Neuroscience and Autism.* Oxford: Wiley-Blackwell.
Kriegel, U. (2009). *Subjective Consciousness.* Oxford: Oxford University Press.
Krueger, J. (2011). Extended Cognition and the Space of Social Interaction. *Consciousness and Cognition* 20(3): pp. 643–657.
Krueger, J. and Michael, J. (2012). Gestural Coupling and Social Cognition: Möbius Syndrome as a Case Study. *Frontiers in Human Neuroscience* 6(81): pp. 1–14.
Lewis, M., and Ramsay, D. (2004). Development of Self-recognition, Personal Pronoun Use, and Pretend Play during the 2nd Year. *Child Development*, 75(6): pp. 1821–1831.
Mahler, M., Bergman, A., and Pine, F. (1975). *The Psychological Birth of the Human Infant: Symbiosis and Individuation.* New York: Basic Books.
Meltzoff, A. (1990). Foundations for Developing a Concept of Self: The Role of Imitation in Relating Self to Other and the Value of Social Mirroring, Social Modelling, and Self Practice in Infancy. In D. Cicchetti and M. Beeghly, Eds. *The Self in Transition: Infancy to Childhood* (pp. 139–164). Chicago, IL: University of Chicago Press.
Meltzoff, A., and Brooks, R. (2007). Intersubjectivity before Language: Three Windows on Preverbal Sharing. In S. Braten, Ed., *On Being Moved: From Mirror Neurons to Empathy*, pp. 149–174. Philadelphia: John Benjamins.
Meltzoff, A., and Moore, M.K. (1977). Imitation of Facial and Manual Gestures by Human Neonates. *Science* 198: pp. 75–78.
Merleau-Ponty, M. (1945). *Phénoménologie de la perception.* Paris: Éditions Gallimard; English translation: C. Smith. *Phenomenology of Perception.* London: Routledge and Kegan Paul, 1962.

Metzinger, T. (2004). *Being No One: The Self-Model Theory of Subjectivity.* Cambridge, MA: MIT Press.
Mishara, A.L. (2007). Is Minimal Self Preserved in Schizophrenia? A Subcomponents View. *Consciousness and Cognition* 16(3): pp. 715–721.
Moll, H., and Kadipasaoglu, D. (2013). The Primacy of Social over Visual Perspective-taking. *Frontiers in Human Neuroscience* 7(558).
Moll, H., and Tomasello, M. (2007). How 14- and 18-Month-Olds Know What Others Have Experienced. *Developmental Psychology* 43(2): pp. 309–317.
Moll, H., Richter, N., Carpenter, M., and Tomasello, M. (2008). Fourteen-Month-Olds Know What 'We' Have Shared in a Special Way. *Infancy* 13 (1): pp. 90–101.
Moll, H., Carpenter, M., and Tomasello, T. (2010). Social Engagement Leads 2-Year-Olds to Overestimate Others. *Infancy* 16: pp. 248–265.
Mondloch, C.J., Lewis, T.L., Robert Budreau, D., Maurer, D., Dannemiller, J.L., Stephens, B.R., and Kleiner-Gathercoal, K.A. (1999). Face Perception During Early Infancy. *Psychological Science* 10: pp. 419–422.
Murray, L., and Trevarthen, C. (1985). Emotional Regulation of Interactions Between Two-Month-Olds and Their Mothers. In T. M. Field and N. A. Fox, Eds. *Social Perception in Infants*, pp. 177–197. Norwood, NJ: Ablex Publishers.
Neisser, U. (1988). Five Kinds of Self-Knowledge. *Philosophical Psychology* 1(1): pp. 35–59.
Oster, H. (2005). The Repertoire of Infant Face Expressions: An Ontogenetic Perspective. In J. Nadel and D. Muir, Eds. *Emotional Development* (pp. 261–292). Oxford: Oxford University Press.
Perner, J., and Roessler, J. (2012). From Infants' to Children's Appreciation of Belief. *Trends in Cognitive Science* 16: pp. 519–525.
Piaget, J. (1954/1981). *Intelligence and Affectivity: Their Relation during Child Development.* Palo Alto, CA: Annual Reviews.
Premack, D., and Woodruff, G. (1978). Does the Chimpanzee Have a Theory of Mind? *The Behavioral and Brain Sciences* 1: pp. 515–526.
Reddy, V. (2008). *How Infants Know Minds.* Cambridge, MA: Harvard University Press.
Repacholi, B.M., and Gopnik, A. (1997). Early Reasoning about Desires: Evidence from 14- and 18-Month-Olds. *Developmental Psychology* 3: pp. 12–21.
Rochat, P. (1998). Self-perception and Action in Infancy. *Experimental Brain Research* 123: pp. 102–109.
Rochat, P. (2004). The Emergence of Self-awareness as Co-awareness in Early Development. In D. Zahavi and T. Grünbaum, Eds. *The Structure and Development of Self-Consciousness* (pp. 1–20). Amsterdam: John Benjamins.
Rochat, P. and Striano, T. (2000). Perceived Self in Infancy. *Infant Behavior and Development* 23(3–4): pp. 513–530.
Rosenthal, D.M. (1997). A Theory of Consciousness. In N. Block, O. Flanagan, and G. Güzeldere, Eds. *The Nature of Consciousness* (pp. 729–753). Cambridge, MA: MIT Press.
Sartre, J.-P. (1936). *La transcendance de l'ego.* Paris: Vrin; English translation: F. Williams and R. Kirkpatrick, *The Transcendence of the Ego.* New York: The Noonday Press (1957).
Sartre, J.-P. (1943). *L'Etre et le néant.* Paris: Tel Gallimard; English translation: H. E. Barnes, *Being and Nothingness.* New York: Philosophical Library (1956).

Sass, L.A., and Parnas, J. (2003). Schizophrenia, Consciousness, and the Self. *Schizophrenia Bulletin* 29(3): pp. 427–444.
Senju, A., and Csibra, G. (2008). Gaze Following in Human Infants Depends on Communicative Signals. *Current Biology* 18: pp. 668–671.
Sheya, A. and Smith, Linda B. (2010). Development through Sensorimotor Coordination. In J. Stewart, O. Gapenne, and E. Di Paolo, Eds. *Enaction: Toward a New Paradigm for Cognitive Science.* Cambridge, MA: MIT Press.
Smith, A.J.T. (2010). Comment: Minimal Conditions for the Simplest Form of Self-Consciousness. In Th. Fuchs, H. Sattel, and P. Henningsen, P., Eds. *The Embodied Self.* Stuttgart: Schattauer.
Sommerville, J.A. and Woodward, A. (2010). The Link between Action Production and Action Processing in Infancy. In F. Grammont, D. Legrand, and P. Livet, Eds. *Naturalizing Intention in Action.* Cambridge, MA: MIT Press.
Spivey, M. (2007). *The Continuity of Mind.* Oxford: Oxford University Press.
Stern, D. (1985). *Interpersonal World of the Infant.* New York: Basic Books.
Thompson, E. (2007). *Mind in Life: Biology, Phenomenology, and the Sciences of Mind.* Cambridge, MA: Harvard University Press.
Trevarthen, C. (1979). Communication and Cooperation in Early Infancy: A Description of Primary Intersubjectivity. In M. Bullowa, Ed. *Before Speech: The Beginning of Interpersonal Communication* (pp. 321–347). Cambridge: Cambridge University Press.
Trevarthen, C. (1986). Development of Intersubjective Motor Control in Infants. In M.G. Wade and H.T.A. Whiting, Eds. *Motor Development in Children: Aspects of Coordination and Control* (pp. 209–261). Dordrecht: Martinus Nijhoff.
Trevarthen, C. (1993). The Self Born in Intersubjectivity: An Infant Communicating. In U. Neisser, Ed. *The Perceived Self: Ecological and Interpersonal Sources of Self-Knowledge* (pp. 121–173). New York: Cambridge University Press.
Tronick, E. (2005). Why Is Connection with Others so Critical? The Formation of Dyadic States of Consciousness and the Expansion of Individuals' States of Consciousness: Coherence Governed Selection and the Co-creation of Meaning Out of Messy Meaning Making. In J. Nadel and D. Muir, Eds. *Emotional Development: Recent Research Advances* (pp. 293–316). Oxford: Oxford University Press.
Tronick, E.Z., Als, H., Adamson, L., Wise, S., and Brazelton, T.B. (1978). The Infant's Response to Entrapment Between Contradictory Messages in Face-to-Face Interaction. *Journal of the American Academy of Child Psychiatry* 17: pp. 1–13.
Tronick, E.Z., Bruschweiler-Stern, N., Harrison, A.M., Lyons-Ruth, K., Morgan, A.C., Nahum, J.P., Sander, L., and Stern, D.N. (1998). Dyadically Expanded States of Consciousness and the Process of Therapeutic Change. *Infant Mental Health Journal* 19: 290–299.
Varga, S. and Krueger, J. (2013). Background Emotions, Proximity, and Distributed Emotion Regulation. *The Review of Philosophy and Psychology* 4(2): pp. 271–292.
Wilby, M. (2010). The Simplicity of Mutual Knowledge. *Philosophical Explorations* 13(2): pp. 83–100.
Wilby, M. (2012). Embodying the False-Belief Tasks. *Phenomenology and the Cognitive Sciences*, Special Issue: Debates on Embodied Mindreading 11: pp. 519–540.
Woodward, A.L., Sommerville, J.A., and Guajardo, J.J. (2001). How Infants make Sense of Intentional Action. In B. Malle, L. Moses, and D. Baldwin, Eds. *Intentions and Intentionality: Foundations of Social Cognition.* Cambridge, MA: MIT Press.

Zahavi, D. (2005). *Subjectivity and Selfhood: Investigating the First-person Perspective.* Cambridge, MA: MIT Press.

Zahavi, D., and Gallagher, S. (2010). *Phenomenological Approaches to Self-Consciousness.* Available online at: http://plato.stanford.edu/entries/self-consciousness-phenomenological/.

Zeifman, D., Delaney, S., and Blass, E. (1996). Sweet Taste, Looking, and Calm in 2- and 4-Week-Old Infants: The Eyes Have It. *Developmental Psychology* 32: pp. 1090–1099.

# 19 Ego disorders in psychosis
## Dysfunction of pre-reflective self-awareness?

*Andreas Heinz*

### Introduction

Passivity phenomena range among the prominent core symptoms of schizophrenia and include thought insertion and blockade (APA 1994 2013; WHO 2011). In the German psychopathological tradition, Kurt Schneider (1942) called those phenomena "ego disorders" and emphasized their status as criteria for the diagnosis of schizophrenia. He insisted that such symptoms, which are reported by the patients themselves, are much more reliable signs of a schizophrenic psychosis compared to symptoms based on clinical impression, such as thought incoherence or flat affect. Indeed, prejudices and personal experiences of any examiner can substantially interfere with his or her judgment of "coherent" speech or the "depth" of any affective experience of a patient, while symptoms articulated by the patients themselves are supposed to reflect their own experiences, at least to the degree to which psychotic, unusual experiences can be translated into any common language. Schneider (1942) had named such symptoms "first-rank symptoms" of schizophrenia, and he assumed that they should guide clinical diagnosis. In a time when the diagnosis of schizophrenia meant that the patient would be sterilized against his or her will or even secretly murdered, Schneider thus suggested limiting the diagnosis of schizophrenia to patients who actively report core symptoms; while quite far from active resistance against Nazi atrocities, his call for "modesty" in diagnosing schizophrenia still resonates with a public that criticizes excessive diagnoses and pathologization of everyday human experiences.

However, a series of studies suggested that such core symptoms of schizophrenia also occur in affective disorders (Carpenter et al. 1973). Therefore, current classifications of psychotic disorders place considerably less emphasis on Schneiderian first-rank symptoms. However, Schneider's system of classification, as reflected in the disease classification of the World Health Organization (2011), is rather resistant to such arguments: As soon as first-rank symptoms of schizophrenia are present, any affective disorder would be labeled "schizoaffective" and would thus be distinguished from purely affective disorders (WHO 2011).

Beyond such diagnostic struggles, there is little doubt that passivity phenomena indeed describe a core aspect of psychotic experience—the alienation of a person from his or her own thoughts (Swiney and Sousa 2013). However, how are such "ego disorders" to be explained? Can psychotic experiences of "thought insertion" reliably be distinguished from everyday questions such as whether a certain thought or idea is indeed due to one's own creative process or whether it is merely a reflection of any other person's ideas or (more generally) a common discourse? In other words, is thought insertion a common phenomenon, as all subjects continuously reflect public ideas and discourses, and does it only figure prominently in psychotic disorders because of the threatening content of such ideas?

Beyond such empirical questions, philosophically the question of whether thoughts can be "inserted" touches on complex problems of pre-reflective and reflective self-awareness: How do we actually know that we are the author and owner of any thought that occurs in our mind? How do I as the subject of all my cognitive experiences know that a certain thought should be ascribed to "me"? Such questions touch on the fundamental problem of how the subject and object of my own experience (the "I" or "ego") are actively and passively involved and reflected upon in any cognitive process. It has been suggested that the German psychopathological tradition, which places a rather strong emphasize on "ego disorders," was inspired by Kant's dictum that the term "I think" is necessarily required to accompany all of my thoughts (Kant 1982). Indeed, how should I know that a certain thought is not "mine" if it does not appear in my own consciousness? On the other hand, if it does appear in my *own* consciousness, how should I *not* know that this thought is in my mind and hence that this is of course due to my own cognitive activity? Questions like this have complicated any discussion of psychotic experiences (Spitzer 1988; Swiney and Sousa 2013).

In this chapter, we will first discuss ego disorders and distinguish them phenomenologically from related phenomena such as obsessions and hallucinations. We will then describe an attempt to understand thought insertion and other passivity phenomena in analogy with the experiences of alien motor control. We will criticize this model, refer to Plessner (1975) and Frank (2012), and suggest that pre-reflective self-awareness is a core characteristic of human mental experiences and that there are different ways in which it can be disturbed in psychotic disorders. We will finally discuss whether our model is limited to traditional European accounts of psychosis or whether it can indeed be translated into different cultural settings, in which psychosis is today clinically diagnosed.

## Clinical phenomena and their interpretation

The term "thought insertion" refers to a deeply disturbing experience of psychotic patients, in which their thoughts are no longer experienced as their own. Often, it occurs amidst deep psychotic anxiety and formal thought

# Ego disorders in psychosis 441

incoherence, i.e., the grammatical and syntactical structures of articulated messages can be close to incomprehensible for any outside person. This is illustrated in the first statement of "Clinical phenomena I" (Table 19.1). Here, a patient suffered from such a severe thought disorder that it took him considerable time just to utter the quoted sentence, repeatedly interrupted by what he felt to be messages and white noise placed in his head by an unknown flying object.

The third sentence is a statement from a patient in Mali, which shows that, while there is considerable variance in explanations provided by patients of how these alien thoughts are placed in their head (radiation machines in Germany, djinns (spirits) in Mali), there appears to be a considerable overlap in the deeply disturbing experience of thought insertion. Such inserted thoughts, which are experienced as "alien" and under outside control, can regularly be distinguished by patients from hallucinations, as described under "Clinical phenomena II" and shown in Table 19.2.

Traditional psychopathology groups acoustic as well as somatic hallucinations (coenesthesia) under the common label of hallucinations, as they are supposed to be sensory experiences without an outside cause. This classification may be questionable for coenesthesia (see the third example in Table 19.2), at least as far as the aspects of alien control of sensations and movements are implied. We will discuss the question of whether thoughts are more directly associated with a subject's self than somatic experiences when we refer to different traditions trying to interpret ego disorders (see below).

Thought insertion is also distinguished from what can be termed delusional perceptions, a concept describing perceptions that are immediately

*Table 19.1*

*Clinical phenomena I: thought insertion*

"I always feels so impedimented – [krsrskrsrs] there it is again – there is a UFO that places me on a level – it puts thoughts in my head."
"My neighbor has a radiation machine and uses it to shoot foreign thoughts in my head."
"The djinns place thoughts in my head. These are not my thoughts."

*Table 19.2*

*Clinical phenomena II: hallucinations*

"I can hear my thoughts as if they are spoken aloud."
"Doctor, it is not true that I am a murderer, right? These voices from the electric outlet keep telling me that I am."
"With that radiation machine, my neighbour also stimulates me sexually; I feel that effect in certain parts of my body."

imbued by a specific meaning, which turns them into signs or symbols that are threatening or at least highly relevant for the subject (Table 19.3).

Schneider (1942) argued correctly that delusions are hard to identify, particularly if they are complex; indeed, any observer usually lacks some more or less substantial parts of knowledge in order to understand whether this world view is an idiosyncratic way to utter a religious experience or a paranoia. In a paranoia, a patient is usually placed in the center of the (often threatening, condemning, or grandiose) experiences and he or she is usually not willing to abandon this interpretation of the situation in spite of all evidence to the contrary. However, Schneider (1942) quotes examples in which real experiences were mistaken for delusions by psychiatric observers and insists that only "delusional perceptions" of real objects should be considered as first-rank symptoms of schizophrenia: Here, some object that can be assessed objectively is imbued with a delusional idiosyncratic meaning for the person suffering from paranoia, and the observer can check whether this irrevisable interpretation is adequate or not.

Finally, inserted thoughts can be distinguished from obsessions, often very aversive thoughts that occur in one's mind and that can even (as in the case of compulsive impulses) manifest themselves as utterances in specific contexts (see the second quotation in Table 19.4, which was reported by a patient with Tourette's syndrome). Here, in spite of the unwanted and aversive character of these thoughts, subjects suffering from such experiences never deny that these thoughts are their own or at least occurred in their own mind just as other thoughts do. Indeed, the distinction between

*Table 19.3*

*Clinical phenomena III: delusional perceptions*

"I saw dead flowers in the gutter and they clearly indicated that my relationship was over."
"When I meet my ex-classmates, I can hear them whisper about me and I know that they talk about the prophecies I uttered in school, which now come true."
"I always read the Bible but this one day I realized that all I was reading was directly about me."

*Table 19.4*

*Clinical phenomena IV: obsessions and compulsive impulses*

"I thought of God and all of a sudden I had the idea that the devils f***s God. I ran to the toilet to pray, but when I returned the thought was back again and I had to enter the toilet and pray again."
"I stood in line and waited at the post office. In front of me was an African American wearing a purple pullover. I am not a racist, but all of a sudden and to my greatest embarrassment I shouted out 'Purple nigger!'"

"obsessions" and "inserted thoughts" is of key importance when trying to distinguish between obsessive-compulsive disorders and schizophrenia. Only thought insertions are supposed to be first-rank symptoms of schizophrenia.

This last example also shows why thought insertions in schizophrenia should clearly be distinguished from the occurrence of any "thought in my mind" that is of dubious authorship, for example, because it simply reflects common prejudices or (racist) discourses. Even if I lose control over such thoughts, as in the case of obsessions, and they keep occurring although I do not want to experience them, they are still "my" thoughts, i.e., patients who are suffering from obsessions never attribute them to an outside force. Passivity phenomena, on the other hand, in which thoughts are attributed to an outside agent ("inserted thoughts"), appear to refer to a deep disturbance of thought authorship and ownership: not only am I not the active author of this thought (i.e., I do not feel that I have created it or in any way facilitated its creation), it is so alien to me that I deny ownership and attribute it to an outside force, which places such thoughts in my mind (Heinz 2014). But how can such phenomena be explained in a philosophical and anthropological context?

## Privileged access to one's own thoughts? Alien limbs versus alien thoughts

Shoemaker (1996) suggested that there is a privileged access to one's own thoughts. He claimed that it would be paradoxical to utter assertively a statement that you claim not to endorse at the same time; for example, to claim that "It rains but I do not believe that it rains" is a statement that does not make sense (Moore's paradox). If Shoemaker is correct, a statement such as "The thoughts in my head/mind/consciousness are not my thoughts" is also paradoxical. Now patients suffering from schizophrenia cannot be expected to describe their experiences in logical terms. However, is there indeed a privileged access to one's own thoughts but not one's own body? Should therefore passivity phenomena that refer to one's own body be classified under "hallucinations" (coenesthesia), as they are akin to other sensory experiences, while passivity phenomena with respect to one's own thoughts refer to a deeper dysfunction of the subject, because they impair the privileged access to one's own cognitive activities?

One example sometimes quoted in this context is the case of a person who finds herself in a heap of other people's bodies after a traffic accident. Due to paralysis of her arm, this person does not feel her left hand any more and when seeing it among the body parts of the other traffic victims, she cannot identify it as her own hand but instead thinks that this is the hand of somebody else (see also Wittgenstein 1960). This example is supposed to show that one can err when ascribing a certain limb to oneself; however, not so when talking about one's own cognitive activities. However, ego disorders seem to contradict this statement directly and, indeed, both "inserted" thoughts and limbs "under alien control" may best be referred to as passivity phenomena instead of artificially distinguishing them into hallucinations (with respect to body parts) versus ego disorders (with respect to thoughts). Once this distinction is no longer made, mechanisms that contribute to a body "feeling alien" may heuristically be transferred to the explanation of thought disorders. Indeed, Frith and others (Blakemore et al. 2002) suggested that the authorship and ownership of a movement can be disturbed on different levels of performance that help to transform an intention into a movement, and that dysfunctions arising in this process may be of heuristical value to understand thought insertion. Specifically, Frith and others (Blakemore et al. 2002) suggested that any intended movement has to be translated into motor commands, which then start the actual movement and are controlled by sensory feedback. Several comparators can thus assess whether (1) the intended state is correctly translated into a certain motor command by comparing a "forward model" of this motor command with the intended state, and (2) whether the motor command is correctly translated into a certain movement that creates a specific sensory feedback (due to the final position taken when the movement reaches its aim). Finally, the sensory information about this final state can not only be compared with the state predicted by the forward model but also with the original intention. Campbell (1999) suggested that this comparator model can be applied to explain inserted thoughts and hypothesized that any verbal intention has to be translated into "thought generation," which is then embedded in the "stream of consciousness." Again, an efference copy of the generated thoughts (akin to the efference copy generated by a forward model of any motor movement) can be compared to the original intention as well as to the cognitive feedback generated when one experiences his or her own "actual stream of consciousness." Any dysfunction of the comparator that compares the efference copy with (1) the original intention or (2) the cognitive feedback could thus contribute to the experience of thought insertion.

However, Gallagher (2004), as well as Vosgerau and Newen (2007), criticized that the whole model is based on an inadequate analogy between thoughts and movements. While it makes sense to distinguish between a forward model of any intended movement and the sensory feedback that arises from specific sensory organs after the movement has been carried out, it is not clear which aspects of the "stream of consciousness" directly correspond to such phenomena. It can be argued that there is something like an "inner monologue" (or rather an "inner polilogue") in which we can experience our own verbalized thoughts more or less coherently and with various degrees of clarity and loudness, and hence some kind of "ownership" based on the experience of this stream of consciousness may exist. However, it is rather unclear which aspect of thought generation should directly correspond to a forward model of a movement (Heinz 2014). Are there really "intended thoughts" that have to be translated into "words" via a forward model, which are then experienced (akin to sensory feedback) in our stream of consciousness? Moreover, even if we accept that there should be some similarity between movements as physical acts and thoughts as conscious acts, phenomena of aphasia (as occur in certain neurological disorders) should warn us that thought insertion does not appear to be a phenomenon that is directly associated with a disturbance in speech production as occurs in such neurological disorders. Indeed, while there is a "motor" versus a "sensory" aphasia, in which either (as in the case of motor aphasia) fluent speech production is impaired or (as in the case of sensory aphasia) speech production is fluent but rather incomprehensible due to the intrusion of unintended words, patients with aphasia do not tend to report psychotic phenomena such as "thought insertion" or "blockade" in spite of their impairments in language production. What occurs in schizophrenia and related psychoses thus seems to differ fundamentally from alterations in speech production as a consequence of neurobiological dysfunctions of brain regions associated with verbal fluency and speech comprehension (Broca's and Wernicke's brain areas). Instead, psychotic experiences referred to as "ego disorders" seem to touch an even deeper layer of subjectivity. They seem to impair a fundamental awareness of one's own intentions as reflected in one's "mind" or "stream of consciousness."

A deep disturbance of ego functions in schizophrenia has also been suggested by Vosgerau and Voss (2014), who distinguish between the presence or absence of *control* of one's thoughts (as can occur in obsessions, when my thoughts are clearly "my" thoughts, but it is not within my control whether I want to experience them or not), and the *authorship* of a thought (which can be absent if I simply reflect on the utterings of somebody else). *Ownership*, on the other hand, has to be undisturbed according to Vosgerau and Voss, since the thought has to be registered in one's own stream of consciousness before it can be ascribed to some "alien" entity. However, if ownership is indeed undisturbed, how do "inserted" thoughts differ from the thoughts that I currently reflect upon after they have been uttered by someone else? Is it only the degree of control I have when reflecting on the thoughts of someone else or some more distinct alteration in "ownership," which is not lost but changed sufficiently to render the thought "alien" (Heinz 2014)?

In any case, most authors agree that in inserted but not intrusive thoughts, i.e., in the psychotic phenomenon of thought insertion but not in the experience of "intrusive" obsessions, authorship of thoughts is absent. However, how could such a profound absence of thought authorship be explained when it is already paradoxical to claim that there is an alien thought in "my" own mind?

## Pre-reflective self-awareness: dysfunction in thought insertion?

Some authors suggest that thought insertions reflect an impairment in the functioning of a core self, which guarantees that my conscious productions are attributed to "myself" (Sass and Parnas 2003). Indeed, it has been suggested by Sartre (1943) as well as the Heidelberg School of Philosophy that self-attribution always requires a *pre-reflective* self-awareness. Without such a pre-reflective, non-propositional certainty of "myself," any reflective and propositional knowledge can be attributed erroneously (Frank 2012). For example, the editor of the magazine *Science* may know that the editor of this magazine has just been promoted to be president of the American Psychiatric Association; however, any such knowledge *de re* does not guarantee that he knows that this information is about *himself* (e.g., he may be unaware that he himself has just recently been promoted to the position, being the editor of *Science*). Errors of self-reference may thus occur on two levels: a reflective one (I may falsely attribute some quality or information to myself while being very well aware that I am the person who performs this act of attribution), and a pre-reflective one, which guarantees that I always "know" or rather "feel" that any information concerning *myself* is indeed attributed to *me*, i.e., the *subject* of my current stream of consciousness. Philosophical attempts to describe such acts of self-reference have often distinguished between the "I" or "ego" as the subject versus the object of cognition (e.g., see Kant 1983). However, while the self as an object may manifest in some cognitive concepts that I attribute to "myself," according to Kant, the subject of my own experiences is by itself no object of experience. However, how is it then to be conceptualized?

Helmuth Plessner (1975) tried to solve this problem by suggesting that human beings, unlike animals, are not only able to experience their environment as perceived from the center of their bodies. The concentric circle around this living body in the centric position is called centric positionality. Humans and only humans are also able to experience the "world" as well as ourselves from an eccentric position (Figure 19.1).

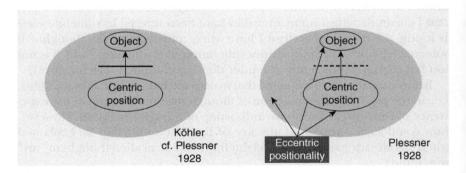

*Figure 19.1* For any animal, an object that is hidden behind a barrier (symbolized by a black line) will either be "out of mind" or only be approached by bypassing the barrier instead of removing it (i.e., the animal does not have a representation of empty space (left), while humans (right) can experience the world from an eccentric point of view and imagine the hidden object.

Plessner's thoughts were stimulated by Wolfgang Köhler's experiments with non-human primates in the 1920s. Such primates would, for example, be unable to move a box out of their way and instead always walk around it, because (as Plessner claimed) they are not able to imagine an empty space. Hence, such an animal experiences its surrounding (here exemplified by an object) from a position that is centered on its momentary location in time and space.

Figure 19.1 illustrates centric versus eccentric positionality. Unlike animals humans can experience the "world" from a position that is eccentric to the momentary location of a subject's body and embodied mind in space and time (eccentric positionality). With this term, Plessner did not claim that this eccentric positionality constitutes a specific point of view—rather, by being eccentric to an individual's position in space and time, it is located "nowhere" and a new dimension (a "world" instead of a simple environment) unfolds. As other persons can also experience this world by partaking in their own eccentric positionality, surpassing centric positions creates a common human experience of a "world" (Figure 19.2).

Plessner argued that centric versus eccentric positionalities, while being categorically different with respect to the "environment" versus "world" they create, never occur in isolation in human life. We may be lost in performing an act (in our centric position) but never lose the ability to surpass this limited centric view (excentrically) and to reflect upon ourselves, cry because of, or laugh at, our failures and mistakes; likewise, we may be lost in thoughts and reflections but, for example, when being physically touched by somebody else, we immediately experience the world from our embodied position in space and time (Figure 19.2). This link between the eccentric and centric positionality, however, is shaky (Plessner 1975), and it is this "shakiness" that may create a vulnerability towards psychotic experiences. Indeed, when lost in thoughts, I appear to need some "pre-reflective self-awareness" to be identified with my centric, embodied position.

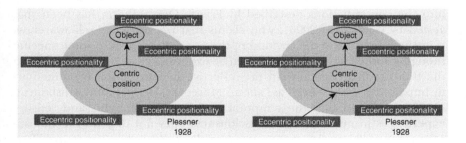

*Figure 19.2* The eccentric position unfolds a human world and includes the perspective of others (left), while direct contact with the environment is always mediated by a person's (centric) embodiment ("vermittelte Unmittelbarkeit") (right).

A temporary or partial failure of such a pre-reflective self-awareness may then promote the experience of "inserted thoughts" or body movements under "alien control." I no longer pre-reflectively experience that all my movements or thoughts belong to me and instead attribute them to an outside agent, who causes the movement or inserts the thought. Plessner argued that only when acting out their intentions ("im Vollzug"), humans are in touch with their environment via their bodies. It is hence only via mediation, i.e., via our embodiment and via acting through the centric position, that humans are able to experience themselves and others: What appears to be an immediate contact with one's environment is thus "mediated" (vermittelte Unmittelbarkeit). This mediation requires pre-reflective self-awareness, and any dysfunction of such a pre-reflective self-awareness may lead to phenomena of alienation such as thought insertion, thought blockade, or alien motor control. All these phenomena are hence an expression of the fundamental gap ("hiatus") between the eccentric and the centric position, i.e., between reflexivity or any other form of surpassing an ego-centric world perspective on the one hand and a centric embodied perspective on the other. However, if I am indeed lost in psychosis in an eccentric position, which alienates me from my own thoughts and enlived body, how can I know that this is the case? How do I know that "I" am alienated from myself?

Manfred Frank (2012) has argued that any attempt to explain such psychotic experiences as a *total* loss of pre-reflective self-awareness goes astray. If I am indeed absolutely unable to ascribe any thoughts to myself, how do I know that some thought that I experience as alien is indeed occurring in "my" mind or my "stream of consciousness"? At least, the alien thought has to be distinguished from "my own" thoughts, which shows that there can be no absolute loss of pre-reflective self-awareness, otherwise I would not be able to feel that some thoughts are indeed still "my own" and that some other psychotic experiences (the "inserted thoughts") differ from my own thoughts and can hence be attributed to some outside force.

There are several ways to explain such phenomena without running into the contradictions described by Frank. One solution has been suggested by Gallagher (2000), who claims that pre-reflective self-awareness is just impaired for some fraction of time or with respect to some specific thoughts. Other thoughts would then be experienced as "one's own," while the thought that occurs when pre-reflective self-attribution is momentarily impaired is experienced as "alien." Moreover, Dennett and Kinsbourne (1992) suggested that the temporal sequence of thoughts and sensory experiences in my stream of consciousness does not depend mechanistically upon their occurrence in the outside world but rather is modified by experience and plausibility. Therefore, small temporal shifts between the "alien" and the "own" thought process may occur, and nevertheless the "alien" thought can be consciously represented as "coinciding" with my own cognitive productions (when in fact the "alien" thought process occurred a little earlier or later than the process experienced as being my "own" thought). Any comparator may thus briefly be impaired but function well a moment later, and "alien" as well as "own" thoughts are nevertheless consciously experienced as occurring simultaneously.

However, why do most authors who try to conceptualize ego disorder rule out that subjects simply make a cognitive error and reflectively misattribute thoughts not to themselves, but instead claim that there is a much deeper disturbance of pre-reflective self-awareness? The answer to this question refers again to the metaphor of "the depth" of psychotic experience. As discussed above, psychotic thought insertions appear to carry a deeply disturbing and unusual character, which patients try to explain by referring to some very powerful and strange outside forces, such as "aliens," "unknown flying objects," or "witches." While all human beings commonly experience erring when attributing certain qualities or characteristics to themselves and to others, experiencing alien control of one's own thoughts and movements seems to interfere with core experiences of the subject's "ego activity" and "vitality." Even when lost in thoughts or in activity, e.g., either in the eccentric or centric position, we can always relocate and dislocate ourselves into and out of our momentary (centric) position. This active ability to creatively change our point of view requires pre-reflective self-awareness and appears to be impaired in psychosis, when our own thoughts and movements no longer seem to be the result of our own vital acts and intentions. This being said, thought insertions may also be experienced at least briefly when subjects are simply confused or anxious, even in the absence of some psychotic disorder; however, when occurring continuously over a longer period of time, such experiences appear to interfere deeply with vital abilities to express one's own thoughts and ideas. Such deep alterations of thought experience due to the impairment of pre-reflective self-awareness may, as we suggest, suffice to render a thought so alien that it neither feels "authored" nor "owned" by the subject who experiences it.

## Ego disorders – a universally valid criterion for psychosis?

A racist colonial psychiatry suggested that certain complex mental disorders are only found in Europeans, but not e.g., in (at that time so-called "primitive") Africans (Carothers 1951). Against such prejudices, Lambo observed that ego disorders do indeed occur in Yoruba psychotic patients living in Nigeria—however, they were limited to patients with a Western upbringing (Lambo 1955). These observations suggest that cultural traditions can play a role in the experience of thought insertion. Such cultural patterns may include certain practices of self-monitoring, e.g., of asking the question whether a certain experience was indeed generated by the subject him- or herself in any active way (Sass 1992). On the other hand, we and others observed ego disorders and other first-rank symptoms all over the world, including patients in Mali and Afghanistan (Napo et al. 2012). Indeed, the WHO study of schizophrenia suggested that first-rank symptoms occur worldwide at comparable levels (Sartorius 2008). In contrast,

Lambo's observation that West African psychotic patients with traditional upbringings do not report ego disorders suggests that social and cultural practices play an important role in the generation of such phenomena. Altogether, there is a considerable lack of worldwide studies on the exact phenomenology of psychotic disorder, which, as we are afraid, will not be promoted by the recent abandonment of specific psychotic symptoms in the *Diagnostic and Statistical Manual of Mental Disorders*, 5th edition (DSM-5) (APA 2013). If Plessner (1975) is correct that being able to experience our environment and the world from an eccentric as well as from a centric position is a general human trait, then psychotic alterations of such functions can be experienced by subjects all around the world. However, how this is articulated will depend on the respective cultural context, which not only influences the degree of self-observation but also provides specific concepts and terms for its expression (Whorf 1956). As frightening as psychotic experiences can be, our considerations suggest that they are deeply human, as they are an expression of our fragile status in the world. As humans, we always have to bridge the hiatus between centric embodiment and eccentric positionality, between standing in the center of our environment and surpassing it when crying, laughing, or reflecting upon our place in the world.

## References

American Psychiatric Association (APA) (1994). *Diagnostic and Statistical Manual of Mental Disorders. DSM-IV*, 4th Ed. Washington, DC: American Psychiatric Association.

American Psychiatric Association (APA) (2013). *Diagnostic and Statistical Manual of Mental Disorders. DSM-5*, 5th Ed. Washington, DC: American Psychiatric Association.

Blakemore S. J., Wolpert D. M. and Frith C. D. (2002). Abnormalities in the Awareness of Action. *TRENDS in Cognitive Sciences* 6: pp. 237–242.

Campbell J. (1999). Schizophrenia, the Space of Reasons, and Thinking as a Motor Process. *The Monist* 82: pp. 609–625.

Carothers J. (1951). Frontal Lobe Function and the African. *Journal of Mental Science* 97: pp. 122–148.

Carpenter W. T. Jr, Strauss J. S. and Muleh S. (1973). Are There Pathognomonic Symptoms in Schizophrenia? *Archives of General Psychiatry* 28: pp. 847–852.

Dennett D. and Kinsbourne M. (1992). Time and the Observer; the Where and When of Consciousness in the Brain. *Behavioral and Brain Sciences* 15: pp. 183–247.

Frank M. (2012). *Ansichten der Subjektivität*. Frankfurt a. M.: Suhrkamp.

Gallagher S. (2000). Philosophical Conceptions of the Self: Implications for Cognitive Science. *Trends in Cognitive Sciences* 4: pp. 14–21.

Gallagher S. (2004). Neurocognitive Models of Schizophrenia: A Neurophenomenological Critique. *Psychopathology* 37: pp. 8–19.

Heinz A. (2014). *Der Begriff psychischer Krankheit*. Berlin: Suhrkamp.

Kant I. (1982). *Kritik der reinen Vernunft*. Stuttgart: Reclam.

Kant I. (1983). *Anthropologie in pragmatischer Hinsicht*. Stuttgart: Reclam.

Lambo A. (1955). The Role of Cultural Factors in Paranoid Psychosis among the Yoruba Tribe. *Journal of Medical Science* 101: pp. 239–266.

Napo F., Heinz A. and Auckenthaler A. (2012). Explanatory Models and Concepts of West African Malian Patients with Psychotic Symptoms. *European Psychiatry* 27: pp. 44–49.

Plessner H. (1975). *Die Stufen des Organischen und der Mensch* (1928). Berlin: Walter de Gruyter.

Sartorius N. (2008). What did the WHO studies really find? *Schizophrenia Bulletin* 34 (2): pp. 253–255.

Sartre J.-P. (1943). *L'être et le néant. Essai d'ontologie phénoménologique.* Paris: Librairie Gallimard.

Sass L. (1992). *Madness and Modernism. Insanity in the Light of Art, Modern Literature, and Thought.* New York: Basic Books.

Sass L. and Parnas J. (2003). Schizophrenia, Consciousness, and the Self. *Schizophrenia Bulletin* 29: pp. 427–444.

Schneider K. (1942). *Psychischer Befund und psychiatrische Diagnose.* Leipzig: Thieme.

Shoemaker S. (1996). *The First-person Perspective and Other Essays.* Cambridge, UK: Cambridge University Press.

Spitzer M. (1988). Ichstörungen: In Search of a Theory. In Spitzer M., Uehlein F.A., Oepen G. et al. (Eds.), *Psychopathology and Philosophy.* Berlin: Springer, pp. 167–183.

Swiney L. and Sousa P. (2013). When Our Thoughts are not Our Own: Investigating Agency Misattribution Using the Mind-to-Mind Paradigm. *Cousciousness and Cognition* 22: pp. 589–602.

Vosgerau G. and Newen A. (2007). Thoughts, Motor Actions, and the Self. *Mind and Language* 22: pp. 22–43.

Vosgerau G. and Voss M. (2014). Authorship and Control Over Thoughts. *Mind and Language* 29(5): pp. 534–565.

Whorf B. (1956). Language, Thought, and Reality. In Caroll J (Ed.). *Selected Writings.* Cambridge, MA: Massachusetts Institute of Technology.

Wittgenstein L. (1960). *The Blue and Brown Books.* Oxford: Basil Blackwell.

World Health Organization (WHO) (2011). *International Classification of Diseases,* 10th revision (*ICD 10*). Geneva: WHO.

# PART V
# Historical philosophical background

# 20 Radical *Epokhè*

## On Sartre's concept of "pure reflection"

*Raoul Moati*

In 1934, during a stay in Berlin, Sartre wrote The *Transcendence of the Ego*. It was during this stay that Sartre discovered Husserl's phenomenology, specifically *Ideas for a Pure Phenomenology* (1913/2014). This text radically informed Sartre's own approach to phenomenology, sharpening and refining his conception of the relationship between the transcendental consciousness and the ego. We can read the work of Sartre not so much as a complete rejection of Husserl's phenomenology, but as a radicalization of Husserl's phenomenology of consciousness. For Husserl, indeed, the transcendental consciousness must be understood as fundamentally *egological*, as the consciousness of an ego, or, to say that otherwise, as inhabited by a transcendental subject, which is presented by Husserl as the source and principle of the unity of the intentional consciousness. Sartre, in contrast, thinks that the principle of intentionality, discovered by Husserl, must be radicalized—the ego is a worldly object constituted by the intentional consciousness when such a consciousness becomes reflexive. The ego, according to Sartre, can indeed claim, "It is a transcendent pole of synthetic unity, like the object-pole of the unreflected attitude. But this pole appears only in the world of reflection" (Sartre 2004, p. 21). On Husserl's view, the field of the transcendental consciousness becomes reachable as a "new region of being," to the phenomenological investigation, after an act of suspension of our natural attitude toward the world. This natural attitude designates our natural and spontaneous belief in the existence of an external world. The suspension of this belief (or, to use Husserl's Greek terminology, "*thesis*") Husserl—taking a concept belonging originally to Ancient Skepticism—names "*Epokhè*." Through the *Epokhè*, Husserl presents the philosopher as "parenthesizing" or "putting out of action" our main existential belief towards the world. The "*Epokhè*" is then supposed, in the Husserlian perspective, to make the field of transcendental consciousness reachable to the phenomenological investigation, as a "region of being" that is offered to the phenomenological reflection once our acts of "positing" the world are suspended.

One fundamental claim in the *Transcendence of the Ego* is that, contrary to Husserl's approach, the suspension of our belief on the world *is only complete* when consciousness is able to appear to itself as impersonal. Sartre, indeed, presents the ego as an object of the world. For that reason, in Sartre's perspective, such an ego must be included into the suspensive brackets of the phenomenological reduction. The ego is understood by Sartre as an object of the world constituted by intentional consciousness and, because of this, Sartre thinks that there is no reason to exclude it, as Husserl does, from the brackets of the phenomenological reduction. For Sartre, the ego is nothing other than an object of the world—in the phenomenological terminology a "noematic unity"—that appears and is constituted when consciousness takes itself as its own object in reflection: "this pole appears only in the world of reflection" (Sartre 2004, p. 21).

Such a thesis seems to present a number of problems internal to Sartre's own approach. For, if it is possible to radicalize Husserl's *Epokhè*, as Sartre claims it is, such a radicalization would imply the possibility for consciousness to reflect itself as *impersonal*. But such a possibility is at the same time denied by Sartre as fully conceivable. Sartre explains in *The Transcendence of the Ego* that there is no reflection towards consciousness that *does not imply* the apparition of an ego within the field of the reflected consciousness. We will see that, even when he speaks about "pure reflection," Sartre insists upon the fact that such a reflection, although "pure," cannot avoid the apparition of an ego within the field of the reflected consciousness. This point has been perfectly emphasized by the French Sartrean scholar, Philippe Cabestan. On Sartre's conception of reflection as unavoidably involved with the ego, Cabestan claims:

> Here we would like to perhaps recover something like an echo of what Husserl described as the impossibility of putting into brackets the pure ego as (a non-constituted) transcendency, within immanence, as if Husserl had never known how to interpret this persistence of the Self.
> (Cabestan 2004, p. 304)

This means that, even if, against Husserl, Sartre claims that there is no ego within consciousness, such a claim seems to be phenomenologically impossible to experience, since there is no reductive or reflective act which does not imply the apparition of the ego within the field of the reflected consciousness. Any reduction necessarily reveals, because of the very structure of reflection as such, a personal consciousness (a consciousness in which an ego dwells).

The main goal of our article will be to demonstrate that the unavoidable apparition of the ego within the field of the reflected consciousness *does not* imply the impossibility of modifying Husserl's *Epokhè* in a way that leads consciousness to face its own actual impersonality. We will defend, through Sartre's texts and main hypothesis, the claim of a possible radicalization of the transcendental reduction without denying the unavoidable apparition of the ego within the field of consciousness once it is posited in an act of reflection. Our question will be the following: how a reduction, if by its constitutive reflective nature implies necessarily the apparition of the ego within the field of the reflected consciousness can, at the same time, not prevent the possibility for consciousness to appear to itself *as impersonal*? Such a seeming paradox can be resolved only through analysis of what Sartre calls "pure reflection" both in its formal and existential meanings.

## Position of the problem (I): Sartre's radicalization of Husserl's principle of intentionality

What Husserl calls the "transcendental reduction" entails the suspension of the psychological ego—as belonging to the transcendent world that is the object of the suspensive act of the reduction. At the same time, the Husserlian reduction leads to the discovery of another ego, no more psychological but transcendental, that appears within the field of transcendental consciousness as its structure. This second ego posited by Husserl became a necessary structure of consciousness *only* after the transcendental turn of phenomenology. Before such a turn, Sartre reminds us, Husserl remained skeptical of any idea that considers the presence of a transcendental ego within the field of consciousness necessary in order to unify and individualize it. In the *Transcendence of the Ego*, Sartre summarizes Husserl's evolution toward the question of the ego the following way:

> Having considered that the Me was a synthetic and transcendental production of consciousness (in the *Logische Untersuchungen*) he reverted, in the *Ideas*, to the classical thesis of a transcendental I that follows on, so to speak, behind each consciousness, as the necessary structure of these consciousnesses, whose rays (*Ichstrahl*) fall on to each phenomenon that presents itself to the field of attention. Thus transcendental consciousness becomes rigorously personal.
>
> (Sartre 2004, p. 5)

In *The Transcendence of the Ego*, Sartre seeks to radicalize the phenomenological approach of the transcendental consciousness in order to depersonalize it. For Sartre, the presence of an ego within the sphere of the reduced transcendental consciousness indicates the incompleteness of Husserl's phenomenological reduction. In order to substantiate this claim, Sartre examines Husserl's account of the transcendental ego. In *Ideas*, Husserl suggests that the transcendental ego we discover after the transcendental reduction is not be understood as an immanent "moment" of consciousness, but rather as a permanent and identical structure defined by Husserl as "a transcendence of a peculiar kind—one which is not constituted" (Husserl 1913/2014, p. 105, modified).

Such a claim means that the transcendental ego, "a necessary structure of consciousness" (Sartre 2004, p. 5), is given to the phenomenological reflection as a *transcendence* that dwells in pure consciousness. Husserl claims indeed that it is a transcendence that *must not* be thought of as a transcendence *constituted* by the transcendental consciousness (a worldly transcendence). Husserl presents the transcendence of the ego as a "transcendence of a peculiar kind" insofar as it mustn't be understood as belonging to the sphere of the transcendent real (as the very field of what is aimed at and constituted by the transcendental consciousness). On account of its peculiar character, Husserl claims that it is not subject to the transcendental reduction. Insofar as it is, in an important sense, free from the transcendental reduction, the transcendence of the ego is for Husserl "a *transcendence in immanence*" (Husserl 1913/2014, p. 105; original emphasis).

It is this understanding of the ego as a transcendence which is exempt from the transcendental reduction Sartre takes to be disputable. That the transcendence of the ego is a "special transcendence which is not that of the object" (Sartre 2004, p. 14) signals a problematic understanding of the ego. For Sartre, there is no reason to recognize the ego as a transcendence that does not share in the same features of any other transcendence. In this sense, the type of transcendence of the ego must be recognized as a transcendence of the world amongst others: "The Ego is a noematic, and not a noetic, unity. A tree or a chair does not exist in any other way" (Sartre 2004, p. 39).

For Sartre, the essential inadequacy by which the ego is given to intuition (as "the object of neither an apodictic nor an adequate evidential certainty") proves that it cannot be an immanent element of consciousness. It can be neither an origin nor a structure, but, as Sartre concludes, "every bit as much as the world, a relative existent, i.e. an object for consciousness" (Sartre 2004, p. 5). Sartre's conclusion is that all transcendence must be considered as an object for the intentional consciousness, that is, all transcendence is *outside consciousness*. Through the fundamental discovery of intentionality, phenomenology must recognize that "everything is finally outside: everything, including ourselves" (Sartre 1970, p. 2).

Consciousness, by its radical ecstatic nature, *has no inside*. "If, impossible though it may be, you could enter 'into' a consciousness, you would be seized by a whirlwind and thrown back outside, in the thick of the dust, near the tree, for consciousness has no 'inside'" (Sartre 1970, p. 2). For Sartre, then, the ego is *also* the object of an ecstatic act of intentional consciousness, when consciousness becomes reflective. The ego is indeed, "a transcendent pole of synthetic unity, like the object-pole of the unreflected attitude. But this pole appears only in the world of reflection" (Sartre 2004, p. 21). The ego experienced as a subjective pole of intentionality is then nothing other than *a concealed objective pole* of intentional consciousness, an object constituted by reflective consciousness, *but simultaneously given to the reflective consciousness as a non-constituted entity. It is given indeed* as a subjective substractum, an "inhabitant" of consciousness, a "necessary structure of consciousness" (Sartre 2004, p. 9). The radicalization of the Principle of Intentionality proposed by Sartre leads necessarily to a radicalization of the phenomenological reduction insofar as the reduction must reach transcendental consciousness as an impersonal constituting field: "The sure and certain content of the pseudo-'cogito' is not '*I* am conscious of this chair', but '*there is* consciousness of this chair'" (Sartre 2004, p. 16).

The transcendental field must be purified of the ego, since the ego itself is constituted by consciousness like all other objects in the world. There is thus no reason to exclude it from the sphere of the phenomenological reduction.

## Position of the problem (II): Sartre's radicalization of phenomenological reduction

For Husserl, the transcendental reduction *cannot lead* to an impersonal consciousness. For Sartre, on the contrary, the very idea of a "special" transcendence, a non-constituted yet *constituting* transcendence that belongs to the sphere of immanence, is, from a strictly phenomenological point of view, a contentious claim. For Sartre, the Husserlian notion of a non-constituted transcendence contains a conceptual contradiction. It identifies it as a dogmatic metaphysical position, which has no phenomenological justification: "How are we to explain this privileged treatment of the I if it is not by metaphysical or critical preoccupations that have nothing to do with phenomenology?" (Sartre 2004, p. 14).

Here, we see, once again, Sartre remaining faithful to some of Husserl's intuitions coming from his earlier work. For example, in *Logical Investigations* (1900–1901), Husserl, in a move against Natorp, identified the transcendental ego as a suspicious entity possessing no phenomenologically intuitive evidence: "I must frankly confess, however, that I am quite unable to find this ego, this primitive, necessary center of relations" (Husserl, 1901, quoted by Sartre 2004, p. 56, note 12). Husserl subsequently modified his own position toward the ego; more and more, its phenomenology through its transcendental turn becomes explicitly egological. In the second edition of the *Logical Investigations*, published in 1913 (date of publication of *Ideas*), Husserl discusses his own position toward the ego: "I have since managed to find it, i.e. have learnt not to be led astray from a pure grasp of the given through corrupt forms of ego-metaphysic" (Husserl 1901, quoted by Sartre 2004, p. 56, note 12).

In 1913, Husserl presented his own evolution as the very condition of possibility of reaching the transcendental consciousness. This is the reason why he posits a limit to the transcendental reduction in *Ideas*: "We cannot suspend transcendencies without limits; transcendental purification cannot mean suspension of all transcendencies, since otherwise there would remain, to be sure, a pure consciousness but no possibility for a science of pure consciousness" (Husserl 1913/2014, p. 107). For Husserl, the transcendantal reduction is coincident with the inhibition of what Husserl calls the "natural attitude," which means an inhibition of our spontaneous activity of positing the existence of the world. Such an inhibition or phenomenological *Epokhè* aims at reaching transcendental consciousness as the origin of the transcendent reality. In *The Transcendence of the Ego*, Sartre does not defer to the Husserlian distinction of the natural attitude on the one hand and the phenomenological one on the other; he instead displaces radically its meaning in such a way so as to denounce Husserl's transcendental reduction *as still remaining trapped in the very natural attitude*. Indeed, for Sartre, the Husserlian passage from the empirical ego to the transcendental one *does not suspend entirely* the natural attitude since natural attitude consists precisely in the identification of *consciousness* as a the product of an ego: "the 'natural attitude' appears in its entirety as an effort that consciousness makes to escape from itself by projecting itself into the me" (Sartre 2004, p. 49).

The Husserlian transcendental ego conceived not as a *content* but as the very *form* of the transcendental consciousness is interpreted by Sartre as a "contraction" of the empirical (worldly) ego:

> Indeed, the *I*, with its personality, is—however formal and abstract one may suppose it to be . . . It bears to the concrete and psycho-physical me the same relation as does a point to three dimensions: it is an infinitely contracted *me*.
> (Sartre 2004, p. 8)

"For Kant and for Husserl, the I is a formal structure of consciousness . . . an I is never purely formal, that it is always, even when conceived in the abstract, an infinite contraction of the material me" (Sartre 2004, pp. 16–17).

This means that, for Sartre, there are not two egos—the transcendental ego and the empirical/material one—*but one and the same ego*. The empirical ego is understood by Sartre as a formal modification of the transcendental one. Since, for Sartre, the Husserlian transcendental ego is a contraction of the psycho-physical ego, the egological form of Husserl's transcendental consciousness *contradicts necessarily* the claims Husserl makes in the *Cartesian Meditations*:

> Consequently for me, the meditating ego who, standing and remaining in the attitude of epoche, posits exclusively himself as the acceptance-basis of all Objective experiences and bases, *there is no psychological Ego* and there are no physical phenomena in the sense proper to psychology, i.e., as components of psychophysical men.
> (Husserl 1999, quoted by Sartre 2004, p. 55, note 10, my emphasis)

If the Husserlian reduction coincides with the act of bracketing off the transcendent world to which the empirical/psychological ego belongs,

Sartre believes that it follows from this that the Husserlian version of the phenomenological reduction *does not break entirely* with the natural attitude. His version fails to detach itself fully from the natural attitude since it maintains an egological form of the transcendental consciousness even after the transcendental reduction. Because Sartre identifies the Husserlian transcendental ego with a formal modification of the empirical ego, the transcendental ego is, on Sartre's view, a transcendence amongst others—an objective transcendence posited by intentional consciousness that *Epokhè* must suspend in order to open access to the only form of consciousness that can be the remainder of the suspension of the world: *impersonal consciousness as such*.

For this reason, *The Transcendence of the Ego* does not seem so much to depart from Husserl, but to aim at a radicalization of its very purpose in freeing transcendental consciousness from its metaphysical residuum embodied by the ego. There is then no such thing, for Sartre, as a "special transcendence"—all transcendences are constituted by consciousness, *including* the transcendental ego (since it is nothing but another version of the psycho-physical ego). It is for this reason that "all transcendence must fall under the scope of the *Epokhè*" (Sartre 2004, p. 4). A phenomenological project, according to Sartre, is insufficient if it does not achieve the transcendental reduction in suspending *in totality* the psychological ego, for the following reasons:

1 The transcendental ego is nothing other than a formal modification of the empirical ego.
2 As a transcendence that is maintained by Husserl despite the reduction, it implies the non-achievement of the suspension of the natural attitude.
3 As remaining a modified form of the natural attitude, the phenomenological attitude remains incomplete, *impure* and *unsure*.

If transcendental reduction must lead from the natural attitude to the phenomenological attitude, it must then necessarily bracket off the *totality* of the transcendent: "All the results of phenomenology are in danger of crumbling away if the I is not, every bit as much as the world, a relative existent, i.e. an object for consciousness" (Sartre 2004, p. 9). In other words, it must be constitutive of the transcendental reduction that it leads to the transcendental field of consciousness as *an impersonal field* in order to overcome fully the natural attitude and enter into the phenomenological one: "the transcendental field becomes impersonal, or, if you prefer, 'pre-personal', it is *without an I*" (Sartre 2004, p. 5; original emphasis). And to a similar end: "The transcendental field, purified of all egological structure, recovers its former limpidity" (Sartre 2004, p. 43).

> The sure and certain content of the pseudo-"cogito" is not "I am conscious of the chair," but "there is consciousness of this chair." This

content is sufficient to constitute an infinite and absolute field for the investigations of phenomenology.

(Sartre 2004, p. 16)

Upon extending the scope of the transcendental reduction to include the ego thereby overcoming the natural attitude, other problems begin to emerge. One problem raised indirectly by Sartre in the *The Transcendence of the Ego* lies in the nature of reflection. That is, the ego seems to appear inexorably in the transcendental act of reflection not only for metaphysical reasons, but also in virtue of the very nature of *reflection as such*. On the one hand, it seems that the suspension of the transcendental ego would lead only to the complete achievement of the transcendental reduction— the access to transcendental consciousness as an impersonal field. On the other hand, such an achievement remains unreachable on account of the very *constitutive nature of reflection* as such. Sartre reminds us that, indeed, "reflection *modifies* spontaneous consciousness" (Sartre 2004, p. 13). Even when Sartre speaks about the possibility of a pure reflection, he reminds us that "But it may happen that consciousness suddenly produces itself on a pure reflective level. *Not perhaps without an ego*, but overflowing the ego on all sides" (Sartre 2004, p. 48, my emphasis).

Does this not mean that any reduction, because of its reflective nature, is condemned to imply the apparition of an ego within the field of the reflected? Might there be no reflection upon consciousness that would not lead to grasping consciousness as egological? The affirmative answer to this question would imply the impossibility of overcoming the natural attitude. If there is no such thing as a pure transcendental reduction, Sartre would then necessarily have to submit to Husserl's point of view of reduction as leading necessarily to an egological consciousness.[1]

Such an apparent pitfall gains further ground in the fact that Sartre reaches impersonal consciousness in using precisely *non-reflexive* means— what Sartre calls "non-thetic memory" (Sartre 2004, p. 11) of a past spontaneous consciousness. The methodology adopted by Sartre in this passage of the *The Transcendence of the Ego* in order to reach consciousness in its originary impersonality is fundamentally focused on how *to avoid the contamination of the non-reflexive memory by the reflection*. In other words, how to remember a consciousness *without* reflecting on it, without imposing the egological surplus implied by the reflective attitude: "This consciousness is not to be posited as an object of my reflection," which is only possible if "I . . . maintain a sort of complicity with it, and draw up an inventory of its content in a non-positional way" (Sartre 2004, p. 11). Sartre speaks of a "non-reflexive grasp of a consciousness" (Sartre 2004, p. 11): "while I was reading, there was a consciousness *of* the book, *of* the heroes . . . but the I did not inhabit this consciousness" (Sartre 2004, p. 12). It seems here that Sartre abandons reflection as a method to reach consciousness in its impersonality. What remains to be shown is how Sartre's conception of "pure reflection" is possible if it implies, insofar as it is *a reflection*, the apparition of an ego, that non-reflective memory prevents from appearing.

## Pure reflection: beyond Husserl's phenomenology

In contrast to impure reflection, pure reflection is not of the kind that frees consciousness totally from the ego. It is rather a reflection in which consciousness *no more* appears to itself as an emanation of an ego. Sartre claims then that "pure reflection" must be distinguished from the (impure) phenomenological reflection: "the pure reflection . . . is . . . not necessarily phenomenological reflection" (Sartre 2004, p. 23).

The Sartrean alternative to the Husserlian reflection on consciousness consists in what Sartre calls "pure reflection." In order to elaborate upon the various degrees of reflection, it is necessary to distinguish between pure and impure reflection as according to Sartre. We will begin with his definition of impure reflection, which has two main dimensions that must be explored: *transgression* and *inversion*.

### Impure reflection: transgression and inversion

Impure reflection is determined by the tendency *to posit too much*, that is, to *constitute transcendent* objects through an act of transgressing what is *actually and really given* to reflection. To transgress, in this sense, is to distort what is really given through an act of projection. In the example given by Sartre in which an *I* looks upon a man Peter, it is in seeing Peter that a consciousness of revulsion occurs: "I see Peter, I feel a kind of profound upheaval of revulsion and anger on seeing him (I am already on the reflective level); this upheaval is consciousness" (Sartre 2004, p. 22).

In this example, what is actually given to reflection, *as an absolute and certain content, is the consciousness of revulsion*. Sartre follows Husserl's conception of immanent perception as originary, absolute, and apodictic; it is given in totality and adequately. (See Husserl 1913/2014, § 38.) This is not, for Sartre, the case—the *state* of hatred for Peter that "appears to me at the same time as my experience of revulsion" (Sartre 2004, p. 22) is not an immanent content of consciousness but a *transcendent object* constituted by an *impure* act of transgressing all that is actually and indubitably given to reflection: a revulsion.

This act of misjudging, of distorting what is actually given, can be explained in the following way: insofar as a consciousness of revulsion, once reflected, appears as an "adumbration" (*Abschattung*) of hatred, it becomes tempting to posit beyond what is just an adumbration of a hatred (revulsion actual given), the state of hatred itself. Such a positional shift coincides with the act of constitution of a state, as a way to posit more than what is actually given. By positing a transcendent object where there is only an adumbration of a transcendent object, the positing subject tacks more on to reality than is actually there. It's the kind of thing occurring, for example, when, instead of perceiving what is actually given in perception, few adumbrations (*Abschattungen*) of an inkwell, I *perceive/posit* an inkwell as such: "So, to say 'I hate' or 'I love' on the occasion of a singular consciousness of attraction or revulsion is to perform a veritable infinitization, somewhat analogous to the one we carry out when we perceive an inkwell or the blue of the blotter" (Sartre 2004, p. 23). This overstepping of the bounds of what is given, this sort of procedure of projection, is how Sartre understands transgression.

Such a transgressive disposition is nevertheless constitutive of our natural way of perceiving. As a matter of fact, we take ourselves not to be perceiving aspects of things, but things themselves, although *what we are actually perceiving* are *aspects of things*. The passage from perception of aspects (or adumbrations) of things *to the perception of transcendent things* is considered by Sartre *an act of the constitution of transcendent objects* through a transgression of the limits of what is actually and really given: an adumbration of a transcendent object, *not the transcendent object as such*—which indeed coincides with hatred—"Hatred is a letter of credit for an infinity of angry or revulsed consciousnesses, in the past and the future" (Sartre 2004, p. 23).

Sartre calls such a transgression an "infinitization." When impure reflection posits the existence of a state of hatred instead of remaining faithful to what is *actually and really given* (an intuition of an adumbration of hate, a revulsion, not hate as such), it goes beyond the given in order and constitutes a state *from which* the consciousness of revulsion is supposed to emanate. This *emanation* constitutes the second dimension of impure reflection, which Sartre names inversion.

This inauthentic tendency constitutive of impure reflection must be defined as follows: a way to affirm more than what is immanently and instantaneously given (first dimension: transgression) in order to reflect consciousness *as a manifestation* of a state produced by an ego (second dimension: inversion). In impure reflection, consciousness sees its own revulsion as a manifestation of hatred, which means as *conditioned* by the prior existence of a state of hatred. Impure reflection coincides then *with the very constitution* of the state through a transgression—what Sartre names "infinitization"—of the actually given. At the same time, however, it implies a *radical inversion* of the real order of constitution of the state: "The order is reversed by a consciousness that imprisons itself in the World in order to flee from itself" (Sartre 2004, 34).

> It is a virtual locus of unity, and consciousness constitutes it as going in completely the reverse direction from that followed by real production; what is *really* first is consciousnesses, through which are constituted states, then, through these, the Ego.
>
> (Sartre 2004, p. 34)

"To flee from itself" means for consciousness to flee not so much from its spontaneity but its *impersonal* spontaneity. Reflection, when it becomes pure, should attempt to grasp consciousness as a "non-personal spontaneity." That is to say that impure reflection does not conceal so much the *spontaneity* of consciousness than *the impersonality* of such a spontaneity. As a matter of fact, as Sartre says: "There is no case in which reflection can be mistaken about the spontaneity of reflexive consciousness" (Sartre 2004, p. 14). This is why, in its activity of constituting the state in an inverted way, impure reflection has to deal at the same time with two seemingly contradictory requirements:

> The relation between hatred and the instantaneous consciousness of disgust is constructed in such a way as to cope simultaneously with the demands of hatred (the demand to be first, to be the origin) and the sure and certain data of reflection (spontaneity).
>
> (Sartre 2004, p. 25)

In impure reflection, consciousness perceives itself as an emanation of a state, which originates from the ego, *instead of* reflecting itself as an *impersonal consciousness*, which is actually *prior* to the state. This latter view would lead consciousness to see itself as independent of any psychological determinism—as being revealed by reflection as "creation ex nihilo" (Sartre 2004, p. 46), which is precisely what our natural impure attitude attempts to thwart. On account of its impersonal spontaneity, consciousness "is what it produces" (Sartre 2004, p. 33). If consciousness is conceived by reflection as coming first, consciousness can then no longer see itself as having an origin, a foundation, *outside* itself in the state of an ego that Sartre presents as what impure reflection considers "to be first" and as the "origin" (Sartre 2004, p. 25). The idea here is that the state is *constituted* and *posited* by reflective consciousness *as prior to consciousness*, as the "origin" whence consciousness is supposed to come from: "hatred appears through it as that from which it emanates" (Sartre 2004, p. 26). Further, because the ego is constituted as "the unity of states and actions" (Sartre 2004, p. 21), every state lived by consciousness is seen as the state of one and the same ego. The (inauthentic) inversion produced by reflective consciousness implies indeed the constitution of the ego given to consciousness as "the producer of conscious spontaneity" (Sartre 2004, p. 42), as an inhabitant of consciousness. In other words, as sharing the very nature of consciousness, as an element of consciousness—a source, a structure, an origin. An authentic reflection would, on the contrary, see the ego as something that is not "a relative existent, i.e. an object *for* consciousness" (Sartre 2004, p. 9). Sartre here, again, remains faithful to Husserl's distinction between the absolute and unsubstantial being of consciousness demonstrated by the fact that consciousness does not depend on the existence of the world to be and also by the fact that the relative and substantial being of the world *requires* consciousness in order to be. (See Husserl 1913/2014, § 49.) In the impure reflection, the irreducibility of consciousness toward the world is lost: consciousness contains worldly elements that *are not recognized as such*, since consciousness tries to conceal its own *impersonal* spontaneity in perceiving its spontaneity as having its origin in a (supposedly) *prior* psychological state. Against such a "natural attitude" that Husserl's transcendental reduction does not dissolve, Sartre reminds us that the ego cannot "be part of the internal structure of *Erlebnisse*" (Sartre 2004, p. 13). For this reason, Sartre claims that the only way to remain faithful to Husserl's fundamental idea (following which, the being of pure consciousness has nothing in common with the being of the world, since the former is "absolute" and the latter "relative") is to achieve Husserl's phenomenological reduction in excluding outside consciousness of the ego. This is because, as a worldly element not belonging to the immanency of consciousness, it implies a substantialization and a naturalization of consciousness that contradict directly the Husserlian discovery of the non-substantial absoluteness of the transcendental consciousness. This gives Sartre the ground on which to make the claim, "All the results of phenomenology are in danger of crumbling away if the I is not, every but as much as the world, a relative existent, i.e. an object for consciousness" (Sartre 2004, p. 9).

### *Pure reflection: from methodological inhibition to anguish*

There are two different accounts of pure reflection in *The Transcendence of the Ego*: a minimal, more formal version, which is described at the very beginning of the second part of the book, and a second, more developed version, which is to be found in the conclusion.

We will describe first of all the minimal and formal version that the second description will serve to enrich. In both cases, pure reflection (or pure *Epokhè*) is defined by Sartre as doing exactly *what impure reflection does not do*. In the first description of pure reflection, it is characterized by Sartre as an attitude that contrasts with the spontaneous natural tendency of reflection to constitute a state beyond the given immediate consciousness (revulsion).

Pure reflection is primarily described by Sartre as a non-positing attitude. It limits itself to what is currently given to it; it recognizes its revulsion as an "adumbration" of the hatred, *not as hatred*. Hatred, indeed, belongs to the field of the *dubitable* transcendence, since *only one* adumbration of it is given to me—my very repulsion—and never "the transcendent unity" of "an infinity of angry or revulsed consciousnesses, in the past and the future." To quote Sylvie Le Bon—"Every object, as an object for consciousness, whether it be my hatred or this table, will also remain dubious, since no intuition will ever be able to deliver it to me once and for all in its totality" (Sartre 2004, pp. 62–63).

Insofar as revulsion is an adumbration of hatred, "my hatred appears to me at the same time as my experience of revulsion" (Sartre 2004, p. 22), but precisely as a *transcendent limit* of my own experience, *not as the actual content of it*. In this sense, contrary to what happens in impure reflection, where I posit from the *only fact* that I have an immanent intuition of *one* adumbration of hatred (and never an intuition of the totality of them) that "I hate Peter," pure reflection "stays with the given without making any claims about the future" (Sartre 2004, p. 23). Pure reflection does not claim or posit anything beyond the current given: "I have a revulsion against Peter in this moment." It does not, *through* the current living revulsion, constitute a permanent state, an existing feeling that is supposed to recur after my current experience of revulsion in a new revulsion or in a feeling of disgust when I see Peter again. Pure reflection does not assert *more* than what it knows with certainty, which is simply what consciousness is currently living (a revulsion, not a state): "Reflection has *de facto* and *de jure* limits. It is a consciousness that posits a consciousness. Everything that it affirms about this consciousness is certain and adequate" (Sartre 2004, pp. 21–22). In pure reflection, consciousness does not look for an origin *of its own spontaneity* outside itself, in a transcendent object (improperly) constituted *as a psychological origin* of its current living experience: "Phenomenology has taught us that states are objects, that a feeling as such (of love or hatred) is a transcendent object" (Sartre 2004, p. 44). Insofar as, in impure reflection, these objects are constituted in "the reverse direction from that followed by the real production," a state is given to the reflective consciousness as a psychological origin of a current (reflected) consciousness. So, instead of perceiving its own being as coming first and never being preceded by anything else (itself as a "creation ex nihilo"), in impure reflection, consciousness flees from its originary impersonality by conceiving itself as an emanation of a state produced by an ego:

> It is thus exactly as if consciousnesses constituted the Ego as a false representation of itself, as if consciousness hypnotized itself before this Ego which it has constituted, became absorbed in it, as if it made the Ego its safeguard and its law.
> (Sartre 2004, p. 48)

This is, for Sartre, what explains the radical irrationality of the notion of the ego as a *derived instance* appearing to the reflective consciousness as a *principle*. As a matter of fact, "what is really first is consciousness" (Sartre 2004, p. 34). On the contrary, we can say that, in pure reflection, revulsion does not appear any more as *coming from* a source that would not coincide with consciousness as such—as a self-determining spontaneity: "transcendental consciousness is an impersonal spontaneity. It determines itself to exist at every instant, without us being able to conceive of anything before it" (Sartre 2004, p. 46). In pure reflection, the inversion of the real process of constitution is suspended since no egological state is constituted: the ego then *still appears* but it *no more appears* as the precise origin of consciousness:

> The reflexive attitude is expressed correctly by the celebrated phrase by Rimbaud (in the letter of the seer), "I is the other." The context proves that he merely meant that the spontaneity of consciousness cannot emanate from the I, it goes toward the I, it meets it.
>
> (Sartre 2004, p. 46)

What this quotation demonstrates is that pure reflection is not absolutely freed from the ego—it is not absolutely non-egological. It does indeed imply the *apparition* of the ego. Nevertheless, in the pure reflection, the ego is no longer improperly given as an origin, but as a *transcendent horizon* drawn by the current reflected consciousness: "The Ego doubtless appears, but on the horizon of spontaneity. The reflective attitude is expressed correctly. It allows to be glimpsed under its limpid thickness but it is given above all as an *individuated* and *impersonal* spontaneity" (Sartre 2004, p. 46).

In pure reflection, the current consciousness perceived, "meeting the I," *is nothing other than an adumbration of the ego*: one adumbration of what appears as its very horizon, a distant totality of consciousness, which coincides with the ego itself.

Consciousness cannot be identified with the ego that appears ("I is the other" ("Je est un autre")) in reflection, whereas the ego only appears *through consciousness, as a secondary and implicit apparition occasioned by the explicit apparition of consciousness*. The ego appears then as the horizon toward which consciousness is directed. Insofar as it functions as a horizon, it appears in pure reflection as remaining *other*—it no more appears as an inhabitant of consciousness nor as an *a priori* source of consciousness. The ego appears through the current consciousness perceived as a transcendent object standing *beyond* consciousness and that consciousness only *joins*—which means that it appears through consciousness as a horizon — ("it allows to be glimpsed under its limpid thickness but it is given above all as an individuated and impersonal spontaneity").

The only difference between the pure and the impure reflective act is thus: the impure reflection *posits and constitutes* the appearing ego as the very origin of consciousness. Pure reflection, on the other hand, *lets the ego draw itself* as a distant horizon, which reflected consciousness only "joins." To this extent, we can see how much the ego finds its condition of possibility in the reflection, since it appears as a horizon, a potential object that can be constituted, *but that pure reflection refrains itself from constituting*. In this sense, we could say that the condition of possibility of the ego depends upon reflection, because it is only in reflection that it appears. At the same time, however, what differentiates pure and impure reflections is the way in which they relate to the ego: impure reflection posits the ego as a permanent object *from which* consciousness comes, whereas pure reflection maintains the appearing ego *as a pure and absolute potentiality that it refrains from positing*. Pure reflection would be then defined by this restraint, remaining faithful to the pure and absolute given *without constituting what appears through it*, in other words, without succumbing to the temptation of converting a horizon into an origin. In remaining a pure and distant horizon of consciousness, instead of an origin, the ego is maintained by this way in its very transcendent alterity ("I is the other").

In order to understand his concept of "pure reflection," we must follow carefully Sartre's explanation of it. As a matter of fact, in what we called the formal presentation of pure reflection, Sartre presents the pure reflection as a kind of ascetic restraint, an attitude based on self-inhibition: "Pure reflection stays with the given *without making any claims about the future*" (Sartre 2004, p. 23, my emphasis). Pure reflection lies in "this *refusal* to implicate the future" (Sartre 2004, p. 22, my emphasis). By contrast, impure reflection is presented as an attitude, which does not observe such a seemingly methodological prudence: "These two reflections have apprehended the same, certain data but the one reflection has affirmed *more* than it knew" (Sartre 2004, p. 24, my emphasis). Later, Sartre speaks about impure reflection this way:

> The unifying act of reflection links each new state in a very special way to the concrete totality me. It is *not limited* to grasping it as joining that totality, as melting into it; it intends a relation that crosses time backwards and gives me the source of the state.
> 
> (Sartre 2004, p. 32, my emphasis)

These two formal presentations of the two kinds of reflections might lead the reader to suppose that pure reflection is defined as a deliberate, prudent attitude of non-positing transcendent objects that appear through it: states and ego. This dimension is formally accurate, but only *formally*. Such a preliminary presentation of the pure reflection remains, at this stage of Sartre's text, entirely formal and theoretical, since pure reflection never occurs in our life as a *deliberate* act, faithful to a methodological prudence. It occurs rather as an accident, a non-desired and unpleasant event that unhinges our natural beliefs. In fact, our natural and spontaneous attitude remains mostly inauthentic, "impure and complicitious" (Sartre 2004, p. 23). It does not seem possible to exercise any kind of self-restraint within the realm of our concrete experience. We are rather, it seems, in spite of ourselves, radically constrained by our experience insofar as it is necessary to endure "pure reflection" which occurs, in its true concrete form, with *anguish*:

> It may happen that consciousness suddenly produces itself on the pure reflective level. Not perhaps without an ego, but overflowing the ego on all sides, dominating it and supporting it outside itself by a continuous creation. On this level, there is not distinction between the possible and the real, because the appearance is absolute. There are no more barriers, no more limits, nothing that can disguise consciousness from

> itself. Thus consciousness, realizing what might be called the fate of its spontaneity, suddenly becomes filled with anguish.
>
> (Sartre 2004, p. 48)

Consciousness discovering its impersonal spontaneity is then never an experience that can be decided. It happens rather as an accident of our natural experience, which suspends our natural attitude. Such an *Epokhè* of our natural attitude occurs precisely at the moment when consciousness appears to itself as *overflowing the ego*. In other words, when it manifests itself as realizing an existence that *cannot any more* find its origin and determinate source in the ego: "There is something that provokes anxiety for each of us in thus grasping, as it occurs, this tireless creation of existence of which *we* are not the creators" (Sartre 2004, p. 46; original emphasis). In pure reflection concretely experienced as anxiety the ego still appears, but because *of the form that is taken by the reflected consciousness*, such an ego *can no longer be posited* as its producer. The *I* as embodying the principle of consciousness is *suspended*. The ego is no more constituted as the source of consciousness, which means that it is no more constituted at all. In the experience that consciousness makes of itself in anxiety, the thesis inherent to the natural attitude is entirely suspended.

In fact, in pure reflection as anxiety, consciousness appears in its *impersonal* dimension, which means, appears as something occurring *independently of the nature of one's personality*: "On this level, man has the impression of eluding himself ceaselessly, overflowing himself, surprising himself by a richness that is always unexpected" (Sartre 2004, pp. 46–47).

Sartre thinks that such a non-controllable self-creativity of consciousness—the fact that *I* don't play any actual role in the production of our "conscious lives" (Sartre 2004, p. 47) and that *I* cannot do anything against such a creation since *I* am overflowed by it—gives to the reflected consciousness what Sartre calls a "monstrous" dimension (Sartre 2004, p. 47). This, as the name suggests, refers to the inhuman aspect of pure consciousness since, indeed, "The I appears only on the level of humanity" (Sartre 2004, p. 5). Such a monstrous dimension is presented by Sartre as the cause of anxiety and as the origin of psychasthenia discovered by Janet and (mostly) psychoanalysis. Sartre refers to the example of Janet:

> A young bride suffered from a terror that, when her husband left her alone, she would go over to the window and hail the passers-by as prostitutes do. Nothing in her upbringing, in her past, or in her character can serve as an explanation for such a fear. In my view, it is simply that a circumstance of no importance (reading, conversation, etc.) had caused in her what might be called a vertigo of possibility. She found herself monstrously free and this vertiginous liberty appeared to her *on the occasion* when she was free to make this gesture that she was afraid of making. But this vertigo can be understood only if the consciousness

suddenly appears to itself as infinitely overflowing its possibilities the I that ordinarily acts as its unity.

(Sartre 2004, p. 47)

What Sartre calls here the "vertigo of possibility" (Sartre 2004, p. 47) coincides with the following existential event: after a contingent and meaningless happening ("lecture," "conversation," etc.) the young bride found herself overflowing with all the possibilities offered by its radical freedom. In her case, there were some behaviors, for example, acting like a prostitute, that she would be unlikely to pursue because she took them to be incompatible with the sort of person she is. Those types of actions appear to her now, after a pure and meaningless contingent event, as behaviors *that nothing can prevent her from adopting*. She discovers, it seems, her own freedom in a "vertigo" because "consciousness suddenly appears to itself as infinitely overflowing in its possibilities the I that ordinarily acts as its unity" (Sartre 2004, p. 47). In the case of the young bride, the "vertigo" of the discovery of her absolute freedom—the pure and positive discovery of the fact that *she can* adopt behaviors radically incompatible with her personal identity—becomes manifest to her "on the occasion when she was free to make this gesture that she was afraid of making" (Sartre 2004, p. 47). In other words, in pure reflection, the individual exhibits a behavior *that cannot be the behavior of her ego*. Her ego cannot prevent her from performing actions that fall outside the scope of actions her ego would be able to create. What this woman becomes aware of is the fact that, despite the fact that *she does not have* the personality of someone who could make these kinds of gestures ("go over to the window and hail the passers-by"), her personality, the nature of her ego, *cannot* prevent her from making them, because of the impersonal self-production of consciousness that she discovers in anguish. Such a situation can be explained only if her *ego is not* the *actual* source of her behavior. Indeed, "If the I of the 'I think' is the primary source of consciousness, this anguish is impossible" (Sartre 2004, p. 49).

## The modification of the phenomenological Epokhè

The transcendental reduction Sartre describes as "a pure reflective act, which would present itself to itself as a non-personal spontaneity" (Sartre 2004, p. 42). Such an act differs in its Sartrean version from the original Husserlian version in four fundamental ways. First, as we have seen, Sartre's reduction shares one aspect with Husserl's—in both cases, an ego is appearing in the field of the reflected. Contrary to Husserl's views, however, in the version presented by Sartre of the phenomenological *Epokhè*, the ego is given not as the principle of the unity of consciousness, but *as what is overflowed* by consciousness: "It may happen that consciousness suddenly produces itself on the pure reflective level. Not perhaps without an Ego, but overflowing the Ego on all sides, dominating it and supporting it outside its continuous creation" (Sartre 2004, p. 48). In Husserl, the reduction was presented as an act of freedom, an unmotivated act, an act accomplished with no prior motives or reasons: "As you will know, in his *Kant-studien* article, confesses not without melancholy that, so long as one remains in the 'natural' attitude, there is *no reason*, no 'motive', for performing the *Epokhè*" (Sartre 2004, p. 49).

Insofar as the phenomenological reduction becomes an accident of ordinary life for Sartre, it cannot be identified as an act that the subject would deliberately and freely perform. On Sartre's account, we are, sometimes and by accident, exposed and *condemned* to the reduction. The purification of the field of consciousness from any egological character is then obtained in the experience of anguish, which coincides with *Epokhè* in its concrete and existential mode: "It is this absolute and irremediable anguish, this fear of oneself, that in my view is constitutive of pure consciousness" (Sartre 2004, pp. 48–49).

Third, the Sartrean reduction coincides with the experience of the anxiety as such. It is therefore not, as it is in Husserl's phenomenology, "an intellectual method, a skilled procedure" (Sartre 2004, p. 49). Contrary to Husserl's reduction, it is an ordeal that is universally experienced and existentially rooted; it is no more a *philosophical* act, but an *existential* ordeal. In this sense, we could say that Sartre was the first to interpret the phenomenological experience of anxiety, as it has been described by Heidegger in *Being and Time* (1962, § 40), as the very name for the phenomenological reduction as such. *Epokhè* "is no longer an intellectual method, a skilled procedure. It is an anxiety that imposes itself on us and that we cannot avoid" (Sartre 2004, p. 49).

Fourth, Sartre introduces a radical modification in the phenomenological concept of *Epokhè* when he claims that *Epokhè is a motivated act*. In Husserl's phenomenology, the reduction is accompanied by a *philosophical conversion*, that is, a change of attitude, from the natural attitude where we posit the world as *being-there*, to the phenomenological attitude where the presence of the world as *being-there* is suspended. What defines such a modification of attitude is the fact that it is entirely non-motivated, that there is no reason to perform the suspension of the world or to change our attitude toward it (Husserl qualifies in the § 31 of *Ideas* as a "radical alteration of the natural Thesis": Husserl 1913/2014, p. 52). In other words, there is no reason to leave the natural attitude, to suspend its fundamental thesis. It is for this reason that Sartre presents Husserl's *Epokhè* as a "miracle." In the alternative concept of the phenomenological *Epokhè* that Sartre proposes, it is no more a miracle, insofar as "we possess a permanent reason for effecting the phenomenological reduction" (Sartre 2004, p. 49). Indeed, insofar as the ego is not *really* at the principle of consciousness, nothing can prevent consciousness from appearing under a *non-egological* form. In other words, anxiety remains a constant possibility of our experience. Unlike Husserl's account, Sartre's account gives a reason for *Epokhè*.

Since *Epokhè* is a way to break with the natural attitude and since such a break is always for Sartre "an accident that is always possible in our daily lives" (Sartre 2004, p. 49).

Husserl claims that, if there is no reason to move from our natural attitude to the phenomenological one, it is because "this natural attitude is perfectly coherent and one can find in it none of those contradictions which, according to Plato, led the philosopher to carry out a philosophical conversion" (Sartre 2004, p. 49). For Sartre, contra Husserl, the natural attitude *is* precisely an *incoherent* attitude. It attaches to "an effort that consciousness makes to escape from itself by projecting itself into the me and absorbing itself in it" (Sartre 2004, p. 49). In order to remain in the natural attitude, consciousness has to constitute the ego "in completely the reverse direction than that followed by real production" (Sartre 2004, p. 34). This is to say that it constitutes the ego in a way *that does not unite* with the real order of its production. Such a reversion of the real, constitutive of our natural attitude, is sometimes compared by Sartre to an artificial construction, a fake montage (for example, when Sartre says that "the relation between hatred and the instantaneous consciousness of disgust *is constructed* in such a way as to cope simultaneously with the demands of hatred and the sure certain data of reflection": Sartre 2004, p. 25). This is why Sartre defines the relation between the states and the consciousness as an *illogical* and *magical* relation: "We readily acknowledge that the relation of hatred to the particular *Erlebnis* of repulsion is not logical. It is, to be sure, a magical link" (Sartre 2004, p. 26).

What this means is that the relation between the state and the consciousness, because of the reversal implied by the impure reflection, *has no logical coherency*. It, indeed, makes the *passive* object (the ego) appear erroneously as a source of *spontaneity*:

> The link between the Ego and its states thus remains an unintelligible spontaneity. It is this spontaneity that was described by Bergson in *Time and Free Will: An Essay on the Immediate Data of Consciousness*, it is this spontaneity that he takes for freedom, without realizing that he is describing an object and not a consciousness and that the link he is positing is perfectly irrational because the producer is passive vis-à-vis the thing created. However irrational it may be, this link is nonetheless the one that we observe in the intuition of the ego. And we grasp its meaning: the ego is an object apprehended but is also constituted by reflective knowledge. It is a virtual locus of unity, and consciousness constitutes it as going in completely the reverse direction from that followed by real production; what is really first is consciousnesses, through which are constituted states, then, through these, the Ego. But, as the order is reversed by a consciousness that imprisons itself in the World in order to flee from itself, consciousnesses are given as emanating from states, and states as produced by the Ego. As a consequence, consciousness

projects its own spontaneity into the object Ego so as to confer on it the creative power that is absolutely necessary to it. However, this spontaneity, represented and hypostatized in an object, becomes a bastard, degenerate spontaneity, which magically preserves its creative potentiality while becoming passive.

(Sartre 2004, pp. 34–35)

For Sartre, our natural attitude is an illogical attitude based on relations of magic. It is an attitude internally inconsistent and therefore impossible for us to maintain. The move from one attitude to another—from our natural attitude to anxiety—as the very phenomenological name for the transcendental reduction, is unavoidable. We are necessarily exposed, in spite of our efforts, to accidental moments of anxiety in which we are condemned to the suspension of our natural attitude. Sartre defines the natural attitude as a constant effort to avoid the truth of our being, and he specifies that such an effort is "never completely rewarded" (Sartre 2004, p. 49). Our natural impulse to flee from our own freedom is evident from the constitution of illogical relations between consciousness and the ego. The internal incoherence of the natural attitude exposes the fundamental impossibility of remaining always in such an attitude; it brings to light the impossibility of non-being sometimes exposed to the radical suspension of the natural attitude in anxiety.[2]

## Notes

1 This point has been well demonstrated by Philippe Cabestan (see Cabestan 2004, pp. 304–305).
2 I would like to thank all the participants of the seminar "Radical Immanence," held at the University of Chicago during the Fall of 2014, especially my colleague David Finkelstein.

## Bibliography

Benoist, Jocelyn (1994). *Autour de Husserl, l'ego et la raison.* Paris: Vrin.
Cabestan, Philippe (2004). *L'être et la conscience.* Paris: Ousia.
Coorebyter, V. (2003). "Introduction" to Sartre J.P. *La Transcendance de l'ego.* Paris: Vrin.
Heidegger, M. (1927). *Being and Time.* Trans. J. Macquarrie and E. Robinson. New York: Harper and Row, 1962.
Husserl, E. (1900–1901). *Logical Investigations.* Vol. 1 and 2. Trans. J.N. Findlay. New York: Routledge, 1970.
Husserl, E. (1913/2014). *Ideas.* Trans. Daniel O. Dahlstrom. Indianapolis, IN: Hackett.
Husserl, E. (1999). *Cartesian Meditations.* Trans. D. Cairns. Dordrecht: Kluwer Academic.

Mouillie, Jean-Marc (2000). *Sartre: conscience, ego et psyche*. Paris: PUF, Philosophies.
Sartre, Jean-Paul (1970). A Fundamental Idea of Husserl's Phenomenology: Intentionality. *Journal of the British Society of Phenomenology*, 1 (2): 4.
Sartre, Jean-Paul (1984). *Being and Nothingness*. Trans. H. E. Barnes. New York: Washington Square Press, 1943.
Sartre, Jean-Paul (2004). *The Transcendence of the Ego*. Trans. A. Brown. New York: Routledge.

# 21 Sartre and Kierkegaard on consciousness and subjectivity

*Iker Garcia Plazaola*

According to Jean-Paul Sartre, "that which should be called subjectivity properly speaking is consciousness (of) consciousness" (*BN*, p. 17).[1] Various reasons account for the philosophical significance of this claim.[2] First, Sartre's claim concerns subjectivity and consciousness, two concepts that philosophers since Descartes have taken to be central in a philosophical understanding of reality and which, more contemporarily, philosophers in the analytic tradition have taken to be central in philosophy of mind.[3] Second, Sartre's claim *relates* subjectivity to consciousness; Sartre doesn't make a claim about subjectivity that, additionally, happens to be also about consciousness: Sartre relates the former to the latter in a prima facie philosophically interesting way. Third, more strongly, Sartre's claim *identifies* subjectivity with consciousness (i.e., a mode thereof): Sartre says that subjectivity *is* consciousness. Assuming that Sartre has a philosophically interesting way to unpack this identification, the fact that what is being identified is two concepts that philosophers since Descartes have taken to be central in a philosophical understanding of reality makes this identification philosophically interesting, whatever our ultimate assessment of it turns out to be.[4] Since in this chapter I will examine Sartre's claim in some detail, it will be helpful to have a name for it. Let's stipulate that in what follows "the $S = Cc$ thesis" or (for short) "$S = Cc$" refers to the claim: "That which should be called subjectivity properly speaking is consciousness (of) consciousness" or (ironing out emphasis and grammar) "Subjectivity is consciousness (of) consciousness."[5]

In this chapter I investigate whether $S = Cc$ can be found, in one formulation or another, in Kierkegaard's writings. In so doing I will construe a case for the common relevance of Sartre and Kierkegaard for locating blind spots in third-person approaches to consciousness and subjectivity defended in current analytic philosophy.

## Introduction

Before discussing $S = Cc$, let's quickly review the reasons why an investigation of this claim in connection to Kierkegaard has philosophical interest.

First, assuming that $S = Cc$ is philosophically defensible (and further assuming per my first paragraph that $S = Cc$ is philosophically significant, pending an elucidation of what $S = Cc$ is really claiming in the first place), it would be good to know whether, and if so, how, $S = Cc$ is endorsed in the context of a philosophical program significantly, if not radically, different from Sartre's. Putting aside in-depth considerations about the semantics of philosophical theses, it is plausible to hold that there is more to the meaning of a philosophical thesis than the meaning of the thesis asserted in isolation.[6] By investigating whether $S = Cc$ (in the same or an analogous formulation) is found in Kierkegaard's writings, we can elucidate the meaning of this thesis and assess its philosophical relevance (and, more ambitiously, its truth).

Second, Sartre's and Kierkegaard's philosophical programs are interesting in their own right,[7] and a comparative analysis is likely to be interesting in its own right too. It's difficult to summarize in a few sentences the interest of Sartre's and Kierkegaard's programs, but the umbrella concept that arguably does the job is *existentialism*. Kierkegaard is the so-called "father of existentialism," and Sartre is one of the movement's foremost twentieth-century representatives, along with Martin Heidegger. Existentialism is important because of its challenge to traditional ways of understanding human beings ("man" in traditional terms). In its most succinct form, the chief tenet of existentialism is that a human being ("man") is ontologically distinguished from the rest of entities in a way that has implications for (what can be called) meta-ontology: the *concepts* we employ in ontology to account for the ontologically distinguished character of a human being vis-à-vis the rest of entities need to be sharply distinguished from the concepts we employ in ontology to account for the type of being of the rest of entities. (This formulation of the chief tenet of existentialism is Heideggerian in inspiration. One can say, following Heidegger, that a human being is not only factually distinguished, but also ontologically, i.e., meta-ontologically, distinguished.[8]) This general idea has variations, among them the idea that a human being is not defined by *what* a human being is but by the fact *that* a human being is (of course, this formula needs unpacking). Another variation is that a human being is never an instance of a kind, but something irreducibly individual (I'll get back to this). In a popular exposition of existentialism,[9] Sartre follows Kierkegaard in attacking the idea that "Man possesses a human nature; this 'human nature', which is the concept of that which is human, is found in all men, which means that each man is a particular example of a universal concept – man" (Sartre 1947, p. 17) (again, this is the idea that Sartre *attacks*). Elsewhere in the same text, Sartre connects existentialism to the concept of subjectivity as follows: "Man is nothing other than what he makes of himself. This is the first principle of existentialism. It is also what is referred to as 'subjectivity'" (Sartre 1947, p. 18).[10]

This quote encapsulates what I'll take Sartre and Kierkegaard to suggest about consciousness and subjectivity in this chapter, i.e., that they are pivotal concepts in a philosophical characterization of a human being, a claim that, combined with the claim that the human being is an entity that is ontologically distinguished from the rest of entities, gives us the conclusion that consciousness and subjectivity are pivotal concepts in a philosophical characterization of entities in general (in ontology). Given that analytic philosophers typically see consciousness and subjectivity as concepts of "local" importance in philosophy (i.e., as related to the mental; see below for discussion), one can conclude that, if Sartre and Kierkegaard are right, analytic philosophers must be missing something important about these two concepts.

Third, and finally, consciousness and subjectivity are interesting philosophical topics in their own right, and an elucidation of these two concepts, as well as how they relate to each other, is likely to be interesting in its own right too. This is the place to expand on my footnote 2 and indicate that the concepts of consciousness and subjectivity can vary significantly for Sartre and Kierkegaard, on the one hand, and for analytic philosophers, on the other (complications arise from the fact that also for Sartre and Kierkegaard these two concepts vary; for the purposes of this chapter, I'll treat them as equivalent). This doesn't mean that an approach of the two sides is not possible (of course, given its purpose, this chapter assumes otherwise), but we need to be careful not to assume that whenever Sartre and Kierkegaard, on the one hand, and analytic philosophers on the other, use the word "consciousness" or "subjectivity" they are talking about the same thing. The chief difference is that when analytic philosophers talk about consciousness and subjectivity they typically refer to a trait of the mental, whereas when Sartre and Kierkegaard talk about consciousness and subjectivity, they refer to something more difficult to characterize, but certainly more general and not circumscribed to the mental. I'll capture this difference by saying that analytic philosophers talk about consciousness and subjectivity as concepts of "local" importance in philosophy, whereas Sartre and Kierkegaard talk about consciousness and subjectivity as concepts of "global" importance.

## The phenomenological tradition

Let's start examining $S = Cc$ as defended by Sartre. $S = Cc$ is defended in Sartre's *Being and Nothingness, Introduction*, V. *Being and Nothingness* (*BN*) is Sartre's magnum opus,[11] his most systematic attempt at developing a theory of consciousness.[12] One can summarize *BN*'s overall thesis by saying that consciousness and the world are ontologically primitive but radically asymmetrical: consciousness and the world cannot be reduced to each other, but whereas the world is something self-identical, i.e., something that (in Sartre's formulation) "is what it is," consciousness is something non-self-identical, i.e., something that (in Sartre's formulation) "is what it is not,"[13] and indeed radically so.[14] (This metaphysical thesis deserves a discussion of its own.) The upshot of this position is an ontological dualism with strong implications for what it means to be conscious (which for Sartre is synonymous with to be human), i.e., to be free, and indeed by necessity.[15] In this chapter I will put freedom aside, but I'll keep in mind that, for Sartre as well as for Kierkegaard, discussions about consciousness and subjectivity are not easily divorced from issues in ontology and metaphysics.

Sartre's elucidation of consciousness and subjectivity follows the lead of the phenomenological tradition started by Husserl[16] and developed most notably by early Heidegger (*Being and Time*, 1927). As suggested above, it's characteristic of this tradition to see in consciousness a concept of "global" rather than of "local" importance in philosophy. Generally, a theory of consciousness is supposed to answer the question what consciousness is, which includes a host of other questions, including: what are the features of consciousness? (the descriptive question), how can consciousness exist? (the explanatory question), and why does consciousness exist? (the functional question) (Van Gulick 2014). Approached from this perspective, consciousness is seen as an object of philosophical study, certainly a puzzling one, but (at least in principle) not essentially different from other objects of philosophical study such as God, freedom, knowledge, morality, beauty, and so on.

The phenomenological tradition, to which Sartre belongs, takes consciousness to be something significantly different. While phenomenologists do attempt to provide a theory of consciousness (or at least they assume one in their praxis), which certainly involves taking consciousness to be an object of study alongside other objects, they additionally take consciousness to be something more special and fundamental. For phenomenologists of the Husserlian brand,[17] the most primitive fact (*not* about consciousness, but *simpliciter*) is that no object is given to us unless it is given to consciousness. Moreover, phenomenologists hold that we need to examine how exactly objects are given to consciousness if we want to investigate philosophically interesting traits of these objects. Consciousness for phenomenologists of the Husserlian brand is thus an object of study that is located at a far more fundamental level of analysis than for philosophers in the analytic tradition: consciousness is both the fundamental object of study in philosophy and the locus where objects of study of interest to philosophy are given to us in the first place.[18]

For Sartre then, following Husserl, consciousness is not a trait of the mental or a special sort of knowledge or self-knowledge, but a special and philosophically fundamental part of reality (here I take "reality" to cover what there is at the most abstract level of generalization): "Consciousness is not a mode of particular knowledge which may be called an inner meaning or self-knowledge; it is the transphenomenal dimension of being in the subject" (*BN*, p. 7).

While Sartre has many things to say against Husserl in *BN*, he is here following Husserl, who in his first and most comprehensive exposition of phenomenology (i.e., *Ideas Pertaining to a Pure Phenomenology*, 1913) claims the following: "[Consciousness] remains as the 'phenomenological residuum', as a *region of being* which is of essential necessity quite unique and which can indeed become the field of a science of a novel kind: phenomenology" (Husserl 1913/1982, pp. 65–66, my emphasis).

Sartre's quote is important because he connects the concept of consciousness to that of subject, a preliminary step to connecting the concept of consciousness to that of subjectivity. We will see in a minute that Sartre draws a distinction between subject and subjectivity: intuitively, whereas the subject is the knower of reality (thus a concept that belongs to epistemology), subjectivity is the ontological constitution of the subject (whatever this exactly means) (thus a concept that belongs to ontology).

## Phenomenon and being

In consonance with Sartre's suggestion that consciousness is a concept that belongs to ontology (and indeed, to general ontology), and with the circumstance that Sartre's theory of consciousness belongs to the phenomenological tradition started by Husserl, Sartre's *BN* is, as indicated by its subtitle, an essay on "phenomenological ontology." Husserl's concept of *phenomenon* is *BN*'s starting point, and the way this concept connects to Sartre's notions of consciousness and subjectivity is through the concept of *being*.

Intuitively, we contrast being to appearing. Assuming that "phenomenon" is a (somewhat technical) synonym of "appearance," it's natural to say that a phenomenon is something that appears but might not be (i.e., exist), or (predicatively) that appears to be *x*, but might not be *x*. One can say, for instance, that Santa Claus appears (for instance, children meaningfully talk about him) but is not (i.e., Santa Claus doesn't actually exist), or that, e.g., this piece of metal appears to be gold but it's not actually gold; and so on. If for philosophical reasons we decide to suspend ontological commitments and investigate how things are given to consciousness (an investigation that is the chief theme of phenomenology, according to Husserl), the concept of phenomenon arguably experiences a modification and, instead of opposing itself to being, it becomes, in Sartre's words, "the measure of being," a criterion of being. Something *is*, one can argue, as Sartre does, to the extent that it *appears*.[19] Speaking in terms borrowed from analytic philosophy, one can define the concept of being in terms of the concept of appearing; according to phenomenologists, appearing is a *primitive* concept, not further analyzable. Modern philosophy, according to Sartre, can be seen as an ongoing attempt to replace the concept of being by the concept of appearing.[20] Does this mean that under this picture the distinction being–appearance collapses and *everything* is appearance? According to Sartre, saying that appearing does not oppose itself to being leaves up in the air what's the sort of *being* of appearing itself; indeed, this is the big philosophical problem that Sartre sees Husserl's phenomenology as raising: "If the essence of the appearance is an 'appearing' which is no longer opposed to any being, there arises a legitimate problem concerning *the being of this appearing*" (*BN*, p. 4).

Furthermore, Sartre comes to the conclusion that being and appearing cannot entirely coincide: "The being of the phenomenon although coextensive with the phenomenon, cannot be subject to the phenomenal condition" (*BN*, p. 6).

However, and this is what I'll take to be Sartre's first chief insight behind S = Cc, consciousness as a region of being is special insofar as for it appearing and being *do* coincide: "[Consciousness] thus remains a 'phenomenon' in the highly particular sense in which 'to be' and 'to appear' are one and the same" (*TE*, p. 8).[21]

This is a claim that, interestingly enough, Sartre shares with a number of philosophers in the analytic tradition (one could try to trace the agreement further back to modern, medieval, and ancient philosophy). For instance, Saul Kripke and John Searle argue that "with mental phenomena there is no distinction between surface appearance and real essence" (Melnick 2011, p. 45). As we have just seen, Sartre agrees: "Consciousness has nothing substantial, it is pure 'appearance' in the sense that it exists only to the degree to which it appears" (*BN*, p. lvi).

One can argue that this claim by Sartre has a phenomenological thrust. I take Sartre to be claiming that what-it's-like-to-be-conscious for a conscious being exhausts what it is to be conscious for that being. What we need to see now is that, according to Sartre, consciousness being conscious of itself is a necessary and sufficient condition for there being what-it's-like-to-be-conscious. Moreover, I will show, the primary mode in which consciousness is conscious of itself is pre-reflective, and only secondarily reflective.

## Consciousness (of) consciousness and pre-reflective consciousness

We know that subjectivity (the same as consciousness) is not for Sartre what analytic philosophers take it to be, i.e., a trait of the mental. Rather, subjectivity for Sartre is a concept that belongs to ontology. Sartre claims that this ontological foundation is consciousness (of) consciousness. What does "consciousness (of) consciousness" mean? To answer this question we need first to ask ourselves what "(of)" means. Sartre is using here a typographical device (brackets surrounding the "of") to indicate what he calls non-positionality. The concept of non-positionality refers to that of positionality, which in turn refers to "position" or "to posit," from Latin *ponere*. The Greek equivalent is *tinesthai*, from which we get "thesis" and the adjectival form "thetic" or "thetical," and hence "non-thetic" and "non-thetical" as the negative forms. According to Sartre, consciousness is positionally conscious of an object when the object is targeted explicitly as an object of consciousness. For instance, if I take a look at the Statue of

Liberty to describe it, I am positionally conscious of the Statue of Liberty. One might be tempted to say "object of attention" instead of "object of consciousness," but it's unclear whether attention is a concept that covers enough to include *any* possible consciousness of something (for instance, if I remember the Statue of Liberty, my consciousness is according to Sartre positionally conscious of the Statue of Liberty; but it's unclear whether we want to say in this case that the Statute of Liberty is my center of attention). According to Sartre, there isn't any consciousness that is not positional, since any consciousness explicitly takes an object or another as its object of consciousness (both "explicitly" and "object" should be understood here in a maximally broad sense): "[A]ll consciousness is positional in that it transcends itself in order to reach an object, and it exhausts itself in this same positing" (*BN*, pp. 7–8).

What Sartre is doing here is to give an ontological twist (some philosophers or historians say "existential") to Husserl's concept of intentionality.[22] If Sartre is right, consciousness is that sort of "entity" that exhausts itself in being intentionally related to other objects; it does so by being *conscious* of those objects.

Moreover, Sartre wants to argue now, consciousness cannot be conscious of other objects without being *conscious of itself* (as being conscious of those objects). In other words, every consciousness of any object is by the same token and *eo ipso* conscious of itself:

> [T]he necessary and sufficient condition for a knowing consciousness to be knowledge of its object, is that it be consciousness of itself as being that knowledge. This is a necessary condition, for if my consciousness were not consciousness of being consciousness of the table, it would then be consciousness of that table without consciousness of being so. In other words, it would be a consciousness ignorant of itself, an unconscious—which is absurd. This is a sufficient condition, for my being conscious of being conscious of that table suffices in fact for me to be conscious of it. That is of course not sufficient to permit me to affirm that this table exists *in itself*—but that rather that it exists *for me*.
>
> (*BN*, p. 8)

Sartre's conclusion, to put it in a slogan-like formulation, is simple: consciousness entails self-consciousness (by necessity, both phenomenological and ontological): "Every positional consciousness of an object is at the same time a non-positional consciousness of itself" (*BN*, p. 9).

Notice the contrast part "positional" vs "non-positional" in Sartre's formulation. Sartre elaborates on the difference in this way:

> This consciousness of consciousness . . . is not positional, i.e. consciousness is not its own object. Its object is outside itself by nature, and this is the reason why, in one and the same act, consciousness can posit

and grasp its object. Consciousness as such knows itself only as absolute inwardness. I will call such a consciousness "first order" or *"unreflective"* consciousness.

(*TE*, p. 8)

While Sartre, therefore, agrees with Descartes and Husserl that the starting point of philosophy is consciousness (of oneself), according to Sartre it's a mistake to think that reflection makes consciousness (of oneself) available to oneself for the first time:

> [R]eflection has no kind of primacy over the consciousness reflected-on. It is not reflection which reveals the consciousness reflected-on to itself. Quite the contrary, it is the non-reflective consciousness which renders the reflection possible; there is a pre-reflective cogito which is the condition of the Cartesian cogito.

## Kierkegaard and philosophy

A focus on Kierkegaard in a discussion of Sartre and philosophy of mind needs some justification, as it's not clear that Kierkegaard has something significant to contribute to this discussion. Indeed, a number of well-known facts about Kierkegaard's work seem to suggest the opposite. Kierkegaard is self-professedly a religious author,[23] specifically Christian, and he makes it clear that this circumstance dictates not only his philosophical concerns, but also the strategies he uses to communicate his chief philosophical insights.[24] While a religious orientation isn't necessarily incompatible with the defense of claims of interest to philosophers who don't assume that orientation, these claims are expected to be defensible on grounds independent from that orientation, something that arguably doesn't happen in the case of Kierkegaard. In an important intellectual-biographical text, *The Point of View* (*PV*), Kierkegaard contends that "to come to know [what Christianity is] thoroughly" is "in the interest of every human being" (*PV* 16), and he explains that the chief topic of his entire output is what he calls "becoming a Christian," specifically becoming a Christian "in Christendom."[25] It turns out that the task of becoming a Christian has, according to Kierkegaard, a philosophically interesting connection to the task of becoming oneself, which in turn requires an adequate answer to the question what the self is, a goal in the vicinity of understanding what consciousness and subjectivity are. This is how, at a first pass, Kierkegaard connects with Sartre and the analytic tradition in the present paper.

However, there are some hurdles in the way. Not only are Kierkegaard's philosophical concerns and claims dictated by his religious orientation, but his overall goal in developing these analyses is practically—rather than theoretically—oriented. Crudely, Kierkegaard's goal isn't to make his reader accept the belief that *p* (say, that the self is relational), but rather, assuming the truth of *p*, that his reader come to have the proper *stance* towards *p* (however this is exactly spelled out). Something along these lines is what Kierkegaard's claim "truth is subjectivity" means (although a lot of interpretative work is required to establish the exact connection). (Two other formulations of the same claim are "truth is inwardness" (*CUP*, p. 77) and "objectively there is no truth, but the appropriation is the truth" (*CUP*, p. 77).

With claims along these lines Kierkegaard is not advocating "subjectivism," if by that is meant the thesis that the truth value of some propositions is relative to different subjects. This position locates truth in propositions (assertions, beliefs, etc.), and thereby assumes truth to be chiefly an object of *knowledge*. Rather, Kierkegaard locates truth in the *relation* of the subject towards a proposition (assertion, belief, etc.), as well as in the relation of the subject towards *herself* in so relating to that proposition, and thereby assumes truth chiefly to be an object of *ethics* or *religion*. More precisely put, Kierkegaard locates (what he calls) *essential* truth (i.e., truth that has a direct and philosophically interesting connection to how one lives one's life) in the relation of the subject towards a proposition. The reader should be aware that Kierkegaard does not deny that there is truth that is located, and correctly so, in propositions, and which is an object of knowledge. This is what Kierkegaard calls "objective truth." What Kierkegaard wants to do is open logical space for a sort of essential knowledge whose truth is "subjective." The chief trait of this sort of knowledge is that it relates to one's own individual existence: "All essential knowing pertains to existence, or only the knowing whose relation to existence is essential is essential knowing" (*CUP*, p. 197).

This idea goes hand in hand with the idea that individual existence is the subject of philosophy. In order to investigate individual existence we need to endorse the idea that (what Kierkegaard calls) the *single individual* is a central category within a philosophical understanding of reality. In consonance with what I indicated in my previous paragraph, Kierkegaard connects this idea with a defense of his religious, in particular Christian, concerns. According to Kierkegaard: "*The single individual*—from the Christian point of view, this is the decisive category, and it will also become decisive for the future of Christianity" (*PV*, p. 121).

Or, more dramatically: "*The single individual*—with this category the cause of Christianity stands or falls" (*PV*, p. 122).

One may wonder what claims like these have to do with consciousness and subjectivity as a trait of the mental, but my contention is that Kierkegaard's concept of the single individual (abstracted away from religious considerations) is what is behind Sartre's theory of consciousness.

## Kierkegaard on consciousness and subjectivity

Kierkegaard is not interested in consciousness as discussed neither in contemporary philosophy of mind or in the phenomenological tradition to which Sartre (and Husserl) belongs. More generally, Kierkegaard is not interested in the mental or the mind, at least as a self-standing topic of philosophical reflection. As suggested, Kierkegaard's philosophical reflections are dictated by his Christian concerns (i.e., how to become a Christian in Christendom). However, many of the claims that Kierkegaard defends about being-human concern what we would call "the mental" if we were doing philosophy of mind. Kierkegaard's philosophical analyses, when they touch on aspects of the mental, have always an ethico-religious perspective. Kierkegaard of course assumes the existence of God, indeed of the God of Christianity (he assumes the truth of Christianity), and all his writings (with a few exceptions) have the normative goal to make the reader "become a Christian" (this expression needs spelling out; as suggested, it doesn't mean to pass from being a non-Christian to being a Christian; rather, it means adopting the right attitude towards Christianity assuming one already *is* a Christian). Given these circumstances, it's hard to see the interest of Kierkegaard for philosophy of mind (which of course ignores God and has no religious concerns). There are two aspects that make Kierkegaard's work potentially interesting for contemporary philosophy of mind: (i) phenomenological; and (ii) ontological.

## *Phenomenological*

Kierkegaard's focus on aspects of being-human that have a bearing on his Christian (or meta-Christian) agenda results in many instances in a description of those aspects from a phenomenological perspective (crudely, what-it-is-like for a human being to experience those aspects); one can plausibly construe these descriptions as being descriptions of the mental (broadly construed). Kierkegaard himself supports this reading with his insistence that there are three aspects to human being—the physical, the psychical and the spiritual, the psychical corresponding to the mental.

## *Ontological*

One of the focuses of Kierkegaard in both *The Concept of Anxiety* and *The Sickness unto Death* (see below) is what sort of being being-human has if something like an experience of anxiety and of despair is possible (one can call this investigation "transcendental" in a somewhat loose, Kantian sense, i.e., an investigation of the "conditions of possibility" of a given phenomenon, which typically targets the world as a whole).

Generally speaking, Kierkegaard objects against accounts of consciousness and subjectivity that, while taking the phenomenological and first-person aspects of consciousness and subjectivity seriously, think of these aspects in generic terms, not as applying to irreducibly *singular* individuals:

> An objection must first be made to modern speculative thought . . . by its having forgotten . . . what it means to be a human being, not what it

means to be human in general, for even speculators might be swayed to consider that sort of thing, but what it means that we, you, and *I and he, are human beings, each one on his own.*

(*CUP*, p. 120, my emphasis)

"Every human being has a strong natural desire and drive to become something else [than subjective] and more" (*CUP*, p. 130).

Remember that, according to Sartre, consciousness is conscious of *itself* by the same token that it is conscious of something. Analogously, according to Kierkegaard,

An individual in despair despairs over *something*. So it seems for a moment, but only for a moment; in the same moment the true despair or despair in its true form shows itself. In despairing over *something*, he really despaired over *himself*, and he wants to be rid of himself.

(*SD*, p. 19)

To despair over something is still not despair proper. It is the beginning, or, as the physician says of an illness, it has not yet declared itself. The next is declared despair, to despair over oneself.

(*SD*, pp. 19–20)

In order to understand what consciousness and subjectivity are for Kierkegaard, one needs to understand his philosophical anthropology. Kierkegaard's philosophical anthropology is a theory about what human being is, from a theological perspective. The chief tenet of Kierkegaard's philosophical anthropology is that the human being is a synthesis of psyche and body that is sustained by spirit (*CA*, p. 48). In order to spell out Kierkegaard's views on consciousness and subjectivity it all comes down to spelling out this chief tenet.

Kierkegaard's *Concept of Anxiety* (*CA*) (1845/1981) is an investigation of (what Kierkegaard calls) anxiety[26] as a condition of original sin (also called ancestral sin). This investigation is obviously theological in nature and it's difficult to see how it connects with the topics of consciousness and subjectivity in connection to contemporary philosophy of mind. I contend, however, that Kierkegaard's theological presuppositions (the existence of God, the existence of sin, the possibility of salvation, etc.) can be methodologically "suspended" without substantial loss (at least for the purposes of this chapter) to the interest of his insights about the topic at hand. For starters, a great deal of what Kierkegaard wants to accomplish in *CA* is of a psychological nature:

The present work has set as its task the psychological treatment of the concept of "anxiety," but in such a way that it constantly keeps *in mente* [in mind] and before its eyes the dogma of hereditary sin.

(*CA*, p. 14)

Kierkegaard's project in *CA* is to find out the relation between the particular individual and the human race. Kierkegaard's response is the *denial* of the natural response, i.e., that the particular individual relates to the human race as an instance of a kind refers to its kind. The concept of hereditary sin (also called original or ancestral sin) is important in conceptualizing the step from innocence to sinfulness, i.e., in explaining how one goes from innocence to sinfulness. The chief two options Kierkegaard considers are (i) through a continuum (a human being is innocent, but little by little he becomes less and less so until at some point he becomes sinful) and (ii) through a leap (there's an unbridgeable gap between innocence and sinfulness, and only a qualitative leap can explain the transition from one to the other).

"At every moment, the individual is both himself and the race" (*CA*, p. 28).[27] "Through the first sin, sin came into the world. Precisely in the same way it is true of every subsequent man's first sin, that through it sin comes into the world" (*CA*, p. 31).[28]

Therefore, Kierkegaard is interested in elucidating how Adam goes from being innocent to being sinful, because this is how every subsequent particular individual goes from being innocent to being sinful (*CA*, p. 29). Adam may be numerically the first individual, but ontologically speaking there is no important difference between him and subsequent human beings. "[Adam] is not essentially different from the race ... He is himself and the race. Therefore that which explains Adam also explains the race and vice versa" (*CA*, p. 29).

Kierkegaard's target is "traditional concepts" (*CA*, p. 29) of the difference between Adam's first sin and the first sin of every other man. Under the traditional account, Adam sinned, and as a consequence every subsequent man is in a state of sinfulness. According to the traditional account, when every subsequent man sins for the first time, he does so (strongly) because he is in a state of sinfulness or (weakly) under the assumption that he is a state of sinfulness. (The weaker account doesn't establish a specific tie between being in a state of sinfulness and sinning for the first time, but it is assumed that being in a state of sinfulness makes us have the disposition to sin.) Kierkegaard rejects this traditional account on the grounds that it cuts the connection between Adam and the race; the thrust of this rejection is that, under this picture, Adam is thought of as a human being abstracted away from his human condition.

> To explain Adam's sin is therefore to explain hereditary sin. And no explanation that explains Adam but not hereditary sin, or explains hereditary sin but not Adam, is of any help. The most profound reason for this is what is essential to human existence: that man is *individuum* and as such simultaneously himself and the whole race, and in such a way that the whole race participates in the individual and the individual in the whole race.
> 
> (*CA*, p. 28)

Kierkegaard rejects the view that sinfulness results from a quantitative progression in a continuum going from innocence to the occurrence of the first sin, either in Adam or in any subsequent individual: "It is . . . a logical and ethical heresy to wish to give the appearance that sinfulness in a man determines itself quantitatively until at last, through a *generatio aequivoca*, it brings forth the first sin in a man" (*CA*, p. 31).

Kierkegaard's formulation of the idea that every individual is wholly responsible for the occurrence of her first sin is that every individual is both himself and the race (*CA*, p. 31).

On a different order of things, the occurrence of sin is grounded on the existential circular structure of the very concept of sin: "Sin came into the world by a sin" (*CA*, p. 32).

I claim that this thesis is analogous to Sartre's thesis that the occurrence of consciousness is grounded on the existential circular structure of consciousness. Recall that, according to Sartre, consciousness has to exist in order to be conscious, but it has to be conscious of something in order to exist.

Similarly, Kierkegaard is suggesting that sin has an ontologically circular structure: one has to be in sin before one sins, but to be in sin is only possible if *one* (not Adam) has sinned. Crudely, then, sin presupposes itself. Since I take sin to be a concept that, according to Kierkegaard, has a philosophically interesting connection to the concepts of consciousness and subjectivity, it's reasonable to contend that, according to Kierkegaard, consciousness and subjectivity presuppose themselves:

"This is the profound secret of innocence, that it is at the same time anxiety" (*CA*, p. 41).

According to Kierkegaard, then, there is for human beings an experience whose ontological structure is circular, and whose experiencing reveals itself pre-reflectively and only subsequently reflectively. "The concept of anxiety is almost never treated in psychology. Therefore, I must point out that it is altogether different from fear and similar concepts that refer to something definite, whereas anxiety is freedom's actuality or the possibility of possibility" (*CA*, p. 42).

According to Kierkegaard, some categories (especially those of interest to ethics and religion) are intrinsically qualitative, which for the purposes of this chapter can be translated as "phenomenological." Thus for instance, Kierkegaard complains about attempts at explaining the concept of innocence in a way that approximates it to the concept of immediacy as dealt with in Hegel. "Innocence is a quality" (*CA*, p. 37).

Sin is a peculiar phenomenon (again, we take the concept of sin as a body of religious doctrine–Christianity, in this case–presents it, without assuming its truth). Sin comes into being from freedom, not from necessity. Sin doesn't draw on any reality whatsoever, only on *possibility*. This means that Kierkegaard is interested in how we experience possibility as possibility; and this involves analyses of relevance to the notions of subjectivity and consciousness. To start with, using Sartrean terminology, we can say that Kierkegaard assumes that there can't be possibility without consciousness (of) possibility.

## Conclusion

One can construe Sartre and Kierkegaard[29] on consciousness and subjectivity as a challenge to first-person approaches to consciousness and subjectivity that (to their eyes) fail to develop a sufficiently robust concept of first-personhood.[30] This idea would require substantial spelling out, but it probably should be presented with the help of the concept of individualization (not to be confused with individuation), which should be presented in turn with the help of the concepts of instance and kind. One can say that a philosophical approach to consciousness and subjectivity fails to develop a sufficiently robust concept of first-personhood if, despite adopting a first-person stance towards consciousness and subjectivity (i.e., despite taking seriously the idea that consciousness and subjectivity must be accounted for from a first-person perspective), the philosophical story that results from this approach presents consciousness and subjectivity as being entities (in a maximally broad sense) that can be thought of as *instances of a kind*. This can be called a "soft" concept of first-personhood. By contrast, Sartre and Kierkegaard emphasize, whatever consciousness and subjectivity ultimately are, they are *never* an instance of a kind. Individual existence (the category created by Kierkegaard and whose ultimate ontological locus is, *pace* Sartre, consciousness) is something ontologically primitive. We typically think of the concepts of instance and kind as interrelated: an instance of a kind is an individual item that belongs to a given category that includes (if not factually, at least conceptually) further individuals. Conversely, a kind is precisely a kind insofar as it applies to several individuals. In the case of consciousness and subjectivity, I take Sartre and Kierkegaard to argue, this doesn't hold: they constitute an ontological category of its own that undercuts the interrelation between instance and kind.

Given that Sartre and Kierkegaard attack first-person approaches to consciousness on the grounds that they fail to develop a sufficiently robust concept of first-personhood (or, under an alternative reading, that develop a sufficiently robust concept of first-personhood but fail to elucidate the ontological structure of first-personhood), a refinement must be introduced in the traditional landscape of philosophical approaches to consciousness and subjectivity. We can think of philosophical approaches to consciousness and subjectivity as traditionally divided into two big groups, third-person and first-person approaches. Whereas the former typically thinks of consciousness and subjectivity as being explainable or analyzable in terms of, respectively, non-conscious and non-subjective entities, properties, events, or the like, the latter denies that this is the case: consciousness and subjectivity cannot be explained or analyzed in terms of non-conscious and non-subjective entities, properties, events, or the like, but rather (using jargon taken from current analytic philosophy), they are "primitive" concepts (concepts we cannot analyze in terms of concepts that are more basic).[31] Alternatively worded, under a third-person approach, consciousness and subjectivity are taken to be reducible to non-conscious and non-subjective entities, properties, events, and the like, whereas under a first-person approach, consciousness and subjectivity are taken to be irreducible. One of the results of this chapter is that Sartre and Kierkegaard make a further division in the latter group, in virtue of which first-person approaches to consciousness can be seen as "soft" or "hard" first-person approaches. The idea here is that many approaches to consciousness (for instance, classically, Descartes') are first-person in a way that fails to individuate consciousness *radically*, i.e., individuate consciousness in the way indicated in my previous paragraph.

## Notes

1 J.-P. Sartre, *Being and Nothingness* [1943] (2003) = *BN*.
2 Pending a clarification of the expression "consciousness (of) consciousness"; see below for discussion.
3 Philosophy of mind is a core area of philosophy in the analytic tradition of philosophy which investigates the mind and its place in nature (McLaughlin et. al. 2009, p. 1). We will see in a minute that both "consciousness" and "subjectivity" mean significantly different things in Sartre and in the analytic tradition of philosophy. One of the purposes of this chapter is to show that, after expository and interpretative work, one can discuss these two terms in a way that puts in contact Sartre and Kierkegaard on the one hand and analytic philosophy on the other.
4 It can be argued that Sartre's identification of subjectivity and consciousness can't be particularly interesting, as these two concepts are many times used roughly synonymously in analytic philosophy (this point connects with the point made in my previous footnote). Sartre's claim, however, is meant to be non-trivial; see below for discussion.
5 My stipulation includes the requirement that this thesis be understood throughout in Sartre's sense. For what the thesis asserts, see the sections from The phenomenological tradition to Consciousness (of) consciousness and pre-reflective consciousness.
6 It's out of the scope of this chapter to address this issue in depth. By focusing on $S = Cc$ in Sartre and Kierkegaard, a side goal of this chatper is to make a partial case for the claim that the philosophical program within which a philosophical thesis is asserted makes semantic contributions to that thesis in a way that is probably systematic.
7 This is an assumption I make, but not defend, in this chapter.
8 "Dasein is ontically distinctive in that it *is* ontological." (Heidegger 1927/1962, p. 32)
9 Sartre (2007) (English translation of Sartre's famous 1945 lecture, *L'existentialisme est un humanisme*).
10 Sartre elaborates: "The word subjectivism has two possible interpretations, and our opponents play with both of them, at our expense. Subjectivism means, on the one hand, the freedom of the individual subject to choose what he will be; and, on the other, man's inability to transcend human subjectivity. The fundamental meaning of existentialism resides in the latter" (Sartre 2007, p. 22).
11 This is true of Sartre's early, existentialist period. Sartre's magnum opus of his later, Marxist period is *Critique of Dialectical Reason* (1960/2004).

12 In consonance with what I said in footnote 2, the expression "a theory of consciousness" means for Sartre something significantly different than for analytic philosophers.
13 See below for an elucidation of this claim.
14 A distinction should be drawn between *x* being non-self-identical (simpliciter) and *x* being *radically* non-self-identical. Intuitively, the latter adds to the former a "self-made" component: *x* being radically non-self-identical means that *x* makes itself non-self-identical, indeed that making itself non-self-identical is *itself* a component of what it means for *x* to be non-self-identical. We will see below, additionally, that Sartre draws the notion of radical non-identity from Kierkegaard's theory of the self.
15 Here's a first point of agreement between Sartre and Kierkegaard, as Kierkegaard also defends the view that man is "free by necessity" (this is not Kierkegaard's phrasing). Needless to say, substantial claims relating consciousness to freedom are at odds with basic assumptions in analytic philosophy, which takes for granted that consciousness and freedom are (pending an argument proving it otherwise) unrelated topics. The connection of consciousness and freedom has been defended by a host of modern philosophers, including Descartes, Kant, Hegel, and Heidegger.
16 Chief works: *Logical Investigations* (Husserl 1900/2001), *Ideas Pertaining to a Pure Phenomenology* (Husserl 1913/1982), and *Cartesian Meditations* (Husserl 1931/1995).
17 The qualification "of the Husserlian brand" is necessary, because some phenomenologists (most notably Heidegger) accept Husserl's thesis that the chief object of philosophical study is the phenomenon (i.e. what appears) without accepting that the chief locus of appearance of the phenomenon is consciousness.
18 If one wants an analogous object of study in the analytic tradition of philosophy, one can think of *language,* because in the analytic tradition of philosophy language is typically taken to be the field of study that makes possible the investigation of other fields of study within philosophy.
19 "[I]f we no longer believe in the being-behind-the-appearance, then the appearance becomes full positivity; its essence is an 'appearing' which is no longer opposed to being but on the contrary is the measure of it. For the being of an existent is exactly what it *appears*. Thus we arrive at the idea of the *phenomenon* such as we can find for example in the 'phenomenology' of Husserl or of Heidegger" (*BN*, p. 2). It might be contested that many things appear but are not, e.g., the rainbow; therefore it must be flawed to draw conclusions about what sorts of things there are (exist) based on what sorts of things appear. The answer is, again, that in this philosophical scenario ontological commitments are suspended: at this stage of analysis, we are not concerned with which things are (exist), but with which and especially *how* things appear.
20 "Modern thought has realized considerable progress by reducing the existent to the series of appearances which manifest it" (*BN*, p. 1).
21 *The Transcendence of the Ego* (henceforth *TE*) 8 (Sartre 1936/2004a).
22 Underlying these three theses is Sartre's idea that consciousness is defined, both phenomenologically and ontologically, by its intentionality. Once again, Sartre is following Husserl on this score. According to Husserl "universally it belongs to the essence of every actional cogito to be consciousness *of* something" (Husserl 1913/1982, p. 73) ("actional cogito" is Husserl's term of art for

any consciousness of something). Husserl sees intentionality as defining consciousness in general: "Intentionality is an essential peculiarity of the sphere of mental processes taken universally in so far as all mental processes in some manner or other share in it... Intentionality is what characterizes *consciousness* in the pregnant sense and which, at the same time, justifies designating the whole stream of mental processes as the stream of consciousness and as the unity of *one* consciousness" (Husserl 1913/1982, p. 199). "Under intentionality we understand the own peculiarity of mental processes "to be consciousness *of* something""(Husserl 1913/1982, p. 200). In *The Transcendence of the Ego* (*TE*), Sartre's first significant philosophical publication, he states that "the essential principle of phenomenology [is] 'all consciousness is consciousness *of* something'" (*TE*, p. 10). Thus, Sartre says, "consciousness is defined by intentionality" (*TE*, p. 6), "the essential principle of phenomenology [is] 'all consciousness is consciousness *of* something'" (*TE*, p. 10). "Through intentionality, Sartre elaborates on, consciousness "transcends itself, it unifies itself by going outside itself" (*TE*, p. 6). These claims are repeated in *BN*: "All consciousness, as Husserl has shown, is consciousness *of* something" (*BN*, p. 7).

23 *The Point of View* (*PV*): p. 23.
24 Kierkegaard has a philosophically interesting story to tell about why special strategies are needed to communicate the theses he wants to defend. Kierkegaard's key concept in this regard is "indirect communication," the idea that when it comes to the task of becoming a Christian, it would be ineffective to assert $p$ in the hope that the reader will come to believe $p$ and thereby change her life stance towards $p$. For instance, in *Concluding Unscientific Postscript to Philosophical Fragments* (*CUP*: Kierkegaard 1846/1992), Kierkegaard says: "Thus there is not a question about the truth of Christianity here in the sense that if this was decided the subjective individual would then be ready and willing to accept it. No, the question is about the subject's acceptance of it" (p. 129).
25 What the expression "becoming a Christian in Christendom" exactly means in Kierkegaard deserves a discussion of its own.
26 The qualification "what Kierkegaard calls" is necessary because "anxiety" is (or so I contend) a quasi-technical term in Kierkegaard: it partially overlaps with, but significantly differs from, "anxiety" in an everyday sense.
27 See also: "Adam also is himself and the race" (*CA*, p. 29).
28 See also: "Every individual... by his own first sin brings sinfulness into the world" (*CA*, p. 34).
29 In this chapter I have limited myself to early Sartre, that is, works produced between 1936 (*The Transcendence of the Ego*) and 1948 (*Notebooks for an Ethics*). As for Kierkegaard, I have focused on his two texts that had a biggest impact on twentieth-century existentialism: *The Concept of Anxiety* (1844) and *The Sickness unto Death* (1849).
30 Of course, there are many ways in which one can construe the philosophical interest of Sartre's and Kierkegaard's programs, and the one I propose is just one of them.
31 For non-specialists we can give the following example: we can analyze the concept of triangle by appealing to the more basic concepts of straight line and number three (a triangle is a geometrical figure made up of three lines), which in turn can be analyzed in terms of even more basic concepts (a straight line is

the shortest line between two points). If it turns out that the concept of, e.g., point can't be further analyzed in terms of something more basic, we say that the concept of point is "primitive" with respect to the concepts of line, number three, and triangle.

## Bibliography

### Primary references

Kierkegaard, S. A. (1845/1981). *The Concept of Anxiety: A Simple Psychologically Orienting Deliberation on the Dogmatic Issue of Hereditary Sin* (*Kierkegaard's Writings, VIII*). Princeton, NJ: Princeton University Press.
Kierkegaard, S. A. (1846/1992). *Concluding Unscientific Postscript to* Philosophical Fragments (*Kierkegaard's Writings, XII.1*). Princeton, NJ: Princeton University Press.
Kierkegaard, S. A. (1849/1983). *The Sickness Unto Death: A Christian Psychological Exposition for Upbuilding and Awakening* (*Kierkegaard's Writings, XIX*). Princeton, NJ: Princeton University Press.
Kierkegaard, S. A. (1859/1998). *The Point of View* (*Kierkegaard's Writings, XXII*). Princeton, NJ: Princeton University Press.
Sartre, J.-P. (1936/2004a). *The Transcendence of the Ego*. London: Routledge.
Sartre, J.-P. (1940/2004b). *The Imaginary*. London: Routledge.
Sartre, J.-P. (1943/2003). *Being and Nothingness*. London: Routledge.
Sartre, J.-P. (1946/2007). *Existentialism is a Humanism*. New Haven, CT: Yale University Press.
Sartre, J.-P. (1948/1992). *Notebooks for an Ethics*. Chicago, IL: University of Chicago Press.
Sartre, J.-P. (1960/2004). *Critique of Dialectical Reason Volume 1: Theory of Practical Ensembles*. London: Verso.
Sartre, J.-P. (1948). Conscience de soi et connaissance de soi. *Bulletin de la Société Française de Philosophie*, 42: pp. 49–91; English translation: Consciousness of self and knowledge of self. In N. Lawrence and D. O'Connor (Eds.). *Readings in Existential Phenomenology*. Englewood Cliffs, NJ: Prentice-Hall, pp. 113–142.

### Secondary references

Antony, M. V. (2002). Concepts of Consciousness, Kinds of Consciousness, Meanings of 'Consciousness'. *Philosophical Studies* 109 (2): pp. 1–16.
Burge, T. (2007). *Foundations of Mind. Philosophical Essays, Volume 2*. Oxford: Oxford University Press.
Chalmers, D. (1996). *The Conscious Mind: In Search of a Fundamental Theory*. Oxford: Oxford University Press.
Dahlstrom, D. (2010). Freedom Through Despair: Kierkegaard's Phenomenological Analysis. In Hanson, J. (Ed.). *Kierkegaard as Phenomenologist: An Experiment*. Evanston, IL: Northwestern University Press.
Gallagher, S. and Zahavi, D. (2010). Phenomenological Approaches to Self-Consciousness. In *The Stanford Encyclopedia of Philosophy* (Spring 2015 edition), Edward N. Zalta (Ed.). http://plato.stanford.edu/archives/spr2015/entries/self-consciousness-phenomenological/.

Hanson, J. (Ed.) (2010). *Kierkegaard as Phenomenologist: An Experiment.* Evanston, IL: Northwestern University Press.
Heidegger, M. (1927/1962). *Being and Time.* New York: Harper and Row.
Husserl, E. (1900/2001). *Logical Investigations.* London: Routledge.
Husserl, E. (1913/1982). *Ideas Pertaining to a Pure Phenomenology and to a Phenomenological Philosophy. First Book: General Introduction to a Pure Phenomenology.* Boston, MA: Martinus Nijhoff.
Husserl, E. (1931/1995). *Cartesian Meditations: An Introduction to Phenomenology.* Dordrecht, Netherlands: Kluwer Academic Publishers.
James, W. (1961). *Psychology: The Briefer Course.* Edited by G. Allport. New York: Harper and Row.
Kriegel, U. (2004). Consciousness and Self-Consciousness. *Monist* 87: pp. 182–205.
Kriegel, U. (2009). *Subjective Consciousness: A Self-Representational Theory.* Oxford: Oxford University Press.
Lewis, C. I. (1929). *Mind and the World Order.* New York: Charles Scribner's Sons.
Lippitt, J. and Pattison, G. (Eds.) (2013). *The Oxford Handbook of Kierkegaard.* Oxford: Oxford University Press.
McLaughlin, B., Beckermann, A., and Walter, S. (Eds.) (2009). *The Oxford Handbook of Philosophy of Mind.* Oxford: Oxford University Press.
Melnick, A. (2011). *Phenomenology and the Physical Reality of Consciousness.* Philadelphia, PN: John Benjamins.
Miguens, S. and Preyer, G (2013). Are There Blindspots in Thinking About Consciousness and Subjectivity? pp. 9–35. In Miguens, S. and Preyer, G., Eds. *Consciousness and Subjectivity.* Berlin: De Gruyter.
Miguens, S. and Preyer, G. (Eds.) (2013). *Consciousness and Subjectivity.* Berlin: De Gruyter.
Pseudo-Mayne, (1728/1983). *Über das Bewußtsein* (An Essay on Consciousness), edited by R. Brandt. Hamburg: Meiner Publisher.
Rosenthal, D. (1986). Two Concepts of Consciousness. *Philosophical Studies* 49: pp. 329–359.
Rosenthal, D. (2005). *Consciousness and Mind.* New York: Oxford University Press.
Sturm T. and Wunderlich F. (2010). Kant and the Scientific Study of Consciousness. *History of the Human Sciences* 23 (3): pp. 48–71.
Theunissen, M. (1993/2005). *Kierkegaard's Concept of Despair.* Princeton, NJ: Princeton University Press.
Tugendhat, E. (1979). *Selbstbewusstsein und Selbstbestimmung. Sprachanalytische Interpretationen*, English translation: Stern. *Self-Consciousness and Self-Determination.* Cambridge, MA: MIT Press.
Van Gulick, R. (2014). Consciousness. In *The Stanford Encyclopedia of Philosophy* (Spring 2014 edition), Edward N. Zalta (Ed.) http://plato.stanford.edu/archives/spr2014/entries/consciousness/.
Velmans, M. (1997). Definining Consciousness. Conference Paper (unpublished).
Welz, C. (2013). Kierkegaard and Phenomenology. In Lippitt, J. and Pattison, G. (Eds.). *The Oxford Handbook of Kierkegaard.* Oxford: Oxford University Press.
Wunderlich, F. (2005). *Kant und die Bewußtseinstheorien 18. Jahrhunderts.* Berlin: De Gruyter.

# 22 Invisible ghosts

## *Les jeux sont faits* and disembodied consciousness

*Jeremy Ekberg*

In Frank Capra's movie *It's a Wonderful Life,* George Bailey gets a second chance at living after his attempted suicide. With the help of his guardian angel he realizes how dismal life would be for his loved ones and his home town had he never existed. This epiphany makes George realize that suicide is not the answer to his problems and the film ends happily on Christmas with its protagonist shouting "Merry Christmas" in the streets of Bedford Falls. As joyful friends and neighbors pour into his home offering money, his adorable daughter declares, "Every time a bell rings an angel gets his wings" (Capra 1946). Just two years after this classic film was released, another with a similar premise debuted in France, entitled *Les jeux sont faits.* In the latter film, star-crossed lovers Pierre and Eve are also given a second chance at life, but in characteristically Sartrean fashion, things do not end happily for the protagonists. What both films have in common is an exploration of what could have been, as their protagonists embark on their mystical journeys of possibility and choice. At a sort of nexus of time and facticity, these characters are given a magical advantage over others, though only George Bailey makes it work in his favor. Jean-Paul Sartre's characters Pierre and Eve, on the other hand, remain too focused on their personal projects to love each other enough to save themselves. The two lovers are each faced with the terrible and impossible choice of having a perfect love versus saving themselves and the people they care for.

The film also investigates the limits of the Cartesian duality between body and mind and how this duality fits into Sartre's conceptions of consciousness. Sartre's characters are, for at least part of the film, deprived of their physical bodies and transformed into ghost-like, floating consciousnesses. This deprivation of the physical precludes any chance of physical illness or injury, but also renders them incapable of touching physical matter or being seen or heard by the living. Although their disembodiment gives them magical powers of invisibility, this clear demarcation of facticity limits their abilities to pursue their projects. Sartre tells us that the force of facticity is so strong that, "without facticity consciousness could choose its attachments to the world in the same way as the souls in Plato's *Republic* choose their condition" (Sartre 1984, pp. 131–132).

*Les jeux sont faits* is a film about consciousness but is about many things other than consciousness—love, rebellion, second chances—but is ultimately a film about failure. The dead tell Pierre, "Of course our lives were failures. Everybody's life is a failure" (Sartre 1948, p. 58). The old man who introduces Pierre to the world of the dead proclaims, "A man's life is always a failure in as much as he dies. He always dies too soon—or too late" (Sartre 1948, p. 59). Despite being mystically given a second chance to live their lives and find love with each other after their initial deaths, Pierre and Eve fail and in the end die a second death much earlier than they might have. But the entire project is a set-up: without their physical bodies and the concomitant pre-reflective consciousness, Pierre and Eve stand no chance of success in their endeavors. To have any chance of a meaningful existence, they and every subject must have a balance of reflective and pre-reflective consciousness. Sartre writes that human existence itself is in a sense a failure. "Human reality is a perpetual surpassing toward a coincidence with itself which is never given." This reality is a surpassing toward what it lacks. It surpasses itself toward what it would be if it were what it is (Sartre 1984, p. 139). Because each subject must necessarily pursue his projects and because this pursuit is always a surpassing, every in-itself is constantly in a state of failure.

Pierre and Eve struggle to love each other enough to save themselves while fighting their personal battles individually. Pierre leads a band of disgruntled and untrusting revolutionaries while Eve must contend with a homicidal, manipulative husband who wants to kill her and marry her sister. The two don't meet until after their deaths as they attempt to adjust to the afterlife, which for Sartre consists of wandering around and struggling futilely to interact with the living. At this point they are magically given a second chance at life because of Article 140, which states that if, because of an error by management, a man and woman destined for each other fail to meet during their lives, they may return to earth to fulfill their love and live together (Sartre 1948, p. 90). And the couple is given yet another advantage: they retain all their memories of their previous lives and their experiences in death; however, they have only 24 hours to prove their love for each other. Unfortunately for Pierre and Eve, they are too distracted with a world of facticity and with their loss of pre-reflectivity to love each other truly and their efforts end in bitter failure because they are deprived of their pre-reflective consciousnesses and are therefore limited in their abilities.

Colin Davis lists the themes of the film as freedom, responsibility, choice, the role of the individual in history, and the self's opacity to itself (Davis 2005, p. 222). *Les jeux sont faits* is a love story gone wrong, one in which second chances are ultimately squandered and its characters defeated by the powers beyond their control. The film also explores the process by which a single consciousness reflects upon itself, its habits, and its existence in a world of revolution and betrayal and how pre-reflective consciousness is associated with the body in accordance with Sartre's theories. Although

Pierre and Eve are given a second chance at life through some fantastic organization with the power to segue between life and afterlife, they are unable to change themselves and go against the habits which led to their deaths in the first place. They are able to reflect on their own consciousnesses but are unable to save themselves and the people around them at the end of the film.

The movie also explores the power of reflective consciousness in determining one's own reality. René Descartes vows in *Discourse on Method* to "conquer myself rather than fortune, and to change my desires rather than the order of the world, and generally to accustom myself to believing that there is nothing that is completely within our power except our thoughts" (Descartes 1998, pp. 14–15). Many philosophers see this statement as a major turning point in the history of philosophy, because, as Mark Taylor comments, "the distinguishing characteristic of modern philosophy is its tendency to think Being in terms of subjectivity" (Taylor 1987, p. 37). The main characters in the film are unable to conquer themselves. This power each individual possesses over his thoughts is what Sartre would later consider the radical and subjective freedom to which each subject is condemned. And it is only because of this radical freedom that each subject is able to create his own essence and his own reality. This concept seems untenable to the two lovers in the film, however, as they strive outwardly against facticity in their vain attempts at their projects, rather than striving to conquer themselves, as Descartes pledged to do. This subjective power each individual possesses has its origin in the soul, according to Descartes, while Sartre would have consciousness as that which is separate from the body. "Thus this 'I,' that is to say, the soul through which I am what I am, is entirely distinct from the body and is even easier to know than the body, and even if there were no body at all, it would not cease to be all that it is" (Descartes 1998, p. 19). With this, Descartes establishes the primacy of the soul over the body, though he also contends that both are necessary sine qua non of the subject. This is proven in the film when its two protagonists lose their bodies through death but retain their thinking selves.

Martin Heidegger built on Descartes's self-reflective process, as he theorized that self-consciousness is empowering for the ego. This is the key to the subject's realization that he is thereby further empowered over all things in his unique universe. Taylor writes in his commentary on Heidegger that "through the subjection of the object, the subject exercises its mastery over everything other than itself. Nothing can be present to self-consciousness unless it is represented by the subject's *own* representative activity" (Taylor 1987, p. 39). As a result, each subject filters through reflection every perception, every stimulus, through his own unique consciousness, which in turn makes every subject the master of his own reality. But, as Davis argues, consciousness is ghost-like in that it is both there and not there. "However, the knowledge that the *pour-soi* can never coincide with itself cannot prevent it from attempting to realize its desires, because its destiny is to try and to fail" (Davis 2005, p. 224). This inescapable failure is the same one the dead warned Pierre about. Unfortunately for Pierre and Eve, these concepts elude them. They remain disempowered when disembodied and incapable of overcoming facticity when finally given their second chance. They are unable to master themselves in relation to the world around them, unable to abide by the stipulations of Article 140, and unable to retain the balance of their two types of consciousnesses because they are caught in an existential trap of living death.

This balance is necessary not only for meaning creation for each subject, but for life itself. In *The Transcendence of the Ego,* Sartre argues that the body is the illusory fulfillment of the I-concept (Sartre 1960, p. 91) and that the body can serve as a visible, tangible symbol for the I (Sartre 1960, p. 90). What this means is that, while the body is distinct from the mind, to the individual, the body in a sense represents the mind to the outside world and in some ways to the self. But for at least part of the film, Pierre and Eve are essentially disembodied ghosts, as they walk around as conscious as anyone else, though invisible and intangible. In this state, they are limited physically as they are unable to open doors or perform other simple, physical activities. Their bodies are separated from them, and they see that this is so. In a sense, when the characters realize they are dead for the first time, it is a culmination of the process by which, according to Sartre, the concrete I is degraded. "[T]he body and bodily images can consummate the total degradation of the concrete I of reflection to the 'I-concept' by functioning for the 'I-concept' as its illusory fulfillment" (Sartre 1960, p. 90). In short, the body is not the self and never could be by itself. The body serves as a symbol for the I. Sartre continues, "I say: 'I' break the wood and I see and feel the object, 'body,' engaged in breaking the wood" (Sartre 1960, p. 90). Sartre insists that the I exists on both the reflected and unreflected levels of consciousness (Sartre 1960, p. 89), but that on the latter, the I loses its intimacy (Sartre 1960, p. 90). The subject, especially during the performance of physical tasks or during illness, is unable to consider himself simply his body. Sartre sees the unreflected I as having its focus more on external, factic elements of consciousness, rather than on reflective thought.

What all this means for Pierre and Eve is that, when they see their dead bodies, they are no longer those dead bodies at all, but are new beings. With each moment of consciousness, each subject has the power to choose and re-choose who he will be and must do so because condemned to freedom. Sartre's theories on this subject are outlined in his treatment of the café waiter (Sartre 1984, pp. 101–103). The waiter is a waiter but this is not all he is. When he goes home, he is a father or husband or whatever else he is. Just like Sartre's waiter, Pierre and Eve continually choose who and what they are based on their projects and how to pursue them. They are, after all, for-itselfs and must be what they are not and not be what they are. As Eve's dead body lies on her bed, her disembodied self, her "I," phantom leans against the wall watching her sister Lucette mourn for her as her husband

André comforts Lucette (Sartre 1948, pp. 66–67). Her dead body is merely a symbol of her former self, just as Pierre's dead body is a symbol of what he used to be. Sartre tells us in *Being and Nothingness* that "for the unreflective consciousness pain *was* the body; for the reflective consciousness the illness *is* distinct from the body, it has its own form, it comes and goes" (Sartre 1984, pp. 442–443). So the Cartesian demarcation between body and soul is akin to Sartre's distinction between reflective and pre-reflective consciousnesses because each distinction divides each thinking subject in two: the physical and the psychical selves.

Pre-reflective consciousness is more associated with the body in the sense that this type of consciousness comprises the subject simply doing or being, rather than reflecting. In *The Transcendence of the Ego,* Sartre uses the example of chopping wood as an activity closely associated with pre-reflective consciousness. But when the two protagonists of *Les jeux sont faits* are deprived of their bodies through death, their pre-reflective consciousnesses are limited. They are no longer able to see their bodies as symbols. As essentially ghosts, the pair must rely on their reflective consciousnesses to pursue their goals until they are inexplicably given a second life to live. As Sartre writes, "All consciousness is positional in that it transcends itself in order to reach an object" (Sartre 1984, p. 11). If a consciousness is capable of reaching an external object, it is also able to reach itself via reflection upon itself.

But Sartre insists that the I does appear on the unreflected level of consciousness (Sartre 1960, p. 89). He lists simple tasks, including trying to hang a picture and repairing a tire, as examples of conscious tasks which do not transport a subject to the level of reflection (Sartre 1960, p. 89). These simple tasks are qualities of the world and not unities of consciousness (Sartre 1960, p. 90). They do not require reflection, but call for unreflective, physical activity performed in facticity. The body serves as a symbol of the I in these moments of conscious and physical activity. Disembodied Eve and Pierre lose this symbol in a way no for-itself ever could in the real world and are as a result disempowered.

When Pierre and Eve realize they are dead, they lose their bodies and are forced into a state of being in which their reflective consciousnesses dominate and their pre-reflective consciousnesses render them all but helpless as they are unable to communicate or touch the living. As ghost-like phantoms, the couple becomes invisible to the living, which forces them to become disembodied reflective consciousnesses. The loss of their bodies gives Pierre and Eve special powers of a sort, as they are invisible to the living and can, for example, spy on Eve's husband and Pierre's enemy the Regent without their knowledge. The elderly dead man who befriends Pierre sees being dead as a good thing. He declares that in death there are "no responsibilities. No material worries. Complete liberty. Choice diversions" (Sartre 1948, p. 75). On the other hand, both characters are disempowered in the physical world because they are unable simply to grasp objects, etc. In their failed attempts to protect Lucette from André and stop the rebel uprising which results in the group's decimation, the two protagonists of the film are forced to exert more energy in their reflective consciousnesses, as they use their wits rather than their physical bodies, in their efforts. They are unable to adjust to their lives after death in the manner the old man has. They remain attached to the people they knew in life and thereby to the world of the living.

The distinction between the two types of consciousness and the importance of each is established early in the film. In the opening scene of the film, Eve's fingers claw at her fur coverlet as she tosses and groans (Sartre 1948, p. 7). Here, Eve is not consciously reflecting but is unreflectively being her body. She is existing in her body in the sense that she at that moment *is* her body more than a reflecting consciousness. Sartre writes that a consciousness exists in its body, but that "there is on the level of the unreflective consciousness no consciousness *of* the body. The body belongs then to the structures of the non-thetic self-consciousness" (Sartre 1984, p. 434). Pre-reflective consciousness is also characterized by its involuntary qualities, while reflective consciousness is by its nature required for voluntary acts (Sartre 1984, p. 581). In the same scene of the film, however, her duplicitous husband André is reflecting, as he looks at his wife with cold scrutiny, suggesting that he is plotting something, thinking how best to be rid of her while keeping her money and marrying Eve's sister, Lucette.

As Eve sleeps, she relies on her pre-reflective (involuntary) consciousness while at the same moment André reflects, as he places poison in her glass (Sartre 1948, p. 8). As André is plotting Eve's death, he constantly reflects on his projects: to kill his wife, marry Lucette, and take a second dowry. As Eve sleeps, she does not reflect, although all the major characters engage in reflective thought at some point. Pierre, for example, plans his insurrection while Eve attempts to save her sister from her husband's clutches. As part of Pierre's reflection, he observes the habits of not only himself, but of others. He calls Lucien—the man who later shoots and kills him—a "dirty little squealer" (Sartre 1948, p. 18), passing a sort of judgment on that character's habits. Meanwhile, Eve accuses André of marrying her for her money and of manipulating Lucette (Sartre 1948, p. 20). These accusations are based on Pierre's and Eve's reflective (voluntary) observations of, and interactions with, the other characters.

In many ways *Les jeux sont faits* is a film about the decisions its characters make, and these decisions can only be voluntary, that is, reflective (Sartre 1984, p. 606). But as a film about failure, its characters make many mistakes and the efforts of at least Eve and Pierre are mostly in vain. According to Davis, the film suggests that second chances are not real and that every subject is destined to repeat his mistakes (Davis 2005, p. 226). But this view raises questions about the absolute freedom of Sartre's theories. Simply because they are forced to focus their conscious energies on reflection does not mean their reflections are any better or more effective than when they were alive. It is possible for them to make so many errors because, as Sartre explains, the for-itself can make decisions which are actually opposed to the fundamental ends which it has chosen. The pre-reflective level, on the other hand, is a spontaneous, involuntary self-projection toward its possibilities and can never be deceived by itself (Sartre 1984, p. 606). This spontaneous, involuntary quality is what makes pre-reflective consciousness what it is as opposed to its reflective counterpart.

Sartre uses the English title of the film in *Being and Nothingness* to clarify his theories on the will: "If, therefore, the will is in essence reflective, its goal is not so much to decide what end is to be attained since in any case the chips are down; the profound intention of the will bears rather on the *method* of attaining this end already posited (Sartre 1984, p. 582). And it is precisely the methods of attaining their goals which go wrong for the protagonists. Sartre writes in *Sartre on Theater* that man is free in a given situation and that in and through that situation he chooses what he will be (Sartre 1976, p. 4). His characters choose what they will be through their decisions as they struggle with others, with facticity, and with their own methods of attaining their goals. They do not choose to die, but they choose the methods of attaining their projects, and this, in turn, results in their deaths.

When Eve is poisoned to death and Pierre fatally shot, it is their pre-reflective selves that cease to be. They actually see their bodies, what Sartre called the symbol of the I, sprawled out dead. Their bodies are denied them by André and Lucien respectively. Their reflective selves, on the other hand, continue to exist, as both characters go on thinking and planning, existing in their disembodied states; in short, pursuing projects. Eve sees the proof that her pre-reflective, bodily self has ceased to exist when she looks in the mirror and sees no reflection (Sartre 1948, p. 27). This is because her body is dead, though her thinking self continues to live. Pierre, for his part, begins to realize what has happened to him when he has no shadow (Sartre 1948, p. 31) and he receives a concierge's bucket of water all over his trousers, though they remain perfectly dry, symbolizing his disembodiment (Sartre 1948, p. 29). This lack of physicality in a world of facticity represents the loss of their pre-reflective selves and their bodies.

As Eve meets with the elderly lady who acts as a clerk for the dead, she is told, "the dead are free" (Sartre 1948, p. 45). The freedom available to Eve at this point in the film is more than that to which all subjects are condemned. In a sense she is more free because unrestrained by physical limits, though she is also less free because so limited without her body. Despite not having a body, Eve still has her will and her projects. "Tomorrow, your will of today will have fallen into the past, outside consciousness; it will have become ossified, and you will be entirely free with respect to it: free to adopt it once again as your own or to commit yourself against it" (Sartre 1999, p. 35). Both Eve and Pierre choose to adopt their wills again and again as they choose to get involved with the world of facticity and otherness rather than ignoring the outside world to focus on loving each other enough to save their lives.

This latter option seems to be condoned by the author himself, although ultimately he proves that the decision itself is impossible and the protagonists of the film are destined for failure.

The two main characters have their first meeting in a sort of test of their new but physically powerless states of existence. In a scene of pathos and futility, Eve attempts to warn a young girl on the street that she is about to be pickpocketed by a young tough. Unfortunately for the girl, she cannot hear Eve's warning, "Look out, little girl, he's stealing your purse" (Sartre 1948, p. 47). The destitute and pitiful girl is robbed because she is unable to hear the cries of a dead woman who exists as a specter with no body. The scene typifies the powerlessness with which the two lovers struggle, powerlessness over the physical world of facticity. It also foreshadows their powerlessness over the existential world of their wills and their reflective selves, as the crestfallen Eve declares, "It's awful . . . awful not to be able to do anything" (Sartre 1948, p. 49).

She experiences even more heartbreaking feelings of powerlessness as she watches Lucette mourn over her dead body while falling more and more into the clutches of the pernicious André. In the scene in which her deceased father appears and speaks to her, Eve realizes that her father is angry over André's manipulations of Lucette, but that he has accepted this powerlessness and seems almost indifferent to his youngest daughter's plight. "One quickly forgets the living," he flatly declares. "You'll see" (Sartre 1948, p. 71). But Eve's father has been dead presumably for several years and has become accustomed to his own futility, his powerlessness against the facticity of the world. He advises Eve, "Don't come back here if it makes you unhappy" (Sartre 1948, pp. 72–73).

But in the next scene, Pierre takes advantage of being physically powerless as he uses the opportunity of his new state of existence to spy on his enemy, the Regent. In the form of a disembodied phantom, Pierre glides through the Regent's elegant palace undetected by his enemy's henchmen. As he stands with a dozen or more dead, many of whom were the Regent's enemies, Pierre confidently reveals to them the planned insurrection against the Regent. "It's three years we've been working at it, me and the others. It can't go wrong" (Sartre 1948, p. 56). But Pierre sees and hears troubling things when Lucien, the man who shot and killed him, is brought into the room. By eavesdropping on Lucien, the chief of police and the Regent, Pierre learns that the Regent "wanted them to have their insurrection. With all the information in our possession," he says, "it was a unique occasion. All the leaders liquidated at one stroke and the League crushed for ten years" (Sartre 1948, p. 62). With this, Pierre learns that his death was a mistake, a crucial mistake made by his enemies. As a result, he resolves to pursue his project of defeating the Regent, though in the end this project fails.

In an act of complete futility, Pierre goes to the hideout of his fellow conspirators in a vain attempt to warn them of the Regent's treachery. He has his first taste of facticity when he is unable to alert his fellows to the Regent's plans as he has no voice; instead, he can only eavesdrop. He is disempowered, so he listens and learns that his raggedy band of revolutionaries plans to go through with the uprising despite his death and despite the fact that a trap is set for them (Sartre 1948, p. 65). In yet another futile act, he pounds on the door and shouts "it's a trap, men! Hold everything. It's a trap." For the first time since his death, he knows the futility of his efforts and suffers from them (Sartre 1948, p. 66).

The protagonists of *Les jeux sont faits* are powerless because denied their pre-reflective selves. They are also limited by a horrible choice: focus their projects on the people in their former lives by attempting to aid the living, or ignore the world around them, love each other, and live happily in accordance with Article 140. But this is an unfair and impossible choice, as Pierre and Eve are unable to stand by and watch others perish and are unable to aid the living. They are tempted to let the world go on without them, especially as they dance together for the first time and become enraptured with each other. Pierre even remarks that dancing with Eve would be better than life itself (Sartre 1948, p. 87). But they are ultimately unable to give up on the world. Pierre had earlier declared, "the docility of the dead is beyond me" to the nameless old man who befriends him (Sartre 1948, p. 75). So their dance is a farce and they know it. They are unable to touch each other in their disembodied, disempowered states and their joyous union becomes tragic as they admit this to each other (Sartre 1948, p. 88).

In the same scene, the two lovers express their agony at their loss of pre-reflectivity. "My God," Pierre says, "but it would be sweet to touch your shoulders. I want to breathe your breath when you smile at me. But I've missed that, too. I have met you too late." Eve's reply is as poignant as it is astute: "I would give my soul to live again for an instant and to dance with you," she says. "It is all we have left" (Sartre 1948, p. 88). The characters make a clear distinction between their thinking, reflective selves (what both Descartes and Eve call the soul) and their pre-reflective bodies and they lament the loss of the latter. It acts as an impediment to their love as they are unable to touch each other. Despite this inability, Pierre and Eve are challenged in the next scene to overcome this disability and love each other enough to save themselves from death in accordance with the stipulations of Article 140.

The mysterious article dictates that the couple will return to life while retaining their memories, though there is a catch. The elderly clerk quotes the article, "if at the end of twenty-four hours you have succeeded in loving each other with perfect confidence and with all your might, you will have the right to an entire human existence" (Sartre 1948, p. 92). Furthermore, as part of their second chance, their lives return to the moments they died and none of their acquaintances are the wiser: they are magically ignorant of what has happened to the two lovers and time goes back to just before they died. This seems like a miraculous advantage for the couple in their pursuit of their goals, though ultimately, it is a farce, with one notable exception, in which the two lovers are able to make a difference in the world.

It is because of this inexplicable miracle that the protagonists are able to carry out an act of kindness and use their experience with the dead for a good cause. As Pierre and Eve joyously leave the room at the back of the shop where they are granted their second chance at life, a deceased workman named Astruc makes a request of them: that they rescue his young daughter from the abuse of his wife's lover. They do so, and this act of kindness constitutes the couple's only successful project in a story in which all their other endeavors end in failure. "*Les jeux sont faits* offers a filmic vehicle for Sartre's uncompromising vision of human reality as conflict and failure. Freedom is a terrible given and a doomed project" (Davis 2005, p. 231). While Davis is astute in his contention that failure is a major theme of the film and all of Sartre's work, the protagonists' rescue of poor Marie Astruc stands as a small exception to this, as the two main characters succeed in removing the girl from a life of squalor and abuse.

But it is only after they receive their second chance and effectively come back to life and regain their balance of pre-reflective and reflective consciousness that the protagonists are able to rescue Marie Astruc, their only success in any of their projects. When they are disembodied, intangible, and invisible, all their projects, all Eve's warnings to Lucette and Pierre's to his comrades, end in futility. The protagonists insist on being involved in the world around them but are unable to change it until they regain their bodies. Even then, their projects end in futility for both of them, except when they rescue poor Marie.

As soon as Eve comes back to life, she warns Lucette of André's machinations, but to her horror her sister refuses to listen. The facticity constituted by the stubbornness of another eventually distracts Eve from what should be her primary project: to love Pierre enough to save herself. This she is ultimately unable to do, as is Pierre. He refuses simply to stand by and remain neutral in the conflict between his friends and the Regent's forces. Both characters insist on remaining involved in the situation and this ends in their second and permanent deaths.

The return of their bodies and thereby the balance of reflective and pre-reflective consciousnesses somewhat empowers the two lovers. They are resurrected, get their bodies back, and are finally able to be seen and heard. Furthermore, they can touch and manipulate physical matter in the mode of other for-itselfs. Once again able to immerse themselves in a world of facticity and projects, Pierre and Eve become even more resolute in the pursuit of their goals. Soon after their rescue of Marie Astruc, Pierre becomes restless and declares, "Eve, I've got to see my friends. When I was . . . on the other side, I learned certain things. We've been betrayed . . . I must go and warn them" (Sartre 1948, p.142). With their pre-reflective selves returned to them via their bodies, Pierre and Eve have a chance at being complete subjects, but are in the end unable to abide by the rules of Article 140.

Pierre warns his fellow insurgents that the Regent knows of their plans and will use that knowledge to crush their organization once and for all. Unfortunately for all involved, the other rebels no longer trust Pierre because he is romantically involved with Eve, who they have learned is the wife of André, the secretary of militia. Eve takes this failure as the ultimate disappointment in their project to love each other. The terrible choice they are given is an impossible one: for them truly to love each other and be awarded a long and happy life together, they must ignore the mortal danger their friends and family members are in and remain uninvolved. Eve realizes this before Pierre, as she declares they will die because they have failed to love each other sufficiently. "Admit, Pierre, admit . . . it wasn't for me that you wanted to live again. It was for your insurrection. At present that it's misfired, you don't mind dying. You know that they are coming to kill you, and you stay" (Sartre 1948, pp. 154–155). Pierre does not deny this and Eve admits that "perhaps" she came back to her embodied life for the sake of Lucette and not for Pierre and their love.

With this, the couple realizes that they are doomed to failure because of their impossible choice, though they still pretend otherwise for a short while. Pierre implores Eve, "Eve, there's nothing in the world but you and me. We are alone in the world. We have to love each other. We must love each other. It is our only chance" (Sartre 1948, p. 157). For a brief moment, it seems as though the lovers might just be able to stay together and love each other happily for the rest of their lives. But mysterious antagonists arrive at Pierre's door, though they do nothing to threaten the two paramours. The intruders leave and Pierre and Eve declare that they are out of danger, that their enemies on the stairs have left because they have begun to love each other and have earned the right to live, though they both know this is not true (Sartre 1948, p. 159).

Eve again says that they two are alone in the world (Sartre 1948, p. 161). But of course, this is impossible. According to Sartre, and in accordance with Heidegger's conceptions of "thrownness," a human consciousness is thrust into a situation in the world. Each one, through its attainment of consciousness, finds itself existing without knowing why. For Heidegger, the subject is something thrown into existence and something which exists as an entity which has to be as it is and as it can be (Heidegger 1985, p. 321). So the two characters have been thrown into a situation but have also made their current situation what it is. They have a choice, but it is a terrible, impossible choice and Pierre makes it: He resolves to abandon the woman he loves because he is unable to detach himself from the world into which he has been thrown, the world he has subsequently made for himself based on his freedom. Eve realizes that she cannot stop Pierre from pursuing his projects, and resolves to pursue her own and attempt to rescue Lucette from André.

As Pierre meets with his comrades and resolves to halt their uprising, he has a "moment of intense reflection" (Sartre 1948, p. 177). He realizes that time has run out, that he has lost Eve forever. As a result, he vows to stay with his fellow insurgents, but is shot by Lucien for a second time and dies, this time permanently. Eve dies too, and in the final scene in the film the lugubrious dead couple is seen discussing their failed projects, although they also finally realize that the world is too factic to become involved with. There are too many forces against them and too many people beyond their control. They comfort themselves that everyone they know will be dead before too long and that therefore their failures are unimportant. Eve says of her helpless sister, "in a few dozen years she'll be one of the dead like us . . . a little moment to be lived through" (Sartre 1948, p. 183). They realize the chips are down, that they will receive no third chance at life, that their project was impossible in the first place, and that it simply doesn't matter anyway.

Although the two main characters regain their bodies near the end of the film and become thereby more empowered than when they were disembodied, their projects end in failure and they are unable truly to love each other and save themselves because they are unable to ignore the world in which they want to live. Unlike George Bailey, who learns that the world really is a better place with him in it, Pierre and Eve are doomed to failure because they are unable to strike the balance between their pre-reflective and reflective selves and unable to abide by the impossible stipulations of Article 140. Their lives seem unimportant to the world as it goes on without them. The world is not a better place because these two characters were in it. It goes on and their efforts at attaining their projects are immaterial and soon forgotten. There is no happy ending like the one in *It's a Wonderful Life* because the entire endeavor is a set-up and failure is one of the few things in the world every subject can count on.

## References

Capra, F. (1946). *It's a Wonderful Life.*
Davis, C. (2005). Sartre and the Return of the Living Dead. *Sartre Studies International* 11(1–2): pp. 222–233.
Descartes, R. (1998). *Discourse on Method.* Indianapolis, IN: Hackett.
Heidegger, M. (1985). *Being and Time.* Trans. John Macquarrie and Edward Robinson. Oxford: Basil Blackwell.
Sartre, J.-P. (1948). *The Chips Are Down (Les jeux sont faits).* New York: Lear.
Sartre, J.-P. (1960). *The Transcendence of the Ego.* New York: Hill and Wang.
Sartre, J.-P. (1976). *Sartre on Theater.* Ed. Michel Contat and Michel Rybalka. New York: Random House.
Sartre, J.-P. (1984). *Being and Nothingness.* New York: Washington Square Press.
Sartre, J.-P. (1999). *War Diaries: Notebooks from a Phoney War 1939–40.* London: Verso.
Taylor, M.C. (1987). *Alterity.* Chicago, IL: University of Chicago.

# Index

access approach 343–5
accessory reflection 368, 370–1 *see also* impure reflection
acquaintance 77, 78–84, 91, 93–5, 171 n.4, 318, 323–5, 328–35
action: acts vs objects of consciousness 107–8, 117, 248; ego as unity of states and actions 301, 310–12; vs passivity 428, 430; and perception 400–1, 426–7; vs sensation 392–4; vs states 300–1
Act-Object model 34
acute pain 365, 373–4, 376–7
adumbrations (*Abschattungen*) 222 n.3, 292, 294–5, 463–4, 466, 468
adverbial interpretations 96 n.12, 101–19, 335–7, 358
adversity, coefficient of 401–2
affection 19, 128, 429
affective disorders 439
agentive phenomenology 150–4, 165–7
alienation 369, 413, 415, 419–20, 433, 443–4, 448–9
alterity 81–2, 91, 469
ambiguous I 306
amnesia 266
anaphora 55–6
anguish 113–14, 469–72
Anscombe, E. M. 38, 56, 209
anti-separatists 32–5
anxiety 170 n.1, 198 n.9, 370, 470, 472–4, 485–6, 488
apodictic judgments 67, 86, 89–90, 180, 193, 265, 463
appearance vs phenomena: being 480–1, 491 n.19; consciousness 36–7; pain 374; perception 405 n.16; physical phenomena 281–4, 292–6; transcendence 68, 78–9, 85–6, 288; translucence 210
Aristotle 282
Aron, R. 259–60
artificial intelligence 162
attention 85–90, 92–3, 324, 351, 374
attitude vs content 253–61
authenticity 220–1, 373, 464–5, 469 *see also* inauthenticity
awareness-content model 126
Aydede, M. 365, 375, 376, 377, 378

bad faith 84, 87, 186, 198 n.9, 220, 221, 380 n.11
Barnes, H. E. 118 n.2, 137 n.1
Barwise, J. 93
Bayne, T. 96 n.7
Beeh, V. 44 n.4
*Being and Nothingness* (Sartre, 1956): acquaintance 80, 82–3, 94; attention 86; bad faith 220; body 385, 386–90, 394–9, 400, 407–21; cogito 5; dialetheia 90; free will 501; interiority 221; introspection 180, 181–2; *for-itself* 296; Law of Identity 66–7; no-content thesis (NCT) 106–9, 111–14; non-egological theory of consciousness 298, 309–12; ontological proof 81, 294; pain 366–74; positional/non-positional consciousness 68, 71, 72, 75, 79, 321, 358; *pour-soi* and *en-soi* 49; pure vs impure reflection 123; "quasi-knowledge" 88; reflection 89, 91–2, 200 n.17, 289, 423–4, 446; regress

320–1; S = Cc thesis 478–81; secondary awareness approach 356; subjectivity 476; time-consciousness 120, 122, 125
beliefs: attitudinal account 253–61; belief fixation 157–8; Kierkegaard 483–4; perception/imagination distinction 253–61, 265; sensory experience 246
Bergson, H. 23 n.3, 188, 473
Berkeley, G. 20, 43
*Bernauer Manuscripte* (Husserl, 1917–18) 127–9
Bernecker, S. 198 n.11
Blakemore, S. J. 444
Blanke, O. 92, 200 n.16, 426
blob theory 305
Block, N. 32, 41, 145, 343
body: bodily coupling 423, 427–30; body-mind problem 181–2, 242, 375, 379, 495, 497–9; body-subject 310–11; body uncanny 374; ego disorders 446–8; embodiment of pre-reflective consciousness 385–406; language-like structure 407–21; *Les jeux sont faits* (Sartre, 1948) 498–506; *for-me* 426–7; pain 366–9
Boyle, M. 176
Brandom, R. 77, 79
Bratman, M. 168–9
Brentano, F.: attitudinal account 255, 260–1, 264–5; Descartes' Cogito 279–87, 295; intentionality 2, 19–20, 107, 109, 318, 350; secondary awareness 344; self-representationalism 351; unconsciousness 337; unified mental states 424
bundle theory 305
Buras, T. 328
Byrne, A. 75, 251, 267 n.4, 268 n.9, 270 n.25, 332

Cabestan, P. 456
Campbell, J. 18, 171 n.4, 444
caresses 418, 420
Carruthers, P. 31, 34
Cartesian freedom 293–5
*Cartesian Meditations* (Husserl, 1999) 460–1
Cassam, Q. 18

Castañeda, H-N.: *esse est percipi* 43, 58; first-personal states 143, 226; guise theory 20, 243 n.1; inner framework of the mental 21; perspectival arrays 60; self-representationalism 31, 38, 59; stream of consciousness 19
Catalano, J. S. 387–8
catharsis 86, 87–8, 124, 291
Cavell, S. 221–2
centric vs eccentric positions 446–9
chains of events 73–4
Chalmers, D. J. 32, 36, 42, 172 n.15, 178, 196, 338 n.4, 404 n.1
character 310–12
*Chips are Down, The/Les jeux sont faits* (Sartre, 1948) 22, 495–506
Chisholm, R. 24 n.11, 38
chronic pain 365, 370, 372–3, 378
circularity 30, 34, 92–3, 94, 488 *see also* regresses
Clark, A. 385
co-awareness 425, 432–3
co-creation 402–3
coefficient of adversity 401–2
cogito: anguish 471; Brentano on 280–7; Cartesian freedom 293–5; ego 234; pre-reflectiveness 3, 21, 104, 122, 287–91; projection errors 186–7; radicalization of 2; reflective 483; thought insertion 440
cognitive science: cognitive dissonance 84; cognitive phenomenology debate 96 n.7; embodied cognition 379; enactivism 385–6; and HOT theory 326–7, 337; introspection 176–8; mental representation 349, 357; pain 375; transcendence 181; zero point representations 159–69
Cohen, L. J. 255
comparator models 165–7
comprehension 193–4
Comte, A. 177
conceptualization: conceptual vs nonconceptual awareness 51; knowledge 83; non-positional consciousness 71, 75; perception 246; reflection 85–90
concurrent protocol analysis 163–5
*connaissance* 3, 4, 41–3, 67, 72, 83
Contat, M. 247, 260

contingency 5, 36, 58, 122, 135, 191, 193, 198 n.9
core-optionality 151–4
Cramer, K. 31
cultural phenomenology 373, 378, 449

Dainton, B. 128, 129
data: attention 85; attitudinal difference 262; continuity of 127–9; indexical thought 55–9, 60, 62; inner/outer sense 126 *see also* sensory data
Davidson, D. 23 n.7, 24 n.23
Davis, C. 496, 497–8, 500
daydreams 199 n.13
death 6, 419, 498–503
deceptive existence 281
decision making 161–5
De Coorebyter, V. 72
deferred/indirect awareness 52, 59, 146, 216, 325, 389
deixis 58, 62 n.3
Delacroix, H. 247
delusions 442
Dennett, D. 448
*de re* 37, 38–40, 446
derealization 92
derived intentionality 109–14, 467
de Sausurre, F. 62 n.1
Descartes, R. 2, 3, 186–7, 202 n.26, 280, 287, 291, 483, 490, 497
*de se* problem 20, 21, 35, 37, 38–40
desire 4–5, 154–6, 255–6, 415–20
determinism 151–2, 198 n.9, 465
developmental perspective 422–38
dialetheia 84, 90
diaphanous consciousness 187, 201 n.22
diasporic consciousness 73
direct acquaintance 77, 93–5
direct awareness 52, 146, 157, 216, 324
disease 371–2
dissociation 167
doubt, reflective vs pre-reflective 186
dreams 199 n.13, 268 n.10, 283
Dretske, F. 33, 75, 118 n.12, 270 n.25, 348
Dreyfus, H. L. 59
dubitability 68–9, 81, 289–90, 293, 466
duress 152

dynamic process, consciousness as 56, 120–2, 422, 425–7
dys-appearance 373–4

eccentric vs centric positions 446–9
ecstatic being 3, 5, 374, 458
Edelman, G. 327
ego: character 310–12; ego disorders 22, 439–51; egolessness 233; egological descriptions (ED) 214, 216–17; egological dimensions of consciousness 212–16, 455, 468; and the empirical self 135, 136–7; historical background 455–75; intimacy of the ego 218–19; opacity of the I 208–9; "outside" consciousness 232–5; and reflection 49, 86, 87, 186–7, 462, 468; Sartre's non-egological theory 298–316; and the "self" 49; superfluity of the ego 215, 235, 302; time-consciousness 124; transcendence 180, 301–9, 457–63
*ekstatic* dimensions 124, 364–74, 377–8
emanations 87, 368, 464, 465, 467
emotion 58, 66, 69, 74–6, 78, 107, 377, 428–9
*Emotions, The* (Sartre, 1939) 66, 74, 86
emphatic self-knowledge 38
empirical self 135, 296
"emptiness" 70
empty intentions 326
enactivism 385, 389–404
encapsulation 43
engrossment 182, 213
*en-soi (in-itself)*: acquaintance 80–4; body 388; Cartesian freedom 294; definition 4–5; identity 42–3; For-Itself approach 353–8; no-content thesis (NCT) 111–12; reflection 43; self-awareness 196; sensation 391
environment: and the body 375, 397–9, 426–7; eccentric personality 446–7; enactivism 386; I* and me* 163; P-properties 391; self-representationalism 32–3; spatial thinking 239; zero point 148
*Epokhè* 455–75 *see also* pure vs impure reflection

*Erlebnisse* 44 n.1, 62 n.6, 232, 292, 315 n.32, 368, 466, 473
error: ego disorders 449; error theory of introspection 176–203; perceptual errors 68–9, 76, 81; projection errors 185, 186–7; reification errors 186, 188; reversal errors 200 n.17; standpoint errors 186, 190–4
*esse est percipi* 43, 58
Evans, G. 62 n.4, 212
existentialism 477
explanatory gap 21, 172 n.15, 344
externalism 4, 22, 32, 75, 145, 201 n.22 *see also* representationalism

facticity: body 374, 415–17, 419; definition 22; freedom 402–3; *Les jeux sont faits* (film, 1948) 495, 499, 502; ontological proof 82; transcendence 108
faith 84 *see also* religion
Fales, E. 90
fear 74–5, 270 n.29, 309, 333, 470–1, 488
feedback loops 327
feeling it good/true 255–6
Fichte, J. G. 20, 30–1, 34, 36, 41, 91
field of consciousness 239–40, 455–6
filtering 169
finiteness 5–6
first-order representationalism 343–4, 348
first-person subjectivity: first-person pronouns 221–2, 226, 229, 299, 424; first-person status 59–60; I* representations 159–69; impersonality of consciousness 214–16; indexical thought 52–9; ipseity 61–2; Kierkegaard 489–90; modes of consciousness 51–2; perception/imagination distinction 249–50, 262; vs third-person 178–9; zero point 144–69
flow 73–4, 121–2, 124, 128, 134
Fodor, J. A. 347
*for-itself* (*pour-soi*): access approach 344; anti-separatistism 32; *Being and Nothingness* (Sartre, 1956) 296; body 386, 388, 396, 498; definition 4–5;

*de se* problem 37; first-person status 61; freedom 401–3, 501; ghost-like consciousness 497; identity 42; For-Itself approach 353–8; no-content thesis (NCT) 111–12; nothingness 354; and the Other 6; pain 366–7, 371; pre-reflective consciousness condition (PRCC) 101; reflexivity 50; self-awareness 196; self-reference 21–2; time-consciousness 122–5; transparency 355
*for-me*: access approach 344–5; acquaintance 329; anti-separatistism 32; bodily coupling 427–30; Kriegel on 35; *mine*-ness 21, 117, 147, 226, 329, 336; phenomenal subjectivity 146–8; positional/non-positional consciousness 482; pre-reflective bodily foundations 426–7; prospection and recollection 154; secondary awareness 345–53; self-representationalism 159; thought insertion 440
*for-others* 191–2, 366–9, 371–3, 387, 408–14, 417, 430
forward models 165–7, 444
Frank, M. (also author of chapter 1) 61, 70, 91, 120, 123, 329, 440, 446, 448
freedom: anguish 113–14; bad faith 198 n.9; Cartesian freedom 293–5; core optionality 151–2; facticity 401, 402–3; finiteness 5–6; free will 500–3; and Marxism 23; radical freedom 497; vertigo of possibility 470–1
Frege, G. 2, 62 n.2
functionalism 32, 377
future, the 122–3, 128–9, 130, 133–5, 265, 402–3

Gallagher, S. 50, 147, 165, 178, 200 n.16, 423, 444, 448
Garro, L. C. 373, 380 n.13
Gennaro, R. (also author of chapter 13) 31, 34, 356, 357–8
Gergely, G. 428
Gertler, B. 323–4
ghost-like consciousness 497, 498, 502
Gibson, J. J. 427
Gilson, E. 261

Gilson, L. 261
given, the 89–90, 122, 130, 401
God 78, 293–4, 346, 485
Graham, G. 145
granularity of consciousness 63 n.8
Gruenheck, S. 406
Grunbaum, T. 63 n.11
guilt 216–17, 309
guise theory 20, 243 n.1
Gunderson, K. 314 n.21
Gurwitsch, A. 19, 70, 312 n.1, 380 n.8

Haggard, P. 166
hallucinations 170 n.3, 269 n.19, 441, 443–4
Harman, G. 33, 75, 253, 270 n.25, 355
Hart, J. 31–2
hatred 213–14, 300, 368, 419–20, 463, 465
Hatzimoysis, A. 70, 198 n.8
Hayne, H. 167
heautoscopy 92
Hegel, G. F. W. 3, 23, 42, 44
Heidegger, M. 2, 3, 6, 424, 472, 477, 479, 497
Heidelberg School 31–2, 40, 446
Hellie, B. 323, 330–5, 337
Henrich, D. 23 n.9, 30, 31, 38, 40–1, 91, 329
higher dimensional projective geometry 93
higher-order theories of consciousness: empirical self 135; failure of 32–5; higher-order perception theory 345–6; HOT theory 21, 70, 118 n.8, 317–18, 319–38; intentionality 285–6; reflective cogito 289–91; secondary awareness approach 345–53; unconsciousness 105, 424
Hill, C. 197 n.2
Hintikka, J. 55
hodological space 392, 396–7, 401
Hölderlin, F. 33
Hopp, W. 95 n.5
Horgan, T. (also author of chapter 6) 32, 39, 145
human nature 477
Hume, D. 19, 127, 187–8, 195, 246, 250–1, 354

Husserl, E.: absolute vs unsubstantial being 465–6; adumbrations 222 n.3, 292, 294–5, 463–4, 466, 468; attention 86; certainty of reflective act 290; cogito 291–3; content vs object 281; embodiment 426; empirical self 135; empty intentions 199 n.14; *Epokhè* 455–75; first-personal experience 424; hyletic data 80–4, 91, 262, 279, 288, 292, 293–4; I-knowledge 20; immanence 68, 458, 463; influenced by Brentano 260, 279; influence on Sartre 2, 180, 209–10, 244 n.7, 253, 259–60, 318; inner perception 292; intentionality 212–13, 482; knowledge 83; naturalism 378; neutrality modification 262; non-objectual consciousness 35; phenomenology 261, 479–80; positional/non-positional consciousness 69; pre-predicative conceptualizations 77; principle of simultaneous awareness 129; protention 5; reflection 84, 89, 471–4; self-consciousness 483; time-consciousness 74, 120, 125–9; transcendental reduction 457, 459–60; transversal consciousness 72; zero point 144, 148–59
hyletic data 80–4, 91, 262, 279, 288, 292, 293–4
Hyman, J. 382 n.24
hypnotic states 337

I* and me* 143–4, 159–69, 226
identification as mode of consciousness 51–2, 55, 58
identity 42
I-knowledge 20
illness 371
illusions 87, 95, 186–8, 219, 283, 308–9, 331–3
*Imaginary, The* (Sartre, 1940): attention 85; belief/desire 256; "ontological proof" 81; perception/imagination distinction 252; positional and non-positional consciousness 68, 69, noe; psychology 181; publication of 247; reflection 87; spatial thinking 201 n.23

imagination 245–76
*Imagination, The* (Sartre, 1936) 68, 247, 248–53
imaging awareness 256–7
immanence: adumbrations 467; cogito 292; death of consciousness 235; hyletic data 80–2; illusion of 87, 186, 188; memory 69; no-content thesis (NCT) 115; perception 463–4; vs transcendence 68–9; transcendence 458; transversal consciousness 72
impersonality of consciousness 214–16, 456–7, 459, 465, 470
implicit awareness 52, 184–9, 192–4
impressions 127, 136, 288–9, 354
impure vs pure reflection: apodictic judgements 67, 180; body 368; cogito 290–1; conceptualization 66–7; degrees of self-presence 84–90; ego 219; historical background 463–75; implicit awareness 185; positional consciousness 124; standpoint errors 192–4; third-person perspectives 178–9
Imuta, K. 167
inattentive awareness 52, 70, 78, 289, 291, 324
inauthenticity 220, 221, 464–5, 469 *see also* bad faith
indexical concepts 20, 52–9, 143, 155, 347
indirect/deferred awareness 52, 59, 146, 216, 325, 389
indirect realism 385, 389–90, 391
infallibility 73, 242, 250, 267, 286, 323–4, 327, 331–2
infants and self-consciousness 422–38
infinite regress problem 104–5, 189, 195, 285, 317
infinitival constructions 155
infinitization 464
informational/nomic-covariation approach 346
*in-itself (en-soi)*: acquaintance 80–4; body 388; Cartesian freedom 294; definition 4–5; identity 42–3; For-Itself approach 353–8; no-content thesis (NCT) 111–12; and reflection 43; self-awareness 196; sensation 391

inner monologue 444
inner perception 19–20, 22, 279, 280–1, 285–6, 292
instantaneity 123–4, 368
instrumental things 397, 403
integrated information theory 197 n.6
intensity of physical phenomena 254, 284
intentionality: acquaintance 80; attitudinal account 253–61; Brentano 19; cogito 287–91, 292, 295; derived 109–14, 467; empty intentions 326; first-person status 63 n.10; higher-order theories 347; hyletic data 279; inner perception 285–6; Intentionality Thesis (IT) 107, 109, 110; longitudinal vs horizontal 72; naturalization 346; no-content thesis (NCT) 109–14; non-intentional relation of awareness (NIRA) 330–5; "overloading" intentions 169; pain 374, 376; perception vs imagination 262; perceptual errors 76; phenomenality 144–6, 147; planning theory 168–9; positional/non-positional consciousness 102, 236, 318; radicalization of 457–9; rationality 156–8; reflexivity 328; representation 318, 334–5; secondary awareness 344; self-concealment 221; sensory-perceptual experience 149; translucence 209–11, 218; transparency 355; transversal intentionality 74; voluntary-action experience 150–4
intentional objects: acquaintance 80; ego 298; introspection 184–6, 189; no-content thesis (NCT) 107–9; vs object consciousness 21; physical phenomena 281, 295; secondary awareness approach 350; transparency 212–14; unconsciousness 105
internalism 32, 375, 379
interpretation, consciousness as 110
interpretive thought processes 53–4, 114, 233
intimacy of the ego 218–19
intrinsic glow 35

introspection: vs adverbial constructs 116–17; concurrent protocol analysis 163–5; error theory of 176–203; HOT theory 317, 319–25, 327, 331, 333; metaphysical theory 305; perception/imagination distinction 251–2, 262; reflective consciousness 356; secondary awareness approach 358; voluntary-action experience 150
intuition 83, 112–13, 458
inversion 463–6
ipseity 50, 61–2, 202 n.26
Ireland, J. 379 n.2
ir-reflectivity 237–41
irreflexive expressions 44 n.4
irreversibility 121
*It's a Wonderful Life* (Capra, 1946) 495, 506

James, W. 62 n.5, 63 n.8, 167
Janzen, G. 328, 337
*Jeux sont faits, Les* (film, Sartre, 1948) 22, 495–506
judgment: apodictic judgments 67, 86, 89–90, 180, 193, 265, 463; cognition without me* 161–5; feeling it good/true 255–6; judgments of observation 131–2; as modality 71–2, 78; perceptual judgments 77, 79, 246, 248; pre-predicative conceptualizations 77, 84–5; reflection 19, 87

Kadipasaoglu, D. 432
Kant, I.: ego 446, 460; Fichte on 30; "I think" 41, 440; regulative ideas 4, 5; time-consciousness 126, 128, 129, 131, 135, 136; transcendence 179
Kapitan, T. (also author of chapter 2) 31–2, 53, 199 n.14
Kierkegaard, S. A. 476–9, 483–90
Kleinman, A. 373, 381 n.14
knowledge: acquaintance 19, 83–4, 323; vs comprehension 193; *connaissance* 3, 4, 41–3, 67, 72, 83; distinctiveness of knowledge 250; I-knowledge 20; illusion of primacy 186, 188; knowledge by acquaintance (KBA) 83; perception/imagination distinction 249–50; quasi-knowledge 88–9; reflection 103–6, 192–3; self-knowledge 208–24
Köhler, W. 446–7
Kriegel, U. (also author of chapter 10): acquaintance 328–9; anti-separatistism 32; introspection 177–8; reductionism 351; self-representationalism 29, 32, 33, 34–6, 37, 39, 195, 318, 324, 325, 338 n.6; simultaneous observer–observed 195; transcendence 70
Kripke, S. 36, 42, 481
Krueger, J. 429

Lambo, A. 449–50
language: body as 407–21; indexical language 52–9; LOT (language of thought) 161–2; protoconversations 428–9; and reflection 86; reflexive phrases 41, 42, 49–51; transcendence 408, 412–14; zero point 161
La Rochefoucauld, F de. 217
"Law of Identity" 66, 93
Le Bon, S. 466
Leder, D. 367, 368, 370, 373–4
Lehrer, K. 96 n.8
Leibniz's law 102
*Les jeux sont faits* (film, Sartre, 1948) 22, 495–506
Levin, J. 377
Levinas, E. 68
Levine, J. (also author of chapter 14) 33, 35, 37, 42–3, 58, 135, 172 n.15, 325–6
Lewin, K. 404 n.8
Lewis, D. 38–9
logic 200 n.20
LOT (language of thought) 161–2
love 70, 217, 285, 300, 418, 502
Lowe, E. J. 196 n.1
Luhmann, N. 24 n.20
Lycan, W. 332, 345, 377
Lyons, J. 62 n.3

Mach, E. 38, 50
magical concepts 311–12, 371, 408, 473–4
Marcel, A. 63 n.9

marginal awareness 52, 60, 62, 70, 78
Marie Antoinette characters 228, 229
Marty, A. 271 n.34, 271 n.35
Marxism 22–3
materialism 5, 21, 343
McGinn, C. 4, 145, 245
me* and I* 143–4, 159–69, 226
memory: amnesia 266; as cognition that needs me* 167–8; immanence 69; mnemonic experiences 247–8, 258, 264–5; perception/imagination distinction 264; recollection 154, 167–8; reflection 84–90
mental illness 166, 200 n.16, 439–51
mental imaging 108, 110, 116, 248, 251–2, 389
mental paint 253, 355
Merleau-Ponty, M. 268 n.12, 378–9, 386, 387, 399, 426
metapsychological thought (MET) 319, 321–3, 326–30
Metzinger, T. 96 n.15, 426
mind-body problem 181–2, 242, 375, 379, 495, 497–9
*mine*-ness 21, 117, 147, 226, 329, 336
minimal self 422, 425, 426, 427–30, 433, 445–6
minimal sensibilia 250–1
Mirvish, A. 392
misidentification 210–11
misrepresentation 325–7, 331, 346
mnemonic experiences 247–8, 258, 264–5
modalities 96 n.12, 135, 149–50, 265
modes of consciousness 51–2, 68–80, 239
Moll, H. 431
Montague, M. 339 n.8
Moore, G. E. 80, 187
moral obligations 152, 216–17
Moran, D. 380 n.6, 387, 388
Morris, K. J. (also author of chapter 15) 313 n.6, 387
Morris, P. S. 70, 289, 309–12
Moss, L. 93
multi-layer models 34–5, 39 *see also* higher-order theories of consciousness
multi-modal sensory experience 149–50

Murray, L. 429
mysticism 35, 39
"Myth of the Given" 79

Nagel, T. 317, 342
Narcissus characters 227, 229, 233
natural attitude 455, 460–2, 466, 470, 472–3, 474, 487
naturalism 375, 378–9
naturalization 342–3, 346
nausea 198 n.9, 372, 419
NCT (no-content thesis) 106–14
negation 91–3
*negatité*s 112–13
negativity of theories 4, 40, 44, 151, 211–12, 293
neurology 94, 326–7 *see also* cognitive science
neurophenomenology 385
neutral concepts 86–7
neutrality modification 261, 262–3
nihilation 4, 112–13, 122, 395
NIRA (non-intentional relation of awareness) 330–5
Nisbett, R. E. 177
no-content thesis (NCT) 106–14
Noë, A. 386, 389–404
noemata 21, 69, 74, 456, 458
noeses 69, 74, 458
nomic-covariation/informational approach 346
non-analyzability thesis 40
non-conceptual representation 71, 75–6
non-intentional relation of awareness (NIRA) 330–5
non-objectual consciousness 35
non-positional/positional consciousness: direct vs indirect awareness 52; HOT theory 319–23; intentionality 115, 184, 318; positing attitudes 69, 91; reflection 68–80, 102, 103–6, 211, 229–30, 356, 466, 481–3; Sartre's concepts of 2–4; secondary awareness 126, 358; self-awareness 235–6; standpoint errors 190–1; time-consciousness 123; transcendence 108–9
non-reflexivity 462

non-representational self-presence 146–8
non-thetic consciousness *see* non-positional/positional consciousness
no-self theory 302
*Notebooks for an Ethics* (Sartre, unfinished) 289
nothingness 89, 106–9, 112–13, 293, 354
Novalis (F. von Hardenberg) 30, 41
Nunberg, G. 63 n.7

object-consciousness 33, 40
objectivity 390
obsessions 442–3, 445
occurrent conscious thoughts 145–6, 246
Ockham, William of 30, 136
Oizumi, M. 197 n.6
one-place models 34–5
ontological naturalism 375
ontological proof 4, 80–4, 112, 294
opacity of the I 208–9, 217–20, 303
open future diagram 133–5
optionality 151–2
origin of negation 67, 80, 93
Other, the: facticity 22; I is the other 468–9; introspection 182, 190; language 408–14, 415–20; objectification by 193–4; *for-others* 191–2, 366–9, 371–3, 387, 408–14, 417, 430; pain 373, 378; phenomenology 88; psychic body 369; self-awareness 195, 242; social concepts 6; social perspective taking 430–3
outer account of self-knowledge 211–13

pain 36, 42, 189–90, 331, 365–84
PANIC theory 343
Papineau, D. 375
passivity: body 416; infants' 428; passive consciousness 300–1; passivity phenomena 439–40, 443–5; perception 75–7, 79, 391–2; phenomenology 151; visual experiences 252
Peacocke, C. 144
Peckitt, M. 381 n.21

Peirce, C. S. 63 n.7
perception: action 394–9; aspects of things 464; body 392–9; enactivism 386; environment 426–7; imagination 245–76; inner perception 19–20, 22, 279, 280–1, 285–6, 292; intentional objects 295; knowledge 83–4; metaphysical theory 305; pain 376, 377–8; passivity 75–7, 79, 391–2; perceptual errors 68–9, 76, 81; perceptual judgments 77, 79, 246, 248; phenomenal subjectivity 146–7; psychic body 369; as relation 389–90, 392–4, 397–9; sensation 391; social perspective taking 430–3; subliminal perception 343–4
peripheral consciousness 70, 78, 227–9, 231, 237, 324–5, 329
Perky experiment 269 n.16
Perry, J. 53, 143, 162–3
personality 234, 236, 460, 470–1 *see also* impersonality of consciousness
perspective: body 367; enactivism 386; indexical thought 54–9, 61; intentional translucence 210; introspection 178–9, 185; multivocality 410; perspectival arrays 57–8, 60, 61–2; P-properties 391, 401; reflective cogito 290; situation 401–2; social perspective taking 430–3; standpoint errors 186, 190–4; third-person perspectives 157; and transcendence 68; zero point 144, 148–59
"Peter" example 213–15, 300, 463, 467
*petitiones principii* 128
phantasmagoric experiences 247–8, 252, 258, 263–4
phenomenological reduction *see* reductionism
phenomenology: access vs phenomenal consciousness 343; acquaintance 91–2, 94; agentive phenomenology 150–4, 165–7; body 388; Brentano 281, 424; cognitive science 181; cultural phenomenology 373, 378, 449; disease 372; ego 87–8; enactivism 385; first-order representationalism 344; historical background 2; HOT theory 331, 337;

Husserl 455; indirect realism 391–2; introspection 178; Kierkegaard 485, 488; metaphysical theory 305; pain 377; perception 246–7, 259; phenomenal concepts 76–7; phenomenality 382 n.25; primacy of pre-reflection 425; S = Cc thesis 478–80; subjectivity 143–59; transcendence 458, 467; transphenomenal dimensions 4, 68–9, 294
physicalism 375
physical phenomena 281–5, 292, 295, 346
Pitt, D. 145
place 402
planning 168–9
pleasure 42–3, 71, 86, 320–1, 416, 418
Plessner, H. 440, 446–8, 450
Pollack, M. 169
positional/non-positional consciousness: direct vs indirect awareness 52; HOT theory 319–23; intentionality 115, 184, 318; positing attitudes 69, 91; reflection 68–80, 102, 103–6, 211, 229–30, 356, 466, 481–3; Sartre's concepts of 2–4; secondary awareness 126, 358; self-awareness 235–6; standpoint errors 190–1; time-consciousness 123; transcendence 108–9
*pour-soi* (*for-itself*): access approach 344; anti-separatistism 32; *Being and Nothingness* (Sartre, 1956) 296; body 386, 388, 396, 498; definition 4–5; *de se* problem 37; first-person status 61; freedom 401–3, 501; ghost-like consciousness 497; identity 42; For-Itself approach 353–8; no-content thesis (NCT) 111–12; nothingness 354; and the Other 6; pain 366–7, 371; pre-reflective consciousness condition (PRCC) 101; reflexivity 50; self-awareness 196; self-reference 21–2; time-consciousness 122–5; transparency 355
P-properties 391, 401
PRCC (pre-reflective consciousness condition) 101, 103–6, 111

pre-ontological self-understanding 75
pre-predicative conceptualizations 77, 79
presentational representations 146, 153–4, 281–4, 285, 295
Preyer, G. 24 n.16, 24 n.18, 329
Priest, G. 90
primitive concepts: *Being and Nothingness* (Sartre, 1956) 49, 478; co-awareness 433; Fichte 20; first-person status 51, 63 n.11, 422, 430–1; infants' self-awareness 423, 425–7; ipseity 61–2; *for-itself* 353, 356; minimal vs higher self-awareness 229, 348; non-intentional relation of awareness (NIRA) 334; phenomenology 479, 489–90; representationalism 1; secondary awareness 356–7; visual experiences 423
principle of persistent givenness 130
principle of simultaneous awareness 129
projection errors 185, 186–7
pronouns: anaphora 55–6; first-person pronouns 221–2, 226, 229, 299, 424; reflexive pronouns 19, 42
propositional attitudes 155
propositional theory of self-knowledge 39
prospection and recollection 154, 159, 170, 173 n.20, 173 n.22
protention 5, 73–4, 126–35, 172 n.11
psychiatry 22, 439–51
psychic body 368–9
psychofunctionalism 377
psychology 19, 22, 181, 255–6, 367, 390
psychosis 439–51
pure vs impure reflection: apodictic judgements 67, 180; body 368; cogito 290–1; conceptualization 66–7; degrees of self-presence 84–90; ego 219; historical background 463–75; implicit awareness 185; positional consciousness 124; standpoint errors 192–4; third-person perspectives 178–9

"qualities" 313 n.8
quasi-knowledge 88–9

rationality 156–8, 218
realism 21, 22, 87, 129, 385, 389–90
*réalité humaine* 4–6
recollection 154, 159, 167–8, 170, 173 n.20, 173 n.22
reductionism, phenomenological: access approach 344; acquaintance 328; anti-reductionism 337; higher-order theories of consciousness 345, 348–52; intentionality 330, 334, 335; perception 261–4; phenomenology 355, 459–63, 472; representationalism 320, 335; secondary awareness 357; transparency 355
*reflet-reflétant* distinction 4–5, 43, 122, 123, 290
reflexive phrases (language) 19, 41, 42, 49–51
reflexivity 328–30, 462
regresses: acquaintance 94; extensive vs intensive 34; Fichte-Shoemaker 91; harmful vs non-harmful 30; HOT theory 317, 319–20, 347–8; infinite regress problem 104–5, 189, 195, 285, 317, 346–8; multi-layer models 35; secondary awareness approach 350–2, 357; transcendence 189
regret 159, 309
regulative ideas 4, 5
reification errors 186, 188
Reisman, D. 368, 381 n.20
relation: acquaintance 82, 324; bodily coupling 427–30; body 388; concsiousness relata 81; consciousness as 354; and identity 42; non-intentional relation of awareness (NIRA) 330–5; opacity of the I 303; orienting relations 56–7; perception as 389–90, 392, 397–9; primacy of pre-reflection 425; reflexive relations 91; relative-absolute phenomena 294; relativity of sensations 390; and representation 33, 36; secondary awareness approach 350; situation 401; social perspective taking 433
religion 84, 483–4 *see also* God
representation: acquaintance 80, 328; anti-realism 129; desire 155; false representations 220; higher-order theories 33–4, 349; immanence 69; intentionality 318, 334–5; misrepresentation 325–7, 331; non-conceptual representation 71; non-positional consciousness 70–1; orienting relations 56–7; perception/imagination distinction 252–3; phenomenal subjectivity 146–8; "pictures in the mind" 398; presentational representations 146, 153–4, 281–4, 285, 295; protention and retention 73; rationality 158; time-consciousness 137; zero point 148, 159–69
representationalism: anti-representationalism 389–92; body 385; first-order representationalism 343–4, 348; HOT theory 330, 337; intentionality 335; non-conceptual representation 75; pain 376–7; PANIC theory 343–4; primitive pre-reflectivity 1; reductionism 320; self-representationalism 1, 31, 32–40, 159–69, 324, 325, 332
repugnance/revulsion 300–1, 463–4, 466–7
response-dependent properties of the object 32
retention 5, 73–4, 126–35, 172 n.11
reversal errors 200 n.17
Rey, G. 143, 161–2
Richmond, S. 380 n.11
Rochat, P. 425, 430, 433
Rosch, E. 385
Rosenthal, D. 31, 34, 319, 324, 326, 331–2, 334, 345, 346–7, 348
Rowlands, M. (also author of chapter 4) 318, 335–6
Russell, B. 19, 77, 83, 268 n.6, 274 n.57, 323
Ryle, G. 359 n.5

Sacks, O. 92, 393
salience 52, 62
*Sartre on Theater* (Sartre, 1976) 501
Scanlon, J. D. 302, 304
scenario content 144
Schelling, F. W. J. 43
schematism of time 131–2, 135

schizophrenia 166, 200 n.16, 439, 443–4, 445
Schneider, K. 439, 442
Schwitzgebel, E. 177, 196 n.1
Searle, J. R. 37, 481
secondary awareness approach 344, 345–53, 356–7
*Selbstbewusstsein* 41, 42
self-acquaintance 77–84, 91, 93–5
self-ascription 135, 346–7
self-as-source 151–4
self-concealment 220–2
"Self-Consciousness and Self-Knowledge" (Sartre, 1948) 66, 74, 91
self-deception *see* bad faith
self-given, the 89–90
self-identifications 38, 90–3
self-interpretation 349
self-knowledge 41, 43, 137, 208–24, 323–4
self-love 217
self-observation 184 *see also* introspection
self-presence 146–8
self-reference 3, 20, 74, 446
self-reflexivity 324, 328
self-registration mechanisms 41
self-representationalism 1, 31, 32–40, 159–69, 324, 325, 332, 351
Sellars, W. 156–7
semantic duality 54
sense of ownership 116
sensory data: anti-representationalism 389–91; attention 52; cogito 295; cognitive science 145; conceptualization 87; hyletic data 82, 94; imagination 255; indexical thought 59; infants 428; judgment 131; *mine*-ness 336; multiple sensory modalities 55, 58; pain 376–7; passivity phenomena 444; perception 246, 248, 389–91, 398; reflexive awareness 50; representation 75; sensorimotor knowledge 165–7, 393, 398–9, 428–9, 444; sensory-perceptual experience 149–50; transcendence 80; vectors 55–6
separatists 32–5
shame 193, 372, 431

Shear, J. 329
Sheya, A. 429
Shoemaker, S. 31, 91, 443
Siewert, C. 145, 325, 337, 344, 348, 350
simultaneous awareness 121, 129–30, 185–7, 195, 251, 299, 303, 352, 458
sin 486–8
Singer, M. 373
single-layer/same-order models 34–40
situated cognition 381 n.23, 385
situation 401–3
social concepts 6
social perspective taking 430–3
social pressures 193–4
solipsism 242
space of causes vs space of reasons 156–7
spatio-temporal concepts: field of consciousness 239–40; immanence 186, 188; indexical thought 54–6; perspective 149, 400; representation 87, 128–30, 134; retention 126–7
Spinoza, B. 78
spontaneity 252, 465, 467, 471, 473–4
standpoint errors 186, 190–4
states vs actions 300–1, 310–12
state vs creature consciousness 317, 336–7
Strawson, G. 19, 63 n.9, 145, 330
stream of consciousness 63 n.8, 293, 299, 302, 309, 444–5, 448
structural coupling 385
subliminal perception 336, 343
suffering 372, 391
Sukale, M. 302, 304
superfluity of the ego 215, 235, 302
Svenaeus, F. 372
symbolism 110–11

tactile experience 149 *see also* sensory data
Tănăsescu, I. 260, 271 n.36
Taylor, M. 497
telicity 374
Tepley, J. (also author of chapter 12) 136
Thau, M. 332
thetic and non-thetic consciousness *see* positional/non-positional consciousness

thingism 248
think aloud protocols 163–5
third-person perspectives: cognitive science 178–9; mental states 1, 22; perspective 56, 155–7, 181–2, 489–90; self-concealment 221–2; standpoint errors 186, 190–4
Thomas, A. 318, 336
Thomasson, A. 318, 350, 359 n.1
Thompson, E. 385, 386
thought insertion 440–3, 445–9
Tienson, J. 145
time-consciousness: argument from opacity 303–4; cogito 3; ego disorders 448; Husserl 74, 125–9; perception/imagination distinction 264; reflection 5, 43–4, 78–9; Sartre's theory of 120–5; schematism of time 131–2, 135; static vs dynamic time 120–5; unity of consciousness 41–2
Timmons, M. 172 n.12
Tinnitus characters 227–8, 233
Toombs, S. K. 380 n.13
transcendence: acquaintance 80–4; body 396; cogito 287–91; conscious experiences 212; desire 415–17; ego 136, 218, 298, 301–9, 455, 457–9; vs immanence 68; intentionality 2–3, 180; introspection 180–1; ir-reflectivity 238; Kant 131, 135; Kierkegaard 485; language 408, 412–14; no-content thesis (NCT) 107–8, 112, 115; pain 371; position/non-positional consciousness 68; psychic body 369; transcendental reduction 457–9
*Transcendence of the Ego* (Sartre, 1957): body 498, 499; definition of ego 299–300; egological descriptions (ED) 217, 218, 219; as focus of book 23; historical background 455; impersonality of consciousness 456; infinitization 464; nature of reflection 462; non-egological theory of consciousness 298, 301–9; non-positional consciousness 211, 212, 213; opacity of the I 208; positional and non-positional consciousness 69, 74, 78; pre-reflective vs reflective consciousness 200 n.17; psychic body 368; pure reflection 466–71; pure vs impure reflection 199 n.12, 219; reflective cogito 289; reflective vs non-reflective thinking 49; regress 319; self-awareness 225–44; time-consciousness 125; transcendental reduction 457, 461; transparency 1–2
transgression 463–6
transitivity principle 331, 336–7, 345, 348
translucence of conscious phenomena 210, 212, 218, 238
transparency 1, 43, 212–14, 354–5
transphenomenal dimensions 4, 68–9, 294
transversal consciousness 72
Trevarthen, C. 428–9, 430
Trump characters 228–9, 230, 234–5, 241
truth 255–6, 294, 484
Tugendhat, E. 31, 39
Tulving, E. 268 n.9
two I's argument 306–8
Tye, M. 33, 75, 118 n.4, 343, 377

unconsciousness 105
"unity" (*en-soi* identity) 42
unity of consciousness 20, 42, 55, 73, 136, 471
unity of states and actions, ego as 301, 310–12
utterance-reflexivity 53

*valeur* 4, 5–6
van den Berg, J. H. 381 n.21, 381 n.22
Varela, F. J. 385, 394
vectors 56–9, 60, 62
vertigo of possibility 470–1
visual experiences: attention 52; infants' self-awareness 425, 430; judgment 398; mental imaging 116, 248, 251–2, 389; modalities 56; perspective 55–8, 148–50, 153; reflexivity 50; secondary awareness approach 350–3; self-awareness 307; vs social perspective taking 430–3; transcendence 108, 116; zero point 148

voluntary acts 150–4, 156–8
Von Hardenberg, F. (Novalis) 30, 41
Vosgerau, G. 444, 445

warping of thought 186, 188
Webber, J. 69, 71, 75, 181, 200 n.15
Weber and Fechner's Law 284
"what is it like" 41, 317, 326, 342, 343, 348, 481
Whitehead, A. N. 56, 63 n.8
"wide intrinsicality view" (WIV) 319, 321–3, 324–5, 326–30
Wider, K. (also author of chapter 16) 66, 83–4, 89, 192–4, 317
William of Ockham 30, 136
Williford, K. (also author of chapter 3) 21, 34, 35, 36, 39, 125, 137, 187
Wilson, T. D. 177
Wittgenstein, L. 110
Woodruff Smith, D. 187, 201 n.21

Zahavi, D.: acquaintance 329; anti-reductionism 337; awareness-content model 126; externalism 201 n.22; first-person status 424, 433; inattentive awareness 70; intentionality 225, 227, 318, 325; ipseity 50–1, 61; phenomenology 147, 178; positional and non-positional consciousness 74, 91, 118 n.6; reflection 423; self-representationalism 32, 39; simultaneous awareness 129; zero point 147
Zaner, R. M. 374, 381 n.21
zero point: cognitive architecture 159–69; phenomenal subjectivity 148–59
Zheng, Y. 87, 96 n.14, 200 n.15, 202 n.25
zombies 172 n.16, 337